THE CENTURY PSYCHOLOGY SERIES
*Richard M. Elliott, Gardner Lindzey &
Kenneth MacCorquodale, Editors*

FOUNDATIONS OF CONDITIONING AND LEARNING

I. P. Pavlov at the International Congress of Psychology, New Haven, Connecticut, 1929.

Foundations of Conditioning and Learning

Edited by

GREGORY A. KIMBLE
Duke University

 New York
APPLETON-CENTURY-CROFTS
Division of Meredith Publishing Company

158.423
K569f

Copyright © 1967 by
MEREDITH PUBLISHING COMPANY

All rights reserved. This book, or parts thereof, must not be used or reproduced in any manner without written permission. For information address the publisher, Appleton-Century-Crofts, Division of Meredith Publishing Company, 440 Park Avenue South, New York, N. Y. 10016.

6106–1

Library of Congress Card Number: 67–10442

PRINTED IN THE UNITED STATES OF AMERICA

E51076

Preface

As the pages of any standard textbook will testify, the amount of material in the field of learning has grown to unmanageable proportions in the past several years and, when such books attempt to describe even a major segment of the subject, they must resort to a summary style that sacrifices depth to achieve some breadth of coverage. The particulars of investigative procedure and theoretical development essential to a true understanding of the subject matter are largely lost in such a presentation. My aim in preparing this volume has been to provide a partial remedy for this state of affairs by presenting a collection of somewhat extensive treatments of a limited number of basic topics.

This book began as a conventional set of readings but gradually took on a somewhat different character. It soon became clear that no suitable papers existed in certain of the areas I wanted to cover. As a solution to this problem I wrote some new chapters myself and dragooned colleagues and former students into writing others with the result that about half of the chapters in the book have some previously unpublished content and, in turn, about half of these are entirely new.

Certain characteristics of this book developed from the fact that our journals presently enjoy the mixed blessing of receiving more publishable articles than their pages will hold. As a consequence, our editors have been forced to insist that papers be written in a style that makes them too brief for the uninitiated to comprehend. The assumption that such writing is not optimal for a book of readings intended largely for undergraduate and graduate students has found several expressions in the content of this volume: I have frequently chosen an older article where the style of communication is somewhat relaxed in preference to a newer and briefer treatment. In two or three cases I decided to reprint a dissertation rather than its published version when I considered the latter to have been too seriously damaged by the editor's red pencil. In other cases I have selected an article from an out-of-the-way journal which allows the author more space for his presentation than our more familiar standard publications.

One problem arising out of these decisions involved the citation of references. The variety of forms of citation suggested that I adopt the present-day APA style throughout the book and include all references at the end of the volume. I have done this but, in so doing, have had to deal with a host of problems raised by personal communications, articles cited as "in press" (which often seem to have been published under a different title, or in another journal, or not at all), and references that make sense only as an expression of *noblesse oblige*. The latter problem most commonly arose in articles from older APA journals where citation was by number. In these papers it was not uncommon to give a dozen references to document a single point. Translated into the new style of citation, by author(s) and dates, this sometimes required the space of a small paragraph. This fact, together with the consideration that the references in older articles frequently are irrelevant today, led me to edit many of them out of the presentation along with most of the other references mentioned above.

Having exercised my editorial prerogatives this much already, it was probably inevitable that I would express my prejudices even further. In any event I have done so, writing occasional evaluative footnotes, supplying summaries for some of the articles where there was none, and one seemed desirable, and, with the authors' permissions, revising certain articles extensively. Beyond this many of my own chapters, in part or entirety, are reactions to certain trends in psychology that distress me greatly. The reference here is chiefly to the growing willingness of theoretical psychologists to accept personal experience, especially personal perceptual experience, as a basic datum—as if such experience were somehow not a concept but a *thing*. I regard this notion as a uniquely unpromising mixture of foolishness and confusion. At various points in the book, but most directly in Chapter 5, I have restated the alternative.

In a rough way the sequence of chapters parallels the organization of my revision of Hilgard and Marquis' *Conditioning and Learning*. And the majority of the selections deals with topics that captured my interest during the preparation of that book.

I am very deeply indebted to Mrs. Edna S. Bissette and Mrs. Verble Roberts who typed most of the manuscript for this book and contributed their very special talents to solving the numerous awkward problems brought on by the decision to maintain uniform style throughout this volume. I am also indebted to the several publishers who granted permission to reproduce materials. The first footnote to each chapter published with such permission provides an acknowledgment.

G. A. K.

Contents

Preface   v

I. HISTORICAL FOUNDATIONS

1. Sechenov and the Anticipation of Conditioning Theory   3
   Gregory A. Kimble

   The life of Sechenov, 3. The general characteristics of Sechenov's psychology, 5. The concept of reflex, 6. The development of voluntary behavior, 12. Summary, 19.

2. Pavlov and the Experimental Study of Conditioned Reflexes   22
   Gregory A. Kimble

   Biography, 23. Pavlov's work on digestion, 26. The direct study of the conditioned reflex, 34. Summary, 42.

3. The Objectivist Climate: Bechterev, Watson and Tolman   44
   Gregory A. Kimble

   Excerpts from Bechterev, 45. Objectivism in American psychology, 50. Summary, 55.

4. A Functional Interpretation of the Conditioned Reflex   57
   Clark L. Hull

   Redintegration and experimental extinction, 58. Patterned stimuli and conditioned inhibition, 60. The anticipatory tendency and inhibition of delay, 64. The dilemma of the conditioned defense reaction, 66. Editor's summary, 67.

II. METHODOLOGICAL BACKGROUND

5. The Basic Tenet of Behaviorism   *Gregory A. Kimble*   73

   Fact and inference from fact, 73. Operational behaviorism and S-R psychology, 76. Summary, 80.

6. The Definition of Learning and Some Useful Distinctions 82
Gregory A. Kimble

Definitions, 82. Learning versus performance, 85. Reinforcement, 86. Practice, 87. Operations necessary to demonstrate learning, 93. Learning versus transfer, 94. Summary, 98.

7. Conditioning as an Artifact   Kendon Smith   100

Author's reflections, ten years later, 100. The argument and a specific instance, 103. Applications in other instances, 104. The pupillary response, 106. Tests and testability, 108. Related notions, 110.

8. A Magnitude Measure of the Conditioned Eyelid Response   112
Henry S. Pennypacker

9. Human Salivary Conditioning: A Methodological Study   117
Ben W. Feather

Review of human salivary conditioning experiments, 118. Purpose of the present studies, 124. Experiment I, 125. Experiment II, 136. Conclusions, 141.

10. The Concept of Reflex and the Problem of Volition   144
Gregory A. Kimble

Skinner's position, 145. William James' theory, 147. Summary, 153.

11. The Effect of Deafferentation on Instrumental (Type II) Conditioned   155
Reflexes in Dogs   T. Gorska and E. Jankowska

III. IMPORTANT THEORETICAL POSITIONS

12. Hull's Version of S-R Theory   Gregory A. Kimble   171

Habit formation, 172. Generalization and stimulus compounding, 181. Primary motivation and reaction potential, 183. Extinction and inhibition, 184. Oscillation and threshold, 187. Summary, 188.

13. The Determiners of Behavior at a Choice Point   190
Edward Chase Tolman

The role of theory, 196. Thorndike, 197. Hull, 199. Programmatic theory of the author, 202. Individual differences, 209. Vicarious trial and error, 211.

14. Formalization and Clarification of a Theory of Learning   218
Virginia W. Voeks

Four postulates, 219. Association, 219. Postremity, 221. Response probability, 224. Dynamic situations, 227. Definitions, 227. Some further theoretical implications, 230. Summary, 238.

Contents ix

15. An Introduction to Two-Process Theory   Gregory A. Kimble   239

16. The Relationship Between Success and the Laws of Conditioning   249
                                                          Harold Schlosberg

Contradictions in the literature, 249. Classical conditioning and S-S contiguity, 251. Instrumental conditioning and reward, 251. Applications of the distinction, 255. A consideration related to type of response, 257. Summary, 258.

17. An Experimental Approach to the Problem of Mechanism of Alimentary Conditioned Reflex, Type II   W. Wyrwicka   260

Historical and biographical statement by Konorski, 260. Associations between stimuli and motivational centers, 263. Associations involving the motor center, 266. Summary, 268.

IV. BASIC PHENOMENA AND PARAMETERS

18. The Role of Absolute Initial Response Strength in Simple Trial and Error Learning   Paul S. Siegel   271

19. Eyelid Conditioning as a Function of the Interval Between Conditioned and Unconditioned Stimuli   279
                                      Gregory A. Kimble and Bradley Reynolds

20. Effects of Conditioned Stimulus Intensity on the Conditioned Emotional Response   Leon J. Kamin and Ronald E. Schaub   288

21. Changes in Response Strength with Changes in the Amount of Reinforcement   Robert H. Dufort and Gregory A. Kimble   298

22. The Gradient of Delay of Secondary Reward in Avoidance Learning Tested on Avoidance Trials Only   Leon J. Kamin   308

23. The Dimensional Bases of Stimulus Generalization   320
                                                            Wayne O. Evans

Absolute versus relational theories, 320. Experimental studies, 326. General discussion, 334. Summary, 335.

24. The Generalization of an Instrumental Response to Stimuli Varying in the Size Dimension   G. Robert Grice and Eli Saltz   337

25. A Study of the Transposition Gradient   David Ehrenfreund   346

26. Prediction of Preference, Transposition and Transposition Reversal from the Generalization Gradients   Werner K. Honig   354

V. MOTIVATION AND REWARD

27. The Effects of Training and Motivation on the Components of a Learned Instrumental Response   *Richard Austin King*   383

28. The Effectiveness of Drives as Cues   *Clark J. Bailey*   399

29. A Quantitative Comparison of the Discriminative and Reinforcing Functions of a Stimulus   *James A. Dinsmoor*   408

30. Strength of Fear as a Function of the Number of Acquisition and Extinction Trials   *Harry I. Kalish*   428

31. Experiments on Motivation: Studies Combining Psychological, Physiological and Pharmacological Techniques   *Neal E. Miller*   440

   Some studies of hunger, 441. Studies of thirst, 452. Learning motivated by electrical stimulation of the brain, 456. Aggression and sex, 461.

32. Some Psychological Studies of Motivation and of the Behavorial Effects of Illness   *Neal E. Miller*   465

   When is a reward reinforcing? 465. Hunger elicited by electrical stimulation of the brain, 470. Variety of effects from ventromedial nucleus of hypothalamus, 473. Chemical coding in the brain, 475. A method for studying the behavioral effects of illness, 479.

VI. EXTINCTION AND THE VARIETIES OF INHIBITION

33. "Inhibition of Reinforcement" and Phenomena of Experimental Extinction   *Carl Iver Hovland*   487

34. Quantitative Studies of the Interaction of Simple Habits: Recovery from Specific and Generalized Effects of Extinction   *Douglas G. Ellson*   491

35. A Comparison of Two Methods of Producing Experimental Extinction   *Gregory A. Kimble* and *John W. Kendall, Jr.*   509

36. The Effect of Random Alternation of Reinforcement on the Acquisition and Extinction of Conditioned Eyelid Reactions   *Lloyd G. Humphreys*   514

37. External Inhibition of the Conditioned Eyelid Reflex   *Henry S. Pennypacker*   528

Contents

38. External Inhibition of the Conditioned Eyelid Reflex as a Function of 545
    the Temporal Locus of the External Inhibitor
    Henry S. Pennypacker and William R. Fowler

39. Does the Interval of Delay of Conditioned Responses Possess Inhibitory 551
    Properties?   *Eliot H. Rodnick*

40. Conditional Diminution of the Unconditioned Eyelid Reflex   567
    Gregory A. Kimble

41. Pathological Diminution of the Eyelid UR in the Squirrel Monkey: 572
    Some Anecdotal Observations
    Henry S. Pennypacker and William A. Cook

VII. RELATIONS TO COMPLEX PROCESSES

42. Thomas M. French on the Relationship Between Psychoanalysis and 581
    the Experimental Work of Pavlov   *Gregory A. Kimble*

43. Contributions of Conditioning Principles to Psychiatry   587
    Wagner H. Bridger

    The Pavlovian model, 587. Experimental evidence, 588. Conditioned versus unconditioned responses, 589. The Pavlovian signal systems, 591. First signal system activity, 592. Interaction of first and second signal systems, 593. Conditioning and psychopathology, 595. Pavlovian basis for therapy, 597.

44. Pain-Aggression   *Roger E. Ulrich* 600

    General method, 601. Shock-elicited aggression, 603. Other conditions that elicit aggression, 606. Other variables relating to pain-elicited aggression, 608. Generality of pain-elicited aggression, 611. Conditioned aggression, 613. Pain-elicited aggression and reinforcement theory, 614. Possible relations to human aggression, 621. Summary and conclusion, 621.

45. The Goal-Gradient Hypothesis Applied to Some "Field-Force" Prob- 623
    lems in the Behavior of Young Children   *Clark L. Hull*

    Choice of the shorter of two paths to a goal, 624. Effect of incentive magnitude, 626. The habit family hierarchy and the effect of direction of the goal, 631. Approach-avoidance conflict, 634. Summary, 638.

46. Attitudinal Factors in Eyelid Conditioning   *Gregory A. Kimble* 642

    Method, 642. The effect of instructions, 643. Ready signals and conditioning, 646. Attitudinal factors and schedule of reinforcement, 651. Development of attitudinal questionnaire, 655. Conclusion, 658.

47. A Stimulus-Response Analysis of Anxiety and Its Role as a Reinforcing   660
    Agent   O. H. Mowrer

    Evidence for the learnability of fear, 660. Freud's position, 661. Relevance of Pavlovian conditioning to the issue, 662. Biological utility of anticipatory reactions to signals of danger, 662. Anxiety as drive, 663. Anxiety-reduction as reinforcement, 664. Summary, 667.

References   668

I

HISTORICAL FOUNDATIONS

1

Sechenov and the Anticipation of Conditioning Theory

GREGORY A. KIMBLE

Although there were anticipations of the study of the conditioned reflex in earlier literary sources, the most important historical antecedents of conditioning are to be found in Russian physiology. The influential contributors were Ivan Michailovich Sechenov and Ivan Petrovich Pavlov. These men, both physiologists, placed an indelible stamp upon Russian interpretations of the conditioned reflex. At this writing, almost exactly a century after the publication of Sechenov's *Reflexes of the Brain,* Russian investigators of the conditioned reflex still begin their articles with a tribute to Sechenov. And Pavlov's word is still sacred in Russian physiology. The conclusion implicit in these facts may have a significance which extends far beyond the realm of science. The Russians do not easily abandon what they regard as a good idea.

THE LIFE OF SECHENOV[1]

Ivan Michailovich Sechenov was born on his father's estate in what is now the Middle Volga district on August 1, 1829. Sechenov was the son of a retired army officer who had married a peasant woman whose education he had arranged before they were married. Ivan himself was the youngest boy. His older sisters, after the Russian custom in those days, were taught French and German by a governess. Ivan acquired a fair mastery of these languages indirectly from his sisters. In addition, the parish priest gave him a smattering of Russian literature and grammar, Latin, and arithmetic.

[1] This account of Sechenov's life is based on Shaternikov's biography in Sechenov's (1935) *Collected Works,* which seems to have appeared in some printings as *Selected Works.* Another (undated) selection of Sechenov's writings (*Selected Physiological and Psychological Works*) is also available.

At the age of 14, Sechenov went to the Military Engineering School in Petersburg. After a conflict with the head of this school, he was transferred, in 1848, to military service, as an ensign of the Second Reserve Sapper Battalion stationed near Kiev. Military life did not agree with young Sechenov, however; and some 18 months later he retired from the army at the age of 20 with the intention of entering medical school at Moscow. After a year's preliminary study, he was accepted by the medical faculty. In medical school, Sechenov found the clinical courses dull but was attracted by the basic scientific courses, particularly comparative anatomy. During this same period Sechenov acquired some acquaintance with psychology through the study of Beneke's works, *Psychologische Skizzen* and *Erziehungslehre*. He became a medical doctor in 1856.

Following the completion of his course work in medicine, Sechenov went to Germany where he came in contact with Johannes Müller, DuBois Reymond and Karl Ludwig. In the laboratory of Hoppe-Seyler he began a study of the physiology of intoxication which he eventually submitted as a thesis to Professor Glebov in physiology at Moscow. Having collected most of the data for his thesis in 1859, Sechenov moved on to Heidelberg to work in the laboratories of Bunsen and Helmholtz. He developed an enormous admiration for Helmholtz which is reflected directly and indirectly in Sechenov's later writings, especially in his use of the concept of unconscious inference. It was probably at this same time that Sechenov met Mendeleyev with whom he became very friendly.

In 1860 Sechenov returned to Russia, presented his thesis to Glebov, and was appointed Assistant Professor of Physiology in the Medico-Surgical Academy at Petersburg. In this position, which Sechenov retained until 1870, he was extremely successful. Apparently he was a brilliant lecturer. His lectures typically involved demonstrations, as was the German practice, and an excellent use of illustrative examples. He was fired with enthusiasm for his subject and utterly convinced of the ability of science and reason to solve every problem of nature. Sechenov also seems to have had a special talent for stimulating young investigators to carry on research.

Early in his career (1862) Sechenov returned briefly to Western Europe, working in the laboratory of Claude Bernard where he conducted research on the frog involving neural centers which inhibited reflexes. It was probably during this period that his views of greatest interest to psychology took definite form. This work led, by analogy, to the concepts that all movements whether voluntary or involuntary are reflex in nature, that the inhibition of reflexes takes place through the arousal of neural centers through sensory stimulation, that thoughts are reflexes with an inhibited end, and that emotions are reflexes with augmented ends.

Upon his return to Russia, Sechenov published his most significant work, *Reflexes of the Brain,* in 1863. Some 10 years later, ideas developed in *Reflexes of the Brain* were expressed again in the important article, *Who Must Investigate the Problems of Psychology and How.* Similar concepts were developed in *The Elements of Thought* revised as late as 1901. From about 1870 until his death in 1905, however, Sechenov worked primarily on problems related to circulatory physiology. His contributions to psychology reside mainly in the three publications mentioned above, with occasional items of interest appearing in his more strictly physiological studies.

THE GENERAL CHARACTER OF SECHENOV'S PSYCHOLOGY

Given that he was a physiologist and that, writing in the early 1860's, he could not have had the benefit of the insights of Sherrington, Freud and Pavlov, Sechenov's dealing with the problems of psychology is remarkable. He seems to have been much in advance of his era and to view these issues in terms which have a very contemporary appeal. Sechenov was interested in truly psychological problems—the development of perception, memory, the acquisition of moral values, the nature of thought and voluntary control over involuntary behavior—all of which we recognize as matters of interest and importance today. On this point, Sechenov's views actually resembled those of modern psychology more than those of Pavlov who, some seven decades later proclaimed (as Sechenov had) that the problems of psychology *must* be subjected to physiological analysis. The problems considered by Pavlov, however, were much more limited than those of Sechenov.

For one thing Sechenov was methodologically sophisticated in a way that Pavlov was not. While Pavlov routinely failed to discriminate between fact and interpretation of fact, Sechenov never confused the two, clearly distinguishing between what was fact and what hypothesis. To illustrate this, Sechenov, in anticipation of Sherrington, had entertained what amounts to the concept of synapse. But he also commented that the notion of neural connection had never been verified directly and that as yet the microscope had been of no help in directly verifying a hypothesis which had to be accepted out of logical necessity. Similarly, Sechenov regarded language as a major obstacle to scientific progress. He complained about "ready made patterns of thought which are impersonated in speech."

Statements such as this last one touch upon a major commitment of Sechenov to the empirical basis of knowledge. He knew Locke's ideas and was much impressed by them, arguing, for example, that ". . . the principal fallacy of metaphysics is the unwarranted assumption that man can acquire knowledge of the outer world by means of pure mental speculation" (*Collected Works,* p. 377).

Sechenov was also a thoroughgoing empiricist in his interpretation of man's behavior, holding that all psychical life begins with stimulation of the senses and that what man is today depends upon his history of previous experience. These points were sometimes stated bluntly:

"The real cause of every human activity lies outside man" (*Collected Works,* p. 334).

". . . 999/1000 of the contents of the mind depends upon education in the broadest sense, and only 1/1000 depends on individuality" (p. 335).

In the same vein, Sechenov advocated a sophisticated use of analogy. Although the final appeal for him was to fact, he did not hesitate to interpret the facts of, for example, human psychology in terms of those of the reflex activities of the decorticate frog. As this implies, Sechenov found nothing at all to recommend contemporary psychological interpretations. The faculties of Will, Judgment and Habit appear in Sechenov's psychological writings but seem to be introduced only as familiar figures of speech inevitably to be translated into more mechanistic conceptions.

Sechenov was a mechanist whose match has never been met in Western psychology, even in the person of J. B. Watson. Sechenov was well acquainted with the science of his day, particularly biological science and chemistry, and he believed that the techniques of science could be used to explain all human activity. In this explanation there would be no need to appeal to vitalistic forces, impalpable faculties or mysterious psychic energies. The account, instead, would be couched in terms of reflexes and the effects of inhibition and excitation upon these reflexes.

THE CONCEPT OF REFLEX

Sechenov believed that all behavior could be understood in terms of the concept of reflex; by this he meant *all* behavior, voluntary or involuntary, simple or elaborate, episodic or of long duration, overt or covert, rational or insane. At the same time Sechenov asserted that human reflex behavior was so complex that the appropriate strategy was to begin with the study of animal behavior. This belief presumably explained in part the nature of his responses to the question, "Who must investigate the problems of psychology and how?" Sechenov answered: The physiologist and by purely physiological methods. Is it not clear (1) that psychology must deal with behavior which occurs only in organisms with brains (the study of which belongs to physiology); (2) that much behavior develops, from conception onward, from a purely material substratum; (3) that important aspects of behavior are inherited (and the study of inheritance is the province of physiology); and (4) that there are important similarities between psychic processes in man and neural processes (which can only be studied by the methods of physiology)? Moreover, Sechenov argued that history proved that the only route to success in science is along the road from simple to complex. If the problems of psychology are to be solved, it will be necessary for the physiologist to begin with the study of isolated reflexes in lower organisms.

Nobody will doubt that the study of psychology will henceforth fall into good hands, for modern physiology is characterized by its sound principles and good judgment. Being a science concerned with real facts, physiology will begin by separating psychological reality from the mass of psychological fiction which even now fills human minds. Strictly adhering to the principle of induction, physiology will begin with a detailed study of the more simple aspects of psychical life and will not rush at once into the sphere of the highest psychological phenomena. Its progress will therefore lose in rapidity, but it will gain in reliability. As an experimental science, physiology will not raise to the rank of incontrovertible truth anything that cannot be confirmed by exact experiments; this will draw a sharp boundary-line between hypotheses and positive knowledge. Psychology will thereby lose its brilliant universal theories; there will appear tremendous gaps in its supply of scientific data; many explanations will give place to a laconic "we do not know"; the essence of the psychical phenomena manifested in consciousness (and, for the matter of that, the essence of all other phenomena of nature) will remain an inexplicable enigma in all cases without exception. And yet, psychology will gain enormously, for it will be based on scientifically verifiable facts instead of the deceptive suggestions of the voice of our consciousness. Its generalizations and conclusions will be limited to actually existing analogies, they will not be subject to the influence of the personal preferences of the investigator which have so often led psychology to absurd transcendentalism, and they will thereby become really objective scientific hypothesis. The subjective, the arbitrary and the fantastic will give way to a nearer or more remote approach to truth. In a word, *psychology will become a positive science.*

Only physiology can do all this, for only physiology holds the key to the scientific analysis of psychical phenomena (Collected Works, pp. 350–351).

The concept of reflex which Sechenov proposed as containing the entire explanation of human conduct consisted of three elements: a sensory nerve, a central connection, and a motor nerve. The reflex begins with the firing of the sensory nerve through the stimulation of a sense organ and terminates in motor action. In his studies of decorticate frogs, Sechenov had been impressed with the machine-like dependability of the reflex: a given stimulus always seemed to produce exactly the same response.

The contrast between such stereotyped reactions and the variability of human and other behavior raised a problem for Sechenov and also suggested the general outline of an answer. The problem obviously was to account for the differences between the behavior of the decorticate frog and the intact higher organism. The crude answer to which Sechenov first arrived was that behavior is governed by processes at more than one neurological level.[2] Simple behavior, such as is observed in decorticate animals or a sleeping man, is mediated by processes mainly at the spinal level. The more variable actions of the intact animal or waking man involve, in addition, higher nervous centers whose function may inhibit or augment (excite) the reflex, producing a degree of undependability which is not found in the pure reflex. Thus, Sechenov argued, reflexes at the spinal level are always machine-like; those involving higher processes sometimes are, but more often are not. Could it be that the rare cases where the behavior of the fully awake, intact organism behaves in a machine-like fashion do exemplify the rule? Sechenov's theory held that this is indeed the case.

In discussing simple reflexes, Sechenov made other important points: (1) He noted that the reflex might or might not intrude upon consciousness, depending upon its mode of elicitation. Random eyeblinks, for example, are not conscious; yet a blink elicited by blowing into the eye is. When such consciousness of the reflex occurs, Sechenov believed it to be associated with the central element of the reflex. (2) Are reflexes inborn or learned? Sechenov believed that they could be either; but that it was often very difficult to tell whether a particular reflex was innate or "extremely habitual." (3) Reflexes (of the simplest sort) are always "expedient" or adaptive. For example, blinking, sneezing, and coughing all expel injurious foreign objects from the body. (4) Reflexes are controlled to a degree by their sensory consequences (feedback). Thus, walking depends primarily upon stimulation provided by contact of the feet with the ground and the weight carried by the leg, but also to a degree upon visual feedback. "Should an adult be deprived of [his motor] sense, as in the case of people suffering from so-called ataxia, not only will he be unable to make a single step when his eyes are closed, he will fall [although he] is capable of walking when they are open. This means that the normal regulator—the muscular sense—can be replaced by vision. And this replacement is possible in all cases when the eyes can follow the movement performed" (*Selected Works*, p. 482).[3]

---

[2] A conception that still dominates Pavlovian theorizing. See Konorski (in Jasper and Smirnov, 1960).

[3] This idea was also advanced by James some years later and still more recently by von Holst in the theory of reafference. See pp. 147 to 152, this volume.

The inhibition of reflexes

In his studies of reflex behavior in the frog, Sechenov had come to two conclusions which were of great importance for his later thinking: (1) That the inhibition of reflexes was an active process in which an inhibitory center exercised control over the excitatory pathways controlling the reflex. (2) These inhibitory centers are aroused by the stimulation of definite sensory pathways. Therefore inhibition is as much a reflex as the more positive excitatory mechanism.

To illustrate something of the mechanism of reflex action as well as of the inhibition of reflexes, Sechenov used this example. Suppose, with her consent, we perform the following experiment on a nervous lady: Warning her that we are about to do so, we knock sharply on the table with our fist. Although she is prepared for it, she starts at the sharp sound. Continuing the experiment, and maintaining the knock at the same intensity, leads to complete adaptation of the startle reaction. Now, and again warning the nervous lady of our intention, we increase the intensity of the sound. Again she starts; but again continuation of the experiment produces adaptation. From this simple experiment, Sechenov derived two basic principles of reflex action: (1) The essential condition for the elicitation of a reflex is strong stimulation. (2) Unexpected stimuli affect only the center for the reflex but expected stimuli excite, in addition, an inhibitory center, . . . "if a person is prepared to undergo any kind of external influence, this means that the influence will be counteracted, no matter whether it finally leads to an involuntary movement or not" (*Collected Works,* p. 270). This second point anticipates discussion of the typical relation between voluntary (prepared-for) and involuntary (startle) behavior to be introduced later.

The augmentation of reflexes

Presumably, it is obvious that, in Sechenov's opinion, the experiment described above would not have worked as it did had it been conducted following decortication of the nervous lady. In that event the stimulus would always have been followed in a machine-like way with a reflex of a predictable magnitude. The inhibition of the reflex required the presence of the cerebral cortex. Beyond this it is quite likely that the initial magnitude of the startle reflex in the nervous lady was somewhat greater than it would have been in a more stolid person. This is because Sechenov looked upon emotion as an intensifier of reflex action and seemed to regard fear (nervousness) as the most potent of such influences, although pleasurable stimuli were thought to have the same effect. Sechenov believed, on the basis of limited evidence, that midbrain structures were involved in such augmentation. In one study he and a colleague had shown that electrical stimulation of a midbrain area simultaneously with the stimulus for a reflex intensified the reflex.

The Sechenov reflex in the abstract

From the preceding description it is possible to assemble a schematic model of the reflex as Sechenov saw it. Such a model appears in Figure 1-1. In a general way that diagram tries to make these points: (1) Reflexes may sometimes be elicited by a relatively direct path leading from stimulus through a 3-neuron path to response. (2) Under the influence of other stimuli, however, the reflex may be augmented. (3) Under still other conditions, the reflex may be inhibited. These last two effects involve the contributions of higher neural centers.

Voluntary behavior as reflex action

Having made for simple involuntary reflexes the point that they were characteristically machine-like and dependable, Sechenov sought to extend this way of thinking to more complex voluntary acts and to destroy the usual distinction between voluntary and involuntary action. His most careful effort in this direction appears in *Reflexes of the Brain* which he originally wrote and attempted to publish (under the title, *An Attempt to Establish the Physiological Basis of Psychical Processes*) in a popular journal. The censorial department, however, found the conclusions of the article so objectionable that it was allowed publication only in a technical medical journal. Moreover, the same organization found the offensive conclusions so plainly anticipated in the title that it was changed to *Reflexes of the Brain*.

Sechenov began his analysis of voluntary and involuntary behavior by presenting what he believed to be the traditional opinion of the differences between the two types of act. The major differences were these:

1. According to traditional theory, an involuntary act always begins with an obvious external stimulus, but a voluntary act proceeds from no obvious stimulus. Indeed, more often than not there is no discoverable stimulus at all. The behavior is considered to be caused by a thought.

2. The attributes of involuntary reflexes are directly related to the attributes of the stimulus: their intensity is proportional to the intensity of the eliciting stimulus; their duration is almost exactly that of the eliciting stimulus; they occur as immediate reactions to the stimulus. But the attributes of voluntary behavior are independent of the stimulus. The intensity of the reaction may or may not correspond to that of the stimulus (if one can be demonstrated); duration may or may not be that of the stimulus; the response may occur at once or with a great delay.

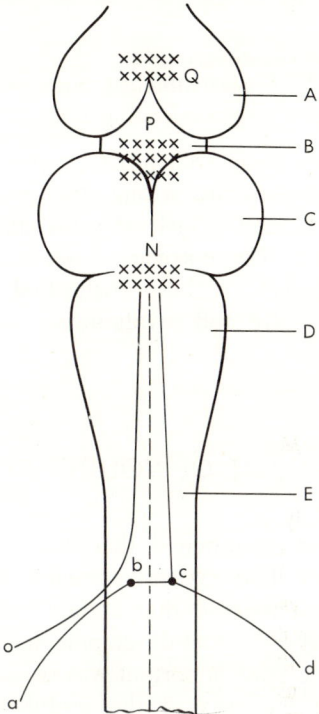

FIGURE 1-1. Sechenov's conception of the structure of a reflex (*Selected Works*, p. 45). Legend: A—hemispheres; B—visual chambers; C—corpora quadrigemina; D—medulla oblongata; E—spinal cord. In the text, Sechenov has this to say: "In the decapitated animal the reflex apparatus for each point of the skin consists of the cutaneous nerve a . . . entering the spinal cord and ending in cell b of the posterior horns; this cell is connected with another cell c, situated in the anterior half of the spinal cord and, together with cell b, forms the so-called reflex center; the motor fiber d issues from cell c and ends in the muscle. . . . As to the reflexes of the brain, they are effected by a mechanism consisting of the following parts: cutaneous fiber o terminating in the nervous centers N . . . ; path N_c along which the voluntary motor impulses proceed from the brain; and finally components c and d. . . ." P refers to an inhibitory mechanism activated by cortical mechanisms (Q).

3. Involuntary behavior is expedient, adaptive. But voluntary behavior is determined by the highest motives, sometimes even negating the instinct of self-preservation.

4. Involuntary behavior is mechanical, machine-like. But voluntary behavior proceeding as it does from Will and Judgment is infinitely flexible.

5. Involuntary reactions may be either conscious or unconscious, de-

pending upon the intensity of the stimulus. But voluntary reactions are always conscious.

6. Involuntary reflexes are grouped and operate together in unlearned ways determined by the neuroanatomical structure of the organism. But voluntary acts are grouped into cooperating units as a result of learning.

Except for the last two, Sechenov's proposal was that these intuitively reasonable distinctions are wrong, that no real distinction exists. Obviously he had set himself a task of some difficulty in assuming this bold mechanistic stance. The essence of Sechenov's view was that all human acts, including man's highest intellectual and moral accomplishments are, in fact, reflexive and involuntary.

THE DEVELOPMENT OF VOLUNTARY BEHAVIOR

We have already mentioned that Sechenov was very much interested in problems of development. Actually, the matter goes deeper than that, for Sechenov believed that certain behavior could be understood only after an analysis of the developmental history of the responses in question. Of these the most important was so-called voluntary behavior. Sechenov thought that the crux of the problem lay in the first point in the list of items contrasting voluntary and involuntary action: If it can be proved that voluntary behavior, after all, actually occurs in response to stimulation and not to thoughts, the rest of the list can be dealt with quickly.

"Is it really true that there is no sensory excitation at the basis of voluntary movement? And if there is, then why is it so difficult to discover this sensory excitation in typical cases of voluntary movement?

"Let me warn the reader that the answer will take a long time, because I shall have to begin with the analysis, not of the highest type of volition, but of its development from the cradle . . ." (*Collected Works*, p. 292). The answer does take a long time (45 pages) leading the author into such related problems as the learning of perception, the development of the ego and the acquisition of emotional control.

Man is born, according to Sechenov, without voluntary behavior, even as that term is developed in the list above. The infant has only a limited number of reflexes which tend to be elicited *en masse* by appropriate stimuli. The sensory capabilities of the infant are also minimal; this is partly because it has not yet learned to use its musculature in response to stimulation. At this point it will be important to note that much of what modern physiological psychology treats as maturation Sechenov attributed to learning.

Sechenov and the Anticipation of Conditioning Theory

In the case of seeing, for example, the infant has only a sensitivity to visual stimuli and a reflexive tendency to be attracted to brightly colored objects. Thus, when such an object appears in the visual field, the child will try to keep the object in view: "Therefore it is clear that without any judgment, i.e. quite involuntarily, the child will strive to keep the eyes in the position that gives the most pleasant sensation." The pleasant sensation, in turn, leads reflexly to the "widely irradiated" set of muscular movements. The child ". . . screams, laughs, moves its arms, legs and body; it is clear that the child is capable of reflexes from the optical nerve in all the animal muscles of the body" (*Collected Works*, pp. 293–294).

The concept of association

The importance of the previous point to Sechenov's theorizing was enormous. Bolstered by a concept of association, it implied the possibility of learned groupings of responses in terms of the stimuli evoking them. As a result of occurrences such as that just described, Sechenov believed that the child developed a wide set of associations to particular visual stimuli. Moreover, the same mechanism allowed for the establishment of of cross-modal associations. Thus, the sight of an object in the hand led to a complex set of associations in which visual, tactile and kinesthetic stimuli all became associated. It is probably fair to say that Sechenov's account of the establishment of associations was somewhat indefinite on the question of how the associated elements became related, but he was clear on the matter of what was associated: they were pairs (or chains) of reflexes.

An association is . . . an uninterrupted series of contacts of the end of every preceding reflex with the beginning of the following one. The end of a reflex is always a movement; and a movement is always accompanied by muscular sensations. Therefore, if we regard the association as a series of central activities, we may define it as an unbroken series of sensations. Indeed, the middle members of every two consecutive reflexes . . . are separated from each other only by movements; and the movements are in their turn accompanied by sensations. Consequently, *an association* [*is*] *a sensation* quite as much as any purely optical or purely acoustical sensation . . . ." (*Collected Works*, pp.: 312–313 italics added)

Diagrammatically what this appears to mean is this:

	Central	
Reflex I	*Association*	*Reflex II*
$[S_1 \rightarrow R_1 \rightarrow s_1]$	....	$[S_2 \rightarrow R_2 \rightarrow s_2]$

In short, what Sechenov advocates is a form of S-S connectionism and, as he says, the reflex is entirely sensory.

Although Sechenov does not provide a clear statement of what he believes to be happening at a neuroanatomical level when an association takes place, he is quite explicit on the necessary conditions. The most important is repetition. Sechenov speaks of ". . . the importance of frequent repetition of one and the same act for psychical development," and says further that "Repetition is the mother of learning, i.e., of the definition of psychical formations." Sechenov also added an interesting complicating element to his concept of repetition. As we saw above, Sechenov specifically stated that he intended no distinction (except in intensity) between an overtly elicited reflex and an association, memory, or image: "I repeat once more: *as far as the process is concerned, there is not the slightest difference between an actual impression (including its consequence) and the memory of this impression.* . . . *I see a man* because his image is actually pictured on my retina; *I remember him* because my eye has caught the image of the door near which he stood" (*Collected Works,* p. 315). On this basis Sechenov argued that the calling up of an association was just as much practice, or repetition, as the actual direct experience. Thus, in Sechenov's thinking, repetition and the strengthening of association could be overt and direct or covert and at the level of images. In what appears to anticipate the concept of generalization, Sechenov also believed that the elicitation of a related association could serve as a strengthening force.

The nature of memory

Sechenov's theory of memory, or the retention of associations, was patterned after the model of visual afterimages which he had learned about in Germany. The traces of experience, he said, are somehow laid down in the nervous system where they undergo a gradual fading and weakening unless they are strengthened by repetition. He referred to this as "the law of latent traces," an expression that seems to capture the meaning of the modern distinction between the storage of memory traces and their retrieval. Sechenov went on to deal with one question relating to the availability of these traces. Childhood experience, he argued, should be more available than it is if the only important consideration were repetition, for many of these experiences were repeated thousands upon thousands of times. Yet it is not so; the memories of childhood fade and disappear. Reflection suggested to Sechenov that this is because the traces are in no way organized. They are like a library in which the books are not catalogued. Finding a particular volume (remembering a particular experience) is nearly impossible although it is there in exactly the same form as it would be in an organized library (or nervous system) where retrieval would be much simpler.

Learning to perceive

The end product of the development of intra- and intermodal associations for Sechenov was the acquisition of perception as the adult knows it. The developmental sequence which Sechenov envisioned involved the establishment of an ever-widening associative (therefore, sensory) network. Illustrating with an example which begins with vision, Sechenov described the development of such perception as beginning with nothing more than sensitivity to light and the ability of the eyes to converge and focus directly upon objects at a distance. The exercise of these elementary talents leads next to a clear visual impression of objects and to appropriate motions of the hands and feet which bring the infant into tactual contact with objects. As we have seen, further experience develops a texture of associations such that the sight of an object elicits not only visual experience, but unconsciously, images of its tactile, auditory, olfactory, and other attributes. Clearly, what Sechenov had in mind was Helmholtz' concept of unconscious inference. Perception, for Sechenov, involved not only the immediate effect of the object, but also the images called out by association.

The emergence of ego

One of the important facts associated with perceptual learning is this: At times, one and the same visual impression will occur in the context of self-produced stimulation; at other times such stimulation will be absent. The context of stimuli (and therefore the collection of possible associations) is quite different when the child sees a toy in his own hand as opposed to the case in which he sees the toy in the hand of the mother. Sechenov knew that learning is capable of improving the differentiation among similar stimuli as is illustrated by the fact that the two-point limen can be improved by practice. Thus, the child is capable of learning to differentiate and does learn to differentiate between self and not-self, the former concept relating to stimuli produced in or by his own body or actions. This corresponds to the psychological concept of ego.

Emotional learning

As the reader will have anticipated, Sechenov interpreted emotional behavior in terms of reflexes and believed that modification of the emotions was a matter of shifting associations. In his treatment of emotions, he probably came closer to a modern conception of conditioning than at any other point in his theorizing. Again the historical, developmental, approach was central. We may illustrate Sechenov's thinking in this area by dealing once more with the reflex reaction of the human infant to colored objects. This response, it will be recalled, consisted of an instinctive turning of the eyes toward the object and a widely irradiated and vigorous motor response. This vigor marked the reaction for Sechenov as a reflex with an "augmented end." For Sechenov all reactions of the infant were emotional; that is, reflexes with augmented or intensified final motor elements. In the course of growing up, however, the emotions are modified and attenuated as a consequence of several important processes: (1) Although emotions are established and strengthened by association, they are also subject to a second law of repetition which is of greater importance: repeated elicitation of an emotional reaction leads to its dulling and disappearance. The only means of maintaining emotional behavior is through the experience of constant change. Thus, the child grows weary of colored objects and, by exactly the same process, the man and wife married for two years have seen their passion subside (sources of possible variation being exhausted) and replaced by a gentler, longer-lasting emotion. (2) As this last point suggests, emotional reactions are established by association (which accounts for the affection of the child for his mother or nurse) and are easily shifted from one stimulus to another. Thus, this passion evoked in the child by colored objects transfers successively to the colored picture of a knight in a storybook, to the experience of himself in the bright clothing of a knight, to the generalized actions of the self and finally to the abstract attributes of these actions—love of truth, human sympathy, self-restraint, and maturity of judgment. Thus what began as the uncoordinated reflex reactions of the infant to brightly colored objects evolves into the highest forms of human conduct. We must not lose sight of the fact that this evolution is, for Sechenov, an evolution of reflexes—nothing more. (3) Other influences lead to the inhibition of emotional reflexes. Thus a parent says, "Do not do this or that, otherwise this or that will happen." And the child learns to inhibit the action which is threatened, including the expression of emotion. Speaking in a very modern way, Sechenov goes on to say, "For the edification of the child, these admonitions are often accompanied by the infliction of physical pain; this burdens terribly the future of the child: under such a system of education, the morality of the motive,—which should alone direct the activities of the child,—is concealed by the much stronger feeling of fear, and in this way the sorrowful morale of fear is brought into the world" (*Collected Works,* p. 319).

Thought and emotion

The last example proved for Sechenov that reflexes of all types are subject to inhibitory action, a conception which leads to the idea that reflexes of all types may be initiated (thought about or imagined) but never carried to completion. Thus Sechenov referred to thought as "the first two-thirds of a reflex" meaning by this that the initial and central components take place but that the end (overt expression) is inhibited. Similarly with emotion, the occasion for, and the feeling associated with, an emotion may occur without overt reaction, because of the inhibitory influence of other circumstances. Sechenov recognized, however, that such control is difficult and seldom perfect.

The evocation of voluntary behavior

We have now reconstructed the psychological machinery which Sechenov employed to reduce volition to reflex. The mechanism may now be obvious: (1) The process of association, starting at birth, produces in the individual a network of associations such that the perception of one item calls up all those related items which repetition has left in the nervous system in the form of latent traces. (2) The association is between reflexes, a fact which means that an association may, unless inhibited, eventuate in behavior. (3) This associative elicitation of behavior usually happens without awareness of the associative process by a process of unconscious inference, although the proprioceptive consequences of an act may intrude upon consciousness. (4) Having developed a sharp discrimination between self and environment, the elicitation of the associate (image) may also elicit the concept of self and engender the false impression that the idea was self-produced. Thus Sechenov's explanation of voluntary behavior is that external stimuli elicit associations which, being indistinguishable from stimulation, in turn elicit behavior in a purely reflex way. The process also encourages the fiction that the behavior was voluntary. "All psychical acts without exception . . . are developed by means of reflexes. Hence, all conscious movements (usually called voluntary), inasmuch as they arise from these acts, are reflex, in the strictest sense of this word" (*Collected Works,* p. 316). ". . . the *initial* cause of behavior lies, not in thought, but in external sensory stimulation, without which no *thought* is possible" (*Collected Works,* p. 322, italics added).

RESIDUAL CONSIDERATIONS RELATED TO THE VOLUNTARY-INVOLUNTARY DISTINCTION

The problem that Sechenov originally considered turned on the question of whether voluntary and involuntary behavior differ in the nature of their causes. He finally arrived at the answer that no legitimate distinction exists, and that both forms of behavior, in the final analysis, derive from external sensory stimuli. There remain, however, the other distinctions between voluntary and involuntary behavior which must now be considered.

The first of these, that the physical attributes of the two kinds of reaction differ, requires no special treatment. All that is involved is the extent to which higher nervous processes participate in the reflex. Where the participation of such processes is large, the form of the reflex may be considerably distorted—augmented by emotion, inhibited completely, or delayed by the occurrence of a chain of associations—all reflex activities.

A second difference, that involuntary behavior is expedient, but voluntary behavior is sometimes maladaptive, Sechenov attempted to remove but did not do so very convincingly:

> .... You are compassionate but you cannot swim. You are walking near a river and see a person drowning. [Seemingly] without stopping to think, you jump into the water to help, and are drowned yourself. People [who do not understand the mechanism of voluntary acts] will say: this was an involuntary movement on your part; but that would be wrong. You jumped into the water because you were compassionate; consequently a thought [reflex produced stimulus for the act] must have passed through your mind before you acted (*Collected Works,* p. 279 n).

Sechenov's point, thus, was that such self-negating acts are subject to the same sort of regulation as ordinary reflexes and that an understanding of the history of the behavior would reveal a basis in involuntary, expedient behavior. But, as we have said, this argument is not overwhelmingly convincing, in part because it is not clear that the basic reflexes are expedient. Startle reactions, sexual reflexes, reflex freezing in fear, the knee jerk, and the achilles reflex are all involuntary reactions whose adaptivity can at best be demonstrated only for the species. In the last two cases, even this is difficult.

Sechenov handled the third distinction—that involuntary behavior allegedly is mechanical whereas voluntary behavior is not—by an argument that made voluntary behavior mechanical. The fourth criterial distinction (in terms of consciousness) remains to be considered. Sechenov's view on this point will be developed in the next section.

Voluntary-involuntary distinction

Although to his way of thinking, Sechenov succeeded in destroying the voluntary-involuntary distinction at the level of mechanism, he maintained the distinction in one form and sought to establish the basis for the separation of two forms of behavior as we tend to do in everyday life. In *Who Must Investigate the Problems of Psychology, and How,*

Sechenov reviewed the attempts at such classification which were current at his time. In turn he discarded a differentiation based on striate versus smooth muscular control and one based on a distinction between actions which are essential or nonessential for existence; but he accepted a distinction in terms of sensory consequences: "In a word, all those movements are voluntary acts which [are] accompanied by distinct sensations even if these movements are not directly visible" (*Collected Works,* p. 380).

The most important implication of this distinction was that it cut across lines defined by the topography of reactions because, by it, one and the same response would sometimes qualify as voluntary and sometimes as involuntary. What Sechenov accomplished by this was an account of certain well-known facts associated with learning. Everyone has had the experience of learning something so well that it became automatic, unnoticed and, therefore, involuntary. For Sechenov this meant that, as the reaction became more habitual, the stimulational consequences were somehow suppressed. Such considerations led Sechenov one step further, to the conclusion that all of what we call voluntary is also learned or habitual. "Does it not follow [that voluntary] movement has been acquired under the influence of circumstances created by life?" (*Collected Works,* p. 381). This strong conclusion (which would place much of what we regard today as inborn automatic reflex behavior into the category *voluntary* because of its sensory consequences) was not so illogical for Sechenov as it might seem. It simply meant that Sechenov was willing to regard most such acts as learned.

SUMMARY: SECHENOV'S CONTRIBUTION TO THE THEORY OF CONDITIONED REFLEXES

We now come to questions of special contemporary interest: What directly or indirectly has been Sechenov's influence upon modern work in conditioning and what additional contributions might it make? This type of question provides a projective device which allows different readers to place different evaluations on a man's impact. The following seven points seem most significant.

Sechenov's influence on Pavlov. A connection between Sechenov and Pavlov is easy to discern, although it is not so easy to say how much of this connection constitutes a direct influence of Sechenov upon Pavlov's thought and how much is merely a reflection of ways of thinking inherent in Russian culture. Pavlov himself, however, confesses to have been very much impressed with *Reflexes of the Brain.* Thus it seems likely that the influence was, at least in part, direct. In a sense what follows in this summary statement is a catalogue of the items where the similarities of thought are most conspicuous.

Sechenov's definition of the field of physiology. Several points are important here. First, there is the fact that Sechenov was willing to bring into physiology problems which hitherto had belonged exclusively to psychology. In fact, he argued that these problems *must* be treated as physiological problems if progress on them is to occur. Beyond this he advocated the analysis of psychological problems in terms of reflexes and proposed that all aspects of human conduct could be reduced to such terms. This wide interpretation of the value of physiological concepts remains imbedded in current conditioning theory.

In Sechenov's hands, however, the concept of reflex was much broader than is typical in physiology. Where traditional physiology tends to concentrate on events within the reflex arc, Sechenov stressed the importance of exterior influences. This was a part of a pattern of extreme environmentalism which characterized Sechenov's thought. Although the connection is remote, modern S-R psychology probably benefited indirectly from this aspect of Sechenov's approach.

Sechenov's stress on the scientific approach. Although it was couched in terms of an attempted justification of the idea that only physiology was "fit" to study the problems of psychology, it is important to note that Sechenov developed, and passed on to Pavlov, the concept of a machine-life organism whose activities could be studied by the techniques of natural science. In his advocacy of this view, Sechenov took the bold position that all human activities are amenable to such investigation—that none can be reserved for the antiscientific humanist.

The concept of association. This conception, of course, came to psychology from more than one source. Only Sechenov, however, made one of the main associated elements a movement (reflex) rather than an idea. It seems obvious that the Pavlovian idea of conditioned reflex would develop more readily from this conception than from the theory of association of *ideas* advocated by the British empiricists.

Excitation and inhibition. The reader will recall that Sechenov leaned very heavily upon these concepts, particularly that of inhibition, in his account of the variability of behavior. Similar emphasis upon the interplay of excitation and inhibition remain in Pavlovian theory and in its derivatives. Two additional points in which Sechenov clearly anticipated Pavlov were these: (1) He assumed that excitation and inhibition were closely related. The evocation of a reflex almost always entailed the mechanism of its own inhibition. (2) The assignment of these influences to the cortex (higher nervous activity) was of great importance and remains a dominant influence in contemporary Pavlovian physiology.

The historical-developmental strategy. This aspect of Sechenov's theorizing seems to require no comment other than: (1) in this regard Sechenov anticipated such later figures as Freud and Piaget and (2) here, more than anywhere else, Sechenov used a conception of reflex which is much more liberal than that entertained by most physiologists.

Specific contributions. In addition to the very general influences detailed above, Sechenov contributed a number of other ideas which we need only list: the concept of feedback as contributing to the control of reflex behavior, the idea that perception is learned, the idea of irradiation, the notion of the modification of emotion by shifting associations, the concept of orienting reflex ("adaptive locomotor reactions of the body which help to increase the sensations" [*Collected Works,* p. 423]), and finally a mechanism for the development of stimulus-stimulus associations which still figure in the physiology of the East.

There is little doubt that, had the writings of Sechenov been more accessible to the West, this early physiologist would have been regarded as one of the giants in the history of psychology.

2

Pavlov and the Experimental Study of Conditioned Reflexes

GREGORY A. KIMBLE

Years ago, there was a ~~little~~ fable which parents sometimes read to their children about how the birds learned to build their nests. According to this story, there was a time when only one bird knew how to make a nest; but its nest was a marvelous thing, carefully constructed and complete with roof. In due course the other birds asked this bird to teach them to build their own nests, and the bird who knew how agreed to do so. In their impatience to get on with it, however, not a single bird stayed for the entire lesson. Each, at some point, assumed that it had seen enough and departed to build a partial nest which it continues to build to this day. The situation of psychology, relative to the Pavlovian investigation of classical conditioning is not unlike that of one of the impatient birds. It has adopted a few simple Pavlovian ideas and treated them as if they were the entire discipline.

The reasons for the failure of psychology to incorporate more of the Russian work on conditioning are not hard to find. For one thing, not very many Americans know Russian, the language which originally contained most of the basic literature on conditioning. Second, judging from the intelligibility of available translations, there is also a form of cultural barrier to communication in that the Russians seldom present the kind of information a behavioristically oriented psychologist needs in order to "understand" a piece of research. The typical journal article begins with a tribute to Sechenov and Pavlov, states a problem in theoretical terms, gives a brief description of method and proceeds directly to an interpretation of results in terms of traditional Pavlovian brain processes. Such an article omits the details of procedure and the quantitative statement of results which our thoroughly introjected operational dicta demand of a scientific article. To the ordinary Western reader it is simply impossible to understand or believe such an article. Finally, there is the consideration that Pavlovian theory is complex. Incorporating everything contained in the theory without more organization than any available statement provides is not easy.

To a degree, these difficulties are not so great now as they were a few decades ago: (1) A considerable amount of Pavlovian literature is now available in translation. And the degree of redundancy in what is available suggests that probably almost all of the essential ideas can be ferreted out of such translated materials. (2) There has been some improvement in the degree to which the Russians provide us with facts, as we understand this term. The several colloquia and conferences in which Russian and American investigators have collaborated (e.g. the "Moscow Colloquium"; Jasper and Smirnov, 1960) have been particularly useful in this connection. Thus it now is possible to present an account of Pavlov's work in a degree of detail that was impossible a few years ago. This chapter attempts such a presentation.

BIOGRAPHY

Even before his work on the conditioned reflex, Pavlov's reputation in physiology was secure. He had done basic work on the circulation of the blood and the innervation of the heart. His work in the digestive system had won him international acclaim and (later) a Nobel prize. Considering Pavlov's work on conditioning, it will be of value to look briefly at Pavlov's biography and to review certain aspects of his work on the digestive glands.

There are several biographies of Pavlov available in English which range in length from a short autobiographical note prepared by Pavlov in 1904 to a much more detailed (365-page) biography by Babkin (1949). By all odds the most interesting are the latter book and a briefer biography by Asratyan (1949). The factual materials covered in these two volumes are so similar as to suggest that they were probably derived from identical sources. At that point, however, the resemblance ends. Babkin's book, *Pavlov, A Biography,* is a somewhat disorganized, sincere, scientifically oriented work which is highly laudatory, but nevertheless makes some effort at objective evaluation of Pavlov's contribution. Asratyan's small volume, *I. P. Pavlov, His Life and Work,* presents a contrast. The book is beautifully written (by the standards set by typical Russian translations), politically inspired and extravagantly positive in its tribute to Pavlov. It is a scientific, rags-to-riches biography which stresses Pavlov's struggle against the idealists and his ultimate confounding of the Western bourgeois reactionary scientists. Pavlov's advocacy of the inheritance of acquired characteristics is presented as an example of Pavlov's forward-looking environmentalist thinking. In spite of all this (in part, because of it), Asratyan's book is worth reading. Most of what follows in this report comes from Babkin's and Asratyan's books.

Pavlov was born in the Russian town of Ryazan on September 14 (old calendar), 1849. He was the son of a poor village priest and the eldest of eleven children, six of whom died in childhood. Pavlov seems to have acquired from his father a love of physical exercise and of learning.

Pavlov had learned to read by the age of seven; but he was seriously injured in a fall from a stone wall at about that age, and did not go to school until four years later. He attended the Ryazan church school and, upon graduation, entered the Ryazan Ecclesiastical Seminary, expecting to follow his father's footsteps and enter the ministry. There was, however, an official arrangement between the Seminary and the University of St. Petersburg which made it possible for students to enter the University before completing their work in the Seminary. Pavlov took advantage of this opportunity.

By his own accord, Pavlov became much interested during the 60's in natural science, an interest which he attributes to reading the works of the popular writer, Pisarev (in an article describing the work of Darwin influenced Pavlov particularly), Sechenov (*Reflexes of the Brain,* 1863) and G. H. Lewis (a Russian translation of *Physiology of Common Life,* 1859). Presumably it was this interest which led to his leaving the seminary and entering the university. At the university, Pavlov was particularly impressed by Cyon (Tsyon), professor of physiology who seems to have stimulated and to have guided Pavlov's first efforts at research.

Following his graduation in 1875, Pavlov continued his study at the Military-Medical Academy with the intention of obtaining the MD degree, not to become a practicing physician but to qualify himself for an appointment in physiology. At the academy, he served for two years as assistant to Professor Ustomovich and began the work on the circulatory system which formed the basis of several early publications and his dissertation. While still a student, in 1878, Pavlov took charge of the laboratory of Professor S. P. Botkin, a position which he retained for about 12 years. During this period, at least four important attributes of Pavlov's later work developed: (1) He acquired a life-long dedication to the proposition that the internal organs of the body are under neural control. (2) More specifically, he came to regard this control as involving excitatory and inhibitory mechanisms. (3) He developed the view that the function of the heart maintains a constant level of blood pressure within narrow adaptive limits, an idea which (a) reflects a Darwinian influence and (b) anticipates the concept of homeostasis. (4) He became impressed with the importance of studying the intact organism for long periods of time following physiological surgery aimed at the construction of fistulae or pouches designed to aid observation.

Pavlov received his MD degree in 1883 submitting a thesis dealing with the innervation of the heart. During the years 1884–1886, he spent two years in Western Europe working in the laboratories of Heidenhain at Breslau and Ludwig at Leipzig. At the time, Heidenhain was interested in studying digestion with the aid of an exteriorized section of stomach. He had actually developed an operation to produce such a pouch, but had not solved the problem of maintaining its nerve supply. Somewhat later, Pavlov perfected the operation which, in his laboratory, was referred to as the Heidenhain-Pavlov pouch. Work with this and similar preparations was a very important antecedent of later studies of the conditioned reflex.

In 1890 Pavlov was appointed Professor of Pharmacology at the Medical-Military Academy; and in 1891 he was invited to organize the department of physiology in the newly formed Institute of Experimental Medicine. In 1895 he was appointed to the chair of physiology in the Medical-Military Academy. It was during this period that Pavlov conducted his work on digestion. The first book-length report of this work appeared in 1897. An English translation was published in 1902 (revised and enlarged in 1910). Pavlov received the Nobel prize for this work in 1904.

In 1902, the same year that the English translation of *Lectures on the Work of the Principal Digestive Glands* appeared, Pavlov began his work on conditioning. By 1903, he had decided to devote himself exclusively, for the next several years, to the study of the conditioned reflex; in 1904 he described some of his work in a lecture given in Stockholm as Nobel Laureate. Pavlov continued this work to the end of his life.

Following the October Revolution of 1917, Pavlov's situation took a considerable turn for the better. Although he was critical of the revolutionists until the early 1930's, his international reputation as well as the nature of his teachings prevented reprisal. The Bolsheviks saw that Pavlov's concept of the conditioned reflex implied the possibility of radically retraining an entire people. In 1921, the Soviet of People's Commissars issued a decree which created a committee directed "to create as soon as possible the most favorable conditions for safeguarding the scientific work of Academician Pavlov . . . [to print] an *edition de luxe* of the scientific work produced by Academician Pavlov . . . to supply to Academician Pavlov and his wife special rations equal in caloric value to two academic rations [and] to assure to Professor Pavlov and his wife the perpetual use of the apartment now occupied by them, and to furnish it and Pavlov's laboratory with the maximum conveniences." Later Pavlov was provided with a special laboratory on which the Soviet government spent some five million rubles in the three years following Pavlov's death (Babkin, 1949, p. 165). In 1923, the work authorized by the decree was published under the title, *Twenty Years of Study of the Higher Nervous Activity (Behavior) in Animals*. The work was translated into English by Gantt in 1928, and published under the title *Lectures on Conditioned Reflexes*.

The last years of Pavlov's life were marked with success. He continued his work on the conditioned reflexes and extended it to include instrumental behavior and problem solving in anthropoid apes. Pavlov made his peace with the Soviet government, apparently about the time that Hitler came to power in Germany. In 1935, at the Fifteenth International Physiological Congress, he was proclaimed the foremost physiologist of the world. Pavlov died of pneumonia on February 27, 1936.

On February 29, 1936, the Russian government took steps to preserve the memory of Academician Ivan Petrovich Pavlov by issuing a decree which required:

... that a monument be erected to Pavlov's memory on one of the central squares in Leningrad. . . .

... that the name of the First Leningrad Medical Institute be changed to that of the Pavlov Institute.

... [that Pavlov's collected works be published] in four languages—Russian, French, English and German.

... that Pavlov's brain be kept in the Brain Institute in Moscow.

... that the laboratory and study of I. P. Pavlov . . . be kept as a museum.

... that Pavlov's widow . . . be given a personal pension of 1,000 rubles per month.

... that the government will furnish the expenses connected with Pavlov's funeral and the perpetuation of his memory.

Pavlov was buried on March 1, 1936, in Volkov cemetery beside the graves of Mendeleev and Pavlov's son (Babkin, 1949, p. 182).

PAVLOV'S WORK ON DIGESTION

It is now generally recognized that Pavlov's work on conditioning stems directly from his study of digestion (Kimble, 1961). What is perhaps not so well known is the degree of detail with which the process had been worked out in the earlier context. In addition, this work contains certain suggestions which do not figure prominently in Pavlov's later work, suggestions which seem to offer promising leads for investigation. This, in addition to the fact that the early work helps to place the later in perspective, indicates the value of at least a brief look at Pavlov's studies of digestion.

Although work in Pavlov's laboratory covered the entire digestive system, connections to psychology are most obvious in his investigations of gastric and salivary function. This account will, therefore, be limited to Pavlov's study of these two systems and their interrelations.

The study of gastric secretion

Experimental work on gastric secretions, with chronic physiological preparations, seems to stem directly from an early nineteenth century report by an American physician of a patient in whom a gunshot wound had created an opening directly into the stomach. In 1842, the Russian, Bassov, and in 1843, the Frenchman, Blondlot, independently thought of creating such a fistula surgically in lower animals. Both performed the indicated operation on a dog by opening the abdominal wall and inserting a metal tube directly into the stomach. The tube remained in place for a long time, allowing direct examination of the contents of the stomach. Unfortunately, the gastric fistula, by itself, was less valuable than had been originally hoped because (a) unless the animal had just eaten, little gastric juice came from the fistula; and (b) when substantial amounts could be obtained, the secretion was mixed with food and difficult to subject to quantitative evaluation.

Pavlov attempted to solve these problems in two ways. First, working with Madam Schumova-Simanovskaia in 1889, he developed a technique of severing the esophagus so that (a) food eaten by the animal did not reach the stomach or (b) when experimental purposes required, food could be placed directly into the stomach. As is suggested in Figure 2-1, this procedure made it possible to study the secretion of gastric juice, stimulated by the act of eating without contamination by food in the stomach. There remained, however, the problem of obtaining a valid picture of stomach activity when food was in the stomach. This problem led to the creation of the Heidenhain-Pavlov pouch, more commonly called the Pavlov pouch.

The manner of constructing the Pavlov pouch is illustrated in Figure 2-2. Approximately one-tenth of the stomach is isolated with nerve

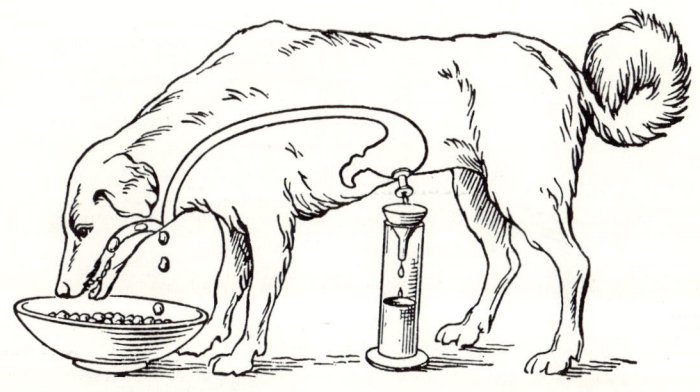

FIGURE 2-1. Dog with esophageal fistula and gastric fistula (Asratyan, 1949).

and blood supply intact, and formed into a miniature stomach with a fistula leading to the exterior of the body. In its action, this small separate stomach mirrors the function of the rest of the organ but, since food does not reach it, the problems left unsolved in animals with an ordinary stomach fistula do not arise. Gastric secretion can be measured, uncomplicated by the presence of food. The only question which may arise is whether the activity of the pouch does actually match that of the intact stomach. Pavlov made direct comparisons of the two forms of activity and obtained results which indicated that the action of the pouch was exactly like that of the rest of the stomach. Because of its smaller volume, however, the

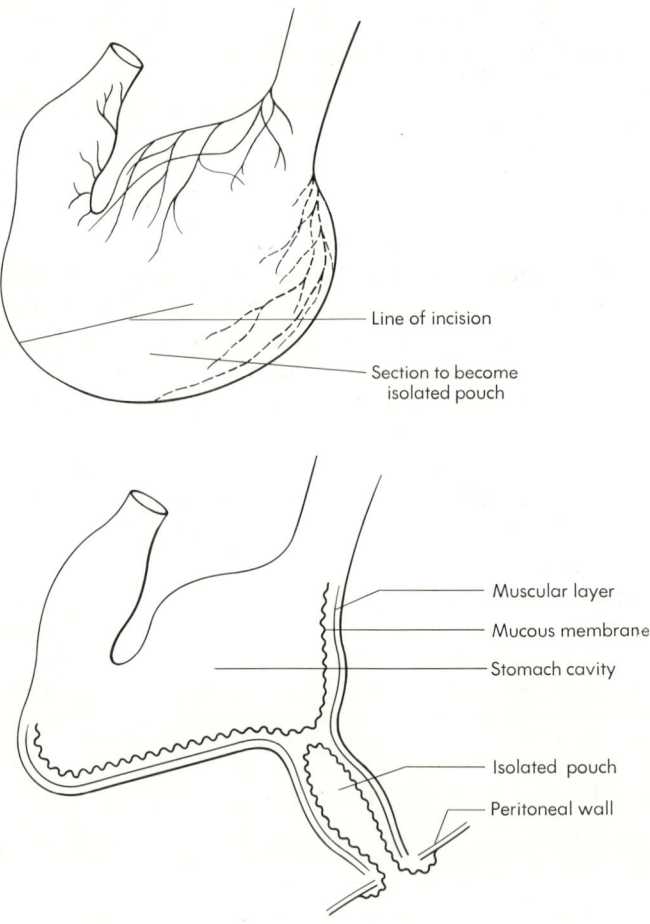

FIGURE 2-2. The Pavlov pouch.

pouch yielded only about one-tenth the amount of gastric juice secreted by the rest of the stomach.

In studies of dogs prepared in these ways, investigators in Pavlov's laboratory made a set of observations which reappear in conditioning studies. In general, the impressive fact about gastric secretion was the subtle, delicate and adaptive way in which it met the physiological needs of the organism: (1) the total amount of gastric juice secreted was found to be proportional to the *amount of a particular food eaten;* (2) there was, in addition, a variation in the amount of gastric juice which depended upon *the kind of food to be digested;* (3) the quantity of pepsin in the gastric juice was found to be directly proportional to the square of the rate of digestion; (4) the rate of secretion was a dependable decreasing function of time since eating (see Fig. 2-3, p. 32). This meant that large amounts of gastric juice were available just after eating, when the amount of food to be digested was large, and progressively less as the need diminished.

The study of salivation

Similar, but more complex interrelationships emerged from a study of the reflex of salivation. Different foods elicited different amounts and different kinds of saliva; other substances, such as acid and sand blown into the mouth, also produced salivation; in addition, the two major salivary glands (submaxillary and parotid) reacted differently to different substances. The picture which emerges from all of this is that of a much more complex, much more adaptive, adjustment of the gastric and salivary secretions to digestive requirements than had previously (or, in many quarters, has since) been recognized.

In addition to all of this, it became increasingly obvious to Pavlov that a "psychic" component was of unexpectedly large significance in the content of digestive secretions. As early as 1852, Bidder and Schmidt (Pavlov, 1910) had reported that the mere sight of food called out gastric secretion in the dog. In *The Work of the Digestive Glands,* Pavlov was able to show that this effect also occurred in the case of salivation and had all of the subtlety of reflex salivation. With one dog, Pavlov demonstrated that the animal salivated when he displayed food, or a familiar bottle of acid, or pretended to throw sand in the dog's mouth. The pretense of dropping pebbles in the dog's mouth produced no salivation. In the same demonstration Pavlov showed that the "psychic" reflex based on the different stimuli produced differences in the kind of saliva which could be detected even in casual examination (Pavlov, 1910, pp. 83–84).

Pavlov's early investigations also led him to the discovery, in their general form, of many of the most important principles of conditioning.

In *The Work of the Digestive Glands,* he formally relegated the concept of "psychic reflex" to the category of metaphor and proposed instead the use of the terms *conditional* (or *conditioned*) *reflex* and *unconditional* (or *unconditioned*) *reflex*[1] for what had previously been called "psychic" and "physiological" reflexes. In addition, Pavlov noted the following facts about conditioned reflexes:

1. The conditioned reflex based on food can be elicited only when the dog is hungry. It is not the animal's "desire" which is essential, however, but the availability of a strong unconditioned reflex to *reinforce* (Pavlov, 1910, p. 86) the conditioned reaction.

2. Repeated elicitation of the conditioned reaction by the presentation of food led to the disappearance of the conditioned response, especially if the presentations occurred in rapid succession.

3. This disappearance was not caused by fatigue, however, because allowing the animal to eat restored the reflex.

4. Moreover, the inhibition of one conditioned reflex did not necessarily arrest all condition reflexes. The inhibition of a reflex conditioned to food had little or no effect on the strength of a reflex conditioned to acid.

5. In addition to these "natural" reflexes, in which (using modern terms) the conditioned stimulus was the sight of the unconditioned stimulus, it was possible to form conditioned responses to neutral stimuli, such as a tone, presented simultaneously with food.

6. Sometimes the elicitation of a strong reflex led to the inhibition of a relatively weak one. For example, a response conditioned to the sight of bread might be completely obliterated by the presence of another dog in the laboratory room.

During this early period, Pavlov also developed the general outline of a quasi-neurophysiological theory of conditioning. Pavlov's supposition was that the intense activation of the neural center for, say, salivation served to make this center a focus of attraction for the activity of all other centers, a state of affairs which serves temporarily to "connect" these centers.

"The connection, however, is a loose one, easily interrupted and needs constant repetition of the associated stimuli to preserve it. But nevertheless, the establishment in this way of temporary relationships between external objects and important life processes, as well as the ease with which they are lost are matters of very considerable value to the organism" (Pavlov, 1910, p. 86).

---

[1] Thompson's translation actually used the adjectives *conditional* and *unconditional*. These terms are still preferred by the physiologists because they convey Pavlov's original idea of relative dependence upon, or independence of, the details of the environment somewhat better than the alternative expressions. Psychological usage of *conditioned* and *unconditioned* is so firmly entrenched, however, that there seems to be little point in launching a crusade against the practice. Accordingly, the psychological terms are used in this volume.

One of the facts which this theory accounted for was the demonstration mentioned in item Number 6 above, that the presence of another dog in the laboratory inhibited a well-established conditioned reflex. What this meant was that the neural center exerted by the presence of the second animal was activated more strongly than that for conditioned salivation, so that excitation was attracted away from the latter center toward the former, rendering the salivary center inactive.

The relationship between salivary and gastric secretion

A great misinterpretation of Pavlovian thinking, which appears to be widespread among psychologists, is that Pavlov viewed the organism as a disjointed aggregate of unrelated reflexes. Nothing could be further from the truth. The reason that Pavlov went to the extremes he did in the preparation of animals with chronic fistulae was that he believed that only intact organisms could be counted on to reveal the true nature of the physiological functioning of the organism. Acute preparations or animals in pain, according to Pavlov, gave distorted reactions warped by the effect of a variety of inhibitory mechanisms. Moreover, Pavlov's research had indicated that many of the internal organs were innervated by branches of the same nerve and thus would be expected to react together. Beyond this, evidence accumulated rapidly that reactions in one organ had an influence upon those of other organs. An excellent example of this is provided by the influence of ingestive reactions upon gastric secretion.

The point of departure for this line of investigation, again, is to be found in the work of Bidder and Schmidt who had demonstrated that a dog will secrete gastric juice at the mere sight of food. This demonstration raises a basic question: Since it is known that the sight of food also produces salivation, is the production of salivation the condition essential to the stimulation of gastric secretion? In one of the lectures in *The Work of the Digestive Glands,* Pavlov began by showing that salivation produced by acid, pepper or sand in the mouth was not associated with gastric secretion, whereas salivation produced by the sight of food was. This led Pavlov to the generalization that substances which the animal would normally accept will produce gastric secretion; whereas those which the animal normally rejects will not.

In search of a better understanding of the cases in which there was an association between salivation and gastric secretion, Pavlov turned to the study of dogs prepared with gastric and esophageal fistulae, and studied the effect of sham feeding (fictitious feeding, imaginary feeding) upon gastric activity. In sham feeding the food which the animal eats does not reach the stomach. This makes it possible to determine the influence of the act of eating upon the secretion of gastric juice. Two rather different kinds of evidence suggest that the effect is great.

The first of these demonstrations involved a comparison of the effect of gastric secretion of the complete act of eating, sham feeding and direct placement of food in the stomach. The data obtained in this comparison appear in graphic form in Figure 2-3. Note that the left-hand panel of Figure 2-3 shows the course of gastric output for four hours after a meal of 200 grams of meat. The next two panels present the same data for the effect of the direct placement of 150 grams of meat directly into the stomach and of sham feeding. The fourth panel shows the effects obtained when the separate effects of direct placement and sham feeding are added (experiments of Khizhin and Lobasov. Pavlov, 1910, p. 100). Two conclusions appear to be warranted by these data: (1) The total amount of salivation consists of two components contributed by influences localized in the mouth and in the stomach. (2) The magnitudes of the two separate influences are about equal.

The second line of evidence mentioned above involved placing food directly into the stomach without the subject's knowledge, perhaps during sleep. The food was strung onto a cord so that any undigested food could be retrieved and weighed later on. Then different animals were allowed to sham feed or not, the loss in weight of the food after a constant period of time providing a measure of the influence of sham feeding upon digestion. In one demonstration of this sort on two dogs, 100 grams of food were placed in the stomach of each. After 90 minutes, 94 grams remained

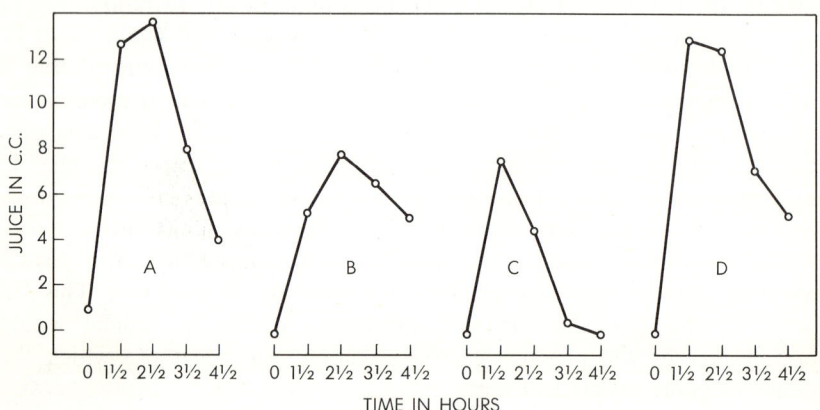

FIGURE 2-3. Gastric secretion as a function of time. Panel A depicts the pattern of secretion after normal feeding. Panels B and C, respectively, show the pattern of secretion after placing food directly into the stomach and after sham feeding. Panel D is the sum of the values in panels B and C. The similarity of the relationships in panels A and D suggested that total secretion normally consists of two additive components. Data from Pavlov (1910).

in the stomach of the control animal; only 70 grams remained in the animal which had been sham fed. In addition to demonstrating the importance of feeding upon digestion, this demonstration went against a then popular theory that the stomach was stimulated to secrete by the physical stimulation of food, a position which Pavlov referred to as "an unfortunate misconception degenerated into a stubborn prejudice" (Pavlov, 1910, p. 104).

Organismic variables that influence conditioning. Finally, in this brief account of Pavlov's early work, it seems important to note that anticipations of the later emphasis upon physiological types are already detectable in Pavlov's observations of the conditions which determined the success of these experiments. We have already seen (1) that Pavlov recognized the importance of hunger as an essential condition for the demonstration of the important facts of digestion, and (2) that he regarded general health as a precondition for the determination of the exact nature of the digestive process. This led to the heavy emphasis upon chronic as opposed to acute physiological preparations in the Pavlovian studies. Two other kinds of organism-centered variables to which Pavlov paid practical attention, in the sense that they played an important part in the planning of experiments, were these: (3) Pavlov believed that there were important differences in the temperaments of animals. Some he said were "Positively indifferent" and poor subjects; it was necessary to use "impressionable and excitable" animals for success in the experiment. (4) Finally Pavlov said that one "has to reckon with the understanding and cunning of the dog" (Pavlov, 1910, p. 91). For example, it was important not to allow the animal to get the impression that it would be tricked or disappointed; otherwise the regularities in the animal's behavior would disappear. This last set of variables refers to a collection of "attitudes" developed within the experimental setting. It seems particularly important to call attention to them, because (except for studies of human conditioning) almost no attention has been paid to them in experiments or theories of conditioning.

The reason for the neglect of such considerations is not hard to find. For the Russians, such attitudinal states would be difficult to deal with because they suggest mentalism and dualism; for the Americans they smack of the anthropomorphic. Yet there is nothing intrinsically wrong with the postulation of such intervening variables because there is nothing in principle which prevents their translation into operational terms. To illustrate, in their discussions of their experimental studies, the Pavlovians very frequently note that an experimental subject entered the conditioning chamber with apparent reluctance or eagerness. Such evidence, and other like it, might easily be used to define the "attitudes" of animal subjects toward an experiment. As we shall see later, such matters probably cannot be ignored in the study of conditioning.

THE DIRECT STUDY OF THE CONDITIONED REFLEX[2]

As the previous sections show, Pavlov's work on conditioning had a direct historical connection with his earlier research. Much the same can be said of his theoretical ideas. They, too, grew directly out of his conceptions of the proper interpretation of other physiological phenomena. The major difference was that, in the study of the conditioned reflex, Pavlov turned to what he regarded as the direct study of brain function which had played merely a contributing role in connection with other physiological processes.

Looked at in one way, the Pavlovian conception of operation of the cerebral hemispheres which emerged from these studies is fairly simple; it has been criticized in the past as too simple. There are only four major theoretical concepts (temporary connection, excitation, external inhibition and internal inhibition) and the properties possessed by these. Looked at in another way, Pavlovian theory is exceedingly subtle and complex and might be criticized, in common with Freudian theory, as possessing the flaw of having an *ad hoc* explanation for almost all behavior and predictive power for almost nothing. This latter statement is nearer the truth than the statement that Pavlovian theory is overly simple. For the purpose of completing a presentation of Pavlov's contribution, we turn now to a brief discussion of the major aspects of Pavlovian experimentation and theory on the topic of conditioned reflexes.

Temporary connection

In *Work and the Brain,* Frolov (n. d.) describes the Pavlovian theory of conditioning in simple terms:

"A conditioned reflex can be formed by combining an indifferent stimulus, say the flash of an electric bulb with an unconditioned stimulus, for instance, food. In this experiment the stimulation goes from the retina along the afferent nerve to the visual center in the cerebral hemisphere and a focus of visual excitation is formed in the cells of the visual center. Since this is accompanied by feeding, another stronger focus of excitation is produced in the animal's nervous system, the nervous system being diverted from the weak center of excitation to the stronger, the dominant one. Gradually, in the course of several days, or even sooner, a *path* between the two centers is paved, and a temporary contact, a conditioned salivary reflex, is formed" (pp. 71–72).

[2] It seems unnecessary, in this chapter, to deal with the standard conditioning procedures or with well-known phenomena. A brief review of these materials can be found in Kimble (1961, especially pp. 44–108).

In more general terms, Pavlov's concept of the ultimate nature of conditioning was that intense (*dominant*) activity (excitation) set up in one neural center by the unconditioned stimulus (US) attracted to itself the weaker activity (excitation) initiated by other stimuli present at approximately the same time. Later on, he postulated that the activity in these two centers *irradiated* and met somewhere in between the two centers. In either case the essential idea is that, under these circumstances, a temporary connection is formed which makes it possible for these other (conditioned) stimuli, presented alone, to arouse excitation in the center corresponding to the unconditioned stimulus and, consequently, the response.

Paramount among the properties of the conditioned response was that Pavlov viewed the connection as *temporary*. Unless the CS was consistently reinforced by the US, the connection was lost. Second, Pavlov thought of the connection as occurring at more than one physiological level. Thus, the connection was not just one cortical connection, as much Pavlovian writing appears to suggest. Subcortical pathways were always implicated and, in addition, the exact cortical locale of the highest connections depended upon the kind of association involved. In particular, connections involving the *second signalling system* (language) were considered to occur in the frontal regions of the cortex.

Figure 2-4, adopted from Asratyan (1953), presents one version of the Pavlovian theory of the development of conditioned connections. Note

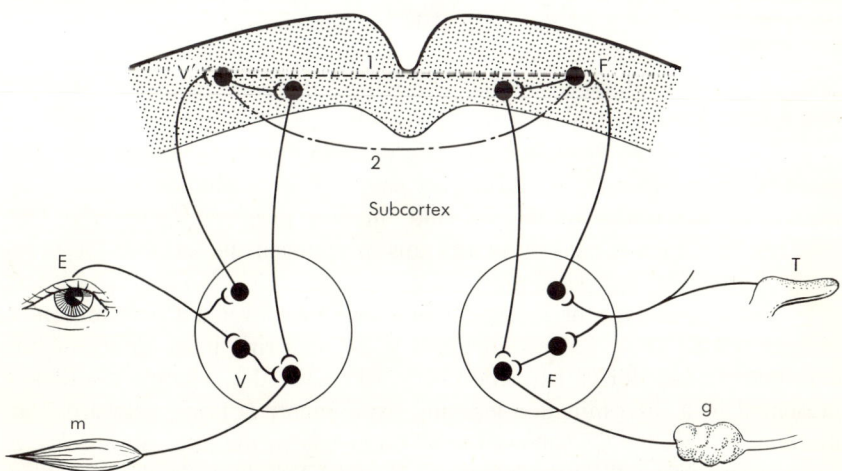

FIGURE 2-4. Pavlov's conception of the conditioned salivary reflex. Note especially that: (1) the conditioned reflex connects two elementary reflexes and (2) the connection occurs at cortical and subcortical levels which are numbered 1 and 2, respectively.

that the association is between two *reflexes,* as Sechenov had originally proposed (p. 13). One reflex is an orienting reflex involving, in the example shown, two separate pathways from eye to muscle, for example neck muscle. One of these two pathways is cortical, the other subcortical. Similar sets of pathways are involved in the reflex elicited by the US, in this case the salivary reflex from tongue to salivary gland. Note finally that the conditioned connection also occurs, theoretically, at two levels, cortical and subcortical.

Excitation and inhibition

Although they are separate hypothetical entities, excitation and inhibition are so closely related in Pavlovian theory that there is little point in attempting to treat them separately. Indeed Pavlov himself regarded the two processes in this way. He often referred to them metaphorically as the Greek god, Janus, whose two faces looked simultaneously in opposite directions. Thus excitation and inhibition are inseparably connected in Pavlovian thought; but they have opposite implications for behavior. Excitation tends to evoke the reflex; inhibition tends to restrain it.

For a variety of reasons, Pavlov assumed the existence of two forms of inhibition. The first is *external inhibition* which Pavlov also called *passive inhibition* or *unconditioned inhibition*. The prototypical example of the function of this type of inhibition is provided by the case in which a novel stimulus presented just before, or during, a conditioning trial prevents the occurrence of the CR. This phenomenon (*external inhibition*) supplied the name for the first type of inhibition. The mechanism for the occurrence of conditioned inhibition involved the concept of the *orienting reflex*. The presentation of a novel stimulus was assumed to arouse the neural center for an "exploratory" or "orienting" reflex. This arousal, depending on its strength, would attract some of the excitation normally attracted by the center of the CS and, in that measure disrupt the CR. Modern Pavlovian theorizing makes this mechanism the basis of the processes of attention and perception.

The second type of inhibition develops whenever a CS is presented without a US. Thus, Pavlov imagined it as occurring in a variety of circumstances: (a) during extinction; (b) whenever the negative stimulus is presented in a discrimination-learning experiment; (c) in backward conditioning, where the CS follows the US; and (d) in the interval of delay in experiments where the time between CS and US is long. In this last case, the CS is nonreinforced for a portion of its duration. In all of these cases, what develops is more than just a tendency not to respond. It is, rather, an active blocking of the response. For this reason, Pavlov sometimes called this form of inhibition *active inhibition;* because of its dependence upon a sequence of nonreinforced trials, he called it *conditioned inhibi-*

tion; to distinguish it from the first type of inhibition which depended upon a novel external stimulus, the second type of inhibition is most frequently called *internal inhibition*. It is important to note that Pavlov regarded internal inhibition as (a) involving a temporary connection which was (b) just as fragile as the connection of excitatory elements. Where nonreinforcement destroys the excitatory connection, reinforcement destroys the inhibitory one.

Properties of excitation and inhibition

The two most important properties of excitation and inhibition are theoretically shared by the two processes. They are (a) irradiation and concentration and (b) mutual induction. To illustrate the irradiation and concentration of inhibition, suppose that a dog is conditioned to salivate in equal strength to a tactile stimulus applied to any of three points on the body (those indicated as points b, c and d in Figure 2-5) but not to respond to similar stimulation applied to the shoulder (point a in Figure 2-5). This would be accomplished by following stimulation of points b, c and d with reinforcement, but withholding reinforcement following stimulation at point a. Now suppose that the following experiment is performed: stimulation at point a on trial N is followed by stimulation at point b, c, or d on trial N + 1. The independent variable in the experiment is the temporal separation of trials N and N + 1. According to the results of Pavlovian conditioning experiments, the strength of the tendency to re-

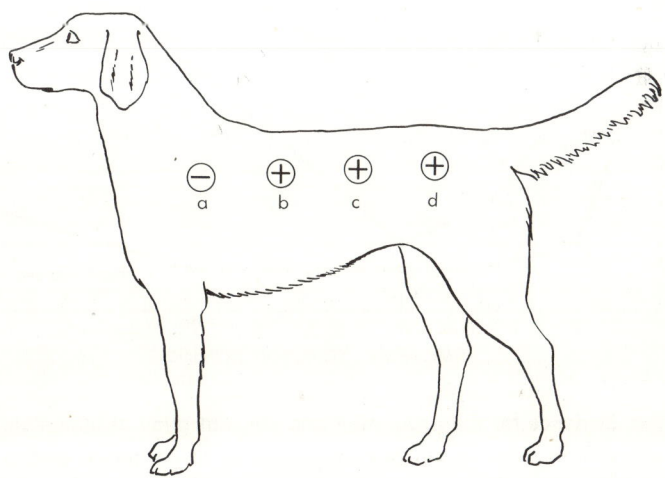

FIGURE 2-5. The location of stimuli for the study of the irradiation and concentration of excitation and inhibition. (Asratyan, 1949).

spond to the previously reinforced stimuli shows a tendency, at first to *decrease* (illustrating the spread or irradiation of inhibition) followed by a return to normal excitability (indicating the subsequent return or concentration of inhibition on the point of its initiation).

This sequence of events is illustrated in Figure 2-6 with data from an experiment by Ivanov-Smolensky (Konorski, 1948). An exactly comparable picture is assumed to hold for excitation; but to demonstrate it, the experiment would have to be the reverse of that suggested in Figure 2-5. That is, point a would be reinforced and points b, c and d nonreinforced. Then the tests would consist of stimulating one of these latter points at various times after stimulation at point a, which in this example would be positive. A demonstration of the irradiation of excitation would consist in showing an initial tendency for stimulation at points b, c or d to elicit a CR. Theoretically this would be followed by a return to an inhibitory state indicating the concentration of excitation. It should be noted specifically that the data which support the postulation of irradiation and concentration are all behavioral data, not neurophysiological as the reified concepts imply.

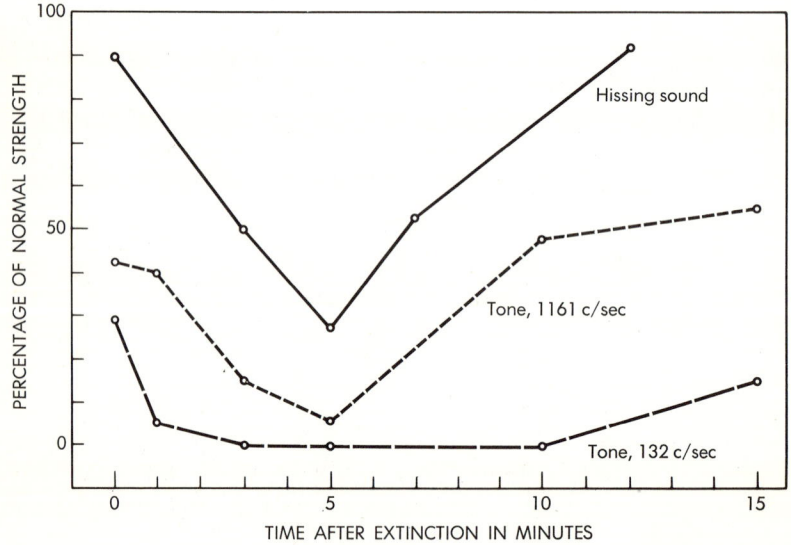

FIGURE 2-6. Evidence for the irradiation and concentration of inhibition. Following the conditioning of a salivary response to three tones and a hissing sound, the CR to the lowest tone was extinguished. Tests were then carried out with the other stimuli. Note that the degree of inhibition depends upon the similarity of the test stimulus to the CS and that the inhibitory effect increases and then decreases with time.

The concept of *induction*, stated briefly, is that either mechanism, excitation or inhibition, leaves in its wake the opposite process and also produces this opposite process in neighboring cortical regions. Thus immediately following arousal the neural centers corresponding to the CS should be inhibitory, as should those corresponding to neighboring stimuli. Identical effects are assumed to operate in connection with irradiation. The wave of excitation emanating from the center representing a positive CS is followed by an induced wave of inhibition; the wave of inhibition spreading from the center corresponding to a negative CS is followed by an induced wave of excitation. A diagrammatic representation of these ideas appears in Figure 2-7 (Frolov, p. 87).

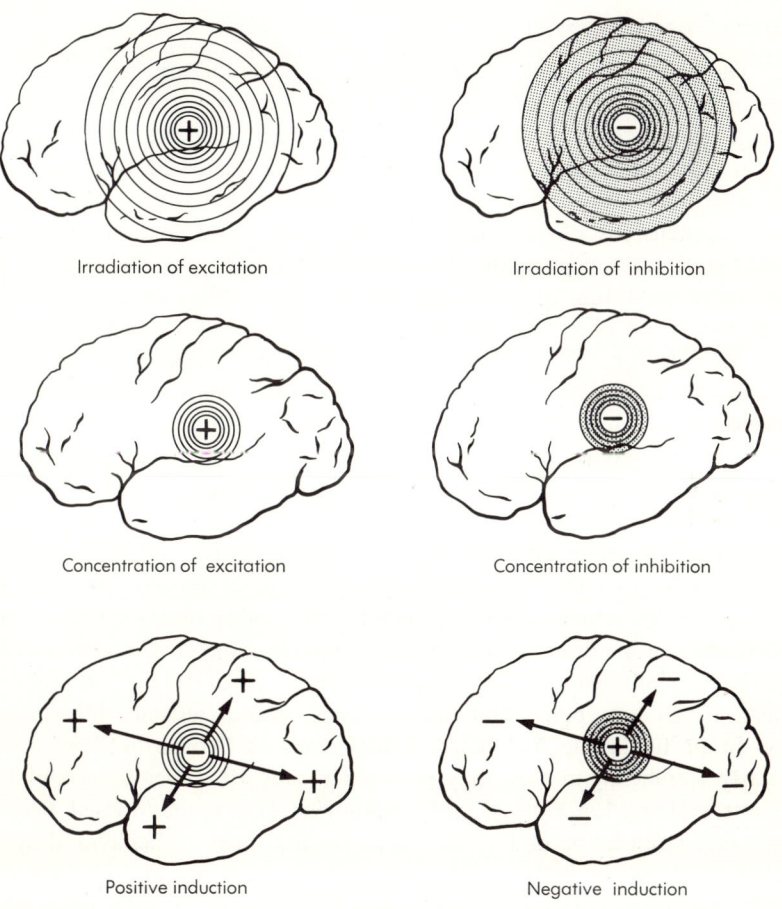

FIGURE 2-7. Schematic representations of irradiation, concentration and induction.

Pavlov's theory of irradiation and, to a lesser extent, induction depends intimately upon his view of the *cortical mosaic*. This concept is that there is a point-for-point correspondence between physical stimuli and areas of the brain. Stimuli that are very similar are thought to be represented by closely adjacent cortical areas. On this basis, stimuli similar to any reference stimulus should be affected more strongly by processes such as irradiation and induction than by very different stimuli. Konorski (1948, p. 12) has pointed out the important consequences of this idea for conditioning phenomena. In general, the more similar a test stimulus is to an inhibited stimulus, the stronger and more lasting should be the effect upon it.

Types of nervous system

The general concepts of excitation and inhibition are included in one more important aspect of Pavlovian theory. Pavlov, as we have already seen, was impressed at the outset of his study of conditioning with individual differences in his experimental subjects. Later he developed this idea somewhat more formally, hypothesizing the existence of three fundamental dimensions of variation: (1) the absolute strength of the basic neural processes of excitation and inhibition, (2) the balance of the strength of excitation to inhibition, and (3) the lability of excitation and inhibition in the particular nervous system. Obviously these three dimensions provide for the existence of a great range of individuality among animals if one believes (a) that many gradations may exist within each dimension and (b) that the values within each are uncorrelated. In practice, however, Pavlov tended to limit his discussion to a small number of types, often those corresponding to Hippocrates' four types of temperament: choleric, phlegmatic, sanguine and melancholic.

Before outlining the hypothetical neural dynamics of these types, it will be useful to consider more general aspects of Pavlov's theory. Nowhere is Pavlov's view of the significance of conditioning expressed more clearly than in his discussion of types of nervous system. Considerably before the development of the typology presented above, Pavlov had proposed others based on behavioral observations made outside the laboratory. In particular he had believed that signs of "cowardice" were particularly significant in that they were diagnostic of a weak or inhibitory nervous system. Later these early typologies had to be revised because dogs considered to be of the same type on the basis of behavioral symptoms turned out to be very different in their reactions to various conditioning procedures. For example, it was found that cowardly dogs might have either strong or weak nervous systems. This led Pavlov to begin to develop a distinction between "character" and "temperament." The former he regarded as the result of experience or "upbringing" whereas the latter referred to the true strength, equilibrium, and mobility of the nervous processes. Cowardice, in these terms, was a symptom, not of temperament, but of character. It is clear, of course, that, having arrived at this distinction, Pavlov would be most interested in the dog's temperament because of its close relationship to physiological functioning.

The distinction in question received empirical support from a study by Virzhikovsky and Mayorov, one of the early investigations of the effect of early experience upon later behavior. Virzhikovsky and Mayorov divided the puppies from two litters into two groups of four each. One group was confined to cages from birth. The other was reared in a free environment. After two years it was found that dogs in the confined group were all cowardly (had strong "passive-defensive reflexes") whereas the others did not. None of the cowardly dogs was of a weak, inhibitory type, however, when tested in conditioning experiments. Thus Pavlov's new view that cowardice was a character trait rather than a true symptom of a weak nervous system was confirmed.

With this type of experimental support for his new theory available, Pavlov set out to discover the identifying marks of the three important neural processes as they appeared in the conditioning situation. Some of the symptoms considered to be diagnostic of these processes were as follows. (1) The *strength* of the nervous system was revealed by the ease with which positive (excitatory) and negative (inhibitory) conditioned reflexes could be elaborated. (a) Strength of the excitatory process was associated with the easy establishment of a positive CR, especially to strong conditioned stimuli. (b) Strength of the inhibitory mechanism was associated with the easy development of conditioned inhibition in extinction, a long delayed CR or differentiation. Pavlov looked specifically upon the strength of the nervous system as the total of the strengths of the excitatory and inhibitory processes. (2) *Equilibrium* depended upon the relative strengths of the excitatory and inhibitory mechanisms. (3) *Mobility* was exhibited by the ease with which a given CS could be transformed from positive or excitatory to negative or inhibitory and back again.

In the description of types of temperament, Pavlov relied much more upon the criteria of strength and equilibrium than he did upon mobility. The four types of nervous systems which Pavlov believed to be most common, identified in terms of Hippocrates' categories, were as follows: (1) *melancholic*—weak both in inhibitory and excitatory processes, so weak that considerations related to equilibrium and mobility were of no importance; (2) *choleric*—strong, but unequilibrated, excitatory processes being dominant; (3) *phlegmatic*—strong and equilibrated with calm external behavior; (4) *sanguine*—strong and equilibrated with lively external behavior. Pavlov showed some tendency to believe that the calmness and liveliness displayed in the everyday behavior of the phlegmatic and sanguine dogs was related to the mobility of the nervous processes and regarded this as an important matter for future investigation and systematization.

SUMMARY: PAVLOV'S VIEW OF THE NERVOUS SYSTEM

Throughout his scientific career Pavlov emphasized the importance of the nervous system in the control of all physiological activity. There was, however, a considerable development in the nature of his views and, especially, in the detail of their elaboration. Originally Pavlov looked upon the nervous system as serving primarily the function of *conduction*. This was the conventional perspective and Pavlov's original opinions were distinguished only by the fact that he placed greater stress than most physiologists of his time upon this neural process in the control of various physiological mechanisms.

The most important change in Pavlov's thinking occurred when he began to conceive of the nervous system as serving, in addition, a *connecting* function. This conception, according to Pavlov (1928, p. 296), entailed the operation of six principal nervous phenomena: (1) excitation, (2) inhibition, (3) irradiation of excitation and inhibition, (4) reciprocal induction of excitation and inhibition, (5) the making and breaking of temporary connections, and (6) analysis and synthesis of environmental events.

The preceding discussion has covered Pavlov's thinking on all of these topics, but a little additional comment on the last may be useful. For Pavlov the cerebral hemispheres consisted of a vastly complex collection of centers, corresponding to elements of environmental influence, *environment* being defined in terms of all energy external to the nervous system. These centers comprised the *cortical mosaic* which Pavlov thought of as constantly undergoing changes which could be described in terms of excitation and inhibition. These processes enabled the organism to develop discriminations (analyses) and recombinations (syntheses) of environmental events in terms of the requirements of the environment.

This brings us, finally, to Pavlov's basic commitment to the view that the functions of the nervous system are, above all, adaptive. At the most basic level, it is obvious that the majority of the unconditioned reflexes are adaptive in that they allow the organism to make adjustments to critical occurrences in the environment. It can easily be demonstrated that such reflexes as salivation, blinking, pupillary action, and so on, provide the organism with a set of reactions which are important to survival. It is equally easy to prove, however, that the survival value of the unconditioned reflex is severely limited by two of its features: (a) it occurs in response to a limited number of stimuli and (b) it occurs, as has been said, to critical events in the environment. This means that the reaction often occurs too late to be of maximal adaptive value.

Conditioned reflexes are more adaptive in that they correct both of the defects in the unconditioned reflex mechanism: (1) They can be connected to any detectable stimulus and, if the facts of interoceptive conditioning are as advertised (Razran, 1961), some that are undetectable. (2) The essence of the conditioned reflex is its anticipatory character which permits the organism to "foresee" critical events and react appropriately. The subtlety of this adaptation is increased still further by the fragility of the conditioned connection. The result of this is that serviceable (reinforced) CRs remain whereas useless (unreinforced) CRs disappear. Obviously, these points are the same as those that Hull (1929) also made in his important article, "A Functional Interpretation of the Conditioned Reflex."

Finally, Pavlov made much of the adaptive value of inhibition. This value came about in two rather different ways. First, inhibitory mechanisms served a timing function, allowing the animal to deal adaptively with the long intervals which sometimes intervened between *signal* (CS) and what was *signalized* (US). The initial phase of inhibition prevented the occurrence of a CR too far in advance of the stimulus to which the process was appropriate. Second, inhibition prevented the damage of the cortical cells by stimulation that was too strong or too frequent. The period of *induced* inhibition which followed stimulation prevented immediate refiring and preserved the cortical cell from the damaging consequences of too frequent activity. Similarly, very intense stimulation induced a *protective inhibition* which kept the cell from firing too intensely. Stimulation of the cortical cell *immediately or almost immediately* caused a countering inhibition to modulate the reaction of the cortical cell.

Pavlov widely extended the idea of inhibition as adaptive in this sense. He held that sleep was in reality a widespread irradiation of inhibition which allowed the cells of the cerebral cortex to rest and recover normal function. For similar reasons, he advocated sleep as therapy for nervous and mental disease. Toward the end of his life Pavlov had become very interested in the problems of psychiatry and intended to apply his physiology to this particular art.

3

The Objectivist Climate: Bechterev, Watson, and Tolman

GREGORY A. KIMBLE

As is well known, the Pavlovian discovery of classical conditioning and its attendant theorizing were readily received by American psychologists because they fitted in so well with the essential aspects of American psychological thought (Kimble, 1961). In general, both Pavlovian interpretations of conditioning and the dominant forms of American psychology early in this century were: (a) analytic at the level of general strategy, (b) associationistic in their view of the major process underlying behavioral change, committed to a point of view which was (c) physiological and (d) more broadly, biological (in the emphasis upon the adaptability of behavior) and (e) opposed, at the level of method and interpretation, to everything subjective, mentalistic, anthropomorphic and introspective. The principles of conditioning had a special appeal to a psychology attempting to break the bonds of mentalistic subjectivism. The operational techniques we now possess for protecting ourselves from getting involved with the unreal, and in this sense fantastic, were not available. Thus a set of methods with objectively statable procedures for obtaining objectively measurable results met an important need of early 20th century psychology.

The Russian physiologists and psychologists, of course, had their own struggles with "idealistic" thinking. Around the turn of the century Pavlov had decided to abandon all psychic interpretations of behavior and to rely entirely, as Sechenov had advised, on objective physiological analyses. Similarly Bechterev, Pavlov's opponent in many ways, joined with him in a rejection of nonobjective methods. Perhaps because Bechterev was particularly interested in psychological problems, he found it necessary in his *General Principles of Human Reflexology* to state the objectivist position at some length. We shall present a series of excerpts from this book, a brief statement of a similar position typically voiced by Watson, and a summary of some of the early views of E. C. Tolman, a particularly effective advocate of the objectivist position.

EXCERPTS FROM BECHTEREV

"In order to assume such a strictly objective standpoint in regard to man, imagine yourself in the position of a being from a different world and of a different nature, and having come to us, say, from another planet. This being, appearing on earth and meeting man, would occupy himself with studying this living individual, who utters apparently unintelligible sounds. He would observe that man, compared to all other terrestrial beings, is endowed with a more varied and complex expression of activity, and expresses himself in movements and other reactions in two ways: some expressions are correlations, which are [quite simple and closely related to] the external stimuli acting on the organism, for immediately after some given external stimulus a certain outer reaction always ensues, even in new-born infants . . . . These are phenomena which we call simple or ordinary reflexes. But in addition to these innate reflex actions, there are exhibited, on the part of the man, other outward expressions, which may be found, too, in other terrestrial living beings, though in much less complex forms, and which are not so simply correlated to the external stimuli as are the ordinary reflexes, but are found correlated not so much to present stimuli as to those of the past, and sometimes even the very remote past.

"So this visitor from another planet would see that man, in selecting his eatables, not only gathers berries and fruit from wild trees, but, guided by past experience, tills the soil in a certain way, grows vegetables and fruit trees, sows corn, and prepares it suitably by thrashing and grinding, and by baking from flour bread which is eaten daily. . . .

"Continuing his observation of human life, this visitor from another planet would see that man, in order the better to struggle with his environment and secure food and shelter, lives in communities, and that his social life impels him, for the purpose of uniting forces, to use means of communication with others in the form of facial expressions, gestures, voice, and speech, the latter exhibiting a multitude of varieties in the form of national languages, which consist of symbolic signs or words, combined in a definite way, and composed of separate sounds. So language makes it possible for different individuals to exchange their personal experiences, and makes practicable the transmission of this experience, by means of education and culture, from one generation to the other, and thus piles up the collective experience of the ages. . . .

". . . . I should like to ask you now: Observing human life in all its complex expressions, would this visitor from another planet, of a different nature, ignorant of human language, turn to subjective analysis in order to study the various form of human activity and those impulses which evoke and direct it? Would he try to force on man the unfamiliar experiences of another planetary world, or would this being study human life and all its various manifestations from the strictly objective point of view and try to explain to himself the different correlations between man and his environment, as we study, for example, the life of microbes and lowly animals in general? I think there can be no doubt about the answer.

"It is quite obvious that a being of a higher nature can study all the various expressions of human personality only from the strictly objective standpoint, without turning to a subjective analysis of suppositions inner experiences and using for their explanation the analogy with himself, which, in the present case, is absolutely excluded.

"In the same way, we, too, can and must study the various activities of man, i.e., his deeds, speech, facial expressions, gestures, and his so-called instinctive activities, or, rather, inherited-organic behavior from the strictly objective point of view, and that in the light of the external and internal stimuli, without our turning to subjective analysis and to the analogy with ourselves. In following this method, obviously we must proceed in the manner in which natural science studies an object: in its particular environment, and explicate the correlation of the actions, conduct, and all other expressions of a human individual with the external stimuli, present and past, that evoke them; so that we may discover the laws to which these phenomena conform, and determine the correlations between man and his environment, both physical, biological, and, above all, social.

"It is regrettable that human thought usually pursues a different course—the subjective direction—in all questions concerning the study of man and his higher activities, and so extends the subjective standpoint to every department of human activity" (Bechterev, 1933, pp 33–34).

"The same holds good also of the infant's inner life. See how the subjectivists evolve their scientific theories of the development of the child's ego. 'The child's first step in this direction is to learn to distinguish the objects of the external world as things existing independently of himself. How this step is achieved we need not stop to inquire. But we must note that all those features of the child's experience that are not thus extruded or referred to a world of external reality remain to constitute the nucleus of his idea of himself. The parts of his body, especially his limbs, play a very peculiar and important part in this process, because they are presented in consciousness sometimes as things of the outer world, as parts of the non-self, sometimes—when they are the seats of pain, discomfort, heat, or cold, or muscular sensations—as parts of the self. Thus the conception of the bodily self is in large part dependent on the development of the conception of things as persistent realities of the external world; and the conception of those things is in turn completed of movement and of resistance to pressure" (W. McDougall: *Introduction to Social Psychology*).

"It is scarcely possible to doubt that here, as well as in further discussions, creative phantasy is put forward as science, because there is question of the first hours and days of the life of the infant, whose subjective world is necessarily inaccessible even to indirect self-observation. Subjective psychology and also animal psychology are full of similar fictions.

"The works of such reliable investigators, as e.g., Romanes, are saturated with these anthropomorphic views. [There] is an example of this in a work of Romanes', in which we find mention of a feeling of penitence in a Spanish mule which has been punished for disobedience, and whose coronal

The Objectivist Climate

and bells have been given to another mule; and of a feeling of pride in the rams and bulls which wear bells and other ornaments given them as leaders of the herd.

"It is true that this subjectivism is gradually being ousted from animal psychology and, from being a universal and all-embracing principle, is becoming more and more restricted, for at the present time nobody will, for example, place on an equal footing with his own ego the inner life of lower animals such as the snail or, still less, the microbe; yet, even now, there is no lack of support for the establishment of an analogy between the ego and the inner life of the higher animals.

"It is not necessary to mention that, in the exploration of the inner world of another man, psychologists still use, as a fully admissible method, the so-called indirect method of self-observation, a method based on the analogy with oneself.

"The fact is that present-day psychology, although it has become richer during recent decades through its adoption of the experimental method of investigation, still remains a thoroughly subjective science, in the sense that consciousness is regarded as the fundamental and inalienable stamp of the psychic activity not only of oneself, but also of others; and that psychology universally uses the so-called introspective method as fundamental in the investigations of inner or psychic processes" (Bechterev, 1933, pp. 39–40).

"One fact is indubitable: there are no suitable methods to direct us unerringly in the study of the psychic life of others. The gist of the matter is this: that the subjective may be directly known only by subjective analysis of oneself and in no other way. If the great lights of subjective psychology are ultimately led into solipsism, it is clear what [little] value the subjective method in general has. Still, subjectivism permeates not only subjective psychology, but also such an applied science as experimental pedagogics. To prove this let us mention the following passage from Meumann's introductory work (*Lectures in Experimental Pedagogics*).

" 'As has been shown long since by general psychology, all our observations of others consist in drawing conclusions leading to psychic experiences from the outer indications of psychic life, i.e. in our case—from the external indications of individuality. These external indications we regard, consequently, as symptoms of an inner life. They are either certain activities or the relations of the individual regarding which we must explain to ourselves what psychic processes and psycho-physical qualities of the individual lie at their root. But an explanation of this kind is always formulated somehow on the basis of analogy with our own inner life and its manifestations which we notice in ourselves; and this means only that every observation (objective or external), made by us in regard to others, is founded ultimately on self-observation. From this, for the practice of observation, there results an important principle which we should never have ignored: we must, if possible, try to trace in ourselves all these individual phenomena which we find in others—trace them and attempt perhaps only to imagine an analogous development of the same qualities in ourselves. But this applies still more to experimentation, which is no more than intensive and accurate observation.'

"I must apologize to the reader for this long quotation, but it is pertinent to the discussion, and not to quote it fully would mean to evade an exhaustive exposition of the views of the subjectivist school. But the question is: How can we trace in ourselves the individual peculiarities of an external person, if nature has not given us these peculiarities? Obviously, there is here a serious and radical error resulting from the subjective method of investigation.

"From this it is clear that, by the use of objective data, it is not possible to have a completely accurate and quite appropriate idea of the subjective world of an external person and of an external living being in general. Of course this does not at all mean that, guided by his own experiences, man cannot reproduce the subjective world of others by means of so-called identification. That such reproduction occurs is proved by the works of the best artists of every age; but this is the problem of artistic creativeness, consequently a creativeness that deviates from reality, and is not scientific analysis, and to be led by it would mean coming to the same logical constructions as if we judged of the real correlation of things from the creations of artists, say painters, or, for instance, accepted a theatrical representation as real life" (Bechterev, 1933, pp. 48–49, paragraphing slightly altered).

"Some of those infected by subjectivism overvalue the importance of the subjective method in another direction. So Woltmann, in his work, *Die Darwinsche Theorie und der Socialismus* (p. 8, Düsseldorf, 1899), says that "' in his personal concerns, man has created, as it were, a mirror, in which, by means of analogy, he observes and comes to know the external world. Man had first to become conscious of his own development, and only then could he recognize evolution as a scientific principle necessary for the explanation of the universe. Before the investigation of the creative force of the struggle for existence in the animal and vegetable kingdoms, this struggle had been already recognized in the world of man,' " etc.

"I must, however, decisively contradict this statement. The progress of thought met the greatest obstacles precisely when man made his own mirror his starting-point. The abandonment of the Ptolemaic system, according to which the earth, on which man lives, is the centre of the movement of all the celestial bodies, the rejection of the absolutely free will of man, the discarding of the idea of a deity externally similar to man, and the abandonment of subjective factors as important have been considerably delayed in the history of mankind, just because man looked, and still looks, into his own mirror, projects his own ego on to the external world, and thus retards the progress of human thought.

"Lastly, it may be thought that the narration of subjective experiences guarantees the accuracy of the reproduction of one's own inner world. But, as we have already said, a word is only a symbol, a sign, and, therefore, here too, we are far from the truth. This refers in still greater measure to those cases in which the narration does not occur immediately after the experiencing of the external event, but only after some time has elapsed, for the narration is then inevitably incomplete in its transmission of subjective experiences, is distorted, and is supplemented by products of the imagination, as has been proved in a number of experiments carried out in our laboratory.

"The experiments of Binet, the later investigations of Stern, and, especi-

The Objectivist Climate

ally, the experiments of Claparède on adults, the object of which was to discovery the rôle of testimony, are particularly instructive in this respect. They disclose the striking unreliability of testimony and its being supplemented by products of the imagination, while, in certain cases, false testimony is rather the rule than the exception. . . .

"It is clear that, on the basis of narration alone, we shall miss the truth; and, in general, we cannot be even more or less accurate in regard to the investigation of the subjective experiences of another man, if the narration is not accurately recorded in writing immediately after the external event, and, in addition, with full attention on the part of the narrator to his inner experiences. . . .

"We shall be still farther from the truth when we aim, by such a method, at the investigation of the subjective experiences of children, psychopaths, and such speechless beings as animals and infants. Here the beloved analogy with oneself will help us still less, for the inner world of these beings is, in its development and manifestations, too remote from our inner ego" (Bechterev, 1933, pp. 57–60, paragraphing slightly altered).

Earlier (p. 55) Bechterev had made the point that individual differences in human reactions are an obstacle to effective use of the subjective method of analogy. A vast range of personal characteristics resulting from heredity and from "upbringing and education pose the following question: How can such a varied set of individuals arrive at a consistent (leaving aside the question of correctness) account of human behavior?" The following passage amplifies this point.

"Finally, if we do not know the psychical experiences of others, but are conscious only of our own, which we put into the heads of others, and if, in the degree of emotion and in the character of the associations, our psychical experiences, as belonging to us as peculiar individuals, cannot be identified with the experiences of some other individual, it is obvious that we understand each other each in his own way, exchanging signs and constructing, according to these signs, our own conscious experiences, which doubtlessly diverge more or less in degree, as well as in character, from the conscious experiences of others. After all of this, can the subjective method satisfy scientific precision? The answer is, undoubtedly, in the negative.

"Everything we have said leads us to the conclusion that objective science not only can, but also should, be built up exclusively on the objective method and without any help from the subjective method.

"The question is: Shall we exclude the latter altogether from the realm of science? Not at all, but it finds its place only in conjunction with the data of the objective method and under its control. . . . In any case, the use of self-observation is possible only on oneself and only at the moment of the experiencing of the event, or just after it.

"Referring to the applicability of the method of self-observation only to the self, I admit that it can be applied not only by myself, but also by others, but each one of those who use this method is an independent observer of his own experiences, and must himself immediately write down the results of his observations, or dictate them to another who records them. These results I can later compare one with the other, so as to note their individual peculiarities, or explicate the most significant points. . . .

"Let us suppose that several subjects are shown an impressive picture, e.g., the picture of John the Terrible's murder of his son. They are required to describe in writing both the picture itself and their inner experiences. Their notes will give me purely objective material, which will be expressed in the more or less accurate description of the picture, in the pointing out of certain characteristics in that description, in the character of the description itself, etc. These same descriptions may also serve me to estimate the subjective states of the subject while looking at the picture, and I can also compare the data of their respective inner experience evoked by seeing the given picture. But, in the last two cases, I shall have judgments, as I have mentioned already, which have for their special aim to investigate the inner or psychical experiences of the subjects, but for objective knowledge, the strictly objective evaluation of the material which I derive from the notes of those who have looked at the picture is sufficient for me; and my objective material will not gain anything if I add to it the subjective evaluation of the same material in the sense of a judgment concerning the subjective experiences of the subjects, but, rather, it will lose to a greater or lesser degree" (Bechterev 1933, pp. 82–83).

OBJECTIVISM IN AMERICAN PSYCHOLOGY

In America subjectivism took a very specific form, the introspective method of Wundt and his followers. Many psychologists, particularly the animal psychologists and those interested in the psychology of infancy, opposed this method. J. B. Watson who was interested in both of these fields was one of those who strongly objected to the introspective method. He maintained a consistent stance in this regard, beginning with a paper in 1913. A briefer statement, taken from a 1925 publication, follows:

"From the time of Wundt on, consciousness becomes the keynote of psychology. It is the keynote of all psychologies today except behaviorism. It is a plain assumption just as unprovable, just as unapproachable, as the old concept of the soul. And to the behaviorist the two terms are essentially identical, so far as concerns their metaphysical implications.

"To show how unscientific is the concept, look for a moment at William James' definition of psychology. " 'Psychology is the description and explanation of states of consciousness as such.' " Starting with a definition which *assumes* what he starts out to prove, he escapes his difficulty by an *argumemtum ad hominem*. Consciousness—Oh yes, everybody must know what this "consciousness" is. When we have a sensation of red, a perception, a thought, when we *will* to do something or when we purpose to do something, or when we desire to do something, we are being *conscious*. All other introspectionists are equally illogical. In other words, they do not tell us what consciousness is, but merely begin to put things into it by assumption; and then when they come to analyze consciousness, naturally they find in it just what they put into it. Consequently, in the analyses of consciousness made by certain of the psychologists you find such elements as *sensations* and their ghosts, the *images*. With others you find not only sensations, but so-called *affective elements;* in still others you find such elements as *will*—the so-called conative element in consciousness. With some psychologists you find many hundreds of sensations of a certain type; others maintain that only a few of that type exist. And so it goes. Literally hundreds of thousands of printed pages have been published on the minute analysis of this intangible something called 'consciousness.' And how do we begin work upon it? Not by analyzing it as we would a chemical compound, or the way a plant grows. No, those things are material things. This thing we call consciousness can be analyzed only by *introspection*—a looking in on what goes on inside of us.

"As a result of this major assumption that there is such a thing as consciousness and that we can analyze it by introspection, we find as many analyses as there are individual psychologists. There is no way of experimentally attacking and solving psychological problems and standardizing methods" (Watson, 1925, pp. 5–6).

Watson coupled such criticism with a plea, not unlike Bechterev's, that psychology abandon the introspective method and attempt a more objective approach to the field. In particular, he believed that the method of the conditioned reflex offered great promise for an objectification of the field.

It was not Watson, however, but rather E. C. Tolman who expressed the argument for objectivism in psychology most effectively. It seems to me that the current methodological condition of the psychology of learning is mainly the responsibility of Tolman and K. W. Spence. Although these two men argued about almost every detail of the nature of the learning process, they nevertheless were in essential agreement on matters of grand strategy. In a series of papers which overlap little or not at all in time, these two men developed the implications of the operational-behavioristic position. Tolman's writings in this general vein began in the very early 1920's and culminated in what may be the most important methodological paper in the history of American psychology, "The Determiners of Behavior at a Choice Point" (Tolman, 1938). Spence, writing first with Gustav Bergmann, carried on the tradition in a series of articles beginning in 1941. Spence's contribution is so well known as to preclude the necessity for any presentation here. It may, however, be of interest to review the contribution of Tolman—especially his early contribution—to the development of psychological methodology.

It may be surprising to find Tolman referred to as a behaviorist.

Perhaps because of the kind of vocabulary he used, Tolman is often erroneously identified with the Gestaltist or phenomenological group. There is no doubt, however, about Tolman's own perception of his position. In 1935 he said bluntly: "I am a behaviorist. I hold that psychology [seeks] . . . the objectively stateable laws and processes governing behavior." Earlier (1927) he had said, ". . . so great is my faith that behaviorism must ultimately triumph that I should rather present even the following quite doubtful hypothesis [about the nature of consciousness] than hold my mouth and say nothing. If we behaviorists cannot present good theories, we can at least present as many bad ones as possible in order that by their successive refutation we may be forced finally either into discovering the correct theory, or, if there be none, into abandoning our behavioristic adventure altogether." Tolman's variety of behaviorism, however, was definitely non-Watsonian. Tolman considered himself a molar behaviorist or an operational behaviorist.

Although Tolman's behaviorism was different from Watson's, Tolman did share with Watson the rejection of the subjective and the method of introspection. Tolman's argument was the same as Bechterev's (p. 46): The stated goal of the introspective psychologist was the scientific understanding of private experience. Logic indicates that this objective contains a basic contradiction. Experience is private but science is a public enterprise. The attainment of a scientific understanding by one individual of the private experience of anyone else is a logical impossibility. Beyond this, Tolman with others noted that the introspective method applied at best poorly to the developing areas in psychology devoted to the study of mental tests and animal psychology.

At the same time, Tolman found it impossible to accept Watson's program of reducing all behavior to physiology, if only because of the practical problems. In 1925, Tolman put his position this way: "Eventually we will undoubtedly have to reduce and explain our more immediate categories of goal-seeking and object adjustment in terms of physiological categories. But the date at which this last will be possible is far distant. And, practically, it seems that the current tendency to talk and think primarily in terms of such inadequate and premature physiological concepts as are now on hand is in part responsible for some of the barrenness of our present animal research."

Having decided as early as 1922 that he could accept neither the old introspective psychology nor the new physiological psychology advocated by the Watsonian revolutionists, Tolman offered "a new formula for behaviorism." The new formula was a nonphysiological, molar, operational behaviorism. The key to much of Tolman's thinking is in his (1926) definition of behavior: "Behavior for me is not as it is for many, probably most, behaviorists primarily a matter of mere muscle contraction and gland secretion. . . . I conceive behavior rather as presenting a new and unique

The Objectivist Climate

set of descriptive properties all its own,—new properties which, as such, can be described and known, irrespective of whatever muscular or glandular activities underlie them. This new set of properties of behavior *qua* behavior is, of course, correlated with and probably completely dependent upon physiological motions, but descriptively and *per se* it is different from these motions.

"A rat running a maze; a cat getting out of a puzzle box; a man riding home to dinner; a beast of prey stalking its quarry; a child hiding from a stranger; a woman doing her washing or gossiping over the phone; a pupil marking a mental test sheet; a psychologist reciting a list of nonsense syllables; myself and my friend telling one another our thoughts and feelings: these are behaviors. And it is to be noted that in mentioning no one of them have I referred to, or, I blush to confess it, for the most part even known, what were the exact muscles and glands, sensory nerves and motor nerves involved. For these responses somehow had other sufficiently identifying properties of their own. And it is these other properties in which, as a behaviorist, I am interested."

In its first version, the "new formula for behaviorism" offered by Tolman (1922) involved four concepts: stimulating agency, behavior cue, behavior object, and behavior act. These correspond approximately to what we respectively call today distal stimulus, proximal stimulus, perceived object, and response. As Tolman envisaged the task of behavioristic science in 1922, the province of psychology consisted in the discovery of three sets of relationships: "those of (1), given the stimulating agency, determining the behavior cues, (2), given the behavior cues, determining the behavior object, and (3), given the behavior object, determining the behavior act. The first of these problems is the well-known one of older physiological psychology of determining the relations between sensory and image qualities and their underlying physiological conditions. The second problem, that of the relation of behavior object to behavior cue, is the old one of perception and apperception. . . . Finally, the problem of the relation of behavior act to behavior object is the extremely important problem of *motive*. It is the problem of desire, emotion, instinct, habit, determining set."

It is also to be noted that, even at this early date, the concept of intervening variable was already implicit in Tolman's thinking. In discussing the nature of the concept *behavior cue,* for example, Tolman began by relating such study to experimental work on sensory discrimination in animals and then goes on to say; "In such work the results, when strictly interpreted, are found to tell us nothing but the possibility of differences of behavior as a result of different stimulating agencies. If, for example, we find that a mouse can learn to behave differently as a result of blue and yellow stimuli but not as a result of red and green stimuli, we do not conclude anything as regards the animal's consciousness of these colors, as such, but merely something as regards the behavior cues which these colors are capable of evoking in him. That is, blue and yellow wavelengths are capable of producing in him two different behavior cues, whereas red and green wavelengths are capable of producing in him only one. In other words, where the older psychology talked about sense qualities our new behaviorism will talk about behavior cues.

"The new concept is identifiable with the older one insofar, but only insofar, as the latter explained the possibility or lack of possibility of differences *of behavior*."

One important aspect of the new approach proposed by Tolman was that he envisaged it as applying to all psychology whether it be the psychology of mental tests, animal behavior, or even the old method of introspection. For Tolman saw very clearly as had Bechterev (p. 48) that all that was objective about the results of introspective experiments was the statement of conditions under which the introspection occurred and the report of experience. These reports he regarded as "a form of behavior and therefore like all other behaviors the basis for an investigation of the objective laws and processes underlying it. . . . Experience *qua* experience, while of concern and interest to the man in the street, the philosopher and the poet, does not enter as such into the laws and equations of psychology—insofar, at any rate, as psychology is to be considered a science."

Armed with this logical arsenal, Tolman sallied forth in an attempt to deal with the categories of "private experience" identified in the old introspective psychology in purely behavioristic terms. One of his earliest and most successful efforts of this kind (1923) involved his behavioristic account of the emotions. The article is at the same time an acceptance of the factual basis of Watson's theory of the emotions and a criticism of its logic. Tolman lists the stimuli and responses employed to identify the primary Watsonian emotions, fear, rage and love. He then proceeds to show that the meaning of a term like *fear* depends upon a knowledge of both stimulus and response. In this sense, his position is not unlike that of Skinner (cf. p. 145) who raised similar issues in dealing with the concept of reflex. To illustrate, the meaning of the term *fear* cannot be understood merely in terms of its stimulational antecedents, a loud sound, suddenly removing all means of support, etc., or in terms of characteristic responses, a sudden catching of breath, crying, etc. The meaning of the term *fear* involves a recognition of both. Again, in this example, we see a clear anticipation of the concept of intervening variable to be stressed so heavily in Tolman's later writings.

In his discussion of the emotions, Tolman also fully realized that it would probably never be possible to reduce an important psychological concept to a single set of stimulus and response operations. He saw that a possible criticism of his behavioristic account of the emotions was for example, that it dealt only with the "impulsive phase" of emotions and had nothing to say about their "more or less passive mental presentations." Tolman's answer to this hypothetical criticism is that sensations, of which these "mental presentations" would be an example must, "in the last analysis, be defined in behavioristic terms only."

Other mentalistic concepts to which Tolman turned his behavioristic attention were purpose, idea, and consciousness. In some of these efforts, especially those devoted to the analysis of cognition and ideas, Tolman began the development of the psychological theory with which he is identified. In others, he stuck more closely to the problems associated with giving objective meaning to the concepts in question. Purpose, for example, he identified with a discriminable feature of behavior which he referred to as "persistence until." His treatment of consciousness was similar: "Whenever an organism at a given moment of stimulation shifts then and there from being ready to respond in some relatively less differentiated way to being ready to respond in some relatively more differentiated way, there is consciousness. For example, let us assume that our rat has up to some given occasion been responding in an undifferentiated fashion to the black and white alleys [in a discrimination-learning situation]. He may, perhaps, have been treating them both as distinct from some third chromatically colored alley, but as between these two, the white and black themselves, his behavior has not distinguished. On this particular occasion, however, we assume that something internal happens such that he then and there switches from not being ready to respond to them as undifferentiated to being ready to respond to them as differentiated. The moment of this switch is the moment of consciousness."

SUMMARY

The unifying theme which underlies the positions of Bechterev, Watson, and Tolman is the rejection of subjectivism. Each saw that the scientific study of the private experience of another person is a logical (not just a practical) impossibility. Bechterev made effective use of the Man-from-Mars metaphor to make his point. Moreover, he as well as Tolman recognized that certain aspects of the introspective method were admissible in a scientific psychology if one took the position that the verbal (and other) expressions of the subject in the introspective experiment had the same factual status as any other objective action of the organism.

But for a psychology developing an interest in animal behavior, psychopathology, child development and mental deficiency, it was obvious that this reformulation of older procedures could not provide a complete methodology. This led to a search for new methods of more general applicability. For Bechterev and Watson the techniques of Pavlov seemed, perhaps, to contain the entire answer. Both of these men, however, entertained a concept of conditioned reflex that was broader than the procedures themselves actually warranted. Watson failed to distinguish between the classical methods of Pavlov and the instrumental methods which he as well as other American psychologists were beginning to develop. Bechterev went even further and advocated the application of the conditioned reflex conception to all psychological phenomena.

A second important aspect of the theorizing of Bechterev and Watson was the (sometimes implicit) hypothesis that the methods of conditioning were in some way closely related to physiological mechanisms and that the study of conditioned reflexes provided a fairly direct means of investigating the functions of the nervous system. Tolman differed from these other two early objectivists in that he rejected this item of Pavlovian naïveté. Tolman saw two things: (1) that the reduction of behavior to physiological mechanisms was difficult and far in the future and (2) that, as used by Pavlov, Bechterev and Watson, physiological mechanisms were concepts, inferences from behavior.

In particular, the second of these astute perceptions of Tolman had far-reaching consequences. It suggested a new formula for behaviorism in which concepts would be introduced into the science ("operationally defined" in contemporary language) in terms of identifying behavioral symptoms. "Purpose," for example, would refer to that aspect of behavior which led to its persistence until some goal was attained. This was very different from the position of Watson who rejected many such terms because of their seeming affinity to introspective psychology. Tolman, in the early 1920's, laid the foundation for treating such terms as intervening variables, a strategy which made it possible to consider studying the laws of such processes. Tolman's later work consisted very largely in the development of a series of programs for such work. There was a certain amount of experimental work, but Tolman's most important contribution seems now to reside in the development of a methodology rather than in any empirical contribution.

4

A Functional Interpretation of The Conditioned Reflex[1]

CLARK L. HULL[2]

The experimental evidence now available shows quite clearly that the conditioned reflex is a two-phase phenomenon. One phase is obviously primary and the other is definitely secondary. Viewed physiologically, the primary phase is positive or excitatory in its nature; the secondary phase is negative or inhibitory. Functionally regarded, the primary phase appears to be a tentative trial, or first-approximation aspect of an adaptive process, while the secondary phase is the selective, corrective, or precision-insuring aspect. These two phases of the conditioned reflex, operating jointly, thus stand revealed as an automatic trial-and-error mechanism which mediates, blindly but beautifully, the adjustment of the organism to a complex environment.

The primary or excitatory phase of the conditioned reflex is the one which is best known and which has been employed most extensively as an explanatory principle. The knowledge of certain aspects of it, indeed, is as old as associationism itself. A much more comprehensive view of the process has recently been exploited to considerable advantage by H. L. Hollingworth under the name of *redintegration*. As applied to the conditioned

---

[1] *Psychological Review,* 1929, Vol. 36. Reprinted by permission of the American Psychological Association.

[2] Whereas for the Russians the conditioned reflex was considered to be a tool for studying the higher nervous activity, for the Americans the conditioned reflex seemed important mainly because it provided a source of concepts to be used in the development of theories to explain behavior other than that represented by the simple conditioned reflex. Pavlov himself saw this difference in approach very clearly and was extremely critical of the Western use of his work. Of all of those who put the concept of conditioned reflex to the use of which Pavlov so thoroughly disapproved, the most effective was Clark L. Hull who, for a period of over 30 years, devoted himself to an analysis of learning in terms of the conditioned reflex. The idea of the adaptive significance of behavioral processes was very characteristic of Hull's thinking. This point of view receives a forceful statement in this article. It is important to note that the paper presents a functionalist interpretation derived from Darwin. Although Hull is often considered a Watsonian type of behaviorist, this is a mistake. As this article makes clear, Hull was basically a functionalist [Ed.].

reflex, this term represents the fact that all elements of a stimulus complex playing upon the sensorium of an organism at or near the time that a response is evoked, tend themselves independently and indiscriminately to acquire the capacity to evoke substantially the same response. For our present purposes the indiscriminateness of the tendency is particularly to be noted.

But the redintegrative aspect is only one of at least four which are discernible in the primary phase of the conditioned reflex. A second significant tendency is an almost total lack of responsiveness to the patterning of the stimulus complex. A third is a remarkable lack of specificity of the conditioned reactions as regards the conditioned stimuli which may evoke them; the reflexologists call this *irradiation*. A fourth characteristic of great significance is the curious tendency, where the conditioned stimulus precedes the unconditioned one in the conditioning process, for the reaction to be attracted forward toward the former. Under certain circumstances the reaction (after a number of reinforcements) may begin a considerable interval before the delivery of the unconditioned stimulus. In the case of certain defense reactions this may even result in the organism not receiving the nocuous unconditioned stimulus at all.[3]

The secondary or inhibitory phase of the conditioned reflex appears to be less widely appreciated. For the most part this phase is not open to ordinary observation, only becoming manifest as the result of ingenious experimental procedures. Corresponding to the four aspects of the excitatory phase, each to each, we find here four parallel inhibitory aspects. They are: (1) inhibition from experimental extinction, (2) conditioned inhibition, (3) differential inhibition, and (4) inhibition of delay. In this connection it is to be noted that a given inhibitory tendency can only be developed on the basis of a corresponding excitatory tendency which must previously have been established.

We may now proceed to the consideration of the biological function performed by the several phases of the conditioned reflex process.

REDINTEGRATION AND EXPERIMENTAL EXTINCTION

Of what biological utility is the redintegrative tendency? It clearly results in the multiplication of the stimulus complexes which are capable of evoking particular reactions. With certain limitations, these conditioned stimulus complexes become equivalent to, i.e., substitutable for, the corresponding native or unconditioned stimuli. But just how does this substitution tendency result in augmenting the survival chances of the or-

---

[3] Note the tendency characteristic of early writing in this area not to distinguish between classical and instrumental conditioning [Ed.]

A Functional Interpretation of The Conditioned Reflex

ganism? It is quite clear, for example, that for any and every stimulus complex to have the capacity to evoke any and every response would not be good biological economy. Such an arrangement could lead to nothing but a wild and unadaptive chaos of behavior. No doubt many psychologists and biologists with a vitalistic leaning will urge that, if the process be really blind and automatic as assumed, we should expect exactly such a chaos. The problem deserves serious consideration.

The solution of the problem is seen perhaps most readily in the conditioning of defense reactions. The unconditioned stimuli for such reactions are ordinarily genuine injuries. With such unconditioned stimuli the organism will rarely or never make an unnecessary defense reaction for the reason that a defense will always be needed. Such certainty could hardly be attained with any other type of stimulus. This is a characteristic example of biological conservatism. The trouble with this particular type of arrangement is that, in order for the defense reaction to take place, the organism must always receive an injury. This is bad biological economy. Clearly a corrective accessory mechanism is needed. This exists in the substitution-of-stimulus tendency characteristic of redintegration.

Now the nature of nocuous stimuli practically limits them to such as involve actual contact with the organism before being effective. But if, as will usually be the case, the nocuous stimulus is of such a nature as also to stimulate a distance receptor like the eye, this latter stimulus is likely to get conditioned to the defense reaction. Here we have a means whereby effective defense behavior may be evoked without always being preceded by an injury. The retinal image of the threatening object when at a moderate distance will be sufficiently like that which is received when it is close enough to deliver the injurious stimulus, to evoke the defense reaction (withdrawal, flight) early enough for the organism to escape the injury altogether. Indeed it may very well be that the frequency among primitive conditioned reflexes of the substitution of distance receptors for contact receptors is due to this combination of circumstances.

Granting the tremendous biological advantage and occasionally being able to substitute certain stimulus complexes for certain others we still are pursued by the threat of a behavior chaos. There remains, in short, the difficulty presented by the indiscriminateness of the redintegrative tendency. Quite irrelevant stimulus elements will almost certainly find their way into every stimulus complex. By the principle of redintegration alone these irrelevant ones must get conditioned exactly as do the relevant. Why does not this produce the blind chaos of behavior previously suggested?

The answer is found in the corrective principle of experimental extinction. Stimulus elements which are not biologically relevant will not accompany a given unconditioned stimulus with any regularity, whereas the truly significant elements must do so. The latter, of course, will develop ordinary conditioned reflexes. The former, also, will tend to do so during their first accidental reinforcements or occasional short unbroken sequences of reinforcements. In so far as this accidental reinforcement takes place there may be realized a genuine unadaptiveness of behavior. Presumably this mechanism is responsible for a certain amount of human and other animal error.

Fortunately complete functional conditioning usually does not take place until after repeated combined stimulations. Except for very unusual runs of chance coincidences of stimuli, the irrelevant stimulus would appear one or more times *unaccompanied* by the unconditioned stimulus before the accidentally initiated redintegrative tendency should have risen above the functioning threshold. Such failures of reinforcement at once produce a tendency to experimental extinction. In this connection it must be remembered that experimental extinction is not a mere passive failure to strengthen an excitatory tendency according to the so-called "law of use." Instead it is a very potent tendency to repress existent excitatory tendencies, particularly the one from which it has taken its origin. Since chance alone will ordinarily present the irrelevant stimulus without reinforcement much more frequently than with it, the resulting inhibitory tendency will very soon become much more potent than the positive redintegrative tendency. Even if by some chance the false conditioned tendency should have gotten above the reaction threshold, the combination of circumstances just referred to would very soon convert it into a permanently inhibited and impotent state.

PATTERNED STIMULI AND CONDITIONED INHIBITION

After observing the utter indiscriminateness of the primary phase of the conditioned reflex as to the components of the stimulus complex which it tends to endow with action-evoking powers, we should not be greatly surprised to find a similar obtuseness as regards sensitivity to the particular combination or patterning of such complexes. Extensive experiments show, as a matter of fact, that the primary conditioning tendency leaves the components of the conditioned stimulus in an essentially unorganized state as regards the evocation of response. It is true that, if only a part of the original stimulus complex be presented, the intensity and promptness of the response will be reduced. This, however, is an addition-subtraction type of reaction rather than a sensitivity to organization or pattern. Barring accidental variability in the potency of the several components of the conditioned stimulus, this reduction in the magnitude of the response closely parallels the reduction in the number of the conditioned stimulus elements. With the same reservation, it may be said that one combination of stimulus elements from an original conditioned stimulus

A Functional Interpretation of The Conditioned Reflex 61

complex, will evoke the same response (both qualitative and quantitative) as any other combination having the same number of elements. Similarly, if two distinct stimuli which have been independently conditioned to a given response be presented together, the intensity of the resulting response is likely to approach closely the arithmetical sum of the responses to the two stimuli if presented separately.[4] It is accordingly clear that, except for characteristic differences in potency, the individual components of a primarily conditioned stimulus complex are completely interchangeable and appear to have little or no functional individuality. Under such circumstances there is naturally no differential sensitivity to any particular combination or pattern of stimulus components.

Now it is evident to ordinary observation that the simple addition-subtraction relationship obtaining among the components of a conditioned stimulus in the primary phase of the conditioning process, is a fairly adequate first approximation for many life situations. Indeed, if the vertebrate organism were to be dependent upon but a *single* stimulus mechanism, it is doubtful whether any other conceivable one would be more conducive to successful environmental adjustment and survival. In the long run, where fewer signs of danger appear, the less danger there is likely to be. Similarly, where two signs of danger appear, both of which independently are tolerably reliable, the organism is pragmatically justified by the law of chance alone in making unusually prompt and vigorous defense reactions. The same may be assumed to hold for positive reactions such as those involved in food getting.

Even so, innumerable life situations arise where the simple addition or subtraction of the potencies of the several components of a stimulus complex is not adequate. In many situations a particular combination or pattern of stimulus components (either simultaneous or temporally extended) is the very essence of the stimulus. To change a single minute component of certain stimuli will completely change the nature of the appropriate response. A telegram is an example of such a patterned stimulus complex. If a single letter in it be changed, the reaction of the receiver may be made either one of joy or of despair.

Numerous experimental examples of differential sensitivity to the patterning of stimuli are found in the conditioned reflex literature. We reproduce from Pavlov (1927, p. 146 ff.) one involving a temporal pattern:

The following is an experiment by Dr. Ivanov Smolensky. The positive conditioned alimentary stimulus was made up of a hissing sound (H), a high tone (hT), a low tone (lT), and the sound of a buzzer (B), ap-

---

[4] The evidence is that, more often than not, the sum of the two response strengths will be *less* than the arithmetic sum (Kimble, 1961, p. 87). Obviously there could be no increment in response strength if the response to one stimulus were at a physiological limit. Probably some form of "exponential addition" is involved [Ed.].

plied in that order, namely H-hT-lT-B. The inhibitory stimulus was made up with the order of the two middle components reversed, namely H-lT-hT-B.

Time	Conditioned stimulus	Secretion of saliva in drops during 30 seconds	Remarks
3:10 P.M.	H-hT-lT-B	4	Reinforced
3:17 P.M.	H-lT-hT-B	0	Not reinforced
3:27 P.M.	H-hT-lT-B	3	Reinforced
3:32 P.M.	H-hT-lT-B	4	Reinforced
3:38 P.M.	H-lT-hT-B	0	Not reinforced
3:46 P.M.	H-hT-lT-B	2	Reinforced

The formation of these inhibitory reflexes usually required a great deal of time; although a relative differentiation could sometimes be observed quite early, absolute differentiation was obtained in extreme cases only after more than one hundred repetitions without reinforcement.

How is this obvious inadequacy of the primary phase of the conditioned reflex met? As in the case of the primary redintegrative tendency, a corrective appears in the corresponding inhibitory phase, i.e., in experimental extinction. This was implied in the example just cited.

A special case of this is known in the literature as *conditioned inhibition*. This is of particular interest because it reveals in some detail one of the simplest mechanisms by which sensitivity to the patterning of a stimulus is mediated. Again we choose an example from Pavlov (1927, p. 68).

A positive conditioned stimulus is firmly established in a dog by means of the usual repetitions with reinforcement. A new stimulus is now occasionally added, and whenever the combination is applied, it is never accompanied by the unconditioned stimulus. In this way the combination is gradually rendered ineffective, so that the conditioned stimulus when applied in combination with the additional stimulus loses its positive effect, although when applied singly and with constant reinforcement it retains its full powers.

IRRADIATION AND DIFFERENTIAL INHIBITION

One of the most clearly marked of the primary tendencies of the conditioning process is that of spontaneous generalization. When a conditioned reflex has been set up in the usual manner, it is found that many other stimuli of a somewhat similar nature will also evoke the response.

This is particularly common where [the test] stimulus operates through the same sensory analyzer as the true conditioned stimulus. Under certain circumstances this vicarious spreading of the conditioned tendency may extend even into entirely different sense fields such as from the skin to the senses of the eye and the ear. This primitive tendency to generalization is known among the reflexologists as *irradiation*.

It is evident upon only a little reflection that irradiation is a tendency of enormous importance. Indeed it is hard to conceive how any organism requiring very complex learned adjustments could survive without it. It is a commonplace observation about the animal world that stimuli varying within a rather wide range may require substantially the same reaction. Take, for example, a simple command. Physical analysis of sound shows that the particular stimulus complex constituting a vowel sound such as ä is largely different as spoken by a man and a woman, and even as spoken by the same person at different pitches or different persons of the same sex at the same pitch. Similar variability is found among all sorts of other stimuli which, for most purposes, are considered the same. Indeed it is doubtful whether, in a strict sense, a given stimulus is ever exactly repeated. It follows that if the conditioning process were to be based upon a principle of strictly exact repetitions of the conditioned stimulus, even within the differentiating limits of the analyzer, rarely or never would a sufficient number of such identical repetitions accumulate to raise the conditioning tendency above the functioning threshold.[5] But even if by some miracle of chance a conditioned reflex should get set up under such conditions, of what biological value would it be? Without the principle of irradiation, it could never function except on the rare chance that the organism should encounter the particular shade of the stimulus upon which the conditioned reflex tendency was originally based. All of the innumerable other shades of variability of the stimulus biologically requiring the reaction could be of no adaptive value to the organism. To be so, each possible shade of the stimulus would need to be separately conditioned. But since the number of such differences would be indefinitely great, the organism might well consume the better part of its life in perfecting the conditioning process of a single response. It is very clear that irradiation is an indispensable principle of learned adjustment.[6]

There is, however, a decided disadvantage in the unlimited tendency to irradiation. If irradiation were extended to its logical limit, it would ultimately bring about a state in which any stimulus whatever would tend to evoke, with little or no distinction, every conditioned response possessed by the organism. This would indeed produce an unadaptive behavior chaos. But just as we have observed in the two preceding aspects of the primary phase of the conditioning process, an inhibitory tendency enters

[5] Later, Hull (1943) referred to this as the "stimulus-learning paradox."
[6] This is what Hull later (1943) called the stimulus-evocation paradox.

e biological situation. In this third case the corrective tendency as *differential inhibition*.

us suppose that a conditioned alimentary reflex has been set up to a bell of a certain pitch. Our knowledge of the irradiation tendency makes it quite safe to assume that another bell of a pitch and quality measurably different from the first will also evoke the response. We will assume that the second bell is not a biologically relevant stimulus. In this case it will not, when presented, receive reinforcement. This in turn (assuming an adequately discriminative analyzer mechanism) will gradually develop an inhibition for the pseudo-conditioned stimulus. Meanwhile the true bell will be steadily reinforced which will preserve the biologically valuable conditioned tendency intact. Thus the two tendencies, working jointly, bring about a most excellent adaptation which neither alone could conceivably effect.

THE ANTICIPATORY TENDENCY AND INHIBITION OF DELAY

Pavlov (1927, p. 40) describes an experiment in which a dog was given a tactile stimulus continuously for one minute, after which there was a pause of one minute, whereupon some dilute acid was introduced into the dog's mouth. Such an introduction of acid is always followed after a brief interval by a flow of saliva—an unconditioned reflex. Pavlov seems not to have interested himself in the phenomenon here emphasized, so that the detailed timing of the process is not given in his report. It is plain, however, that at the beginning of the experiment the flow of saliva could not have taken place until some seconds *after the termination* of the one-minute pause. After the procedure described above had been repeated a number of times, a significant change takes place. The saliva begins to appear during the one-minute pause, i.e., *preceding* the introduction of the acid. The first time there was only half of a drop, presumably appearing just at the close of the period. Ten minutes later, ten drops appear during the pause. Since each drop requires some time for secretion, the first of these drops must have preceded the acid by a considerable part of the one-minute pause. A later repetition yielded fourteen drops during the pause, the first drop of which presumably preceded the introduction of the acid by a still longer interval. This experiment illustrates very nicely a most interesting and significant aspect of the excitatory phase of the conditioned reflex. It is the tendency of the reaction to creep forward in time toward the conditioned stimulus in such a way as to lessen the interval originally separating the two and to make the reaction antedate the presentation of the unconditioned stimulus.

We can now ask what may be the survival value of this anticipatory characteristic of the conditioned reflex. The writer ventures a fairly confident prediction that this primitive mechanism will be found intimately connected with the "short circuiting" so essential a part of the more complex forms of learning. By *short circuiting* is here meant the tendency of a significant or critical reaction in a learning behavior sequence, to move forward in the series in such a way as to antedate (and thus eliminate) useless and irrelevant behavior segments formerly preceding it. But quite apart from this possibility, the shortening of the time interval between the conditioned stimulus and its response has a most obvious and immediate biological significance. As usual this is most easily seen in the case of defense reactions, particularly those involving withdrawal and flight. If the conditioned defense reaction were to preserve unchanged its temporal distance from the conditioned stimulus, the organism would (assuming the conditioned stimulus to be related in a constant temporal manner to the unconditioned stimulus) encounter the injurious stimulus on every occasion. It would thus in no wise profit by the conditioning of the defense reaction, say, to a distance receptor. This would obviously be very bad biological economy. Clearly, for a defense reaction to be wholly successful, it should result in a complete escape from injury. The only way this can be effected is to have the flight reaction antedate the possibility of the impact of the nocuous stimulus. This the basic anticipatory tendency of the conditioned reflex brings about.

But not all reactions are defensive in this sense. Certain behavior acts such as the various delayed reactions, require for their success in mediating biological adjustment that the period of latency or delay, instead of being reduced to a minimum, shall be separate from the stimulus by a quite definite and fairly prolonged period. This *inhibition of delay,* as it is called, has been studied experimentally by the reflexologists. By special techniques they have been able in dogs to condition periods of delay up to thirty minutes, with considerable precision. These experiments yield convincing evidence that the delay results from an inhibition which represses what would otherwise be an overt tendency for the reaction to follow the conditioned stimulus at once. The following report taken from Pavlov (1927, p. 41) describes one of the more illuminating of these experiments:

This animal can be given food regularly every thirtieth minute, but with the addition, say, of the sound of a metronome a few seconds before the food. The animal is thus stimulated at regular intervals of thirty minutes by a combination of two stimuli, one of which is the time factor and the other the beats of the metronome. Further, if the sound is now applied, not at the thirtieth minute after the preceding feeding, but, say, at the fifth or eighth minute, it entirely fails to produce any alimentary conditioned reflex. If it is applied slightly later, it produces some effect; applied at the twelfth minute the effect is greater; at the twenty-fifth minute greater still. At the thirtieth minute the reaction is of course complete. If the sound is never combined with food except when applied at the full interval, in time it ceases to have any effect even at the twenty-ninth minute and will only produce a reaction at the thirtieth minute—but then a full reaction.

Once more, then, we observe the primary excitatory phase and the secondary inhibitory phase of the conditioned reflex combining . . . to bring about a type of biological adaptation which neither tendency could possibly produce alone. . . .

THE DILEMMA OF THE CONDITIONED DEFENSE REACTION

In connection with that aspect of the conditioned reflex last considered, a curious and rather sharp distinction appears between positive reactions such as those involved in the taking of food, and defense reactions such as involve withdrawal or flight. In the case of an alimentary reaction, a successful response would ordinarily be followed each time by the consumption of food. This means, of course, that the conditioned tendency is continuously reinforced, which will keep it up to full strength. In this respect the case of the defense reaction is quite otherwise. As pointed out above, for a defense reaction to be wholly successful, it should take place so early that the organism will completely escape injury, i.e., the impact of the nocuous (unconditioned) stimulus. But in case the unconditioned stimulus fails to impinge upon the organism, there will be no reinforcement of the conditioned tendency which means (one would expect) that experimental extinction will set in at once. This will rapidly render the conditioned reflex impotent which, in turn, will expose the organism to the original injury. This will initiate a second cycle substantially like the first which will be followed by another and another indefinitely, a series of successful escapes always alternating with a series of injuries. From a biological point of view, the picture emerging from the above theoretical considerations is decidedly not an attractive one.

The sharpness of the conflict here, invites speculation as to how the problem is met by nature. One possibility which suggests itself is that the greater potency of the defense reaction tendencies may make them less subject to the weakening tendencies of experimental extinction. Another possibility is that the tendency to experimental extinction may be more or less in abeyance where defense reactions are concerned. But as soon as the principle of experimental extinction becomes inoperative, the organism is exposed to the dangers resulting from accidentally conditioned irrelevant stimuli. There is thus presented a kind of biological dilemma apparently not at all the product of misplaced ingenuity on the part of the theorist. If experimental extinction operates fully the organism seems doomed to suffer the injury of the nocuous stimulus periodically in order to renew the strength of its conditioned defense reactions. If, on the other hand, experimental extinction does not operate, the organism seems doomed to dissipate much of its energy reacting defensively to irrelevant stimuli.

It is suggested on the basis of mere casual observation that what might be called a kind of organic compromise may be operating in this curious situation. It may be that experimental extinction becomes progressively in abeyance as the gravity of the injury increases. Thus slight injuries would suffer considerably from experimental extinction and would consequently require more frequent nocuous reinforcement. Reactions to grave injuries would be affected relatively little by experimental extinction but for this reason would be very prone to become attached to irrelevant stimuli. This last, indeed, may account for the prevalence of phobias which appear, at least superficially, to be more or less accidental conditionings of irrelevant stimuli to strong emotional reactions. On the other hand very mild punishment is very likely to require frequent repetition. The problem presents a fascinating field for experimental investigation.[7]

EDITOR'S SUMMARY

This paper has asked, in the case of the classically conditioned reflex, the functionalist question: What is the adaptive significance of this phenomenon?

It has been shown that the conditioned reflex displays two characteristic attributes which we have called excitatory and inhibitory phases. The excitatory process possesses at least four aspects: redintegration (the capability of components of a stimulus situation to evoke the conditioned reaction), the absence of specific reactions to patterning, irradiation or stimulus generalization, and a tendency for the conditioned reaction to move forward in time and to antedate the unconditioned stimulus. The inhibitory phase of the conditioned reaction takes four forms which appear to parallel those of the excitatory phase: experimental extinction, conditioned inhibition, differential inhibition, and inhibition of delay. All of these aspects of conditioning contribute to the survival value of the process.

The redintegrative feature of conditioning is of basic significance in that it allows the organism to act adaptively in anticipation of dangerous situations. For example, the perception of a dangerous object at a distance contains enough of the elements of the object itself to evoke a con-

[7] Note the anticipation of the hypothesis of "irreversibility" later developed by Solomon and Wynne (1954).

ditioned defense reaction, thus keeping the organism from pain and perhaps death.

The chief difficulty with this state of affairs is that redintegration *could* lead the organism to respond defensively to any stimulus that contained only a few of the elements of a situation of danger, clearly a maladaptive possibility. The principle of experimental extinction provides the necessary corrective mechanism: reactions to components of stimuli that are not associated with unconditioned stimuli undergo extinction. In this way the organism comes to respond defensively only to stimuli that realistically demand such reactions. Moreover, the organism is prevented from acquiring inappropriate conditioned reactions by the fact that conditioning is a gradual process. Accidental pairings of normally unrelated conditioned and unconditioned stimuli will seldom occur with sufficient frequency to raise the level of such inappropriate conditioning above a reaction threshold.

Although the biological value of conditioning is quite obvious in these examples, there remains to be explained that the behavior of organisms is much more delicately adapted to reality than the simple processes of redintegration and experimental extinction would appear to allow. The correct differentiation of situations on the basis of patterns of stimuli is an important case in question. Conditioned inhibition provides the solution to this problem, for it has been shown by Pavlov that dogs (albeit with great difficulty) can learn to respond positively to a given set of stimuli presented in one sequence and negatively to the very same stimuli presented in another.

The relationship between the indiscriminateness of excitation and the operation of conditioned inhibition is not unlike the relationship between irradiation (stimulus generalization) and differential inhibition. The former process predisposes the organism to react in the same way to any and all stimuli of a given class; differential inhibition effectively limits the range of such reactions.

Something very similar connects the anticipatory characteristic of the conditioned reflex and inhibition of delay: since the conditioned reflex tends to move forward in time, it potentially could occur too soon, that is, before it is required to deal with an event of primary danger or benefit. The development of inhibition of delay leads the organism to postpone its reaction until the appropriate moment to respond.

Thus, in four cases we see the same pattern emerging. To summarize:

1. Redintegration leads the organism to the (adaptive) tendency to respond to components of situations but also to the (maladaptive) tendency to respond to sitiuations containing too few such components. Experimental extinction checks this tendency.

2. Irradiation leads to the (adaptive) tendency to respond to situations resembling a situation with significance for survival but also to the

(maladaptive) tendency to respond to situations that only remotely resemble situations of such significance. Differential inhibition provides the adaptive remedy.

3. The indiscriminateness of the conditioned response and a process of summation lead the organism to the (adaptive) tendency to react to assemblages of stimuli without regard to patterns but to the (maladaptive) tendency to ignore such patterns when they are important. Conditioned inhibition makes it possible for the organism to discriminate different patterns of identical stimuli.

4. The tendency of the conditioned reflex to move forward in time allows the organism to deal (adaptively) with situations before they eventuate in moments of crisis but also to a (maladaptive) premature occurrence of such responses. Inhibition of delay provides a mechanism by which the organism may time its reactions adaptively.

Thus the conditioned reflex, with its opposed excitatory and inhibitory phases and its more specific opposed aspects, stands revealed as an automatic trial-and-error mechanism which mediates, blindly but beautifully, the adjustment of the organism to a complex environment.

II

METHODOLOGICAL BACKGROUND

5

The Basic Tenet of Behaviorism

GREGORY A. KIMBLE

My purpose here is to describe certain very general commitments which I believe are held by the majority of theorists of learning, whatever their differences of opinion on more specific matters. My argument is that the only sound methodological basis for psychology derives from an operational-behavioristic approach of the type espoused by Tolman (p. 52, this volume). The fundamental point in support of this position is that if one is careful to separate observation from inference in psychology, the behavioristic position becomes a matter of epistemological necessity. In order to start somewhere, let us begin with an example.

At the 1963 meetings of the American Psychological Association in Philadelphia, a dozen fortunate psychologists and I had the opportunity to discuss conditioning with Professor Jerzy Konorski for the better part of an afternoon. For most of the time the American psychologists questioned Konorski on such matters as the difference between classical and instrumental conditioning, the role of kinesthetic feedback in the control of behavior and the surgical problems associated with the deafferentation of a limb. At the end, Professor Konorski had a question for us. Paraphrasing slightly: "Why is it that you, who are interested in these problems, are not physiologists? Or if you are really psychologists, why do you refuse to go about your proper business—studying the workings of the mind?" Readers of this volume will recognize at once that this query was Professor Konorski's way of asking the same two questions that the Russians have been asking for us over a century, that is, since Sechenov: "Who shall investigate the problems of psychology, and how?" and, by implication, suggesting the traditional Russian answers: "The physiologists and by strictly physiological methods."

FACT AND INFERENCE FROM FACT

A century ago, when Sechnov advocated the position reiterated by Konorski in the paraphrased questions above, these points were well taken. Psychology had not yet achieved the status of a separate discipline; metaphysical issues loomed large, ties to religion were close, and the concept of soul was explicit in many psychological writings. It was to rid the field of inhibiting influences such as these that Sechenov argued that physiology *must* investigate the problems of psychology. Otherwise psychology seemed doomed to an eternal preoccupation with such conceptions as mind, will, judgment and desire, all of which were impalpable, soul-like entities somehow endowed with reality. In the last half century or so, however, the situation has changed markedly. We are now free of philosophy and religion, except for such ties as we choose to establish. And despite the feet-dragging of a humanistic minority, psychology has now advanced from the introspective to the experimental, from the subjective to the operationistic, and from an orientation defined in terms of "mind" to one defined in terms of "behavior." Indeed it could now be argued that the American behavioristic psychologist understands objectivity better than the contemporary Pavlovian physiologist, in that he perceives the difference between fact and interpretation of fact (e.g., the distinction between generalization and the irradiation of some hypothetical brain process) more clearly.

Perhaps this matter needs no elaboration, but adequate understanding of the most elementary aspects of the situation seems to have eluded all of the Russian conditioners (Konorski is Polish) and a good many of the American physiological psychologists. Thus Lashley writing to Babkin (1949, p. 322) held it to be unfortunate and paradoxical that the concepts of conditioning have been employed most consistently by the American psychologists who most actively advocate the exclusion of physiological concepts from psychology (e.g., Hull, 1929, pp. 57 to 69, this volume). Comments such as these suggest that some further elaboration of the point may not be out of place.

The point missed in all such comments, of course, is that *as concepts* the Pavlovian processes are not physiology no matter what they are called. They are, rather, inferences drawn from the behavioral facts observed in experiments.

One of the few Eastern physiologists who actually understand the matters we have just been discussing is Professor Jerzy Konorski (in spite of his tongue-in-cheek question). He alone of these physiologists appears to feel no guilt at using psychological terminology when it is convenient. Now and then he has been criticized for this tendency by his colleagues. Thus, Grabhchenkov (Jasper and Smirnov, 1960, p. 88) says: "My last remark in connection with the communication of Professor Konorski concerns the necessity strictly to adhere to neurophysiological terminology; the usage of purely psychological terms and concepts should be avoided because they belong to the subject and methods of quite another science." The trouble with this observation, of course, is that the expression "quite another science" implies a type of evidence rarely available to the Pavlovian. In spite of such insistence, the term "irradiation" differs in no important respect from the term "generalization." Both are inferences drawn from the fact that conditioned responses transfer to stimuli resembling the CS. These terms would refer to concepts of separate sciences only if they were drawn from different types of evidence.

The Russian conditioners usually *talk* as if such different types of evidence existed. Thus the standard account of the effect of the CS upon the organism is that it affects the receptors and that, as a result, neural energy is transmitted to the cortex where it establishes a focus of excitation (or inhibition in the case of negative CSs). This excitation or inhibition spreads to neighboring cortical areas and subsequently reconcentrates in the original focal area.

We must not allow the fact that this interpretation is probably wrong (even when evaluated in terms of the evidence originally advanced in its favor) to cloud the issue. Instead, we must ask the more basic questions: What should a scientist have done to earn the privilege of talking this way? Had the early Pavlovians done these things? In considering these questions, it seems fairly clear that the Pavlovian theory implies evidence of the following sort. Upon the presentation of a stimulus, there is *physiological* evidence (obtained perhaps with implanted electrodes) that the first thing that happens in the brain is a concentrated focus of activity in a particular area. With time, this activity spreads and activity is detectable in adjacent brain areas. Still later, the activity gradually recedes to the original focal point before it disappears altogether. Obviously such evidence would provide powerful support for the conception of irradiating and concentrating waves of excitation and, in the parallel case, of inhibition.

But had the early Pavlovians done this kind of experimentation? As we have seen in the presentation of Pavlov's ideas, the answer to this question is "No." The observations which underlie the conception of irradiation are entirely behavioral: amounts of salivation which occur to stimuli of varying degrees of similarity to some CS, are considered as a function of time. The evidence differs in no important respect whatsoever from that obtained in behavioristic investigations of stimulus generalization and it follows that the two concepts, stimulus generalization and cortical irradiation, are the same. They are the same, that is, except for the promissory note implicitly issued in the assignment of a neuroanatomical locale in the case of the latter concept. Until this debt to science is paid, by direct physiological demonstrations of the alleged neural events, it is important to recognize this, and other, Pavlovian concepts for what they are: "strictly behavioral" in spite of all the insistence on "purely physiological."

OPERATIONAL BEHAVIORISM AND S-R PSYCHOLOGY

The main point to be drawn from this discussion is that the distinction between fact and inference from fact is basic. Although subtleties do arise, the situation is also simple. If one discusses the distinction with an intelligent first-year class of graduate students and then asks, "Just what are the *facts* of psychology?" he will get the right answer with almost zero latency: "Descriptions of behavior and accounts of the circumstances under which behavior occurs." From here it is but a brief step to a recognition that these "facts" are what we more typically call *responses* (descriptions of behavior) and *stimuli* (the circumstances under which behavior occurs). Thus the facts of psychology turn out to be Ss and Rs, a state of affairs which suggests with a certain insistence that the laws of psychology must be reducible to these terms and that an S-R psychology is an inevitability.

This conclusion raises two questions: (1) Why has it not been reached by everyone in psychology who has ever thought about such matters? And (2) why does it strike so many psychologists as a shocking conclusion and somehow wrong in spite of the logic behind it? Once more I think the answer reveals a failure to ask seriously about the referents of the words in our technical vocabulary. The terms *S, R,* and *S-R* law involve extensive connotations or implications. The common, but violent, negative reactions to their use are almost certainly because of their implications and not their basic meanings. One or two of the important aspects of these reactions are discussed in what follows.

The S-R formula vs. the S → R formula. Albeit implicitly, the formula S-R is translated with some frequency into the relatively stronger expression, S → R. Whereas the S-R formula merely suggests that behavior (R) is to be understood in terms of environmental influences (S), the statement S → R has more powerful implications. These reside in the suggestion that the *cause* of R is somehow exclusively in S, where S refers to some immediately present and identifiable stimulus. Obviously no one but the most out-of-date critic, in need of an S-R straw man to set afire, a dead S-R horse to beat, or both, would suggest in this day and age that S-R psychology is committed to exactly this. But even the sympathetic critic is apt to see validity in some of it. For this reason, there appears to be some virtue in stating where a behavioristic psychology stands on the several aspects of this statement. Much of this turns out to be a statement of where S-R psychology does not stand.

1. Behavioristic psychology does not hold that the sole cause of a given response is a specific S. Suppose a mouse runs through the room

The Basic Tenet of Behaviorism 77

where a dozen ladies are convened for an evening of bridge. Half of them will probably show signs of agitation, in the extreme case climbing up on the bridge chair and screaming. Could the mouse, which weighs only a few ounces, *cause* all of this kind of behavior in a 120-pound lady? Certainly in one sense it did; but not in the obviously ridiculous physical sense which the $S \rightarrow R$ translation of the S-R formula may seem to imply. There must have been other causes to be found in the things (Ss) that have happened to the lady in the past. Here is a related example from the laboratory. Suppose we deprive a rat of food for 24 hours and find, at the end of that time, that it presses the bar in a Skinner box 100 times in an amount of time during which it emitted only 5 responses prior to the period of fasting. Did 24 hours of food deprivation *cause* the increased energy apparent in the rat's behavior? Again, in one sense it did, but not in the physical sense which the $S \rightarrow R$ translation of the S-R formula may seem to imply. The situation in this case is particularly clear because deprivation (taking away food) obviously cannot, in a physical sense, supply the animal with energy.

2. The behavioristic psychologist does not mean by S only some presently identifiable discrete environmental object or event. The laboratory example above is instructive here. The sympathetic reader probably has arrived at this point without even stopping to puzzle over the question whether the example is appropriate, because the idea of treating food-deprivation as an S is so familiar. The unsympathetic reader, by now, has been reminded of an old query: "What do you S-R people mean by stimulus? And how can you expect to develop an S-R science of psychology when your concept S is hopelessly ambiguous embracing objects and events as diverse as a mouse and 24 hours of food deprivation?"

To question basic concepts, especially if it is done in a somewhat sepulchral tone of voice, can be a very effective argument against the position to which the concepts are basic. This is largely, no doubt, because these concepts tend to be accepted on faith and have only rarely (Koch, 1954) been subjected to critical analysis. Since the concepts of stimulus and response have recently been criticized by highly visible psychologists in essentially the terms used above, it may be important to deal with the criticism: by a stimulus we mean any independently identifiable event within the range of an organism's receptors. Obviously this is an oversimplification. The term *event* needs definition, a matter which would take us deeply into epistemology. But this does not seem to present any problems that are basically unsolvable.

In fact, the immediate reaction of the reader may not be to that aspect of the definition at all; his first reaction is apt to be that the definition is rather sterile. "Obviously," one might say, "not all stimuli, thus defined, are stimuli in any meaningful sense. Radiation derived from nuclear fallout is a stimulus by this definition, but it has nothing to do with behavior. Your purely operational specification has quite plainly put you in the position of defining as stimuli events which are irrelevant to your scientific purposes." The essential consideration in the answer to this criticism seems to me to be that the critic has unwittingly changed the subject. Two points: (1) obviously I can define stimuli in any way I choose, so long as I do not violate the basic rule that definitions must be circular; (2) my definition does not answer questions of lawfulness, nor is it intended to. The fallout example used above was selected because it is particularly instructive. The definition of stimulus offered above would indeed define fallout or X-radiation as a stimulus. It is also true that it defines as a stimulus an event which, a priori, most of us would not expect to enter into S-R laws. This expectation, however, is wrong. In a recent experiment, Garcia *et al.* (1955) seem to have proved beyond doubt that X-radiation can serve as a conditioned stimulus for other reactions. Thus it becomes clear that our critic, in subtly changing from questions of definition to questions of lawful relationships, has clouded an issue that the operational approach left perfectly clear.

It should be clear, of course, that psychology's main interest is in stimuli that have an effect upon behavior: a part of psychology's mission is to discover which stimuli have such an effect as well as the circumstances under which the effect occurs. But it seems wise to consider such matters under the heading of lawfulness rather than under the heading of definition. It is important, for example, to allow for the case in which a stimulus, defined as above, has *no* effect upon behavior. No doubt X-radiation usually belongs in this category. But to consider it sometimes a stimulus and sometimes not seems to me to be more awkward than to have a relatively clear definitional statement and to treat the functions of stimuli separately.

One additional point: within the context of an experiment, the meaning of the term *stimulus* (and *response*) is usually perfectly clear. Stimuli are events of the kind defined above as stimuli; responses are measurable consequences of the organism's activity. The little progress psychology has made in the century of its official existence has come about by paying careful attention to stimuli in these terms; psychology has benefited (rather than suffered) from refusing to debate the cosmic significance of the term (as we have been doing in this section).

3. The behavioristic approach need not limit itself to independent variables defined in terms of stimuli, even as the term is used here. The reference is in part to the inclusion, in behavioristically oriented theories, of R-R hypotheses which have a behavioral measure as an independent variable. A particularly clear example of this is provided by Spence's work on classical conditioning. On the one hand, such environmental (S) variables as N (the number of reinforced trials), I_{US} (the intensity of the unconditioned stimulus) and t_{CS-US} (the

The Basic Tenet of Behaviorism

interstimulus interval) are postulated as contributing to the level of conditioning. On the other hand, Spence also assumes that one response-inferred variable, anxiety, as measured by the subject's score (R) on the Taylor Manifest Anxiety Scale, also participates in the determination of the rate of conditioning. Thus, in Spence's theory, we see that there are two kinds of laws:

A. A set of S-R laws of the general form:
$R_C = f\ (N, I_{UCS}, t_{CS-US})$, where R_C refers to the level of conditioning.

B. At least one R-R law:
$R_C = f\ (R_{MAS})$, where R_{MAS} refers to score on the Taylor Manifest Anxiety Scale.

In his recent writings, Spence has also made much of the importance of one additional subject-centered variable, set or attitude. Does this concept figure in S-R or R-R laws as those terms were used above? In Spence's theory *set* is an S-inferred concept because the attempt has been to link it to the conditions of the experiment. Thus, for example, when the US is omitted for the first time in extinction (S), it is assumed that this tends to produce a set to resist responding. It is quite clear, however, that the concept of set could as easily be inferred from behavioral measures. An investigator might ask his subjects at the end of the experiment how they reacted to the procedures. If the subjects responded (R) that they noticed the change in conditions when the US was omitted and resisted responding, it would then be possible to define *set* in terms of these responses. In this latter case the law of conditioning involving the concept of *set* would be like the law involving anxiety, whereas in Spence's present usage, it is like the laws involving other environmental (nonresponse) variables.

The S-R approach is also more flexible in another way than its critics usually take it to be. The term *S* has gradually become so general as to be roughly synonymous with the concept of *cause*. In a sense this is unfortunate because it means that, in practice, we tend to lump with the term *stimulus* events that clearly do not meet the definition. The practice is so well established, however, that it seems useless to attempt to change it. In any event, it is important to recognize that the word *stimulus,* in addition to referring to specific physical objects, also includes such independently specifiable circumstances as the number of trials in a learning experiment, the time since the last trial in a study of spontaneous recovery, instructions to subjects, and so on. I would prefer to see psychology use the term *antecedent condition* for all such events, reserving the term *stimulus* for a more particular class of operations. It seems unlikely that psychology will soon adopt the practice, however, and in the meantime something may be gained by recognizing that the meaning of the term changes with changing contexts. Given this recognition, the ambiguities in the term *stimulus* seem less damaging to the S-R point of view that they seem at first.

4. Behavioristic S-R psychology is not committed to the proposition that learning is gradual (or sudden) to a drive reduction theory of reinforcement or to a stance in opposition to physiological psychology. Although the word *behaviorism* tends, for many psychologists, to call up such associations, there is nothing in the term itself that necessarily implies any of this.

SUMMARY

The essential idea which I have tried to develop in this chapter is that the most basic question presented by any psychological statement is whether the statement is one of fact or one of interpretation. Obviously, these alternatives have been put more sharply than they need to be, or perhaps should be. Almost all statements are partly statements of facts and partly records of inference from these facts. But this does not eliminate the importance of being sensitive to such matters; it simply makes the problems somewhat more difficult.

In this chapter, we have considered two main examples: the Pavlovian theory of conditioning and American behavioristic psychology, discovering in each case that the implications of the basic distinction have something to contribute. In the case of Pavlovian theory, the situation is fairly simple. It is clear that, despite the position almost reflexly adopted by the orthodox Pavlovian, Russian physiology deals with concepts that are surprisingly like those of American behavioristic psychology. In other words, the operations involved in the Pavlovian concepts are not usually directly physiological. Thus, these concepts have the same status as those employed in psychology.

The analysis of S-R psychology involves more subtle matters but, hopefully, it is demonstrated that, in the most basic sense, all psychology must become an S-R psychology as a matter of logical necessity. If they can be led to an understanding of this last sentence, even the most hostile critics of S-R theory should be able to accept it. They must be able to see that the concepts of S, R and S-R law apply in a basic sense to the raw materials with which we all deal. How a given psychologist uses these raw materials is up to him. He can be as wholistic, physiological, "dynamic," personalistic, or even humanistic, as his conscience will allow—so long as he continues to deal with the materials that go to make up psychology rather than those that are basic to neuroanatomy, poetry or religion.

The Basic Tenet of Behaviorism

There are several other applications of these ideas that deserve a brief mention.

1. Elsewhere (pp. 82 to 84) I have dealt with the distinction between classical and instrumental conditioning in basically these same terms. On the one hand, these terms refer to different operations so that the two forms of learning experiment can be distinguished on procedural grounds. On the other hand, they deal with processes (inferred consequences of these operations) which not everyone accepts as different for the two forms of learning. Settling the latter issue may be hastened if we maintain a certain clarity of thought, recognizing when we are talking about procedures and when we are talking about processes.

2. The concept of reinforcement has also been subjected to a similar analysis (p. 86). It also has one meaning in terms of operations and several others in terms of imputed essential nature.

3. Mowrer (1960) has recently proposed the introduction into our vocabulary of four highly anthropomorphic terms *hope, fear, relief* and *disappointment*. Although there are good reasons to object to the use of these words and even better reasons to doubt the scientific value of one or two of them, the most important considerations do not reside in the use of the words themselves. The operations implied by each are actually quite clear. Thus, in each case the word refers to the hypothesized reaction to a stimulus that has been associated in the past with the onset or termination (physical events) of positive or negative reinforcers, determinable by independent indicator experiments as Thorndike (1911) clearly saw. The point is that the operations are perfectly specifiable and raise interesting questions about behavioral consequences. They should not be laughed out of court on grounds that are verbal and nothing else.

6

The Definition of Learning and Some Useful Distinctions

GREGORY A. KIMBLE

It may be possible to secure general, if occasionally reluctant, agreement among psychologists of learning that the term *learning* can be defined as follows: *learning* is a relatively permanent change in a behavioral potentiality which occurs as a result of reinforced practice. This definition is of the type referred to as a factual or empirical definition (Kimble, 1961, p. 2). The term *reinforcement* need have no theoretical significance. It refers only to events which may be employed to insure the occurrence of learning.

There are several considerations which make a definition of this type easy to accept. In the first place, it identifies learning as a concept or as an intervening variable and prepares us for an important distinction between learning and performance. Figure 1 illustrates the methodological

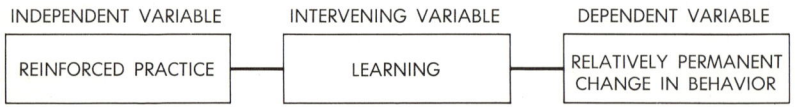

FIGURE 6-1. The status of the concept, learning, as an intervening variable.

status of the term *learning*. The definition above also fairly clearly separates learning from other changes in behavior with which it might be confused. In addition, it provides a way of introducing a number of basic issues related to the definition of learning.

DEFINITIONS

Behavior

First, the definition refers to changes in *behavior* (or a potentiality for behavior), a point that probably should be taken more literally

The Definition of Learning

than it usually is. This consideration has particular significance for the numerous instances where it is alleged that reinforcement, inhibition or motivation is "learned," "acquired," "conditioned," or "secondary." The absence of anything like a response in such references suggests that the question be raised. It is not that these references are necessarily wrong, but rather that the term *learning* usually implies the existence of responses. One cannot help wondering whether the ignoring of possible responses is not an important oversight.

To illustrate with the concept of secondary reinforcement, the more or less standard definition of this concept is that "stimuli regularly associated with primary reinforcement acquire reinforcing properties themselves." On the basis of this definition, which *does not* mention behavior, one might expect that studies of secondary reinforcement would proceed by attempting simply to operationalize the definition. That is, these procedures would consist in pairing a neutral stimulus with reinforcement, and nothing else. This has *not,* however, been the typical method employed in studies of secondary reinforcement. Instead, the neutral stimulus has been presented and reinforcement has been *made available.* Virtually without exception in these studies, the subject is required to perform some motor response (e.g., approach a food tray or run a straight alley) in preliminary training to obtain the reinforcer.

The immediate significance of this point is that it is easy to see that the procedure actually employed is the same as that required for the establishment of a discriminated operant in which the instrumental responses are those involved in securing reinforcement. Thus what studies of secondary reinforcement may actually accomplish is merely the conditioning of these reactions to the previously neutral stimulus the experimenter is trying to endow with secondary reinforcing powers. If this were true it would mean that the most important case in which a *state* of the organism has allegedly been conditioned is called into question because of the fact that only its responses have been involved.

Now assume (perhaps incorrectly) the validity of this argument, at least for the moment. Certain other possibilities suggest themselves. It may be that the difficulty routinely encountered in producing convincing demonstrations of "conditioned hunger" is related. The procedure is that of presenting a neutral stimulus to an organism when it is hungry on the hypothesis that this stimulus will later elicit the *state,* hunger. But if only responses can be conditioned and if hunger produces no consistent responses to be conditioned, it would be extremely difficult to demonstrate any effect of such training. In a similar way it seems possible that the difficulties in demonstrating conditioned "relief" (Mowrer, 1960) by pairing neutral stimuli with the termination of noxious stimulation derive from the same source. The cessation of pain may not be associated with responses to be conditioned. Thus, if only responses, and not states of the organism, can be conditioned, this may account for (1) the relative ease of obtaining secondary reinforcement and conditioned fear and (2) the difficulties associated with obtaining conditioned hunger and relief.

Relative permanence and the learning-performance distinction

The inclusion in the definition of learning of the criterion of relative permanence makes it possible to distinguish learning from changes in behavior brought on by such factors as fatigue, habituation and motivational changes. These latter changes are all quite temporary and disappear spontaneously with variables not ordinarily associated with learning.

The application of this aspect of the definition of learning to experimental data has led to the development of the factorial method of separating effects upon learning from those upon performance. Consider any experiment of the following type. Each of two groups of subjects is trained under one of two values of some variable. Then, half of each group is continued under its original condition and the other half is switched to the other condition. Measures obtained *after the switch* can be analyzed for an answer to the question of whether the effect of the variable is on learning or on performance. Effects that are permanent, in the sense that they survive the change in conditions, are attributed to learning. Those that are temporary and do not survive are performance effects.

The most instructive experiment of this type included in the present volume is that of Kamin and Schaub (pp. 288 to 297) on the effects of the intensity of the CS on a conditioned emotional response in rats. These investigators paired a weak or strong CS (tone) with electric shock and then subdivided each group for extinction, using a strong CS for one-half of the subjects and a weak CS for the other. The measure obtained was an index of the extent to which presenting the CS suppressed the rate of bar pressing for food. The details of procedure and measures need not concern us here except to note that the "suppression index" was obtained during extinction and that low indices mean greater suppression and, therefore, a stronger effect.

The diagram below spells out the factorial procedure and indicates possible types of analysis for the Kamin and Schaub experiment.

This diagram shows the following. (1) A comparison of row means reveals any effect of training intensity under conditions where the two cells in each row contribute a group extinguished with weak and strong intensities. In short, the test for the effect of training intensity occurs under conditions where the groups are balanced for extinction intensity. (2) a similarly balanced test is possible for extinction intensity by com-

The Definition of Learning

	EXTINCTION INTENSITY	
	Weak	Strong
TRAINING INTENSITY — Weak	Trained or weak; extinguished or weak (unchanged)	Trained or weak; extinguished or strong (changed)
TRAINING INTENSITY — Strong	Trained or strong; extinguished or weak (changed)	Trained or strong; tested on strong (changed)

Comparing row means tests for effect on learning

Comparing column means tests for affects on performance

Comparing diagonal means tests for generalization decrement —effect of changed stimulus conditions

paring column means. (3) The means that can be computed from the two cells that make up the diagonals provide a test of the effect of a change in intensity between training and extinction. Data from Table 3 in the Kamin and Schaub paper (the data for day 1) appear in Table 6-1, together with each of the three types of mean (row, column and diagonal).

TABLE 6-1

		EXTINCTION		
		Weak	Strong	
TRAINING	Weak	.13	.10	.115
	Strong	.16	.01	.085
	.130	.145	.055	.070

Recall that small numbers indicate great response suppression. Although the means in Table 6-1 do not meet the accepted criteria of statistical dependability, they suggest the following lines of interpretation. (1) The suppression ratio is larger (suppression is lower) for subjects *trained* with a weak CS than with a strong one. This is the relatively permanent type of effect required to state that a variable influences *learning*. (2) Subjects extinguished with a weak CS show less suppression than subjects tested with a strong CS. This type of result assigns a variable the role of a *performance* variable because the effect is produced by immediately present conditions. (3) The left-hand diagonal mean is larger than the right-hand diagonal mean. These differences show that more conditioned suppression occurred in subjects extinguished with the same CS intensity as was used in training than occurred in subjects for whom CS intensity was changed. This result illustrates the phenomenon of *generalization decrement* emphasized by Kamin and Schaub in their discussion.

It should be emphasized that these analyses rest on inadequate statistical foundations. What is important are the type of analysis, the lines of interpretation suggested and, just possibly, the notion that an experiment with a larger number of subjects in each cell might produce reliable results of the sort just described.

Potentiality

Learning is commonly defined as simply a "change in behavior." This statement seems incomplete, however, because it is obvious that learning may occur when there is no change in behavior. We learn from school books, motion pictures, demonstrations, lectures, maps, and the gossip of our colleagues, but there is no immediate translation of such learning into performance. Technically, we say that such learning is *latent* and in accordance with this idea, we make the distinction between a state (learning) and the manifestation of that state (performance).

Reinforced practice

Starting again with the most common definitions, they usually define learning merely as something that happens as a result of practice. This statement, however, without the specification that the practice is reinforced, does not differentiate between learning and extinction—extinction is also a change in a behavioral potentiality which occurs as a result of practice. The source of psychologists' unwillingness to include the term *reinforced* in their definitions is not difficult to find. The accidents of history have led to an unfortunate equation of the term *reinforcement* with Thorndike's law of effect or with the most popular modern derivative of Thorndike's position. Thus, the inclusion of the term *reinforcement* may *seem* to imply the acceptance of some version of drive-reduction theory. For this reason, it is important to recognize the error in this way of looking at the problem and to recognize as well that the term *reinforcement can* (and in the definition above *does*) refer to a purely empirical set of operations.

In fact, the situation is even muddier than could result from the single confusion between the fact of reinforcement and hypothetical mechanisms. With "reinforcement" equated with "drive reduction," there has been a further unfortunate tendency for "reinforcement theory" to be equated with all of the other aspects of the most important theory of this type (Hull, 1943). Thus, the term *reinforcement theory* has become surrounded by illegitimate and illogical connotations. For many psychologists, reinforcement theory seems to imply S-R theory, continuity theory, and mechanistic interpretation of behavior as well.

Practice

There are relatively permanent changes in behavioral potentiality which are the result of circumstances other than what would be considered practice. The inclusion of the term *practice* in the definition of learning is intended to exclude other processes such as maturation and physiological change. This point is commonly understood. Including *practice,* however, often has a variety of additional consequences: some are excluded from the concept *learning* by the criterion of "relative permanence"; others pose difficult problems for anyone attempting to use the term *learning* in an unambiguous way.

Habituation. It can be demonstrated that a reinforcer loses some of its effectiveness with repeated application. Thus, in studies of GSR conditioning and finger withdrawal, it is a common practice to increase the intensity of the shock employed as US in order to counteract such habituation. Similarly the food or water used as reinforcers in appetitively reinforced learning may partially satiate the subject and produce a similar effect. The suggestion that satiation is a form of habituation seems plausible on the face of it, although this equation is not commonly employed in the psychology of learning.

Pseudoconditioning and sensitization. Sometimes exactly the same procedures employed to produce habituation have the opposite effect and lead to a heightened reaction to stimulation. The studies of *pseudoconditioning* fall into this category as do those of *alpha conditioning* (Kimble, 1961, p. 477). Similarly, there are demonstrations that prefeeding a rat with just a taste of food prior to a maze run increases the speed of running. This last type of demonstration suggests that the critical variable determining whether presentations of the reinforcer lead to sensitization or to habituation may be the number of applications. Possibly very few such applications lead to sensitization, many to habituation. Whatever the status of these ideas, the phenomena mentioned above raise an important question: Are they or are they not learning? In the past the usual answer to this question has been in the negative, but, more recently, an occasional investigation has suggested that we reconsider.

Inhibition. Conceptually separate from habituation are the various kinds of inhibition known to develop as a function of practice in the learning situation. Most students of inhibitory phenomena agree that these effects are complex and involve at least two types of inhibition which Pavlov (1927) called external or passive and internal or active.

Multiple habits. The common intuition that practice acts on one single process called *learning* or *habit* is an oversimplification. Even in the most limited learning situation the organism learns many other things. These include secondary reinforcement (even if it reduces to a modification of unmeasured responses, as suggested above), secondary drive (which raises the same problems of basic nature) and incentive. In addition, the subject may learn more subtle things such as the fact that the US is present on every trial or omitted on some, the pattern of reinforced and nonreinforced trials if there is a pattern, or the fact that it is random if no pattern exists. The human subject can usually verbalize such knowledge after a very few trials. The occurrence of the first conditioned reaction, however, may not take place until many trials later. It is quite obvious that the recognition of the general conditions of the experiment and the acquisition of the conditioned response are two very different forms of learning, both of which occur in the conditioning situation.

It may be worth noting that this distinction does not apply only to verbalizing subjects. Behavioral evidence that the subject recognizes the sequence of events on a typical trial is very often obvious in lower animals. The posture of "expectancy" which the dog assumes when the CS comes on in a classical salivary conditioning experiment is a good example. Obviously with careful observation or elaborate instrumentation, the development of such reactions could be traced as objectively as the development of the salivary CR. The main point here is that these two forms of learning are discriminable and that it is probably important to keep them separate. Indeed, one suspects that the classic arguments between expectancy theorists and S-R theorists were possible only because members of the former group tended to look upon learning exclusively in terms of the development of what I have called the recognition of the conditions of the experiment and the latter group have tended to restrict their attention exclusively to the development of the conditioned response.

One point that may need further discussion is whether some of these changes are actually learning. What potentialities for altered behavior are being established when the subject acquires an "attitude of expectancy"? This type of question is crucial because it is clear that the usual experiment does not provide for the measure of the tendencies in question. But it is equally clear that methods could be found that would yield the necessary indices. Human subjects can be interviewed about their general reactions and more detailed observations of the behavior of lower animals may provide partial information along similar lines.

There is also this incidental point: assuming that evidence eventually becomes available for the many behavioral changes occurring in a learning situation, it will add nothing but confusion to state that this proves that *the* CR is complex. Such evidence seems rather to support the idea that the subject learns many different things that must be analyzed separately.

Changes in details of the response. As the subject learns in even the most elementary conditioning situation, there are marked changes in the various quantitative features of the reaction. Latencies often become shorter and the vigor of the response becomes typically greater. Although it is easy to find exceptions to these generalizations, they will adequately serve our purposes here. The usual attitude taken by the theorist of learning is that these changes in latency and vigor reflect alterations in the strength of an underlying reactional tendency, and that all responses of a given type are to be considered the same response.

The basic nature of this assumption is well illustrated in Boneau's (1958) discussion of the problems involved in defining an eyelid CR. In his experimental work, Boneau had run groups of subjects in an eyelid conditioning experiment where the interstimulus intervals were 0.5, 1.0 or 1.5 seconds. Previous work had demonstrated that eyeblinks occurring in the interstimulus interval could be of several varieties: random blinks, unconditioned responses to the CS, and conditioned responses. The problem obviously was to identify conditioned responses and, to as large a degree as possible, to avoid counting as CRs the other varieties of reaction. The general criterion which Boneau used was latency: responses shorter than a particular latency were not counted as CRs. The application of this criterion was complicated, however, by the fact that identical latency criteria would not work for all interstimulus intervals. This was partly because the longer intervals increased the probability of obtaining a random blink and partly because the latencies of true CRs depend somewhat upon the interstimulus interval. In the face of this difficulty, Boneau turned to the basic definition of learning for his criterion and counted as CRs only those which showed a tendency to increase with practice. The following excerpt from Boneau's paper illustrates his reasoning in greater detail.

. . . . Since the latency characteristics of responses to different intervals are different . . . , the problem of the definition of a CR for the specific intervals employed had to be faced at the outset of the analysis of results. In dealing with this problem the assumption was made that CRs will tend to increase with increasing numbers of trials. [Thus] a CR was defined as a response in any range of response latencies which shows a consistent increase in level of responding as conditioning proceeds. Operationally, the distribution of responses by latencies for an early stage of conditioning is compared with that for a later stage or stages. That part of the distribution which increases from one stage to the next constitutes a range of response latencies which is used to define the CRs for the interstimulus interval involved. Such a procedure automatically compensates for the larger number of random blinks expected in the interval between CS and US as its length increases by tending to eliminate them from consideration as CRs.

Because of the importance of the latency distributions, they are presented in Figures 6-2, 6-3, and 6-4 for the .5-, the 1.0-, and the 1.5-sec. interstimulus intervals, respective. For all interstimulus intervals, the responses are presented as a set of five separate distributions representing successive fifths of the conditioning trials. . . . In the figures, the columns represent the number of responses for latency ranges in .05-sec. steps. The designating number below each bar indicates the maximum response latency (measured

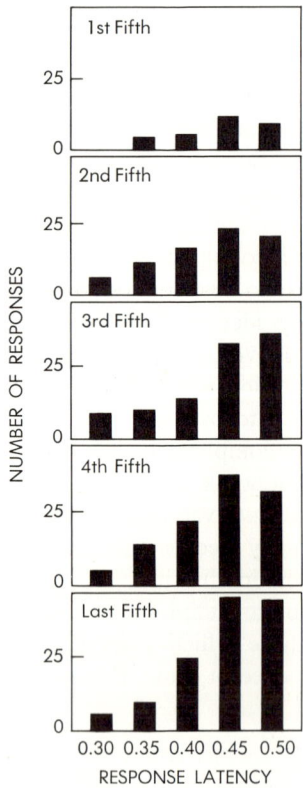

FIGURE 6-2. Latency distributions of responses to 5-second interstimulus interval.

The Definition of Learning

in .01 sec.) in that column. Distributions are truncated at .25 sec. since a negligible amount of responding occurred before that point.

Characteristic of the course of responding as shown by the sets of distributions is a progressive increase in the number of responses in the region immediately adjacent to the point of application of the US. . . . This is paralleled by a shift of the median response latency as indicated by the arrows. Another expression of this tendency is seen, at least for the .5- and 1.0-sec. interstimulus intervals, to be a successive narrowing of the range of response latencies which shows an increase in level of responding when compared with the first fifth of trials. This suggests that the anticipatory

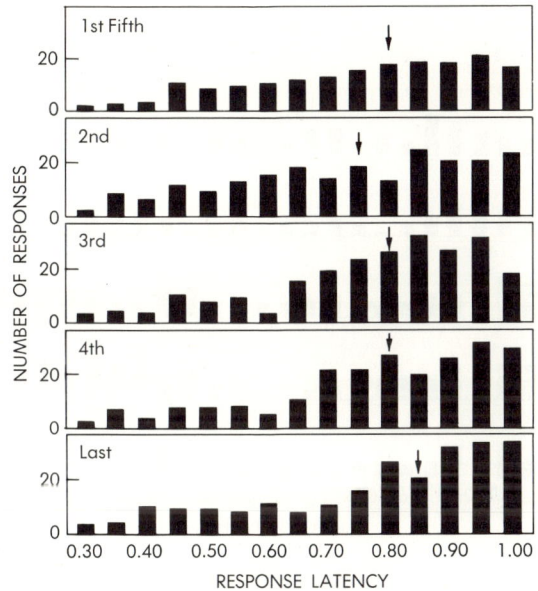

FIGURE 6-3. Latency distributions of responses to 1.0-second interstimulus interval.

blinks tend more and more closely to approximate the onset of the US. Data of a different kind illuminate this process. The records . . . permitted an examination of the temporal relationship between blink and puff. Specifically, it was possible to determine whether or not the blink preceded the puff and whether its duration was long enough to overlap the puff. Typically, the records revealed that blinks lasted approximately .2 sec., that a sizeable number did *not* overlap the puff and thus did not successfully avoid it. Analysis of the records for the 1.0 Control Group showed a progressive increase in the percentage of avoiding CRs from 70% for the first fifth to 90% for the last fifth of conditioning. Of the 12 subjects showing a change in percentage of avoiding CRs 11 increased, an event whose occurrence by chance has a probability of less than .01.

Thus there is evidence that, as conditioning proceeds, there is an increase in the percentage of CRs, and also an increase in the precision of the timing of the blink so that it tends more and more to overlap the puff, presumably vitiating its effects. Such a finding complicates the attempt to establish a simple definition of the CR since the region of increased responding progressively narrows with increasing numbers of trials. Rather than use a sliding criterion, the following ranges were rather arbitrarily decided upon as definitions of CRs appropriate to their respective interstimulus intervals: .31 to .50 sec. for the .5-sec. interstimulus interval, .66 to 1.00 sec. for the 1.0-sec. interval, and 1.01 to 1.50 sec. for the 1.0-sec. interval. As reference

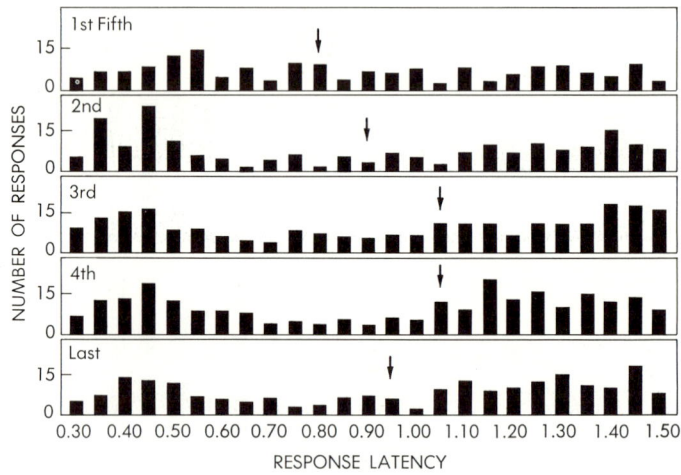

FIGURE 6-4. Latency distributions of responses to 1.5-second interstimulus interval.

to the latency distributions will show, these ranges fairly adequately satisfy the principle which designates as CRs only those responses which show a *consistent* increase in level of responding with practice. (Boneau, 1958, pp. 465–467)

The operation of different processes at different stages of practice. A final complexity facing the scientist who seeks a clean definition of the process of learning stems from the fact that very different events may take place at different stages of practice. To illustrate, let us continue with a discussion of eyelid conditioning. In this simple form of learning the factors responsible for the very first CR in an experiment are not

The Definition of Learning

understood but, once the first conditioned eyeblink has occurred, the situation changes markedly: now the conditioned response can be reinforced in a way that was not previously possible. Since the conditioned blink partially protects the eye from the air puff commonly used as the US, the response can be strengthened by the reduction of noxious stimulation. Boneau's data presented above show that the timing of the CR changes as this conception would suggest it should. Similarly, once the first salivary CR has occurred, it can be rewarded by dilution of the acid US or an increase in the palatability of food if that is used as the US.

This fact has not gone unnoticed in the psychology of learning. Hebb (1956), for example, used it to advocate the position that so-called classical salivary CRs are really instrumentally conditioned. Others (Jones, 1962; Liu, 1964) have advanced stage theories of classical conditioning, proposing that the mechanism of reinforcement changes with the progress of classical conditioning and that something like contiguity learning accounts for the occurrence of the first CR and that reward learning occurs later on. One direct implication of this position is that the person who wants to study classical conditioning in its simplest form might take as his measure of conditioning the number of trials required to elicit the first CR and, for certain purposes, such as studying the generalization of classical CRs, he might be wise to run subjects to a very low criterion of learning (perhaps a criterion of one CR) and then to initiate the test of interest.

METHODOLOGICAL CONSIDERATIONS

Operations required to demonstrate learning

One implication of the foregoing materials is that even a careful definition of learning raises many problems. Another implication is that it will be important, early in the study of any form of allegedly learned behavior, to institute procedures designed to rule out the various alternatives. The standard operations for producing a classical CR involve the pairing of CS and US at some fixed relationship in time. But if conditioning occurs, how is one to know that just presentations of the CS or US alone might not have had the same effect? Or that the mere passage of time did not produce the change? Or that random presentations of CS and US, unpaired in time, might not have had the same effect?

Jensen (1961) has raised questions of this type and has argued that, for an adequate demonstration that a change in behavior is learned, an investigator should run four control groups: CS-only, US-only, CS, US unpaired and a group in which there is only a lapse of time. If, after these treatments, only the experimental group which received CS and US paired were to give CRs to the CS, the demonstration that conditioning had taken place would be quite convincing. If other groups responded similarly, but less, the effectiveness of CS or US presentations could be assessed. In actual experimental practice only the CS, US unpaired control group is commonly used on the assumption that it alone controls for everything the other groups do—presentations of CS, US and the lapse of time. This assumption may not be sound, however. The CS, in the CS, US unpaired procedure, may come to stand for the *absence* of the US, a position advocated by Pavlov (1927) and Mowrer (1960).

All of the procedures recommended by Jensen for justifying the assertion that a particular response is a learned response might be called "between-subjects" procedures. There is, in addition, a "within-subjects" procedure that is occasionally used for the same purpose. This procedure involves conducting a discrimination experiment: two stimuli are used; one is paired with a reinforcer, the other is not. Particularly if the two stimuli excite the same sensory modality, it appears justifiable to refer to an increase in the tendency to respond to the reinforced stimulus as learned if no comparable increase occurs to the nonreinforced stimulus.

Learning versus transfer

In certain of the examples considered in previous sections it seemed likely that two processes, the learning of sequences of events and the strengthening of some response, occurred together in the same situation. It seems equally likely, however, that in other situations only one of these processes (the first) has been involved in any important way and that, by implicit analogy to the more conventional learning situations, responses have been considered as representing the second kind of process when they were really something quite different. A possibly relevant example involves the studies of "verbal conditioning" in which a subject is reinforced by the experimenter for the use of a particular pronoun such as "I" or "we," or for the emission of plural nouns. In these studies the typical result has been an increase in the frequency of emission of the reinforced verbal category. Such an increase does not, however, prove that the subject has *learned* to use these responses. In fact, the details of the evidence suggest quite the opposite. It is entirely possible that the changes in question reflect only the *learning* of the contingencies that apply in the experiment and that the *performance* of the reinforced response represents nothing more than the transfer to this situation of responses already available to the subject. Thus it is possible to view these experiments as ones in which the subject first learns that the experimenter says "good" whenever he says "I" or "we," or gives a plural noun. The subject may decide to go along with the obvious little game the experi-

The Definition of Learning

menter wants to play, or he may not if he is offended by this type of group activity. In brief, the possibility offered here is that the subject learns the contingencies in the situation and that changes in the measured response are not learning but transfer.

If the analysis of the verbal conditioning situation is correct, many psychologists would probably consider such learning and the theoretical issues which surround it as trivial. Thus, it may be worthwhile to apply the same type of analysis to questions that are definitely not trivial: Is learning without responding possible? Although no poll of competent psychologists of learning with respect to this question exists, it seems fairly safe to say that if such a poll were conducted, the results would indicate that these psychologists do believe that learning without responding is possible. In particular, it would be possible to cite the experiments on learning under curare-like drugs. Support of this idea (Kimble, 1961) has been found in the work of Beck and Doty (1957). These investigators immobilized the flexion response to shock in various ways (including injections of bulbocapnine) and paired a .2-second shock with a tone to determine whether conditioning would occur. When the subjects, cats, were tested in a normal state, seven of the eight animals showed substantial levels of conditioning. This evidence could be interpreted as showing that learning without responding had taken place.

The same results could also be interpreted, however, in quite a different way. Under the influence of the drug which immobilized the limb, the cats could make certain responses, specifically the autonomic responses of the fear reaction. Similarly, while under the influence of the drug, these responses could be conditioned to the tone. When the effects of the drug had worn off, the presentation of the CS would elicit the fear conditioned in the drugged state. The animal, then, might very well react with the responses previously acquired under the motive of fear. It would probably surprise no one to discover that these responses included leg flexion (perhaps as a component of a general flight reaction) or that this response was actually a highly dominant reaction to fear. In this way, it is possible to interpret the results of these experiments as demonstrating the conditioning of the responses which could be made under the immobilizing drug and the transfer of responses acquired previously to the test situation in the service of this conditioned fear. Looked at in this way, the results demonstrate the opposite of the conclusion usually drawn from them. They suggest that the responses acquired were those which occurred and that the rest of the results reflect the influence of transfer.

The most radical application of the learning-transfer distinction is to the process of conditioning itself. Specifically there is reason to suspect that the behavioral changes presented as conditioned responses in *some* conditioning experiments are not conditioning at all but are really instances of transfer or generalization. Human salivary and GSR conditioning seem to fit best into this category. Somewhat surprisingly, the former case supplies the stronger evidence. Although human salivary conditioning is difficult to obtain (Feather, pp. 117 to 143, this volume), when it does occur it displays a very suspicious pattern of acquisition. The probability of occurrence of a CR reaches its maximal value in the early trials (see the article by Feather, p. 133 for the evidence). It may be that human salivary CRs, alone among all CRs, display one-trial learning. This seems unlikely, however. It appears more probable that a single reinforcement calls up a general concept ("sour tastes") and that, from then on the subject produces the responses he has previously learned in the service of that concept.

Although the GSR does not show one-trial conditioning as often as three- or four-trial conditioning, the GSR occurs very quickly, suggesting again that such data reflect something other than the establishment of an S-R connection *de novo*. Stewart et al. (1961), noting the same point, have suggested that these early responses are sensitized responses to the CS. Although it is possible that this interpretation is right, the similarity to the salivary results suggests an alternative interpretation; namely, that a series of very few trials with CS and US (usually shock) is enough to remind the subjects of "things that hurt" and that what are counted as CRs are really transferred reactions mediated by this concept.

As was mentioned at the beginning of this section, the suggestion that some CRs are really transferred responses is a radical suggestion, one that this author would prefer to reject. The evidence provides at least weak support for the idea and nothing constructive seems likely to follow from ignoring such implications.

The identification of types of learning

Subsequent chapters of this volume (chapters 15 and 16) devote additional attention to the question of whether learning is more than a single process. In the present context, however, it may be useful to present the situation in terms of certain methodological considerations. In this chapter, learning was identified as an intervening variable with the methodological status diagramed in Figure 6-1. It is commonly recognized that useful scientific concepts must be anchored to independent and dependent variables, as suggested in Figure 6-1. Similar considerations apply to *distinctions* between concepts. Since it is necessary to make firm distinctions between categories of learning, the distinctions between the independent variables must be identified and related operationally to the different forms of learning. Varieties of learning identified

The Definition of Learning

in this operational way must also, of course, relate to differences on the dependent-variable side of the paradigm.

The diagram in Figure 6-5 is an elaboration of Figure 6-1 and represents an attempt to provide an objective picture of the ideas just presented. As the left-hand side of that diagram shows, it is possible to distinguish between instrumental and classical conditioning in terms of independent variables, the contingency or lack of it between a response and a reinforcer. The materials on the right-hand side of the diagram

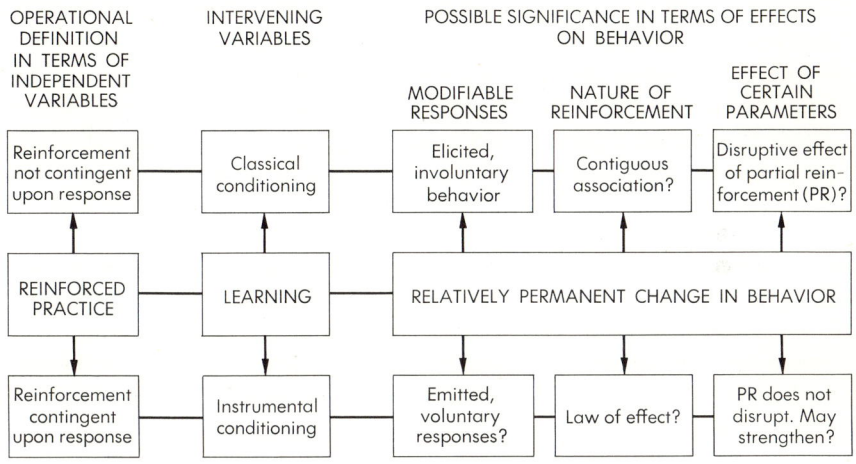

FIGURE 6-5. Diagram to illustrate how the distinction between classical and instrumental conditioning entails the same considerations as the definition of learning.

deliberately raise a series of questions about the possible significance of the operational distinction between classical and instrumental conditioning: Are the responses involved in the two forms of learning different? Do they obey the same law of reinforcement? Do variables such as the schedule of reinforcement have the same effect in partial and in classical and instrumental conditioning? If the answer to these questions is that the two forms of learning are, in every respect, the same, there obviously would be no point, except possibly for purposes of communication, in maintaining the distinction between classical and instrumental conditioning. As has been spelled out elsewhere the two forms of learning seem to this author to involve different types of behavior, different laws of reinforcement and different effects of certain experimental manipulations (Kimble, 1964). Thus it is important to maintain the distinction, at least until these differences are definitely proven to be wrong.

SUMMARY

We have been concerned with the various problems raised directly or indirectly by the definition of learning as "a relatively permanent change in a behavioral potentiality that occurs as a result of reinforced practice." We have found that these problems are more numerous and also more basic than at first seems to be the case. Before turning to a brief review of the issues raised by the definition, however, it may be important to comment on a matter of basic strategy. The definition of learning cited above represents an effort to define learning in ways that limit the term to the meaning we usually give it in everyday speech. There is always a danger in this strategy in that the vulgar use of a term may have the most limited scientific value. It may be that common speech has identified only an approximation to a useful scientific concept and that efforts to capture popular meaning are misguided.

Even recognizing this danger, however, the effort to define learning in a satisfactory way has opened a variety of issues worth discussing.

1. In the case of certain concepts the psychology of learning seems implicitly to have rejected certain elements of this definition. It has described as learned certain states of the organism such as inhibition, motivation and reinforcement which are neither behavior nor potentialities for behavior. A wiser course might have been to pay closer attention to the reactions that serve as symptoms of these states and to consider the possibility that these reactions are those that are learned.

2. The criterion of relative permanence serves the useful purpose of excluding from the definition certain temporary states such as motivation and fatigue. It also provides the basis for the factorial separation of learning and performance.

3. The term potentiality was included in the definition because it is obvious that learning can occur without overt action, although the evidence cited for learning without responding can also be interpreted in terms of generalization of transfer, a distinction to be discussed later.

4. The inclusion of the term *reinforcement* in the definition is necessary if we are to distinguish between acquisition and extinction. The term, however, is an empirical term and need not have the connotations so often associated with it.

5. Although learning may be defined as a function of practice, it is clear that several other processes (some of them producing opposite behavioral effects) are also the result of practice. These include *habituation, sensitization,* at least two kinds of *inhibition,* mechanisms of *motivation* and *reward* and various *changes* in the details of the response. It is also clear that more than one process properly called learning oc-

The Definition of Learning

curs with practice. These include at least the development of a *cognitive* understanding of the conditions of the experiment and the acquisition of the *response* to be learned. Some of our theoretical disputes in the psychology of learning have been the result of a failure to be clear about this distinction.

6. In addition to all of this, it now seems obvious that different processes operate at different stages of training. It is likely that first CRs are produced by different mechanisms than later CRs in experiments on eyelid and other forms of classical conditioning.

7. Some, but not all, of these problems can be handled by performing experiments under proper conditions of control. Other problems demand further clarification of our concepts.

8. Sometimes these clarifications will take the form of maintaining certain distinctions until the necessity for the distinction can be demonstrated no longer to exist. One of these is the distinction between learning and transfer, a distinction which has potential implications for interpreting several controversial matters in the psychology of learning. These include the arguments over learning without awareness and learning without responding. In at least certain instances, the distinction raises questions about the validity of referring to a particular response as "learned."

9. Finally, there is the distinction between definition and law which seems to be valuable in discussing problems related to the differences between classical and instrumental conditioning. Differences exist at the level of definition; whether they also exist at the level of law remains to be discovered.

7

Conditioning as an Artifact[1]

KENDON SMITH[2]

I have always felt a little apologetic about "Conditioning as an Artifact" for two reasons. In the first place, the paper is something of an explication of the obvious. Everyone has known for thousands of years that somatic exertion brings on visceral disturbance; it has been generally recognized for decades that the galvanic skin response can be readily produced by the voluntary contraction of the striate musculature; and anyone in touch with the primary literature knows that light-reinforced pupillary conditioning has never, even after many careful attempts, been satisfactorily demonstrated. The broad idea that autonomic conditioning does not really exist, but that it is merely counterfeited by somatic learning, is suggested so strongly by these considerations that there seems little distinction in being the one to formalize it.

The second reason for being apologetic is mentioned in the paper itself. There, it is pointed out that virtually any attempt to refute the "artifact hypothesis" must find itself in the position of having to prove a negative proposition—namely, that no skeletal muscular activity has occurred during some critical experiment. Inasmuch as it is at least very difficult to establish a negative proposition, the hypothesis accordingly enjoys a logical position which is almost impregnable. The original article expressed regret at this unscientific situation and offered some constructive suggestions concerning it. A recent statement has, moreover, disavowed any intent to seek refuge in logical impregnability (Smith, 1946b).

Original or not, testable or not, the idea that autonomic conditioning might be an artifact has apparently had some tendency to encourage

---

[1] Professor Smith has kindly provided me with a supplementary comment with which this paper begins. After some deliberation I have come to the conclusion that it will be better for the reader to begin with the supplement than with the main body of the article. [Ed.]

[2] The writer wishes to acknowledge with real appreciation the helpful and sustained interest of his colleagues, Professors Joseph H. Grosslight, John F. Hall, and William M. Lepley.

research in the area of the effects of somatic concomitants upon the course of putative visceral conditioning. Without reviewing that research in detail here, it can be said that, on the whole, it has not seemed too threatening to an artifact hypothesis. It has, in fact, appeared to support such an hypothesis. There has been an inclination to focus on respiration as a somatic response (see Malmo, 1963, and Wood & Obrist, 1964, for current examples and for entrance to the literature), and this inclination is understandable and defensible. The existence of somatic contaminants other than respiration is, however, entirely likely; and one would hope that this possibility might be investigated more thoroughly. Also reported have been relevant experiments employing drugs resembling curare to suppress activity of the striate muscles. These experiments have been criticized elsewhere (Smith, 1964a), and the criticism has elicited interesting new data (Black & Lang, 1964).

One always has second thoughts about an article which has been in print for a while, and many of those thoughts are prompted by what the article seems really to have conveyed to others. The principal point which "Conditioning as an Artifact" has failed to communicate, evidently, is the one concerned with the sense in which somatic learning is said to be real, and autonomic artifactual. These are indications that the paper has been understood to say that the somatic learning is "real" because the skeletal response comes first and because neural feedback from this response is the direct cause of the autonomic response. It is true that the paper suggests that a gross mechanism of this sort may operate sometimes (as in the instance of conditioned salivation). It is also true, however, that the paper lays great stress on a more subtle mechanism. Thus, it insists that the somatic response and the autonomic response must be pictured, in the general case, as arising coordinately from a common source; and that the somatic response is the more basic only because it provides the neural feedback required to maintain the entire somato-autonomic *Gestalt* as a response to the conditioned stimulus.

This point may one day be of some significance. If an attempt is made to test the artifact hypothesis by eliminating afferent return from the striate muscles, for instance, one should not expect (on the basis of the hypothesis) the immediate elimination of some correlated visceral response—and thus regard the hypothesis as compromised if the visceral response continues for a number of trials. The hypothesis would actually predict the latter phenomenon, simply as a manifestation of extinction. Only the protracted survival of the acquired autonomic response would be really damning.[3]

The case for a pure reinforcement theory of learning has been

---

[3] What follows is reproduced from the *Psychological Review*, 1954, 61, with the permission of the American Psychological Association and the author.

strongly put by recent papers (Kendler, 1951; Kendler & Underwood, 1948; Miller, 1951; Spence, 1950), and it is difficult now to escape the conviction that such a view is essentially correct.

In spite of its fundamental strength, however, reinforcement theory has remained weak in one respect. It has experienced continual difficulty in handling the problem of autonomic, visceral learning. To be consistent, Hull was obliged to maintain that reinforcement was crucial even in the presumed acquisition of such responses as salivation, alteration of skin resistance, cardiovascular changes, etc. This he did (1943, pp. 76-80), although not as flatly as he is sometimes said to have done. Hull thus arrived at a position that many have regarded as untenable; for, although it is possible to imagine reinforcemental factors at work in some instances of alleged visceral learning, there are many other instances in which the influence of such factors seems to be completely out of the question.

One variant of reinforcement theory that is designed to meet the situation more adequately is the so-called "two-factor" theory. It has been most recently and most vigorously promoted by Mowrer (1947, 1951), but Mowrer's views are in reality quite similar to those previously advanced by Thorndike (1932, pp. 401-412) and Skinner (1938, pp. 109-115). Mowrer differentiates between *conditioning* and *problem solving*. The first term refers to the process of learning by a stimulus-substitution, contiguity principle; the second term, to that of learning by a principle of reinforcement. Conditioning is alleged to occur specifically via the autonomic nervous system, and problem solving to be mediated solely by the "central" (i.e., somatic) nervous system; a sharp distinction between the two neurological divisions is drawn and emphasized.

Such incisive dualism has an undeniable appeal. It suffers, however, from a disquieting lack of parsimony. It is extremely difficult to believe that "visceral learning" and somatic learning, so alike in so many respects, must be accomplished by two different principles (Sheffield, 1951). The resolution of the problem thus appears to lie elsewhere.

As it happens, there exists a rather simple way to save reinforcement, and parsimony with it. One can begin by accepting the notion that somatic learning is reinforcemental learning. He can then go one step further than Mowrer has, and expunge from the viscera not only problem solving but conditioning as well. This procedure leaves the law of effect to rule in monistic majesty. Of course, it also makes the autonomic nervous system totally uneducable; but that, it can be asserted, is as it should be. For it can be argued that every "conditioned visceral response" is in reality an artifact, an innate accompaniment of the skeletal responses inculcated by the conditioning process.

The present paper will, in fact, attempt to defend this general line of thought.

The argument and a specific instance

In the elaboration of this proposal, it might be wise to begin with a concrete example. The galvanic skin response and its "conditioning" would seem to be appropriate.

When an attempt is made to condition the galvanic skin response, the procedure generally pairs a neutral conditioned stimulus with an unconditioned stimulus that is more or less noxious in nature, typically an electrical shock. Several pairings will eventuate, in some subjects, in a new correlation between the GSR and the originally neutral stimulus. "Conditioning"[4] has occurred.

Anyone who has actually carried out this procedure knows, however, that the foregoing account is seriously incomplete. The subject is not by any means a passive hulk during the entire program. In particular, he soon comes to regard the conditioned stimulus as a signal for a muscular "bracing" against the noxious stimulus to come; presumably this bracing, being somatic, is a matter of reinforcemental learning. At any rate, one would expect such skeletal activity to be accompanied by the GSR, simply as a matter of innate neural connections. The occurrence of the conditioned GSR is thus hardly surprising, and it can be explained without recourse to a principle of autonomic learning. It is, in short, an artifact.

Now, at least two objections arise immediately. The first is that a scheme that works so well for one response, the GSR, may not work at all for others: what about salivation, for instance? This is a reasonable misgiving, but it will be reserved for later consideration. The second objection is basic and serious, and it will be faced immediately.

The difficulty is this: although it may seem quite natural to think of somatic responses as somehow "causing" their concomitant autonomic reactions, and although such a notion frequently finds expression in the literature, it is well to remember that the causal sequence is actually most obscure. It is entirely possible, for instance, that the muscular tension and its associated GSR arise as parallel events from a common innervation. The conservative view would seem to be that there is no distinguishable priority as between the two responses. By what right, then, is one considered the "real" response and the other a mere by-product?

Common sense would very likely answer that question rather readily: "The muscular response is the real response, because it is *con-*

---

[4] Inasmuch as this paper ultimately arrives at the conclusion that "conditioning" does not actually exist, the term itself has been treated so far in a rather gingerly fashion. In the interests of clean typography, quotation marks will be omitted from now on; but when conditioning and similar terms are used, they are meant to be read as if quotation marks were still present.

scious; I didn't even know there was a 'galvanic skin response' until you told me about it!" Common sense thus suggests an answer which makes a certain amount of scientific sense too.

The combined, bracing-GSR reaction has already been pictured as a unitary one; and it was agreed to begin with that somatic responses attach themselves to new stimuli according to a reinforcemental paradigm. It follows, therefore, that the combined response, as a unit, gets about by reinforcement. Now, the acquisition and maintenance of a voluntary (i.e., reinforcementally acquired) response is dependent upon the existence of afferent cues (Boring, 1942, p. 524 ff.).[5] The skeletal responses, in the case at hand, provide a wealth of afferent information; but the autonomic reactions generate no regulatory feedback whatsoever. Acquisition of the whole response pattern, therefore, would seem to depend upon the integrity of the somatic component. If it were not for the muscular response, the GSR would not exist; but the GSR could be eliminated, perhaps by sympathectomy, and the bracing response would remain unaffected. The GSR is truly, in this sense, a secondary-phenomenon, a by-product.

The earlier analysis of the conditioned GSR thus appears to be valid. At the same time, examination of this particular instance has generated a logic that can be applied to other instances of alleged autonomic learning. If it can be shown that the development of any new autonomic response is coincident with the growth of a somatic response known to have such an autonomic response as a regular correlate, it is legitimate to label the autonomic response as a secondary effect and the conditioning as bogus.[6]

The question remaining, then, is this: Do other instances of conditioning fit this pattern well enough to permit generalization of the artifact hypothesis?

Applications in other instances

As one might expect, some varieties of conditioning conform to the pattern quite obviously, and others do not. For example, there are quite a few autonomic responses which, like the GSR, are known to be associated with the diffuse skeletal reactions that develop during a conditioning procedure. The foregoing discussion might just as well have

---

[5] It is perhaps possible that this dependence stands as a testimony to the importance of immediate higher-order reinforcement; the afferent cues may constitute particularly prompt rewards and punishments. In any event, the dependence seems to be a fact.

[6] It is true that some visceral responses arouse afferent neural activity. As a class, however, these responses are sluggish, and the afferent information that they provide is greatly delayed in returning to the central nervous system. It can be presumed that there might as well be no return at all.

revolved about the response of vasoconstriction as about the GSR; thus, conditioned vasoconstriction (Beier, 1940; Menzies, 1937; Roessler & Brogden, 1943) fits the theory well. The same might be said for the few reported instances of conditioned vasodilation and for conditioned cardiac deceleration, which was recently observed in animals and human beings (Kosupkin & Olmstead, 1943; Notterman, Schoenfeld, & Bersh, 1952). On the other hand, there are also instances that do not fall into place quite so neatly. Nevertheless (and this is the burden of the paragraphs to come), they do not, on close examination, present the prohibitive difficulties one might expect.

A case in point is that which generated the concept of conditioning in the first place: the salivary reflex. Everyone knows about Pavlov's classical experiments, and everyone knows that Pavlov induced his experimental animals to salivate on signal. It is not quite so widely known, however, that the animals did several other things besides salivating. Of special interest at the moment is the fact that they displayed gross skeletal responses. Pavlov observed movements of the head and "smacking . . . of the lips" (1927, pp. 29–30), the animal appearing ". . . to take the air into its mouth, or to eat the sound" of the conditioned stimulus (Pavlov, 1932). Pavlov spoke frequently of the "alimentary reflex" or the "complex reflex of nutrition" (1927, pp. 13–14), and emphasized the fact that he was dealing with a pervasive pattern of behavior rather than with salivation alone.

These facts are manifestly made to order for the present hypothesis. Further, they have been confirmed by later experimenters. Zener (1937) who also worked with the salivary reflex in dogs, sometimes saw "chewing and licking" responses when the conditioned stimulus was administered; Zener and McCurdy (1939) reported a correlation between rate of salivation and rate of chewing. And Moore and Marcuse (1945) who stoutly undertook to condition the salivary responses of two sows, were explicitly concerned that the observed salivation might be due to oral activity. The records obtained by Moore and Marcuse seemed to give negative indications. These experimenters, nevertheless, had finally recognized the possibility, which had been so curiously neglected until their time, that the salivary responses were not essentially independent of the motor responses in the animal's behavior, but rather that the visceral activity of salivation was a natural concomitant of the acquired somatic activities of chewing, swallowing, etc. In this case, it might be noted, the possibility of concomitance had existed not only in the sense in which it has been developed in the foregoing discussion. It had existed also in the more obvious sense that sheer mechanical stimulation arising from oral activity could be expected to elicit salivation directly.

Of special interest at this point are Razran's reports of conditioned salivary responses in human subjects. Razran's experiments are well known, but it might be emphasized that, here once again, it was a complex process that was under investigation. Early results were rather widely irregular (1935), and Razran (1935, 1936, 1939) soon came to recognize the importance of his subjects' "attitudes." It turned out also that the act of thinking was important in the experimental results: ". . . it is seemingly not mere 'willing' but thinking of some more or less specific stimulus or response that produces a voluntary flow of saliva" (1935, p. 9). Explicit instructions to "form associations" between conditioned and unconditioned stimuli "produced very effective positive conditioning," while instructions to avoid forming associations usually had an opposite effect. It was even possible to substitute the thought of eating for actual eating, as the *unconditioned* stimulus, and still have a successful experiment.

Razran (1935) cautioned his subjects against gross oral movements, and his injunctions were evidently obeyed; thus the skeletal responses that might have evoked salivation were not as obvious in this instance as they were in the case of animal conditioning. Nevertheless, the fact that thought processes seemed so important is quite suggestive. If there is anything at all to a motor theory of thought and imagination, one must acknowledge the possibility of oral activity similar in nature, if not in magnitude, to that of the animal subjects. If such activity occurred, it might well have evoked the measured salivation. To be emphasized, also, is the role of gross bodily tension. Razran's subjects were hungry, and the food signal might well have led to a certain degree of general muscular relaxation in anticipation of ingestion. Such relaxation could be expected to tip the autonomic balance toward parsympathetic dominance and thus toward salivation.

It appears, then, that the conditioned salivary response is not beyond reconciliation with the notions proposed earlier. Attention may now be turned to another standard example of visceral learning: the conditioned pupillary response, which is of special interest in the present context principally because it evidently does not exist.

The pupillary response

It is, perhaps, surprising to discover that pupillary conditioning is even in doubt. The early reports of Cason (1922b) and Hudgins (1933) were optimistic and well publicized. They mentioned not only iridic conditioning but even "voluntary control" of the pupillary response. In 1934, Steckle and Renshaw reported an attempt to condition the pupillary reflex; the attempt was unsuccessful, and the experimenters expressed some skepticism about the earlier accounts. The ensuing discussion in the literature (Hudgins, 1935; Steckle, 1934) made it clear that these earlier studies had been replete with technical difficulties that left considerable room for subjective, judgmental factors. In 1936, in the second of the two papers last mentioned, Steckle again reported negative findings.

In 1938, positive results were claimed once more. Baker described iridic conditioning to "subliminal" and supraliminal sounds. Conditioning was alleged to be particularly rapid and stable when subliminal stimuli were employed. An elaborate repetition of Baker's work by Wedell, Taylor, and Skolnick (1940) failed to confirm his results, as did a careful check by Hilgard, Miller, and Ohlson (1941). A recent and thorough exploration by Hilgard, Dutton, and Helmick (1949) has again produced very little evidence of successful iridic conditioning. Citing similar results with animals as well as with human beings, these latter authors warn that continued negative findings may force a revision of accepted learning theory.

In terms of the matter at hand, the defection of the pupillary response has a double significance. In the first place, it means that no theory need be seriously concerned with accounting for the existence of a conditioned iridic reflex; the present formulation, along with others, thus escapes a certain amount of travail. In the second place, and more importantly, the failure of the pupillary response is materially embarrassing to a conditioning theory of visceral learning. Here, in the hands of competent workers, the principle of contiguity has had ample opportunity to exhibit itself. It has not done so. If "contiguity" and "artifact" are regarded as exhaustive alternatives, the artifact hypothesis appears to be the sole survivor.

It is of some incidental interest to speculate as to why conditioning should fail in the special instance of the pupillary response. It might be suggested that the changes in level of illumination that are customarily employed in iridic-conditioning experiments are of no practical consequence to the subjects, and that, therefore, no anticipatory skeletal responses are acquired. There being no acquired skeletal responses, there is no conditioning.

In this connection, it is worth noting that unexplained failures characterize almost every conditioning experiment. Some subjects condition, and others do not. Such vagaries are much more suggestive of individual differences in personality structure than they are of the presumed essential similarity of fundamental neurological processes from person to person. One thinks of greater and lesser tendencies toward anticipation, anxiety, and (literal) tension as perhaps underlying the personal variations in conditionability. It is evident that the recently reported correlations between anxiety level and conditionability fit in rather neatly with such a conceptualization (Bitterman and Holtzman, 1952; Notterman, Schoenfeld and Bersh, 1952; Welch & Kubis, 1947).[7]

---

[7] Note that in this account the argument is applied only to pupillary conditioning experiments where the US was a strong light. Pupillary conditioning has been obtained a number of times using shock as the US [Ed.].

Tests and testability

The foregoing evidence is taken to be strongly favorable to an artifact theory of conditioning. It hardly suffices to close the matter, however. It seems appropriate now to examine other lines of evidence, formal and informal, actual and potential, which might have a bearing upon the hypothesis at hand.

From everyday experience comes the first datum: it is notoriously possible to forestall an untoward visceral response by "not thinking about it." Stimuli that might otherwise elicit nausea, flushing, or sexual reflexes lose much of their effectiveness when one refuses to dwell on their implications. If thought is somatic, it would thus appear that the autonomic response depends upon the somatic and does not arise independently of it. There are clear and perhaps important implications here for a further understanding of such phenomena as hysterical nausea and psychological impotence.

A somewhat similar argument also rises from everyday experience. Sheffield (1951) has well pointed out the obvious fact that bowel and bladder functions are in some sense subject to reinforcemental training. An equally obvious fact, to be emphasized here, is that such training is conducted in terms of massive somatic responses, and that everyday visceral control is exercised only by virtue of diffuse contractions of the skeletal musculature. Again, it appears that the "real" response is a somatic one.

Both of the preceding arguments bolster the basic contention that learned visceral activity is a by-product of somatic behavior. A crucial test of this contention could be made if one could provide oneself with a subject who is completely passive, and even unthinking. A subject in such a state should not, according to theory, be susceptible to conditioning. Could such a situation be contrived under deep hypnosis? One can imagine a good hypnotic subject, instructed to relax and to "keep his mind completely blank," but to remain awake and aware of such stimuli as bells and shocks; would the conditioned GSR appear in such circumstances?

To the best of the writer's knowledge, such an experiment has not been performed. It must be admitted, however, that a rather similar situation has been reported, and that it does not seem to conform to theoretical expectations. In 1938, Lindsley and Sassaman reported the discovery of an individual who was able to exercise "voluntary control" over his pilomotor responses. The body hair could be erected or lowered upon signal. The subject reported having come upon his talent more or less accidentally. He denied that the basis for his performance was controlled imagery: he imagined nothing in particular; he simply "willed" the response. Neither were there obvious skeletal movements or muscular tensions to account for these hirsute accomplishments. This case, anomalous as it is, presents difficulties for practically any theory of conditioning. The only saving feature, as far as the present hypothesis is concerned, is that there were indications of a very diffuse activity of some sort: cardiac and pupillary effects accompanied the pilomotor responses. The possibility of a covert somatic response was thus considerable.

The tenor of this discussion suggests a well-known animal investigation, that of Harlow and Stagner (1933). Using cats as subjects, these investigators paralyzed the striate musculature by deep curarization. While the animals were under curare, the pupillary response to electrical shock (which could still be elicited) was conditioned to the sound of a buzzer. Here again is ostensibly negative evidence. As it has turned out, however, the effects of curare upon the neuromuscular system seem to be quite complex, and later experiments have found striate-muscle responses even in deeply curarized animals (Girden, 1942; Girden & Culler, 1937). If Harlow and Stagner's animals retained some degree of skeletal responsiveness, the experiment loses much of its crucial aspect as far as the present discussion is concerned.

One final bit of information comes from Mowrer. In a recent defense of two-factor theory (1951), he has quoted incidental observations by Gantt to the effect that when a conditioned-response pattern embraces both motor and cardiac elements, the visceral, cardiac component often persists after the motor has disappeared. Such an observation, if well founded, might also damage an artifact theory. The original passage from Gantt goes on to say, however, that "the respiratory component also accompanies the cardiac" (p. 51). Evidently, then, Gantt means by "motor component" only really gross skeletal behavior. Less spectacular somatic responses not only could occur along with the autonomic responses, but admittedly do.

It begins to appear that an artifact theory is remarkably easy to defend. As a matter of fact, it is almost invulnerable. Unless an experimenter is meticulous in the elimination of skeletal responses, it will always be possible to account for visceral conditioning by postulating undetected somatic activity. And whenever visceral conditioning fails, one can always claim that no effective skeletal behavior was aroused (a stand already taken above with respect to the failure of pupillary conditioning).

This is an unfortunate situation scientifically, but it is not unique. In the current controversy over "latent learning," for instance, the reinforcementalists find themselves in exactly the same logical position. The strategy in that instance has been to attempt to eliminate all conceivable opportunities for reinforcement to operate, expecting thus to minimize "latent learning." Perhaps an analogous attack can be made upon the problem here at hand.

Related notions

The concepts sketched above are not, of course, completely original. There has long existed a general feeling that the conditioned reflex is somehow vaguely fraudulent. Hilgard, who has displayed a lasting interest in the systematic status of conditioning has quite recently taken a position essentially antecedent to the one adopted here. Two excerpts from his 1948 book will define his stand:

> . . . experiments in which autonomic conditioning takes place (salivation, galvanic response) are full of indirect accompaniments of a reinforcemental variety. When the circumstances seem also ideal for demonstrating . . . conditioning, as in attempts to condition pupillary contraction by presenting a tone along with a light, it is extremely difficult to obtain any conditioning at all. The few cases which have found conditioning are in doubt. . . . (pp. 119–120)
>
> . . . there is little evidence that the simultaneous or nearly simultaneous occurrence of an incidental stimulus and an unconditioned response is the sufficient condition for establishing a sensori-motor association between them. (p. 334)

An earlier (1935) and more general expression of somewhat the same sentiment can be found in a note by Foley:

> . . . experimental work on conditioning in complex organisms . . . is often completely vitiated by the fact that certain implicit reactions, with their attendant stimulations, are frequently occurring simultaneously or temporally adjacent to the predetermined stimulations experimentally administered by the investigator. (p. 444)

Foley, however, does not fix his suspicions upon reinforcemental factors as plainly as does Hilgard. Neither did Freeman, who summarized his experiments of 1930, on the GSR, in much the same vein:

> Since the quantitative results were obtained in a manner similar to that of animal experimentation, I have interpreted them as "conditioned responses"; but it seems that they might just as easily be interpreted as physiological accompaniments of the attitudes of expectation and surprise. (p. 534)

Cook and Harris (1937), Lazarus and McCleary (1951), and Mowrer in an earlier paper (1938) have expressed similar opinions on the conditioned galvanic skin response. With respect to salivary conditioning, Razran and Zener have also emphasized motivational and attitudinal factors in quite general terms.

The formulation arrived at in the present paper should not be confused with an already rather common one. A great many theorists have maintained, in one way or another, that what actually develops as a result of stimulus contiguity is an association, a cognition, an expectancy, or, perhaps, a conditioned sensation. At any rate, this general view represents essentially an extension of the contiguity principle to somatic learning (it is not always completely clear how these theorists account for the autonomic phenomena that arise during the conditioning process). Such an extension of the contiguity principle is, of course, quite opposed to the theory at hand, which sets out to obliterate the principle entirely.

The present view welcomes the suggestion that what really happens in visceral conditioning is that an "expectancy" develops. It would insist, however, that such an "expectancy" is a somatic process, inculcated by reinforcemental learning (Woodworth, 1947) and occurring in the skeletal musculature, and that, as an innate by-product of this muscular activity, the observed visceral responses arise.

8

A Magnitude Measure of the Conditioned Eyelid Response[1]

HENRY S. PENNYPACKER

Before any natural phenomenon can be subjected to scientific investigation it is first necessary to devise procedures whereby changes in some quantitative aspect of the phenomenon can be represented numerically—in short, the phenomenon must be measured. Although considerable attention has been focused on this problem in the case of the conditioned eyelid response, the variety of mensurational techniques currently in use attests to the fact that none of them has been found to be entirely satisfactory. Changes in eyelid response strength are currently being inferred from measures of latency, amplitude, or simple frequency of occurrence, the latter index being used most frequently.

The eyeblink differs from most skeletal responses, for which frequency measures are generally appropriate, in that its occurrence is occasioned by the contraction of a sphincter muscle, the *obicularis oculi*. Thus, as one may readily observe by electromyographic monitoring techniques, the period of lid closure in an awake subject corresponds to a period of continuous action of the sphincter. Since the amount of lid closure (momentary amplitude) at any instant may be regarded as reflecting the amount of sphincter contraction at that instant, it follows that the definite integral of momentary amplitude with respect to time, evaluated between the temporal limits set by the time course of the blink, would measure the continuous action of the sphincter muscle and would thus provide a continuous index of the strength of the blink. This measure, which I shall call magnitude,[2] is illustrated for the case of the conditioned anticipatory blink in Figure 8-1.

---

[1] A different report of this study appeared in *Science*, 144, pp. 1248–1249.
[2] The term *magnitude* has previously been used by Humphreys (*J. gen. Psychol.*, 1943, 29, pp. 101–111) to denote the average amplitude (including zeros) of a finite set of responses. Since the present use of the term is with reference to properties of a single response, the likelihood of confusion would seem to be minimal.

A Magnitude Measure of the Conditioned Eyelid Response

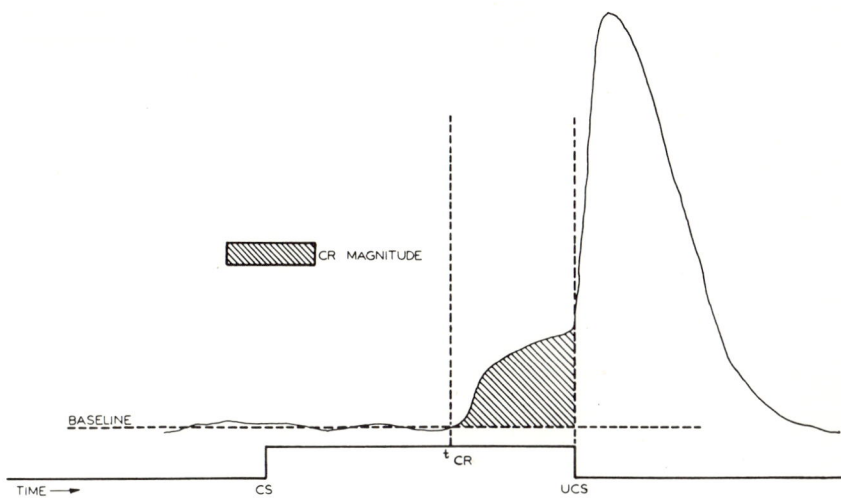

FIGURE 8-1. An idealized tracing of a conditioned anticipatory blink followed by the unconditioned response to the air-puff. The magnitude is defined as the area under the tracing bounded by the extrapolated base line and the occurrence of the UCR.

In order to estimate the concurrent validity of this measure in terms of the conventional indices of conditioned eyelid response strength, 18 college students each received 60 conditioning trials in which the CS was a circular red light, the UCS was a 180 mm. air-puff of 0.10 second duration, and the CS-UCS interval was 1.0 second. A full description of the apparatus and procedure is available elsewhere in this volume (cf. pp. 532-534, Gp. 1); briefly, lid responses were recorded by mechanically connecting the shaft of a microtorque potentiometer to the subject's eyelid by means of a false eyelash. The output of the potentiometer was amplified and recorded on a moving paper record; a separate channel monitored the occurrences of the conditioning stimuli.

For each of the 1,080 trials thus administered, 4 measures of conditioned response strength were obtained: (1) frequency (1 or 0 depending upon whether or not a pen deflection in the direction of closure occurred), (2) amplitude (the maximum distance the pen deviated from the baseline prior to the onset of the UCS), (3) latency (the time between the onset of the conditioning stimulus and the occurrence of the deflection, provided that such time exceeded 600 msec., the arbitrarily defined minimum latency of a conditioned response), and (4) magnitude. The magnitude data were obtained with the aid of a specially constructed rubber stamp which had a tiny raised dot in the center of each square of a grid ruled in millimeters. By stamping the record with this stamp, then counting the dots inside the prescribed area, a measure of the desired area in square millimeters was obtained.

Figure 8-2 compares the descriptions of acquisition performance produced by the four measures individually. In case of all four measures, trials on which a response failed to occur were arbitrarily scored 0, thus making the general form of the function relating latency to the independent variable comparable to that of the other three functions.

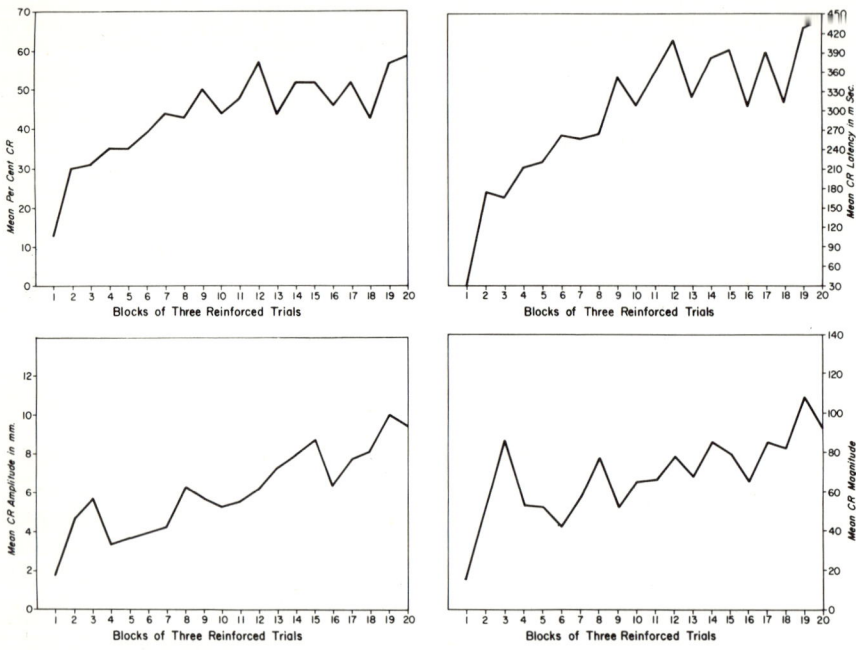

FIGURE 8-2. Performance during acquisition as described by four separate measures of response strength. The unit of magnitude measurement is the square millimeter.

Estimates of the reliability of each of the four measures were obtained by correlating the subject's odd and even trial totals and, with the aid of the Spearman-Brown prophecy formula, adjusting the results to approximate the reliability of the complete measurement session. This procedure produced the following reliability coefficients: frequency, .966; latency, .950; amplitude, .983; and magnitude, .991. It is apparent that the magnitude measure is, by a slight margin, the most reliable of the four measures involved.

Intercorrelations among the various measures are presented in Table 8-1. The non-italicized coefficients involving latency reflect the use of 1.0 as the latency value arbitrarily assigned to those trials on which no response occurred; this procedure was adopted at this point in order to

TABLE 8-1

Intercorrelations among measures of conditioned response strength, frequence, amplitude, latency, and magnitude*

	Frequency	Amplitude	Latency	Magnitude
Amplitude	.688 .000			
Latency	-.792 .000	-.646 -.248		
Magnitude	.587 .000	.856 .767	-.713 -.493	

* The italicized coefficients were calculated after the "non-response" trials were omitted from the data.

eliminate the presence of a discontinuity in the latency distribution which is no longer needed for comparative purposes. The italicized coefficients were calculated after the trials on which no responses were obtained were omitted from the analysis. All intercorrelations in Table 8-1 are corrected for attenuation due to unreliability of measurement of both variables and may thus be regarded as estimates of the "true" relationships among the various response indices, uncontaminated by random errors of measurement.

It is evident from Table 8-1 that the magnitude measure provides a statistically superior description of the physical properties (latency and amplitude) of the conditioned eyelid response than does the commonly used frequency measure. The average of the absolute correlations of frequency with latency and amplitude is .743; the average absolute correlation of magnitude with these two variables is .797, a difference which is significant beyond the .01 level. This difference, coupled with the fact that the correlation between frequency and magnitude is relatively low, indicates that the frequency measure does not account for variance among conditioned responses which would necessarily seem to be related to the physiological processes by which such responses are produced. On the other hand, the magnitude measure appears to exhibit variance which cannot be explained by linear combination of latency and amplitude ($R_{m.al} = .870$). This finding is in line with anecdotal observations; the majority of response tracings exhibit irregularities which cannot be quantitatively described without reference to the continuous changes in amplitude over time.

Use of the magnitude measure as a dependent variable in future eyelid conditioning studies may be fruitful for a number of reasons. The variance which it seems to display uniquely may be lawfully related to unexplored dependent variables. Second, the increased precision of measurement achieved by application of a continuous scale can be expected to make the results of eyelid conditioning procedures quantitatively comparable to results obtained using other response mechanisms (such as the GSR) for which continuous measures have been devised. For example, various inhibitory phenomena which often lack sufficient potency to suppress the response entirely, may now be described and investigated in the eyelid conditioning situation. Finally, and perhaps most importantly, the face validity of the magnitude measure as an indicant of the underlying physiological process by which the eyeblink occurs certainly appears to exceed that of any other measure yet devised. To this extent, its use can only be expected to facilitate the integration of the psychological and physiological phenomena which jointly define classical conditioning.

9

Human Salivary Conditioning: A Methodological Study[1]

BEN W. FEATHER

The first systematic studies of classical conditioning began in the last century with Ivan P. Pavlov's pioneering experiments on conditioned salivation in dogs, although the phenomenon itself was neither new nor revolutionary. As Rosenzweig (1959) has pointed out, the earlier literature contained at least a half dozen observations of naturally occurring conditioned salivation and one experiment by Claude Bernard on conditioned salivation in the horse. Thus Pavlov's contribution consisted in the conception and execution of a comprehensive experimental program on a phenomenon which previously had stirred only passing interest. The theoretical use to which Pavlov put his empirical findings is now well known. In the conditioned reflex, he saw a foundation for the first scientific program of study of higher nervous activity. In Western science, the significance of classical conditioning was evaluated in quite different terms. Learning theorists (e.g., Hull, pp. 171 to 189, this volume) saw the conditioned reflex as a basic form of learning whose laws might apply to more complex behavior.

The writer's interest in classical conditioning developed in this latter tradition and stemmed from Razran's (1961) review of Russian studies on semantic generalization which suggested that subtle thought processes might be revealed objectively by semantic generalization experiments. An increasing familiarity with the problems inherent in these studies, however, led to a rather pessimistic appraisal of the validity of most of them (Feather, 1965a) and to an interest in classical conditioning per se. For several reasons, conditioned salivation seemed a reasonable choice of experimental procedure to develop in the service of this interest.

[1] The investigation reported here comprised the author's doctoral dissertation research, sponsored by Dr. Gregory A. Kimble. I am very grateful to Dr. Kimble for his advice, support and encouragement. The research was supported by a Public Health Service Career Development Award, K3-MH-19, 523, from the National Institute of Mental Health, by the Duke University Council on Research, and by the Research Foundation of the National Association for Mental Health, Inc.

The first reason for choosing the salivary reflex for further study was the belief that it might be influenced relatively little by voluntary and attitudinal variables. This belief was based more on physiological considerations than on experimental evidence, since the direct effect of voluntary factors on salivation in a conditioning experiment is still unknown. A second reason for choosing salivation was the hope (firm evidence again being lacking) that problems of sensitization and pseudoconditioning, so troublesome in other varieties of autonomic conditioning, might be avoided. This hope was based on the fact that the salivary reflex is relatively more specific, being elicitable by a more limited class of stimuli than is, say, the GSR. Finally, there is a large gap between Pavlov's results of conditioning in dogs and human behavior to which these results have been applied. It seemed important, therefore, to examine the basis for extrapolating from animal to human conditioning.

REVIEW OF HUMAN SALIVARY CONDITIONING EXPERIMENTS

With a few exceptions, previous studies of human salivation have been occasional, sporadic, and designed more to study some other phenomenon than systematically to investigate the salivary CR. As a result, there is no information concerning optimal values of any parameter of salivary conditioning. Indeed, very few experiments have adequately demonstrated human salivary conditioning. A further complication is that no accepted standard method has evolved for collecting, measuring, and recording human salivation, much less for specifying the characteristics of a CR. There are at least five different techniques for studying salivary secretion in man. Since the results obtained by these different methods are not comparable, they will be considered separately in this section.

Frequency of deglutitive movements. In order to measure salivation indirectly, Krasnogorsky recorded the number of deglutitive movements. An infant lying on its back will swallow after even a slight accumulation of saliva in the mouth. Krasnogorsky found that sounding a bell and reinforcing it with milk soon began to cause an increase in the frequency of swallowing movements to the bell. Initially Krasnogorsky simply observed and recorded swallowing, but later he used mechanical recording devices. Krasnogorsky also recorded concurrent motor activity, and came to consider motor and secretory responses as two separate reflexes with different characteristics. For example, the first conditioned mouth movement usually occurred earlier in acquisition, and typically was of shorter latency than a secretory response. The possibility that conditioned salivation was dependent upon such motor activity was not investigated. The main value of these early experiments should have been to call attention to the relationship between motor and secretory reflexes. Unfortunately, this relationship has been ignored in most later investigations and is still not understood.

Parotid fistulae and cannulation of Stensen's duct. Pavlov's method of studying salivation in dogs required the surgical formation of an external parotid fistula. While this method is not applicable in man, there have occurred occasional cases of parotid fistulae as a result of disease or trauma. One such subject was studied by Gley and Mendelssohn (1915). They took advantage of this unusual opportunity by attempting to produce conditioned salivation. Using both lights and sounds as CSs and chocolate covered cakes as the US, they found no evidence for conditioning after 40 to 50 combinations. They suggested that their negative results might be due to the intervention of previous associations, memory processes, and simple judgments.

Lashley (1916) reviewed early attempts to obtain human salivation by cannulation of Stensen's duct and concluded that this method was inadequate because of leakage of the secretion around the cannula and the difficulty in keeping the cannula in place. The present writer employed this method on two subjects, but soon gave it up. In order to avoid leakage, the outer diameter of the catheter must be greater than the inner diameter of the undistended Stensen's duct. A catheter this large produces painful irritation, and can be used only for short periods.

Absorbent technique. Razran (1935) devised a simple technique for measuring human salivation. His method consisted of placing a preweighed dental cotton roll under a subject's tongue for a given time, then reweighing and recording the increment as amount of saliva secreted. His general procedure was to divide each experiment into a preconditioning, conditioning, and postconditioning series of trials. In the preconditioning series, salivation was measured after a period of no stimulation and after a comparable period in which the CS (e.g., a metronome) had been presented alone. In the conditioning series, salivation was measured after the US (e.g., eating pretzels) alone and after presentation of combined CS and US. The postconditioning series was identical to preconditioning. The most convincing evidence of conditioning would have been a significant increase in salivation from the pre-experimental to the postconditioning series in the CS test trials compared to control trials. The data were given in this form for only the first preliminary experiment on five subjects. This difference was significant in only one subject.

In his next study, Razran employed eight subjects and used the same procedure as in the preliminary experiment. His results differed markedly from those of Pavlov on dogs, and these differences were summarized as follows:

1. The conditioning was very sporadic and unstable, its appearance and disappearance in trials and sessions seemingly little related to any objective factors and conditions of the experiments.

2. The conditioning was not affected after the first few trials by training or reinforcements of the conditioned by the conditioning stimulus.

3. The conditioned responses suffered no decrements upon the repeated applications of the conditioned without the conditioning stimulus, or, in other words, did not show the phenomenon of experimental unconditioning (extinction).

4. The distributions of the magnitudes of the conditioned responses were not normal, but bi- and tri-modal.

5. The variabilities of the conditioned responses were very large and independent of the magnitudes; they also were comparatively constant, so that the relative variabilities correlated negatively with their respective magnitudes.

6. After a great deal of training, the thought of the conditioned stimulus was a more effective conditioner than the conditioned stimulus itself, although the thought was not specifically associated with the conditioning stimulus [Razran, 1935, pp. 40–41].

In his remaining two experiments, Razran studied the effects of some 20 different treatments in 24 subjects. These included several different conditioned stimuli and unconditioned stimuli and various instructions and sets. He found conditioning to be more substantial and stable in those subjects who were instructed to form associations between the CS and US. Controls for sensitization and pseudoconditioning were not used in any of these studies.

Razran later used the absorbent technique to study many aspects of classical conditioning, such as semantic generalization, configural conditioning, stimulus intensity, and effects of various attitudes and sets. In spite of the number and theoretical importance of Razran's studies, few experimenters have employed his technique for further investigation of conditioning.

Jones (1939) used the absorbent technique to compare human salivary conditioning with the results Pavlov obtained on dogs. She did employ a group of control subjects in which US alone trials and comparable periods of no stimulation were alternated. She concluded that her attempt to condition the human salivary response was generally unsuccessful. A majority of the experimental subjects salivated less to the CS after it had been paired with the US, and the proportion of subjects who salivated more to the CS was about the same in the experimental and control groups.

Bindra, Paterson, and Strzelecki (1955) employed the absorbent technique to study differences in conditioning between high anxious and low anxious subjects. While their experiment has been considered to demonstrate the success of this method (Willett, 1960), it should be pointed out that it actually provided little evidence that conditioning occurred. These authors employed a 1-minute intertrial interval during acquisition, with every ninth trial a test trial in which the US was omitted. Since the unconditioned salivary reflex is known to have a duration considerably longer than one minute, they were undoubtedly considering unconditioned salivation as conditioned, and there was no experimental control for this possibility.

Willett (1960) studied the relationship between personality variables and conditioning, and among other CR measures, used the absorbent technique to measure salivation. He found a high degree of variability in salivary responses, both between subjects and within responses given by any one subject. He did find, however, that there was a significant difference between salivation to the CS and salivation in comparable control intervals. To rule out the possibility that this increase in salivation to test trials was a sensitized response or an unconditioned response to the CS (a blinking light), he carried out a control study on 20 subjects. These subjects were put through the same procedure, except that no USs were given. In this group he also found a greater increase in salivation to the CS than in comparable control periods, although this difference was not as significant as the difference in the experimental group. He concluded that one could not feel very confident that conditioning had occurred, and suggested that the conditioning apparently obtained might well have been an artifact of the stimuli used.

Of these four experiments in which the absorbent technique was used, two were purported to demonstrate human salivary conditioning. These two studies employed no sensitization or pseudoconditioning controls, while two studies which employed such controls yielded little evidence of conditioning.

Electrical activity of the parotid gland. Iwama and Shinjo (1950) reported a method for measuring a change in electrical potential across the parotid gland in intact human subjects. They have described this response in some detail and report that it correlates highly with velocity of salivary flow, and has almost the same latency as the salivary secretory response. Iwama and Abe (1952) have used this electrical activity as a measure of conditioned salivation. Their report, however, was not sufficiently detailed to enable the reader to conclude whether or not conditioning occurred. The present writer, employing their method insofar as possible, made concurrent records of parotid secretion measured by a drop sialometer, electrical potential across the parotid gland, and swallowing and tongue movements monitored by a volumetric transducer. Records of the change in electrical activity appeared quite similar to those reported by Iwama and Shinjo, but were found to parallel motor activity almost as closely as secretory activity. There was no convincing evidence that the measured change in electrical potential was caused by glandular secretion.

Parotid capsule. Lashley (1916) devised a simple means of collecting parotid saliva from the opening of Stensen's duct. It consisted of a small metal disk in which two concentric chambers were cut. The inner chamber fit directly over the duct opening, and was connected to tubing which conveyed the saliva out of the mouth. Drops of saliva were counted as they emerged from the end of the tube. The outer chamber was connected to a source of vacuum and served only to keep the capsule firmly in place.

With this device, Lashley studied the effects of various kinds of stimulation on parotid secretion, although his investigation of conditioned secretion was quite limited. In a single subject, he found that sight of food was inadequate to stimulate salivation; but after this subject was permitted to eat an oyster, he would then salivate upon seeing or holding a chocolate bar or other piece of food. While Lashley did not pursue these studies, several subsequent investigators have used modifications of his apparatus.

Krasnogorsky (1926) independently devised a parotid salivary capsule almost identical to Lashley's. The saliva displaced drops of an electrolyte which closed an electrical circuit and made possible a direct kymographic recording of salivary rate. He used soundproof rooms, which permitted separation of the subject from the experimenter; all stimuli were delivered automatically, and intervals and durations of stimulation were recorded kymographically.

Krasnogorsky also devised capsules for collecting submaxillary and sublingual saliva, but preferred the parotid gland for most of his conditioning studies. He found that the submaxillary gland secreted at a higher rate, regardless of external stimulation. Because of this, and because of the added difficulty of attaching the capsule to the sublingual area, nearly all of his experiments used parotid salivation. Razran (1933) reviewed over two dozen experiments from Krasnogorsky's laboratory. These studies represent a wide range of interests, ranging from external inhibition to the effect of diet on conditioning, and to conditioning in various diseases. The majority of these experiments were carried out on individual subjects, and there were no controls for sensitization or pseudoconditioning.

Lentz (1935) conducted studies of salivary conditioning in normal and feebleminded children. He used a parotid capsule similar to Krasnogorsky's, but recorded salivation by displacement of dye in a graduated cylinder, rather than by counting drops. He reported many similarities between his results and Pavlov's. He was interested in subjects' introspection during conditioning, and the relationship between their reported experience and the development and extinction of conditioned responses. For example, he demonstrated that in a simple discrimination reversal, while the subject is readily aware of the altered contingencies, there is considerable inertia of the conditioned response.

Bernhard (1939), employing Krasnogorsky's method, carried out several experiments on a single subject, a healthy nine-year-old boy. A feature of his experiments was the use of gustatory CSs. He found that a low concentration of sodium chloride (less than .5 percent) could be tasted, but caused very little unconditioned salivation. By pairing the dilute sodium chloride with hydrochloric acid, he was able to show conditioned responses in his one subject.

More recent experiments in human salivary conditioning have been carried out by Finesinger, Sutherland, and McGuire (1942), Finesinger and Sutherland (1939), and Sutherland (1962). Using a modification of Krasnogorsky's method, Finesinger et al. (1942) studied conditioned bilateral parotid salivary reflexes in ten psychoneurotic patients. They used 2 cc. of sweetened lemon juice as US and a metronome (150 beats per minute) as CS. The interstimulus interval varied from 2 to 3 seconds, and they interspersed test trials in which the US was delayed 15 to 20 seconds. Subjects were trained on successive week days, and received from two to six trials daily. The total number of trials per subject ranged from 24 to 269. All ten subjects showed a higher frequency of increased than decreased or unchanged salivary rate during the CS. The mean magnitude of the bilateral CR was 3.6 drops (range 2.2 to 7 drops). There was not a significant relationship between frequency and magnitude of CRs. There also appeared to be no relationship between magnitude of CRs and number of preceding conditioning trials.

Finesinger et al. called attention to a base line problem which is inherent in human salivary conditioning experiments. They commented, as did Lentz, that previous investigators had ignored the fact that salivation occurs in the absence of external stimulation. Finesinger et al. corrected for this basal or nonstimulated salivation by subtracting the average quarter-minute volume preceding the trial. This value was usually low, since they waited for the salivary rate to recede before starting the next trial. Unfortunately, this practice introduces a serious bias because spontaneous salivation occurs in spurts and selecting a momentary period of low secretion in which to begin a trial increases the probability of a rise in salivary rate during the trial. The authors attempted to handle this problem after the experiment by comparing the frequency of change in rate after other periods of low salivation with frequency of change following pre-CS periods. Since the frequency of increases following the pre-CS period was much greater, they concluded that their data presented clear evidence of conditioning. No control groups for sensitization or pseudoconditioning were employed.

This brief review of some earlier experiments on human salivary conditioning highlights several problems of technique, design, and control. Of the five techniques discussed, only two (absorbent technique and parotid capsule) have been used in sufficient numbers of subjects to enable one to evaluate their usefulness. Such an evaluation reveals that there are features of the absorbent technique which greatly limit its value. (1) There is considerable extraneous stimulation involved in inserting and removing the cotton rolls, and it is difficult, if not impossible, to separate these effects from the effects of the conditioned stimulus. (2) This technique does not permit study of the time course of a single CR. (3) The absorbent technique measures the combined secretory activity of all six major salivary glands, including the submaxillary and sublingual glands, which Krasnogorsky showed to have a high unstimulated secretory rate. Including the output of those glands makes it more difficult to demonstrate the effect of specific stimulation. The parotid capsule technique, on the other hand, minimizes the difficulties inherent in the absorbent technique and was the method employed in the present studies.

PURPOSE OF THE PRESENT STUDIES

Few human salivary conditioning experiments have incorporated adequate controls: Neither pseudoconditioning control groups nor the discrimination procedure (pp. 93 to 94, this volume) have been employed. Beyond this there has seldom been an adequate consideration of the fact to which Finesinger *et al.* have called attention, namely that some salivation (usually called "basal responding") does occur in the absence of an immediately preceding stimulus. For these reasons we were not satisfied that salivary conditioning has ever been produced in the laboratory.

The primary purpose of this investigation was to demonstrate conclusive evidence of salivary conditioning in human subjects, with improvements of existing apparatus, with larger groups of subjects than have been used heretofore, and with the incorporation of suitable controls for pseudoconditioning and for prestimulus salivary rates. Further goals were to attempt to clarify the relationship between secretory and motor responses, to study the course of acquisition and extinction of conditioned salivation, and to demonstrate the acquisition and reversal of a simple discrimination. Our strategy was, first, to devise a sensitive and reliable technique for measuring salivation, and then to carry out an extensive series of informal pilot experiments not reported here (see Feather, 1965b). The purpose of these pilot studies was to find some combination of parameter values that would permit a demonstration of salivary conditioning. The information obtained in these studies was used in planning the two experiments described in this report.

EXPERIMENT I

The primary purpose of Experiment I was to demonstrate conditioned salivation in an experiment using an adequate number of subjects and incorporating controls for pseudoconditioning and for prestimulus salivary rate. Secondary goals were to (1) describe the course of acquisition and extinction, and (2) ascertain whether there is a statistical relationship between motor and secretory activity during the interstimulus interval.

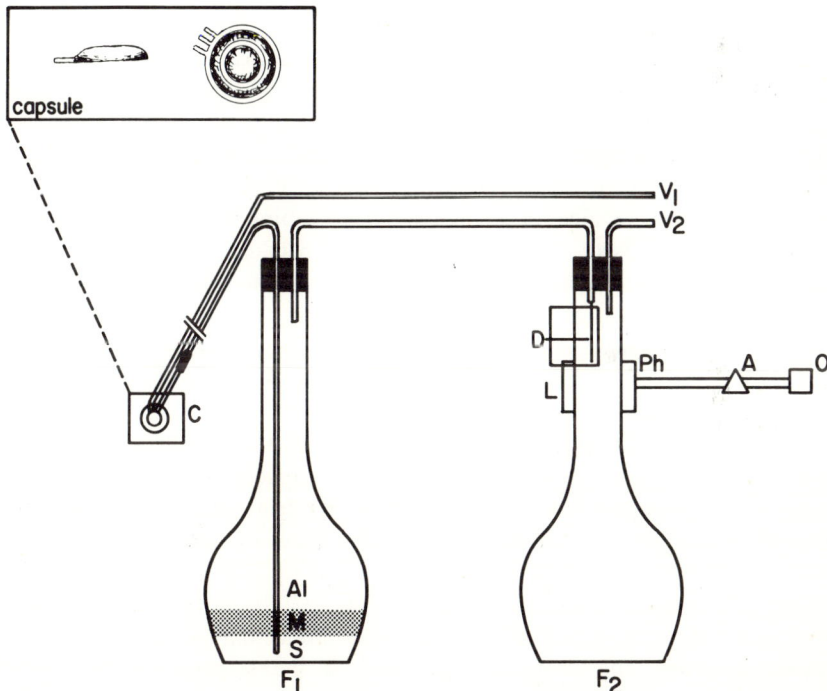

FIGURE 9-1. Schematic diagram of sialometer. This figure shows collecting capsule (C), first Florence flask (F_1) with layers of saliva (S), mineral oil (M), and alcohol (A1). The second Florence flask (F_2) contains the dropper (D); attached to the neck of the flask is a light source (L) and photocell (Ph). (V_1) and (V_2) are separate sources of vacuum.

Apparatus. The sialometer (Fig. 9-1) consists of nine components: collecting capsule (C), two Florence flasks (F_1 and F_2), dropper (D), light source (L), photocell (Ph), vacuum source (V_1 and V_2), amplifier (A), and oscillograph (O). All components except the capsule are located in a control room separated from the subject by a soundproof wall. The capsule consists of a two-chamber stainless steel disk, whose outside dimensions are 20 mm. (diameter) and 3 mm. (thickness). Each chamber is connected to 16-gauge stainless steel tubes which extend 5 mm. beyond the edge of the capsule. A third steel tube is attached to the outside rim of the capsule, and contains a single perforation for the administration of dilute acid into the mouth. The capsule is attached to polyethylene tubing in the following manner: the outer chamber connects to a constant vacuum source, the inner chamber connects to the sialometer, and the perforated tube is connected to a source of dilute acid. In this arrangement, the capsule is held in place by vacuum applied to the outer chamber only. The sialometer and inner collecting chamber of the capsule are connected to a separate source of vacuum which is kept at a level just sufficient to overcome the viscosity and cohesiveness of the saliva.

F_1 and F_2 (Fig. 9-1) are 1-liter Florence flasks fitted with No. 3 rubber stoppers. Saliva is conveyed to the bottom of the first flask under a 0.5-inch layer of light mineral oil. Above the mineral oil, the flask is filled with 95 percent ethyl alcohol. As saliva enters this flask it displaces an equal volume of alcohol via polyethylene tubing to a second Florence flask. Alcohol is used as the displaced liquid because it will form smaller drops than water or saliva and thus provide greater resolution.

Since resolution of the instrument depends entirely upon the size of the drops of displaced liquid, the drops should be as small as possible but should not form a stream at high salivary rates. A needle dropper of very small aperture, say a 24-gauge hypodermic needle, gives fairly small drops (approximately 150 per cc.) but introduces an undesirable time lag into the system. A sudden cessation of flow at the capsule may not be reflected until 4 or 5 seconds later at the dropper. By trial and error, a dropper was designed that did not introduce a long time lag and which provided quite small drops (approximately 300 per cc.). This was simply an 18-gauge intravenous needle that has been altered by lengthening the bevel to 2 cm., thus providing a thin, tapering point that is polished with a jeweler's stone. The dropper is inserted in the stopper of the second Florence flask (F_2), which in turn is connected to a source of constant vacuum (V_2). Five-gallon glass jars, evacuated and connected to the sialometer and capsule by polyethylene tubing, provide independent sources of negative pressure. Mercury manometers (not shown in Figure 9-1) are connected to the vacuum lines. One inch below the point of the dropper, a suitable light source (L) and photocell (Ph) are attached to the outside of the flask. Each drop intercepts the light beam, causing a change in resistance across the photocell. The resulting pulse is amplified and recorded as a vertical pip by a Grass Model 5D polygraph.

Calibration of the sialometer was achieved by using a burette filled with water as a source of liquid. The number of drops per cc. was then determined for the entire range of flow rates to be measured. The results of this calibration appear in Figure 9-2. The volume of the individual drops is affected by the rate, and this relationship is not linear. Small

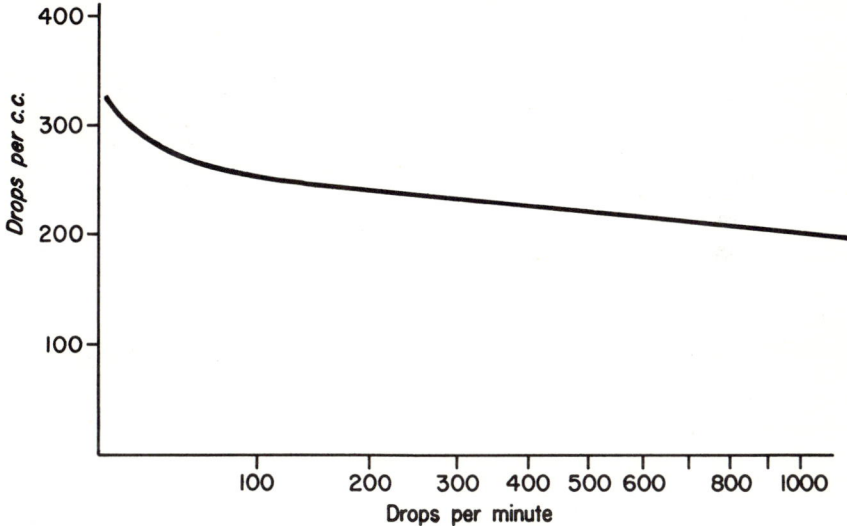

FIGURE 9-2. Drop volume as a function of flow rate.

changes in the design of the dropper affect this curve slightly, but no dropper design tested provided either a constant drop volume or a linear relationship between volume and rate. The dropper described does provide satisfactory resolution and, at all but the slowest rates, a roughly linear relationship between rate and drop-size.

A feature to be considered in evaluating the accuracy of such an instrument is the time lag, or the period of time between a change in flow rate at the input and the subsequent change in rate at the dropper. This lag depends upon the elasticity of the flask and tubing, as well as the aperture of the dropper. The time lag may be determined by starting or stopping flow at the input by opening or closing a solenoid valve and measuring the time it takes for this change to be reflected in the record. The measured time lag has been consistently under 0.5 second.

A final feature to be evaluated is the sensitivity or minimal detectable change in input pressure. This was determined by raising or lowering the calibrating burette or other source of liquid and noting the minimum change which is reflected as an increase or decrease in rate of drop formation. This value has been found to be less than 1 cm. of water.

The unconditioned stimulus delivery system is functionally separate from the sialometer. A reservoir of dilute acid in a 700-cc. volumetric flask is kept under positive pressure of 100 mm. Hg. Positive pressure is obtained from a 5-gallon glass jar that has been filled with air until it reaches the desired pressure. In the polyethylene tubing between the acid reservoir and the capsule is a stainless steel solenoid valve. This valve may be opened for any precise period of time by a suitable timer. The amount of reinforcement and its duration are controlled by adjusting the pressure under which the acid is delivered and by varying the time the solenoid valve is open.

The CS, a 700 c.p.s. tone of approximately 30 db. intensity, was delivered by a tone generator to a speaker placed 6 feet directly in front of the subject. The US was 2 cc. of 0.5 percent HCl, flavored with lemon extract and an artificial sweetener, delivered in 2 seconds to the left lateral margin of the tongue. The US delivery system was described earlier.

Motor activity was monitored by two methods. A small rubber balloon encased in a rigid plastic holder was fitted over the thyroid cartilage and held in place by elastic bands around the neck. The balloon was connected via polyethylene tubing to a Grass Model PT 5A volumetric transducer, the output of which was amplified by a Grass Model 5P1 low-level DC preamplifier and driver amplifier. This arrangement permitted a continuous recording of swallowing and tongue movements. In addition, EMG was monitored by a Grass Model 5P3 integrator, preamplifier, and driver amplifier. EMG was recorded from Grass EEG electrodes placed 1 cm. on either side of the midline of the submental region, and a reference electrode was placed on the earlobe.

A Grass Model 5 C polygraph was used to make continuous recording of salivary drop rate, two measures of motor activity, and duration of all stimuli. The sequence and intervals of trials were preprogrammed on punched paper tape. The durations of CS, US, and interstimulus interval were controlled by Grason-Stadler timers. Figure 9-3 is a polygraph record of a single conditioning trial.

Subjects and design. The subjects were 37 college undergraduates who participated in the experiment for partial fulfillment of a psychology course requirement. There were 23 males and 14 females, and sex was approximately balanced for the two basic conditions. The first seven subjects were assigned to the experimental group and the remaining subjects were assigned alternately to experimental and control groups.

Human Salivary Conditioning

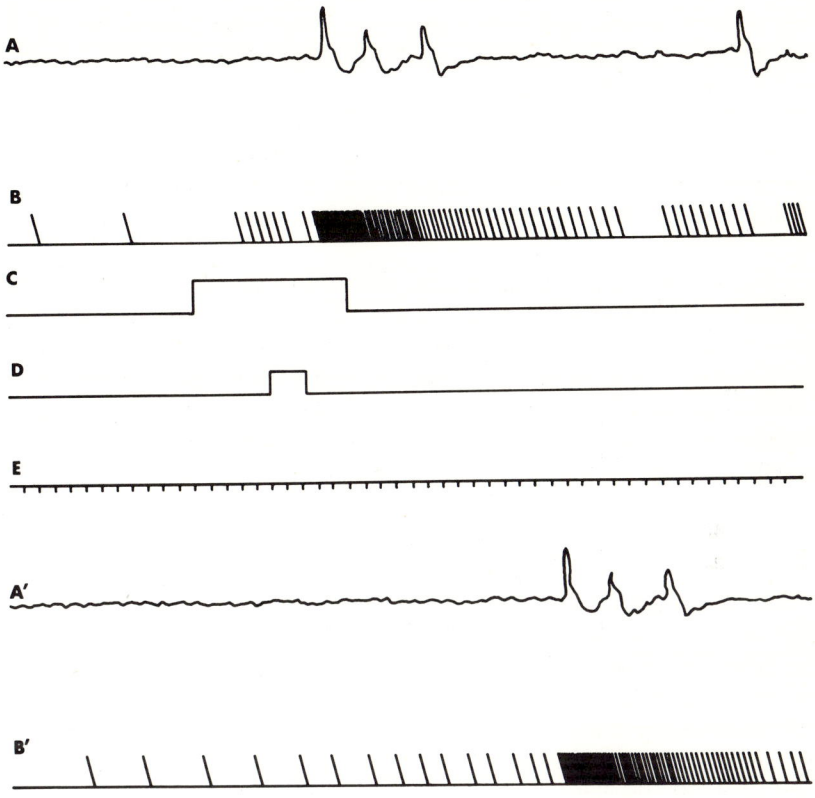

FIGURE 9 3. Polygraph record for a salivary conditioning trial. (A), swallowing and gross tongue movements; (B), salivary record; (C), CS, a 10-second tone; (D), US, 2 cc. of 2 percent citric acid; (E), time in seconds. (A') and (B'), record from another subject, show the effect of delayed swallowing on secretory rate during the UR.

The experimental group ($N = 22$) received five training sessions, one each on consecutive weekdays. The first four sessions consisted of six acquisition trials each, and the fifth session consisted of two acquisition trials and six extinction trials. The CS-US interval was 6.0 seconds. A conditioning trial consisted of an 8-second CS, which overlapped the US in the last 2 seconds. The US was omitted in the extinction trials. The intertrial interval was a nonsystematic sequence of 3, 4, and 5 minutes.

Control subjects ($N = 15$) had the same number of sessions and the same number of CSs and USs within each session. Stimuli, however, were not paired, but presented in a nonsystematic sequence with the following constraints: a US never followed a CS within 60 seconds, and no more than two alike stimuli were presented consecutively. The second and sixth trials in each session for the experimental group were comparable to the second and fourth trials for the control group in that the same length of time (3 minutes) had elapsed since the previous US.

Procedure. Each subject was interviewed briefly in advance of the experiment, but was given only minimal information about the purpose of the study. Subjects were asked to omit the last meal prior to the experimental sessions.

In the first experimental session, the subject was taken to the sound-attenuated experimental room and seated. The experimenter then cleansed the submental area and the left earlobe with alcohol, and attached EEG disc electrodes which had been lightly coated with Grass electrode paste. The balloon was placed over the thyroid cartilage and adjusted until comfortable. The left Stensen's duct was then located visually, and the salivary capsule was put into place. These procedures were explained briefly to the subject, who was then told, "This is an experiment on salivation. From time to time, you will hear a tone, and also from time to time, you will receive some sour lemon juice in your mouth. When the lemon juice comes in, you may swallow it. If you need to talk to me for any reason, I will be in the adjacent room, and will be able to hear you over the intercom. Are there any questions?" If there were no questions, he was then told that he would receive a small amount of lemon juice in a few seconds. The experimenter then delivered 1 cc. of acid in order to make sure the capsule was correctly placed. If the capsule was placed properly, as indicated by a UR, the lights in the experimental room were dimmed, and the door was closed. After 2 minutes, the preprogrammed sequence of trials was begun.

Results and discussion

The first stage of data reduction consisted of counting the number of drops occurring in each second, beginning 6 seconds before and extending 6 seconds beyond the onset of CS. Separate second-by-second counts were made for each CS for both experimental and control groups. Figure 9-4 is a composite graph of the two comparable trials in each session for both groups. Inspection reveals a sharp increase in salivary rate for experimental subjects, beginning in the second second of the interstimulus interval, and reaching a peak in the fourth second. While there is a slight increase in the salivary rate in control subjects, the rates clearly separate in the CS-US interval. Student's t tests (two-tailed) of the significance of the difference between mean pre-CS and post-CS salivary volume were calculated for both experimental and control groups. For this and the following calculations, the pre-CS period was defined as the last 5 seconds

Human Salivary Conditioning

before onset of CS, and the CS period was defined as the last 5 seconds of the interstimulus interval. The 1st second of the CS-US interval was omitted on the assumption that salivary CRs have a latency of at least 1 second. For the experimental group, this difference was significant ($p < .01$), and for the control group the difference was not significant. A t test was then calculated to evaluate the probability of the observed difference in increments of salivation (pre-CS to CS) between experimental and control groups. This difference was significant ($p < .01$).

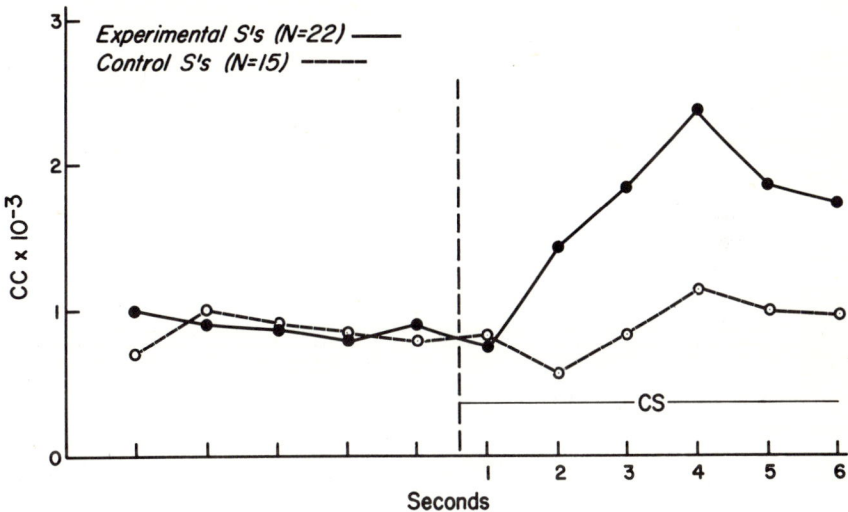

FIGURE 9-4. Salivary rate during comparable acquisition trials.

Figure 9-5 shows a composite graph for all acquisition trials, as well as graphs for each session. These graphs illustrate the early development of salivary conditioning. The higher prestimulus salivary rates for control subjects are due to the fact that in two-thirds of the trials, control subjects had received a US more recently than had experimental subjects.

Figure 9-6 represents the percentage of subjects who showed a pre-CS to CS increment of .003 cc. (one drop) or more on each of the comparable acquisition trials. This measure disregards magnitude of responses, and, for both groups, includes increments due to random variation in salivary rate.

Figure 9-7 presents the extinction data for all five extinction trials plotted separately for experimental and control groups. Inspection reveals increased salivation extending well beyond the CS-US interval. The salivary CR appears to last about 60 seconds.

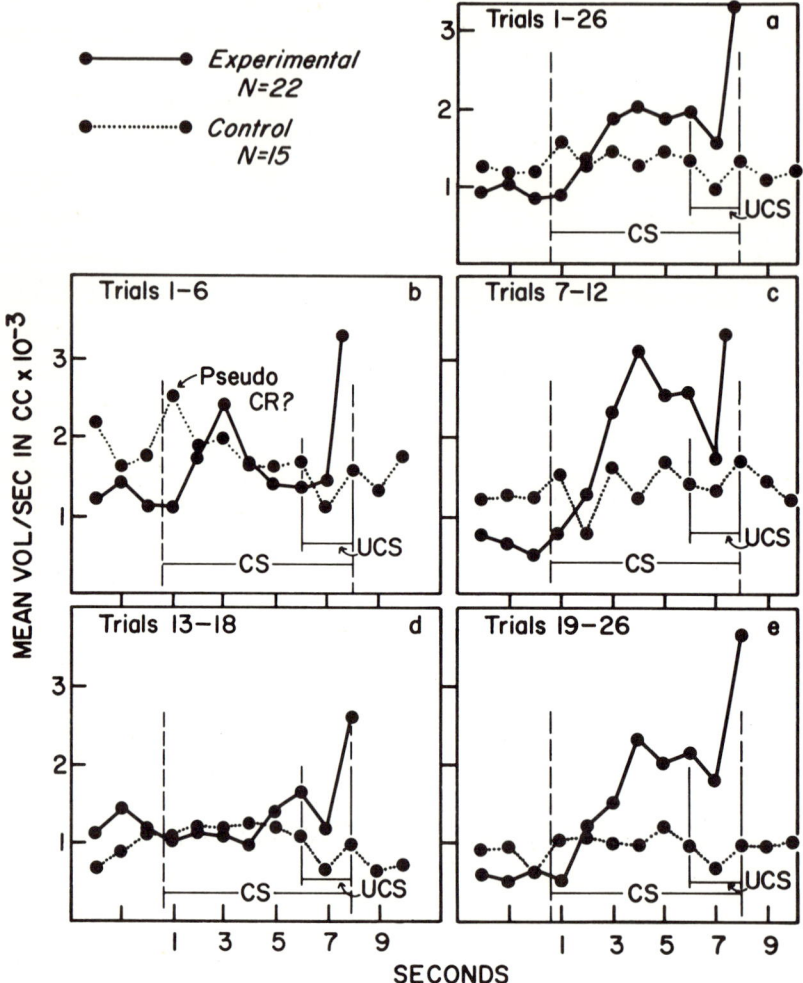

FIGURE 9-5. Salivary rate during all acquisition trials.

Figure 9-8 shows the course of extinction as a function of nonreinforced trials. Each point on the graph represents the pre-CS to CS increment in salivation, using the same 5-second periods described above. Extinction appears to be nearly complete by the fifth extinction trial.

UR latencies and magnitudes varied considerably from subject to subject. A UR was arbitrarily defined as the secretion occurring during the 60 seconds immediately following the US. The mean UR magnitude for control subjects was 89 drops, and the range was from 3 to 470 drops. Figure 9-9 is a frequency distribution of UR latencies for the control

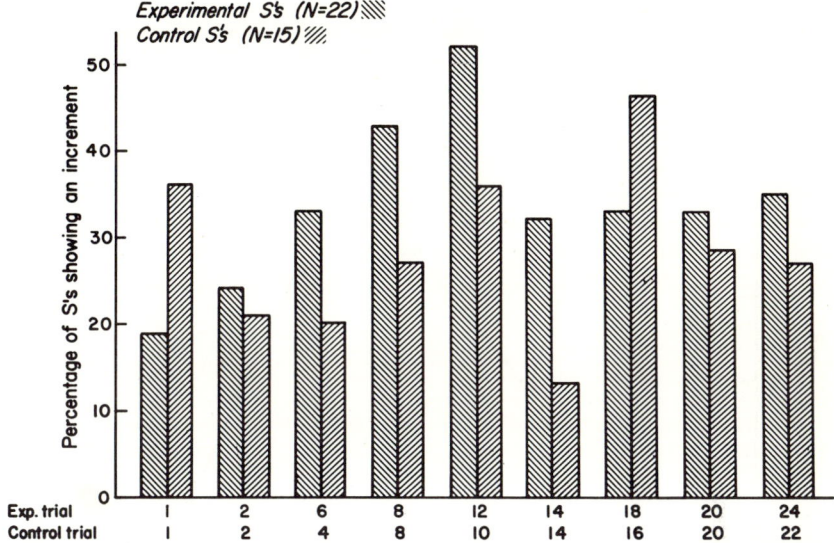

FIGURE 9-6. Percentage of subjects who showed a salivary increment on each of the comparable acquisition trials.

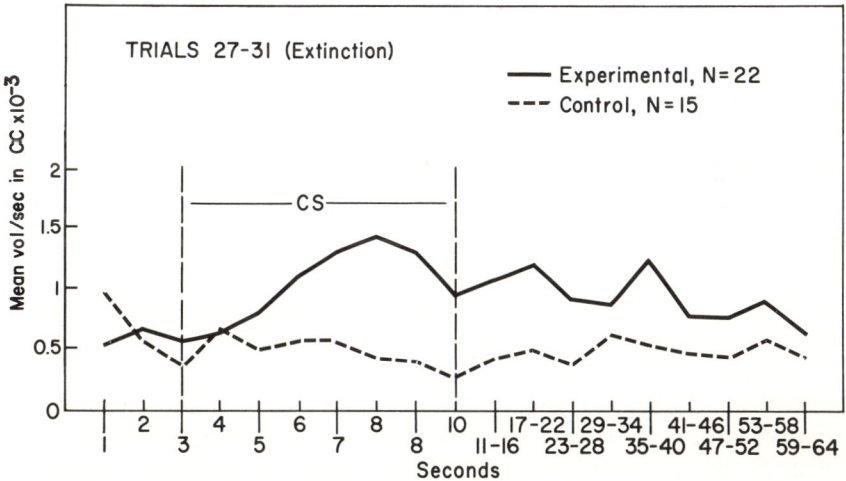

FIGURE 9-7. Salivary rate during extinction trials.

group. The onset of the US was defined as that point in time midway between the first two drops whose period was less than one-half the period of the preceding pair of drops. The mean latency was 3.4 seconds, and the standard deviation was 2.16. The few exceptionally long latency URs

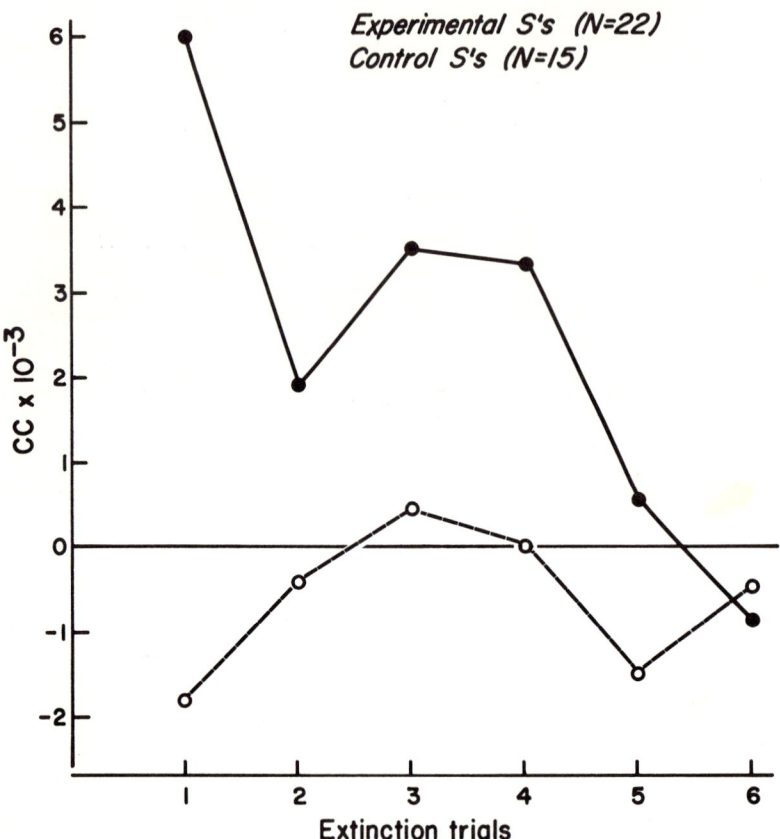

FIGURE 9-8. The course of extinction as a function of the number of extinction trials.

were contributed primarily by subjects who showed a correspondingly long latency motor UR on the same trials (cf. Fig. 9-3).

As stated earlier, one goal of the experiment was to attempt to clarify the relationship between motor and secretory activity in the interstimulus interval. For this purpose, the question was asked: Do pre-CS to CS increments in secretory and motor activity occur together? For this comparison, the last 6 seconds before the CS were taken as the pre-CS period, and the 6 seconds between CS and US were taken as the CS period. Motor activity was defined as any discernible elevation, apart from known artifacts, in the EMG record. Since the two measures of motor activity were in nearly perfect agreement, only the EMG was scored. Each trial for each subject was then scored plus, minus, or zero, indicating an increment, a decrement, or no change for motor and secretory activity respectively.

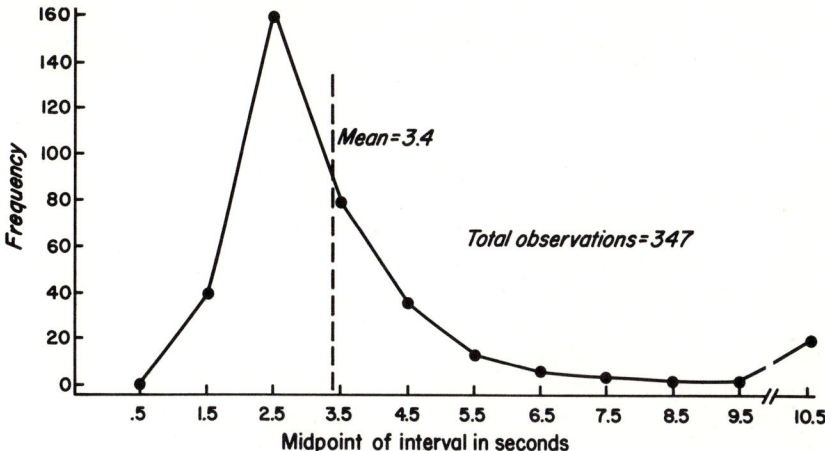

FIGURE 9-9. Frequency distribution of UR latencies for control subjects.

These ratings were carried out by one assistant, and the interobserver reliability was assessed by comparing them with a random sample of ratings on the same records by another assistant. Agreement was found to be 90 percent. The percentage of all acquisition trials showing a pre-CS to CS increment in salivation was 43 for experimental subjects and 34 for control subjects. The percentage of all these trials also showing a pre-CS to CS increment in motor activity was 33 for experimental subjects and 15 for control subjects. The probabilities of this degree of association between motor and salivary increments were evaluated for individual subjects by Tocher's modification of Fisher's Exact Probability Test. These probabilities were significant ($p < .05$) in only two subjects. On the other hand, the earlier observation of salivary bursts related to swallowing *during the UR* was again noted. These results suggest that swallowing and tongue movements intensify unconditioned stimulation by distributing the acid over a larger number of receptors. After the acid is neutralized by saliva and swallowed, further motor activity (e.g., in the CS-US interval) does not have a significant effect on salivation.

One disappointing outcome of this experiment was a marked variability in conditioning, both between subjects and between trials within subjects, which had been described by other investigators. So far we have a tentative explanation only for the intersubject variability: there is a fairly close relationship between total salivation and conditioned increments in salivation, and subjects with a low salivary rate showed few if any CRs. For example, the seven experimental subjects who showed the lowest overall salivary rates contributed virtually no pre-CS to CS salivary increments. This relationship between conditioned and total salivation was unexpected and remains unexplained but the important conclusion was examined directly and validated in the next experiment.

Razran's (1935) observation that salivary conditioning was unrelated to number of acquisition trials was confirmed. Conditioning occurred quite early, and neither magnitude nor probability of a response increased with further trials. It is possible, of course, that had acquisition been carried out for many more trials, a more typical acquisition function might have been obtained. However, Finesinger et al. (1942) gave as many as 245 trials over a period of several months, and, similarly, found no increase in conditioning.

Razran's contention that extinction does not occur in human salivary conditioning is not confirmed. Figure 9-8 shows extinction to be complete by the fifth unreinforced trial.

The following are some incidental observations that were taken into account in planning the next experiment. Several subjects complained of boredom and drowsiness during the sessions, and some asked if they could take a book or magazine into the experimental room. One subject fell asleep, did not hear the CS on one trial, and had to be awakened. Some subjects also complained about the sourness of the acid, and an occasional subject had mild ulceration of the peridontal mucosa where the US was administered. These subjects were given a bicarbonate of soda mouthwash, and in every case the irritation had cleared up by the next session. For these reasons the general procedure and the US were both changed for Experiment II.

EXPERIMENT II

The chief goal of this experiment was to replicate conceptually Experiment I, using the kind of control for sensitization or pseudoconditioning provided by the conditioned discrimination paradigm. Reversal of the conditioned discrimination also was studied in subjects who were informed of all stimulus contingencies. A second goal was to obtain further information about the relationship between the magnitude of the salivary UR and the level of conditioning. A third goal was to compare the effects of 3- and 6-minute intertrial intervals within individual subjects. This third objective was introduced because a reconsideration of the results of pilot studies suggested that the poor conditioning obtained in Experiment I might have been the result of using too brief an intertrial interval.

Subjects. The subjects consisted of 29 college undergraduates who participated for partial fulfillment of a psychology course requirement. There were 24 males and 5 females.

Apparatus. The sialometer was the same as that used in Experiment I. The two CSs were red and white lights placed 3 feet directly in front of the subject. The stimulus panel measured 10.8 by 15.2 cm. and contained two clear, 4-watt bulbs, placed 6.4 cm. apart. The bulbs were covered respectively with a red and a white round lens, 1 cm. in diameter. The US was 2 cc. of 2 percent citric acid, delivered by the method described in Experiment I.

Motor activity was monitored by EMG but the EEG electrodes used previously were replaced by larger silver electrodes measuring 1.5 cm. in diameter.

Recording of salivation was carried out by a Grass polygraph as before. In addition, 20 Grason-Stadler counters were employed to obtain a direct second-by-second count of drops for the 10 seconds preceding and following CS onset.

Design. Except for color of the reinforced stimulus, treatment was the same for all subjects, each subject serving as his own control. From one to two weeks prior to the conditioning sessions, each subject had a 30-minute preconditioning session for the purpose of ascertaining the magnitude of unconditioned salivation. The first four conditioning sessions consisted of 10 discrimination trials, of which 5 employed a reinforced CS, and 5 a nonreinforced CS of the other color. The sequence of reinforced and nonreinforced trials was nonsystematic except that no more than two alike stimuli were presented consecutively, and the sequences were different on alternate days. The sequences were arranged so that, in each session, two reinforced and two sequentially comparable nonreinforced trials occurred 6 minutes after the preceding US. The remaining three reinforced and three nonreinforced trials occurred 3 minutes following a US. These sequences necessitated the administration of one US alone in each experimental session. For half the subjects, the red light was reinforced, for the other half, white. On the fifth session, the contingency between color of CS and reinforcement was reversed.

Procedure. In the initial, pre-experimental interview, subjects were told that this was an experiment on salivary conditioning, and the procedure was explained to them. They were asked to omit the last meal prior to the preconditioning session and all conditioning sessions. The preconditioning session consisted of administering three USs (2 cc. of 2 percent citric acid) 3 and 6 minutes apart and recording both total salivation for the session and the quantity of saliva secreted during 1 minute following each US.

At the beginning of the first conditioning session, after the salivary capsule and EMG electrodes were attached, the subject was told, "From time to time, this red (white) light will come on. A few seconds later, you will receive some lemon juice. From time to time, this white (red) light will come on, but will not be followed by lemon juice. The red (white) light will always be followed by lemon juice, the white (red) light never." The subject was then handed a small box containing two buttons, one red, the other white, and was told: "I would like you to guess each time what color light will come on next. About a minute after a light has appeared, push the red button if you think the next light will be red, push the white button if you think the next light will be white. Also, when the light actually comes on, please push the corresponding button to indicate which light came on." This procedure was introduced in an attempt to make the experiment less boring for the subject. At the beginning of each session, the subject was reminded that "the red (white) light will always be followed by lemon juice, the white (red) light never." At the beginning of the fifth session, he was told that "Today the white (red) light will always be followed by lemon juice, the red (white) light, never." When the subject indicated that he understood the instructions, the experimenter left the room and administered 1 cc. of acid in order to ascertain the placement of the capsule. If there was a satisfactory UR, the door was closed, and after 2 minutes, the preprogrammed sequence of trials was begun.

Results and discussion

Subjects were ranked on the basis of total salivation during the preconditioning session. The same subjects were then ranked on the basis of their average secretion in the 10-second pre-CS period during acquisition, and finally were ranked on the basis of total secretion during the conditioning sessions. There was an apparent relationship between a given subject's preconditioning salivary rate and his subsequent pretrial rate. However, if the pretrial volume is considered the criterion measure, preconditioning volume misclassified eight subjects. Four subjects classified as high (above the median) on preconditioning volume were low on pretrial volume, and four subjects classified as low on preconditioning volume were classified as high on pretrial volume. On the other hand, pretrial volume and total volume secreted during conditioning were more closely related, and the median division yielded high and low groups which were the same except for two subjects. Ensuing references to high or low salivators imply a median split based upon total secretion for all conditioning trials.

Figure 9-10 shows pretrial and CS-US interval secretion to CS+ and CS— for both high and low salivators for Trials 2 through 20. Inspection of this graph confirms the impression gained in Experiment I, that secretory rate is directly related to the level of conditioning. Salivary CRs appear dependably only in the high salivators. Two points may be made about the results for high salivators. (1) The CR latency is considerably longer

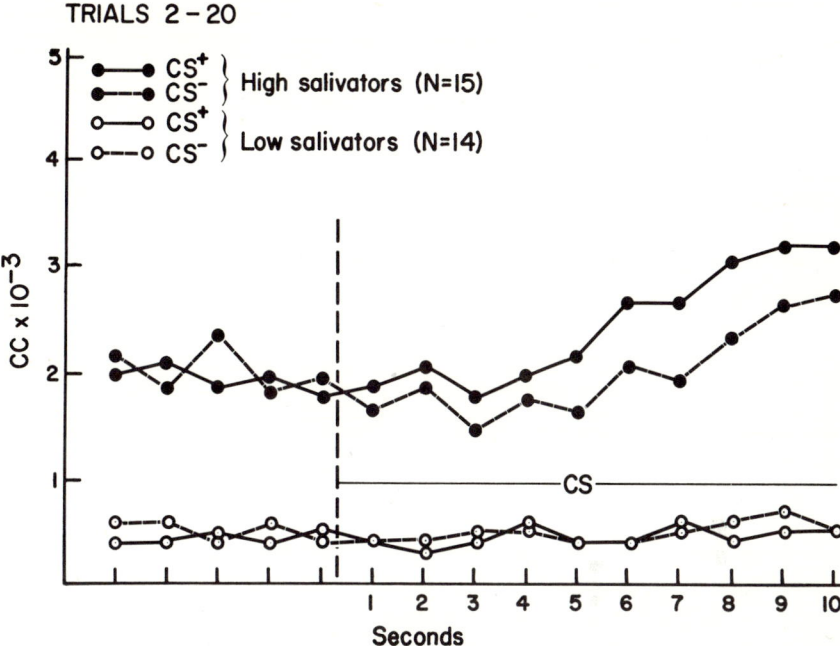

FIGURE 9-10. Salivation during discrimination Trials 2-20.

than in Experiment I, a result we tentatively attribute to the longer CS-US interval, and (2) there is salivation to the nonreinforced stimulus. Figure 9-11 shows the same data for high salivators only, plotted session by session. As in Experiment I, conditioning appears to develop early, and response magnitude does not increase with the number of reinforced trials.

Figure 9-12 shows pretrial and CS-US interval secretion to CS+ and CS− for high and low salivators on Trials 21 through 25. These trials comprise the fifth conditioning session on which the discrimination was reversed. It is readily apparent that discrimination is greater following the reversal of CS-US contingencies than during the initial discrimination.

The preceding graphs (Figs. 9-10, 9-11 and 9-12) were based on all the conditioning trials. Similar graphs were constructed separately for trials which occurred 6 minutes and 3 minutes following a US. These graphs were quite comparable one to another, indicating that the time elapsed since a preceding US had little effect on conditioning.

For statistical analysis 3- and 6-minute intertrial measures were combined and the analysis was limited to the high salivators. The major analysis was a mixed model analysis of variance described in detail in a more complete description of this study (Feather, 1965). This analysis, in sum-

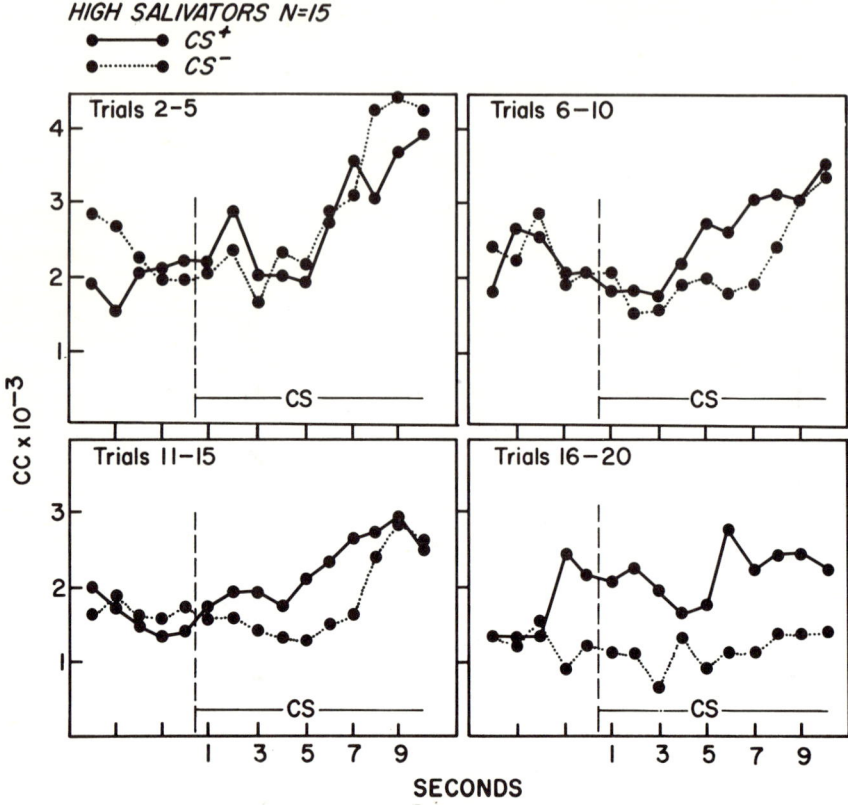

FIGURE 9-11. Salivation during discrimination trials in individual sessions.

mary, supports the point that CRs occurred to CS— as well as to CS+, but the discrimination revealed in the case of the high salivators is significant.

Data obtained during the discrimination reversal phase of the experiment were analyzed separately by means of a t test. The mean volumes secreted to CS+ and CS— during the 10-second CS-US interval differed significantly ($t = 5.06$; $p < .005$).

The relationship between motor and secretory responses was not analyzed separately for individual subjects in this experiment. However, there was less motor responding to the CS in Experiment II than in Experiment I. When all acquisition trials in Experiment I (experimental group) were considered, the probability of an increment in motor activity to the CS was .33. In Experiment II (high salivators only), the probability of an increment in motor activity to CS+ was .18, and to CS—, .24. Thus,

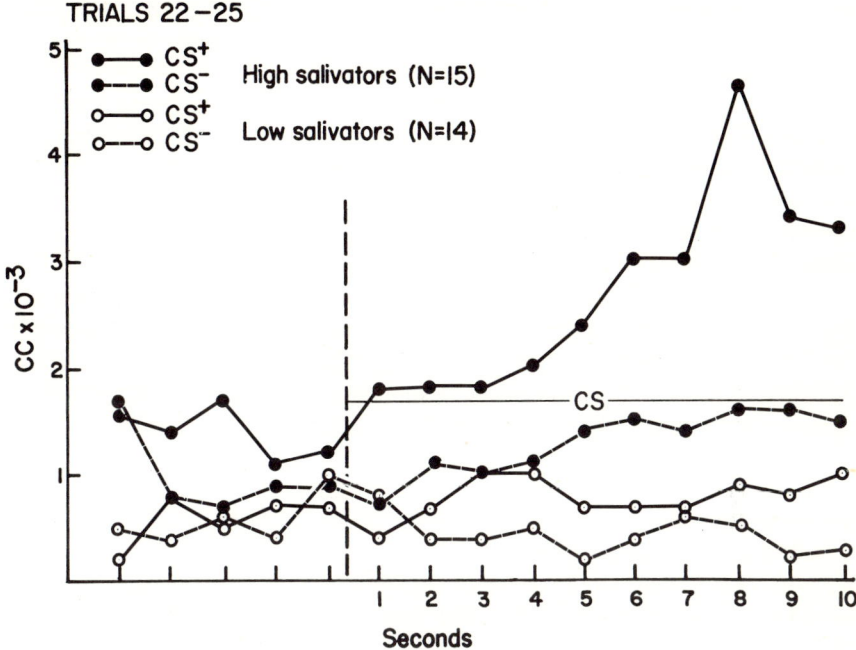

FIGURE 9-12. Salivation during discrimination reversal trials.

the salivary conditioned discrimination clearly was not a result of motor discrimination.

CONCLUSIONS

The major aim of these experiments has been accomplished. Classical salivary conditioning has been obtained with human subjects under adequate conditions of control. In addition, we have demonstrated several of the basic phenomena of conditioning. These include:

1. *Acquisition.* In both experiments conditioning occurred early and did not increase with further trials. As was pointed out in the introduction, this has been the most frequent result in experiments of this type. This fact reminds us of Pavlov's stressing of the importance of the second signal system in man and his guess that instructions might take the place of many paired presentations of CS and US. The experiments presented here confirm Pavlov's prediction for the salivary response and raise the question of why some other responses such as the eye-blink require so

many responses to condition. However this question is eventually answered, an immediate and practical implication of these results is that future experiments on salivary conditioning can be carried out in one or two sessions and with fewer trials.

2. *Experimental extinction.* In Experiment I it was found that the salivary CR extinguished in a very few trials. This result contradicts Razran's assertion that the response does not extinguish easily.

3. *Stimulus generalization.* In Experiment II substantial degrees of salivation occurred to CS—, a result that may be interpreted either as the result of sensitization or as an instance of stimulus generalization. The results seem to favor the interpretation in terms of generalization because the response to CS— showed the same latency and form as the response to CS+. This latency is well beyond the latency of an unconditioned salivary response. For this reason, responding to CS— was interpreted as conditioned rather than sensitized. These observations do suggest, however, that discrimination may not always serve as a control for sensitization unless a conditioned response can be differentiated from a sensitized response on the basis of some criterion or set of criteria other than the antecedent conditions.

4. *Discrimination.* In spite of the presence of generalized responses to CS—, differential responding did develop in Experiment II. This differed from the typical Pavlovian result in that zero responding to CS— was not obtained. In this respect, the results are more like those characteristically obtained in eyelid conditioning.

5. *Discrimination reversal.* The most impressive result of Experiment II was that the reversal discrimination rapidly became more accurate than that obtained with many more trials in the initial phase of the experiment. This, together with the rapid conditioning to reinforced stimuli in both experiments, again points to the probable importance of instructional factors and set in human salivary conditioning. It may even be that such responses are not so free from voluntary control as is commonly supposed. This possibility is currently under examination in the laboratory at Duke University.

6. *Inhibition of delay (?).* The average latency of the CR was greater in Experiment II than in Experiment I. This may mean that we have demonstrated inhibition of delay since the CS-US interval was 10 seconds in Experiment II and only 6 seconds in Experiment I. In any event, it is to be noted that these results again are like those obtained in classical eyelid conditioning (pp. 90 to 92, this volume).

7. *No close relation between motor responses and the CR.* No clear-cut relationship between conditioned salivation and swallowing has emerged from these experiments. The incidence of swallowing to the CS was fairly high in the first experiment (experimental group) and much lower in the second. Although the two responses occurred together on

some trials and consistently together in two subjects in Experiment I, it seems clear to the writer that neither the salivary CR nor discrimination can be interpreted as an artifact of swallowing.

These experiments also raise several questions that badly need answers if classical salivary conditioning is to become an effective experimental procedure. To list what now seem to us to be the two most important:

1. *Sources of intersubject variability.* Probably the most disquieting result in both experiments was the high degree of intersubject variability in salivary rate and conditioning. It was shown in Experiment II that, on the whole, high salivators conditioned and low salivators did not. One possible explanation of the failure of the low salivators to condition is that, for the elicitation of a salivary CR, there is an optimal pretrial salivary rate which is higher than the average rate shown by low salivators 3 minutes after a US. A future experiment is planned in which trials will be given when the salivary rate reaches some arbitrary value, which will be the same for all subjects. Although this will sacrifice some measure of control over the length of the intertrial interval, two advantages might result from this strategy: (1) more low salivators might acquire CRs under these conditions; and (2) analyses will be greatly simplified if the pretrial salivary rate is the same for all subjects.

2. *Optimal values of parameters.* As we have said previously, we have no firm evidence at all as to the experimental arrangements that might consistently produce high levels of conditioning. Results of pilot studies and some internal evidence from Experiment I had suggested that the intertrial interval might be important and optimally longer than 3 minutes. The same informal evidence had suggested that the optimal CS-US interval might be greater than 6 seconds. Accordingly, in Experiment II the CS-US interval was increased to 10 seconds and a comparison of performance at intervals of 3 minutes and 6 minutes was made possible in the design of the experiment. Neither of these manipulations led to anything informative, however. The level of conditioning was about the same in Experiment II as it had been in Experiment I and performance at the two intertrial intervals was also about the same. Obviously we are still badly in need of thorough parametric studies of the intertrial and interstimulus interval as well as other potentially important variables such as type and intensity of CS, type and intensity of US and schedule of reinforcement.

10

The Concept of Reflex and the Problem of Volition

GREGORY A. KIMBLE

The early physiological investigators of the conditioned reflex seem not to have worried much about the question of whether the concept of "conditioned reflex" does logical violence to the more basic concept of "reflex." In discussing the matter, Pavlov (1927) introduces the conception in physiological terms without differentiating in this definition between conditioned and unconditioned reflex: "An external or internal stimulus falls on some one or other nervous receptor and gives rise to a nervous impulse; this nervous impulse is transmitted along nerve fibers to the central nervous system, and here, on account of existing nervous connections, it gives rise to a fresh impulse which passes along outgoing nerve fibers to the active organ, where it excites a special activity of the cellular structures" (p. 7). From this point of departure, Pavlov proceeded in several directions. (1) As Sechenov had emphasized, the concept of reflex implies determinism and necessity in behavior. Pavlov re-emphasizes this point, suggesting that it applies to conditioned and unconditioned behavior. (2) The concept of reflex may readily be broadened to cover most, if not all of what was referred to as instinctive behavior. (3) The innate reflexes provide the foundation of all human and animal activity and (4) for this last reason, especially, it is important to develop a comprehensive inventory of the reflex repertoire of an organism. Pavlov himself had observed behavior which led him to assume the existence of hitherto unrecognized "freedom reflexes" and "investigatory reflexes." The question of whether the new reflexes that developed on the foundation of the innate reflexes were of the same type as the basic reflexes themselves received no specific treatment, but obvious inferences lead to the conclusion that Pavlov saw no difference except in the histories of the two types of reflex.

It is probably true that psychologists as a group are more preoccupied with such matters than physiologists are. In any event, it remained for a psychologist, B. F. Skinner (1931), to subject the concept of reflex to logical analysis.[1]

In matters of this kind, it is often of prime importance to see that there is even a question to ask. As Skinner says in discussing the flexion reflex, "We have been proceeding, of course, upon an unnecessary assumption, namely that there *is* a flexion reflex, which exists independently of our observations. . . . Such an assumption is wholly gratuitous." In other words, the existence in our vocabulary of a word ("reflex") does not mean that there must also be an item of psychological or physiological reality (reflex) to correspond exactly, or even approximately to it. It is clear that the term *reflex* refers not to a fact of physiology or psychology but to a concept, constructed by the scientist from certain types of empirical observations.

Proceeding from this point, Skinner defined a reflex in terms of correlations between stimuli and responses. In the identification of any reflex, we are dealing, he said, with a set of correlations which have certain characteristics in common. The effectors are the same, and the stimuli are grossly similar. The important consideration, however, is the correlation between stimulus and the response: the fact that, given the stimulus, the response invariably ensues. The patellar reflex cannot be defined either in terms of a blow on the patellar tendon or in terms of the knee jerk. The meaning of this reflex involves both of these facts and their interrelationship.

But what of the neurological activity (stimulus reception, afferent neural impulse, central switching, efferent activity and effector action) usually employed in the definition of reflex as Pavlov did above? Here it is essential to make a sharp conceptual distinction between (1) the *reflex* defined in function terms as an S-R correlation and (2) the *reflex arc,* a physiological mechanism allegedly responsible for the production of this correlation. This distinction suggests a division of professional interest between the physiologist and the psychologist: "The one seeks a description of the reflex in terms of physicochemical events, the other a description of behavior in terms of the reflex."

Finally, to what extent does the concept of reflex contain a general formula for the science of psychology? Clearly the definition of reflex in terms of a stimulus response correlation suggests the fruitfulness of seeking laws of the general type, $R = f(S)$, where these terms all have the meanings now conventionally assigned them. On the other hand, any attempt at a rigorous, especially a quantitative, application of this type of law leads to an important additional point and to raising an important question:

---

[1] This analysis has been reprinted in a collection of Skinner's writings (Skinner, 1959). Although our purposes are adequately served by a summary of its contents, the whole paper provides an outstanding example of clear thinking in our field.

(1) The important point emerges even from a study of reflex behavior as physiologists use this concept. The strength of the reflex varies with a set of additional variables (A) such as the frequency of elicitation of the reflex and the recency of its elicitation in the immediate past. Thus, the general form of the law referred to above must become $R = f(S,A)$ to take account of the additional variables.

(2) The important question arises when we leave the level of reflex behavior and attempt to apply the $R = f(S,A)$ formula more widely. Such an attempted application almost immediately encounters the fact that much behavior appears to be spontaneous, self-determined, or *voluntary*. The $R = f(S,A)$ law appears to be inappropriate in these cases, for lack of an identifiable S. How shall we deal with actions like this?

The standard gambit, from Sechenov to Skinner, has been to suggest that the stimuli exist and eventually will be discovered. Skinner cites the Pavlovian discovery of the conditioned reflex as an instance when the stimuli actually controlling behavior previously thought to be spontaneous were discovered, and predicts that this will be the case for all instances of such behavior: *"Given a particular part of the behavior of an organism hitherto regarded as unpredictable* (and probably, as a consequence, assigned to nonphysical factors), *the investigator seeks out the antecedent changes with which the activity is correlated and establishes the conditions of the correlation"* (italics Skinner's).

Unfortunately, projecting such a program and carrying it out are two different things and there remain many types of behavior for which the stimuli are unknown. Skinner himself now refers to such reactions as "operants" to distinguish them from "respondents" where identifiable stimuli evoke the response. He also maintains a parallel distinction between "emitted" and "elicited" behavior to refer to the same classes of reaction. This treatment allows Skinner to proceed with the study of operant behavior and learning involving such behavior. It does not, however, answer the original question raised by the existence of spontaneous, volitional, behavior. Nor does it deal with certain questions raised by various attempts at the theoretical level to provide stimuli for these acts.

As we shall see more concretely in a moment, it was commonly suggested that these stimuli were kinesthetic stimuli that take the form of an "image" of the response to be performed. It was argued that, once this image was formed, the response occurred automatically or reflexly to these stimuli. Without further interpretation, however, this theory is entirely unsatisfactory because it leaves unanswered the essential question: where do these stimuli come from? Sechenov had answered that they were aroused by an associative connection to other stimuli present in the behavioral situation. This solution, although potentially useful, suffers from an undesirable degree of vagueness. Certain of the early behaviorists (e.g. Hudgins & Hunter, 1934) proposed that they were self-initiated. This answer is

The Concept of Reflex and the Problem of Volition 147

even less satisfactory than Sechenov's because it is equally vague and, in addition, begs the question. How is one to distinguish between a self-initiated stimulus and one which arises from an act of volition? Obviously, this explanation begins by accepting, as already understood, what it proposes to explain.

The one individual who offered an interpretation rich enough in detail and objective enough to submit to test (at least in principle) was William James. The theory made the common assumption that the stimuli for volitional acts are mainly kinesthetic stimuli; it builds on Sechenov's hypothesis that they are evoked by way of associative connection to other stimuli. Moreover, James suggested a neurological mechanism for the associative process. So far, in the history of psychology, no one seems to have improved on James' theory, although von Holst (1954) half a century later and apparently independently, developed nearly an identical theory.

WILLIAM JAMES' THEORY

James' chapter on Will (1893, pp. 486–592) is long and covers a great deal of territory that no longer seems germane. On the other hand, James considered the problem at hand with great thoroughness and produced an account of voluntary behavior that deserves more attention than has been paid it in the last several decades. Using now language that is predominantly that of James:

The first point to be understood in the psychology of volition is that "voluntary movements must be secondary, not primary functions of the organism. . . . Reflex, instinctive and emotional movements are all primary performances. The nerve-centers are so organized that certain stimuli pull the trigger of certain explosive parts; and a creature going through one of these explosions for the first time undergoes an entirely novel experience." The organism is in no sense prepared for the effect of the stimulus, not having been subjected to it in the past. In actions properly called voluntary, on the other hand, "the act must be foreseen [and] no creature not endowed with divinatory power can perform an act voluntarily for the first time. . . . When a particular movement, having once occurred in a random, reflex, or involuntary way, has left an image of itself in the memory, then the movement can be desired again, proposed as an end, and deliberately willed. But it is impossible to see how it could be willed before" (p. 487; italics deleted).

Involuntary acts, thus, were presented by James as inborn, automatic, reactions which on their first occurrence could not even be predicted by the organism. They provide the foundation for voluntary action in that an "image" of their consequences (what today we would call "feedback" or "reafference" [von Holst, 1954]) is essential to the occurrence of the reaction in question. The emphasis throughout is on motor movement; James suggests that the mechanism is of wider significance. Considering a common autonomic response, he says: "It is true that the idea of sweating will not commonly make us sweat, nor that of blushing make us blush. But . . . Some can even succeed in sweating voluntarily, by the lively recollection of the characteristic skin-sensations, and the voluntary reproduction of an indescribable sort of feeling of relaxation, which ordinarily precedes the flow of perspiration" (p. 495 n). Several points follow from this brief example: (1) it is obvious that voluntary control over reactions other than motor movements is possible; (2) a part of the image associated with voluntary behavior is not provided by the response, but involves the stimuli preceding the reaction (in this case, the stimuli provided by relaxation but in other cases, the image of a frightening object or situation); and (3) the notion that the stimulational consequences of behavior are not limited to the active effector. This last point is clearer in the case of voluntary movement of the eyes, where some of the feedback is visual.

Having proposed that an image of the act, in the form of a resident impression of its stimulational consequences, is essential for the voluntary initiation of behavior, what evidence could James cite in favor of this position? The most impressive of this evidence involved clinical patients who lack kinesthetic sensitivity. In certain of these cases, the patients apparently were unable to initiate a motion of the anesthetic member at all. In all of them, when blindfolded, great deficiencies in motor coordination appeared. This observation was important because, with the blindfold removed, these patients were able to handle themselves much better. James concluded that they normally relied on visual feedback (see point 3 above) to guide their acts. As a partial validation of this interpretation it is possible to cite the results of simple experiments on normal subjects, which show that, when blindfolded, they are more able to touch a particular location if they have previously seen it than if they have previously reached out and touched it. This seems to mean that such reactions are predominantly instances of motor-visual rather than of motor-kinesthetic coordination and that providing a visual cue allows a more precise execution of the voluntary response than providing the kinesthetic stimuli consequent upon the behavior.

Such evidence led James to the conclusion that it is the idea or image of the consequences of an act, visual, motor, or whatever, that forms the precondition for voluntary action. Again in James' words:

> I trust that I have now made clear what that "idea of a movement" is which must precede it in order that it be voluntary. . . . It is the anticipation of the movement's sensible effects, resident [e.g. kinesthetic] or remote

The Concept of Reflex and the Problem of Volition 149

[e.g. visual] and sometimes very remote indeed. Such anticipations, to say the least, determine *what* our movements shall be. I have spoken all along as if they also might determine *that* they shall be. This, no doubt, has disconcerted many readers, for it certainly seems as if a special fiat, or consent to the movement were required in addition to the mere conception of it, in many cases of volition; and this fiat I have altogether left out of my account. This leads us to the next point in the psychology of the Will. . . .

The question is this: Is the bare idea of a movement's sensible effects its sufficient mental cue. . . or must there be an additional mental antecedent, in the shape of a fiat, decision, consent, volitional mandate, or some other synonymous phenomenon of consciousness, before movement can follow?

I answer: Sometimes the bare idea is sufficient, but sometimes an additional conscious element, in the shape of a fiat, mandate, or express consent, has to intervene and precede the movement. The cases without fiat constitute the more fundamental because more simple, variety . . . .

Whenever movement follows unhesitatingly and immediately the notion of it in the mind, we have *ideo-motor action*. We are then aware of nothing between the conception and the execution. . . . Dr. Carpenter, who first used, I believe, the name of ideo-motor action placed it, if I mistake not, among the curiosities of our mental life. The truth is that it is no curiosity, but simply the normal process stripped of disguise. (pp. 521–522; italics somewhat altered)

Movement is the natural immediate effect of feeling, irrespective of what the quality of the feeling may be. It is so in reflex action, it is so in emotional expression, it is so in voluntary life. Ideo-motor action is thus no paradox, to be softened or explained away. It obeys the type of all conscious action, and from it one must start to explain action in which a special fiat is involved. (p. 527, italics deleted)

[The reason the doctrine implicit in the concept of ideo-motor action] is not a self-evident truth is that we have so many ideas which do not result in action. But it will be seen that in every case, without exception, that is because other ideas simultaneously rob them of their impulsive power. (p. 525)

[In cases of ideo-motor action] the determining condition of the unhesitating and resistless sequence of the act seems to be the absence of any conflicting notion in the mind. Either there is nothing else at all in the mind, or what is there does not conflict. (p. 523)

For James, the mechanism for this inhibition of voluntary behavior involved a conception essentially identical with the later motor theory of thought. "We may lay it down for certain that every representation of a movement awakens in some degree the actual movement which is its object" (p. 526). Obviously, conflicting ideas would elicit incompatible instigations to action. In cases where extended deliberation precedes an act, James believed that many conflicting ideas and incipient movements were taking place.

Although, in what we have now covered, James had made, by argument and available evidence, something of a case for his theory, there remained an enormous gap: how is the impression which evokes voluntary behavior aroused? James recognizes this problem fully and devotes the last dozen pages of the chapter to the development of a physiological model capable of accounting for this process.

Now how can the sensory process which a movement has previously produced, discharge, when excited again, into the center for the movement itself? On the movement's original occurrence the motor discharge came first and the sensory process second; now in the voluntary repetition the sensory process . . . comes first, and the motor discharge comes second. . . . Evidently the problem is that of the formation of new paths; and the only thing to do is to make hypothesis, till we find some which seem to cover all the facts.

How is a fresh path ever formed? . . . I submit as my first hypothesis that [neural] paths all run one way, that is from "sensory" cells into "motor" cells and from motor cells into muscles, without ever taking the reverse direction. . . .

A corollary of this law is that "sensory" cells do not awaken each other connately; that is, no one sensible property of things has any tendency, in advance of experience, to awaken in us the idea of any other sensible properties which in the nature of things may go with it. There is no *a priori* calling up of one "idea" by another; the only *a priori* couplings are of ideas with movements. All suggestions of one sensible fact by another take place by secondary paths which experience has formed.

The diagram [Fig. 10-1] shows what happens in a nervous system ideally reduced to the fewest possible terms. A stimulus reaching the sense-organ awakens the sensory cell, S; this . . . discharges the motor cell, M, which makes the muscle contract; and the contraction arouses the second sensory cell, K [apparently for 'kinesthesis' although the mechanism allows K to refer to any resident or remote feedback]. This cell K discharges into M. If this were the entire nervous mechanism, the movement, once begun, would

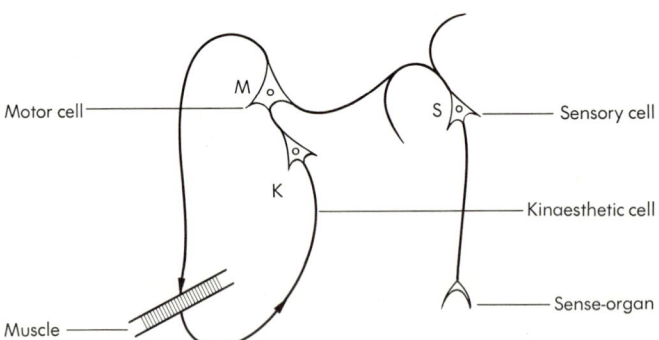

FIGURE 10-1. The nervous system reduced to the fewest possible terms.

The Concept of Reflex and the Problem of Volition

be self-maintaining and .... We should all be cataleptics ... were it not that other processes simultaneously going on inhibit the contraction. Inhibition is therefore not an occasional accident; it is an essential and unremitting element of our cerebral life. ...

Having now considered a nervous system reduced to its lowest possible terms, ... let us turn to conditions under which new paths may be formed. Potentialities for new paths are furnished by the fibers which connect the sensory cells among themselves; but these fibers are not originally pervious, and have to be made so by a process which I proceed hypothetically [this is hypothesis 2] to state as follows: Each discharge from a sensory cell in the forward direction [that is, in the direction toward the motor cells] tends to drain the cells lying behind the discharging one of whatever tension they may possess. The drainage from the rearward cells is what for the first time makes the fibers pervious. The result is a new-formed "path" running from the cells which were "rearward" to the cell which was "forward" on that occasion; which path, if on future occasions the rearward cells are independently excited, will tend to carry off their activity in the same direction so as to excite the forward cell, and will deepen itself more and more every time it is used.

Now the "rearward cells," so far, stand for all the sensory cells of the brain other than the one which is discharging; but such an infinitely broad path would practically be no better than no path, so here I make a *third hypothesis*. ... It is that the deepest paths are formed from the most drainable to the most draining cells; that the most drainable cells are those which have just been discharging or in which the tension is rising towards the point of discharge. Another diagram [Fig. 10-2] will make the matter clear. Take the operation represented by the previous diagram at the moment when, the muscular contraction having occurred, the cell K is discharging forward into M. Through the dotted line *p* it will, according to our third hypothesis, drain S ... and the result is that *p* will now remain as a new path open from S to K. When next S is excited from without it will tend

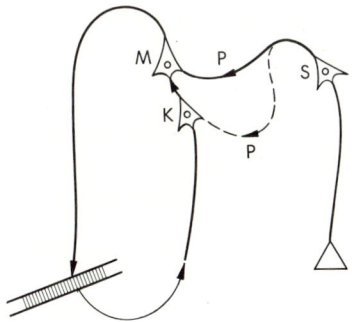

FIGURE 10-2. James' neurological theory to account for the formation of the associations required for the production of voluntary behavior.

not only to discharge into M but into K as well. . . . [Thus] when a sensation has once produced a movement in us, the next time we have the sensation, it tends to suggest the idea of the movement, even before the movement occurs. . . .

Here, then, we have the answer to our original question of how a sensory process which, the first time it occurred, was the effect of a movement, can later figure as the movement's cause [for as we have seen, in the simplest instance the mere image of a movement can initiate the movement itself].

[To illustrate one application of this theory I will] bring back the case of the child and the flame (Vol. I, p. 25). . . . The sight of the flame stimulates the cortical center S^1 which discharges by an instinctive reflex path into center M^1 for the grasping-movement [see Fig. 10-3]. This movement

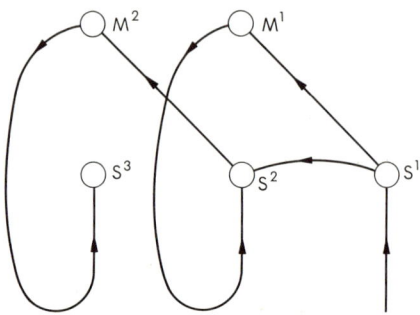

FIGURE 10-3. James' theoretical neural mechanism to account for the fact that the child withdraws its hand before being burned by the candle flame.

produces the feeling of burn, as its effects come back to the center S^2; and this center by a second connate path discharges into M^2, the center for withdrawing the hand. The movement of withdrawal stimulates the center S^3, and this, as far as we are concerned, is the last thing that happens. Now the next time the child sees the candle, the cortex is in possession of the secondary paths which the first experience left behind. S^2, having been stimulated immediately after S^1, drained the latter, and now S^1 discharges into S^2 before the discharge of M^1 has had time to occur; in other words the sight of the flame suggests the idea of the burn before it produces its own natural reflex effects. The result is an inhibition of M^1, or an overtaking of it before it is completed, by M^2—The characteristic physiological feature in all these acquired systems of paths lies in the fact that the new-formed sensory irradiations keep draining things forward, and so breaking up the "motor circles" that would otherwise accrue. (pp. 580–591; italics altered)

The attentive reader, in addition to following the thread of James' argument will have noted the following important points:

The Concept of Reflex and the Problem of Volition

1. Although James speaks of cells, paths, centers, neurons, etc., the anatomical referents of these terms are unimportant to the argument, a fact to which James calls attention by the use of quotation marks.

2. The associative process described by James bears a very close resemblance to Pavlov's theory of conditioning.

3. The activation of a sensory center by any path whatsoever usually has motor and further sensory consequences at the level of images. Thus the child, not only anticipates the feeling of the burn at the sight of the candle, but also withdraws; and withdrawal has its own sensible effects. As a much more impressive demonstration of the same points, James quotes the following passage from Helmholtz' *Physiological Optics*.

When the external rectus muscle of the right eye, or its nerve, is paralyzed, the eye can no longer be rotated to the right side. So long as the patient turns it only to the nasal side it makes regular movements, and he perceives correctly the position of objects in the visual field. So soon, however, as he tries to rotate it outwardly, i.e., towards the right, it ceases to obey his will, stands motionless in the middle of its course and the objects appear flying to the right, although position of the eye and retinal image are unaltered.

In such a case the exertion of the will is followed neither by actual movement of the eye, nor by contraction of the muscle in question, nor even by increased tension in it. The act of will *produced absolutely no effect* beyond the nervous system, and yet we judge the direction of the line of vision as if the will had exercised its normal effects. We believe it to have moved to the right, and since the retinal image is unchanged, we attribute to the object the same movement we have erroneously ascribed to the eye. (p. 507)

SUMMARY

Pavlov made no important distinction between conditioned and unconditioned reflexes, defining both in terms of the physiological mechanism of the reflex arc. It remained for Skinner to deal with the methodological problems associated with the concept of reflex.

An important part of Skinner's contribution lay in his recognition of the facts (a) that a methodological problem existed and (b) that "reflex" is a concept and not a thing. Skinner defined a reflex in terms of a dependable correlation between stimuli and responses and made no mention of physiological connections. He also noted that the extension of this concept to the study of behavior implied a psychology whose laws were of the general type, $R = f(S)$.

Even at the simplest level, however, such laws are an oversimplification because the strength of reflex behavior depends upon additional (A) variables. Thus, even for these cases, psychological laws must take the form, $R = f(S,A)$. These considerations become particularly important in the case of so called voluntary responses that appear to be entirely a function of unspecifiable "A" variables with little or no relation to "S." Skinner's way out of this dilemma was to suggest that S-variables exist for voluntary behavior but that the study of such behavior could proceed in the absence of their specification. As is well known, Skinner has followed this program for over 30 years.

The psychologist who dealt with the problem of voluntary behavior most responsibly was William James. James took the position that voluntary behavior was just as automatic or reflexive as any other behavior, that the fundamental mode of behavior was represented by ideo-motor action in which the "image" of the consequences of a response led automatically to the response in question. This bold proposition, of course, raises the question of how these stimuli are presented. In attempting to answer this question James developed a neurological model in which there was a mechanism by which a signal to respond could arouse the kinesthetic (and other) consequences of a response. These stimulational consequences, in turn, elicited the reaction.

Theories of this type have recently been redeveloped by Konorski (1948), von Holst (1954) and others. One of the critical questions thus raised concerns the role of kinesthetic feedback in the control of instrumental behavior: Can an instrumental act be performed if its sensible consequences no longer follow? This question is put to experimental test in the next chapter.

11

The Effect of Deafferentation on Instrumental (Type II) Conditioned Reflexes in Dogs[1]

T. GORSKA

E. JANKOWSKA[2]

In our previous experiments on cats and rats (Jankowska, 1957, 1959; Gorska and Jankowska, 1961) it was found that the animals are able to perform some learned movements with a deafferented limb in order to obtain food. These results concerned the instrumental scratch reflex and the instrumental reaction of lifting the hindlimb in the cleaning reflex. Both reflexes were established before the operation by food reinforcement of the respective unconditioned reflexes. The mechanism of instrumental reflexes derived from some complex unconditioned reflexes is, in comparison with other simpler conditioned motor reactions, not well understood. The question therefore arose of the effects of deafferentation on instrumental reflexes consisting of a single movement and established by routine methods (e.g., reinforcement of passive movements). Moreover, in our previous experiments the quality of instrumental reactions of the deafferented limb could not be precisely analyzed, owing to the difficulties in recording (the animals moved freely in the experimental cage). In the present series of experiments the effects of deafferentation were studied in dogs, in which well defined, simple motor conditioned reactions have been established and analyzed in a proper way.

MATERIAL AND METHODS

Experiments were performed on 12 dogs. In each animal an instrumental conditioned reflex to an auditory stimulus was established. The instrumental reaction consisted either of high flexion of the hind-

[1] Reprinted, with slight modifications, from *Acta Biologiae Experimentalis*, 1961, 21, by permission of the editor.
[2] The authors are very indebted to Professor Jerzy Konorski for his valuable criticism and helpful advice during the preparation of this paper. We are also grateful to the technical assistants, Mr. Antoni Rosiak and Miss Janina Gawrys, for their careful attention to the health of our operated animals.

limb, or of lifting the foreleg and putting it on a high platform. In 4 dogs the presentation of food was used as reinforcement, in 8 other animals, an electric shock, 50 c/s, applied either to the ear or to one of the legs. In these 8 dogs the instrumental avoidance reflexes were established, i.e., if the dog performed the instrumental reaction to the conditioned stimulus, the nociceptive stimulus was not given, but if the dog did not execute the proper movement during a definite time of conditioned stimulus exposure (5–7 seconds), the electric shock was applied. It was switched off only when the dog performed the learned reaction (so-called escape reaction).

The instrumental reactions were established either by reinforcing the passive movements or the unconditioned defensive flexion reflex. In two of 4 dogs with alimentary reflexes, passive movements were used, in the other two the reinforced motor reaction was provoked by application of the electric shock to the foot at the beginning of training. In 8 dogs with avoidance reflexes, passive movements were used in 5 (in this case the electrodes were fixed either to the animal's ear or to one of his paws, but not to the limb whose movements were trained), and in 3 other dogs, the avoidance reflexes were elaborated from the classical defensive reflexes, i.e., the electric shock was applied to the same limb which was engaged in the execution of the movement. The training of instrumental reflexes was carried on according to the normal procedure of elaboration of type II conditioned reflexes. Experiments were conducted in a typical soundproof conditioned reflex chamber.

The preoperative training lasted for 3–6 months, up to the moment when the instrumental reflexes were firmly established. It consisted in different animals of 35–101 experimental sessions, with 6–8 trials per session, i.e., 235–540 trials with the positive conditioned stimulus. In two dogs (Nos. 16 and 17) the instrumental reflexes had already been previously established.[3] In the final preoperative period (100 trials preceding the operation) the instrumental reactions to the positive conditioned stimulus were present in all the dogs in 97–100 percent of the trials.

In the course of training special attention was paid to the amplitude of instrumental movements. To the conditioned stimulus the animals had to react with fairly high flexion and only such movements, and not those of lesser amplitude, were considered as a correct reaction. This was achieved in the majority of dogs by using a special device which automatically either presented the bowl with food or, in avoidance reflexes, switched off the stimulus only when the animal had raised its limb sufficiently high.

[3] These dogs had been trained by Dr. A. Zbrozyna, and in both animals the prefrontal area of the cortex had been ablated about 2 years before deafferentation. This operation did not affect the positive conditioned reflexes.

Effect of Deafferentation

In 10 out of 12 dogs, in addition to the positive conditioned reflex, an inhibitory reflex was established to another auditory stimulus much different from the positive one. During the entire training the inhibitory stimulus was applied 35–70 times. In the last 20 trials before operation the number of correct reactions to the inhibitory stimulus amounted, in all the animals but one, to 90–100 percent.

Surgical procedure

In all the animals deafferentation of the limb engaged in the movement was performed. For the hindlimb, the extent of deafferentation varied from L_1 or L_3 to S_4 or Coc_1 (9–12 roots), when the foreleg was deafferented all the dorsal roots from C_5 to Th_3 or Th_4 (7–8 roots) were sectioned. The dorsal roots were transected extradurally, proximal to the spinal ganglions. In longer roots a piece of several millimeters was excised and the ganglion was, if possible, crushed. The shorter roots were simply sectioned.

In all animals some ventral roots were also severed in addition to the sectioned dorsal roots. This had to be done with all ventral roots which strongly adhered to the dorsal roots, such as the upper lumbar (L_1, L_2) and lowest sacral (S_3, S_4) anterior roots for the hindlimb, and ventral root C_5 for the forelimb. The number of transected ventral roots varied in different animals from 1 to 4. The extent of deafferentation and the ventral roots additionally cut are shown in Table 11-2.

The operation was performed under aseptic conditions with nembutal anesthesia (40–45 mg./kg. of body weight). The operative technique did not differ from the analogous operation in cats (Jankowska, 1959), except for the fact that in dogs the dorsal roots were cut extradurally, while in cats intradurally.

Macroscopic verification of the sectioned roots indicated that deafferentation within the required limits was complete, and sensory tests (pricking) likewise indicated complete anesthesia.

The general state of the animals after deafferentation

Deafferentation in dogs was followed by a number of symptoms identical with those found in other animals. These symptoms are described here in order to give a better picture of the experimental animals.

1. *Cutaneous sensation.* In all dogs section of the dorsal roots, within the limits described above, resulted in a complete loss of cutaneous sensitivity (reaction to pricking) over the entire surface of the limb. When the hindlimb was deafferented, the limits of the anesthetized area varied, according to the extent of deafferentation, rostrally from 2–6 cm.

in front of the pelvis and caudally 3–10 cm. beyond the base of the tail. For the forelimb, the anesthetized area extended from about 3 cm. in front of the anterior border of the shoulder blade, to about 3–4 cm. to the back of the posterior border of this bone. The typical extent of the anethetized area following deafferentation is shown in Figure 11-1.

2. *Position of the deafferented limb and walking.* The deafferented dogs began to get up and tried to walk within 2–5 days after operation. At the beginning, while standing, they kept the affected extremity contracted and, while walking, they hopped on three legs. After some days, when in an upright position, they put the operated limb on the floor, often on the dorsal part of the toes, and tried to support themselves on it. The normal pattern of movements during walking, i.e., rhythmic and

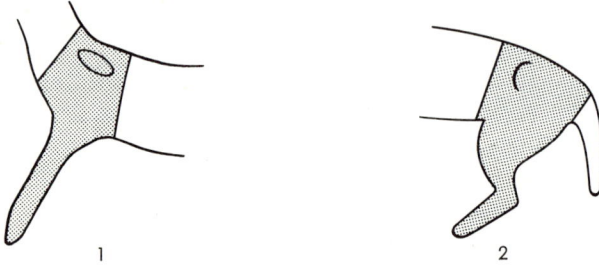

FIGURE 11-1. Area anaesthetized after section of respective dorsal roots in dogs.

alternative flexions of the deafferented extremity, reappeared in the majority of animals 2–3 weeks after operation.

In 5 dogs with a deafferented hindlimb (out of 10) a regression in the process of walking was observed 3–4 weeks after operation. This was due to a strong curving and twisting of the spine towards the normal limb which, in the worst cases, prevented the animals from putting the affected limb on the floor and even from maintaining an upright position (e.g., dogs Nos. 3 and 5). This curving of the spine was the more distinct the more extensive was the deafferentation. In order to partly counteract this process we took special care not to let the animals sit or lie on the deafferented side.

In half of the animals with a deafferented hindleg a marked tendency to keep the affected extremity in extension was observed 4–6 weeks after operation. The deafferented limb, completely flaccid directly after operation, became gradually more rigid and resistive to passive flexion. The extension of the deafferented limb was more marked in the distal than in the proximal joints (cf. Bickel, 1897; Ranson, 1928; Ranson, Hinsey, & Taylor, 1929; Hnik, 1956; Jankowska, 1959).

The tendency to extend the affected limb caused a change in its position during walking and standing. While standing the dogs kept the affected extremity stretched forward and when walking, movements were usually limited to the thigh joint. In the case of deafferentation of the foreleg no tendency to keep the operated limb in extension was noticed, but rather, a tendency to flexion could be observed.

In 4 dogs oscillating movements of the affected leg synchronous with respiration were observed (Orbeli & Kunstman, 1929; Jankowska, 1959). They appeared in one or a few experiments and only in a state of strong emotional excitement (dogs with avoidance reflexes).

3. *Other anomalies.* Trophic skin changes, ulcers, etc. were noticed in 4 dogs. As in cats, they resulted chiefly from mechanical damage, such as abrasion of the leg during walking. In order to protect the animals, the dogs were kept on a rubber floor and wore leather shoes on the affected limb. Nevertheless, in two cases it was necessary to amputate the digits of the deafferented hindlimb.

Results

The types of reflexes established in each dog and their postoperative state are presented in Table 11-1. Below is a more detailed description of the results of deafferentation.

1. In all the dogs the instrumental reflexes established before the operation were also present after deafferentation. During the period of postoperative observation they did not reveal any tendency to disappear.

In 10 out of 12 deafferented dogs postoperative testing continued to at least 100 trials with the positive conditioned stimulus. Since in several animals the experimental sessions were performed only once or twice a week, or were discontinued for some weeks, the period of postoperative observation varied in different dogs from one and a half to three and a half months. On two dogs (Nos. 3 and 5) the instrumental reflexes of the deafferented limb were examined for a very short time only (20 and 24 trials respectively), because the general state of these animals did not permit further observation.

Comparison of the number of instrumental reactions to the positive stimulus before and after operation (Table 11-3) shows that in 8 out of 10 dogs observed for a long time, the instrumental reactions were present in all the trials (3 dogs with alimentary reflexes and 5 with avoidance reflexes). In 2 other animals (Nos. 8 and 14) the instrumental avoidance reactions were present in 81 and 97 percent of trials. If trials

TABLE 11-1

Experimental conditions for individual animals

Dog No.	Kind of reflex	Movement of leg	Kind of movement	Kind of training	Electrode position
2	Avoidance	Left hindleg	Moderate flexion	Classical defensive reflex	Left hindleg
3	Avoidance	Left hindleg	Moderate flexion	Classical defensive reflex	Left hindleg
4	Alimentary	Left hindleg	Moderate flexion	Classical defensive reflex	Left hindleg
5	Alimentary	Right hindleg	High flexion	Passive movements	–
8	Avoidance	Left hindleg	High flexion	Passive movements	Right hindleg
9	Avoidance	Left hindleg	High flexion	Passive movements	Left ear
12	Alimentary	Right hindleg	High flexion	Classical defensive reflex	Right hindleg
13	Avoidance	Left hindleg	High flexion	Classical defensive reflex	Left hindleg
14	Avoidance	Left hindleg	High flexion	Passive movements	Left ear
15	Alimentary	Right hindleg	High flexion	Passive movements	–
16	Avoidance	Right foreleg	Putting on platform, or high flexion	Passive movements	Right hindleg
17	Avoidance	Right foreleg	Putting on platform, or high flexion	Passive movements	Left hindleg

with escape reactions (see under Methods) are also counted, the number of conditioned movements amounts to 96 and 100 percent respectively.

2. The mean latent period of instrumental reflexes remained almost unchanged in all operated animals when compared with the last preoperative period, nor did it show any prolongation during the period of postoperative examination (Table 11-4). The differences were in general less than 1 second, and only in one dog (No. 16) was a twofold increase observed in the latency of movements after operation.

3. The amplitude of instrumental reactions after deafferentation also remained practically unchanged in the majority of animals (Table 11-5). In some animals the percentage of relatively high movements even

TABLE 11-2

Extent of deafferentation and results

Dog No.	Extent of deafferentation	Ventral roots additionally cut	Postoperative character of movements	Remarks
2	$L_1 - S_3$	L_1, S_3	Unchanged during the whole period; marked extension of a limb	
3	$L_1 - Coc_1$	L_1, L_4, S_4, Coc_1	Unchanged for first 20 trials, experiments then interrupted	
4	$L_2 - S_3$	L_4, S_2	Unchanged during the whole period; marked extension of a limb	
5	$L_1 - S_3$	S_2, S_3	Unchanged for first 24 trials, experiments then interrupted	
8	$L_2 - S_4$	L_2, S_3, S_4	Somewhat irregular and lower than before; chiefly in the 1st period marked extension of a limb	Strong neurotic symptoms, which diminished in the 2nd period
9	$L_3 - S_4$	S_3, S_4	Unchanged during the whole period; marked extension of a limb	
12	$L_3 - Coc_1$	S_3, S_4, Coc_1	Unchanged during the whole period; marked extension of a limb	
13	$L_2 - S_4$	L_2, L_3, S_3, S_4	Unchanged during the whole period	
14	$L_2 - Coc_1$	L_2, S_3, S_4, Coc_1	Unchanged during the whole period	Slight neurotic state in 2nd period
15	$L_2 - S_4$	S_2, S_3, S_4	Unchanged during the whole period	
16	$C_5 - Th_3$	C_5	First unchanged, then gradual diminution of amplitude and increase in latency of movements	Chronic inflammation of the limb beginning 4 weeks after operation
17	$C_5 - Th_4$	C_5	Unchanged during the whole period	

TABLE 11-3

Percentage of instrumental reactions to the positive stimulus before and after deafferentation

Kind of reflex	Dog No.	Before operation (last 100 trials)			After deafferentation					
					1-50 trials			51-100 trials		
Alimentary	4	99			100			100		
	5	97			95			–		
	12	99			100			100		
	15	98			100			100		
		Av.*	Esc.	Sum	Av.	Esc.	Sum	Av.	Esc.	Sum
Avoidance	2	100	0	100	100	0	100	100	0	100
	3	99	1	100	100	0	100	–	–	–
	8	100	0	100	70	22	92	92	8	100
	9	98	2	100	100	0	100	100	0	100
	13	100	0	100	100	0	100	100	0	100
	14	100	0	100	100	0	100	94	6	100
	15	100	0	100	100	0	100	100	0	100
	16	100	0	100	100	0	100	100	0	100
	17	100	0	100	100	0	100	100	0	100

* Av. — avoidance reaction; Esc. — escape reaction; Sum — sum of conditioned reactions.

increased after operation, while in others a small decrease was observed. Only in 2 dogs (Nos. 8 and 16) was deafferentation followed by a marked reduction in the total number of high flexions.

4. The instrumental reactions of the deafferented limb, although in principle unaffected, were performed in a somewhat changed manner. They were rather awkward and ataxic and sometimes seemed to be executed by the animals with a greater "effort" than normally. These features were constant and during the period of postoperative observation no changes in the skill of the performed movements were noticed.

In some cases the reaction of the deafferented limb had a more tonic character, i.e., the movement, despite its unchanged latency, was performed more slowly, and, or the animals continued for a while to hold the affected limb in the air after the conditioned stimulus had been switched off, which had never occurred before operation (cf. Teasdall and Stavraky, 1953).

In dogs which kept the deafferented limb in marked extension the flexion movement was largely limited to the thigh joint.

TABLE 11-4

Mean latent period of instrumental reactions before and after operation

Dog No.	Before operation (last 100 trials)	After deafferentation		
		1-50 trials	51-100 trials	Mean
2	1.2	1.0	1.3	1.1
3	1.9	1.5	–*	–
4	1.3	1.8	2.7	2.2
5	1.0	1.1	–	–
8	2.2	4.2	2.0	3.0
9	2.0	1.3	2.0	1.7
12	1.7	1.8	1.7	1.7
13	2.0	1.6	2.6	2.1
14	1.6	1.5	1.6	1.5
15	1.0	1.0	1.0	1.0
16	1.6	2.4	3.8	3.1
17	1.1	1.0	1.0	1.0
Mean	1.5	1.7	2.0	1.8

* In dogs Nos. 2, 3, and 4 the amplitude of movements was not precisely recorded.

TABLE 11-5

Amplitude of instrumental reactions before and after deafferentation (percentage of trials in which high flexion was performed)

Dog No.	Before operation (last 100 trials)	After deafferentation		
		1-50 trials	51-100 trials	Mean
5	96	87	–	–
8	92	32	72	54
9	63	78	98	88
12	98	92	86	89
13	74	74	40	57
14	95	96	96	96
15	100	100	100	100
16	100	86	32	59
17	100	100	100	100
Mean	91	83	78	80

TABLE 11-6

Percentage of trials with no instrumental reaction to the inhibitory stimulus before and after deafferentation

Dog No.*	Before operation (last 20 trials)	After deafferentation (first 20 trials)
8	90	90
9	50	100
12	95	85
13	100	100
14	100	85
15	100	85
16	100	100
17	100	100
Mean	92	92

* In dogs Nos. 3 and 5 the inhibitory stimuli were not applied after the operation.

5. Deafferentation had no effect on the inhibitory reflexes established in the animals (Table 11-6).

6. Acute extinction[4] of the conditioned reflexes of the deafferented limb was performed in 3 dogs. The criterion was 5 successive trials with no conditioned reaction to the positive stimulus. In 2 dogs with alimentary reflexes (Nos. 12 and 15) this criterion was reached after 18 and 7 applications of the unreinforced stimulus respectively. Extinction of the avoidance reflex (dog No. 8) took place after 18 trials. In all these animals a single application of the unconditioned stimulus (food or electric shock) led to an immediate restoration of the extinguished conditioned reflex.

7. The role of vision in the execution of movements with a deafferented limb was investigated in 4 animals. Exclusion of vision did not affect at all the instrumental reactions performed with the hindlimb (dogs Nos. 9, 13, and 14). In the dog which performed the movement with the foreleg (No. 17), movements of high flexion were maintained but the paw was no longer placed on the platform. This fact, however, might have been due to factors other than the exclusion of vision, since the blindfolded animal kept its head very low and probably could not put the foot into the platform in this position.

[4] That is, extinction carried out in a very few sessions; to be contrasted with *chronic extinction* involving a great many sessions [Ed.].

DISCUSSION

The results described above show that firmly established instrumental reflexes consisting of a relatively simple movement are regularly performed with a deafferented limb and do not show any tendency to disappear. Deafferentation produces only a slight impairment in the skill of such movements but does not abolish the capacity to execute them with the same regularity, latency and amplitude as under normal conditions. Results similar to ours were obtained in animals only by Knapp, Taub and Berman (1958).[5]

In the light of our data, the part played by proprioception in the performance of voluntary movements has to be revised. The proprioceptive impulses are generally considered as an indispensable factor in the execution of even the simplest voluntary movements, as well as in the establishment of new instrumental reflexes. For instance, according to the theory of Konorski and Miller (1933, 1936) the active reproduction of passive movements during the training of motor conditioned reflexes occurs on the basis of connections between the pattern of proprioceptive impulses, generated during the execution of a given motor act and proper states of excitation and inhibition of the center of the unconditioned stimulus. According to their theory no voluntary act can be established nor occur without proprioception.

[Thus] our results have shown that the proprioceptive feedback enhances only the skill and precision of instrumental reactions but is not necessary for execution of a simple motor reaction. A question then arises as to how the animal can perform a "voluntary" motor act without knowing which movement is required and whether or not it has been accomplished. It seems that the following explanations of this fact are possible:

1. The deafferentation of one leg does not abolish the proprioceptive feedback from other extremities and the body. Flexion of one leg is accompanied by a simultaneous shift of the body's center of gravity and subsequently by a change in muscle tonus in the other extremities. The pattern of proprioceptive impulses from the unaffected legs when the animal stands quietly on the floor differs from that arising when the deafferented leg is flexed. Therefore, it might be possible that

---

[5] These authors established in monkeys an avoidance reflex of the foreleg to the criterion of 80 percent positive reactions, and then performed deafferentation. They found that in the first period after operation the learned movements did not appear, or were present only in some trials. The reconditioning of these reflexes was, however, possible. As it seems, the temporary loss of reflexes might be due to the shorter preoperative training and, or their earlier postoperative examination, as compared with our experiments.

the unaffected proprioception of the body sufficiently informs the animal what the starting position of the deafferented limb is, and which movement has been executed. In the light of this hypothesis the essential part played by proprioceptive feedback in voluntary movements should not be rejected, provided that afferent impulses of the deafferented leg are replaced by the proprioceptive message obtained from other parts of the body.

Some experimental data, however, seem to contradict this interpretation. First, according to this hypothesis, the deafferented animals should, after operation, relearn to perform the trained movement on the basis of proprioception from other extremities. It seems that in normal animals the afferent impulses from the limb engaged in a definite movement should be more important than those from other extremities. Consequently, the impairment of instrumental reactions should be especially marked in the first period after operation, and then, in the course of postoperative training, a gradual improvement of this movement should be observed, as the animal learns to discriminate the position of the affected limb on the basis of proprioception of the rest of the body. However, our experiments show that the quality of motor reactions was, during all the time of postoperative observation, quite constant, if not best in the first experimental sessions. . . .

2. It may be possible that the motor center activity associated with the execution of the leg movement is also signalled to other brain centers by an intercentral feed-back mechanism other than the one arising in the limb. The recently described (Magni *et al.,* 1959; Jabur & Towe, 1960; Kuypers, 1960) direct nervous connections between the pyramidal tract and the cuneate and gracilis nuclei, as well as the nucleus proprius in the spinal cord, might support this hypothesis.

3. It may be assumed that all concepts emphasizing the essential part played by proprioceptive afferentation in voluntary movements should be restricted to other kinds of motor activity than relatively simple motor acts. According to this view the execution of a simple voluntary movement may not need any proprioceptive afferentation, since the reflex arc for such a reaction does not pass through the appropriate afferent centers. This hypothesis could explain the facts observed in our experiments.

Let us consider the reflex arc of a learned simple motor act. According to the schema of conditioned motor reflexes (Wyrwicka, 1952; Soltysik & Kowalska, 1960) the performance of a learned movements to a given stimulus is due to nervous connections established between the center of the conditioned stimulus and the center of a definite motor reaction. As a result of these connections (both direct, and indirect through the center of the corresponding drive) the application of a conditioned stimulus causes an excitation of the appropriate motor centers and consequently elicits the instrumental reaction. Not only flexion of the leg, but also putting it back on the floor may be attributed to the function of these centers. While the application of the conditioned stimulus activates the definite motor centers, the discontinuation of this stimulus in avoidance reflexes, or the presentation of food in alimentary reflexes, cuts short their excitation. This is followed by a return of the leg to a normal position. Furthermore, the greater the excitation, the stronger be the reaction performed. Hence prolongation of the conditioned stimulus leads to increased flexions. This is comparable to the effects of direct stimulation of the motor cortex, which also results in some simple movements, like flexion or extension, varying in amplitude and latency according to the parameters of the electric current. Experiments with stimulation of the motor cortex (Lassek, 1953), pyramidal tract (Teasdall & Stavraky, 1953) and ventral roots (Lassek, 1953) in normal and deafferented animals have shown that the excitability of the efferent parts of the reflex arc are not diminished after deafferentation. This explains why the learned movements were performed by our operated animals with the same regularity, latency and amplitude as before the operation. It may then be assumed that afferent influx plays only a supplementary function in simple voluntary movement, modulating its character and increasing its precision.

These considerations have only dealt with the role of afferent information in the performance of those voluntary movements which consist of a single and simple motor act, such as movements elicited by direct stimulation of the motor cortex. However, regardless which of the above hypothesis proves to be true, there is no doubt whatsoever that proprioception plays an indispensable part in many kinds of motor activity. The motor behavior of animals usually consists of more complex reactions than those found in laboratory conditions; they are either composed of several successive simple movements, as for example in walking, or need a very subtle analysis of muscle tonus, as in the case of precise movements. In all these chain-like reactions proprioception would be an indispensable factor, since the afferent impulses set up during execution of the first movement should form a conditioned stimulus for the next movement. The reflex arc of such complex motor reflexes would then involve, besides the motor centers for the successive movements, also the sensory centers involved in their performance. Therefore, it is to be expected that deafferentation will completely abolish the possibility of performing such chain-like voluntary movements.

SUMMARY

It was found that deafferented dogs are able to perform some simple instrumental movements with the affected limb, established by preoperative training. Deafferentation of a limb does not abolish the ability to execute them with the same regularity, latency and amplitude as under normal conditions. These results are interpreted according to the following three hypotheses: (1) execution of a voluntary movement with a deafferented limb occurs on the basis of the unaffected afferent influx from the rest of the body; (2) deafferentation does not abolish the afferent feedback based on intercentral connections; (3) performance of a simple voluntary movement requires no afferent information since this feedback is not involved in the reflex arc of type II conditioned reflexes. In view of the last hypothesis proprioceptive information plays only a secondary role in the mechanism of such instrumental reflexes, modulating their character, but not necessary for their execution.

III

IMPORTANT THEORETICAL POSITIONS

12

Hull's Version of S-R Theory

GREGORY A. KIMBLE

During the period 1929–1953, research in the field of learning was heavily dominated by the various theoretical formulations of one individual, Clark L. Hull. Over a quarter of a century, Hull developed several theories which varied in scope and addressed themselves to several different forms of learning. Of all of Hull's theories, the most influential was that described in *Principles of Behavior* (1943).

The influence of *Principles of Behavior* on the psychology of learning was both direct and indirect. In part, the influence of the former type took the form of explicit statements of hypothesized empirical relationships embodied in Hullian theory. These statements provided the stimulus for literally hundreds of experimental studies. In addition, Hull's theoretical position on such matters as the nature of reinforcement, the continuity-noncontinuity issue and S-R vs S-S theories of what is learned, provided the impetus for other studies. Even studies not conducted as direct tests of Hullian theory tended to concentrate on problems which made sense within a Hullian type of system. Thus, there were many studies of the "parameters of reinforcement" (Kimble, 1961) which were not offered as tests of any of Hull's conceptions but were nevertheless related.

To some extent, Hull's influence persists in psychology today, although it is now obvious that the 1943 theory is insufficient in many respects. Unfortunately, the major analyses of Hull's theory have done little to clarify the theory's inadequacies. The first of these (Koch, 1944) was an extravagantly positive statement which glossed over obvious defects in the theory. There was little discussion of logical contradictions, almost nothing about the inadequate factual basis of the theory, and only mild criticism of its transparent lack of generality and the questionable value of many of its concepts. Another major analysis (Koch, 1954) went to the other extreme: the theory was ridiculed and presented as a crime against the science, seemingly committed with malice aforethought. Neither of these expressions contributed anything constructive to the development of the theory. In what follows, an attempt is made to place Hull's theory in better perspective.

Hull's theory is an S-R theory and consists of a chain of intervening variables bridging a logical gap from stimulus to response. Although it is somewhat artificial to do so, for purposes of exposition, it will be convenient to consider the theory as consisting of five major clusters of variables, in order: habit formation, generalization and stimulus compounding, motivation, inhibition, and response evocation.

HABIT FORMATION

As is well known, the pivotal concept in Hull's system is $_sH_R$ or habit strength, the logical status of which may be presented with the aid of a diagram as follows:

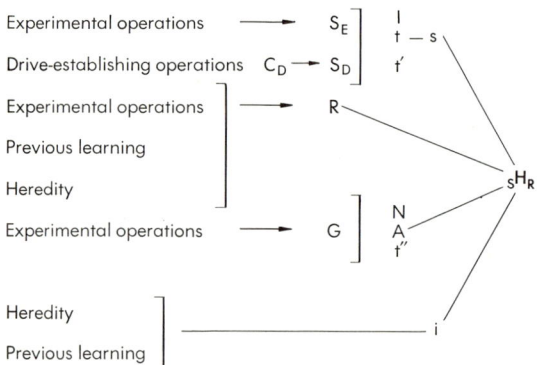

This diagram implies two sets of circumstances, experimental operations and drive-establishing operations, that provide the most important stimulating conditions in Hull's theory. Thus, these operations define the two classes of stimulational independent variables, S_D (drive stimulus) and S_E (environmental stimulus).[1]

These stimulational factors, whether environmental or motivational, have three important characteristics: intensity (I), duration (t) and, in the case of brief stimuli, the time since their cessation (t'). Hull assumed that these three attributes of stimulation combined quantitatively

---

[1] The symbol S_D appears in Hull's writings; S_E does not. I have taken the liberty of modifying Hullian symbolism at several points. In general, this has entailed the addition of symbols to represent steps in Hull's argument that tend to be implicit rather than spelled out. [Ed.]

Hull's Version of S-R Theory

to determine the value of a second-order intervening variable, afferent neural impulse or stimulus trace (s). This trace is one of the important contributors to the value of Hull's major intervening variable, habit strength ($_sH_R$).

The experimental procedures in every experiment on learning also have the effects of favoring the appearance of some response (R) and of providing for reinforcement (G) in the empirical sense of the term *reinforcement*. Hull himself characteristically left the empirical level and spoke in terms of drive- or need-reduction, but this shift in levels of abstractness is not necessary and for our purposes it will be better to remain at the level of facts. Reinforcements for Hull had three significant characteristics: number of previous occurrences (N), time of delay (t″) and amount (A). The significances of these several parameters of reinforcement, however, entered into learning in different ways. The latter two, together with stimulus trace (s),[2] determined the upper limit of habit growth (M) attainable. Thus, $M = f$ (S, t″, A). The first variable, together with an individual differences variable (i) determines the value of $_sH_R$ at any point in learning.

The theoretical combination of these variables proposed by Hull is represented in his well-known equation for habit formation, $_sH_R = M - Me^{-iN}$, where i is the individual difference constant referred to above, N is the number of reinforcements and M is a theoretical limit of habit growth. The limit of habit growth (M) was assumed by Hull to be a positive function of the magnitude of the stimulus trace and the amount of reinforcement, and a negative function of the delay of reinforcement. The individual differences variable (i) was not treated as an intervening variable in *Principles of Behavior,* but presumably it would reflect whatever influences in the organism's heredity and prior experiences affect the rate of habit formation. The equation itself is a simple statement of the proposition that habit strength increases *gradually* as a function of the number of reinforcements, approaching a limit (M).

The effect of number of practice trials

Developing the concept of habit strength in more detail, Hull says:

Having decided to employ the construct $_sH_R$, we proceed at once to the problem of determining the presumptive quantitative nature of its functional relationship to its various antecedent determiners. The first of these

---

[2] The reader acquainted with Hull's theory will recognize that Hull developed the concept of stimulus trace early in the book and then did so again in his chapter on stimulus-response asynchronism. In discussing habit formation, Hull postulated that this latter variable (operationally, the interstimulus interval) determined the upper limit of habit growth. Such redundancy or "conceptual obesity" was a serious defect in the theory. In this discussion I have tried to eliminate this unnecessary overlap by relating $_sH_R$ to stimulus trace directly.

to be considered will be the relationship of $_sH_R$ to the number of reinforcements (N) . . . .

The investigation of the functional relationship of habit strength to the number of reinforcements is so new that the greater part of the trial and error involved in its determination has yet to be performed, . . . Taking our point of departure from extensive observations in the field of habit information [however] it is concluded that very probably:

1. Habit strength is an increasing function of the number of reinforcements.

2. This function increases up to some sort of physiological limit beyond which no more increase is possible.

3. As habit strength approaches this physiological limits with continued reinforcements the increment (Δ_sH_R) resulting from each additional reinforcement decreases progressively in magnitude.

Now, there are numerous algebraic expressions which yield results conforming to the above specifications. One of these [the simple positive growth function] has a rather special promise because it is known to approximate closely a very large number of observable empirical relationships in all sorts of biological situations involving growth and decay. . . .

The basic principle of the simple positive growth function . . . is that *the amount of growth resulting from each unit of growth opportunity will increase the amount of whatever is growing by a constant fraction of the growth potentiality as yet unrealized.* . . .

From the foregoing it is evident that the rate of habit growth is dependent upon three factors or *parameters*:

1. The physiological limit or maximum (M)

2. The ordinal number (N) of the reinforcement producing a given increment to the habit strength (Δ_sH_R)

3. The constant factor (F) according to which a portion (Δ_sH_R) of the unrealized potentiality is transferred to the actual habit strength at a given reinforcement

There must also be devised a unit in which to express habit strength. This is taken arbitrarily as 1 percent of the physiological maximum (M) of habit strength attainable by a standard organism under optimal conditions. In order to make the name of the unit easy to remember, it will be called the *hab*, a shortened form of the word *habit*. Thus under the conditions stated above there would be 100 habit units, or habs, between zero and the physiological limit, i.e., one hab = $\frac{M}{100}$.

We proceed now with [an] example. Suppose that the growth constant (F) in a given reinforcement situation is taken at 1/10. One-tenth of the total possibility of learning (100 units) is 10 habs (1/10 of 100 = 10). The generation of 10 units of habit strength from a base, zero, leaves 100 − 10, or 90 units of growth yet possible of realization. Consequently the habit increment resulting from the second reinforcement must be 1/10 of 90, or 9; i.e., the second $\Delta_sH_R = 9$ habs. Subtracting 9 from 90 we have left 81 units of possible growth. One-tenth of 81 in turn yields our next Δ_sH_R of 8.1

TABLE 12-1

Analytical table showing the theoretical evolution of a typical "growth" function in which each increment to the habit is 1/10 of the potential habit strength as yet unformed

Ordinal number of reinforcements	Increment of habit ($\Delta \dot{S}^H R$)	Total accumulated habit in hab units ($\Sigma \Delta \dot{S}^H R$)
1	10	10
2	9	19
3	8.1	27.1
4	7.29	34.39
5	6.561	40.951
6	5.9049	46.856
7	5.3144	52.1703
8	4.7830	56.9533
9	4.3047	61.2580
10	3.8742	65.1322
11	3.4868	68.6189
12	3.1381	71.7570
13	2.8243	74.5813
14	2.5419	77.1232
15	2.2877	79.4109
16	2.0590	81.4698
17	1.8530	83.3228
18	1.6677	84.9905
19	1.5009	86.4915
20	1.3509	87.8423
21	1.2158	89.0581
22	1.0942	90.1523
23	.9848	91.1371
24	.8863	92.0234
25	.7977	92.8210
26	.7179	93.5389
27	.6461	94.1850
28	.5815	94.7665
29	.5233	95.2899
30	.4710	95.7609

habs, and so on. This process can be repeated as many times as there are successive repetitions of the reinforcement. [Pp. 112–115. The results obtained in a series of such repetitions appear in Table 12-1.]

Now let us turn to an account of some of the variables assumed by Hull to determine the limit of habit growth.

Stimulus reception

After reviewing the literature on the effect of the interstimulus interval on conditioning, Hull developed three empirical propositions:

1. The maximum efficiency of conditioning occurs when the onset of the unconditioned stimulus follows that of the conditioned stimulus by a fraction of a second.
2. As the delay in the onset of the unconditioned stimulus increases beyond that yielding the maximum learning efficiency, the rate of habit-strength acquisition decreases progressively according to a simple decay function of the amount of this additional delay.
3. The value of this function at the limit of its fall is about a third of that at its highest point. This asymptotic value presumably approximates the status in learning situations of static, i.e., non-changing, stimulus elements. [p. 167]

Next, after considering a limited amount of physiological evidence, Hull developed a neurological hypothesis which, with greater generosity than reason, he called the Kappauf-Schlosberg hypothesis. This hypothesis contains a series of propositions:

1. Receptor discharge impulses begin an appreciable interval after the impact of the stimulus energy on the receptor. . . .
2. As the energy impact on the receptor becomes weaker, the discharge latency becomes longer. . . .
3. Following the period of receptor-discharge latency there is a period of relatively rapid recruitment in the frequency of receptor discharge impulses, which usually reach their maximum within a second. . . .
4. The amount of stimulus energy ultimately applied remaining constant, the faster its rate of application, the more rapid will be the rate of recruitment and the greater the maximum frequency of receptor-discharge impulse. . . .
5. If the rate of stimulus impact is relatively abrupt and constant, the greater the stimulus energy applied, the greater will be the maximum frequency of receptor impulse discharge. . . .
6. Following the attainment of the maximum frequency of receptor discharge impulses, the stimulus meanwhile continuing to act unchanged, there ensues a progressive decline in frequency approximately according to a simple decay function. In some receptors, such as touch and those associated with hairs, the frequency quickly fall to zero; in others, such as pressure and those associated with muscle spindle, the frequency becomes constant at a level well above zero. . . .
7. In case the impact of the stimulus energy on the receptor organ ceases before the point of maximum receptor-discharge frequency is reached, there is usually a brief after-discharge which apparently may be prolonged under

certain circumstances by self-propagating central processes (9). This latter perserverative activity presumably declines as a simple negative growth function of the time since stimulus termination, the asymptote of this decline being zero. . . . [pp. 167–168]

On these bases Hull then formulated the Kappauf-Schlosberg hypothesis and offered a series of testable implications:

We now add to this summary of empirical findings a formalized statement of the Kappauf-Schlosberg hypothesis: *Other things equal, the increment to the strength of a receptor-effector connection* ($\Delta_S H_R$) *resulting from a reinforcement is an increasing function of the frequency of the associated receptor discharge, or the intensity of the resulting afferent impulse.*

Our immediate concern here is with the implications of the Kappauf-Schlosberg hypothesis and certain items of the receptor impulse summary presented above, namely, items 3, 4, 5, 6, and 7.

I. It follows from the above hypothesis and empirical item 3 that *in a reinforcement situation there is a temporal relationship of the conditioned to the unconditioned stimulus such that as the onset of the unconditioned stimulus is progressively delayed, the rate of learning will increase.*

II. It follows from the hypothesis and empirical item 4, other factors remaining constant, that *in a reinforcement situation the slower the rate of application of the conditioned stimulus energy, the slower will be the rate of habit-strength acquisition.*

III. It follows from the hypothesis and empirical item 5 that *in a reinforcement situation, temporal relationships of conditioned and unconditioned stimuli remaining optimal, within moderate ranges the greater the conditioned stimulus energy applied, the more rapid will be the rate of habit-strength acquisition.*

IV. It follows from the hypothesis and empirical item 6 that *in a reinforcement situation as the time of the onset of the unconditioned stimulus is further retarded beyond the point of optimal timing, the rate of learning will decline, but at a rate slower than the rate of rise during the recruitment period, the course of the decline following a negative growth function of the amount of delay, with asymptote appreciably above zero in the case of certain receptors.*

V. It follows from the hypothesis and empirical item 7 that *in a reinforcement situation as the time of the onset of the unconditioned stimulus is retarded beyond the optimal amount, the action of the conditioned stimulus having ceased before the maximum rate of receptor discharge impulse is reached, trace conditioned reactions will be generated.* In such cases the rate of learning will decline according to a simple negative growth function of the amount of delay, with its asymptote at zero. [pp. 168–169]

It is to be noted that these deductions concern, in the main, the so-called interstimulus-interval function and the effect of CS intensity. Research prior to the publication of *Principles of Behavior* and more recent experimentation have tended to support Hull's predictions about the interstimulus interval function. Neither, however, has provided much support for the postulated effect of CS intensity.

At the time Hull advanced these propositions the situation with respect to empirical knowledge about the effect of CS intensity was as follows. The best systematic investigation of this variable (Carter, 1941) was a study involving eyelid conditioning. It appeared to indicate that CS intensity contributed nothing to the rate of conditioning. A host of incompletely reported Russian studies, on the other hand, suggested that CS intensity was a very important variable. The reasoning behind Hull's hypothesis was obviously based on the assumption that the Russian data were correct and that Carter was wrong.

Hindsight suggests that Hull would have done well to consider the nature of the evidence more carefully than he did. If he had done so, he might have noted two potentially important differences between the two types of investigation: (1) Carter's study was with human subjects, whereas the Russian experiments were with dogs, and (2) Carter's study employed a between-groups design in which different groups of subjects were conditioned with a single CS intensity, whereas the Russian studies usually employed a within-groups method in which single subjects were conditioned with a range of intensities.

More recently, Grice and Hunter (1964) have shown the between groups-within groups variable to be extremely important in determining the effect of CS intensity upon eyelid conditioning in human subjects. Confirming Carter's finding, these investigations obtained little effect of CS intensity in a between-groups experiment. Using a within-groups design, however, they obtained a large difference in favor of the stronger CS.

No similar comparison exists for lower animals. Kessen's (1953) study, however, does contain two fairly similar experiments employing within- and between-groups procedures in an investigation of the effect of CS intensity upon avoidance learning in rats. An examination of the two sets of results from these experiments suggests that the type of procedure may make much less difference with rats than with human subjects and that CS intensity is an important variable under both conditions with this species. Such a finding is in line with Hullian predictions.

At another level, however, Kessen's results raise serious questions for the Hullian position. There was no difference in resistance to extinction in the rats conditioned with different CS intensities. Since resistance to extinction, according to Hull, is a measure of habit strength, these results indicate that CS intensity is probably a performance variable, rather than a learning variable, a conclusion to which the results of other factorially designed experiments have also led (Kimble, 1961, pp. 118–120).

Reinforcement

In 1943, Hull treated the amount of reinforcement as a variable determining the limit of habit growth, although he briefly considered (pp. 131–132) the possibility that seems more likely today: that this variable has a motivational influence and an effect on performance rather than on habit formation. The main points in Hull's analysis of the effect of the amount of reinforcement appear in the following passage:

> We saw above . . . that the curve of habit strength as a function of the number of reinforcements was dependent upon two constants, (1) the physiological maximum of habit strength (M), and (2) the fractional part (F) of the as yet unrealized potentiality of habit-strength acquisition, which is added to the actual habit strength at each reinforcement. Assuming the soundness of this hypothesis, it is evident that the influence of increasing the amount of the reinforcing agent on the size of the increment of habit strength ($\Delta S^{\text{H}}R$) at a given reinforcement must result from an increase in one, and possibly both, of these parameters. [An inspection of available learning curves suggests] that in habit formation the F-value may be approximately constant for different amounts of the reinforcing agent or reward. The only possible remaining parameter which could produce the slower learning with small amounts of the reinforcing agent is the asymptote or upper limit of the learning curve.
>
> In this connection it will be recalled . . . that the physiological limit of habit strength under absolutely optimal conditions was taken as 100 habs. . . . To this value was assigned the symbol M. The introduction of the presumption that the asymptotes of learning curves may vary below this level, depending on the amount and quality of the reinforcing agent, makes it necessary to employ a separate symbol (M') to represent such limits or asymptotes. We now state the working hypothesis at which we have arrived: *In a learning situation which is optimal in all other respects, the limit* (M') *of habit strength* ($_sH_R$) *attainable with unlimited number of reinforcements is a positive growth function of the magnitude of the agent employed in the reinforcement process.* This tentative conclusion is based on admittedly inadequate grounds and will therefore be subject to reexamination and revision when more satisfactory evidence becomes available. . . .
>
> The meaning of the working hypothesis just formulated may be clarified by indicating one or two of its implications. Let it be supposed [that if one gram of a certain food were used as the reinforcing agent] the maximum habit strength to be expected at the limit of practice would be 23.75 habs [and that] the maximum to be expected from the use of six grams of this food at each reinforcement would be 70.14 habs.
>
> With these maxima available it is possible to calculate the theoretical course of habit-strength acquisition under the respective conditions by substi-

tuting first one of the values for [M'] in the simple positive growth function, and then the other, letting the fractional incremental factor F, equal 1/10. . . .

Let it be supposed that the habit has been reinforced with one gram of the food fifteen times and that the reinforcement is then suddenly shifted to six grams on the next fifteen reinforcements. Neglecting the presumptive perseverating influence of secondary reinforcement in the situation, the outcome is easily calculated. . . . This is shown [Fig. 12-1] by the dotted curve rising from the one-gram curve at the fifteenth reinforcement. A glance at Figure 12-1 shows that according to the present hypothesis an increase in the amount of the reinforcing agent should be followed by a marked increase in the rate of habit-strength acquisition. . . .

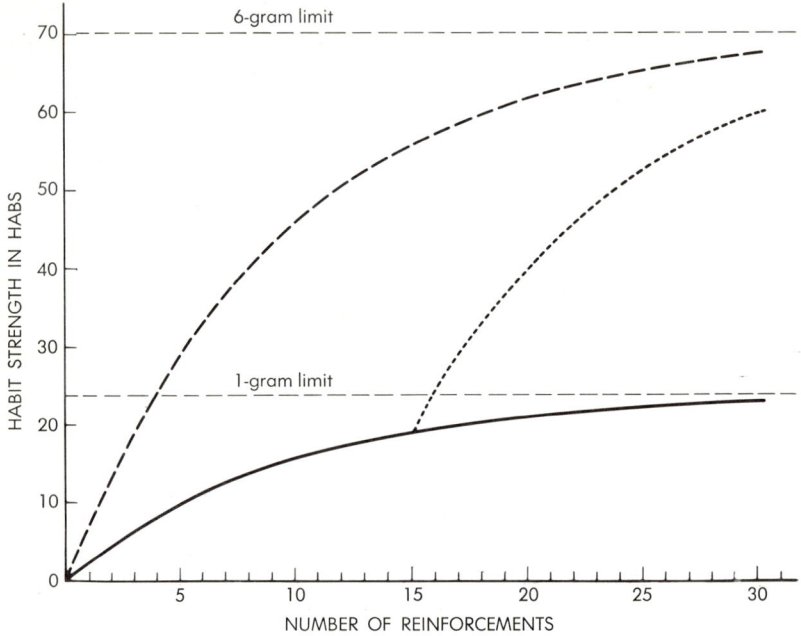

FIGURE 12-1. Graphic representation of the theoretical course of habit growth under three conditions: (a) with a 6-gram food reward, (b) with a 1-gram food reward and (c) with a switch from 1 to 6 grams midway in acquisition. (Hull, 1943, p. 130.)

Finally, an additional case may be mentioned—that in which the six-gram habit would be reinforced ten times. This would generate a habit strength of 45.68 habs, which is considerably above 23.75 habs, the maximum attainable by means of a one-gram reinforcement. Then the reward would suddenly be shifted to one gram. Assuming these conditions, and ignoring secondary reinforcing effects, it is to be expected that successive reinforcements would result in a progressive weakening of the habit. Consideration of this interesting but complex problem must be deferred until the phenomena of experimental extinction have been taken up in detail. . . .

After reviewing the literature relevant to the effect of delaying reinforcement upon performance in the learning situation,[3] Hull came to these important conclusions: (1) that the effect of this variable was upon learning rather than performance, (2) that its specific effect was upon the limit of habit growth and (3) that the specific form of the delay-of-reinforcement function could be determined only in an experiment where secondary reinforcement could be eliminated during the period of delay. In Hull's own words: "On the basis of the direct experimental approaches outlined above, together with certain indirect approaches presently to be disclosed, we formulate our hypothesis concerning the molar functional relationship of habit strength to the temporal delay in reinforcement as follows: (1) *The maximum habit strength (m') attainable with a given amount and quality of reinforcement closely approximates a negative growth function of the time (t) separating the reaction from the reinforcing state of affairs; (2) the asymptote or limit of fall of this gradient is zero; and (3) the more favorable the condition for the action of secondary reinforcement, the slower will be the rate of fall, so that this limit may not be approximated until after considerable periods of delay, though for many conditions less favorable for secondary reinforcement it may be reached in a period of from 30 to 60 seconds.*" This hypothesis set the stage for a series of studies designed to determine the form of this function. An excellent investigation of this type by Grice (1948) shows the function to be shorter than Hull thought. The study by Kamin included in this volume is of special interest because it manipulates delay of reinforcement in the context of an avoidance learning experiment and demonstrates that the function there is much like that obtained by Grice with an appetitive reward.

GENERALIZATION AND STIMULUS COMPOUNDING

In Hull's theory the process of generalization provides a transition from learning to performance. The critical concept is *effective habit strength* ($_s\bar{H}_R$), which Hull considered to be the values of $_sH_R$ *reduced by some function of the psychophysical distance (d) between the con-*

---

[3] The amount of literature available to Hull was very limited but has seen a marked increase since the publication of *Principles of Behavior*. Renner (1964) has published an excellent contemporary review of these studies.

ditioned stimulus (S) and an evoking stimulus (S). In the form of an equation, $_s\bar{H}_R = {_sH_R}\, e^{-jd}$, where d is the difference between $\dot{S}$ and S in psychophysical (j.n.d.) units and j is a determinable empirical constant.

Building on the diagram presented earlier, the status of the concept $_s\bar{H}_R$ is as follows:

$$(\dot{S}-S) = d \longrightarrow \begin{array}{c} _sH_R \\ \searrow \\ \ _s\bar{H}_R \end{array}$$

Presenting all of this in Hull's language,

> . . . the simple notion of habit strength, as indicating merely the strength of connection between the stimulus and the reaction involved in the original reinforcement process, must be radically expanded before the influence of learning on functional activity is to be understood and represented in a realistic manner. It is true that the various principles of reinforcement when perfected will presumably enable us to predict with precision the strength of the connection between the conditioned stimulus and the associated reaction. This is all right so far as it goes, but it represents only a small portion of the zone of reaction evocation potentialities set up by a given reinforcement. The strength of the connections at the other points of the zone can be determined only from a knowledge of the strength of the receptor-effector connection ($_sH_R$) at the point of reinforcement and the extent of the difference (d) between the position of the conditioned stimulus ($\dot{S}$) and that of the evocation stimulus (S) on the stimulus continuum connecting them. Thus there emerges the concept of functional or *effective habit strength*, which we shall represent by the symbol $_s\bar{H}_R$. . . . The symbol $_sH_R$ will be reserved, as before, to indicate the strength of habit at the point of reinforcement; i.e., when d = zero,
>
> $$_s\bar{H}_R = {_sH_R}.$$

It is also convenient to think of the concept of effective habit strength as applicable to the problem of stimulus compounding, that is, to the case in which several stimuli combine to form the conditioned stimulus in a particular experiment. Hull (p. 213) deals with this problem as follows:

If two or more stimulus aggregates, each independently conditioned to the same reaction, impinge simultaneously on the receptors of the organism . . . the effective habit strength borne by the several stimulus aggregates summate to produce a joint habit strength as would the separate effects of the number of reinforcements necessary to produce each, if such reinforcements were to be given consecutively in some standard reinforcement sequence.

Thus suppose that one stimulus aggregate . . . has a habit strength . . . of 34.39 habs, and a second stimulus aggregate . . . has . . . a habit strength of 46.86 habs. . . . Now, by Table 12-1 [p. 175], 34.39 habs would . . . be produced by four reinforcements, and 46.86 habs would be produced by six reinforcements. On the above principle it follows that the physiological summation of the two habit strengths would yield a joint habit strength equal to that which would be produced by $4 + 6 = 10$ reinforcements, which by Table 12-1, equals 65.13 habs.

In the most general terms, this means that the joint effect of combined conditioned stimuli will be less than the arithmetic sum of their separate strengths. Hull cites a variety of evidence to suggest that the strength of an individual stimulus might be something like two-thirds the strength of the compound.

PRIMARY MOTIVATION AND REACTION POTENTIAL

The introduction of an effect of motivation into Hull's system continued the transition from learning to performance. Specifically, Hull defined a new concept, excitatory potential or reaction potential ($_sE_R$), at this point as follows: $_sE_R = f\ (_s\bar{H}_R) \times f\ (D)$, where $_sH_R$ is *effective habit strength* and D refers to *drive*. The concept (D) in this equation requires the following clarifying statements:

1. The symbol, D, refers to a generalized, undifferentiated, drive state.

2. This generalized drive, on the other hand, represents the summated effect of a variety of individual motives. Thus, Hull assumed that the various different motives were functions of their own determining conditions but contributed to a generalized motivational pool.

3. The fact that all motives are not equally effective in arousing or energizing various responses can be dealt with by the concept of drive stimulation (S_D). As we have seen above, these stimuli carry a certain habit loading in any situation and their presence would potentiate reactions associated with that particular drive at the expense of other habits not specifically conditioned to these drive stimuli.

4. The multiplicative relationship between habit and drive specified in the composition of reaction potential seems necessary on logical grounds. Specifically, there needs to be some mechanism for allowing the reaction potential associated with a particular reaction to have a value of zero. The multiplicative relationship means that this state of affairs exists whenever D is zero.

On the independent variable side, Hull thought of various drive-establishing operations or conditions (C_D) as determining the value of various drives, a proposal which we might symbolize in this way $C_D = (D_1 + \ldots + D_N)$, using the plus sign to indicate Hull's further conception that individual drives added to produce a total drive state (D). Returning to our diagrammatic representation of Hull's theory we may schematize these ideas this way:

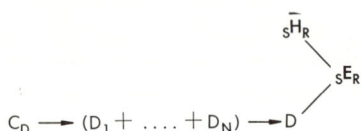

Extinction and inhibition

In order to explain experimental extinction and some of its associated characteristics, Hull developed a two-factor theory of inhibition. The primary concept in this theory was reactive inhibition, I_R. Hull assumed that each reaction left in the organism an increment of I_R which was a fatigue-like state, the value of which depended on the amount of work (W) involved in the reaction and the number of times the reaction was elicited (n). I_R was assigned the property of reducing the magnitude of reaction potential. In addition, Hull assumed that reactive inhibition spontaneously delayed as a function of the time (t''') since the evocation of the reaction. This introduces a third independent variable (t''') controlling the value of I_R. Beyond this Hull assumed that I_R was a negative drive whose goal response was the cessation of the response which produced it. These assumptions together with Hull's commitment to a drive-reduction theory of reinforcement, logically demanded the development of a second inhibitory component which he called conditioned inhibition, $_sI_R$.

The necessity for such an additional inhibitory concept comes about as follows: since I_R is a drive, the reduction of I_R is a reinforcement and, as such, is capable of strengthening any response which precedes it closely in time. In the original development of the I_R concept, a particular response, the cessation of activity, was assumed to occupy such a position. Such reasoning provided the mechanism for the conditioning of a resting response evoked by I_R and reinforced by I_R-reduction. Hull referred to this process as the conditioning of I_R to the stimuli in the learning situation. Hence the name *conditioned inhibition* and the symbol $_sI_R$. Hull's own summary of his theory of inhibition follows:

Hull's Version of S-R Theory

The Mowrer-Miller hypothesis states in effect that all responses leave behind in the physical structures involved in their evocation, a state or substance which acts directly to inhibit the evocation of the activity in question. The hypothetical inhibitory condition or substance is observable only through its effect upon positive reaction potentials. This negative action is here called reactive inhibition. An increment of reactive inhibition (ΔI_R) is assumed to be generated by every repetition of the response (R), whether reinforced or not, and these increments are assumed to accumulate except as they spontaneously disintegrate with the passage of time. The magnitude of the individual increments, and therefore of the rate of accumulation, appears clearly to be in part a positively accelerated increasing function of the amount of energy consumed by the response.

Because of the motivational characteristics of reactive inhibition, or inhibitory potential, it is opposed to reaction potential ($_sE_R$) rather than to habit ($_sH_R$), as is sometimes supposed. Thus effective reaction potential ($_s\bar{E}_R$), the potential actually available for the evocation of action, is the reaction potential less the inhibitory potential.

Since under ordinary learning conditions response and reinforcement occur in parallel, the strengthening of the habit due to reinforcement usually is great enough to over-ride the accumulating inhibition. As a consequence, inhibition of reinforcement is only detected by special means. In case little or no reinforcement follows the reaction evocations, extinctive inhibition soon neutralizes the reaction potential, the stimulus gradually ceases to evoke the response, and there ensues the state known as experimental extinction which thus appears as a secondary or derived phenomenon.

The Mowrer-Miller hypothesis regards reactive inhibition as essentially a need to cease action, i.e., a need for rest; it follows that anything which reduces this need should serve as a reinforcing state of affairs. Since the cessation of action reduces the afferent proprioceptive impulses generated by it in the presence of the inhibiting condition, particularly when many responses have generated a considerable amount of inhibition, it comes about that the cessation of action, rather than action, becomes conditioned to whatever stimuli may be present. In this way we find a plausible explanation of conditioned inhibition ($_sI_R$) and of the stimulus generalization of extinction effects. There are a number of indications that phenomena analogous to conditioned inhibition and stimulus generalization of inhibition occur under conditions of ordinary learning reinforcements, though not all the empirical evidence harmonizes with this *a priori* expectation. For this reason the theory of the origin of S'R must be regarded with somewhat more than the usual amount of distrust.

Because conditioned inhibition ($_sI_R$) is generated as a secondary effect from the accumulation of reactive inhibition I_R, it follows that at least in extinction situations both I_R and $_sI_R$ will result. Assuming that the two summate physiologically, it follows that at complete experimental extinction the excitatory potential ($_sE_R$) will be opposed or neutralized in part by I_R and in part by $_sI_R$. Now, I_R dissipates spontaneously through the passage of time, but $_sI_R$, being a true habit, presumably does not, at least to any great extent. The dissipation of I_R will produce spontaneous recovery of direct extinction effects, but this will naturally result in only partial recovery. On the other hand the second inhibitory component in extinction ($_sI_R$) should be subject to external inhibition. Since $_sI_R$ is responsible for only a portion of the depression of $_s\bar{E}_R$ below $_sE_R$, disinhibition, which presumably operates only on $_sI_R$, also should never produce complete recovery. The slight initial rise in response vigor when extinction follows massed reinforcements is plausibly interpreted as the external inhibition of the conditioned inhibition ($_sI_R$) presumably set up during the reinforcement process. The facts, however, are not wholly in harmony with this interpretation.

In case a reaction tendency ($_sE_R$) is extinguished a good many times, each extinction being performed by massed practice on separate occasions, the gradual accumulation of the relatively permanent conditioned inhibition implies that the time required for the successive extinctions of the reaction tendency should grow less and less, the minimum approaching zero as a limit.

The magnitude of I_R, and also, presumably, of $_sI_R$, generated by a given number of response evocations depends upon the amount of energy consumption or work (W) involved. This implies that of two or more alternative behavior sequences repeatedly executed by the organism in the attainment of an ordinary reinforcement, that sequence will finally come to be chosen which involves the less work or the less tissue injury. This is the important "law of less work," which, as pointed out by James (1934), accounts for the prevalence of "laziness" in the behavior of organisms.

Because reactive inhibition (I_R) dissipates spontaneously through the passage of time, it follows that a part of the "inhibition of reinforcement" will dissipate during the pauses which occur throughout learning by distributed reinforcements or repetitions. The less the I_R, presumably, the less will be the $_sI_R$, and so, certainly, the less the $\dot{I}_R$ and consequently the greater will be the $_s\bar{E}_R$ at the end of the learning process. Thus is explained the well-known empirical law of the economy of distributed repetitions in learning. If, on the other hand, a considerable number of reinforcements are massed and then a pause occurs, the same principle leads to the frequently observed empirical phenomenon of spontaneous recovery of effective reaction potential ($_s\bar{E}_R$) known as "reminiscence."

Formally Hull proposed that I_R added to $_sI_R$ to produce total inhibition, $\dot{I}_R$. This in turn was hypothesized to subtract from $_sE_R$ and to reduce response strength. Thus extinction was conceived as occurring because of the development of I_R, a response-localized temporary inhibitory state, and $_sI_R$, a habit, which would be permanent unless specifically subjected to extinction. In more formal terms, Hull defined a new intervening variable, $_s\bar{E}_R$ as follows, $_s\bar{E}_R = {_sE_R} - \dot{I}_R$. Again in terms of the diagram we have been building, the relationships among these variables are as follows:

Hull's Version of S-R Theory

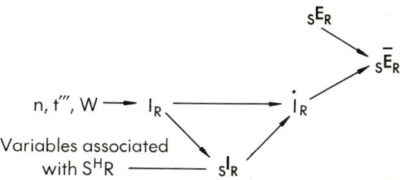

The concepts of oscillation and threshold

The final concepts in Hull's chain of constructs depend heavily upon two response-inferred variables, oscillation ($_sO_R$) and threshold ($_sL_R$). Although there is nothing very specific in the definition of these concepts, it is not true, as Koch (1954) has mistakenly insisted, that they are unrelated to independent variables. The situation simply is that the independent variables involved are response variables rather than stimulus variables which Hull generally employed throughout the rest of his system. Actually, the situation is reasonably straightforward. It is a matter of common experimental experience that the magnitude of a learned reaction varies somewhat from occasion to occasion in the learning situation, hence the conception of an oscillation applied to one of the preceding concepts in the theoretical chain. Spence (1956) applies the idea of oscillation to inhibition, but it could apply to any other of the previous concepts without doing logical violence to the theory.

Similarly, with the concept of threshold, it is again a matter of common experimental observation that several reinforcements are required before the learned reaction occurs, hence the conception that habit strength or excitatory potential must reach some threshold value before the response appears.

When Hull introduced these concepts into his theory, he defined two new constructs, momentary effective reaction potential ($_s\breve{E}_R$) and momentary superthreshold effective reaction potential ($_s\overset{\circ}{E}_R$). The first of these concepts was effective reaction potential reduced by an influence associated with oscillation; the second introduced a further reduction associated with the threshold. Hull defined four attributes of the reaction, probability of occurrence (R_p), latency (R_t), magnitude (R_m), and resistance to extinction (R_n) as a function of this terminal construct.

With these concepts available we may now complete our schematic diagram.

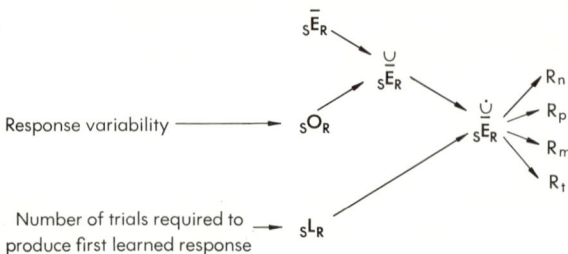

SUMMARY

Hull's (1943) theory of learning consists of a chain of intervening variables connecting a variety of independent, stimulational (S), variables and four measures of response (R) strength. On this basis it is appropriate to refer to Hull's theory as an S-R theory. The important links in the chain of intervening variables are these:

1. The low-level concept, stimulus trace(s) is defined in terms of the intensity, duration, and time since cessation of any stimulus event. The concept applies to traces of environmental stimulation (S_E) and drive stimulation (S_D). These latter terms derive their meaning from statements about certain conditions of a specific experiment: experimental operations and drive establishing operations.

2. The experimental conditions just referred to also favor the occurrence of some response (R).

3. The major circumstance assumed to be necessary for learning to occur in reinforcement (G) a construct whose value depends upon the amount (A), delay (t″) and frequency of previous application (N) of a known reinforcer.

4. The parameters of reinforcement enter into the composition of habit strength ($_sH_R$) in two different ways. The first two parameters, amount and delay of reinforcement together with the value of the stimulus trace(s), determine the upper limit (M) of habit growth. Thus:

$$M = f(s, t'', A)$$

The first parameter, together with a growth constant (i) related to individual differences, determines the value of $_sH_R$ after any number of reinforcements:

$$_sH_R = f(M, N, i)$$

or more specifically

$$_sH_R = M - M_e^{-iN}$$

5. In Hull's system, generalization begins the transition from learning to performance. The strength of the response to any stimulus other

than that involved in actual learning was hypothesized to depend upon the value of $_sH_R$ and to be a decreasing function of the difference (d) between training and test stimuli. The central concept was generalized habit strength ($_s\bar{H}_R$). Formally

$$_s\bar{H}_R = {_sH_{R_e}}^{-jd}$$

6. The next conception in Hull's chain of intervening variables is drive (D) which Hull treated as an additive consequence of all the drives, relevant or irrelevant, possessed by the organism at any moment. The individual drives were hypothesized to be the result of specified drive condition C_D which are also the independent variables for the drive stimuli referred to previously. Total drive (D) was assumed by Hull to interact multiplicatively with $_s\bar{H}_R$ to produce a new construct, reaction potential ($_sE_R$):

$$_sE_R = f\,({_s\bar{H}_R}) \times f\,(D)$$

As this equation implies, Hull assumed drive to be directionless. The directedness of motivated behavior depends upon the existence of drive stimuli.

7. At this point in his theory Hull introduced two inhibitory constructs, reactive inhibition (I_R) depending upon the conditions of work involved in the learning task and conditioned inhibition ($_sT_R$) a learned inhibition generated in the situation. The sum of these two forms of inhibition, $\dot{I}_R$, was to be subtracted from reaction potential to produce effective reaction potential $_s\bar{E}_R$:

$$_s\bar{E}_R = {_sE_R} - \dot{I}_R$$

8. The final two constructs in Hull's system, oscillation ($_sO_R$) and threshold ($_sL_R$), differ from the previous ones in being response inferred. They also differ in being somewhat more informally derived than the previous concepts. The first of these concepts interacts with effective excitatory potential to produce momentary effective reaction potential ($_s\breve{E}_R$):

$$_s\breve{E}_R = {_s\bar{E}_R} - {_sO_R}$$

The second subtracts from $_s\breve{E}_R$ to produce momentary effective suprathreshold reaction potential $_s\dot{\breve{E}}_R$:

$$_s\dot{\breve{E}}_R = {_s\breve{E}_R} - {_sL_R},$$

the final construct in the chain.

9. The dependent variables in Hull's system response probability (R_p), response latency (R_t), response magnitude (R_m) and resistance of the response to extinction (R_n) are specified hypothetical functions of $_s\dot{\breve{E}}_R$.

13

The Determiners of Behavior at a Choice Point[1]

EDWARD CHASE TOLMAN

The question I am going to discuss is the very straightforward and specific one of "why rats turn the way they do, at a given choice-point in a given maze at a given stage of learning."

The first item in the answer is fairly obvious. They turn the way they do because they have on the preceding trials met this same choice-point together with such and such further objects or situations, down the one path and down the other, for such and such a number of preceding trials. Let me, however, analyze this further, with the aid of a couple of diagrams. First, consider a diagram of a single choice-point (Fig. 13-1).

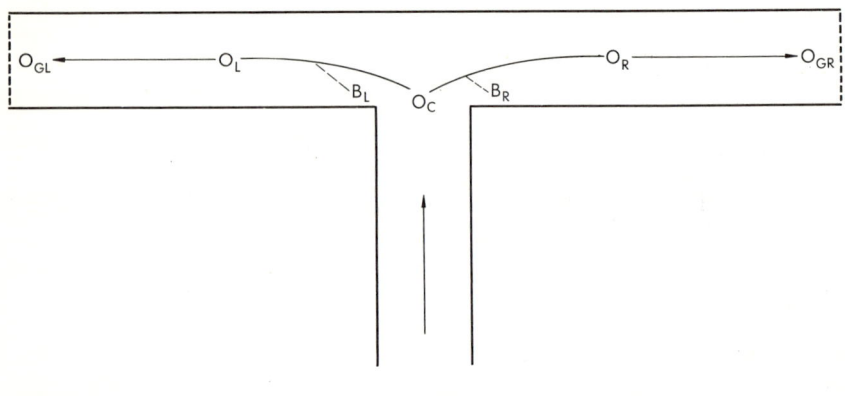

FIGURE 13-1

In this figure the point of choice itself is designated as O_C; the complex of stimulus-objects met going down the left alley, as O_L, that

---

[1] Presidential address delivered before the American Psychological Association, Minneapolis, September 3, 1937. Reprinted from *Psychological Review*, 1938, 45. Somewhat edited; section headings added.

The Determiners of Behavior at a Choice Point

met going down the right alley, as O_R; the goal at the left, as O_{GL}; and that at the right, as O_{GR}. The behavior of turning to the left is represented by the arrow B_L; and that of turning to the right, by the arrow B_R. The point I am now making is that the relative strength of the tendency to turn, say, left (rather than right) will be, first of all, a result not only of the present presentation of O_C but also of all the previous presentations of it together with the O_L, O_{GL}, O_R, and O_{GR} consequences of having behaved by B_L and B_R on all these preceding occasions. In short, I would schematize this feature of the causal determination of the left-turning tendency by the diagram shown in Figure 13-2.

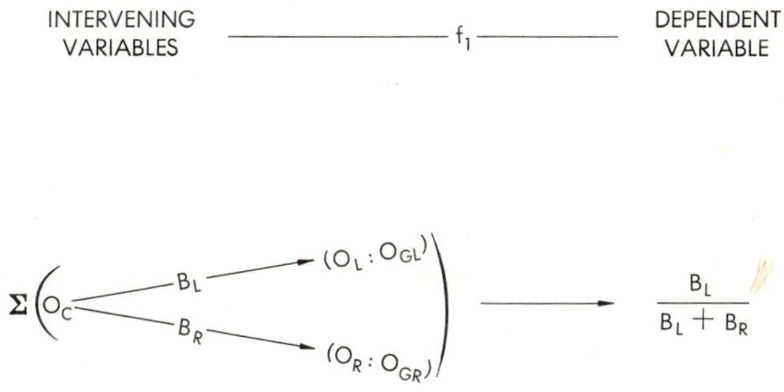

$$\text{INTERVENING VARIABLES} \xrightarrow{f_1} \text{DEPENDENT VARIABLE}$$

$$\Sigma \left(O_C \begin{array}{c} \xrightarrow{B_L} (O_L : O_{GL}) \\ \xrightarrow{B_R} (O_R : O_{GR}) \end{array} \right) \longrightarrow \frac{B_L}{B_L + B_R}$$

FIGURE 13-2

The expression $B_L/(B_L + B_R)$ at the right hand side of Figure 13-2 is the "dependent variable" (we may call it the behavior-ratio). It is the percentage tendency at any given stage of learning for the group as a whole to turn left. And the hieroglyphic at the left hand side of this figure is the "independent variable" which determines this behavior-ratio. This hieroglyphic is to be read as meaning: the *sum* of all the preceding occasions in which O_C has, by virtue of B_L, been followed by O_L and O_{GL} and by virtue of B_R been followed by O_R and O_{GR}. This diagram is thus no more than a schematic way of representing the, shall we say, (to use the term we theoretical psychologists have of late taken so violently to our bosoms) "operational" facts. The expression at the left is an "operationally defined" independent variable and that at the right, an "operationally defined" dependent variable.

For brevity's sake, I shall often substitute, however, an abbreviated symbol for the left-hand term, viz., simply $\Sigma(OBO)$, as shown in Figure 13-3.

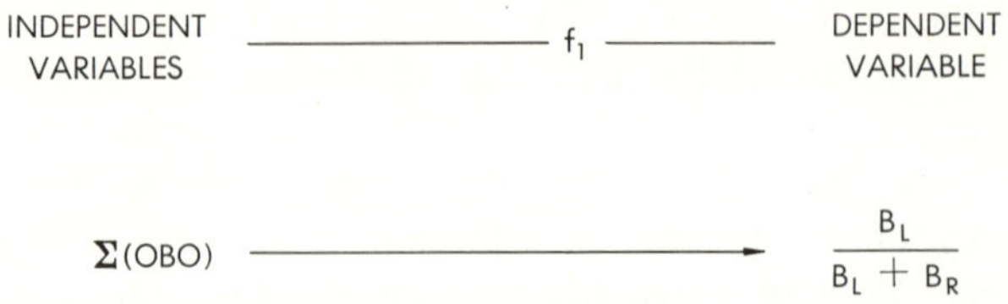

INDEPENDENT   DEPENDENT
VARIABLES   ———————— f_1 ———————— VARIABLE

$\Sigma(OBO)$ ————————————————→ $\dfrac{B_L}{B_L + B_R}$

FIGURE 13-3

One further point—the f_1 in each of these figures indicates merely the fact of the functional dependence of the dependent variable upon the independent variable. To indicate the "form" of this function we would require a more analytical diagram, such as that shown in Figure 13-4.

But this, of course, is no more than our old friend, the learning curve. It results when we plot the independent variable along an X axis and the dependent variable along a Y axis. Nothing very new so far. It seems surprising, however, that in spite of the thousands, not to say millions, of such learning curves which have been obtained in the last four decades in American rat laboratories, there are still a variety of quite simple things about this function which we do not yet know or with regard to which we are still in dispute.

For example, we are still in dispute, first of all, as to the relative

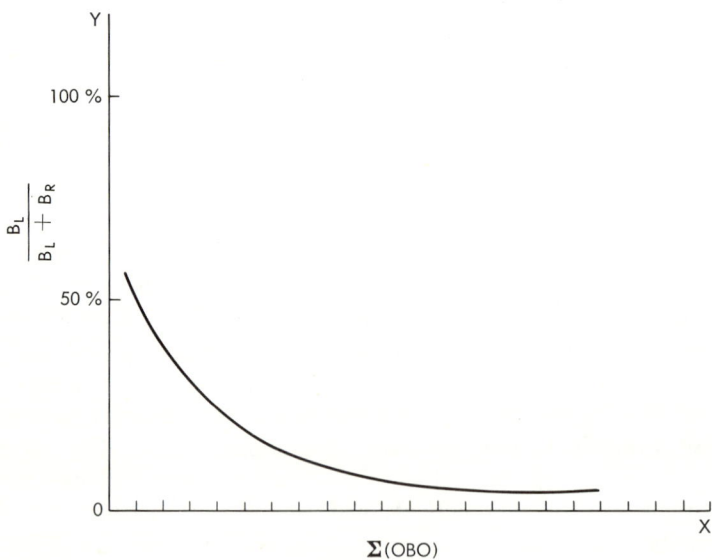

FIGURE 13-4

The Determiners of Behavior at a Choice Point 193

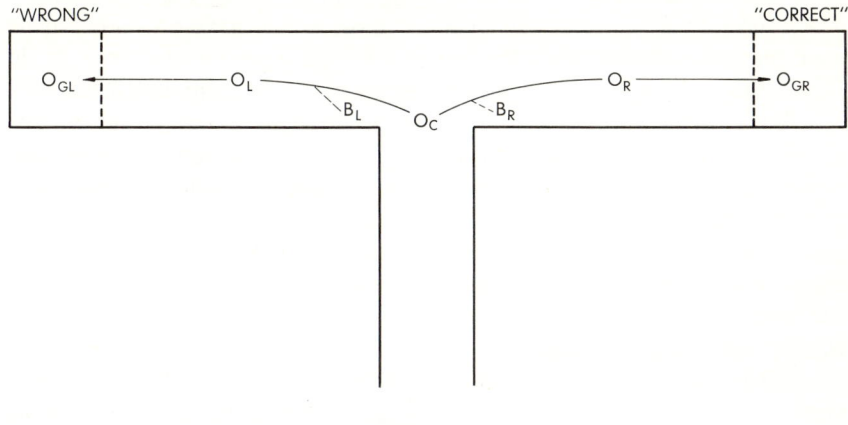

FIGURE 13-5

importance of the occurrences of the two alternative behaviors B_L and B_R, where B_L is "wrong" and B_R is "correct." (See Fig. 13-5.)

Thorndike (1932, 1935) and Lorge (1936) and their coworkers, as you all know, working with human beings in analogous, though verbal, set-ups have now concluded that the occurrence of the wrong behavior has no such general causative effect. They find that learning appears only as a result of the occurrences of the rewarded sequence $O_C \text{———} B_R \rightarrow O_R : O_{GR}$). On the other hand, still more recently, Muenzinger and Dove (1937), working with set-ups similar to Thorndike's have found that the occurrence of the wrong response $O_C \text{———} B_L \rightarrow (O_L : O_{GL})$ does weaken its tendency to reoccur. Also Carr, as a result of a series of experiments done by his students some time since in the Chicago laboratory, was finally forced to conclude that ". . . a certain number of errors must be made and eliminated before the subject is ever able to run the maze correctly. Correct modes of response are established in part by learning *what not to do*" (1925, p. 98, italics mine).

A second point about which we are still surprisingly ignorant is that we do not yet know the importance of the rat's being permitted, or not permitted, to return out of the wrong choice. In some experiments, when the animal takes the wrong alley, he passes through a one-way gate and is started over again. In others, he is allowed to treat it as a blind and back out. But, so far as I know, there has been no carefully controlled comparison between these two procedures.

Third, the question of the relative effects of concentrated versus distributed repetitions has not as yet received the thoroughgoing experimental analysis that it deserves. But I understand that Professor Stone and his coworkers are now directing their attention to it and are getting some very significant findings.

Fourth, we are ignorant concerning the difference between animals which have an initial left-hand bias and those which have an initial right-hand bias. We usually lump the results for both types together in a single curve. But we might well separate them and study them independently.

Fifth, Brunswik has recently brought to light a new point in our ignorance. He has been trying the effect of rewarding on the right and rewarding on the left different proportions of times. In other words, it was no God-given rule but apparently some merely human predilection on our part which made us heretofore tend almost invariably to make one of the alternative behaviors always rewarded and the other always punished. But other frequencies of reward and punishment are equally possible and equally deserving of study.

Sixth, experiments by Krechevsky (1937 a,b,c) seem to indicate that there may be certain general features about the content of the OBO's such, for example, as their containing variable or nonvariable paths, which are very important in determining the resultant behavior-ratios and about which we need more information.

Seventh, a further point which needs more investigation is, as Muenzinger and his coworkers (e.g., 1934) have beautifully brought out, the fact that punishment or obstacles to be overcome, *even on the correct side*, may sometimes seem to aid rather than hinder learning. . . .

Eighth, there is the question of what happens when $\Sigma(OBO)$, the number of trials, has become very great. This seems to induce a special sort of result for which the term fixation has been suggested. And further studies of such "fixations" are needed.

Ninth, the problem as to the effect of temporal intervals between O_C and the resultant O_{GL} and O_{GR} are still by no means altogether completely worked out in spite of all the beautiful work of Hunter and his students, and others who have followed after, on the "delayed reaction" and on "double alternation."

Finally, however, there is a point with regard to which we are not altogether ignorant but the importance of which we usually overlook—namely, the fact that any such function—any such learning curve, actually, is always obtained within the matrix of a larger number of other independent variables in addition to $\Sigma(OBO)$. The following is a tentative list of such other variables together with $\Sigma(OBO)$:

I. Environmental Variables
      M—Maintenance Schedule
      G—Appropriateness of Goal Object
      S—Types and Modes of Stimuli Provided
      R—Types of Motor Response Required
  $\Sigma(OBO)$—Cumulative Nature and Number of Trials
      P—Pattern of Succeeding and Preceding Maze Units

The Determiners of Behavior at a Choice Point

    II. Individual Difference Variables
        H—Heredity
        A—Age
        T—Previous Training
        E—Special Endocrine, Drug or Vitamin Conditions

As you will see, I have divided such independent variables into two groups which I have called: (I) Environmental Variables, and (II) Individual Difference Variables. The *environmental variables* are M, the maintenance schedule, by which I mean time since food, water, sex, parturition, or the like, which in common parlance we would call the drive condition; G, the appropriateness of the goal-object provided at the end of the maze relative to this drive; S, the specific types and modes of stimuli which the maze provides; R, the specific kinds of motor response required of the animal in the maze; $\Sigma(OBO)$, the cumulative sum and manner of trials; and P, the general pattern of the maze, that is to say, the number and sorts of preceding and succeeding units. The individual difference variables are: H—heredity, A—age; T—previous training, and E—any special endocrine, drug, or vitamin conditions.

But if, now, we are to include all these independent variables together with $\Sigma(OBO)$, we must have a new causal picture. I suggest the one shown in Figure 13-6.

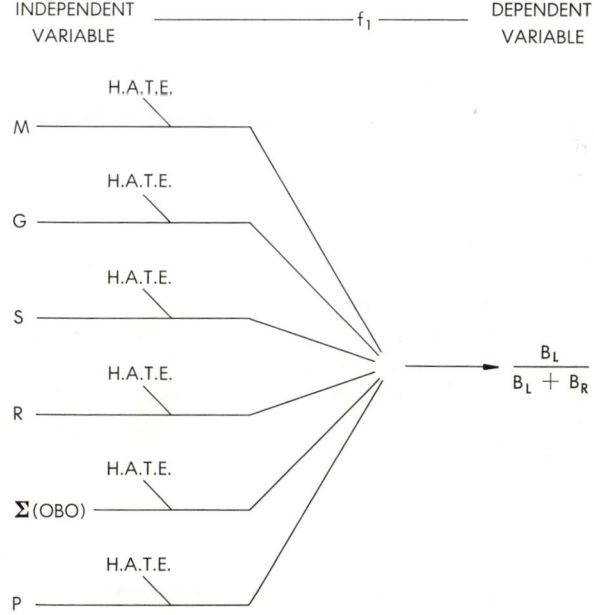

FIGURE 13-6

A main causal line has been drawn, as you see, issuing from each environmental variable. And the individual difference variables, H, A, T, and E, have been arranged as possible modifiers of each such main causal line. And what I have hereby tried to indicate is merely the actual types of experiment which we maze-psychologists go in for.

THE ROLE OF THEORY

I wish now, however, to pass from the above outline of experiments to a consideration of theories. But why, you may ask, can we not be satisfied with just experiments and the 'facts' resulting from them? I find that there are two reasons. In the first place, an entirely factual, empirical establishment of the complete functional relation, f_1, to cover the effects on $B_L/(B_L + B_R)$ of all the permutations and combinations of M, G, S, etc., etc., would be a humanly endless task. We have time in this brief mortal span to test only a relatively limited number of such permutations and combinations. So, in the first place, we are forced to propose theories in order to use such theories to extrapolate for all these combinations for which we have not time to test.

But I suspect that there is also another reason for theories. Some of us, psychologically, just demand theories. Even if we had all the million and one concrete facts, we would still want theories to, as we would say, "explain" those facts. Theories just seem to be necessary to some of us to relieve our inner tensions.

But what is a theory? According to Professor Hull (1937), a theory is a set of definitions and postulates proposed by the theorist (on the basis presumably of some already found facts) from which other empirically testable facts, or as he calls them, theorems, can be logically deduced. These deduced theorems will be new empirical relationships which the theorist—or more often, his research assistants—can, then and there, be set to look for.

For my own nefarious purposes, however, I wish to phrase this matter of the relationship of a theory to the empirical facts out of which it arises and to which it leads in somewhat other terms. A theory, as I shall conceive it, is a set of "intervening variables." These to-be-inserted intervening variables are "constructs" which we, the theorists, evolve as a useful way of breaking down into more manageable form the original complete f_1 function. In short, I would schematize the nature of our psychological theories by Figure 13-7. In place of the original f_1 function, I have introduced a set of intervening variables, I_a, I_b, I_c, etc., few or many, according to the particular theory. And I have conceived a set of f_2 functions to connect these intervening variables severally to the independent variables, on the one hand, and an f_3 function to com-

The Determiners of Behavior at a Choice Point 197

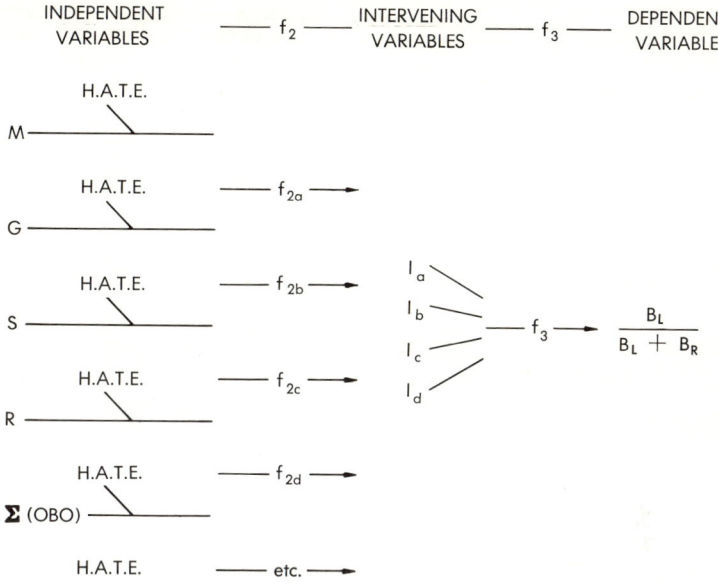

FIGURE 13-7

bine them together and connect them to the final dependent variable, on the other.

But turn, now, to some of the actual theories. I shall restrict myself to the discussion of three—Professor Thorndike's, Professor Hull's, and my own. This, of course, will hardly be a fair survey of the field. There are many other doctrines of learning, as, for example, Professor Guthrie's (1935), and those of the other conditioned reflex psychologists[2] and those of the Gestalt school, which are of as great importance and which have equally affected my own thinking. But I shall have to omit a discussion of them here.

Thorndike

Professor Thorndike's "intervening variables" are quite simple. They are "stimuli," "bonds" or "connections," and "response-tendencies." His theory I would represent, therefore, by the diagram shown in Figure 13-8. It is Thorndike's conception of the nature of the f_2 function which seems to be the crux of his theory. Originally, his statement of this function included both a Law of Exercise and a Law of Effect. But now, as we all

[2] For a superb presentation and summary of all the conditioned reflex theories of learning, see Hilgard (1937).

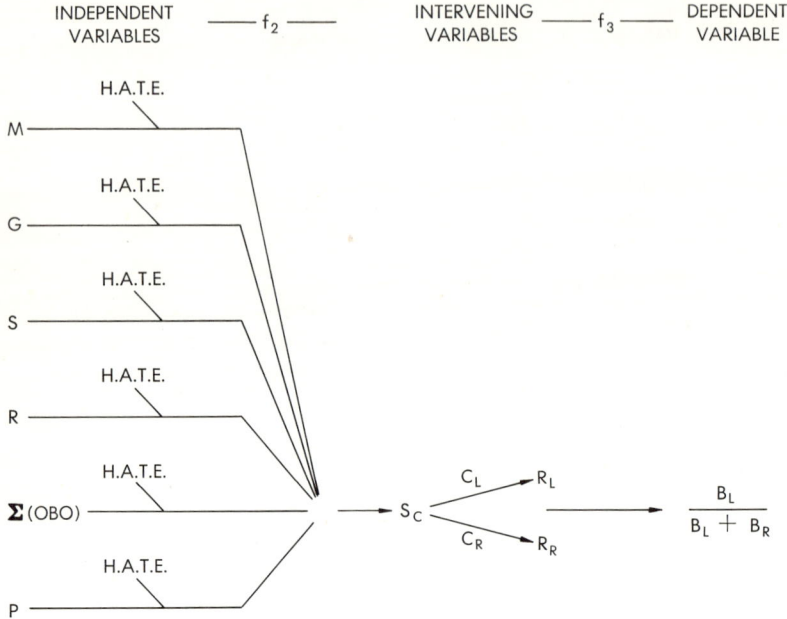

FIGURE 13-8

know, it includes a Law of Effect only, and a truncated law at that. For, as now stated, Thorndike finds that it is the repetitions of the rewarded sequence $O_C \text{———} B_R \rightarrow (O_R : O_{GR})$ which alone are important. These strengthen the C_R connection. The repetitions of the punished $O_C \text{———} B_L \rightarrow (O_L : O_{GL})$ sequence do not, he says, correspondingly weaken the C_L connection.

I have quite a number of quarrels with this theory. I would like to say first, however, that it seems to me that this theory of Thorndike's either in its present or in its earlier form, is *the* theory relative to which the rest of us here in America have oriented ourselves. The psychology of animal learning—not to mention that of child learning—has been and still is primarily a matter of agreeing or disagreeing with Thorndike, or trying in minor ways to improve upon him. Gestalt psychologists, conditioned-reflex psychologists, sign-gestalt psychologists—all of us here in America seem to have taken Thorndike, overtly or covertly, as our starting point. And we have felt very smart and pleased with ourselves if we could show that we have, even in some very minor way, developed new little wrinkles of our own.

Let me now, nonetheless, try to present my criticisms. First, Thorndike's theory, as I see it, identifies stimuli (S's) with gross objects (O's) and identifies specific muscular responses (R's) with gross means-end behaviors (B's). And this procedure seems to me to require more justifica-

The Determiners of Behavior at a Choice Point

tion than he gives it. It raises the problem of "equivalence of stimuli" and "equivalence of response" which Klüver (1933), Waters (1936), and others have been concerned with. It is also probably connected with the problem of perception-constancy which the Gestalt psychologists and other Europeans have dealt with at such length.

My second objection is that the theory as stated by Thorndike does not allow for the facts of "latent learning," or the complementary phenomenon of a sudden shoot-up in errors when a goal is removed, and of the utilization of alternative habits under different motivations. That, to allow for these facts, a distinction must be made between "learning" and "performance" has indeed already been emphasized by Lashley (1929), Elliott (1930), Leeper (1935) and myself (1932, 1933). But Thorndike's theory allows no such distinction.

Finally, my third objection is that the theory does not, for the most part, make anything of the other circumambient variables M, G, S, etc., in addition to $\Sigma(OBO)$. No doubt Thorndike, if this were pointed out to him, would try to work all these other independent variables in as further conditions tending to favor or hinder the respective strengths of C_R and C_L. But my suspicion is that he would have difficulty.

Hull

Turn, now, to Professor Hull's theory. For Hull the intervening variables are "conditionings" of the running responses to successive aggregates of exteroceptive, proprioceptive, and interoceptive stimuli. In order to explain this, first let me present another picture of the simple T-maze (Fig. 13-9).

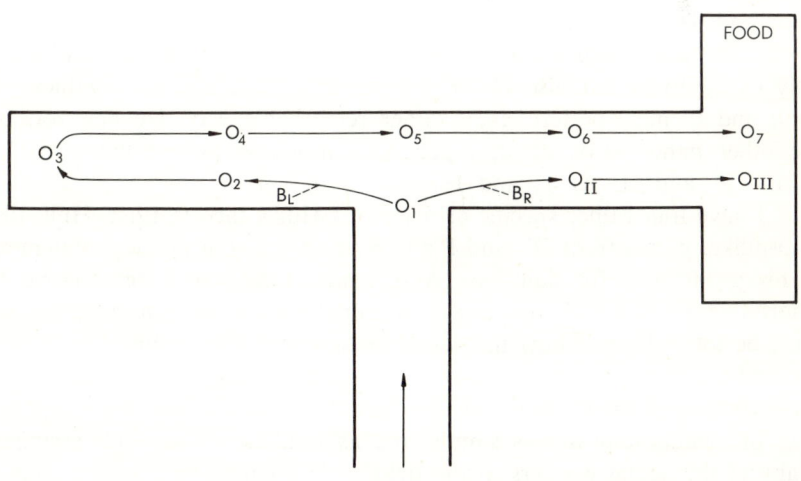

FIGURE 13-9

Two alternative routes are shown—one in which the animal goes directly down the true path and one in which he first chooses the blind to the left. Successive points along these two paths are indicated as successively numbered *O*'s. The true path involves three such O's, the blind alley, seven, and, to explain the tendency which develops in such a situation to go right rather than left, Hull's theory postulates the intervening variables shown in Figure 13-10.

What I have done, as you will see, is to insert one of Hull's *own* diagrams in the middle and to call it his set of intervening variables. You are all familiar with such diagrams. They are very clever and can be invented, as I know to my cost, to explain practically any type of behavior, however far distant from an instance of conditioning such a behavior might at first sight appear. I have, therefore, the greatest respect for them. And, even though I argue against them, I find myself continually being intrigued and almost ready to change my mind and accept them and Hull after all.

It must be noted further, however, that there are certain other concepts besides conditioning involved in these diagrams which help to make them work. These seem to be: (1) anticipatory goal-responses, i.e., the little r_G's with their little resultant proprioceptive or interoceptive s_G's whereby the character of the goal is brought back into the aggregates of conditioned stimuli at the different points along the maze; (2) the continuous drive stimulus S_D which also appears at all points and thus also becomes part of the total conditioned stimulus-aggregate at each point along the maze paths; (3) the goal-gradient hypothesis whereby all conditionings are stronger the nearer they are to the goal; and (4) habit-family hierarchies whereby, if one path or route is blocked, the rat readily switches over to any alternative chain of conditionings which he has at his command. By virtue of these concepts, in addition to that of conditioning *per se,* Professor Hull is able to bring into his diagram the influences not only of $\Sigma(OBO)$ but also of M, maintenance schedule; G, goodness of goal; and P, maze-pattern, in a rather remarkable way. He has not, on the other hand, as I see it, especially considered as yet the variables S, and R, and H, A, T, and E.

I have four rather specific criticisms of Hull's theory. First, Hull, like Thorndike, passes from O's and B's to S's and R's with no clear statement of his justification for doing so. And, again, I feel, as I did relative to Thorndike, that, if such simple S-R formulations are to have cogency, we must be told why and how the actual gross O's can be reduced to simple S's, and the actual gross means-end B's to simple R's.

My second criticism lies in the fact that I doubt that the supposed laws of conditioning are as simple and as well known as Hull assumes. Many of the actual workers in the field . . . seem to find conditioning a very variable and complicated phenomenon. To explain maze behavior by

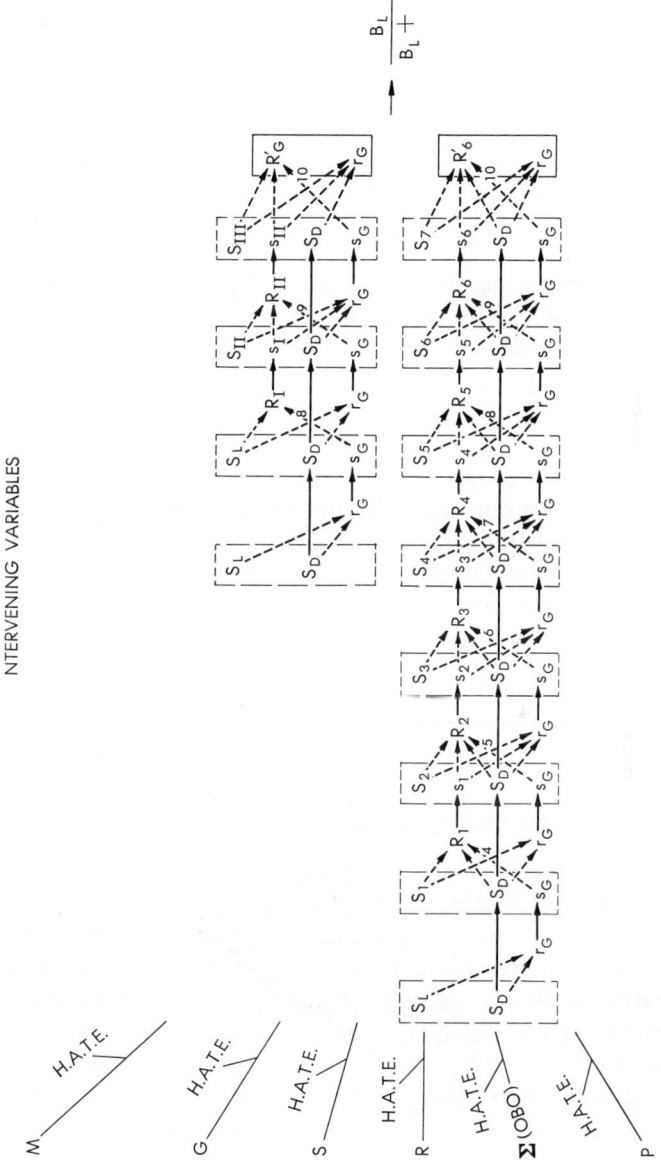

FIGURE 13-10

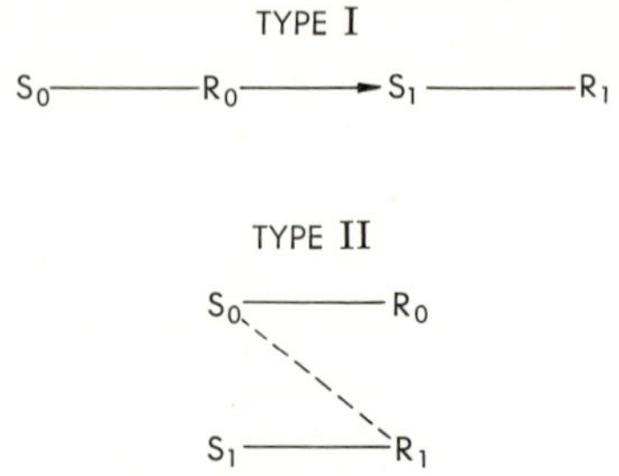

TYPE I

$S_0 \longrightarrow R_0 \longrightarrow S_1 \longrightarrow R_1$

TYPE II

$S_0 \longrightarrow R_0$

$S_1 \longrightarrow R_1$

FIGURE 13-11

conditioning seems to me, therefore, like asking the halt to lead the blind. Or to put this another way, what Skinner (1935) (see Fig. 13-11) calls his Type I sort of conditioning (which for me is not conditioning at all) seems to be at the present stage of the game, just as well and perhaps better understood than the more classical, or what he calls his Type II, sort of conditioning.

Finally, when it comes to using one of Hull's diagrams for actually predicting, on any given occasion, the value of $B_L/(B_L + B_R)$ I find the difficulty of determining the actual strengths to be assigned to the various S-R connections an almost insuperable one. But, then, perhaps an analogous sort of criticism will be raised against my diagrams. So, in conclusion, let me repeat that I have a tremendous respect for Professor Hull's theory and that I am not by any means as yet altogether certain that mine is better.

PROGRAMMATIC THEORY OF THE AUTHOR

I come, now finally, to my own theory. But first, I would like to make it clear that however complicated what I am actually going to present may appear, it will be in reality an *over-simplified* and *incomplete* version. Partly for the sake of simplicity and partly also, I suppose, because I have not as yet completely thought the whole thing through, the diagrams I shall present will not contain as many "intervening variables" nor as complicated interfunctional relations as, I suspect, will finally actually prove necessary. They will, however, indicate the general picture.

Intervening variables: relationships to dependent variables

My first diagram would be that shown in Figure 13-12.

The Determiners of Behavior at a Choice Point

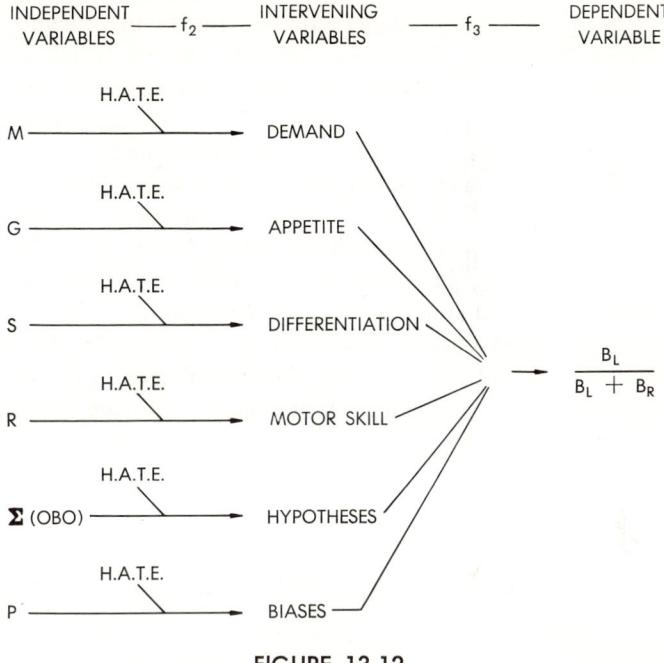

FIGURE 13-12

Note the list of *intervening variables:* "demand," "appetite," "differentiation," "skill," "hypotheses," and "biases." Such concepts are, I am sure, irritating in that they appear subjective and not the sort to be permitted in an honest behaviorism. Each of them is, nonetheless, I would claim, capable of a perfectly objective definition and measurement. Thus, you will note that each is depicted as resulting from its own correlative environmental variable plus the controlling effects of H, A, T, and E. "Demands" result from M's; "appetites" from G's; "differentiations" from S's; "skills" from R's; "hypotheses" from Σ(OBO's); and "biases" from P's. And I am now going to assert that each such "intervening variable" is defined by a standard experiment in which its correlative independent environmental variable is systematically varied. Further, in each such experiment all the other independent variables are held constant while the one in question is systematically changed. Under such conditions the resultant variations in $B_L/(B_L + B_R)$ are, *by definition,* to be said to mirror directly the variations in the one given intervening variable.

For example, the intervening variable—"demand"—(say, for food) shall, by definition, be measured by the variations in the behavior-ratio which occur in a standard experiment when G and S and R and Σ(OBO) and P and H, and A, and T, and E, that is, all the independent variables *other than M,* are held constant at certain "standard" values, while M, itself, is systematically varied. For example, as standard values for these other variables I should probably choose: for G the regular standard living diet of the colony, for S an elevated maze in which all possible visual, olfactory, auditory, tactual and kinaesthetic stimuli would be available, for R a maze which involved running rather than swimming, or climbing, or going hand over hand, or pulling strings, or what not, for $\Sigma(OBO)$, that set-up which makes the left-hand side a blind and a distribution of one trial every 24 hours, and a number of trials which, for an average value of M, would bring the learning curve about down to the base line—say some 10 trials—and for P a single-unit T with no preceding or succeeding units. With such a set-up in which all the other independent variables would thus be given these standard values and held constant, I would then vary M and study the correlated variations in $B_L/(B_L + B_R)$. And the sort of results one would get are shown in Figure 13-13.

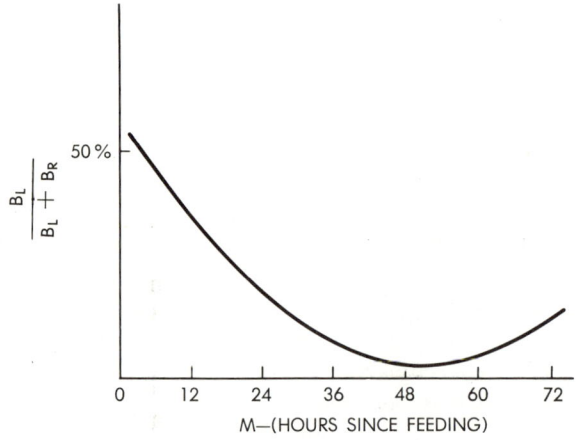

FIGURE 13-13

But the demand should really be defined as inversely related to this $B_L/(B_L + B_R)$ ratio, so that replotting one would have as one's final defining function that shown in Figure 13-14. And having, thus at last, this curve—this f_2 function—between M and "demand" one would use it for defining the to-be-assumed value of the demand for any given value of M on all future occasions.

But this procedure, which I have thus outlined in some detail for demand, could also be used in analogous fashion for defining each of the other intervening variables. For each of them, also, we could set up a defining experiment in which all the independent variables other than the

The Determiners of Behavior at a Choice Point

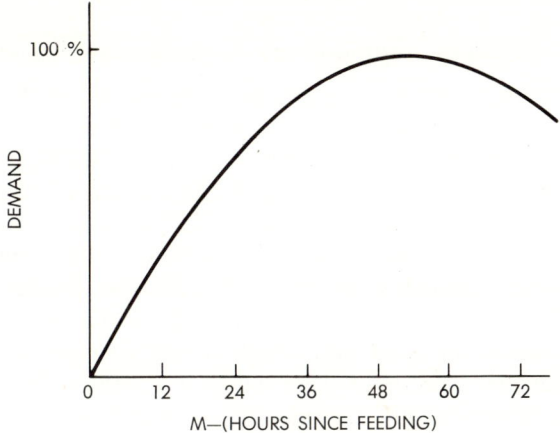

FIGURE 13-14

correlative one, would be held constant while that one was systematically varied. And we would obtain in each case a resultant defining curve or table. Figure 13-15 schematizes the fact of such possible defining procedures.

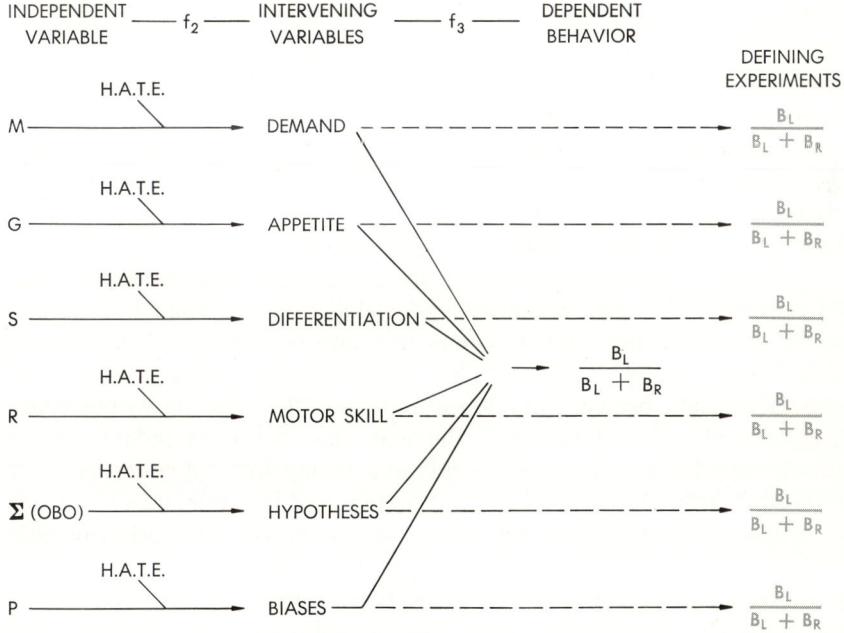

FIGURE 13-15

Intervening variables: relationships to dependent variables

Finally, turn to the f_3 function. It is by means of this f_3 function (if we but knew what it was) that we would be able to predict the final outcome for all possible values of the intervening variables. It would allow us to predict the result of every possible strength of "demand" combined with every possible degree of "appetite," with every possible goodness of "differentiation," and so on. That is to say, the f_3 function, if we but knew it, would provide a set of rules by which to predict for all these million and one possible combinations. It would consist in some equation, geometrical picture, or what not, which would give the way of adding together the different values of these different variables. But here, alas, I confess is the feature of my doctrine about which I am, to date, haziest. I would venture, however a few suggestions.

First, I would assert that the implicit assumption of most other psychologists is to the effect that their f_3 functions are in the nature of simple algebraic summations. That is to say, these others seem to assert that a poor demand would be compensated for by a good hypothesis, a poor skill by a strong differentiation, a poor differentiation by a strong appetite, and the like. Indeed it seems to me that *all* the associationistic psychologies, whether they be of the trial-and-error variety or of the conditioned reflex variety really imply just such simple algebraic summations. What I have distinguished as "demands," "appetites," "differentiations," "skills," "hypotheses," and "biases" the associationistic psychologies have lumped together, one and all, as mere S-R's. If the rat be very hungry (have a strong demand) this, for them, is but an enhancement of some S-R connection; if he have a strong appetite as a result of the type of goal presented, this also is but some S-R, stronger than it otherwise would have been; if the given maze-bifurcation present lots of stimuli (leads to clear differentiations) again, merely some S-R's are stronger; if the maze be constructed to require unusual motor skill from the animal, this again means merely a strengthening (or in this case probably a weakening) of some bond or other; if $\Sigma(OBO)$ has become large—if, that is to say, the hypotheses have become "developed and sure" this also means but better *S-R* connections; and finally, if the maze be shaped to induce, say, a strong centrifugal swing to the right or a strong forward-going tendency to the left, this, also is for them, but a matter of the strengthening of one or another S-R bond. And the final value of the resultant behavior-ratio is then obtained by all such psychologies by a simple toting up of these plus and minus, strong and weak, S-R bonds. But I am very doubtful of the adequacy of any such simple type of additions.

Let me recall again the facts of "latent learning." During latent learning the rat is building up a "condition" in himself, which I have de-

The Determiners of Behavior at a Choice Point

signated as a set of "hypotheses," and this condition—these hypotheses—do not then and there show in his behavior. S's are presented, but the corresponding R's do not function. It is only later, after a goal has been introduced which results in a strong appetite, that the R's, or as I would prefer to say, the B's, appropriate to these built-up hypotheses appear. So long as there is no appetite for what is found at the end of the maze, strong demands, plus strong hypotheses do not add up at all. A strong hypothesis and a strong demand do not compensate for a weak appetite. And a strong demand and a strong appetite cannot in their turn overcome a weak hypothesis. And so on. The ways of combination of the intervening variables do not seem those of simple scalar addition.

Or consider, as another example, the addition of two hypotheses. And suppose that instead of the usual two-way choice-point, we had one such as that shown in Figure 13-16. In this set-up after a long series of preliminary training in which only the two side-paths were open, the middle path was also opened up (I refer here to an actual experiment devised and carried out at California by Mr. R. S. Crutchfield). As a result of the preliminary training the two hypotheses of food to the left and food to the right were built up. It appeared, however, in the test runs, that these then added together in such a way as to make a very strong resultant tendency to go straight ahead when the third central path was opened—

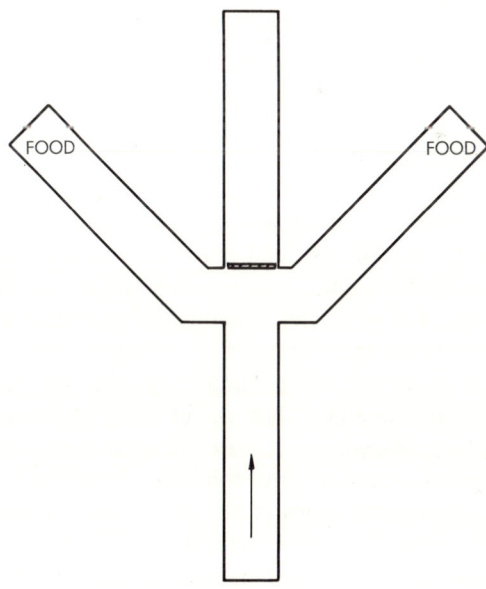

FIGURE 13-16

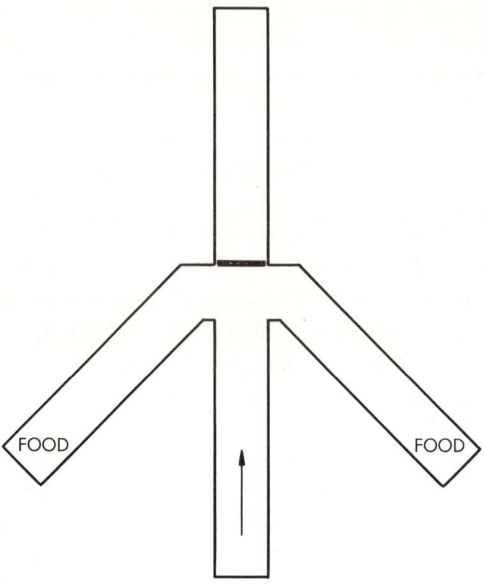

FIGURE 13-17

in short, a very much stronger tendency to go ahead than was found to have resulted from the two hypotheses which got built up when in another set-up the two side paths were as shown in Figure 13-17. The laws of the addition of hypotheses here appeared, in short, not as scalar and algebraic, but as vectorial. . . .

And so I am brought finally to my present confession of faith—namely, that Professor Lewin's topological and dynamic concepts (1935, 1936) now seem to me the best lead that I have at present for conceiving the nature of this f_3 function. I neither understand nor approve them in their entirety. And, if I were clever enough, I should undoubtedly try in many ways to improve upon them. But nonetheless, even as they are, they seem to me by far the most stimulating and important ideas which have appeared in psychology (that is, in pure psychology, as distinct from physiology or embryology) in the past decade.

One final point, concerning my thinking about the f_3 function. I am at present being openly and consciously just as anthropomorphic about it as I please. For, to be anthropomorphic is, as I see it, merely to cast one's concepts into a mold such that one can derive useful preliminary hunches from one's own human, everyday experience. These hunches may then, later, be translated into objective terms. But there seems to me every advantage in *beginning* by conceiving the situation loosely and anthropomorphically. I might never have arrived at this point of view of accepting anthropomorphism as a perfectly proper heuristic procedure all by myself. And I certainly would hardly have dared advance such a view publicly, if it had not been for the counsels of several other psychologists, especially Professors Liddell and Zener. But, in any case, I in my future work intend to go ahead imagining how, *if I were a rat,* I would behave as a result of such and such a demand combined with such and such an appetite and such and such a degree of differentiation; and so on. And then, on the basis of such imaginings, I shall try to figure out some sort of f_3 rules or equations. And then eventually I shall try to state these latter in some kind of objective and respectable sounding terms such as vectors, valences, barriers, and the like (to be borrowed for the most part from Professor Lewin).

Also, of course, I shall try to do experiments similar to those of Lewin and his students in which these intervening variables (as extrapolated from their correlative independent variables) are given such and such supposed values and then the final behavioral outcomes measured.

INDIVIDUAL DIFFERENCES

But many of you must have been asking yourselves all this time: what about the H, A, T, and E variables? In the defining experiments I have suggested so far, which have been concerned primarily with the environmental variables, these "individual difference variables" are assumed to have been given average standard values. We rat-workers have always done this, perhaps unconsciously. We have tried to keep heredity normal by using large groups, age normal by using rats between 90 and 120 days old, previous training normal by using fresh rats in each new experiment, and endocrine and nutritional conditions normal by avoiding special dosages and also again by using large groups.

But suppose, now, our interests *be* in individual differences, per se. What experiments do we carry out then? It seems to me that individual-difference psychologists here tend to do two sorts of things.

On the one hand, they attempt (as do we environmental psychologists) to manipulate their independent variables for whole groups of animals and to get correlated variations in $B_L/(B_L + B_R)$. Thus they vary heredity, H, . . . in controlled ways for large groups and get corresponding variations in this behavior-ratio, for such groups. Or, they vary age, A, as Stone and his students have done, also for large groups and again get corresponding variations in the behavior-ratio. Or, they vary previous training, T, that is, they study the effects of transfer—and here we have all taken pot shots— . . . and again attempt to get corresponding variations in the behavior-ratio. Or, finally, they vary drugs, endocrines and vitamins, E, and get correlated variations in $B_L/(B_L + B_R)$. Here there are too many experiments for me to attempt to list them.

Secondly, however, the individual difference psychologists have also done another *more characteristic* type of experiment. They have accepted from God, and from the accidents of miscegenation and of nursery schools, very large heterogeneous samples of rats and then they have put

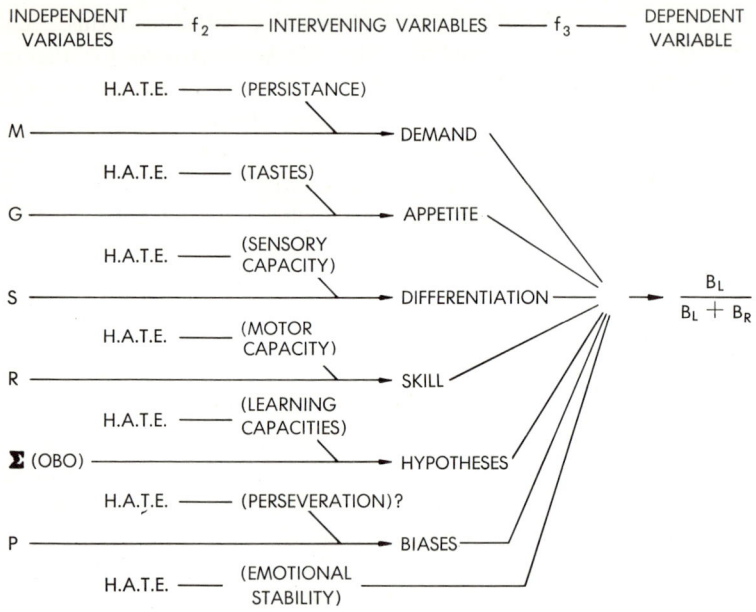

FIGURE 13-18

each such sample through a miscellaneous assortment of experiments (i.e., the different types of mazes that, in American rat-culture, are required of young rats in school, and also the different types of maze, discrimination-box, food, times since eating, and the like, which are required of old rats in polite society); and then they have obtained correlations and worked out factor analyses. And, finally, these individual-difference psychologists have ended up with their notions concerning the number and nature of the fundamental traits or capacities—"The Vectors of Mind" (Thurstone, 1935). These traits or capacities are, of course, but a new type of intervening variable and it would be nice, for me, if they fitted in neatly with the sort of intervening variables already suggested. They could then be put into my diagram as shown in Figure 13-18. But, alas, at present the results of factor analysis do not seem to suggest any such simple or agreed-upon results. You all know how the controversy rages from Spearman's (1927) one or two factors through Kelley's (1928) and Thurstone's (1935) three to nine factors, differing somewhat in each set-up to Thorndike's (1923, 1927b) and Tryon's (1935)—God only knows how many.

VICARIOUS TRIAL AND ERROR

By way of conclusion, I want now, however, to turn to one wholly new point. I want to suggest that there also appear in maze behavior types of activity other than the simple B_L's and B_R's which we have thus far talked about. If these latter be called "achievement behaviors," then these new types of activity which I now have in mind, may be called "catalyzing behaviors." And it seems that we rat psychologists have to date rather pigheadedly (i.e., like Professor Liddell's pigs) ignored such catalyzing behaviors.

I have two instances which I would here like to call to your attention, although I believe that in the future technological advances in recording will bring to the fore many others for study. The first of these two examples consists of those "lookings or runnings back and forth" which often appear at the choice-point and which all rat-runners have noted, but few have paid further attention to. And the second type is that disrupted sort of activity which appears when a previously obtained goal object is removed or blocked. Let me begin with the former.

A few years ago I had the temerity to suggest that such "lookings back and forth" might be taken as a behavioristic definition of *conscious awareness*. This was, no doubt, a silly idea. I would hardly dare propose it now. But, at any rate, such behavior is interesting and deserving of further study. Anthropomorphically speaking, it appears to be a "looking before you leap" sort of affair. Klüver (1933) and Gellerman (1933) have recorded it in connection with the behavior of monkeys, chimpanzees, and children. And, further, I have recently learned that Professor Muenzinger and his students have also been keeping records of it in rats and that they have called it "vicarious trial and error"—or, more briefly, VTE. I shall, therefore, designate such behavior as VTE or B_{VTE} from here on.

First, let me show you some individual rat curves obtained by [Muenzinger and Gentry, 1931]. The one rat had a difficult discrimination—namely, to go left when a tone is sounded; the other had an easy

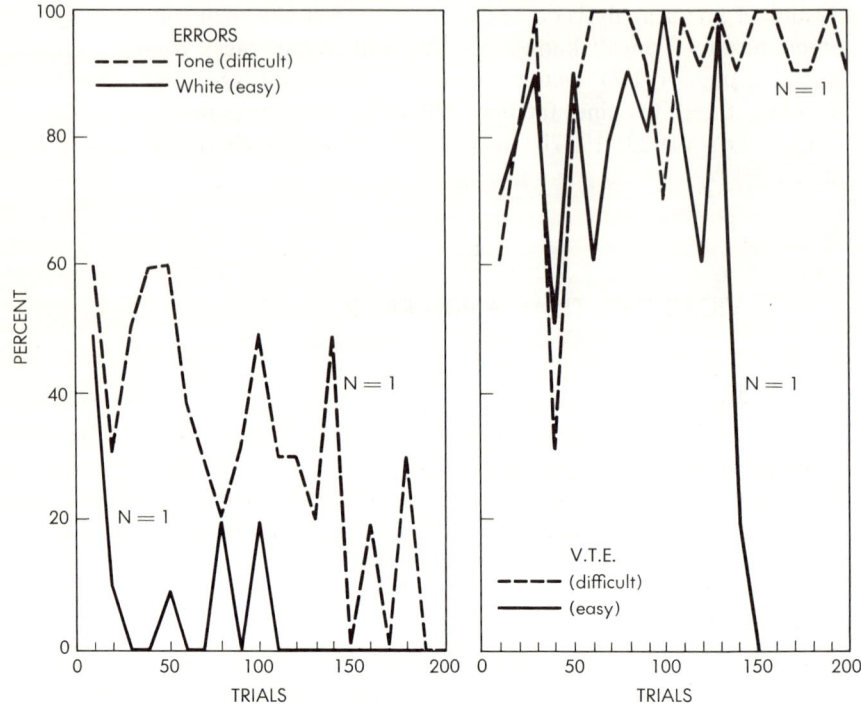

FIGURE 13-19

discrimination—to go towards the white in a white-black discrimination box (Fig. 13-19).

At the left are the error curves and at the right the VTE curves. Whenever the rat looked one or more times before making his overt choice in a given trial that trial was recorded as having involved a VTE. The points on the curves are averages for ten trials. The solid curves are for the easy discrimination and the dash curves are for the difficult discrimination. As you see, there tended to be more VTE and the latter persisted longer for the difficult discrimination than for the easy one.

Next, let me present some recent data on VTE obtained by Mr. M. F. Friedman at California on the effect of moderate amounts of cortical lesion (see Fig. 13-20). The problem was learning to turn left on a simple elevated T where one arm led to food and the other did not. The dash curves are for the brain lesion group and the solid curves are for the control group. Each point is an average of 4 trials. The normal animals exhibited more VTE and learned faster than did those with cerebral insults.

The Determiners of Behavior at a Choice Point

Next, I present some curves obtained by Honzik with an elevated discrimination set-up. The animal had to discriminate between a black and a white face-on door. There was a partition projecting out between the doors. White was the positive stimulus. One group ran over a continuous platform and could run back around the projecting partition if they chose the wrong door first. The other group had to jump a gap of $8\frac{1}{2}$ inches to a 4-inch ledge just in front of the doors. If this jump group chose incorrectly, they had to jump back again to the starting platform and then make a second jump to the correct door (Fig. 13-21). The solid curves are for the jump group and the dash curves for the non-jump group. Each point represents an average of 10 trials. The jumpers made more VTE's and learned faster.

Finally, let me present a set of curves also obtained by Honzik, in a similar set-up, but for two different jump groups (Fig. 13-22). The conditions for the one-jump group were those just described. We may call them here the near-jump group. For the others, which we may call the far-jump group, the farther side of the gap was fifteen inches from

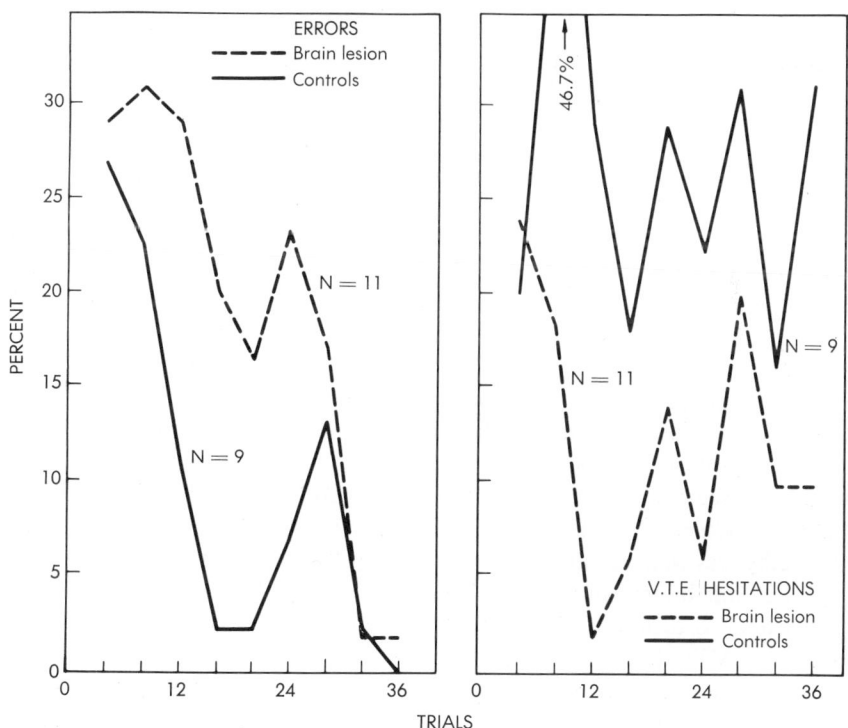

FIGURE 13-20

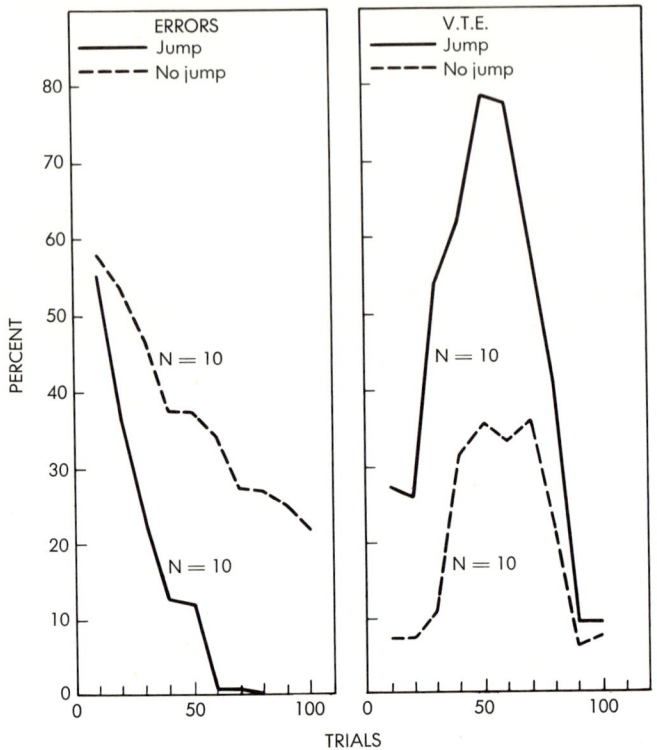

FIGURE 13-21

the to-be-discriminated doors and the taking off platform $23\frac{1}{2}$ inches from these doors. Solid curves are for the near jumpers, dash curves for the far jumpers. Each point represents an average of 10 trials.

The near-jump group learned faster and exhibited more VTE than did the far-jump group. It is to be noted that the far-jump group probably could not see the differences between the two doors at the place of "taking off" very well. Hence their poor error score. Further, because they could not see very well, it did them little good to "go in for" "looking before they leapt." And, in fact, the VTE's for this far-jump group were decidedly less than for the near-jump group.

Let me briefly summarize: (1) For a difficult discrimination such as learning to turn left when a tone is sounded there was slower learning but more VTE than for an easy, white-black discrimination; (2) On a simple T, normal rats showed faster learning and exhibited more VTE than did brain lesion rats; (3) With a near-jump, jump rats learned faster and showed more VTE than did non-jump rats; (4) Near-jump rats learned faster and exhibited more VTE than did far-jump rats.

The Determiners of Behavior at a Choice Point 215

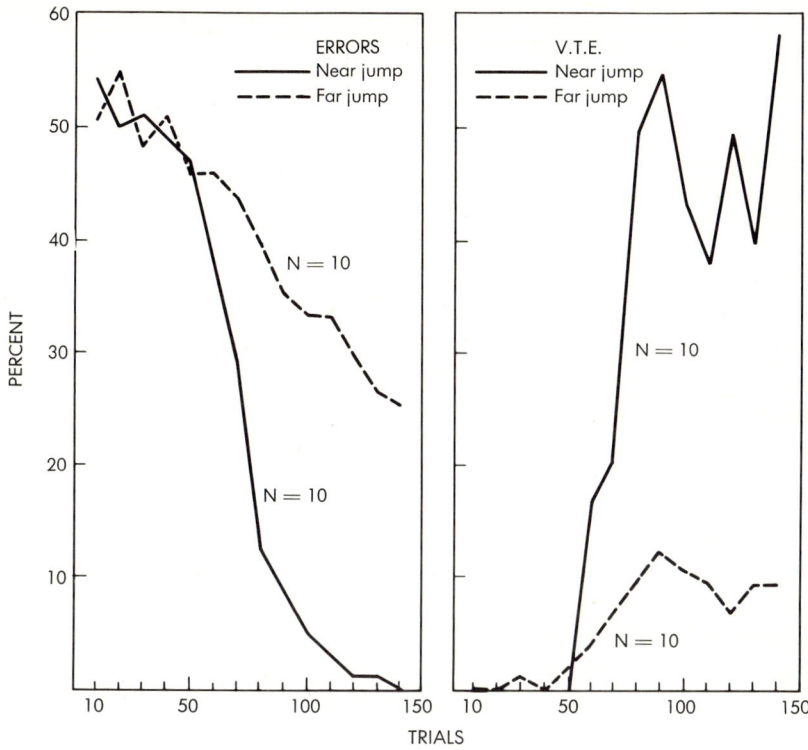

FIGURE 13-22

What, now is to be our theoretical envisagement? Obviously, the question divides into two: (1) what effect do VTE's, when evoked, have upon learning; (2) what are the conditions of learning which favor the evoking of such VTE's?

In answer to the first question I shall postulate that VTE's always aid the learning which they accompany. In the sole case, that of the difficult discrimination, where the poorer learning was accompanied by more VTE's I believe that this learning was nonetheless faster than it would have been if it had not been for these greater VTE's. And in all the other three experiments the greater VTE's did accompany the faster learning.

Turn now, to the second question. What are the learning conditions which tend to evoke VTE's? Here I believe we are not yet ready for any general answer. I shall therefore merely re-enumerate for your benefit the conditions of the four experiments. The conditions favorable to VTE's in these experiments were: (1) a difficult discrimination; (2) a normal brain; (3) a gap to be jumped which induced caution, and (4) a nearness

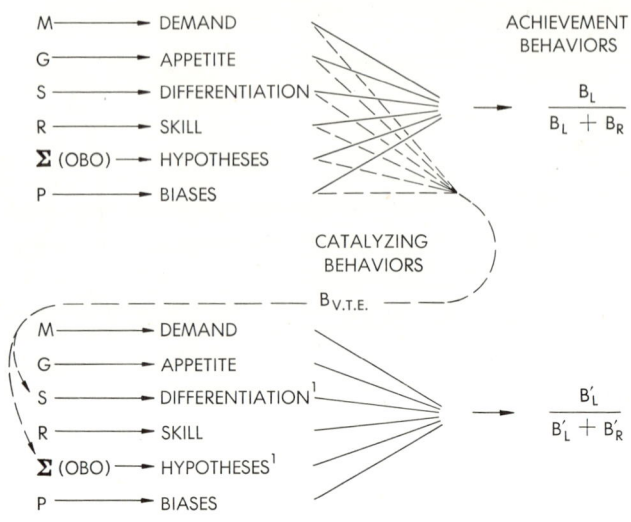

FIGURE 13-23

of the jumping platform such that the extra caution exposed the animal longer to the critical stimuli.

Finally, let me by another figure suggest how I would propose to fit this catalyzing VTE behavior into my general causal diagram (Fig. 13-23). You will note that I have shown the VTE behavior—symbolized as B_{VTE}—as an auxiliary result of the "intervening variables." These latter are to be conceived as tending to produce their usual "achievement behavior" $B_L/(B_L + B_R)$. But, in addition, they produce more or less B_{VTE}, and the further catalyzing effect of such B_{VTE} is, I have assumed, in some way to enhance the values of one or more of the independent variables themselves—in this case especially of S and of $\Sigma(OBO)$—and thus to help induce new values of certain of the intervening variables and a new final value of the achievement behavior. That is to say, as shown in the figure, the achievement behavior takes some new value $B_L'/(B_L' + B_R')$.

Turn now briefly to the case of the disruption behavior which occurs when an expected goal is not obtained. I have as yet no curves or detailed data concerning either the causes or the results of such disruption behaviors. I believe, however, that they also are to be conceived as auxiliary, catalyzing sorts of affair which react back upon the independent variables and make the final values of the resultant behavior-ratios different from what the latter originally would have been.

The rat's disrupted behavior is a surprised sort of hunting about and

The Determiners of Behavior at a Choice Point

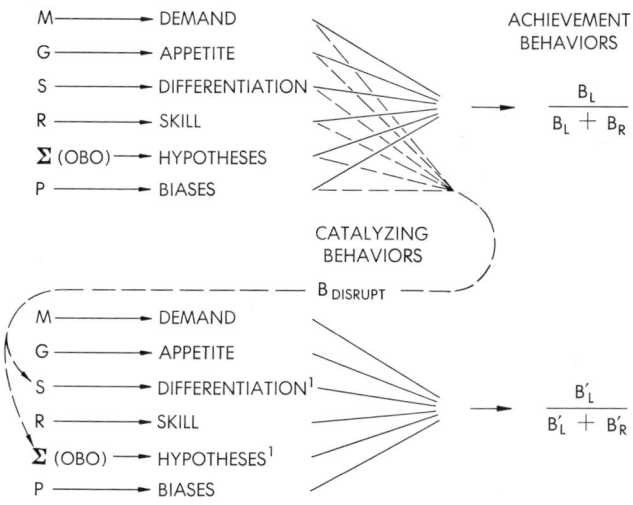

FIGURE 13-24

exploring. And it is my contention as shown in Figure 13-24 that this surprised hunting and exploring brings about new values of the independent variables—especially of G and $\Sigma(OBO)$,—and thus causes a different outcome in the final behavior ratio. The disrupted behavior enhances a new negative aspect in what was originally a positive goal. In short, I am assuming that because of this disrupted searching the rats are better in the next trials about not continuing to go to that side where the goal has been blocked than they would have been if this, their disrupted searching, had not appeared.

Let me close, now, with a final confession of faith. I believe that everything important in psychology (except perhaps such matters as the building up of a super-ego, that is, everything save such matters as involve society and words) can be investigated in essence through the continued experimental and theoretical analysis of the determiners of rat behavior at a choice-point in a maze. Herein I believe I agree with Professor Hull and also with Professor Thorndike.

So in closing let me borrow a verse written by Alexander Meiklejohn in a copy of his book, as he gave it me. He wrote, and I would now repeat:

> To my ratiocinations
> I hope you will be kind
> As you follow up the wanderings
> Of my amazed mind.

14

Formalization and Clarification of a Theory of Learning[1]

VIRGINIA W. VOEKS[2]

INTRODUCTION

In order to test any theory and determine the revisions necessary to bring it into accord with the empirical world, and in order to apply the theory in control and prediction of events, rigorous deductions from the theory are prerequisite. Whatever aids making these deductions is, then, of both theoretical and pragmatic importance. One facilitating factor is clear statement of the fundamental theoretical generalizations.

While writing with great logical consistency, Guthrie never formally presented his postulates and definitions. The basic principles can be induced from his publications; but often that is all, the fundamental aspects of the theory usually being rather more implicit than explicit.

This paper is an attempted remedy—attempted partly because of the considerations mentioned in the opening paragraph and partly because advances in understanding any area of investigation seem highly dependent upon having tightly formulated theories at our disposal. Apparently also, having a multiplicity of such theories aids advancement of any science.

Presented herein is an explicit statement of various postulates and definitions apparently constituting the basis of this theory, some of their implications, and the derivation of eight theorems.[3] The theory is re-

[1] Reprinted from *The Journal of Psychology*, 1950, *30*, pp. 341–362, by permission of the author and publisher.
[2] The importance of this paper derives more than in part from the fact that it states the basic position later developed quantitatively by Estes (1950) and others in the formulation of "statistical learning theory" [Ed.].
[3] These postulates "apparently" constitute the basis of the theory because (a) they are, as mentioned, largely a matter of inference; and (b) it is entirely conceivable that various other hypotheses, consistent too with Guthrie's statements (but which may be deduced from the following postulates), could be taken as postulates instead of those selected, and could be used as bases for deducing some of the present postulates as well as a still greater variety of theorems. If this is the case, such a set would be preferred to the present combination. However, of the various possibilities I have tried, the four given below proved the most satisfactory combination.

Formalization and Clarification of a Theory

flected only as it has been presented in the past and stands at present. It is highly probable that in light of further observation, the postulates may need to be revised or supplemented by additional postulates to mediate deduction of certain established (or to-be-established) empirical phenomena.[4]

POSTULATES

Postulate 1: Principle of association

(a) Any stimulus-pattern which once accompanies a response, and/or immediately precedes it (by $\frac{1}{2}$ second or less), becomes a full-strength direct cue for that response. (b) This is the only way in which stimulus-patterns not now cues for a particular response can become direct cues for that response.[5]

The proposition that association of a response-pattern and stimulus-pattern is established when those stimuli accompany the response is repeatedly presented in Guthrie's writing, for example, in 1930, p. 412, lines 28–29; 1933b, p. 355, lines 18–21; and p. 365; 1934a, p. 200–202; and these two quotations:[6]

"What we can predict is that the influence of the stimuli acting at the time of either satisfaction or annoyance will be to re-establish whatever behavior was in evidence at the time that the stimuli were present. . . . The substitute stimulus is probably always coincident with the response though not with the original stimulus" (1934b, p. 454–455).

"The stimuli present as the response occurs are the future cues for the response" (1935, p. 33).

That Guthrie holds this is the *only* way an S-R association may be set up and also is fundamental to all learning, is evinced by his discussions of serial learning in maze situations and involving nonsense syllables (1933b, p. 361–364; 1936, p. 111 ff.), so-called trial-and-error

---

[4] For example, there probably will need to be some indication of which physical forces are most apt to be stimuli in the psychological sense defined below, when and if that is determined. This is, of course, an aspect of the old problem of the prepotency of stimuli and attention, as well as of the newer problem of the nature of patterns; it is a possible lack of completeness not peculiar to any one theory.

[5] To have any stimulus-pattern become a direct cue for a specified response, Part a states that contiguity or near contiguity of the stimulus-pattern and response is a sufficient condition, and Part b states that it is a necessary condition.

[6] The documentations given herein are not all the relevant sections of Guthrie's treatises, but they are representative in that no statement in the original sources is obviously inconsistent with those present here. These few are given partly to illustrate that these postulates express views forming an integral part of Guthrie's theory, partly to clarify the meaning of the postulates, and finally to show ways in which they may be used.

learning, as for instance in puzzle boxes (1934b; 1935, p. 187 ff.; 1937; 1937b and 1938b—with Horton; 1942a), instrumental conditioning (1936; 1937; 1942b, p. 107), the establishment of voluntary responses (1937; 1938), the effect of reward and punishment in habit formation (1934b; 1935, p. 148 ff.; 1940a), Katona's dichotomization of learning ("repetition" with conditioning being included therein, vs. "understanding"—1940b, p. 822, lines 33–40), and by such comments as:

"This acquisition, when it does occur, is the fundamental mode of learning" (1930, p. 416, after a statement that if stimuli accompany a particular response, a new association between the two is acquired).

"The only generalization applicable to all learning that appears to me acceptable is the general principle of association" (1942b, p. 113), essentially the same point as that elaborated in 1938, p. 33 ff., and 1942a, p. 23.

"That we learn is insured by the association of a stimulus with a response" (1946a, p. 10).

The lucid discussion following the final quotation is to the effect that if a certain stimulus-pattern is present while a response is made, a learned association results; and furthermore, that not only is this a *sufficient,* but also the *necessary* condition of learning (although it is not sufficient, of course, to demonstrate that learning has occurred, since that requires an additional presentation of the newly conditioned stimulus-pattern without the US). This is precisely the same point made in 1946b, p. 286, paragraph 5.

Finally, the *strength* of the association between the stimulus-pattern and the response-pattern is held to be *established fully* through *once* pairing the two (cf. 1930, p. 419, lines 34–37, and p. 420, lines 13–19; 1934a, p. 205, lines 9–13; 1935, p. 98, lines 26–30; 1942a, p. 30, lines 33–34; 1946c, p. 8, line 1, and p. 41, col. 2, lines 3–4).

That this accords with Guthrie's theory is somewhat obscured by his usually combining implications of Postulate 1 (a principle of learning) and Postulate 3 (a principle of performance), and sometimes of Postulates 2 and 4 as well. Thus we read:

"A stimulus pattern that is acting at the time of a response will, if it recurs, *tend* to produce that response" (1942a, p. 23). (Similar statements appear in 1935, p. 26, lines 2–5, and 1938, p. 37, lines 28–29, as well as many other places.)

Such statements may be a bit misleading as they do not mean the association is only partially established when once the stimuli accompany the response.

The statements would be clearer, perhaps, were an explicit distinction made between (a) establishing *association* of a response with a stimulus-pattern and (b) future *elicitation* of that response by a stimulus-pattern. Now elicitation of a particular response upon presentation of certain stimuli (e.g., ones of Pattern S_1) depends in theory upon a variety of factors *in addition to* that of whether the response has become associated with S_1 (Postulate 1). Such additional factors are, for example, (a) whether all stimuli of S_1 are present at the time specified, (b) whether S_1 or a part of S_1 has accompanied some incompatible response in the interim (Postulate 2), (c) whether in addition to S_1, the group of stimulus-patterns presented on the trial specified includes also many others differing from S_1 (which often is the case—Postulate 4), (d) whether these additional stimulus-patterns are cues for the response-pattern in question (Postulate 3), etc.

This aspect of the theory then, as I understand it, is as follows: Through once pairing them, a new association will be established between S_1 and a certain response (say, R_x) and established as strongly as it ever can be. As a result, R_x subsequently would always be evoked by that pattern (if presented alone or with other cues for R_x and before intervening counter-learning) even though some other response has previously accompanied S_1 with indefinitely greater frequency. Nonetheless, according to the theory, there is a *tendency* only for R_x to be elicited on future presentations of S_1 due to the other factors of theoretical importance listed in the preceding paragraph. Prediction of what response will be made depends upon observing the stimulus-patterns present at the time (not upon observing merely the presence or absence of one particular pattern), knowing what responses these various patterns last accompanied, and taking this information and the preceding factors into consideration.

Postulate 2: Principle of postremity

(a) A stimulus which has accompanied or immediately preceded two or more incompatible responses is a conditioned stimulus for only the last response made while that stimulus was present. (b) This is the only way in which a stimulus now a cue for a particular response can cease being a cue for that response.

There is frequent reference to this principle, such statements as the ones below being found throughout Guthrie's writing:

"If the stimulus combination occurs, and the response is prevented by any means, the stimulus combination loses its power to elicit the response" (1930, p. 417).

"An association is continuously destroyed by new associations" (1934b, p. 453), i.e., a stimulus-pattern ceases being a cue for responses formerly made when it is associated subsequently with responses incompatible with the former ones.

"I would not hold that all satisfiers tend to fix the associative connection that has just preceded them. When a satisfying situation involves breaking up the action in progress (i.e., if as a result of the 'satisfier,' some new response incompatible with the former response is made), it will destroy connections between the former CR and CS's acting at the time" (1934b, p. 457).

Although Postulate 2a generally has been referred to as a principle of recency (cf. Guthrie, 1935, p. 114; McGeoch, 1942, p. 537; and Spence, 1942b, p. 301), there are a number of objections to a continuance of this custom. These objections are outlined below, largely in an effort to clarify the meaning of the present postulate.

(a) "Recency" has been used with a great variety of meanings, of which the following are examples.

Brown (1846, p. 372) popularized the term for use in reference to the temporal relationship of a given experience to all other experiences, i.e., to the position on the time continuum of any association. This is essentially the same meaning as one given by McGeoch (1942, p. 569): "The time elapsed between initial fixation and a later measure of retention," and used by Hunter (1934), for example.

A modification in Brown's meaning was introduced by restricting "recency" to the temporal relationship existing among associations of various responses to various stimuli (the different stimuli being associated with different responses) when these associations are established in the same general situation. This is the meaning of the term in the "primacy-recency" discussions. "Recency" here is not a question merely of how long ago some association was formed, but rather of which of the various S-R connections established in the same serial learning situation was last in the series. (For example, in a series such as this: S_{1+g}-R_1, S_{2+g}-R_2, ... S_{n+g}-R_n, the connection S_n-R_n is favored over the others because of "recency.") For cases of this usage, see Warden, 1924; Jersild, 1929; Warden and Cummings, 1929.

A further modification is that of Watson (1914) in which "recency" referred to the relationship between various responses made to the same stimulus, e.g., the relationship of S_1-R_1 and S_1-R_2 to S_1-R_3, the last response to S_1 being the most "recent." Here again, how long ago S_1 was encountered is wholly irrelevant. With respect to these matters (but only these), Guthrie's meaning of recency is the same as Watson's.

The difference between the meaning of Postulate 2a and recency in any of the above senses is clear if one considers this case: S_1 has accompanied R_1 x time ago; S_2 has accompanied R_2, $x + y$ time ago; neither S_1 nor S_2 has since been present. According to any of the above meanings of recency, the strength of the association for S_2-R_2 will be stronger than that for S_1-R_1. But it will *not* be stronger according to Postulate 2a—they will be equally strong if neither S_1 nor S_2 has since been present.

Yet another meaning is one of those given by McGeoch: "The time interval between the terms to be associated" (1942, p. 569).

Formalization and Clarification of a Theory

(b) Not only are there different meanings of the term, but also markedly different rationales for the various principles.

The first of these to be presented in detail was that of Watson, wherein the principle of recency was subordinated to that of frequency, with the "Law of probabilities" tentatively being held fundamental to both. His rationale is this: With the appearance of the last (and correct) response, the S-R series is cut short; and thus certain responses, which otherwise might have been made also, are prevented from occurring. Hence, these other responses have a *decreased frequency,* relative to the frequency of those which did occur, and as a result have a tendency to be eliminated from the animal's repertoire. Similarly, since the response which terminates the situation *does* appear (and must invariably do so), it has an *added frequency* of one, and thus an increased probability of re-occurrence. Hence, due to the supposedly relatively greater frequency of the most "recent" response and the theorized positive correlation between frequency and probability of re-occurrence, "recency" may be a factor determining what response will come to be made invariably to a situation. The effectiveness of "recency," according to Watson's theory, is dependent upon the existence and effectiveness of frequency.

Radically different in this rationale, suggested by Guthrie: At the time each response is made in a situation, it is attached to the stimulus-patterns present, and all preceding responses are wholly detached from them (detached as a result of that one pairing in spite of the possibility that in the past those responses accompanied this set of stimulus-patterns a large number of times). In this manner, all responses made in a situation are successively associated with and then dissociated from those stimuli—all responses except one: the last response in a situation. It remains associated; for after it, no further response can be made with those stimuli present, and so no new responses can be cued to them. Therefore, the last response before termination of any stimulus-pattern will be the only one whose learned association with those stimuli is preserved, and hence it will be the response elicited by them upon their next presentation.

(c) It is difficult of course to achieve clarity of communication or thinking if a variety of meanings exist for the same term. When working with Guthrie's theory, this difficulty is increased by the fact that the most common connotations of "recency" are those of Brown's term. Thus one finds himself confusing in his thinking and observations what the animal did last (connotations of Brown's meaning) with what the animal last did *in the particular stimulus situation* with which one is concerned.

(d) Probably partly because of an early linkage of frequency and recency as factors in learning (viz. Brown, Watson, Thorndike), there is a tendency toward considering the two together (cf. Peterson, 1922; Reed, 1927; Tolman, 1934; Ruch, 1941; McGeoch, 1942). As a result, with elimination of frequency as inadequate or inconsistent with experimental findings (cf. Cuff, 1929; Thorndike, 1927 and 1932; Yoshioka, 1928 and 1930), recency sometimes also has been automatically rejected, whether or not the data have any clear connection with it.

(e) Finally, theoretical arguments (cf. that of Wilson, 1924, and others) have strongly indicated the invalidity of recency with Watson's rationale or the Brownian meanings, and experimental studies have suggested that "recency" in *some* senses is of little or no importance (cf. Peterson, 1917 and 1922; Jersild, 1929; Warden & Cummings, 1929; Yoshioka, 1930; Thorndike, 1932). Through semantic difficulties, such works have been cited as evidence against the validity of *all* principles of "recency," although the various arguments and experiments may be relevant to "recency" in one sense only.

In view of the five points above, it seems advisable to introduce an unambiguous descriptive term for at least one of these principles of recency. "Postremity" (from the Latin adverb *postremo,* superlative of *last*) has been suggested, and it is the term which will be used in the present paper when referring to Guthrie's postulate, reserving the term "recency" for the more traditional principles.

It may be wondered why Postulate 1 is not alone sufficient, and why the "principle of postremity" was included. An answer to these questions is this:

Though Postulate 1 is consistent with Postulate 2, the former does not completely imply the latter. It is not Guthrie's view, but it is conceivable, that precisely the same stimulus could be the cue for not only one response or two compatible responses but for two (or more) incompatible responses; and this is a matter about which Postulate 1 says nothing.

Therefore to Postulate 1 must be added a second, either: (a) the same stimulus cannot be a CS for two incompatible responses (from this plus Postulate 1, we then could derive our present postulate concerning postremity), or else (b) if the same stimulus-pattern happens to be present while two incompatible responses are made, it will be cued to the postreme response only (which directly implies "a" above).

Of these logical alternatives, the latter was chosen as being clearer in its implications, placing the emphasis on a more important aspect of the problem, and being more directly applicable.

Postulate 3: Principle of response probability

The probability of any particular response's occurring (P_{RY}) at some specified time is an increasing monotonic function (x) of the proportion (N) of the stimuli present which are at that time cues for that response (S+). $P_{RY} = (N_{S+})^x$.

This principle often recurs in Guthrie's publications. For instance:

"The 'strengthening' of an S-R connection with repetition may very possibly be the result of the enlistment of increasing numbers of stimuli as conditioners" (1930, p. 420).

"A response conditioned upon two separate stimuli on separate occasions will be . . . more certain if the two conditioners are presented together. Two conditioners generally are more effective than one" (1935, p. 99).

"Why should practice make the effect increasingly certain? Is it not possible that on successive practice periods more and more conditioners are enlisted, so that after twenty pairings there is a high probability that the cue will have enough support from the presence of these additional newly conditioned stimuli to be effective?" (1935, p. 100).[7] Similarly, in discussing why one often finds, as the Freudians have pointed out, better learning under conditions of excitement, Guthrie suggests that it may be due largely to the greater contraction of muscles during excitement, and that this "greater contraction stimulates new fields of proprioceptor sense organs. . . . These added stimuli may become conditioners of movement and hence explain the increased certainty of conditioning" (1935, p. 105; see also 1942a, p. 22). This "explains the increased certainty" if one assumes Postulate 3, that the more cues there are for the response the more likely is the response.[8]

Before leaving this postulate, two of its implications should be clarified: (a) Is it necessary, according to the theory, to change more than half the stimulus-pattern to bring a change in response? (b) What are the conditions under which one will predict a change in reponse?

To the first question the answer is, "No." For any given trial, it is true, the most probable response theoretically is R_Y if $P_{RY} = 51$ percent. But this does not mean that R_Y should occur on *every* trial when $P_{RY} = 51$ percent. Rather according to the theory, the proportion of trials on which R_Y will occur is equal to P_{RY} (Postulate 3); and therefore, if $P_{RY} = 51$ percent for each of 100 trials, R_Y should occur on only 51 of those 100.

Postulate 3 states also that $P_{RY} = (N_{S+})^x$. From this it follows directly that regardless of what value x may have, changing *any* part of

---

[7] As the reader conversant with these publications knows, other factors are also suggested to explain why repetition sometimes is efficacious in learning. For example, it may take many trials before one succeeds in once eliciting the response one wishes to establish as the CR to certain stimuli while those stimuli are present; it may be necessary to cue the response to many stimulus-patterns, not all of which can be present on one trial; and, the learning may be of such a nature that many sets of stimulus-patterns and response-patterns must be associated (as in learning a maze, other serial learning problems, or skills).

[8] A further cause suggested for better learning with excitement is that the "movements during excitement are more complete and vigorous than movements during unexcited states" (*ibid.*), so the response-to-be-learned is made more completely.

the stimulus-pattern to non-cues for R_Y will bring a change in response—in *some* instances (which is a part of the answer to Question 2 above). In other words, unless $N_{S+} = 1.00$, R_Y will not invariably appear. Suppose the changes in N_{S+} are so slight that $P_{RY} = 99$ percent for each one of some set of trials; out of 100 such trials, on the average one trial will be an instance in which R_Y is *not* made.[9] But for a set of instances in which N_{S+} has a value such that $P_{RY} = 80$ percent out of five of these, one will be an instance in which R_Y is not made. It is obvious from this that when any part whatsoever of the stimulus-pattern is changed to n (non-cues for the response in question), there should be a change in response in at least some cases.

To predict in *how many* cases, out of say 20, R_Y will fail to occur, our knowing only N_{S+}[10] will be insufficient; for the number of trials on which the response should appear is not directly proportional to the amount of the stimulus-pattern which is unchanged or, though changed, still composed of cues for the response in question, but is proportional rather to P_{RY}. Hence, for this we need also to know the value of x. Consider these two cases in which N_{S+} for R_Y equals .80: If $x = \frac{1}{2}$, $P_{RY} = .89$ and R_Y should fail to occur two times out of 20; but if $x = 2$, then $P_{RY} = .64$ and R_Y should fail to occur seven times out of 20.

Without knowing x, but assuming it remains constant for the set of cases being considered, we can make these predictions from the theory: (a) Introduction of any non-cues for R_Y will result in a change in response in some cases. (b) The greater the change in the stimulus-pattern to non-cues for R_Y (and hence the smaller the value of N_{S+}), the smaller will be the proportion of times on which R_Y occurs. (c) A very small change in the stimulus-pattern can result in a substantial number of shifts from R_Y to some other response. For instance, when one changes to Category n even 10 percent of the total stimulus-pattern, in 5 percent of such cases (if $x = \frac{1}{2}$) or in 19 percent of such cases (if $x = 2$) some response other than R_Y will occur.

---

[9] By this theory, any one of the 100 is as apt to be the trial with the non R_Y as any other trial.

[10] N_{S+} is the proportion of the total stimulus-pattern present on any specified trial which is composed of stimulus-patterns cued to the response in question. N_{S+} is *not* necessarily, therefore, the proportion of the total pattern which is the same as that present on some previous trial. For example, the value of N_{S+} may *change* even though the same pattern was present on two successive trials; on one trial N_{S+} may equal .60, but on the next trial (if R_+ occurred on the preceding trial) that same stimulus-pattern will now have an N of 1.00. Further, the value of N_{S+} may remain the *same* from one trial S_+ to another, although the stimulus-pattern has been changed; this would be the case if, for example, a certain proportion of S_+ stimuli were dropped but the same proportion of other S_+ stimuli were added from one trial to the next, or if non-S_+ stimuli were dropped and other non-S_+ stimuli replaced them.

Postulate 4: Principle of dynamic situations

The stimulus-pattern of a situation is not static but from time to time is modified, due to such changes as result from the subject's making a response, accumulation of fatigue products, visceral changes and other internal processes of the subject, introduction of controlled or uncontrolled variations in the stimuli present.

This postulate stresses that changes in stimulus-pattern go on virtually continuously, and emphasizes certain factors of theoretical importance which will bring about such changes (viz., the fact that there always will be a change in the stimuli as a result of making a response, since any response results in the introduction of new proprioceptive stimuli as well as in other internal modifications perhaps and results also in a change in the external stimulus-patterns acting on the subject). For a few of the places where this matter is stated explicitly or else assumed in Guthrie's discussions, one may consult the following references: 1935, p. 10; 1937a, p. 527, lines 13–22; 1938a, p. 39; 1942a, p. 31, last 2 paragraphs, and p. 32, paragraphs 2 and 3, as well as pp. 39–43; 1946c, p. 40, lines 24–27. This completes the present set of postulates, and we turn to the definitions.

DEFINITIONS

As most of these reflect to a considerable extent the conventional usage, no complete glossary of terms will be presented. The meaning of a few, however, differs somewhat from other accepted definitions; and since these differences constitute a unique and fundamental part of the theory, they are given below.

1. *Stimulus* (S) to an individual: Any change in physical energy or chemical state activating a receptor of some specified individual, thus setting up an afferent impulse to the CNS, and eventually an efferent impulse which elicits some response. It is clear that by this definition not all physical forces are stimuli; nor are energies which may be stimuli to an individual under some circumstances *always* stimuli to that individual. Physical forces must be in the Life Space of the individual to be stimuli for that individual.[11]

---

[11] A bar, for example, does not furnish any stimulus-patterns to an animal on a "trial" when the animal is sitting in a somewhat distant corner with its back to the bar. Nor do curtain rods furnish any stimuli to a baby in another part of the room, looking somewhere else. Number of presentations of stimuli (as others view this) would not necessarily equal number of presentations of stimuli by this definition, for, what constitutes presentation of S's-to-experimenter does not necessarily constitute S's-to-subject.

2. *Cue* (for a response): Any unconditioned or previously conditioned stimulus-pattern for the response in question.

Indirect cue (for some R): A stimulus-pattern which is a cue for that response indirectly, by being a cue for an R which leads to the creation of S's which in turn are cues for the R in question. E.g., in an S-R chain such as this: S_1-R_1—S_2-R_2—S_3-R_3—S_4 . . . S_n-R_n, each R brings into existence other stimuli, these stimuli are cues for other responses, and all stimuli of that chain are indirect cues for R_n (except S_n which is a direct cue for R_n).

3. *Response* (R): The contraction of any group of muscles or the secretion of any gland or glands. It will be noticed that gross *movement* is not necessary in order that something may be classed as a response. If many muscles are contracted (possibly antagonistics), this is a response even though the animal just "sits still." In part, it is this usage which led Guthrie to speak of "the response of not responding," although by that phrase he implies also any response other than that particular one in which the observer is most interested.

4. *Conditioned response* (CR) to some S: Any response different from that which the S originally elicited through the effects of inherited structure and maturation alone.

5. *Indirect conditioned response* to a stimulus-pattern (e.g., S_1): Any response in an S-R chain such as S_1-R_1—S_2-R_2—S_3 . . . , other than R_1 which is the direct CR to S_1.

6. *Postreme response:* The last response made to a particular stimulus-pattern. (If R_1 was the last response to accompany Stimulus-Patterns 1-2-3, and R_2 was the last to accompany Stimulus-Patterns 4-5, there are two postreme responses for the situation of Stimulus-Patterns 1-2-3-4-5, R_1 and R_2, until some response occurs to this combination; then that response is the postreme response for the whole pattern and all parts of it.)

7. *Incompatible responses:* Two or more responses which cannot be made at the same time, either because of reciprocal innervation of the muscles involved or because of the same muscles being used in two different ways in the two responses. Obviously, complex responses may be either partially or wholly incompatible.

8. *Learning:* Any change in response to a situation which is the result of past responses to the same or similar situations and is not nullified to any degree by a period during which neither that nor any similar situation is presented.

This definition excludes fatigue and its effects. It also excludes phenomena which might be classified as learning by one who accepts a theory that effects of learning may partially disappear over a period of time, even when none of the cues has been present during the interim—a theory, in other words, that forgetting can occur in spite of there having been no chance for extinction through the occurrence of the S-R without subsequent reinforcement, and no chance either for counter-conditioning through the occurrence of some of the conditioned stimuli in conjunction with responses incompatible with the learned response in question. This restricted principle of disuse is not however one Guthrie holds, so the definition above excludes no phenomena he would consider "learning."

It includes all phenomena he does consider "learning." Some of these, it is true, would not be included under that rubric by other psychologists who, following the tradition of Hobhouse (1901), Thorndike (1911) and Lloyd Morgan (1930), delimit learning to changes which are an improvement or achievement in accordance with their plans. On this point Guthrie differs. His view is that learning has occurred not only when the animal eventually makes the "correct" response after having made "incorrect" responses, but also when he comes to make an "incorrect" response when he previously made either correct responses or some other error to a similar stimulus-pattern. *"Learning" includes changes in behavior which are not necessarily a betterment* (cf., 1936, pp. 111–113; 1937, p. 526, lines 1–3, and p. 528, lines 13–19; 1942a, p. 58, lines 11–12; 1942b, p. 105, lines 34–37 and p. 106, lines 1–7; 1946b, p. 286, lines 1–12 of col. 2).

Some of the considerations which lead to rejecting the classical definition are epitomized in the following passages:

"This identification of learning with the attainment of a good result is all very well for common sense, but for a scientific understanding of human behavior it will not serve. And the reason that it will not serve is that in the same manner and in the same ways that human beings acquire skills and capacities, they also acquire faults and awkwardnesses and even lose capacities which they once possessed. Since virtues and skills are acquired in the same way that faults and awkwardnesses are acquired, it seems unreasonable to limit the meaning of the word learning to achievement. . . . We have deserted the methods of empirical science if we assume that all learning is good, that every action has its goal" (1935, p. 5).

"It is what gets done that is of practical importance. . . . But to use . . . goal attainment, success, as the essential criterion of learning, and to turn our search for facts to the observation of success and the conditions under which it is attained is analogous to . . . the definition by the physicist of work in terms of useful work or valuable work. . . . We must understand the processes through which behavior is *changed* for better or for worse" (1946a, p. 5).

SOME FURTHER THEORETICAL IMPLICATIONS

In this section are presented certain theorems flowing from the preceding postulates and definitions. In essence, each of these theorems states: when the conditions herein specified exist, then, if the theory is sound, this effect should result. The material in parentheses accompanying every statement in the theorem derivation gives the bases from which that particular statement logically follows.

The question has been raised as to how an animal can ever learn if Guthrie's theory is valid. The various steps in the derivation of Theorem I are an answer to this.

The statement of Theorem I gives the conditions under which a specified stimulus-pattern will come to elicit a response which was not elicited at some previous time by that particular pattern. That these are the *sufficient* conditions is demonstrated in Theorem I; that they are *necessary* conditions is demonstrated in Theorems II, III, and IV. In other words, if a sequence of events has all characteristics stated in a, b, and c of Theorem I, a new response subsequently will be evoked by the same stimulus-pattern; if, on the other hand, the sequence of events has the characteristics stated in Theorem II or III or IV, no new response will come to be evoked by the specified stimulus-pattern.[12]

THEOREM I: After a stimulus-pattern has been temporarily modified by (a) the addition of other stimuli which (b) result in a new response being made while (c) the original stimulus-pattern still is present, on its next presentation the original pattern will evoke a response it did not evoke before the preceding events occurred.

Symbols:[13]

Let R_1 = The response-pattern elicited by stimulus-pattern I at time A
R_2 = Any specified response-pattern not elicited at time A and different from (but not necessarily incompatible with) R_1
$S_1 = S_1 + S_2 + S_3 + \ldots S_n$ = the stimulus-pattern present at time A
$S_{11} = S_1 + S'$

---

[12] As stated, these first four theorems are concerned primarily with the conditions under which the *same* stimulus-patterns will come to evoke a response different from that which it formerly elicited. It is obvious that another way in which a different response may be evoked is by having a different stimulus-pattern present on that test trial. These are the two fundamental causes, and the conditions essential, for an animal's not always doing the same thing.

[13] Symbols are merely a mode of abbreviated expression and in defining them one should make no assumptions nor specify any conditions not given in the statement of the theorem, postulates, or definitions.

Formalization and Clarification of a Theory 231

S' = Any unconditioned or previously conditioned stimulus-pattern for R_2 which, even when presented with S_1 at a time all stimuli of S_1 are cues for R_1, evokes R_2
S_x = Any stimulus-pattern not included in S_1 which does *not* evoke R_2 when added to S_1
A = Any time previous to B, when S_1 is presented
B = The time when S_{11} is first presented subsequent to time A
C = Any time after time B when S is next presented

Deduction:
1) At time A, S_1 elicits R_1 and does not elicit R_2. (Definition 1 and given.)[14]
2) At time B, $S_{11}(S_1 + S')$ is presented and R_2 occurs. (Given.)
3) Immediately after time B, the stimuli of S_{11} are cues for R_2. (Step 2 postulate 1a.)
4) Immediately after time B, the stimuli of S_1 *without* S' have become cues for R_2. (Step 3.)
5) At time C, S_1 is next presented. (Given.)
6) Between time B, and time C, S_1 accompanies no response because not present. (Step 5.)
7) So at time C, S_1 must be cues for R_2. (Steps 4 and 6, Postulate 2b.)
8) At time C, S_1 will evoke R_2. (Steps 5 and 7, Postulate 3.)
9) Thus, the organism now (time C) makes a new response to S_1 which formerly (time A) he did not make to that stimulus-pattern. (Steps 8 and 1.)
10) Hence, after a stimulus-pattern has been temporarily modified by (a) the addition of other stimuli which (b) result in a new response being made while (c) the original stimulus-pattern still is present, on its next presentation the original pattern will evoke a response it did not evoke before the preceding events occurred. (Steps 2 and 9.)

THEOREMS II, III, AND IV: If additional stimulus-patterns are not presented (II) or if they do not evoke a different response (III) or if the specified stimulus-pattern is not still present (IV), the original specified pattern will continue to evoke only that response it formerly elicited.

THEOREM II: Stated above.

Symbols: Same as before, except
Let B = A time after time A when S_1 (with no additional stimuli) is next presented

[14] "Given" indicates that the accompanying statement follows directly from one or more of the conditions specified in the statement of the theorem.

Deduction:
1) At time A, S_1 elicits R_1 (and are cues for R_1), but not R_2. (Given, Postulate 1a.)
2) At time B, S_1 is re-presented with no additional stimuli. (Given.)
3) At time B, R_2 will not be evoked. (Step 2, Step 1 and Postulate 3.)
4) Therefore, at time B, S_1 has not accompanied R_2. (Step 3.)
5) And the stimuli of S_1 have not become cues for R_2. (Step 4, Step 1 and Postulate 1b.)
6) So the stimuli of S_1 remain cues for R_1. (Steps 1 and 5, Postulate 2b.)
7) At time C, S_1 is again presented. (Given.)
8) At time C, S_1 will evoke R_1. (Steps 6 and 7, Postulate 3.)
9) At time C, S_1 will not evoke R_2. (Step 5, Postulate 3.)
10) Hence, if (with the specified stimulus-pattern) additional stimulus-patterns are not presented, that specified pattern will continue to elicit on its subsequent presentations only the response it formerly elicited. (Steps 2, 1 and 8, 9.)

THEOREM III: Even when additional stimulus-patterns are presented with a specified stimulus-pattern, if they do not evoke a new response, the original specified stimulus-pattern will continue to evoke only the response it elicited before the stimulus-pattern had been temporarily modified.

Symbols: Same as before, except
 Let B = Any time subsequent to A at which S_1 is re-presented with the addition of S_x

Deduction: Same as for Theorem II except the following steps should be substituted for the ones of corresponding number in Theorem II.
 2) At time B, S_1 is changed by adding S_x and the combination is presented. (Given.)
 10) Hence, even when additional stimulus-patterns are presented with a specified stimulus-pattern, if this change does not result in a response different from that previously made to the original specified pattern, that pattern will continue to evoke (time C) only the response it formerly elicited (at time A) before the introduction of the change. (Steps 2, 1 and 8, 9.)

THEOREM IV: If the specified stimulus-pattern is not still present when a new response is made, that pattern will continue to evoke only the response which it elicited previous to the change.

Formalization and Clarification of a Theory

Symbols: Same as before, except
   Let B = The time at which S' is presented but S_1 is not present

Deduction:
1) At time A, S_1 elicits R_1. (Given.)
2) At time B, S' is presented and R_2 is made; but S_1 is not present. (Given.)
3) Therefore, S_1 does not accompany R_2 at time B. (Step 2.)
4) So immediately after time B, S_1 will not have become cues for R_2. (Step 3, Postulate 1b.)
5) And the stimuli of S_1 remain cues for R_1. (Steps 1 and 3, Postulate 2b.)
6) S_1 is next presented at time C. (Given.)
7) At time C, R_1 will be evoked by S_1. (Steps 5 and 6, Postulate 3.)
8) At time C, R_2 will not be evoked by S_1. (Steps 4 and 6, Postulate 3.)
9) At time C, S_1 elicits the same response, and only that response, which it elicited before the change in stimulus-pattern. (Steps 1 and 7, 8.)
10) Hence, even when a change is made in stimulus-pattern so that a new response is evoked, if the original specified stimulus-pattern is not present at that time, the original pattern will continue to evoke on its presentation only the response it elicited previous to these events. (Steps 2, 9.)

The preceding theorems specify the condition under which an animal comes to make *new* responses to the same stimulus-pattern. However, under those conditions, that stimulus-pattern not only will come to elicit a new response but *may continue to elicit the old response as well.*

The conditions under which a specified stimulus-pattern will cease to elicit its old response are given in the theorem following; i.e., this theorem gives the necessary and sufficient conditions for extinction to occur.

THEOREM V: A stimulus-pattern which now elicits a particular response will cease eliciting that response *when and only* when the stimulus-pattern subsequently (a) has been present while (b) some additional stimulus-pattern is presented which (c) elicits a new response incompatible with the old response.

Symbols: Same as before with this addition
   Let R_3 = Any response not only different from but incompatible with R_1

Deduction:
1) At time A, S_1 evokes R_1. (Given.)
2) At time A, R_1 is cued to S_1. (Step 1, Postulate 1.)
3) S_1 will cease being cues for R_1 when and only when S_1 subsequently has accompanied an incompatible response, R_3. (Step 2, Postulate 2a and 2b.)
4) Therefore, S_1 will cease to evoke R_1 when and only when S_1 subsequently has accompanied R_3. (Step 3, Postulate 3.)
5) S_1 does not evoke R_3 at time A. (Step 1, definition of "incompatible response"—Definition 7.)
6) S_1 will never evoke R_3 unless Conditions a, b, and c have been fulfilled. (Step 5, Theorems II, III, IV.)
7) S_1 will evoke R_3 when Conditions a, b, and c have been fulfilled. (Step 5, Theorem I.)
8) Therefore S_1 will come to evoke R_3 when and only when Conditions a, b, and c have been fulfilled. (Steps 6, 7.)
9) So S_1 will cease to elicit R_1 when and only when Conditions a, b, and c have been fulfilled. (Steps 4 and 8.)
10) Hence, a stimulus-pattern which now elicits a particular response will cease eliciting that response when and only when it subsequently (a) has been present while (b) some additional stimulus-pattern is presented which (c) elicits a new response incompatible with the old response. (Step 9.)

For the remaining theorems, three additional definitions are needed, the symbols used in these definitions being those listed for Theorem VI.

9. *Alternation:* R_x occurring on the trial following a trial on which R_1 occurred; or R_1 occurring on the trial after one on which R_x occurred.

10. *Stable situation:* A set of stimulus-patterns on successive trials having the following characteristics (a) all stimuli that are present on Trial X are present on all succeeding trials, (b) none of the stimuli present on Trial X is present between trials, (c) none absent from Trial X is added on succeeding trials.

11. *Relatively more unstable situation:* Compare to some other series of trials, a set having the following characteristics (a) a smaller proportion of those stimuli present on the various trials, ones which were present on a preceding trial when R_x was made, (b) a larger proportion of the stimuli present on the trials, either ones which were present last between trials, or else ones which were not present on any previous trial when R_x was made and are largely non-cues for R_x.

Formalization and Clarification of a Theory

THEOREM VI: For any given individual in a situation which is completely stable at least after the trial on which the new CR first is made, the new CR after once occurring will consistently occur, regardless of the past frequency with which that stimulus-pattern may have accompanied some other response or responses, i.e., P_{RX} will jump from 0 to 100 percent.

Symbols:
Let R_x = The response E is interested in establishing as the CR to the experimental stimulus-patterns
R_i = Any response incompatible with R_x
X = The trial on which R_x first occurs
S_x = The stimulus-patterns present on Trial X

Deduction: For any given individual
1) On trial S, R_x occurs for the first time. (Given.)
2) Therefore, immediately after Trial X, all stimulus-patterns of S_x have become full-strength cues for R_x, regardless of how frequently they have been associated with some other response. (Step 1, Postulates 1a and 2a.)
3) And immediately after Trial X, all stimulus-patterns of S_x (which may have been cues for R_i) cease being cues for R_i. (Step 1, Postulate 2a.)
4) Between Trial X and Trial X + 1 (and between any other succeeding trials), none of S_x is present. (Given.)
5) So between trials, none of S_x can become a cue for R_i. (Step 4, Step 3, and Postulate 1b.)
6) Therefore, at the time that Trial X + 1 is given, all stimulus-patterns of S_x will be cues for R_x. (Step 2, Steps 3, 5, and Postulate 2b.)
7) On trial X + 1, S_x and only S_x is presented. (Given.)
8) So on Trial X + 1, P_{RX} = 100%. (Steps 6 and 7, Postulate 3.)
9) Therefore on Trial X + 1, S_x will elicit R_x. (Steps 7 and 8, Postulate 3.)
10) Immediately after X + 1 (or any other trial on which R_x occurs), all stimuli of S_x are cues for R_x. (Step 9, Postulate 1a.)
11) Between Trials X + 1 and X + 2 (and any other trials), no stimuli of S_x can cease being cues for R_x. (Steps 4 and 5.)
12) On Trial X + 2 (and all succeeding trials), S_x and only S_x is presented. (Given.)
13) Therefore when Trial X + 2 is given, 100% of the stimulus-pattern is composed of cues for R_x. (Steps 10, 11, 12.)
14) Therefore, on Trial X + 2, R_x will be evoked. (Step 13, Postulate 3.)

15) Similarly on all succeeding trials, R_x will be evoked. (Step 14, and Steps 10, 11, 12, and Postulate 3.)
16) Hence, for any given individual in a situation which is completely stable at least after the trial on which the new CR is first made, the new CR after once appearing will consistently do so, regardless of the past frequency with which some other response may have accompanied that stimulus-pattern. (Steps 9, 14, 15.)

THEOREM VII: Assuming (1) not more than one-half the total stimulus-pattern after the first CR is consistently composed of patterns which are not cues for the response in question (R_x), and (2) that the response between trials is R_i, in any specified number of trials after Trial X there will be, on the average, more alternations for a group of subjects in a relatively less stable situation than a group in any relatively more stable situation.

Symbols: Same as for Theorem VI, with these additions
Let L = Any situation relatively less stable than Situation M
M = Any situation relatively more stable than Situation L

Deduction:
1) Compared to M, on the trials for L a smaller proportion of stimulus-patterns are ones that were present when R_x occurred. (Given, and Definition 11.)
2) Therefore, the total pattern of L contains from this source a smaller proportion of cues for R_x than that of M. (Step 1, Postulate 1.)
3) Compared to M, a larger proportion of the stimulus-patterns presented during the trials in L are patterns which were last present between trials. (Given, Definition 11.)
4) Stimulus-patterns present between trials are, at the beginning of the next trial, cues for R_i and no longer cues for R_x. (Given, Assumption 2, Postulate 2a.)
5) Therefore, L has a larger proportion of cues for R_i than does M. (Steps 3 and 4, Postulate 2a.)
6) Compared to M, in L a larger proportion of stimulus-patterns present on various trials are patterns not present before, and most of these are not cues for R_x. (Given, and Definition 11.)
7) So, in general, L has a lower P_{R_X} than has M. (Steps 2, 5, and 6, Postulate 3.)
8) For each individual, the occurrence of R is a function of P_{R_X}. (Postulate 3.)
9) Therefore, in any specified number of trials, more of the responses

will be R_i for a group of subjects in situation L than for one in M. (Steps 7 and 8.)
10) P_{RX} for both L and M is above fifty percent for the majority of trials after Trial X. (Given, Assumption 1.)
11) So for subjects in either L or M, on the average more than one-half the responses after Trial X will be R_x. (Step 10.)
12) Therefore, in any specified number of trials after Trial X, more alternations will occur on the average for the group in Situation L than that in Situation M. (Steps 9 and 11.)
13) Hence, assuming not more than one-half the total stimulus-pattern is consistently composed (after the first CR) of patterns which are not cues for the response in question (R_x), and that the last response between trials is R_i, in any specified number of trials after the first CR there will be, on the average, more alternations for a group of subjects in a relatively less stable situation than a group in any relatively more stable situation. (Step 12.)

THEOREM VIII: In any specified number of trials following the first R_x, on the average there will be longer consecutive series of R_x's for a group under relatively more stable stimulus conditions than for a group under relatively less stable conditions.

Symbols: Same as for Theorem VII.

Deduction:
1) On Trial X, R_x occurs. (Given.)
2) to 7) Same as Steps 1 through 6 for Theorem VII.
8) Therefore on Trial X + 1 and subsequent trials, P_{RX} is higher on the average for subjects in Situation M than for the group in Situation L. (Steps 2 through 7.)
9) The higher is the value of P_{RX}, the more likely is R_x. (Postulate 3.)
10) So for each trial after X, R_x is more likely for subjects in Situation M than for ones in L. (Steps 8 and 9.)
11) Therefore, unless the number of trials following X is less in M than in L, there will be on the average longer consecutive series of R_x in M than in L. (Step 10.)
12) Hence, in any specified number of trials, following R_x, on the average there will be longer consecutive series of R_x's for a group under relatively more stable stimulus conditions than for a group under relatively less stable conditions. (Step 11.)

SUMMARY

For the advancement of our science, and to meet other theoretical and pragmatic considerations, we must have precise formalization of as many theories (conceivably correct syntheses of information) as possible.

An effort was made to systematize and clarify one theory of learning (that of Guthrie) by more explicit formulation of the postulates and definitions apparently constituting the basis of that theory, presentation of certain aspects wherein this theory differs from others, and discussion of some questions concerning the theory. It is entirely possible these postulates will need to be revised in light of further observation and almost certain they will need to be supplemented by others.

Also, eight theorems and their derivation from the present system were presented. These show some implications of the theory, give an answer to various questions, and are open to experimental tests. (In fact, the writer is preparing a report of an experiment testing them.) They are but a few of the theorems which may be deduced from the postulates as they stand.

It was suggested that "postremity" be used as the descriptive term for the Guthrian postulate and rationale stressing the importance of the response made last to a specified stimulus-pattern. This suggestion was made in view of the variety of meanings and rationales for "recency," the nature of various connotations of the term, a rather confusing linkage of recency and frequency, and the results of this state of affairs.

15

An Introduction to Two-Process Theory

GREGORY A. KIMBLE

In this chapter, we turn to the discussion of an issue which has been a matter of controversy for some years and may soon replace the "reinforcement" issue as the most hotly disputed point in theories of simple learning. The question involved is whether learning is a single process or whether there are two or more subvarieties of learning.

As we have already seen (pp. 96 to 97) this issue arises from the fact that operationally it is possible to make a clear distinction between the procedures employed in classical and instrumental conditioning. Classical conditioning is a situation where the US is delivered without respect to the organism's behavior, while in instrumental learning, there is a definite contingency between response and reinforcer. This operational separability inevitably suggests that the forms of learning which take place under the two procedures may also be different, hence the development of two-process theories.

Before taking a position with respect to the validity of this distinction, we will discuss the terms in which its validity will be decided. The general situation is this: If, for all its operational clarity, the distinction between classical and instrumental conditioning has no associated differences in consequences for behavior, there is no point in making the operational distinction. The difference between classical and instrumental conditioning, in that event, would be a difference that makes no difference and there would be no point in maintaining the distinction.

Obviously the arguments between multiprocess and uniprocess theorists of learning turn on this last point. The latter group of theorists maintain, in effect, that the distinction does not relate to differences in the laws of learning; the multiprocess theorists take the opposite view that the classical-instrumental distinction is a valid one in that it is related to the kind of behavior that can be manipulated, to the nature of reinforcement or to something else.

It is important to recognize that, although multiprocess theorists agree that there is more than one form of learning, they do not necessarily agree on the particular features that differentiate classical and instrumental conditioning at the process level. In this chapter we shall review several suggestions from a variety of theorists. As a matter of general perspective it is important to keep the following in mind: that all of these theorists (in company with the uniprocess theorists whom they oppose) accept the fact that it is possible to make a reasonably clear *operational* distinction between classical and instrumental conditioning, but their suggestions vary as to the exact significance of this distinction. In other words, there is agreement that there is an operational difference between the two forms of learning but a variety of opinions as to what else this distinction implies.

Let us begin with these general points. (1) What follows adopts, for the sake of the argument, the two-process view. The reader interested in a more detailed exposition of one-process theory might well consult Hull (1943) and Guthrie (1935) or the chapters describing the positions of these theorists in Hilgard (1956). (2) There is no dispute as to the essential difference in procedure which defines the distinction between classical and instrumental conditioning. It is the contingency or lack of it between response and reinforcer. (3) Certain theorists, for example Konorski (1948), Tolman (1938), Mowrer (1947), Kimble (1961), and Grant (1964) have offered analyses which involve subdivisions of one or both of the main categories of learning. These finer differentiations are not to be considered here. (4) Most authors who have considered this problem recognize that the classical-instrumental dichotomy is difficult to realize in experimental practice and believe that most learning even in the laboratory is a composite of classical and instrumental conditioning. (5) The student who reads widely in this area will encounter an annoying heterogeneity in terminology. In some of the most important primary sources, the classical-instrumental distinction has taken these forms, with the first item referring to classical conditioning: Type S versus Type R conditioning, respondent versus operant conditioning, conditioning of the first type versus conditioning of the second type, Type II (sic) conditioning vs. Type I conditioning and conditioning versus problem solving. (6) The sources used in this section are chosen, from many possible treatments, from those which overlap least in content. They are Kimble (1964), Konorski (1948), Mowrer (1947), Schlosberg (1937), Skinner (1935), and Turner and Solomon (1962). French (1933), summarized in Chapter 43 of this book, offers an interesting, novel suggestion that leads in the direction of a two-process theory. To the best of my knowledge, no one has followed this suggestion through with any systematic persistence although Konorski* entertains similar ideas. (7) Unexpectedly, it is convenient to organize these materials in terms of the categories proposed by Miller and Dollard

---

* In a personal communication.

An Introduction to Two-Process Theory

(1941), to present an analysis in terms of drive, cue, response and reward.

A consideration related to drive

Skinner (1935) may have been the first psychologist to diagram classical and instrumental conditioning as they are below.

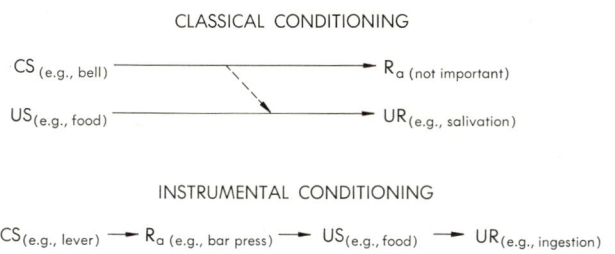

In these diagrams, the symbols CS, US and UR have their usual meanings; R_a is a response to the CS that exists prior to the experiment. These two diagrams will be useful in discussing several of the differences proposed by Skinner and others as differentiating between classical and instrumental conditioning. Before turning to these distinctions, one preliminary point needs to be made. Note that neither the term, conditioned reflex, nor its common abbreviation, CR, appears in these diagrams. In instrumental learning, the conditioning process is hypothesized to consist of the *strengthening* of the reflex CS-R_a, which existed at the beginning of the experiment at least in minimal strength. More of this later. In classical conditioning, Skinner hypothesized that learning consists of the *creation* of the reflex CS-UR.

One of several distinguishing features proposed by Skinner was that, in classical conditioning, the drive at work is always identified by UR, whereas in instrumental conditioning, the drive cannot be so specified. For Skinner, the name for a particular drive (e.g., hunger) referred to a concept inferred from the fact that some operation (e.g., food deprivation) increased the strength of an entire set of reflexes (e.g., those involved in obtaining food). Salivation, whether conditioned or unconditioned, is one such set of reflexes, those potentiated by hunger. The GSR is a reflex associated with anxiety as are the eyeblink, pupillary dilation, etc. Skinner's proposal was that the close relationship between these reflexes and particular drives identifies them as classically conditionable reflexes. Instrumentally conditionable responses, by contrast, bear no dependable relationship to certain drives, and the instrumental conditioning of CS-R_a can take place in the service of any motive whatsoever. For example, hunger, thirst, fear, and whatever motivates responding for brain stimulation have all been used experimentally as the motives for bar pressing.

The value of this distinction depends upon considerations whose implications are not clear. In particular, it is not clear (at least to me) what the implications for Skinner's position would be if motivation had actually nothing directly to do with classical conditioning. Although this may seem an extreme view, there is some reason to suspect that it is correct. For one thing, it now seems obvious that, in instrumental learning, motivation is strictly a performance variable (Kimble, 1961, p. 416). And some motivational variables (e.g., anxiety) appear to energize classical eyelid conditioning in the same way as hunger energizes an instrumental reaction.

Beyond this, at least some classical conditioning raises questions of whether motivation is even necessary for such learning. The Russian studies of interoceptive conditioning (Razran, 1961) provide the most impressive examples, but the conditionability of a blocking of the alpha rhythm of the brain and recent demonstrations that cortical evoked potentials can be conditioned to cortically delivered CS's raise similar problems.

Thus, with respect to Skinner's argument, we may say that it is surely true that instrumental reflexes ($CS-R_a$) may be conditioned on the basis of a wider collection of motives than any of the usual classically conditionable Rs, but the meaning of this fact depends upon decisions (partly factual and partly definitional) that cannot be made in isolation from the whole topic of conditioning.

The cues associated with classical and instrumental conditioning

Skinner also suggested another criterion for differentiating the two forms of learning. In classical conditioning the CS is typically presented suddenly and intermittently while the CS in instrumental conditioning is very often a stable feature of the environment. For example, the lever in the Skinner box is an ever-present stimulus, but the bell used as the CS in the salivary situation is abrupt. This distinction is more important for its further implications, however, than as a differentiator of classical and instrumental conditioning. Skinner had to consider the fact that there are obviously some cases of instrumental learning where the stimuli are presented suddenly and intermittently. In what we now call a discriminated operant, for example, a bar press may be reinforced only in the presence of a particular stimulus, such as light. The animal learns to respond only when the light is on. Skinner calls such discriminated reactions, whether based on classical or on instrumental conditioning, a *pseudo-type* of conditioned reflex, since the reaction, actually to the lever, appears to be controlled by the light. The light merely provides the occasion for the occurrence of the reflex ($S_{lever} \rightarrow R_{bar\ press}$).

The basic process involved in the establishment of a conditioned reflex of the pseudo-type is the extinction of responses to irrelevant features of the environment—to the bar, for example, when the absence of the discriminative stimulus indicates that such reactions will not be reinforced. For this reason, classically conditioned reflexes are always partly conditioned reflexes of the pseudo-type. The CR initially appears to features of the general environment but, as the process of conditioning proceeds, a discrimination develops so that responses occur only in the presence of the CS.

It is also to be noted that any experiment concerned with the influence of an attribute of a conditioned stimulus (such as its pitch, hue, rate of onset, or intensity) must be an instance of conditioned reflexes of the pseudo-type. In these cases, the organism first learns to react to the stimulus as a unit and only then to react to the specific feature.

If these ideas were to be generalized and offered as differentiating classical from instrumental conditioning, a criterion might be stated somewhat as follows. In classical conditioning, the CS is presented suddenly, and the organism must learn in part to discriminate between the environment with this relevant feature and the environment without it. In true (that is, not pseudo-) instrumental conditioning, however, the relevant feature of the environment is always present, and no discrimination of the type required in classical conditioning is necessary. Again, however, such a difference seems to be one of degree. Some discrimination takes place in instrumental learning even in the free responding situation. The animal no doubt learns to respond to the lever as the significant aspect of the environment rather than to anything else.

There is different criterion involving the cues for the two kinds of conditioning. It has often been proposed (Turner and Solomon, 1962; Konorski, 1948) that the responses involved in instrumental learning provide more massive proprioceptive feedback and also more exteroceptive feedback (since the environment is often manipulated) than classically conditioned responses. As in several of the points discussed above, this defines only a quantitative difference between the two forms of learning. It is important to question the significance of this distinction, particularly if it is connected to the voluntary-involuntary distinction to be discussed in the next section.

Classically and instrumentally conditionable responses

The criteria discussed in the last two sections have not been considered as significant by two-factor theorists as the two remaining topics are: the types of responses which may be conditioned classically and instrumentally, and the law of reinforcement applicable to each. In this area several authors have proposed strict dichotomies, making the claim that certain responses are conditionable *only* classically and others are conditionable *only* instrumentally.

Mowrer (1947), for example, proposed that responses of the autonomic nervous system are conditionable only classically and responses of the skeletal nervous system are conditionable only instrumentally. This bold assertion could be refuted either by demonstrating the instrumental conditionability of an autonomic reaction or the classical conditionability of a skeletal response. Both demonstrations have been attempted. Many authors have reported successful instrumental conditioning of the GSR. Kimmel and Hill (1960), for example, demonstrated an increase in the rate of spontaneous emission of GSRs of large magnitude by making a reward contingent on such a response. These results are suspect because of the ease with which a GSR may be produced as an artifact of skeletal movements, but they illustrate one type of experiment which might refute Mowrer's view. Things are clearer in the case of the classical conditioning of skeletal responses. Several responses of this type have been conditioned classically: the eyeblink and finger withdrawal are common laboratory procedures; the knee jerk can, with difficulty, be classically conditioned; a tensing of the vocal cords revealed by a rise in pitch of the voice was conditioned in a clever experiment by Taylor (1933). The bulk of the evidence, thus, suggests that Mowrer's distinction is not exactly right.

Turner and Solomon (1962) began their study of human avoidant conditioning with the concept of a *dimension* of reflexiveness which they thought would be related to the *ease* of conditioning a response classically or instrumentally. They ended their discussion proposing a *dichotomy* related to the *possibility* of conditioning a response classically or instrumentally. Responses which would be called reflexive or highly reflexive (depending on whether the discussion is couched in terms of the dimension or the dichotomy) have these characteristics: short latency, confined to a limited part of the body, delivers little proprioceptive or exteroceptive feedback, and typically has a high probability of occurrence. After a detailed examination of their data, Solomon and Turner make a good case for the proposition that responses characterized by these features can be conditioned only classically and that responses lacking these features can be conditioned only instrumentally. They raise, but do not answer the question of whether a response which is reflexive in one situation may become nonreflexive in another.

Another cluster of theorists have offered dichotomies related to the mode of evocation of classically and instrumentally conditionable responses. Skinner (1938) distinguishes between *elicited* (*respondent*) and *emitted* (*operant*) behavior. Elicited responses are reactions to identifi-

An Introduction to Two-Process Theory

able stimuli; emitted responses occur spontaneously and as reactions to stimuli whose existence we may want to postulate but cannot demonstrate in fact. Skinner proposes that reactions of the first type participate only in cases of classical conditioning (in Skinner's terms, *respondent conditioning* or *Type S conditioning*); responses of the latter type are subject to instrumental learning (*operant* or *Type R conditioning*).

Skinner also proposed that certain related features distinguish between respondents and operants: (1) respondents (e.g., salivation) may be described without reference to external objects whereas operants (e.g., seizing, chewing, swallowing *food*) require reference to an external object. (2) At the outset of conditioning, the S-R correlation (reflex) is normally zero in the case of respondents; in instrumental conditioning, the reflex has an appreciable value. Thus (3) operant conditioning involves a modification of the strength of the reflex whereas in respondent conditioning there is the establishment of a reflex *de novo*.

Other writers have suggested additional distinguishing criteria. Hilgard and Marquis (1940) and several others have noted that, in classical conditioning, the CR and UR are of the same general kind, but that in instrumental conditioning they are normally different. It has also been suggested that there is a true separation of the responses that can be conditioned classically and instrumentally and that these classes of reaction correspond to what we call "voluntary" and "involuntary" reactions (Kimble, 1964). This position is not unlike Skinner's, but it has the virtue of a blunt use of these terms which may force psychology to deal with an issue which it has refused to face for decades.

Voluntary vs. involuntary responses

Some responses, such as the eyeblink, appear to be elicitable in either of two ways, reflexly or involuntarily as an automatic response to an external stimulus, and voluntarily through some other mechanism. A question that arises almost at once is this: Is the *conditioned* form of the eyeblink

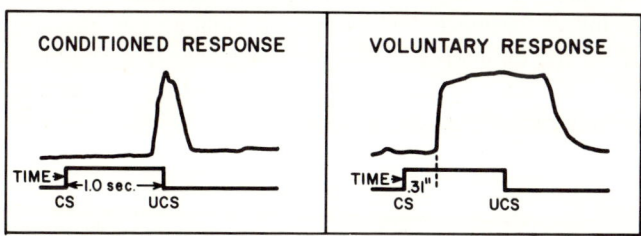

FIGURE 15-1. Characteristic forms of involuntary and voluntary responses.

a voluntary response or an involuntary response? One group of investigators (e.g. Kimble, 1964; Spence, 1964) maintain that there are two different forms of response which can be distinguished by the shorter latency and altered form of the voluntary response (see Figs. 15-1 and 15-2). Although this point seldom comes through strongly in discussions of this problem, it seems obvious that voluntary responses (assuming for the moment the validity of the distinction) are instrumentally rather than classically conditioned.

The importance of coming to a decision about the validity of the voluntary-involuntary distinction is that a basic matter of experimental practice is at stake. If the distinction is sound, it seems very likely that the two forms of reaction will not figure in exactly the same way in the psychology of learning. Thus, one should limit experimental observations to one form of reaction or the other and not consider these two forms as the same reaction. This reasoning has led certain investigators (Spence and Ross, 1959; Kimble, 1964) to exclude from their data responses of the voluntary type, as well as "voluntary responders" whose "conditioned" reactions are predominantly of the voluntary form. Obviously the procedure is proper if the initial assumption of two forms of response is correct.

Another group of investigators (Moore & Gormezano, 1961) maintain that the original distinction is *not* correct, that there is only one form of reaction in eyelid conditioning, and that the discarding of data on the basis of this false dichotomy is indefensible. These latter writers hold that the shortened latency and particular form of the so-called "voluntary" response in Figure 15-1 are to be treated as quantitative indexes of the strength of the response. What others call voluntary responses are nothing more than particularly strong CRs of the same type as all others.

The latter point of view has two points in its favor. (1) It is difficult to provide general rules that distinguish sharply between the two forms of response. (2) The concept of volition is not easy to operationalize and seems to bring back to psychology an impalpable spirit-like entity which the field strove for decades to eliminate. On the other hand, to eliminate a concept or a distinction just because there are practical problems or because the distinction violates our prejudices is obviously not to the long-term good of the science. It is important at least to keep an open mind on the matter and to allow the argument to be settled by facts rather than by polemics.

Reinforcement

Several theorists (e.g. Skinner, 1935; Schlosberg, 1937) have noted that classical and instrumental CRs appear to serve different biological

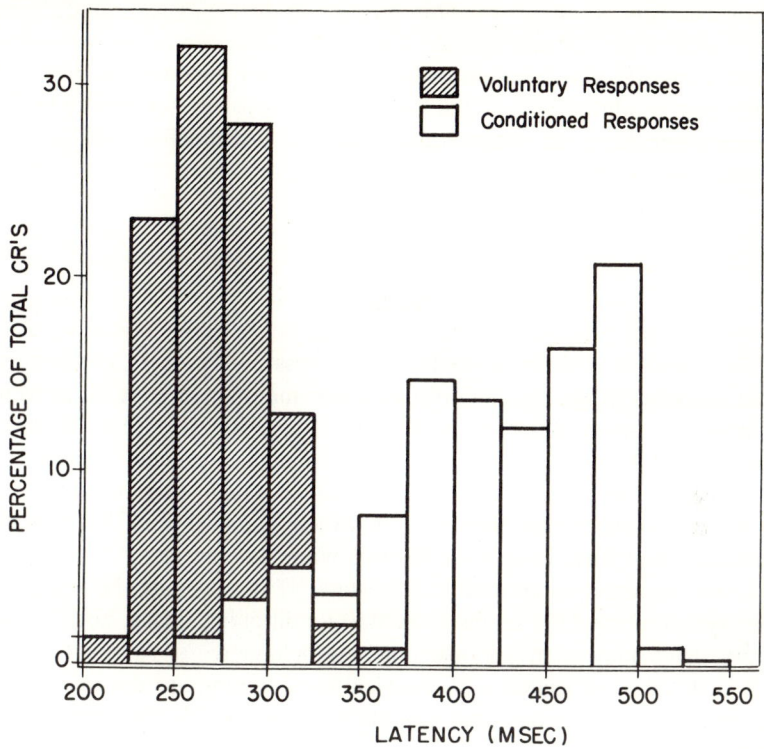

FIGURE 15-2. Distribution of latencies of instructed (voluntary) and uninstructed (involuntary, conditioned) responses. [*Unpublished data, G. A. Kimble.*]

functions. Classical CRs serve a "signalizing" function, that is, they prepare the organism for the appearance of a biologically significant, or "reinforcing" stimulus; instrumental CRs produce these stimuli and allow the organism to cope with them. It has often been alleged, in addition, that the signalizing function is more primitive and less demanding on the nervous system than the adaptive function of instrumental acts.

The concept that classical conditioning serves a signaling function leads fairly naturally to the hypothesis that it is the onset of US that provides reinforcement in such learning. If one takes the position that the US has motivational significance, this means that the postulated mechanism of reinforcement for classical conditioning is an increase in drive or *drive induction*. Drive induction, of course, is exactly the opposite of the mechanism of *drive reduction,* commonly regarded as providing reinforcement for instrumentally conditioned responses. These statements suggest the theory of reinforcement most commonly advocated by two-process theorists. This position is that classical conditioning entails a mechanism of *contiguity,* that conditioning occurs as a result of the mere temporal juxtaposition of conditioned and unconditioned stimuli. Instrumental conditioning, on the other hand, involves tension reduction or some other form of satisfaction. That is, instrumental conditioning obeys the *law of effect.*

SUMMARY

This chapter is devoted to the uniprocess-multiprocess controversy. Certain theorists (e.g., Hull, Guthrie) have maintained that all learning is basically the same; others have held that there are two (e.g., Skinner) or more (e.g., Tolman) forms of learning. The two-process position has been presented here. The theorists who have taken this position have most often maintained a distinction between classical and instrumental conditioning and have proposed the following differentiae:

1. In classical conditioning the state of drive may be identified by the nature of the UR. In instrumental conditioning this is not the case and any drive may motivate instrumental behavior.

2. The cues associated with classical conditioning are discrete events; those involved in instrumental conditioning are stable features of the environment.

3. The responses that are classically and instrumentally conditionable differ. Classically conditionable responses are reflexive, elicited, involuntary and largely autonomically mediated. Those that are instrumentally conditionable are nonreflexive, emitted, voluntary and largely mediated by the skeletal nervous system.

4. The basic principle of reinforcement is suggested to be (CS-US or CS-UR) contiguity in classical conditioning and the law of effect in instrumental learning.

None of these distinguishing criteria has gone uncriticized, however, and each point represents a focus of experimental and theoretical dispute.

16

The Relationship Between Success and the Laws of Conditioning[1]

HAROLD SCHLOSBERG

The purpose of the present paper is to differentiate between two types of learning, namely, that involving simple conditioning, and that involving the law of effect. First, I shall describe the particular results which brought the question to my attention, and show that these results are related to two different sets of "laws" of learning. I shall then survey a number of classical conditioning experiments in an attempt to see how well the differentiation has been made in the past. Next I shall develop the thesis that there are two somewhat different types of learning:

(1) Simple conditioning, which applies particularly to diffuse, preparatory responses.

(2) "Effect" learning, which applies particularly to precise, adaptive responses, and makes greater demands upon the nervous system than does simple conditioning.

Finally, I shall discuss the original experiments in light of this tentative distinction, and point out the implications.

In a series of three papers (Schlosberg, 1934c, 1936; Kappauf & Schlosberg, 1937) and several abstracts (Schlosberg, 1932, 1934a,b; Schlosberg & Kappauf, 1935), a number of experiments on conditioned responses in the white rat have been described. The animal was always restrained in a holder, while auditory or visual stimuli were presented in conjunction with a shock to the tail or to the foreleg. One of the most notable results to emerge from these experiments was the greater effectiveness of an unavoidable shock, as compared to one that could be avoided or terminated by the appropriate response. These results are consistent with traditional laws of conditioning, and may be attributed to differences in the duration and frequency of shocks involved in the two methods. In the first place, the duration of the unavoidable shock was set by a timer at either .16 second or .33 second. The duration

[1] Reprinted from the *Psychological Review*, 1937, 44.

of the avoidable shock was determined by the latency of the withdrawal movement, and usually fell below .1 second. With such short intervals the difference in duration was roughly equivalent to a variation in the strength of the shock, so that the unavoidable (fixed) shock would be expected to be more effective as an unconditioned stimulus. The results indicated that this was true, since breathing, tail and leg responses were conditioned more readily with the fixed than with the avoidable shock. In the second place, if the conditioned stimulus preceded the shock by a moderate interval (.33 second) a prompt conditioned leg movement would actually prevent the shock. Thus, "reinforcement" ceased as soon as a conditioned flexion reflex started to develop and "extinction" might have been expected. This is exactly what did happen (Schlosberg, 1936). One rat that had already developed a stable conditioned flexion with a shock of fixed duration was changed to the avoidable shock situation. The first few responses avoided the shock, and the response waned as extinction set in. This led to additional reinforcement, which built up the response, until the rat was again avoiding the shock. This sequence was repeated over and over again, through six sessions of 16 buzz-shock stimulations each. Thus, it seems clear that the response established in these experiments closely followed the usual laws of conditioning.

These results are in marked contrast with those reported by Hunter (1935), and by Culler.[2] Hunter studied the white rat in a circular alley. A light or buzzer preceded the charging of the floor of the alley by 2 seconds. Much more rapid "conditioning" occurred if the shock was omitted every time the animal ran in response to the buzzer or light than was obtained when the animal was shocked every time, regardless of its response. Culler reported that Brogden found comparable results with the use of a rotating device, similar to an activity cage. Why are these results in complete contrast to mine?

It is immediately apparent that the difference between the two sets of results is not peculiar to the experiments described above. Indeed, the contradiction seems to be between two different sets of laws of learning, namely, those of conditioning, and those of trial and error learning. Many attempts have been made to reduce both sets to a single system. It is not our present concern to decide whether or not such reduction can ultimately be made. The important points are that there are two different methods of modifying the behavior of an animal through experimental stimulation, and that there are certain marked differences between the generalizations which are drawn from the two methods. A complete description, whether operational or otherwise, must not neglect these differences. Perhaps the most important difference is that which

[2] Culler reported the work of Brogden in his symposium paper at the 1936 meetings of the American Psychological Association.

Success and the Laws of Conditioning

is often formulated as the Law of Effect. This law was proposed to account for the fixation of successful responses and the elimination of unsuccessful ones. It has been seriously criticized on the grounds of circularity and of embracing several different elements. . . . [In spite of these criticisms, however,] the law seems to refer to certain phenomena that are important. In other words, the concept of effect, despite its inadequacies, seems to be an essential one in the description of trial and error learning, at least at the present stage of our knowledge.

Fortunately, no reference need be made to effect in our statement of the laws of the conditioned response. The first of these laws would indicate that paired presentation of a new (conditioned) and old (unconditioned) stimulus, under certain intensive and temporal conditions, leads to the development of a conditioned response. A second major law would indicate that the repeated presentation of the conditioned stimulus without the unconditioned one leads to a weakening of the conditioned response (experimental extinction). These two laws were first proposed by Pavlov, and have received repeated verification. If one wished to plan an experiment to study the detailed operation of these laws, he would be particularly careful to control the intensive and temporal characteristics of the stimuli which he planned to present to the animal. He would, therefore, arrange his apparatus so that the conditioned response *could not* increase or decrease the effectiveness of the unconditioned stimulus. In dealing with shock, for example, he would deliver the unconditioned stimulus without regard to the "success" or the "failure" of the animal to withdraw the forepaw. For a response which prevented the shock would be expected to lead to extinction (Hull, 1929; Schlosberg, 1936), and a response that shortened the duration of the shock should make it less effective as a conditioning agent. This is exactly opposite to what one would expect from the law of effect, in which "successful" responses are fixated.

Theoretical consideration, therefore, would lead us to avoid any possibility of success or of failure in a conditioning situation. To what extent has this practice been followed in the large number of experiments that have supposedly been carried out by the conditioning method? Let us make a survey of such studies, and attempt to see whether or not "success" is relevant in each of them. Our criterion of success or failure of the conditioned response will be the effect the response has on the unconditioned stimulus. Further, whether or not a response is to be called "successful" will depend upon the nature of the unconditioned stimulus. Thus, a conditioned response will be considered successful if it prevents or terminates a "nociceptive" unconditioned stimulus, or if, on the other hand, it leads to, or increases, a "beneceptive" unconditioned stimulus. Conditioned responses will be "unsuccessful" in the reverse cases. Unfortunately there is no very good way of deciding whether a given stimulus is nociceptive or beneceptive. These terms are used because they are a bit less objectionable than others that might be employed. Despite the lack of objectivity of the terms, it is quite clear that careful observers would agree on extreme cases, such as the successfulness of a response that avoids or lessens a shock, and of the reaction that obtains food (or more or less food) for a hungry animal. There will also be cases in which observers would be less willing to agree on the adaptive value of the response, and perhaps some on which many would agree that the concept of success is quite irrelevant. With these facts in mind, we may now proceed to examine the conditioned response experiments, and make somewhat tentative judgments as to whether or not the conditioned response influences the unconditioned stimulus in a way that most observers would characterize as "successful."

The conditioned eyelid reflex, as studied by Hilgard and Marquis (1935), would be judged quite successful in avoiding the puff of air that served as the unconditioned stimulus. It is also probable that a conditioned closure of the lid would decrease the stimulating value of a tap delivered to the lower lid, which served as the unconditioned stimulus in experiments performed by Switzer (1930) and by Shipley (1933). It is more difficult to see the adaptive value of the conditioned lid reflex in the specific situation utilized by Cason (1922a), where a shock to the cheek served as the unconditioned stimulus. Finally, most observers would probably agree that the conditioned lid reflex in Hilgard's original experiment (1931) was nonadaptive as far as that situation was concerned. Closure of the lid in response to the conditioned stimulus, a light, could certainly have had no effect on the unconditioned stimulus, a sharp sound. It is not implied that the conditioning process which makes such reaction possible has no adaptive value in general, but rather that, in this particular situation, the conditioned response developed can be called neither successful nor unsuccessful. In other words, one cannot say that the law of effect, as stated above, is pertinent to this experiment.

The knee jerk has been conditioned by a number of experimenters. The successfulness of the conditioned knee jerk would seem to be as near zero as one could imagine. As a matter of fact, I chose this reflex for my first study of the conditioning process (Schlosberg, 1928) because it seemed unlikely that human subjects would complicate the situation by verbal decisions as to what they should do. I have suggested, however, in another paper (1932) that such complications do come in and obscure the conditioning process. We must consider not only the effect of subtle attitudes and self-administered instructions but also the fact that the conditioned response may either increase the effectiveness of the tap on the tendon, by making it more taut, or may decrease its stimulating value by causing the hammer to hit the shin of the extended leg, depending upon the height of the early kick. Considering these complications, most observers would agree that the law of effect is not unambiguously applicable to the conditioned knee jerk.

Now let us turn our attention to the so-called "alimentary" reflexes. In Pavlov's laboratory and in the others in which his technique is used, the organism under investigation receives food whether it salivates or not. In this sense the conditioned response is neither a success nor a failure. But it is possible that the copious conditioned secretion of saliva enhances the stimulating value of the dry meat powder usually used as the unconditioned stimulus. In that respect, the CR might be called adaptive. However, we would probably find our observers in disagreement as to whether or not this conditioned response should be called successful. They might be more nearly willing to agree to the adaptive value of conditioned salivary secretion based upon acid as the unconditioned stimulus, for the saliva dilutes the acid and decreases its stimulating value. They might also be willing to agree to the *lack* of adaptive value of conditioned feeding responses as established by Krasnagorski (1926), Mateer (1918), and Marquis (1931), since the preparatory movements of the jaws, etc., did not determine whether or not the child was to be fed.

The conditioned iris reflex, as established by Cason (1922), might be said to be successful in that it did prepare the eye for the change of illumination that served as the unconditioned stimulus. But the same cannot be said, without fear of contradiction, for the second- and third-order conditioned reflexes established on the same unconditioned reflex. And when we consider some of the other unconditioned reflexes that are related to the autonomic nervous system such as vomiting, urination, diuresis, defecation, and immunity reactions, it becomes quite futile even to attempt to evaluate the effects of the conditioned response on the unconditioned stimulus.

Let us turn now to a discussion of the conditioned reactions based upon shock. The papers devoted to experiments with these responses probably outnumber those devoted to all other types of conditioned reactions. The responses to shock may be grouped under two classes, namely, those responses, usually of skeletal muscle, that would remove the member from the locus of the shock, and those reactions of muscle and gland that result from the shock but are not specific to the shocked area. The former are called "withdrawal" or "flexion" reflexes or responses and are sometimes classified as "defense" reactions. The less specific reactions have no convenient generic name. They include various changes in the breathing rhythm, pulse rhythm, electrical skin resistance, body volume, pitch of voice, and tonic change. Such responses may be referred to as emotional, attentional, anticipatory, or preparatory. They "condition" rather readily. But they probably do not materially modify the effectiveness of the unconditioned stimulus, even though they may occur as conditioned responses before the unconditioned stimulus. Their success is debatable, in the particular situation in which they are elicited. It may be true that increased tonus makes it possible for the organism to react more promptly to the shock, but increased tonus, of itself, does not prevent the shock. As a matter of fact, the work of Jacobson (1929) makes it seem likely that increased tension or tonus actually increases the effectiveness of the shock. Therefore, the writer believes that these reactions do not offer a really clear-cut example of "effect."

If we turn, however, to the actual withdrawal of the stimulated member, the situation is very different. A conditioned withdrawal, if it occurs soon enough, may completely prevent the shock, *if* the electrodes are not attached to the stimulated member. The organism has been free to remove its member from the shocking grill in practically all of the conditioned response studies utilizing the withdrawal response with human subjects. Bechterev (1932) used a key with two electrodes to deliver the shock. Watson (1916), who introduced the method to this country, designed an apparatus with an indifferent electrode under the palm and a stimulating electrode at the fingertip. The numerous experimenters who have followed these pioneers continued to use electrodes from which the hand would be withdrawn in response to the shock. The law of effect seems quite pertinent to these studies, for the conditioned response is successful if it prevents or terminates the shock. This is especially true if the conditioned stimulus is presented soon enough to permit the withdrawal of the member before the stimulating current flows through the electrodes. Then there is the further consideration of symbolic processes. The human subject may integrate the instructions, the immediate stimuli, and the possible responses at a verbal level, and then decide on the response to be made. . . .

If we turn to the consideration of this reflex in animals, we no longer have the same difficulties with instructions. But we do find two distinct methods of presenting the shock. A number of studies have been made in which the shock is delivered through a grill from which the animal may withdraw its shocked, or to-be-shocked, member. In these experiments, the law of effect might be expected to operate. The same is true for the experiments in which the electrode is attached to the animal, but the shock is terminated by the response through the use of a switch. This latter method has been used by the present writer (1934c), by James (1934), and by Culler (1934). In other experiments, the electrode is attached to the leg and the shock is presented whether the animal responds to the conditioned stimulus or not. In the latter experiments the law of effect seems irrelevant. It seems to the writer that these latter experiments are more in accord with the usual definition of the conditioned response. For example, in Warren's dictionary we find the following: "conditioned response = a response, whether simple or elaborated, which, though originally not arousable by a given stimulus, has come to be arousable by it as a result of simultaneous or nearly simultaneous presentation of the latter along with some stimulus that had been potent to arouse the response in question."

According to this definition, which is quite typical, temporal contiguity of stimulus and response is the significant factor in describing the conditioned response. It would seem, therefore, that any situation in which the conditioned response materially affected the unconditioned stimulus, thus involving additional factors, would not be a typical conditioned response. This distinction has not often been made.[3] The present writer has already suggested it briefly (1934c, p. 322).

Skinner, in a recent paper (1935), has clearly analyzed two types of simple stimulus-response situations and differentiated between them. His Type II conditioned response is clearly *the* conditioned response as defined above. Skinner also described a situation in which one response leads to another stimulus response sequence. He chose to call the behavior resulting from such situations conditioned response Type I. The present writer would prefer to call such situations by some other name, such as "problem-solving," to avoid confusion. But he is completely in agreement with Skinner in separating the two types of situations. Both Skinner[4] and the present writer believe that a situation such as that used to establish the conditioned withdrawal response in man and that used by Culler and by Hunter for animals are composites of both types of situations described above. That is, to say the original withdrawal is a result of simple conditioning, but it is fixated by its success in avoiding the shock. That this fixation occurs is demonstrated by Culler's and Hunter's reports that learning develops more rapidly under the avoidable shock situation than it does under the fixed shock of more typical conditioning situations. Thus, "effect" seems to mask or counterbalance the extinguishing effects of the omitted reinforcements, to such an extent that the response is actually fixated more rapidly than it is under regular reinforcement.

---

[3] It is worth noting that most experimenters who have used flexion as the unconditioned reflex have tacitly assumed something akin to the law of effect by using an unattached (and hence avoidable) electrode. On the other hand, those who have been most interested in breathing, galvanic skin reactions, etc., have tended to use an attached electrode, administering the shock regardless of the response. This is most clearly illustrated in the work of Watson (1916). When he studied the withdrawal of the hand or foot, he used an unattached electrode and even referred to the shock as "punishment." But when he studied only breathing reactions, as in birds, the electrodes were firmly attached to the animal, and the shock was delivered every time. But, to the writer's knowledge, no experimenter had even mentioned that these two techniques were different, much less demonstrated the advantage of either, prior to the first paper of this series (Schlosberg, 1934c).

[4] According to private communication.

In some experimental situations, then, the conditioned response cannot be considered either successful or unsuccessful, since it cannot affect the unconditioned stimulus. This would seem to be the conventional type of conditioned response. But in other experimental situations the response has the possibility of being successful, and of modifying the unconditioned stimulus (gaining a reward, or avoiding a punishment).

It will be noted from what has been previously stated that those conditioned responses to which the law of effect seemed most clearly irrelevant were largely of a tonic or diffuse nature, and that in general they prepared the organism for future action. It is these responses that seem to condition most readily and regularly as has been proven in the conditioning of breathing, glandular secretions and galvanic skin responses. (Indeed, this idea was held by Pavlov, as shown by his use of the term "signal reflex" as a synonym for conditioned reflex.) For example, Razran, in his excellent review of conditioned responses in children, concludes (1933, p. 99), "A response involving wide-spread bodily action (emotional?) is faster conditioned than a response concentrated in few effectors." This conclusion is based upon a fairly large number of studies. Liddell finds that "When a new conditioned reflex is being established, movement of the head, in conjunction with the respiratory and psycho-galvanic reactions to the approaching shock, is always observed before the anticipatory movement of the foreleg appears" (Liddell, James, & Anderson, 1934, p. 45). He also indicates that the diffuse responses are more susceptible to experimental extinction than are the more specific ones. Similar results for the rat have already been reported (Schlosberg, 1934c).

Other points in favor of this view can easily be found. Thus, the fact that the conditioned response tends to occur before the unconditioned stimulus almost invites one to call it "anticipatory." Finally, the differences between conditioned and unconditioned responses argue in the same direction. . . .

Now consider those responses to which the law of effect seems most relevant. They are all of the type in which the organism does something to the reinforcing stimulus. Thus, in a maze the animal actually approaches food, or gets off a charged grill. This type of behavior may conveniently be called "problem-solving." The present writer would place the experiments of Hunter and of Culler and Brogden in this class.

It is thus possible to make a rough, and perhaps superficial distinction between diffuse preparatory responses, to which the laws of conditioning apply in a direct fashion, and precise adaptive responses, in which the law of effect seems relevant. The distinction, in common with most of those that are drawn in the biological sciences, is not to be construed too rigidly. Further, it is quite possible that the distinction is not an ultimate one, and that the facts referred to under the law of effect may eventually be reduced to terms of conditioning. . . . But the distinction has some merit in ordering certain of the experimental results obtained in the field of learning.

If the distinction is applied to the conflicting results that were described at the beginning of this paper, it becomes apparent that *all* of the responses in the writer's experiments must be classed as tonic or diffuse. For breathing, tail lashing, and squealing, this is a very satisfactory description as far as the present writer is concerned. The nature of the leg withdrawal is not so obvious. It would seem at first glance to be specific, and the question immediately arises as to why the rat cannot learn to "solve the problem" of avoiding the shock by a foreleg flexion. The clue to the answer may be found in some observations made by James (1934). He reported that there was great difficulty in establishing a foreleg flexion in guinea pigs, but that they learned to run from a shock with relative ease. It seems difficult in the rodents studied to isolate the foreleg flexion from its larger whole, running away. If the rat is restrained in a holder, it cannot run, and becomes frightened and excited. The foreleg response remains a response preparatory to running away, instead of being isolated as a precise adaptive response. The rat can develop specific foreleg responses in other less exciting situations (cf. Skinner's lever situation). Higher mammals, such as dogs, can develop precise foreleg reactions even when restrained in a holder, and the law of effect seems to apply as well in these situations as it does to those where rats are free to run.

Further light is shed on the problem by the results of Culler, [Girden and their] associates (1934, 1936) on conditioning in dogs. A normal dog passes through two stages in his training. At first the conditioned response is diffuse, widespread, and violent. Gradually the precise foreleg response develops, just strong enough to avoid the shock. The authors refer to this final stage of conditioning as "adaptive." A decorticate dog is not able to reach this stage, never getting beyond the level of diffuse, "massive" conditioning. Thus, the behavior of a decorticate dog seems to resemble rather closely that of the normal rat in the writer's experiments. This immediately suggests that a certain degree of cortical development is necessary for the formation of precise adaptive responses. The rat has a cortex which is adequate for the development of adaptive behavior of the whole animal, such as running to avoid shock. But it is not sufficiently differentiated to permit the breaking up of this behavior into segmental responses, such as the lifting of a single fore-paw to prevent the shock. The fore-paw movement remains part of the larger response, and cannot function separately as an adaptive bit of behavior.

The implications of this discussion are worthy of some brief attention. In the first place, it has indicated that there is a type of modification of behavior which depends solely on the paired presentation of a conditioned and an unconditioned stimulus. The progress of this modification will depend upon the number of pairings, their temporal and intensive characteristics, and upon the condition of the organism. Further, this modification may be broken down by the repeated isolated presentation of the conditioned stimulus. This type of modification makes rather meager demands on the nervous system, and may even be established in decorticate animals. But in certain situations, higher animals may show behavior which is superficially inconsistent with these principles. A second process seems to cut across, preventing extinction, and resulting in the rapid fixation of the successful response. This second process is covered by the law of effect. It seems to be dependent on a more highly developed nervous system than does simple conditioning. Since this latter type of modification shows certain "operational" differences, it is suggested that it be given a separate name, as "trial and error learning," or "problem-solving," and should not be called "conditioning."

A second general implication of this discussion may be pointed out, although this is not the place to develop it further. It seems quite possible that the diffuse anticipatory responses which result from conditioning of the sort carried out by the writer are the correlate of the "expectancies" of Tolman (1934), and of comparable concepts developed by others. Indeed, after explaining the experiments to his non-professional friends, and describing the conditioned inspirations, squeals, and leg movements, the writer has often been told, "You mean that the animal comes to expect the shock." Thus, it seems possible that the distinction between the diffuse conditioned responses, and the more precise adaptive responses established by trial and error, may well give an objective basis for the distinction between learning and performance which has been proposed by certain writers. This is, of course, suggested as a very tentative hypothesis, and not as an essential part of the present paper.

SUMMARY AND CONCLUSIONS

1. In certain shock situations "success" seems to fixate the response which prevents the shock. In other situations, successful avoidance of the shock leads to extinction. One result is consistent with the law of effect, while the other agrees with the laws of conditioning.

2. A large number of different conditioning situations were surveyed. In many cases the concept of success seemed quite irrelevant, since the conditioned response could not modify the unconditioned stimulus. These are examples of simple conditioning. In other experiments there was the possibility that the "law of effect" would cut across the simple conditioning. These experiments might well be referred to by a different name, as trial and error learning, or problem-solving.

3. Conditioning is particularly effective for diffuse anticipatory responses, and apparently demands a less complicated nervous mechanism than does the precise adaptive behavior involved in problem solving.

4. Since these two methods of modifying behavior seem markedly different, at least at a superficial level, clarity of contemporary thought demands that they do not both receive the name of "conditioning."

17

An Experimental Approach to the Problem of Mechanism of Alimentary Conditioned Reflex, Type II

W. WYRWICKA[1]

This article is representative of the type of theorizing currently being done within the Pavlovian tradition by such investigators as Asratyan, Konorski and their associates. Without question, the present-day Pavlovian investigator whose interests are closest to those of American psychology is Professor Jerzy Konorski of the Nencki Institute in Warsaw. Konorski was among the first to recognize the operational distinction between classical (Type I) and instrumental (Type II) conditioned reflexes. Much of the work of Konorski's laboratory has been directed at the development of a neurophysiological theory of the latter type of conditioning. Professor Konorski has graciously prepared and granted me permission to publish a brief biographical sketch. Slightly edited, it follows:

I was born in Lodz, Poland, in 1903. From 1922 I studied medicine in the University of Warsaw, where I obtained my M.D. degree in 1929. My close colleague and friend was Stefan Miller, murdered by the Nazis in 1942. We decided to become psychiatrists with the vague idea of understanding in this way the mental processes in man.

In 1927 we came across the classical book of Pavlov on conditioned reflexes which had been just issued. We hadn't heard before about Pavlovian studies in this field—hardly anybody in Poland had. From the very first moment we became immensely fascinated by this book; we studied it again and again, and knowing a bit of Russian, we read the original papers of Pavlov's associates. And so, after some time, we became quite well acquainted with Pavlov's work and ideas which seemed to us the only scientific approach to the understanding of mental phenomena of animals and man.

---

[1] The author is very grateful to Prof. J. Konorski for his interest in this work, many discussions and valuable criticism. Many thanks are due to Dr. E. Fonberg, Mgr. W. Lawicka and Mgr. I. Stepien for critical reading of the manuscript as well as to Dr. M. Mishkin for helpful discussion and correction of the English translation.

However, after some time we began to realize that there was an omission in the Pavlovian work on conditioned reflexes, since it did not take into consideration the motor behavior of animals, which to our mind could not be reduced to Pavlovian conditioning [and thus constituted a different variety of conditioned reflex, conditioned reflexes of the "second type"]. We planned a number of experiments designed to prove our concepts, and the practical problem arose to find the laboratory in which we could perform them.

In that time there was in Warsaw beside the regular university the so-called "Free Polish University," in which Dr. Jacob Segal was a professor of psychology. He showed a full understanding of our troubles and allowed us to carry out our experimental work on a dog in his department. And thus we established a very modest laboratory on conditioned reflexes, in which we performed the crucial experiments in which four varieties of motor conditioned reflexes were separated. We have called these reflexes Type II CRs to distinguish them from Pavlovian CRs which we called Type I. We published the first two papers on the subject in *Comptes Rendus de Soc. de Biol.*, 1928, vol. 99, and wrote a letter to Pavlov telling him about our results.

Pavlov was, undoubtedly, much impressed by our work, although he totally rejected our ideas concerning the distinctness of Type II CR from Type I. However, he proposed that we should come to Leningrad to discuss with him the whole problem, and he invited us to work for some time in his laboratory.

We succeeded in going to Leningrad in the end of 1931, and I remained there for nearly two years [Dr. Miller was obliged to leave earlier because of his duties as a psychiatrist]. During that time I became thoroughly acquainted with the methods and achievements of the Pavlovian school, and the work in close contact with Pavlov was for me a unique and unforgettable experience. Although I later came into opposition to a number of particular Pavlovian concepts, I consider myself his follower in all his basic ideas.

After my return home in 1933, Dr. Miller and I established a small laboratory of conditioned reflexes in the Nencki Institute of Experimental Biology where we continued to work on Type II conditioning. Unfortunately, a great part of the results of our work was destroyed during the bombardment of Warsaw.

Already in the period preceding the war it became more and more clear to me that although the *general* Pavlovian approach to the phenomena of animal behavior was sound and fruitful, his neurophysiological theory of the functioning of the brain was rather foreign in respect to the modern ideas of the functioning of the nervous system. Moreover, I became convinced that it was possible to resystematize the huge experimental material gathered by the Pavlov school, and to make it congruent to, and a regular part of, the contemporary neurophysiology. This attempt was undertaken by me, and the monograph "Conditioned Reflexes and Neuron Organization" published in 1948 by the Cambridge University Press was the result of my considerations.

As soon as the war came to an end, a small group of the former scientific workers of the Nencki Institute who survived decided to restore our Institute. This was done with the wholehearted support of the Polish Government and the Polish Academy of Sciences. A new building was erected in Warsaw in the place of the destroyed one, and the Department of Neurophysiology of which I was a head was set up. A group of young scientific workers was selected and trained in neurophysiology, and particularly in the physiology of higher nervous activity. In this way, our common work on conditioned reflexes began.

This period of my studies is fairly well known to American scientists because of my and my colleagues' frequent visits to the U.S.A., and distribution [unfortunately still too limited] of our journal *Acta Biologiae Experimentalis* in which our papers are published. We continue to be mainly concerned with the problems of physiological mechanisms of Type II conditioning, a field in which great progress was made from the pre-war period, and with the problems of the physiological role and organization of particular parts of the brain.

In the present period I am preparing a monograph in which an attempt is made to present a synthesis of our work on conditioned reflexes and to give an idea of the integrative activity of the brain based on the contemporary achievements in this field.

Unfortunately, at this writing the monograph referred to above has not become available. It seems likely, however, that the paper of Wyrwicka, one of Konorski's associates at the Nencki Institute, will provide some feel for the style, at least, of Konorski's theory. [Ed.][2]

When a given movement performed by the animal is followed by presentation of food (or any other "rewarding" agent) then it tends to be repeated again and again till the animal [is] satiated. On the contrary, if the movement is followed by some noxious stimulus ("punishment"), its performance tends to be suppressed. These well-known types of behavior were first subjected to precise experimental investigation by Thorndike (1911) at the turn of the century. [Many years later Konorski and others] made an attempt to analyze these responses from the physiological point of view and to elucidate their neural mechanism. They have shown that the behavior based on "reward" or "punishment" can be expressed in a rigorous conditioned reflex form, i.e., as definite acquired reactions elicited by definite stimuli. They have also shown that the physiological structure of these reflexes is different from, and more complicated than that of classical Pavlovian conditioned reflex. Therefore they denoted this form of conditioned reflex as Type II in contradistinction to Type I, i.e., Pavlovian conditioned reflex. Similar responses were later called operant behavior by Skinner (1938) and instrumental responses by Hilgard and Marquis (1940).

[2] What follows is reprinted with modification from *Acta Biologiae Experimentalis,* 1960, 20, with permission of the editor. I have added a brief introductory statement relating this paper to the work of Konorski with which it must be associated [Ed.].

In recent years we have been engaged in studying the inter-central structure of conditioned reflexes Type II, using the same general experimental procedure as that applied by Konorski and Miller [see Konorski, 1948, Ch. 13]. We were concerned with alimentary conditioned reflexes Type II and were not interested so [much] in the process of their elaboration [as] in their mechanism after they had already been firmly established. . . . And so we exclusively concentrated on the problem of what is going on in nerve centers involved between the moment of application of a conditioned stimulus and the moment of appearance of the instrumental reaction. As our results seem to throw some light on this problem, we present here in short all our data collected so far, which were partly published in detail before (Wyrwicka, 1952, 1956, 1958).

It is well known that an alimentary conditioned reflex Type II reaches its full value only in a hungry animal which shows a sufficiently high level of alimentary excitability [and that instrumental reactions are diminished or completely absent when the experiment takes place when the animal is satiated just before the experiment, i.e., when its alimentary excitability is reduced]. Therefore if we consider the conditioned reflex a process brought about by the acquired connections between certain brain centers, the conclusion may be drawn that the pathway of the instrumental reflex goes through a hypothetical alimentary center. A corresponding scheme may be written as in Figure 17-1. In this scheme S is the center corre-

FIGURE 17-1. Scheme I of supposed connections between the center of conditioned stimulus (S), the alimentary center (A) and the center of instrumental reaction (M), active in the course of alimentary conditioned reflex type II.

sponding to . . . a sporadic conditioned stimulus and its situational background (experimental situation), or an experimental situation alone when sporadic stimulus is not used; "A," represents the alimentary center considered as a compound of centers responsible for a state of "alimentary excitation"; "M," is the center of instrumental reaction including all motor and sensory centers responsible for accomplishment of this reaction.

The above scheme allows us to understand and even predict the following experimental facts:

1. In dogs, not previously used in experiments, the alimentary instrumental conditioned reflex of putting the foreleg on the food-tray was established to an acoustic stimulus. Then a new stimulus, the smell of ether, was introduced and, in spite of absence of the learned instrumental reaction, food reinforcement was given after 10 seconds. After several

daily experiments during which the smell of ether reinforced by food was applied twice daily, a salivary reaction at first was obtained and then the learned movement "spontaneously" appeared. In the following days the instrumental reaction to the olfactory stimulus became the same as that to the acoustic stimulus. In the same way the conditioned instrumental reaction to visual and tactile stimuli was established in these and other dogs.

According to our scheme these facts can be explained as follows. Reinforcement of the new stimulus by food causes at first the establishment of the connection $S \rightarrow A$ (Fig. 17-1) so that the new stimulus raises the excitation of the alimentary center A; the latter having been connected by previous training in the same situation with the center M, sends excitatory impulses to it and the instrumental reaction is evoked.

2. An alimentary conditioned reflex of putting the foreleg on the food-tray was established in dogs (as well as in goats and rabbits) to the experimental situation; every learned movement performed in this situation was reinforced by food. After some days of training the extinction of the reaction was performed, i.e., the learned movement ceased to appear as a result of nonreinforcement by food. When, afterwards, a portion of food was given, the instrumental reaction reappeared immediately.

It may be supposed that the lack of food reinforcement in the course of extinction makes the connection $S \rightarrow A$ "weaker," so that the conditioned stimulus (the experimental situation in this case) is no longer capable of raising the excitation of the alimentary center to a suitable level. Giving food after the extinction renews the connection $S \rightarrow A$ and then the instrumental reaction can again be evoked through the alimentary center.

3. In a dog which, on account of heat, showed a very low alimentary excitability, the conditioned stimulus was without effect, i.e., the dog did not perform the learned movement to it. When, in the absence of the instrumental reaction, the food reinforcement was given each time to the conditioned stimulus, the learned movement appeared after several trials.

This fact may be explained as follows. Giving food raises the excitation of the alimentary center and this leads to a rise of excitation of the center of the learned movement; as a result the instrumental reaction appears.

4. The movement of putting the foreleg on the food-tray to the loud bubbling of water was always reinforced by food while the same reaction to soft bubbling was never reinforced. In consequence, the soft bubbling became an inhibitory differential stimulus which did not evoke the learned movement. When, however, the inhibitory stimulus had been reinforced by food several times, it evoked the instrumental conditioned reaction though this reaction was delayed and smaller than to the positive stimulus. After several days of consistent reinforcement, the soft bubbling

elicited a conditioned reaction of normal value (Wyrwicka, 1952). A similar experiment was also performed with other inhibitory stimuli, e.g., with so-called "primary inhibitor," i.e., a stimulus different to the others and not reinforced from the very beginning (Konorski and Szwejkowska, 1952), and the same result was obtained.

In these cases the connection $S \to A$ is inactive on account of non-reinforcement of the stimulus by food (Konorski, 1948). When we change the procedure and reinforce the inhibitory stimulus, the connection $S \to A$ is renewed (or arises) and therefore this stimulus can excite the alimentary center and through it the center of the instrumental reaction.[3]

The existence of the connection $S \to A \to M$ was also shown with other methods of investigation. As is known, a center of food intake [has been] discovered in the lateral hypothalamic area. The properties of this center suggest that it corresponds to our alimentary center. According to our scheme, destruction of the feeding center resulting in aphagia [refusal to eat] should abolish all alimentary conditioned reflexes in the animal. Such experiments (Wyrwicka, 1957) were performed on 5 rabbits in which 2 instrumental conditioned reflexes were established (i.e., pushing a ring with teeth, reinforced by carrot, and scraping the food-tray with forelegs, reinforced by potatoes). Bilateral coagulation of the lateral hypothalamic area resulted in aphagia lasting 1–2 weeks and in the complete disappearance of both conditioned reflexes for a longer time. In one rabbit the conditioned reflexes did not reappear at all for 3 months, after which time the animal was sacrificed.

Our scheme suggests on the other hand that electrical stimulation of the feeding center, which causes hyperphagia, should excite the center [A] and thus evoke the instrumental reaction. Corresponding experiments were performed on unanaesthesized goats (Wyrwicka, Dobrzecka and Tarnecki, 1959). Using Hess' method (Hess, 1949) adapted for goats by Andersson (1951), weak stimulation (about 1 V, 50 imp./sec.) of the lateral hypothalamic area, i.e., the feeding center, in completely satiated goats evoked the previously established conditioned reaction of putting the left foreleg on the food-tray and eating food given as reinforcement. A prolonged stimulation evoked learned movements and eating alternately up to interruption of the stimulation. Similar stimulation of the hypothalamic "drinking center" (Andersson, 1952, 1953) evoked the instrumental reaction which in previous training was reinforced by water (Andersson and Wyrwicka, 1957). Analogous facts were described by Miller (1957)....

---

[3] It is especially to be noted that the concept, excitation of the alimentary center, is hypothesized in this account to be a function of two very different sets of experimental operations: Those capable of producing what we would call hunger and those defining what some have called incentive. Extinction is thus attributed to a reduction in incentive. [Ed.]

The scheme presented in Figure 17-1 concerns the case when only one instrumental reaction is established in the animal in a constant experimental situation. It cannot explain and predict the behavior of an animal trained to perform various movements to various stimuli, e.g., to raise the foreleg to a visual stimulus and the hind leg to an acoustic stimulus; [nor can it explain the well-known fact that an animal in free surroundings is able to perform many varied movements connected with finding food in various circumstances and different seasons.] If merely $S \rightarrow A \rightarrow M$ connection exists, every conditioned stimulus connected with feeding should evoke all these movements. Yet this is not so. Therefore it is reasonable to admit that there is also a direct connection $S \rightarrow M$ (Fig. 17-2). If we take into account that, according to the principle of forma-

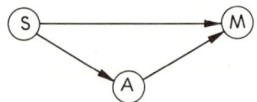

FIGURE 17-2. Scheme II of probable interrelations between brain centers in the course of an alimentary instrumental conditioned reflex. S—center of conditioned stimulus; A—alimentary center; M—center of instrumental reaction.

tion of the conditioned connections, the latter arise between all the brain centers excited at the same time, the relation $S \rightarrow M$ seems to be quite natural because the instrumental movement is performed during the action of the conditioned stimulus.

Admitting the existence of this connection we can easily explain the appearance of two different movements to two different conditioned stimuli respectively (Fig. 17-3). Each stimulus elicits only that movement which is directly connected with it by training. The assumption of the direct connection $S \rightarrow M$ is supported by the following experiments.

1. An alimentary instrumental conditioned reflex of putting the right foreleg on the food-tray to an acoustic stimulus was established in dogs in the usual experimental chamber. When the same stimulus was applied in an empty room quite unlike the chamber, the instrumental reaction did not appear; even when the acoustic stimulus was reinforced several times by pieces of meat which were eaten voraciously by the dog, the learned movement was not elicited and even a simple raising of the right foreleg was not observed. Only when the food-bowl was placed on a low bench somewhat similar to the food-tray, did the instrumental reaction appear (Wyrwicka, 1958).

This result indicates that the instrumental reaction cannot be evoked merely by excitation of the alimentary center (caused by food). Other

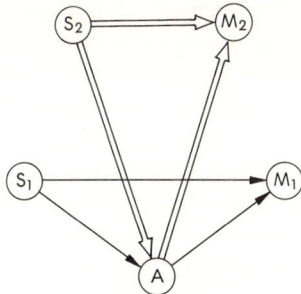

FIGURE 17-3. Schematic representation of probable connections between brain centers in the case of 2 different instrumental conditioned reflexes. S_1, S_2—centers of conditioned stimuli; A—alimentary center; M_1, M_2—centers of learned movements.

components of the training situation are also needed. This seems to support the view about the direct connection between the center of conditioned stimuli and the center of the instrumental reaction.

2. Dogs were trained for about a year to put their right forelegs on the food-tray to various stimuli and the reaction was very firmly established. The animals were completely satiated before entering the experimental chamber and the conditioned stimuli were tested. It was found that the acoustic stimuli which were considered as "strongly motogenic" (Konorski & Wyrwicka, 1952) evoked the instrumental reaction in spite of the fact that the animals refused to eat food (Wyrwicka, 1950).

This finding shows that the learned movement can appear as a result of the direct connection $S \rightarrow M$ alone, since lack of alimentary excitation has made the connection $S \rightarrow A \rightarrow M$ inactive.

3. In a dog the instrumental conditioned reflex of putting the foreleg on the food-tray was established to three stimuli: tactile stimulus applied to the same leg, tactile stimulus applied to the dog's back and sound of metronome. Then the animal was completely satiated and all the stimuli were tested. It was found that the metronome and the tactile stimulus on the back evoked the conditioned reaction in the first trials only and then were without effect, while the tactile stimulus applied to the paw elicited putting this leg on the food-tray much more permanently. However the learned movement to this stimulus was more and more delayed and finally ceased to appear. The animal refused to take food during the whole experiment despite the fact that it was presented after each application of the conditioned stimulus. It must be stressed that the appearance of the reaction cannot be considered as a defensive reflex to the tactile stimulus on the leg because the movement elicited was the pre-

viously learned complexed movement of putting the leg on the food-tray and not a simple raising leg.

This result indicates that the appearance of the learned movement of the leg to a tactile stimulus acting on the same leg does not depend on the high excitability of the alimentary center. This fact is easy to understand: the impulses from the tactile stimulus excite the center of this stimulus which is localized in the area close to the motor centers of the same leg; therefore there is a natural facilitation of the conditioned movement and a preponderance of the direct pathway $S \rightarrow M$ over the indirect one $S \rightarrow A \rightarrow M$.

SUMMARY

Impulses generated by the center of the conditioned stimulus run to the centers connected with it by training, i.e., the alimentary center as well as the center of learned reaction. In turn the alimentary center sends impulses to all centers connected with it, among them to the center of the learned movement which already is partly excited. Only then does the excitation of the center of the learned movement reach a supraliminal level and the motor reaction appear. The impulses running through the indirect pathway $S \rightarrow A \rightarrow M$ thus give the general "direction" of the reaction, i.e., alimentary in our case; however the final determinant of which movement is performed depends on the excitation of the direct pathway $S \rightarrow M$. As we see, however, the two connections under discussion do not always function equally and simultaneously, and under certain circumstances one of them can predominate.

IV

BASIC PHENOMENA AND PARAMETERS

18

The Role of Absolute Initial Response Strength in Simple Trial and Error Learning[1]

PAUL S. SIEGEL

This paper deals with the following problem. Suppose that in some learning situation, one group of subjects has two equally strong incompatible reaction tendencies, both of them *weak,* and that another group of subjects has the same two competing reaction tendencies, but both of them *strong.* Now suppose that the subjects must learn to respond with only one of the competing reactions. Which group will learn more rapidly?

In more concrete terms suppose that the situation is a simple T-maze and that two groups of rats are given different amounts of preliminary training designed to establish equally strong tendencies to turn right and to the left on any particular trial. Specifically, suppose that one group (W) receives only 4 preliminary trials, 2 forced to the right and 2 forced to the left; the other group (S) receives 80 such trials, 40 to the right and 40 to the left. Now suppose that all subjects are reinforced for a right turn but not for a left turn. Which group will learn more quickly to turn consistently right, the group (W) with two *weak* habits developed by the small number of reinforcements or the group (S) with the two *strong* habits developed by the large number of reinforcements? This experimental study seeks an answer to this question. The method is also essentially that just suggested.

Hull's (1943) theory makes a definite prediction for the outcome of this experiment. Recall (see p. 175) that the habit-growth curve proposed by Hull implies (a) the continuous development of habit strength as a function of the number of reinforcements and (b) that the increment in habit strength ($\Delta_S H_R$) is greater with each further reinforcement at low initial levels of $_S H_R$ than at higher levels. The second point assumes that habit strength develops as a simple positive growth function of the number of reinforcements.

In his dealing with the interaction of competing response tendencies, Hull assumed that the probability of occurrence of the stronger of two such tendencies depended upon the absolute magnitude of the difference between

---

[1] Reprinted from the *Journal of Experimental Psychology,* 1945, vol. 4, and revised as indicated by permission of the American Psychological Association and the author.

the strengths of the competing tendencies. It might take a difference of, say, 10 units of strength to produce a consistent response in terms of one habit rather than the other. With the concept of a negatively accelerated habit growth function, this leads to the prediction that the group of subjects with two *weak* competing habits will establish a consistent tendency more quickly than a group with *strong* competing habits since, in terms of absolute strengths, weak habits (after few reinforcements) increase more rapidly than strong habits (after many reinforcements).

The argument above does not allow any extinctive effects of nonreinforcement to be involved in the experiment. Consideration of the probable effects of such extinction, however, only reinforces the conclusion already arrived at. With low and moderate levels of learning, at least, strong habits resist extinction more than weak habits, and it should be harder to extinguish an incorrect strong habit than a weak one. Thus, for two reasons, the prediction is that the establishment of a consistent tendency to respond in a particular way will be easier when the conflicting response tendencies are weak than when they are strong. [Ed.]

Method

SUBJECTS. The experiment employed 64 albino rats, with ages ranging from 60–85 days at the beginning of the experiment. This population was drawn at random from the departmental colonies of Duke University and the University of North Carolina. In the past several years considerable inter-colony breeding has been permitted between these two laboratories.

Group W was comprised of 32 animals, 18 females and 14 males. Group S duplicated this distribution with respect to age, sex, weight, and number.

Daily rations consisted of Purina checkers with an occasional supplement of lettuce. Water was available in the home cages at all times.

APPARATUS. A conventional T-maze was employed with animal-operated push-up type retrace prevention doors. The two doors were located one at the beginning of each arm of the T. In operation they required an upward pressure of approximately 10 gm. The start box door (guillotine type) was manipulated by the experimenter by means of a short length of twine. Illumination was afforded by a 150-watt bulb suspended three feet above the center of the maze. The maze measured three feet along the arms of the T (overall) and two feet along the approach alley (including the start box). The alleys were three inches in width.

The maze was situated in a quiet part of the building and a noisy electric fan served as a sound screen at all times. Runs were conducted only during the evening hours. In the free-choice series and the learning series (see procedure, stages 3 and 4), the reward mixture was liberally scattered beneath both compartments to control odor cues.

PROCEDURE. Four convenient stages may be designated.

1. *Orientation Period:* All animals were given two weeks' experience in a straight alley situation. During this time they learned to manipulate retrace doors. They were run in a hungry condition and rewarded on crushed Purina.

2. *Preliminary Training:* By this time a temporal feeding rhythm had been well established. Throughout this stage and those that followed, both groups were run under conditions of 20 hours food deprivation (plus or minus ½ hour). A 10-second reinforcement interval was uniformly observed, and the reward mixture, presented in a small round tin pan, consisted of pulverized Purina (dry). The 10-second interval marked confinement in the reward compartment. After the initial trial all animals fully employed this time in eating.

During this stage, the two groups were treated differently. Group W received 4 forced runs in the T. Group S received 80 forced runs in the T. Forcing was effected by the addition of a stop or block at the region of choice. This served to seal off one or the other compartment while permitting entry of the opposite arm. The two running schedules are presented in Table 18-1. This stage was introduced for the purpose of establishing in Group W the two equal but weak reaction tendencies; in Group S, the two equal but strong reaction tendencies. The selection of two reinforcements and 40 reinforcements merely represents a choice of two extremes of the strength continuum. The random order of successive runs was designated to obviate recency factors, i.e., again, to establish equally strong competing tendencies in each group.

3. *Free-Choice Series:* To furnish a baseline for the final stage, both groups were given six free-choice trials during one nightly session. Both compartments of the T were accessible and the choice of either turn was followed by reinforcement. The trials were given in succession. When the animal had made a choice and had been permitted to feed for 10 seconds, he was immediately returned to the start box for another trial. Caution was exercised throughout to see that the animal had ceased chewing before his introduction to the start box. He was then placed in the box and when he had oriented in the direction of the door, it was raised quietly by the experimenter. In this manner, all animals were given six trials during this nightly series.

Running times as well as choices were recorded. The running time was defined as the interval that elapsed between the raising of the start box door by the experimenter and the closing of a retrace door behind the animal.

Essential to the experimental design was an equality of strength

TABLE 18-1

Running schedules of Group W and Group S

GROUP W

Night	Reinforced side	Number of runs
1	L	1
2	R	1
3	R	1
4	L	1
	Totals	2L
		2R

GROUP S

Night	Reinforced side	Number of runs
1	L	4
2	R	4
3	R	6
4	L	6
5	R	6
6	R	6
7	L	6
8	L	6
9	R	6
10	L	6
11	L	6
12	R	6
13	L	6
14	R	6
	Totals	40L
		40R

between the two reaction tendencies *within* both groups. For this reason, those animals that yielded a 6–0 or a 5–1 distribution of choices were discarded. That is, a 6–0 or a 5–1 distribution was regarded as indicative of a strength imbalance in favor of the more frequently occurring response. Further, this imbalance would be exaggerated by the differential reinforcement that occurred during this series. Only those animals yielding a 4–2 or a 3–3 distribution were retained. Twenty-six animals of Group W and 21 of Group S met this criterion during the free-choice series. Of the 26 in Group W, 15 yielded 3–3 distributions and 11 yielded 4–2 distributions. In Group S, there were 9 animals giving 3–3 distributions and 12 giving 4–2 distributions.

The average running time for all six trials was computed for each subject in these two selected populations. For the 26 animals of Group W, the mean of these individual averages was 21 seconds. The mean of the 21 animals of Group S was 8 seconds. The difference between these two means is 13 seconds and the t of this difference is 2.77. With 45 degrees of freedom, a t of 2.69 is significant at the one percent level.

The selection of the two populations assures approximate equality of strength between the two reaction tendencies *within* each group. A difference *between* groups in absolute level of reaction tendency strength is indicated by the difference in running times. This assumes, of course, that running time is inversely related to the strength of a reaction tendency (a commonly accepted operational definition). This fulfilled the two major demands of the experimental design. The two selected groups were then introduced to the experiment proper, the trial-and-error learning stage.

4. Learning Series: During the learning series, both compartments of the T were accessible, but the choice of only one was followed by reinforcement. When the animal took the opposite turn, he was confined in the empty compartment for a period of 10 seconds (nonreward).

To obviate idiosyncracies possible to the setup, a special control was introduced during this stage. Approximately one-half of Group W was reinforced for right turns and approximately one-half for left turns, i.e., the correct choice was made right for one-half and left for the other. These two sub-groups were designated on the basis of the distribution of choices yielded during the free-choice series. Those animals that gave a 3–3 distribution were arbitrarily assigned half right and half left. Those animals that yielded 4–2 distributions were divided between the right and left subgroups in such a way that the to-be-correct response averaged for the *entire* group approximately .50, i.e., a 50 percent or chance level of occurrence of the *correct* response was established at the outset. For example, if an animal making four left turns and two right turns during the free-choice series was placed in the to-be-reinforced on the right subgroup, there was also included an animal that had made four right choices and two left choices. In this way, the frequency of occurrence of the correct response was made to originate at a 50 percent level. This point, representing the results of the free-choice series, is referred to in the results (Fig. 1) as Session o.

Group S was similarly treated.

Both groups were then given six nightly sessions of eight trials each or 48 massed learning trials. The trials were again given in succession. The conditions of motivation and reinforcement have been indicated earlier (stage 2).

Results

Our interest centers upon the difference in learning rate between the two groups, i.e., in the speed of acquisition of the correct response

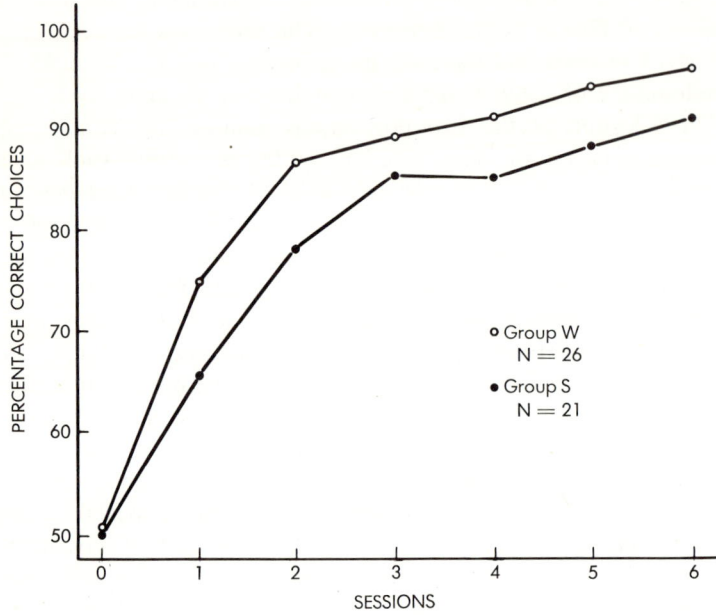

FIGURE 18-1. Mean percentages of correct choices at each session.

during the trial-and-error learning series. This interest is best served by a comparative analysis of the two curves that express the frequency of occurrence of the correct response as a function of number of trials.

Figure 18-1 depicts the growth of the correct response within each group. The points on the two curves represent simple means. Each point is the mean percentage of occurrence of the correct response for the group during a nightly session of eight trials. The initial point (Session o) has been discussed earlier. The analysis of that point is in terms of the to-be-correct response since both responses were reinforced during the series.

Discussion

Inspection of Figure 18-1 reveals a marked difference in the speed of learning of the two groups. The curve of Group W is seen to rise

The Role of Absolute Initial Response Strength

more rapidly. Every point (beyond Session 0, the baseline) exceeds the corresponding point for Group S.

An evaluation of the overall significance of this difference was made. For the 48 critical learning trials, the average number of correct responses was computed for each group. For Group W this mean was 43, sigma, 2.5; for Group S, 39, sigma, 4.1. The difference in means is 4 and the t of the difference is 3.96. Again, with 45 degrees of freedom, a t of 2.69 is significant at the one percent level. We conclude that Group W responded with a significantly larger total number of correct choices.

These results rather strongly suggest that the speed of acquisition of the correct response in a simple trial-and-error situation is some inverse function of the initial level of *absolute* strength that prevails among equally strong competing reaction tendencies. . . .

[As was mentioned briefly in the introduction to this paper, Hull's prediction of the outcome of this experiment depends upon the type of habit-growth equation proposed. Table 12-1 (p. 175) contains a more complete statement of this habit-growth function. The entries in the table show the increments of habit strength produced by several different numbers of reinforcements. Now suppose that one habit is consistently selected in preference to another when there is an absolute difference of 10 habs between them. After two reinforcements ($_sH_R = 19$) it will take only 2 reinforcements of one habit to achieve this difference, whereas after 15 reinforcements ($_sH_R = 79.4$) it will take 6 additional reinforcements. After 20 reinforcements ($_sH_R = 87.8$) it will take 15 reinforcements to produce a difference of 10 habs (values not included in the table were calculated). This increasing difficulty of learning to choose one of two equally strong habits as the individual members of the pair become stronger is consistent with the outcome of this experiment.]

SUMMARY

Sixty-four albino rats were employed in a simple T-maze under motivational conditions of hunger-food reward. Group W (32 animals) was subjected to a preliminary training period during which each animal was given four forced runs, two to the left and two to the right. Group S (a matched group) was given 40 reinforcements of the right-turning habit and 40 reinforcements of the left-turning habit. Both groups were then given a free-choice series of six trials to establish a baseline. Those animals that yielded a 6–0 or a 5–1 distribution of choices were discarded. Twenty-six animals of Group W and 21 of Group S met the criterion of response strength equality, a 3–3 or a 4–2 distribution of choices. The two selected groups were then introduced to the trial-and-error learning stage. Choice of one compartment was followed by reinforcement during the series and choice of the other was followed by a 10-second interval of confinement in the empty compartment (nonreward). During this stage, 48 trials were given, eight per night on six nightly sessions.

The learning curve (average percent of occurrence of the correct response as a function of number of trials) was seen to rise more rapidly for Group W. Statistically, a significantly greater total number of correct choices was made by Group W.

It was concluded that the speed of learning in a simple trial-and-error situation is some inverse function of the initial level of *absolute* strength that prevails among competing reaction tendencies.

19

Eyelid Conditioning as a Function of the Interval Between Conditioned and Unconditioned Stimuli[1]

GREGORY A. KIMBLE

BRADLEY REYNOLDS[2]

One of the major corollaries of Hull's (1943) theoretical formulation is concerned with the relation of the rate of conditioning to the time interval separating the onset of the conditioned stimulus (CS) and the unconditioned stimulus (US). It states, "In a reinforcement situation, there is a temporal relationship of the conditioned to the unconditioned stimulus such that as the onset of the unconditioned stimulus is progressively delayed, the rate of learning will increase" (p. 168). As Hull goes on to elaborate, this relationship holds only for short intervals, the maximum of the implied function being reached at about 500 msc. Beyond this point, a new or different relationship holds.

Behind the above stated corollary, and apparently considered by Hull as the basis of its derivation, is quasi-neurological hypothesis,

---

[1] Reprinted from Kimble (1947) and modified as indicated by permission of the American Psychological Association.

[2] Two studies published in the late 1940's may be taken jointly as providing a determination of the interstimulus interval function for eyelid conditioning over a considerable range of values. These studies (Reynolds, 1945, and Kimble, 1947) both investigated eyelid conditioning as a function of this variable. In most respects, the procedures were the same. Potentially the most important differences were these: While Kimble used a delayed-conditioning procedure and a visual CS, Reynolds used a trace-conditioning procedure and an auditory CS. On the other hand, these differences seem unlikely to be important at very short intervals. Inasmuch as the Kimble study was confined to such intervals and the Reynolds study concentrated on long intervals, it is probably appropriate to combine the studies and present the results together. This is done in this chapter. The language is that of Kimble with an occasional bracketed comment to indicate important points which relate to the Reynolds study. The results section has been rewritten to present the two sets of data together. [Ed.]

which has been stated as follows. "Other things equal, the increment to the strength of a receptor-effector connection ($\Delta_S H_R$) resulting from a reinforcement is an increasing function of the frequency of the associated receptor discharge or the intensity of the resulting afferent impulse" (p. 168). This afferent discharge is, in turn, postulated to be a function, among other things, of the duration of the stimulus which produces it. This latter assumption is based upon experimental physiological studies which have shown that, when a receptor organ is stimulated, there result, after a brief period (latency), receptor or neural impulses, the frequency of discharge of which increases rapidly to a maximum. It is the frequency of these neural discharges which Hull considers a critical factor in determining the limit and rate of conditioning. Conditioning would be most efficient, according to this conception, when the CS-US interval is such that the receptor discharge from CS is at its maximal frequency at the time of occurrence of the unconditioned response. According to Hull's hypothesis, this maximum is reached somewhere within one second.

A basic fault in this formulation becomes apparent, however, when attention is called to the fact that the physiological data cited by Hull as demonstration of the characteristics of the receptor neural discharge were data obtained from the reactions of cold-blooded animals, e.g., the eye of the eel. It is a well-established fact that the temporal characteristics of the neural activity of such specimens differ markedly from those of warm-blooded animals, being much slower in latency, longer in chronaxie, etc. Riggs (1941), for example, has published electroretinographic records from the human eye which show the receptor discharge reaching a maximum at about 100 msec. Bartley (1941) presents materials which indicate that the afferent neural discharge in the optic nerve of the rabbit has about the same temporal characteristics as the receptor discharge recorded electroretinographically. Both functions reach their maxima in approximately 100 msec. to 200 msec. after the onset of stimulation. On the assumption that conditioning is a function of the receptor discharge or the afferent neural discharge resulting from it, we should expect optimal conditioning to be reached at some point within this interval.[3] This is considerably short of the interval of 450 msec., which is most often cited as being optimal for conditioning. It is probably little more than accident that the afferent discharge pattern resulting from the stimulation of the peripheral organs of these animals is in correspondence

[3] If one assumes that maximum frequency of sensory discharge must coincide with the occurrence of the *response,* the optimal CS-US interval would be even smaller than the above figures indicate, for allowance would have to be made for the latency of the unconditioned response. If the latency were, for instance, 50 msec., the optimal interval would be reached somewhere between 50 msec. and 150 msec.

with results which have characteristically been obtained in conditioning experiments with mammalian subjects.[4]

Furthermore, there is certain indirect evidence which would suggest that the maximum rate of receptor discharge in the case of the human eye is attained considerably before the optimal interval for conditioning. This evidence is to be found in the studies which have been concerned with the increase in apparent (reported) brightness of a visual stimulus as a function of the duration of stimulation. McDougall (1904), for instance, found that for a *threshold* stimulus, maximum apparent brightness was obtained in approximately 200 msc., the apparent brightnesses of more intense stimuli reaching their maximum in even less time. A very extensive and carefully performed study by Bills (1920) resulted in similar findings. The apparent brightnesses of visual stimulations reached their maxima in times ranging from less than 100 msc. to slightly more than 200 msc., depending upon the brilliance and hue of the light stimulus employed. It would seem reasonable to assume that the time taken for the afferent neural discharges from the human eye to reach a maximum would be no longer than that required for the perceptual response to reach its maximum.[5] On the basis of this assumption, at any rate, we would again be led to expect that maximum conditioning to a visual stimulus would occur at a much earlier interval than is at present considered to be the case.

Review of previous experimental studies on optimal CS-US interval

A number of studies have been reported which have attempted to establish the relationship between extent of conditioning and the time between conditioned and unconditioned stimuli. The present status of our knowledge about this relationship seems to suggest that the optimal time interval is somewhere in the neighborhood of 500 msc., and that either longer or shorter intervals are less effective in the establishment of conditioned responses. This generalization is based on the results of several studies.

The first is an investigation by H. M. Wolfle (1930). She found that the maximum degree of conditioning of a finger withdrawal response

---

[4] It should not be concluded, however, that this unfortunate choice of neurological material entirely negates Hull's theoretical formulation. The mathematical part of the theory (which is the essential part of it) does not stand or fall with the proof or disproof of the neurophysiological notions which lie behind it. The critical tests of the theory must eventually come in the form of experimental studies designed to test the theoretical (mathematical) statements either direcly or else in the form of tests of the deductions made on the basis of the theory.

[5] This assumption appears even more plausible when one considers that the perceptual response involves some central process of discrimination which would presumably consume a certain amount of time.

was obtained when the time between CS and US was 500 msc. In this experiment, both longer and shorter intervals were less effective in the establishment of conditioned responses. Hull (1943) has fitted a symmetrical bidirectional gradient to the Wolfle data and, by extrapolation, determined that, in this experiment, maximum conditioning would have been obtained at .44 second had such a time interval been used.

A second relevant study is that of Kappauf and Schlosberg (1937). These investigators conditioned a complex response pattern in rats to the sound of a buzzer, by a delayed conditioning technique, the unconditioned stimulus being an electric shock. Depending upon which part of the response complex was chosen as the response measure, they found that most efficient conditioning occurred when the time between stimuli was either 667 msc. or 1000 msc. Although this study was not set up to answer very specifically the question as to the exact time interval at which most efficient conditioning is obtained, the results do suggest that the optimal interval is probably greater than $\frac{1}{3}$ second and less than one second.

Somewhat different results are to be found in a second study by Wolfle (1932), who, in a situation essentially similar to that employed in her earlier study, ascertained the optimal time interval to be 200 msc. Both longer and shorter intervals were found to be less effective. Still different results have been reported by Bernstein (1934) who obtained most effective conditioning at 300 msc. for eyelid conditioning and found no significant differences between conditioning obtained at that interval and conditioning obtained at longer intervals up to 1480 msc. Intervals shorter than 300 msc. were found to be definitely inferior. Unfortunately, however, no groups were conditioned at intervals between 300 msc. and 500 msc., the exact region where the optimal interval is suspected to occur.

The present investigation was directed at a more precise determination of the nature of the relationship holding between the *rate* and *maximum level* of conditioning and the time interval between the conditioned and the unconditioned stimuli.

Experimental technique

APPARATUS. The apparatus used was the Dodge pendulum-photochronograph which has been described elsewhere (1926).[6] Eyelid movement was recorded by the paper eyelash method. The unconditioned stimulus was an air puff delivered by the fall of a 90-mm. column of mercury in a manometer. The air tube which delivered the puff to the subject's eye was divided so as to activate a plastic reed which recorded

---

[6] The apparatus, with such modifications as are indicated in the text, was that used by Reynolds (1945).

a shadow on the photographic record. Calibration of the moment of arrival of the puff at the subject's eye and the recorded movement of the reed showed no difference between the two within the limits of the recording system used.

The conditioned stimulus was a circular light, six cm. in diameter, reddish in color, and at a distance of 75 cm. from the eye of the subject. Prior to its onset, the subject was barely able to see the white circle which was produced by the milk-glass covering the circular opening of the light box. The apparent brightness of the conditioned stimulus, as measured by the MacBeth illuminometer, was .53 millilambert. The source of light was two GE neon lamps of $1\frac{1}{2}$-watt intensity, chosen because they attained their maximum brilliance in less than $\frac{1}{1000}$ sec. after the application of current to them. This feature seemed particularly desirable since the interval between stimuli in some cases was shorter than the time required for many standard filament lamps to reach maximum intensity. In order to keep CS constant from group to group, some lamp such as the one used seemed necessary. In the conditioning situation, the conditioned stimulus was presented for 1500 msc. on each trial. The unconditioned stimulus was presented at the appropriate interval after the onset of the conditioned stimulus.

The time intervals employed, in milliseconds, were 100, 200, 225, 250, 300 and 400 (Kimble study) and 250, 450, 1150 and 2250 (Reynolds study).

SUBJECTS. Sixty-nine subjects in all were used in the Kimble experiment. They were divided into six groups, each group conditioned at a different CS-US interval. Ten subjects were assigned to each of the three longest interval groups, and 13 subjects were assigned to each of the shortest interval groups. The assignment of subjects to the various groups was controlled to the following extent: from four to seven subjects were first run in each group, the exact number depending upon the number of subjects available at that particular time. When these subjects had been completed, enough subjects were run in each group to bring the total number in each group to ten. Three additional subjects were then run in each of the shortest interval groups. Complete randomization was not used because of the difficulties in setting and calibrating the apparatus that such a procedure would have entailed. There were also approximately 10 subjects in each group in the Reynolds study.

PROCEDURE. Each subject was given 60 reinforced acquisition trials. The number of acquisition trials was selected after an examination of Reynolds' (1945) results had indicated that, for his subjects, conditioning seemed to have reached a maximum after approximately this number of trials under the conditions of distribution used in the present study.

Conditioning was carried out under conditions of relative distribution of practice, trials being separated by an interval of one to two minutes, with a mean intertrial time of 1½ minutes. Each subject served in two sessions given on successive days. The time between sessions varied from 20–28 hours, the average time being approximately 24 hours.

In both acquisition and extinction, photographic records were made only on every other trial (the "even" trials) because of a lack of the necessary materials in sufficient quantity to make records on every trial. On every tenth acquisition trial the unconditioned stimulus was omitted in the Kimble study but not in the Reynolds study. These trials were designated as "test-trials."

Results

Conditioning curves, not presented here, reveal that these functions had reached what appeared to be the limit of acquisition in most conditions by Trials 51–60. Accordingly, percentage of CRs on these trials are plotted as a function of the interstimulus interval in Figure 19-1. In this curve the circles are for the points sampled in the Kimble study and the triangles are for those studied by Reynolds. The reasons for using closed and open circles will become clear in a moment.

The pattern of these points indicates very clearly that there is an

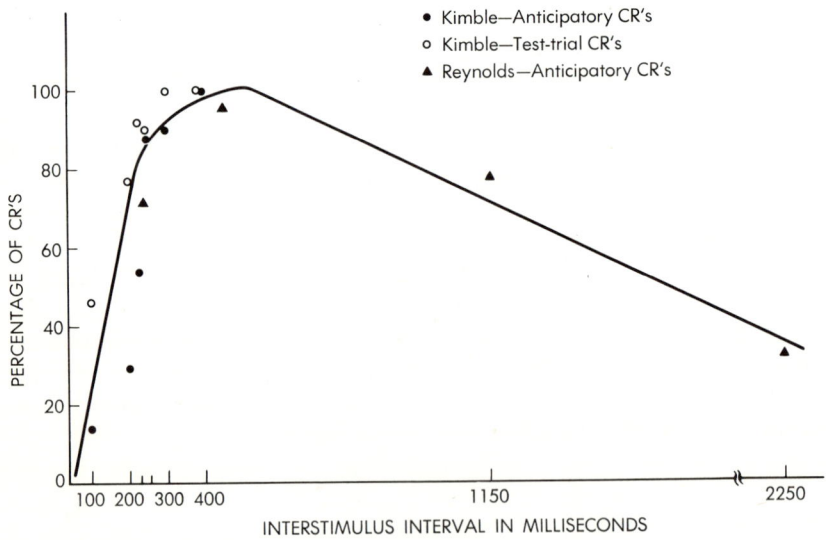

FIGURE 19-1. Idealized interstimulus interval function. [*Based on data from Reynolds (1945) and Kimble (1947).*]

Eyelid Conditioning

optimal interstimulus interval somewhere in the neighborhood of 400–450 msc. The details of the function are somewhat difficult to determine for four reasons.

1. In the case of very short intervals, the convention of counting anticipatory responses as CRs (plotted as closed circles) reduces the probable number of CRs because those with latencies longer than the interstimulus interval would be counted as URs. For this reason, Kimble employed test trials, without the US, in his study. Data obtained on these trials are plotted as the open circles. Clearly this procedure reveals a higher level of conditioning than is suggested by the anticipatory response data, the magnitude of the increase being inversely related to the length of the interval. Probably the test trial data give the more accurate picture of the level of conditioning attained by the different groups. Unfortunately, however, they possess defects of their own. One of these is unreliability. For reasons to which we come in a moment, it is probably inadvisable to give more than one test trial in a series of 10. This was the procedure in the Kimble study. Thus, the percentage of CRs plotted in Figure 19-1 is also the percentage of subjects responding, a very unstable measure. The reason for not using more test trials is that then the experiment employs a partial reinforcement procedure which introduces new problems.

2. The percentage scale in terms of which these data are plotted has an upper limit at 100. It is possible for different conditions to yield a value of 100 percent and yet to differ on other measures such as resistance to extinction. The 300 msc. and 400 msc. groups in the Kimble study, for example, both reached 100 percent conditioning on the test-trial measure, but show a slight difference in extinction, giving 68 and 73 percent CRs, respectively.

3. Unfortunately, in common with other investigations of this variable, these studies did not employ the best possible selection of intervals. It would have been useful if there had been three or four intervals between 400 and 1000 msc.

4. It is very likely that performance at all points is somewhat elevated by the inclusion of beta responses (cf. Kimble, 1961, p. 55).

The smooth curve drawn through the data points in Figure 19-1 was fit by eye in a manner which takes all of these factors except the last into account. The form of the function is that characteristically presented as "the interstimulus interval function."

Discussion

In Hull's theoretical formulation, the time between CS and the response is postulated as one of the many factors determining the asymptote of the habit growth curve. The assumption made is that, when the time between the conditioned stimulus and the response is less than about 500 msc., the limit of rise of the habit curve is an increasing function of the length of this interval.

In general, the present findings confirm this assumption. The fact that different limits of conditioning are attained by the different groups definitely supports Hull's guess that this variable of the CS-US time interval determines the limit to which the hypothetical habit (H) curves grow. Reference to Figure 19-1, however, suggests the possibility that the maximum of this function may be attained before 500 msc., perhaps as early as 300 msc. But it should be noted that our data on this latter point are not decisive. The fact that the 300 msc. and 400 msc. groups had the same maximum value, i.e., 100 percent, does not permit one to conclude that the limits of their hypothetical habit growth curves would necessarily be identical. Unfortunately, in the case of these two groups, we have come to the end of our measuring scale (percentage of response) and hence it is not possible to ascertain by means of this measure any evidence as to possible differences in the limits of their strengths. The data for longer intervals conform quite well to expectations based on Hull's theory.

A major remaining question concerns the specific nature of the function according to which the limit of habit growth is determined by the length of the CS-US interval. Reference to Figure 19-1 indicates that, for short intervals, this function was found to be a negatively accelerated one which reaches its maximum at some point beyond 400 msc. The shape of the function is somewhat different from that fitted by Hull (1943) to the data of one of the Wolfle studies in his discussion of this point. The curve presented by Hull is one such that, as the time interval between CS and US becomes progressively longer or shorter than the optimal interval of 440 msc., the amount of conditioning decreases as a simple negative exponential function from this point. In terms of increasing time intervals, this means that the amount of conditioning is a positively accelerated function of the CS-US time for the portion of the curve between 0 msc. and 440 msc. Although the Wolfle data were obtained in a trace conditioning experiment, the present study involved a delay conditioning technique; there is, at present, no evidence to indicate that there should be any essential difference in the shape of this function for the two different types of conditioning experiment. In general, the available evidence suggests that the segment of the curve between simultaneity and the optimal interval exhibits negative acceleration as the maximum is approached. For example, Hilgard and Marquis (1940, pp. 160–165) have presented temporal gradients for four relevant studies. An examination of these curves shows that every one of them is negatively accelerated during the portion of the curve under discussion, including the Wolfle study, the results of which Hull fitted with a positively accelerated gradient.

Finally, it may be noted that, while the results of the present investigation are in essential agreement with Hull's original mathematical statement of the relationship between stimulus duration and the magnitude of the stimulus trace, they do not confirm his added neurophysiological theorizing about this construct. Instead, they bear out the findings of most previous studies in suggesting that the optimal interval for conditioning is 400 msc. or longer, a value much greater than the time required for either the receptor or neural discharge to reach a maximum in the case of mammalian organisms. The fact that the optimal interval for conditioning is almost identical with the recruitment time of such functions in cold-blooded animals is probably no more than a chance similarity.

SUMMARY

1. Ten groups of human subjects were conditioned in an eyelid conditioning situation at nine different CS-US intervals of 100–2250 msc., with the end in view of investigating the relationship between the level and rate of conditioning and the time between CS and US.

2. The results indicate that, for the range of intervals used in this experiment, the level of conditioning is an increasing, negatively accelerated function of the length of the CS-US interval up to 400 or 450 msc., and a decreasing function beyond that.

3. The simplest interpretation of the results suggests that the length of the CS-US interval is one of the factors which determines the asymptote of the habit-growth curve.

4. These results and other evidence throw doubt upon the value of Hull's neurophysiological interpretation of his construct, stimulus trace, but do support the purely mathematical definition of it.

20

Effects of Conditioned Stimulus Intensity on the Conditioned Emotional Response[1]

LEON J. KAMIN
RONALD E. SCHAUB

The research reported here was designed to explore the effects of CS intensity on the Estes-Skinner conditioned emotional response (CER) in the rat. Presumably, the suppression of operant behavior produced by CER training reflects the Pavlovian conditioning of respondents incompatible with operant behavior. Thus, we assume (Annau & Kamin, 1961; Kamin, 1961) that the CER technique can provide data for the parametric analysis of Pavlovian conditioning, and the present study is designed to contribute toward such an analysis.

There is, in fact, surprisingly little information on the effect of CS intensity on conditioning. Performance of the CR is said to vary both directly (Kimble, 1961, p. 121; Lawson, 1960, p. 55) and inversely (Kimmel, 1959) with CS intensity; other writers (Osgood, 1953, p. 334; Solomon & Brush, 1956, p. 253) conclude that no significant function relating CS intensity to conditioning has been demonstrated.

The available Russian data (Razran, 1957) indicate a positive effect of CS intensity on CR magnitude, at least up to a point, beyond which the function seems to reverse itself. These studies of conditioned salivation in dogs, however, are based upon *within-subject* effects. That is, after the CR has been well established in an individual subject, varying CS intensities are introduced on test trials. This procedure makes comparison and contrast effects (generalization) possible. The American studies are *between-subject* experiments, and do not permit comparison of intensities by subject. The studies, almost all based on the human galvanic skin response or the eyeblink, tend to measure only resistance to extinction. There has been an inconclusive attempt in several such

[1] Reprinted from the *Journal of Comparative and Physiological Psychology*, 1963, *56*, 502–507, with the permission of The American Psychological Association and the authors.

experiments to separate effects of CS intensity on performance from effects on learning.

The major purpose of the present study is to provide data on rate of acquisition of a CR as a function of CS intensity, with CS intensity varied between groups of subjects. The first study provides such data for a delayed conditioning procedure, and then attempts to separate effects on learning from effects on performance. The second study is concerned with the problem of effects of CS intensity with a trace conditioning procedure.

EXPERIMENT 1

Method

SUBJECTS AND APPARATUS. The subjects were 24 experimentally naive male hooded rats from the McMaster colony, approximately 8 months of age. The apparatus consisted of eight standard Grason-Stadler operant-conditioning units, with relay, timer, and counter systems providing for automatic programing and recording. The CS was white noise from a Grason-Stadler Model 901A noise generator, delivered to the experimental box via a loudspeaker. The CS was Strong, Medium, or Weak. To maintain constant day-to-day noise levels, the volume dial of the noise generator was set at a fixed position and standard resistors were connected in series with the generator and speaker as required by the experimental design. The mean background noise level of the eight experimental boxes, with exhaust fans operating, was 62 decibels measured by a General Radio sound survey meter. The CS intensities, measured with the fans disconnected, had mean values of 81, 62.5, and 49 decibels for the Strong, Medium, and Weak CS conditions. The Weak CS was clearly audible through the background noise of the blowers. The variability of intensity values from box to box was relatively small, and was controlled by counter-balancing experimental treatments and boxes. The US was electric shock provided by a Grason-Stadler Model E1064GS shock generator. The US was 1 milliampere of .5 second duration.

PRELIMINARY TRAINING. The subject was reduced to 75 percent of ad lib. body weight, and maintained at that weight on a 24-hour feeding rhythm. Preliminary training concluded with 10 hours (five daily 2-hour sessions) of bar pressing under a 2.5-minute variable-interval food-reinforcement schedule. On the last day of preliminary training (Day P), the appropriate CS was presented alone for four 3-minute periods during the 2-hour bar-pressing session as a pretest.

CER ACQUISITION. The subjects were randomly assigned to three groups of eight subjects each, which differed only with respect to CS intensity (Strong, Medium, or Weak). The CER training began on the day following Day P, and continued for 5 days. Within each daily 2-hour bar-pressing session, four CS-US sequences were programed independently of the food-reinforcement schedule. The CS was of 3-minute duration, terminating simultaneously with the .5-second US. The CS was presented 19, 55, 95, and 115 minutes after beginning of the session.

CER EXTINCTION. The Strong and Weak CS groups were given 3 days of extinction training immediately following CER acquisition. The Medium CS group was not given extinction. The extinction training consisted of four daily CS presentations within the 2-hour session. The two groups studied in extinction were randomly subdivided into halves. There were thus four extinction groups of four subjects each in a 2×2 factorial design. The S-S group received the Strong CS during both acquisition and extinction; the W-W group received the Weak CS during both acquisition and extinction; the S-W group received the Strong CS in acquisition and the Weak CS in extinction; and the W-S group received the Weak CS in acquisition and the Strong CS in extinction.

MEASURE. The magnitude of the CER was measured by computing the "suppression ratio" described by Annau and Kamin (1961). The ratio is $B/A + B$, where B represents number of bar presses made during the 3-minute CS, and A number of bar presses during the 3 minutes immediately preceding the CS. Thus, a ratio of 0 indicates complete suppression of bar pressing during the CS, while .50 indicates no effect of the CS on bar-pressing rate. The ratio was computed daily for each subject by summating responses made during the appropriate intervals of the four CS-US sequences.

Results

There were no differences between experimental groups ($F < 1$) in suppression ratios for Day P. The grand mean (and median) pretest ratio was .52. Thus, the CS did not suppress bar pressing in any group on Day P.

The median suppression ratios for all groups as a function of acquisition day are presented in Figure 20-1. The Strong CS group acquired the CER most rapidly, and the Weak CS group least rapidly. The three groups converged to an asymptote of virtually complete suppression by Day 5. To test the significance of differences between groups, a mean suppression ratio for Days 1–5 was computed for each subject. These data are summarized in Table 20-1. Whitney's extension of the

Effects of Conditioned Stimulus Intensity on the CER

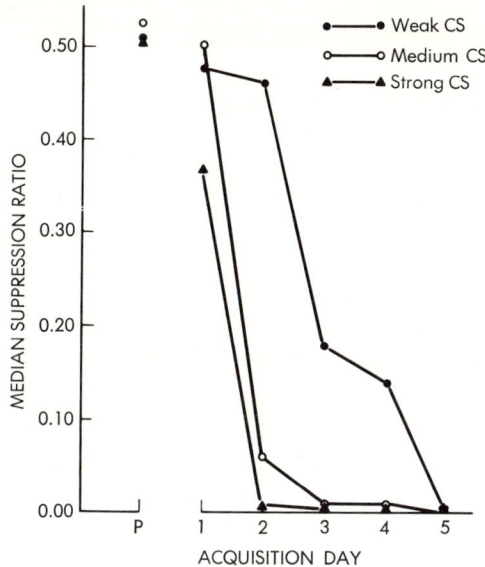

FIGURE 20-1. Median suppression ratios by groups as a function of CER acquisition day.

U test indicated a trend significant well beyond the tabled .01 level; the more intense the CS, the lower the suppression ratio. When Day 2 ratios alone were considered, each group differed significantly from each of the others (U tests, $p < .005$).

The extinction suppression ratios were submitted to an analysis of variance which is summarized in Table 20-2. The factors in this analysis were: CS employed during acquisition, CS employed during extinction, and extinction days. The significant effect of days indicates merely that suppression ratios increase as extinction training progresses. There was no

TABLE 20-1

Mean suppression ratios, days 1-5, as a function of CS intensity

MEASURE	CS INTENSITY		
	Strong	Medium	Weak
Mean	.09	.14	.26
Median	.08	.14	.26
Range	.06-.13	.09-.20	.19-.36

TABLE 20-2

Summary of analysis of variance of suppression ratios during extinction

SOURCE	df	MS	F
Between subjects			
CS during acq. (A)	1	444.08	–
CS during ext. (B)	1	645.33	1.40
Interaction, A × B	1	3104.09	6.74*
Error (b)	12	460.87	
Within subjects			
Ext. days (C)	2	1853.69	30.21†
Interaction, A × C	2	43.27	–
Interaction, B × C	2	27.02	–
Interaction, A × B × C	2	348.27	5.67‡
Error (w)	24	61.37	

* p .05.
† p .001
‡ p .01.

main effect of either acquisition CS or extinction CS, but the interaction between acquisition CS and extinction CS, and the triple interaction, were significant. These interactions are clarified in Table 20-3, which presents mean suppression ratios for each extinction day for all experimental groups.

The simple effects of acquisition CS were examined by analyzing separately the extinction ratios of groups given the Strong and the Weak CS during extinction. With the Strong CS employed in extinction, there

TABLE 20-3

Mean suppression ratios during extinction

GROUP	EXTINCTION DAY		
	1	2	3
S-S	.01	.04	.12
W-S	.10	.27	.46
W-W	.13	.18	.26
S-W	.16	.30	.41

was a significant effect of acquisition CS ($F = 13.82$, $p < .01$), and the interaction between extinction day and acquisition CS was also significant ($F = 4.94$, $p < .05$). That is, subjects trained with a Strong acquisition CS were more resistant to extinction. With the Weak CS employed in extinction, there was no significant effect of acquisition CS.

The simple effects of extinction CS were examined by analyzing separately the extinction ratios of groups given the Strong and the Weak CS during acquisition. With the Strong CS employed in acquisition, there was a significant effect of extinction CS ($F = 13.88$, $p < .01$). The subjects extinguished with a Strong CS had lower ratios throughout extinction. With the Weak CS employed in acquisition, there was no effect of extinction CS but the interaction between extinction day and extinction CS was significant ($F = 4.65$, $p < .05$). That is, though the groups extinguished with Strong and with Weak CS behaved similarly early in extinction, the group extinguished with a Weak CS was more resistant to extinction.[2]

Discussion

The data very clearly indicate that rate of acquisition of the CER is, within the range of values tested, a positive monotonic function of CS intensity. This result is consonant with the observation (Barnes, 1956) that dogs made more conditioned leg movements to an 80-db. tone than to 60 db.

The analysis allows no firm conclusion as to whether CS intensity affects learning, performance, or both. To be sure, if one views *rate* of acquisition of a "stable" CR as an indicator of learning (Lawson, 1960, p. 55; Razran, 1957, p. 3), learning has been affected. The *lowest* Weak CS ratio observed on Day 2 was .43; the *highest* Strong CS ratio on Day 2 was .04. The lowest pretest ratio observed was .41. Thus, no conditioning whatever is exhibited by the Weak CS group on Day 2, when every subject in the Strong CS group has a stable CR.

The more sophisticated factorial analysis would have indicated an effect on learning had CS during acquisition influenced extinction scores. The analysis, however, showed no significant main effect of CS intensity either on learning or performance. The significant interactions and simple effects seem best interpreted in terms of generalization decrement. That is, once the subject has been conditioned to a specific CS intensity, *any* change in the CS ought to accelerate extinction; and in fact, every significant effect in the present data represents more resistance to extinction by a group for which extinction CS is identical to acquisition CS

---

[2] The effect of extinction day was significant ($p < .005$, at least) in all analyses of simple effects.

than by a group for which the CS has been changed. The problem of generalization decrement is of course logically inherent in any design which tests effects of CS intensity *within* individuals.

EXPERIMENT 2

The effect of CS intensity on conditioning is often attributed to the level of neural activity established by the CS. The assumption is made that, the greater the level of neural activity coincident with the US, the more easily is conditioning established (Hull, 1943, p. 167). Presumably, a physically intense CS produces intense receptor and cortical activity.

The neurophysiological viewpoint suggests that CS intensity might be an especially potent variable when trace (rather than delayed) conditioning is examined. The trace conditioning procedure involves termination of the CS at some time appreciably before presentation of the US. Within Pavlovian theory, this "empty" time gap is bridged by a decaying neural trace of the CS. We have assumed that the intensity and duration of neural trace activity are simple positive functions of CS intensity. Thus, suppression during a trace interval should clearly be a function of CS intensity; further, a CS sufficiently intense to establish a delayed CER might produce a trace too weak or short-lived to establish a trace CER.

Method

The subjects were 14 naive rats, randomly assigned to Strong and Weak CS groups. The two CS intensities were identical to those employed in Experiment 1. Preliminary and CER training duplicated Experiment 1, with the exception that the CS was of 2-minute duration, followed, after 1 minute, by the US. These two time intervals are designated as the "CS interval" and "trace interval," respectively. The CER training in Experiment 2 was continued for 10 days.

The CER in this study was measured by two separate suppression ratios calculated daily for each subject. The trace ratio contrasts responding during the 1-minute trace interval with baseline response rate; it was determined by the formula $3T/A + 3T$, when T represents number of responses during the trace interval, and A number of responses during the 3 minutes immediately preceding the CS. The CS ratio contrasts rate during the 2-minute CS interval with baseline rate, and was calculated by $3B/2A + 3B$, with B representing number of responses during CS.

Effects of Conditioned Stimulus Intensity on the CER

The trace and CS ratios are thus equivalent to the suppression ratios of Experiment 1, with 0 representing complete suppression of responding, and .50 no change in response rate during the critical tested interval.

Results

The analysis of data deals separately with trace and CS ratios, focusing primarily on the trace ratios. There was no significant difference between groups on Day P for either trace or CS ratios. The median trace ratios of both groups are portrayed in Figure 20-2 as a function of training day. The results are very clear. The Strong CS group rapidly acquired virtually complete suppression during the trace interval, but the Weak CS group exhibited no sign of a CER. The mean ratio of each subject for Days 1–10 was calculated. The median of these ratios of the Strong CS group was .08, with a range of .05-.29; the median of the Weak CS group was .47, with a range of .42-.50. A single subject in the Weak CS group did give some evidence of acquiring suppression; its ratios on the last 3 days of training were .36, .37, and .24.

The median CS ratios of both groups are presented in Figure 20-3 as a function of training day. The picture is much the same. The Strong CS group was considerably suppressed during the CS interval. The Weak

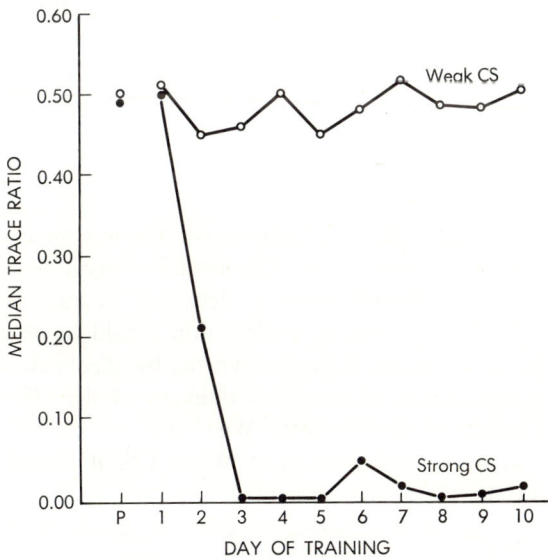

FIGURE 20-2. Median trace suppression ratios as a function of CER acquisition day.

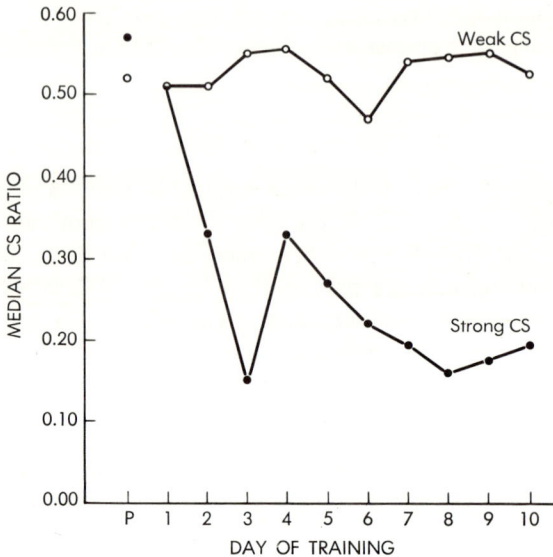

FIGURE 20-3. Median CS suppression ratios as a function of CER acquisition day.

CS group exhibited no suppression. The suppression exhibited during the CS was considerably less severe than that observed during the trace interval. This is in keeping with the one previous study of a trace CER (Kamin, 1961).

Discussion

The data demonstrate that intensity of the CS has an overwhelming effect on acquisition of a trace CER. The results suggest that trace conditioning does, in fact, depend upon a decaying neural trace process initiated by the CS. The alternative explanation would be to postulate a CS-initiated chain of persisting behavior which, by feedback stimulation, provides a cue simultaneous in time with delivery of the US. This view, however, is not adequate to the data. We have not observed, empirically, any such "bridging" behavior. The Weak CS, it should be noted, is a sufficient cue to allow the subject to initiate mediating behavior; for it is the *same* CS which, under a delayed conditioning program, ultimately resulted in complete suppression.

Thus, the simplest interpretation seems to us to be that the decaying neural trace is a positive function of CS intensity, and that level of conditioning is in turn a positive function of the magnitude of neural activity coincident with the US. Presumably, the trace of the Weak CS had diminished below some critical threshold value by the time of US presentation. There was thus no effective CS to be associated with the US.

We think it is worthwhile to emphasize that trace conditioning of the CER can be a very rapid and efficient procedure, which does not require successive approximations to gradually longer trace intervals. The long time gap bridged by the subject in the present study is not at variance with the time intervals employed in Russian conditioning studies on dogs. The CER thus seems to be a remarkably sensitive technique for the study of Pavlovian conditioning, with the very great virtue of high reliability across individual subjects.

SUMMARY

Effects of CS intensity on conditioned emotional response (CER) were explored with 38 rats. CS was white noise. The first study, with a delayed conditioning procedure, produced a positive monotonic function relating conditioning to CS intensity. When extinction was explored with a factorial design (to separate learning from performance), the only effect was a generalization decrement; changing CS intensity accelerated extinction. The second study, with a trace conditioning procedure, resulted in complete suppression to the trace of an intense CS. There was no conditioning to the trace of the same weak CS which produced a CER under delayed conditioning. Trace conditioning seems to depend on the magnitude of a decaying neural trace, itself a positive function of CS intensity.

21

Changes in Response Strength with Changes in the Amount of Reinforcement[1]

ROBERT H. DUFORT

GREGORY A. KIMBLE

In *Principles of Behavior* (1943), Hull attributes decrement in response strength during experimental extinction to the accumulation of reactive inhibition (I_R) and conditioned inhibition ($_sI_R$). Reactive inhibition is a temporary negative motivational state resulting from response evocation; conditioned inhibition is a permanent habit of not responding, reinforced by I_R-reduction during intervals when no response occurs. Both I_R and $_sI_R$ subtract from reaction potential ($_sE_R$) and response decrement results. Extinction is not weakening of habit strength ($_sH_R$) but a performance decrease.

Within the Hullian system, there are several alternatives which might be used to account for extinction in terms of a reduction in $_sH_R$. Of these, the most obvious, as pointed out earlier by Zeaman (1949), would consider extinction to be the result of decreasing the amount of reinforcement to zero. Although Hull never specifically considers the effect upon $_sH_R$ of decreasing the amount of reinforcement, he does treat the case of increasing amounts. His interpretation there is that the effect of increasing the amount of reinforcement (w) is to change the limit (M) of habit growth. Moreover, he presents an equation for describing this change which can presumably be generalized to cover the case of amount decrease as well. The equation is:

$$_sH_R = (M' - {_sH_R}')(1 - e^{-iN}) + {_sH_R}' \quad (1)$$

where $M' = M(1 - e^{-kw})$

and $\quad N =$ number of reinforcements

$\quad$ i, k = constants

$\quad\quad$ w = amount of reinforcement

$\quad\quad$ e = 10

$\quad\quad$ M = the maximum of habit strength, taken as 100

[1] Reprinted with permission from *Journal of Experimental Psychology*, 1956, 51, 185–191.

M' = the maximum of habit strength modified by the amount of reinforcement

$_sH_R$ = habit strength at any given reinforcement after the amount of change

$_sH_R'$ = habit strength developed at the time of the amount change.

The nature of this equation is such that changing the amount of reinforcement alters the limit approached by $_sH_R$. Whether the change is an increase or decrease, $_sH_R$ approaches the new maximum (M') as a growth function of N. If the amount of reinforcement is shifted to zero, the limit of the decreasing function is also zero. The extinction curve thus becomes the limiting case of a family of curves obtained by decreasing the amount of reinforcement. Moreover, Hull's theory demands that the slopes of these functions be the same. That for the extinction curve should be identical with the slopes of other functions obtained with increases and decreases in the amount of reinforcement.

Several studies have demonstrated differences in response strength produced by differences in the amount of reinforcement. Others have shown that response strength increases or decreases appropriately with increases or decreases in amount. These studies have stressed certain emotional (frustration and elation) effects occurring with changes in amount. None has presented a detailed analysis or comparison of curve forms obtained after the change. Nor has any obtained data relevant to the question whether the extinction process can be attributed to a decrease in the amount of reinforcement to zero.

The purpose of this study is to test the prediction that the data obtained for both increases and decreases in amount can be satisfactorily represented by the same curve forms, and that the curve obtained during experimental extinction will differ from such functions only in asymptote.

Method

SUBJECTS. The subjects were 40 experimentally naive male albino rats of the Wistar strain, ranging in age from 100 to 180 days. They were received from the supplier in two groups of 16 and 24, the second group arriving 15 days after the first group had completed the experiment. Upon receipt they were housed in individual living cages and allowed free access to food and water for 4 days. During this time each subject was handled for 10 minutes a day. On Day 5 the subjects were placed on a 23-hour feeding schedule, having access to food 1 hour a day at the time their squad would finish the daily experimental sessions. Each subject continued to have free access to water. Experimentation began on the Day 8.

Twenty subjects ran in a morning (A.M.) squad and 20 in an afternoon (P.M.) squad. Assignment to these squads was at random. In the first group, 6 subjects ran in the A.M. squad and 10 in the P.M. squad; in the second group, 14 ran in the A.M. squad and 10 in the P.M. squad.

APPARATUS. The apparatus was an elevated stand, consisting of a 10- by 5-inch starting platform, an 18- by 2.5-inch straight runway, and an approximately semicircular goal platform 16 inches long and 30 inches wide. The straight runway led into the goal platform at the center of its straight side. The starting platform was separated from the runway by a removable block which prevented the subject from leaving the starting area until he met an orientation criterion.

Five soft drink bottle caps were arranged at equal intervals around the circumference of the goal platform, at a distance of 15 inches from the end of the runway. The center cap was directly in line with the center of the runway. The others were located at 5.75 inches and 11.50 inches on either side of the center cap. Each cap had a slight dent in the top to hold the fluid reinforcement. The goal cap immediately to the right of the center cap was the correct one.

A black cardboard 17 inches high, supported by hardware cloth, was attached to the curved edge of the goal platform. The cardboard prevented the subject from jumping off the apparatus and provided a homogeneous black background, except for a 4- by 5-inch white card, which was directly behind the correct cap. This card remained in place throughout the experiment, except for pretraining, in the belief that it would provide a distinctive cue and facilitate learning. The reinforcement used in the experiment was one drop (.08 ml.) of sucrose solution. To obtain different amounts of reinforcement, the solutions were of 5, 10, and 20 percent concentration. They were prepared by adding to a given amount (e.g., 5 mg.) of sucrose enough distilled water (e.g., 95 ml.) to produce 100 gm. of solution. As Guttman (1953) has pointed out, the advantage of using nutrients in solution is that this avoids confounding the amount of reinforcement with the amount of consummatory activity.

The apparatus provided a measure of the time required for the subject to leave the starting platform and run down the straight alley to the goal platform, a distance of 18 inches. Removing the block separating the starting platform from the runway closed a switch which started a .01-second timer. The timer stopped when the subject broke a beam of light directed at the element of a photocell, located at the end of the runway. In order to reduce the visibility of the beam it was passed through a bottle of household iodine.

PROCEDURE. The experimental procedure involved three stages: pretraining, original learning in which all subjects received the same amount of reinforcement and, finally, a test condition in which the amount of reinforcement varied for different groups.

PRETRAINING. The experiment began with a series of pretraining sessions. The experimenter placed the subject on the starting platform and waited for it to orient toward the goal platform. When this happened, the experimenter removed the block and allowed the subject to explore the apparatus for 10 minutes. On these trials each goal cap contained one drop of 10 percent sucrose solution. The experimenter recorded running time, cap preference, and noted whether the subject drank the solution in each cap. This procedure was followed daily until the subject met two criteria on two successive days: (a) a running time of 20 seconds or less and (b) drinking from all five caps.

ORIGINAL LEARNING. In this stage of the study, the subject learned to run to the correct goal cap, which contained one drop of 10 percent sucrose solution; the other caps were empty. The subject received 10 trials a day for two successive days. In each daily session, trials were separated by about 15 seconds. The procedure followed that used in pretraining. The experimenter removed the block separating the starting platform from the runway after the subject oriented toward the goal platform and recorded running time and the goal cap to which the subject responded. In this latter case the experimenter counted a response if the subject actually touched a cap as if to drink; contacts with the feet and tail did not qualify as responses. If the subject responded to the wrong cap, he was returned to the starting platform for another trial; correction was not permitted.

EXPERIMENTAL TREATMENT. At the completion of the original learning sessions, subjects were subdivided into four groups of 10 subjects each and given four daily sessions of 10 trials each with different amounts of reinforcement. One group continued on the 10 percent solution. The others were switched to 20, 5, and 0 percent conditions. The subjects in the 0 percent (extinction) condition found the goal cap empty. The subjects were assigned to these conditions prior to original learning in a counterbalanced order depending upon when they reached the criteria terminating pretraining.

From preliminary experimentation, it was suspected that in the 0 percent group subjects would cease to run near the end of the 40 trials. In order to prevent interference with the experimental schedule, a criterion of 20 seconds for terminating a trial was imposed on all groups. It was necessary to invoke this criterion only on subjects in the 0 percent group. This meant that there was an artificial upper limit of 20 seconds on the latencies of these subjects.

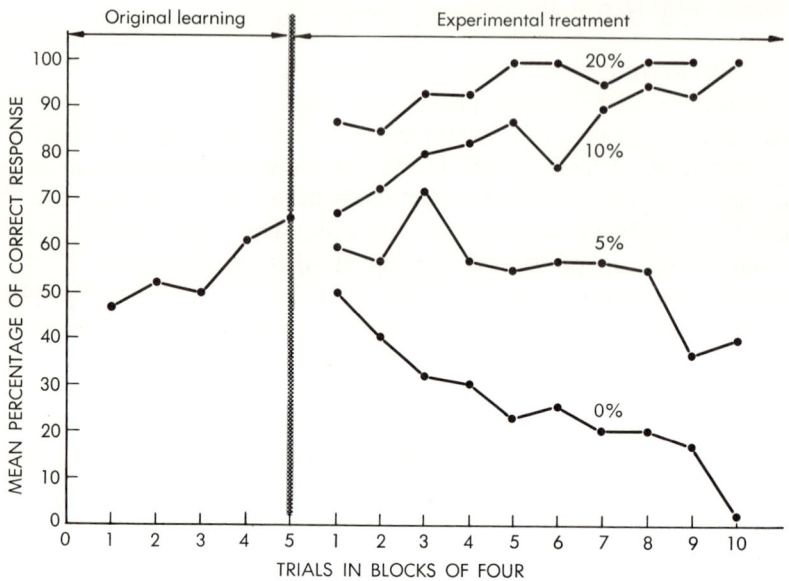

FIGURE 21-1. Mean percentage of correct response as a function of practice. Original learning data are for 40 subjects. For each experimental treatment, N = 10.

Results

The basic data from the experiment appear in Figures 21-1 and 21-2, in the form of learning curves. In each case the trials are grouped in blocks of four to reduce irregularity in the functions. In spite of this, the probability-of-response data in Figure 21-1 are too uneven to justify precise mathematical treatment. The important points concerning these data seem to be as follows. (1) There is a clear separation of the four functions on this measure. An analysis-of-variance testing for over-all differences in the functions obtained after the amount change produced an F of 34.34, $(P = .001)$. (2) Although the 5 percent sucrose solution is well above the reinforcement threshold estimated by Guttman, there is a decrease in percentage of correct responses for this group. (3) The shift from the 10 percent to the 20 percent condition produced an abrupt increase in this measure. (4) At the end of the experiment the 10 percent and the 20 percent groups had reached the same level of response strength. In this respect the results for the probability-of-response measure are different from those for the speed measure.

Figure 21-2 presents the speed measure in learning curve form. The empirical points are means of 100 multiplied by the reciprocal of running

Changes in Response Strength

time. The vertical line separates the data obtained in original learning from those obtained after the change in amount of reinforcement. Renumbering of the blocks of trials after the change is to accommodate the type of function used by Hull to describe changes in $_sH_R$ with changes in the amount of reinforcement.

Although there is a significant difference among the four groups on the first block of trials in original learning ($F = 4.13$; $P = .025$), this difference has completely disappeared at the end of original learning ($F = .39$). On the assumption that the initial significant difference was a sampling error, the data have been combined for purposes of mathematical treatment. In fitting curves to the data, we have fit Hull's curves directly to the speed of running measures. As Spence (1954) has pointed out, this procedure is justifiable if such measures show differences over and above differences in latency or if the learning curves do not reflect the early stages of learning. The length of the runway used in the present study, and the fact that the percentage of correct responses was

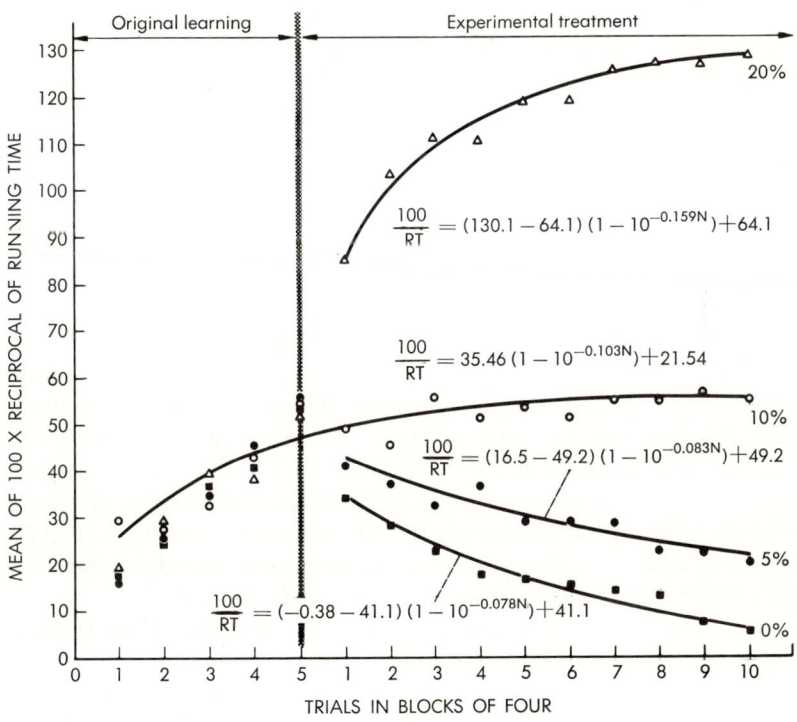

FIGURE 21-2. Speed of running as a function of practice. For an interpretation of the fitted curves, see text.

at 50 percent after only four trials would seem to justify these assumptions. Another consideration which cannot be overlooked is that growth functions fit the data reasonably well.

One of the implications of Hull's theory is that the slopes of the functions obtained with a shift in the amount of reinforcement should be the same as the slope of habit growth obtained without a shift. For this reason, the curve fit to the data for the 10 percent control group is of the form, $_sH_R = M(1 - e^{-iN})$, used by Hull to depict habit growth with no change in reinforcement amount. It covers the entire series of 15 blocks of trials. The curves fit to the other three sets of data, obtained after the change in amount of reinforcement, are of the form of Equation 1. The curve-fitting procedure was that described by Lewis (1948).

With the data in this form, it is possible to evaluate the adequacy of Hull's theory for handling them. First of all it may be pointed out that the growth curves fit the data rather well. For the functions in the right hand portion of Figure 21-2, an F test for goodness of fit reveals that in no case is it possible to reject the hypothesis that the growth curve adequately represents the data. The largest F was 1.26 which is not significant even at the .20 level.

According to Hull's theory, changing the amount of reinforcement should produce new asymptotes of habit strength. The test of this prediction proceeded in a series of steps. To determine whether the functions had reached asymptotic values, a treatments-by-subjects analysis of variance was applied to the last three points on each curve. The largest F produced by this analysis was 2.359 for the 0 percent group. This F is significant at only the .20 level. All other F values were less than 1.0. A second step in this analysis involved t tests to determine whether the empirical asymptotes are different from the asymptotes estimated in the curve-fitting procedure. Comparison of these values for each group showed the t of 114.6 obtained for the 0 percent group to be highly significant. Presumably this was the result of using a criterion latency in the case of this group. The other t values were all less than 1.0. To determine whether the empirical asymptotes are significantly different, an analysis of variance involving the last 3 blocks of trials for all groups was employed. The F of 89.49 is significant at the .001 level. To determine whether adjacent asymptotes are significantly different, t tests were employed on the same measures. The t values obtained were: for a comparison of the 0 percent group and 5 percent group, 3.40; for the 5 percent group and the 10 percent group, 3.29; for the 10 percent group and the 20 percent group, 7.33. These t values are all significant at the .01 level or better. On the basis of this series of tests, the conclusion that groups with different sucrose concentrations reached different asymptotes seems entirely justified.

The remaining question is whether the slopes of the four functions

Changes in Response Strength

are the same. It was predicted that data obtained for both increases and decreases in amount could be represented by Equation 1. The critical value in the fitted equations for testing this prediction becomes that of the constant i, the rate of approach to the asymptote. Within Hullian theory, a change in the amount of reinforcement changes the asymptote of the learning curve, but does not change the rate of approach constant. If the curves are identical, the values of i should be similar. As a test of this, the i values for the 0 and 5 percent curves, which are almost identical ($-.078$ and $-.083$), were averaged and the resulting value substituted in each of the four fitted equations in place of the i values which were obtained from the original curve-fitting procedure. The goodness of fit test applied to the resulting calculated values indicated that the growth functions with the new i values adequately fit the empirical data in all cases but 20 percent. In this case, the hypothesis of adequate fit must be rejected with an F significant at the .001 level ($F = 5.189$); the new calculated curve underestimated the original values at every point on the function.

Discussion

The curve-fitting analysis of the results of this experiment indicates that deductions from Hull's theory describe the data very well except for those obtained from the group shifted from a 10 to a 20 percent solution. In this case the change in behavior strength was much greater and more rapid than would be predicted either from the function obtained early in learning or from the rest of the data obtained after the shift in amount of reinforcement. The general suggestion of the data is that the effects produced by increasing the amount of reinforcement are different from those produced by decreasing the values of this variable. It may be that the rapid increase in speed of responding for the group receiving an increased amount is an exaggerated elation effect of the sort described by Crespi (1942). Since there was no 20 percent control group in this experiment, we cannot say. If the explanation for this feature of the results does ultimately turn out to be of this sort, the indication is that the effect of changing the amount of reinforcement is at least partly on performance rather than habit. Such an account would be more nearly in line with Hull's (1951) recent treatment in terms of incentive motivation (K) than it would be with the theory examined in this paper which treats the results in terms of changing asymptotes of $_sH_R$.

At a more general level the important point of this paper stands. Whether the effect of changing the amount of reinforcement is on habit or performance, it seems quite clear that the effect must, almost of logical necessity, cover a part of the explanation of extinction. There is now ample evidence that increasing and decreasing the amount of reinforcement increases and decreases response strength appropriately. It seems a theoretical extravagance to assume a completely new process to deal with the special case of decreasing the amount to zero. Furthermore, the fact that the slope of the extinction function obtained in this experiment is the same as that for the curve produced by decreasing the amount to 5 percent indicates in a factual way the fruitfulness of considering extinction as a part of the same process as is involved in decreasing amounts of reinforcement.

In Hull's theory there are two other ways to reach an explanation of extinction similar to that developed in this paper. The alternative accounts would view extinction as the result of increasing the CS-UCS interval or the delay of reinforcement to a point where no learning occurs. Hull did not treat the effect upon behavior of changes in these variables. It was largely for this reason that this experiment manipulated the amount of reinforcement. At the same time, it seems likely that changes in either variable would produce changes in performance, and that a large increase could produce experimental extinction. In the case of the CS-UCS interval, there is experimental evidence which points directly toward such an interpretation. McAllister (1953) found that increasing the interstimulus interval from an optimal to a nonoptimal value produced a decline in performance resembling extinction.

SUMMARY

The purpose of this study was to determine whether, as one aspect of Hull's theory would indicate, the slopes of performance curves produced by changes in the amount of reinforcement would be the same whether the change was an increase, decrease or even a decrease to zero (experimental extinction).

The subjects in the experiment were 40 albino rats. They were trained to run down an 18-inch alley to obtain a 10 percent sucrose solution at one of five goal caps. After 20 such trials subjects were divided into four experimental groups which received a 5, 10, or 20 percent solution or nothing.

The different groups behaved differently during this phase of the experiment on both of the measures available in the experiment. Because of an unsatisfactory degree of irregularity in the percentage of response measure, however, the analysis is largely confined to the speed of running data. With one exception these data fit the predictions drawn from Hull's theory very well. As the theory predicts, shifting the amount of reinforcement alters the asymptotes approached by the learning curves.

Moreover, the functions change at the same rate except for the group in which the shift was from 10 to 20 percent sucrose. In this case the increase in performance was much greater than the theory would predict. This finding suggests that the influence may be on performance rather than on learning as assumed in this paper. It does not, however, alter the major conclusion that extinction may be treated as the limiting case of a reduction in the amount of reinforcement.

22

The Gradient of Delay of Secondary Reward in Avoidance Learning Tested on Avoidance Trials Only[1]

LEON J. KAMIN

The major S-R theories of avoidance learning assert that response termination of the CS, and not avoidance of the US, reinforces avoidance responding. The CS, after pairing with a noxious US, is said to have acquired aversive properties (Schoenfeld, 1950); or, alternatively, the CS is said to elicit a conditioned anxiety coterminous with it (Mowrer & Lamoreaux, 1942). Thus, S-R theories regard CS-termination as a secondary reward, or a reduction of secondary drive. Therefore, a delay of CS-termination in avoidance training is a delay of reinforcement; and exploration of this parameter should reveal a gradient of delay of secondary reward analogous to the primary delay-of-reward gradient.

The effects of delay of CS-termination on avoidance learning were explored in a previous study (Kamin, 1957) which reported a marked gradient effect. The significance of this empirical gradient, however, was not clear. The experimental procedure, following the pioneer work of Mowrer and Lamoreaux (1942), delayed CS-termination *both* on escape *and* on avoidance trials. This procedure was found to affect the trial on which the first avoidance response occurred. The subjects trained with a delay of CS-termination during escape trials made the first avoidance on a later trial of training than subjects trained without delay. Thus, differences among groups in total number of avoidances might have been merely a function of differential treatment on escape trials.

The present study, which also explores the effects of delay of CS-termination, accounts for this possibility by delaying CS-termination *on avoidance trials only*. With all groups treated alike on escape trials, any differences among groups will be less ambiguously attributable to the

[1] Reprinted from *Journal of Comparative and Physiological Psychology*, 1957, 50, with the permission of The American Psychological Association and the author.

The Gradient of Delay of Secondary Reward

effects of varying periods of delay of CS-termination during avoidance trials. Thus, a gradient effect, if found, may be interpreted as a demonstration of a gradient of delay of secondary reward and as support for S-R interpretations of avoidance. This paper reports two separate experiments which test for the existence of such a gradient.

EXPERIMENT I

Method

SUBJECTS AND APPARATUS. The subjects were 48 experimentally naive hooded rats, ranging in age from about $2\frac{1}{2}$ to $3\frac{1}{2}$ months. The rats, maintained on an ad lib. feeding schedule, were randomly assigned to experimental groups. The apparatus was modeled after the Mowrer-Miller shuttlebox. The dimensions of the box were: length, 36 inches; width, 5 inches; height, $4\frac{3}{4}$ inches. There was no barrier between the two halves of the box, but a metal molding projected $\frac{3}{8}$ inches into the box from the center of each side wall to demarcate the two halves.

The US (electric shock) was administered through a grid floor. The grid of each half of the box could be separately charged. The intensity of the US was held constant for all subjects, with a current flow to the average subject of about 1.1 ma. The CS was an Edwards Lungen buzzer, damped by mounting on a sponge-rubber pad. The CS was placed on the table on which the apparatus stood, centered to the rear of the shuttlebox. The sound level to which the subject was exposed was 74 db.

DESIGN. There were four experimental groups, with eight subjects in each group. The subjects of each group were trained with a different interval elapsing between avoidance responses and CS-termination. The four intervals studied were 0, 2.5, 5, and 10 seconds. There were also two control groups, each with eight subjects. The first control group was classically trained, never avoiding the US. The remaining group was a backward-conditioning control for sensitization.

PROCEDURE. (1) *Experimental groups*. The subject was placed in the apparatus and left unmolested for 5 minutes. The CS was then presented for the first time, followed 5 seconds after its onset by the US. The CS and US continued to act until the subject (usually very promptly) ran to the opposite half of the apparatus, when both were turned off. This procedure was identical for all groups, and was repeated throughout training on all *escape* trials.

There were, however, many trials during training when the subject responded by running to the opposite half of the box after onset of the

CS and before the scheduled onset of the US. When this occurred, the experiment withheld the US for that trial. The CS, on such avoidance trials, might terminate immediately with the subject's response, or it might continue for an additional 2.5, 5, or 10 seconds. This was of course contingent on the group to which the subject had been assigned.

There were, for all groups, 100 trials conducted in a single session. The interval between trials was set at a fixed, irregular schedule. The intertrial intervals were 50, 60, or 70 seconds, with a mean of 1 minute. The CS-US interval for all groups was 5 seconds. The frequency of escapes and avoidance was tabulated, and response latency was recorded by stop watch to the nearest 0.1 second. The frequency of "spontaneous" intertrial runs across the box was also recorded.

(2) *Control groups.* With both control groups, the number of training trials and intertrial intervals duplicated the experimental group procedure. The "classical" control subjects were shocked inevitably on each trial. When the subject failed to respond before delivery of the US, the procedure was identical with that employed with experimental subjects on escape trials. When the subject did respond by running before delivery of the US, it was nevertheless shocked 5 seconds after onset of the CS. The US on such trials was terminated by the subject's running to the opposite half of the box, and the CS acted uninterruptedly until the subject ran off the charged grid. The subject was credited with a "CR" if it ran in response to the CS.

The backward-conditioning control subjects were on each trial first presented with the US alone. The US was terminated by the subject's running to the opposite half of the box. Then, 5 seconds after onset of the US, the "CS" was presented for a maximum of 5 seconds. The subject was credited with a "CR" if it ran in response to the CS, and the CS was terminated immediately with any such responses. This procedure, it should be noted, provides a base line which includes any responses attributable to sensitization or pseudoconditioning, to mere practice of the escape response from shock, or to inherent noxiousness of the CS.

Results

There were no significant differences among groups for the trial on which the first avoidance occurred, for the latency of the first avoidance, or for the number of spontaneous runs made during the initial 5-minute observation period. This indicates satisfactory random assignment of subjects to groups.

Table 22-1 presents, by groups, data for the number of avoidances recorded, for the maximum number of consecutive avoidances, for the median latency of avoidances, and for the number of spontaneous responses. (The data for the control groups, of course, represent CR's not

TABLE 22-1

Various response measures for experimental and control groups

MEASURE	SECONDS OF DELAY OF CS-TERMINATION				CONTROL	
	0	2.5	5	10	Classical	Backward
Number of avoidances						
Mean	61.5	36.0	19.1	23.8	24.3	6.4
Median	66.5	31.5	22.0	24.0	28.5	4.5
Range	31-83	18-74	6-28	5-49	4-37	0-18
Maximum number of consecutive avoidances						
Mean	20.5	4.5	2.6	2.4	2.5	1.3
Median	18.5	3.5	2.0	2.5	2.5	1.0
Range	6-41	2-11	1-6	1-4	1-4	0-3
Median avoidance latency						
Mean	2.66	2.88	3.19	2.20	2.98	2.97
Median	2.35	3.08	3.25	2.15	2.80	3.40
Range	1.9-4.1	1.9-3.4	2.3-3.7	1.0-3.3	2.2-4.3	1.3-3.5
Spontaneous responses						
Mean	29.0	16.1	11.0	25.1	12.8	13.5
Median	30.0	6.5	11.5	17.5	16.5	10.0
Range	1-57	0-50	1-20	3-59	0-28	1-38

"avoidances.") The acquisition of the avoidance response by experimental group is plotted in Figure 22-1 by blocks of ten trials. The 0-, 2.5-, and 5-second delay groups fall in the expected rank order. There is a minor reversal between the 5- and 10-second groups.

The data for total number of avoidance responses made by the four experimental groups were submitted to an analysis of variance. The effect of delay of CS-termination was highly significant ($F = 13.22$, $p < .001$). The more critical test was Whitney's bivariate extension of the U test, which was employed to test for the presence of trend within the 0-, 2.5-, and 5-second delay groups. This test confirmed a trend in the expected di-

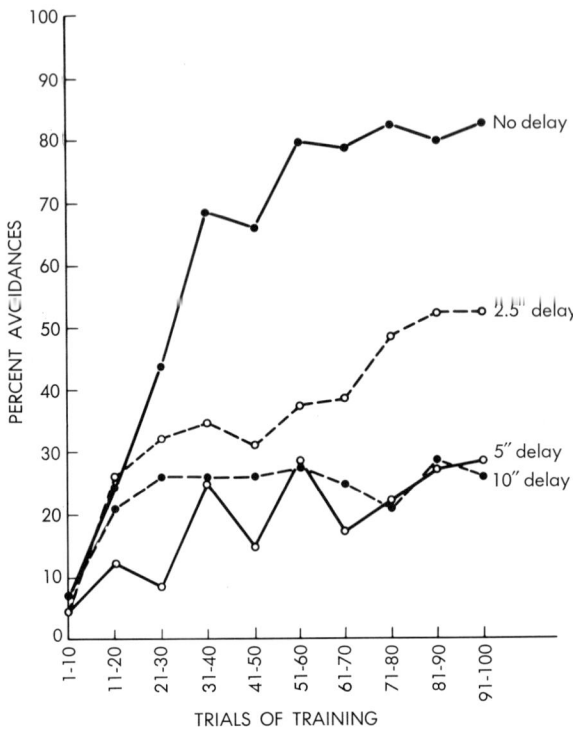

FIGURE 22-1. Acquisition of the avoidance response as a function of trials of training. Parameter is delay of CS-termination.

rection, significant far beyond the tabled .01 level. The small difference between the 5- and 10-second groups, submitted to the U test, was not significant.

The U test was utilized to assess differences between the control and experimental groups. The performance of the classical-control subjects was inferior to that of the no-delay group at much beyond the .01 level; but neither the classicals' inferiority to the 2.5 group, nor their very slight superiority to the 5- and 10-second groups, was significant. The trial-by-trial acquisition curve of the classical subjects (omitted from Figure 22-1) closely approximated the curves of the 5- and 10-second groups. The backward-conditioning control subjects were unequivocally inferior to all others, including the classicals, at beyond the .01 level.

The gradient effect of delay of CS-termination on avoidance learning is presented graphically in Figure 22-2. The figure contrasts the data of the present study with those of the earlier study (Kamin, 1957) which delayed CS-termination on both escape and avoidance trials. The figure also indicates the number of responses made in the present study by the classical- (c) and backward-conditioning (b) control groups.

The avoidance latency data in Table 22-1 are difficult to interpret. The Whitney test indicates the expected trend, for the 0-, 2.5-, and 5-second groups only, to be significant ($p < .01$). The 10-second group, however, reverses this trend sharply. These data are in any event not very reliable, as the median avoidance latency was in some cases derived from a very small number of responses. The very variable data for spontaneous responding suggest no trend whatsoever.

Discussion

The data reveal a pronounced gradient effect of delay of CS-termination on acquisition of an avoidance response. The number of avoidances made and the latency of avoidance are monotonic functions of delay of CS-termination through a range of from 0- to 5-second delay, with the

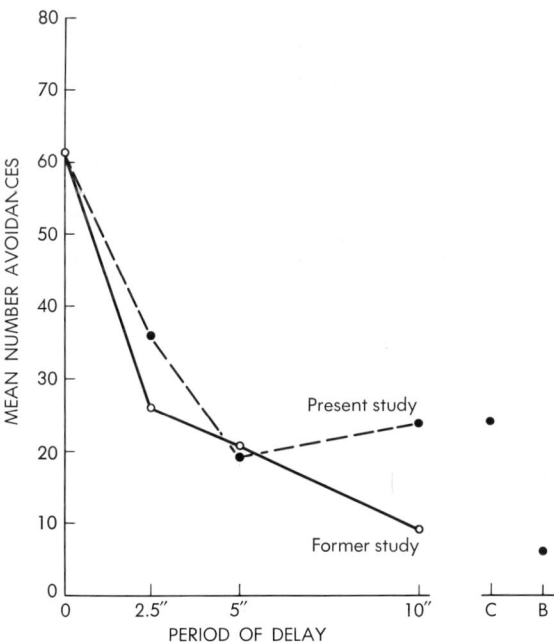

FIGURE 22-2. Total number of avoidance responses, in two experiments, as a function of delay of CS-termination. Reference points for classical- (C) and backward-conditioning (B) control groups are indicated.

performance of the 10-second delay group approximating that of the 5-second group. This gradient effect, since CS-termination was delayed on avoidance trials only, supports S-R interpretations which regard response termination of the CS as the reinforcement for avoidance. The obtained gradient appears to represent the effects of delay of secondary reward.

The gradient obtained in the present study is somewhat flatter than that obtained in the earlier study. This is due to an inhibitory effect of delay of CS-termination during *escape* trials on the appearance of antedating avoidance responses, particularly when CS-termination is long delayed. The 10-second group of the former study is significantly inferior to that of the present study ($p < .05$), and does not differ significantly from the backward-conditioning controls.

The data of the classical controls have some theoretical significance. We had suggested in an earlier paper (Kamin, 1956) that response termination of the CS should have a facilitating effect on the acquisition of avoidance, independent of avoidance of the US. This suggestion was confirmed in a factorially designed experiment; but the performance of a group which avoided shock without response termination of the CS was superior to that of a classically trained group. This embarrassment for S-R theory was evaded with the suggestion that experimental conditions were such that the group which avoided without response termination of the CS, derived reinforcement from CS-termination *shortly after* their avoidance responses. Thus, we predicted that a study of the effects of delay of CS-termination would reveal a gradient of reinforcement, with some period of delay at which performance was no better than that of a classical control group. The present study reveals just such a gradient. When CS-termination is delayed for as little as 5 seconds beyond the avoidance response, performance is in fact not significantly inferior to a classical procedure. These data demonstrate at the least that mere avoidance of the US is not a sufficient condition for the establishment of avoidance learning and that response termination of the CS is necessary for effective learning.

The close agreement between the 5- and 10-second delay groups and the classical subjects in total number of responses suggests that their performance represents some irreducible minimum. This number of responses will probably always occur when escape trials result in response termination of the CS, regardless of whether or not avoidance is permitted and of how much longer CS-termination might be delayed on avoidance trials. There must be, as Mowrer and Lamoreaux observed (1942), some factor at work during the early escape trials which tends to make the escape response antedating; otherwise, the *first* avoidance response would never occur. The fact that avoidance training involves sequential alternation of escape and avoidance trials means that this factor continues to contribute "avoidances" throughout training. Presumably, responses made by the classical and by the 5- and 10-second groups are entirely attributable to this factor.

We know very little about this factor. We do not know that it is not "sensitization," nor is it mere practice at escaping from shock; rather, the CS must precede the US in time for this factor to operate effectively. These facts are shown by the inferiority of the backward-conditioning controls to *all* other groups. We know also that this factor is sensitive to the effects of delay of CS-termination on *escape* trials (Kamin, 1957). While S-R theorists have not hesitated to speculate about this factor, no present theory predicts unequivocally even the few known facts. The S-R theories at this difficult point have no advantage over cognitive views which assign the first avoidance response to some "expectancy" of shock. The difficulty for cognitive interpretations in these data is the demonstration that the *reinforcement* of avoidance is not attributable to *confirmation* of an expectancy that shock will be avoided. When shock is avoided without CS-termination, avoidance is not reinforced.

EXPERIMENT II

There is a fundamental difficulty with parametric studies of avoidance, which is not eluded by the study reported as Experiment I. The structure of avoidance training is such that, when the independent variable under study affects the frequency of avoidance responses, experimental groups differ uncontrollably with regard to a number of confounded variables. Thus, if delay of CS-termination has an initial effect on avoidance frequency, experimental groups soon begin to differ in number of CS-US pairings, in number of exposures to the US, in patterns of partial reinforcement, in degree of practice of the escape response from the US, etc. These confounded variables are each theoretically relevant. Thus, the empirical effect of variation of a single parameter over an extended series of trials becomes a contaminated amalgam.

The variable of delay of CS-termination, however, will lend itself to an almost pure test. With a reasonably large N and with like treatment of all experimental groups on escape trials, the trial of first avoidance should be the same for all groups. Then, on the first avoidance trial, CS-termination can be delayed for a varying period for each of several groups. Then we can count the number of escape responses which occur before the next (second) avoidance takes place, and the experiment can be discontinued at this point.

This procedure means that the experimental groups will have been treated alike in every respect but one. The only differential treatment of groups occurs during the few seconds following the first avoidance.

Prior to this time, all groups will have had an equal number of identical escape trials, and all will have avoided only one US on the immediately preceding trial; after this time, all will again receive identical escape trials. Thus, any gradient which appears will be wholly attributable to the effects of one trial. The procedure in this respect affords a unique opportunity for the assessment of the effects of a single trial on avoidance learning.

Method

SUBJECTS, APPARATUS, PROCEDURE. The subjects were 101 naive hooded rats, of which 80 survived various selection criteria. There were 4 discards due to apparatus failure or experimental error, 8 discards for responding to the first CS-presentation, and 9 discards for failing to make the first avoidance within 25 trials. The last criterion was adopted to make certain that no experimental group contained a disproportion of slow learners.

The various temporal intervals, as well as the procedure for escape and avoidance trials, duplicated the conditions of Experiment I. The present experiment, however, was discontinued when subject made its second avoidance.

DESIGN. The 80 surviving subjects had been randomly assigned to experimental groups, with 20 subjects in each of four groups. The sole difference in treatment of groups was the duration of the CS on the first avoidance trial. The intervals between the avoidance response and CS-termination were 0, 2.5, 5, and 10 seconds for the various groups.

Results

There were no significant differences among groups for the trial on which the first avoidance occurred, for the latency of the first avoidance, or for the number of spontaneous responses. This indicates satisfactory random assignment of subjects to groups. Table 22-2 presents by experimental groups data for the trial and latency of the first avoidance. There was *very* little spontaneous responding, the median subject failing to make a single such response.

Table 22-3 presents data for the number of escape trials intervening between the first and second avoidances, and for the latency of the second avoidance. There appears to be a tendency for both these indices to vary directly with delay of CS-termination. The data for number of intervening escapes were submitted to a simple analysis of variance. The resulting $F(3.89$, with 3 and 76 df) was significant ($p < .025$). Whitney's bivariate extension of the U test was employed to test for trend within the 0-,

TABLE 22-2

Characteristics of the first avoidance response, by experimental groups

MEASURE	SECONDS OF DELAY OF CS-TERMINATION			
	0	2.5	5	10
Trial of first avoidance				
Median	10.00	11.50	9.50	9.50
Mean	11.65	10.50	10.0	10.40
Range	2-24	2-20	2-25	2-24
Latency of first avoidance				
Median	3.10	3.00	3.20	3.40
Mean	2.89	3.05	3.21	3.23
Range	0.8-5.0	0.7-5.0	1.6-4.9	1.0-5.0

2.5-, and 5-second delay groups. The test indicates a trend in the expected direction, significant far beyond the tabled .01 level. The differences between all pairs of experimental groups were tested by the U test, one-tailed evaluation. The no-delay group differed significantly from all others (0 vs. 2.5 seconds, $p < .05$; 0 vs. 5 and 0 vs. 10 seconds,

TABLE 22-3

Characteristics of the second avoidance response as a function of delay of CS-termination

MEASURE	SECONDS OF DELAY OF CS-TERMINATION			
	0	2.5	5	10
Number of escapes intervening between 1st and 2nd avoidance				
Median	1.00	2.50	6.00	6.50
Mean	2.30	5.00	9.75	6.50
Range	0-9	0-27	1-49	1-15
Latency of 2nd avoidance				
Median	2.50	3.50	3.70	3.75
Mean	2.81	3.35	3.32	3.36
Range	0.6-5.0	1.6-4.9	1.8-4.9	1.4-4.8

p < .001). The 2.5-second group also differed significantly from the 5-second group (p < .025).

The analysis of variance of latencies of the second avoidance indicated no significant effect, and differences between pairs of groups for this index were also not significant. There was a suggestion, however, that a real difference may exist between the no-delay group and groups trained with delay. The *ps* of differences between the no-delay and other groups ranged from .15 to .08, while differences among delay groups had *ps* of .50.

Discussion

The data clearly demonstrate a gradient effect. The number of escape trials intervening between the first and second avoidances varies with the delay of CS-termination on the first avoidance trial, with all other variables controlled or randomized. Thus, the data support S-R conceptions which attribute reinforcement of avoidance to response termination of a secondarily noxious CS. The data do not elucidate the factors responsible for the appearance of the *first* avoidance response. The factors operative during early escape trials to produce the initial avoidance must continue to operate during subsequent escape trials. Thus, the trial of *second* avoidance in this study must be the product of two forces—reinforcement of the first avoidance, plus the facilitating effects of escape trials. The *direction* of the gradient, however, is clearly attributable to the varying delays of CS-termination on the first avoidance trial. The data thus indicate that the increment to a tendency toward avoidance responding is a monotonic function of delay of CS-termination on avoidance trials. This is clearly in accord with the notion that CS-termination constitutes a secondary reward.

While the confirmation of a prediction tends to support the theorizing which suggested this study, there are alternative interpretations possible. Thus, it might be argued that delay of CS-termination is not a delay of secondary *reward,* but a lengthening of secondary *punishment*. This view suggests that the no-delay groups are merely not punished for avoidance responses, while delay groups are punished by progressively longer exposures to a secondarily aversive CS. There appear to be no clear data from other studies to support any expectation that length of punishment has a gradient effect on responding. The confounding of delay of reward and "lengthening of punishment" is in any event inevitable when the reward is removal of a noxious stimulus.

Then it might be argued that the effect of delayed CS-termination is not on the *instrumental* avoidance response, but on a *classically* conditioned fear of the CS assumed to underlie avoidance. That is, fear (or acquired aversiveness) of the CS may be diminished not only by the

The Gradient of Delay of Secondary Reward

dissociation of CS and US (a constant for all groups) but also by a prolonged exposure to the CS. There again appear to be no clear data on whether classical conditioning extinguishes in this cathartic fashion. This possibility could be tested experimentally with the use of some independent index of fear.

These data, finally, have a special interest in the fact that they demonstrate the effects on learning of a single trial. The sensitivity of shuttlebox avoidance learning to such an index is perhaps surprising and of particular concern to theories of avoidance which assume that cycles of one or two trials have significant effects. . . .

SUMMARY

With the assumption that response termination of the CS is a reinforcer of avoidance learning, the parameter of delay of CS-termination (delay of secondary reward) was explored in two experiments. The termination of the CS was delayed on avoidance trials only. The apparatus was a shuttlebox, and subjects were 128 hooded rats.

When training was continued for 100 trials, acquisition of avoidance was a declining monotonic function of delay of CS-termination through a range of from 0 to 5-second delay. The performance of a 10-second delay group did not differ significantly from the 5-second group. The groups trained with any period of delay (other than zero) did not differ from a classically trained control group, but all groups were significantly superior to a backward-conditioning control group.

When CS-termination was varied on the first avoidance trial only, and the experiment discontinued with the second avoidance, the number of escape trials intervening between the first and second avoidances was similarly a monotonic function of delay of CS-termination. The data, demonstrating the effects of a single trial, support the assumption that delay of CS-termination is a delay of secondary reward.

23

The Dimensional Bases of Stimulus Generalization[1]

WAYNE O. EVANS

Since an early stage in the development of the psychology of learning the phenomenon of stimulus generalization has been a matter of theoretical and factual interest. In its first demonstration by Pavlov (1927), it was found that a response conditioned to one stimulus transferred, in reduced strength, to a new but similar stimulus. The phenomenon has since been found to be a very general one, occurring in many species and in a variety of experimental situations.

One of the most basic issues raised by the concept of stimulus generalization concerns the description of stimulus similarity (Hull, 1939; Keller & Schoenfeld, 1950). It has been found that the response does not transfer to the same degree to all stimuli; that is, the data obtained in studies of generalization often take the form of a gradient, in which the response strength diminishes with increasing differences between training and test stimuli. This fact leads to the concept that generalization occurs on some graded scale or dimension, which is, in some way, correlated with an independently specifiable dimension from which the training and the test stimuli are selected by the experimenter. In the classical studies of stimulus generalization the dimensions employed (for example, pitch and loudness) were easy to describe either in physical or psychophysical terms. In more recent studies, however, generalization has been demonstrated in contexts where the dimensions involved are not physical ones, semantic generalization being a good example. Such demonstrations have led certain authors to stress different forms of generalization, while others argue that generalization must occur on a variety of dimensional bases. It may be well to examine here some of the most prominent of these positions.

The earliest interpretations of stimulus generalization (Pavlov, 1927;

[1] Based on a dissertation submitted to the Graduate School of Duke University in partial fulfillment of the requirements for the Ph.D. degree. A much abbreviated version has been published elsewhere (Evans, 1961).

Hull, 1939) typically attempted to relate generalization to discrimination. For example, Hull (1943) postulated that the generalization gradient is a decreasing exponential function on a j.n.d. scale of the physical properties of the stimuli. This implies that the more easily two stimuli can be discriminated, the less transfer there should be between them. Shepard (1958) and Kalish (1958) take essentially the same position.

Schlosberg and Solomon (1943) took the logical last step in this direction by proposing that the generalization gradient was a linear function of the discriminability of the physical properties of the stimuli. This proposition suggests that generalization is nothing more than a failure of the organism to discriminate among the stimuli and that the generalization experiment and the psychophysical experiment are essentially equivalent.

Certain facts of stimulus generalization are very difficult to interpret in terms of such a simple theory. First, there is the phenomenon of cross-modal generalization. Pavlov (1927) found that a response conditioned to a bell transferred to a light. It seems unlikely that this occurred because the animal confused the two stimuli. Then there is the fact of semantic generalization mentioned above (Osgood, 1957) in which meaning mediates the transfer of a conditioned response from one stimulus to another. Beyond this, generalization has been shown to occur in substantial amounts between stimuli differing as much as one hundred and fifty j.n.d.s in loudness (Hovland, 1937). Again, an interpretation in terms of the subject's failure to discriminate seems inappropriate. Experiments such as these, as well as evidence from experiments by Guttman and Kalish (1956), make it very difficult to accept the assumption that generalization occurs only as a result of the subject's confusion or a failure to discriminate among the stimuli on the basis of their physical properties.

A second view which has been proposed to explain the evidence of stimulus generalization is the Lashley and Wade (1946) hypothesis. These authors believe that stimulus generalization is not related to the discrimination of the absolute physical properties of the stimuli but rather is established by the organism's learning the relationships among the stimuli. They have stated, "The dimensions of a stimulus series are determined by comparison of two or more stimuli and do not exist for the organism until established by differential training." To these authors the dimensional bases of stimulus generalization are the relationships among the stimuli in a series, which the organism must learn by comparing the stimulus elements.

Although it is attractive on intuitive grounds, this theory fails at the points where a discrimination theory is most successful. Relational theory does not account for the numerous studies in which the subjects have produced generalization gradients when they have not been able to compare the stimuli, nor does it account for the results of experiments in which the stimulus generalization gradients are very similar to the discrimination functions for the same data. These weaknesses are ably summarized by Hull (1947).

A third approach to the question has been proposed by Razran (1949). He identifies his own view as "the categorizing rating position." According to Razran, the Lashley and Wade position is correct, but only part of the story. He calls the data which can be explained by Lashley and Wade "pseudogeneralization." To Razran "true" generalization is the formation by the organism of crude categories of similarity-dissimilarity. In essence, Razran accepts relational generalization, but contends that "true" generalization involves mediational processes, and that the bases of generalization are much cruder than the term dimension seems to imply. An analysis of Hovland's results on pitch generalization provides good support for such a position, in that Razran shows that there is little evidence for a smooth gradient in the data for individual subjects.

As with Lashley and Wade, Razran has difficulty in explaining the results of certain studies. Possibly the most embarrassing are those in which individual organisms produce finely graded generalization functions, such as those found by Guttman and Kalish (1956). It is also difficult to see why the extrinsic relational dimensions of Lashley and Wade are "pseudo" or, why the categorizing behavior proposed by Razran is "true" generalization.

In this paper an attempt will be made to distinguish between different sources of stimulus similarity. The approach resembles that of Dollard and Miller (1950) and, even more closely, that suggested by Hilgard and Marquis. These latter authors have stated, "There are many types of equivalence between stimuli which cause the stimuli to be reacted to as similar, so that conditioned responses formed to one of the stimuli will be generalized to the other. Among these may be mentioned: partial identity, sensory similarity, formal similarity, affective similarity, and mediated similarity" (Hilgard & Marquis, 1940, p. 201).

It is the present author's belief that gradients of stimulus generalization may be produced by the organisms responding to any one of three basic types of dimensions. These three types will be referred to as absolute, relational, and connotative dimensions. The absolute dimension serves as the basis of the transfer of a response when the stimuli are physically similar. This incorporates the partial identity and the sensory similarity types mentioned by Hilgard and Marquis. Such generalization is of the sort described by Schlosberg and Solomon (1943) in which the basic process is the failure of the subject to discriminate physically similar stimuli and in which the more similar the stimuli, the greater will be the amount of transfer. The gradient is, therefore, a confusion gradient produced by the organism which would be expected to show a close resemblance to a psychophysical function.

The Dimensional Bases of Stimulus Generalization 323

The relational dimension is similar to the formal similarity of stimuli mentioned by Hilgard and Marquis. It is not directly related to the absolute physical properties of the stimuli, but is dependent upon the relationships among the absolute properties of the stimuli. The utilization of this type of dimension is dependent upon the ability of the subject to compare stimuli, either with the aid of memory or because two or more stimuli are physically present at the same time. Since the gradient resulting from the utilization of the relational dimension is not caused by the subject's confusion as to the identity of the stimuli, the gradient need have no direct relationship to the discriminability of the stimuli along an absolute physical dimension. A gradient of stimulus generalization of this sort may result when the stimuli are easily discriminable one from another.

Finally, gradients of stimulus generalization sometimes occur along dimensions which are not describable in terms of the physical stimulus situation. Semantic generalization is the most widely studied form of such generalization. This type of dimension might be called a connotative one since it depends upon the meaning assigned to the stimuli presented. Obviously such generalization poses a peculiar problem in connection with the independent specification and scaling of the dimensions (or categories) involved.

Probably it should be mentioned here that the author's belief is that these three basic types of generalization (and perhaps others) may occur simultaneously. It is obvious that even the purest example of an absolute generalization involves at least an element of mediational activity; and that, conversely, the most involved instance of mediated generalization involves physical stimuli. This does not mean, however, that these forms of generalization are in no way separable. The general purpose of this study is to clarify the operation of two types of generalization in a situation involving ·a simple voluntary response.

The dimensions with which this study is most directly concerned are the absolute and the relational ones. Recently, Brown, Clark, and Stein (1958) have presented an experimental study of what they refer to as spatial generalization. In this study the stimuli were lights arranged about 8 inches apart in a horizontal row approximately 6 feet in front of the subject. All of the lights were visible at the same time. The subjects were told that the lights represented race horses and that their task was to guess whether the horse "won" or "lost" in a series of "races." In all there were 210 trials or "races." The "horse" represented by the middle light "won" 80 percent of the races; the other "horses" (lights) "won" 20 percent of the time. The subjects run under these conditions produced smooth gradients of generalization on both sides of the highly reinforced center light. The probability of a "win" response declined symmetrically as a function of distance from the center light. The character of the data led Brown, Clark, and Stein to describe their results as an instance of spatial generalization, an interpretation which we would class as one in terms of absolute generalization.

Such an interpretation, even on common sense grounds, does not seem acceptable. With the lights so far apart, it seems unlikely that the subjects had any difficulty in discriminating among the stimuli; and yet impressive generalization gradients were formed. On the other hand, the procedures used in this study appear to lend themselves to an analysis of the dimension which subjects actually employed. Such an analysis is undertaken in this report.

METHOD

The series of four experiments involved in this report shared certain features in common. In each experiment the procedure, apparatus, instructions, and response measures were similar. For this reason, a general description of the experimental method is given here and the specific alterations of the procedure are described in connection with the experiments to which they apply.

APPARATUS. The apparatus was a modification of the type used by Brown, Clark, and Stein (1958). It consisted of an opaque black screen with seven six-watt lights mounted on it. The lights were arranged in a horizontal line on the side of the screen facing the subject. The lights were mounted eight inches from the top of the screen by a device that allowed them to be moved from one position to another in a horizontal line. This allowed the experimenter to vary the distances between the lights.

On the subject's side of the screen there were two response keys. The key to the subject's right was marked "win" and the key to his left was marked "lose." Pressing either of the response keys illuminated a "win" or "lose" sign to indicate to the subject whether the horse had "won" or "lost" the "race" represented by a particular trial. The sign which came on was determined by the experimenter independently on the subject's response. These signs were used to inform the subject of the correctness of his choice of response; that is, as reinforcers.

PROCEDURE. In all experiments the subjects were seated in a chair at a distance approximately two feet in front of the screen. The following instructions were then read to them. These instructions were similar to those used by Brown, Clark, and Stein.

"In this experiment we are establishing the relationship between intelligence and gambling behavior. The seven lights you see here represent seven different race horses. These horses race at different times and at different parts of the country, but they never race against each other. The

The Dimensional Bases of Stimulus Generalization

lighting of a bulb means that the horse is in a race against other imaginary horses not represented here. Your task will be to guess whether the horse will win or lose the race. You will express your guess by pressing either the win or the lose button when the light comes on. Pressing the button will make a sign come on here which will tell you the actual outcome of that race. At first your bets will be sheer guesses, but as you proceed you will see that each horse wins a certain percentage of the races it is in. Since some of the horses will win a greater percentage than the other horses, this will allow you to bet with an increasing accuracy. At the end of the experiment, I shall ask you the percentages of the time that each horse won and compare it to your betting behavior on that horse. Naturally, the more intelligent a person is the more accurately he will be able to bet. Do not be surprised if the experiment is different from what you might have heard from your friends, since there are many different conditions and the likelihood of you being in the same one is small. This is not a reaction time experiment so there is no need for you to hurry. Just bet without particular haste or delay. Remember the horses never run against each other and your job is to bet as well as you can on each race. Are there any questions? Very well, let's start."

To begin the experiment, the experimenter turned on one of the seven horizontal lights, and set the reinforcement sign selector switch to either "win" or "lose." The subject then pressed one of the response keys and turned on the reinforcement sign previously selected by the experimenter. After a delay of one and one-half seconds the horizontal light and the reinforcement sign automatically turned off and the apparatus reset itself for the next trial.

The order of presentation of the stimulus lights and of the "win" or "lose" trials were predetermined, and were random with certain constraints. The constraints were that no stimulus could be presented more often than any other and that every stimulus followed each other stimulus equally often. Each stimulus light was presented 24 times. This made a total of 168 trials. The reinforcements were arranged so that the horse symbolized by the middle light, i.e., light number four won 80 percent of the time and all other lights won 20 percent of the time. With the constraints already mentioned, the time that a given light "won" or "lost" was random.

The time between trials was approximately three seconds. During the trials the experimenter noted each response made by the subject to each stimulus on each presentation. Following the completion of the experiment the subjects were asked to estimate the percentage of times that each stimulus light had "won."

SUBJECTS. The subjects were 100 male and female students of general psychology at Duke University. Their ages ranged between 18 and 29 years.

Experiment I

The purpose of this experiment was to determine whether the procedure described in the method section produced a stimulus generalization gradient which was based on a dimension of absolute physical space. Previously, Brown, Clark, and Stein (1958) using a similar apparatus and procedure had obtained a generalization gradient which they believed was based on an absolute spatial dimension. The gradient, however, occurred in a situation where the individual stimuli were so far apart that they must have been easily discriminable one from another. In fact, Brown, Clark and Stein mentioned that it was difficult to understand how a stimulus generalization gradient could be formed when the stimuli were so easily discriminable.

In considering this problem the present author noted the possibility that the gradient produced by the Brown, Clark, and Stein procedure might not actually be based on the absolute spatial positions of the stimuli, but rather on the relational spatial positions of the stimuli. This could well have been the case, since the stimulus lights were all simultaneously present and available to inspection, making it easy for the subjects to note the relationships among them. If such relationships, rather than the absolute spatial locations of the stimuli, did provide the basis for generalization, then changing the distance between the lights should not affect either the shape or the height of the generalization gradient, because this distance does not alter such relationships. On the other hand, if the gradient depended on the absolute spatial dimension, then changing the distance between the stimulus lights should sample from different parts of the underlying spatial gradient. This would lead to a flatter gradient, if the stimulus lights were placed closer together. Experiment I was designed to investigate these possibilities.

METHOD. The apparatus and procedure for this experiment was the same as outlined in the method section. Two groups of ten subjects each were used. For the first group, the stimulus lights were placed 3 inches apart while, for the second group they were placed 1.5 inches apart. The first group was called group 3.0-NS. This means that the stimulus lights were 3.0 inches apart, and that there was no translucent screen (used in later experiments) in front of the stimulus elements. The second group was designated 1.5-NS, indicating that the stimulus lights were 1.5 inches apart and there was no screen in front of the lights.

RESULTS. The mean percentages of "win" responses to each stimulus light for both groups are shown in Figure 23-1, which suggests that chang-

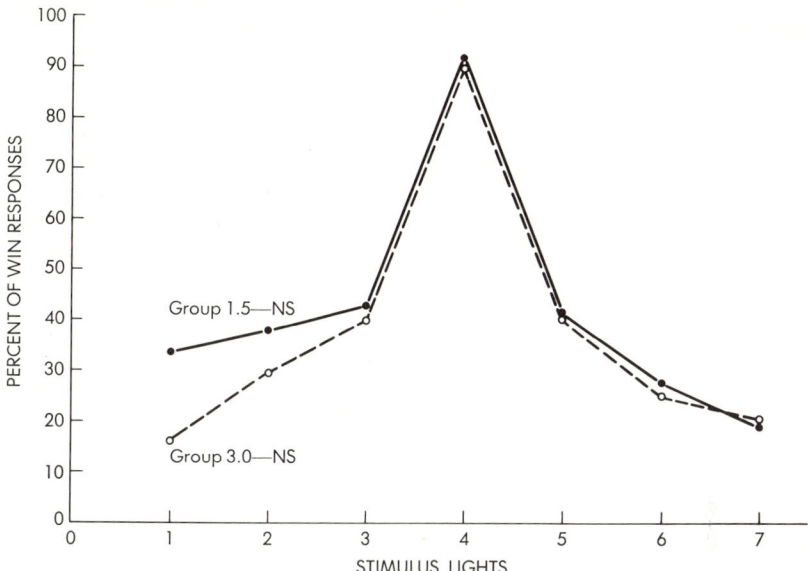

FIGURE 23-1. Comparison of groups 3.0-NS and 1.5-NS (Experiment I).

ing the spatial separation of the lights did not change either the shape or the height of the stimulus generalization gradient.

For the purpose of statistical analysis, the two sides of the gradients were averaged. This was permissible since the gradients seemed by inspection to be symmetrical. The responses to the fourth light, i.e., the 80 percent reinforced light, were not included. This was done to eliminate the elevation due to reinforcement rather than to generalization. A comparison of the two resulting curves was made by an Alexander test of trend (Alexander, 1946). The F value for between group slopes was less than 1.00, and that for between group means was 1.77. Both of these values are well below a confidence level of .05. On the other hand, the F value for overall slope was 24.90 ($p. < .001$).

DISCUSSION. It is clear that the procedure employed in this experiment produces generalization gradients similar to those obtained in other investigations. But it is also apparent that the physical separation of stimuli has little or nothing to do with the production of this gradient. The fact that changing the distances between the stimulus lights had no effect upon the gradient suggests that the gradients obtained depend upon the relationships among the stimuli rather than their absolute positions in space. The following experiments will demonstrate the tenability of this hypothesis.

Experiment II

On the assumption that the gradients obtained in Experiment I depend upon the subject's perception of the relationships among stimuli, it follows that any operation which tends to prevent the perception of the relationships should either destroy the gradient or force the subject to rely on some other dimension than the relational one in the development of a gradient. Experiment II explored these possibilities. In this study the stimulus lights were covered by a translucent screen which prevented comparisons of the locations of the individual lights and again the spatial separation of the stimuli was manipulated.

METHOD. The apparatus and procedure was the same as in Experiment I. In this experiment, however, a translucent screen was placed in front of the stimulus lights. This effectively prevented the subject from seeing any stimulus light except the one illuminated for the particular trial. The instructions were the same as in Experiment I with the exception that there was no mention of the number of "horses." This was done in order to eliminate relational cues based on a knowledge of the number of stimuli present. The subjects were questioned following the experiment as to the number of stimulus lights they believed to have been present.

There were three groups of ten subjects each. For group 3.0-S the stimulus lights were 3.0 inches apart. For group 1.5-S the stimuli were 1.5 inches apart. For group .75-S the stimuli were .75 inches apart. The designation "S" for these groups indicates the presence of the translucent screen. The same procedure was used for all three groups.

RESULTS AND DISCUSSION. Figure 23-2 shows the performance of each group plotted in percentage of "win" responses to each stimulus light. From this graph we see that as the inervals between the stimuli becomes smaller, a gradient becomes more pronounced. No significant trend was found for group slope in group 3.0-S ($F < 1.00$. In group 1.5-S a gradient appears to be developing, although the F value for trend (4.22) was not quite significant at the .05 level of confidence. Group .75-S shows a well developed gradient. The F value for group slope was 27.36 ($p = .001$). A comparison of the slopes of groups 75-S and 3.0-S yielded an F value of 14.69 ($p = .001$).

In order to determine whether the presence of the screen made a difference at wide stimulus intervals, a comparison was made between groups 3.0-S and 3.0-NS from Experiment I. Figure 23-3 presents these curves which suggests that the groups differed both in slope and in absolute level of performance. Analysis of variance supports these conclusions. The F value for between group slopes was 78.79; that for between group means was 34.70 ($p < .001$ in both cases).

The Dimensional Bases of Stimulus Generalization

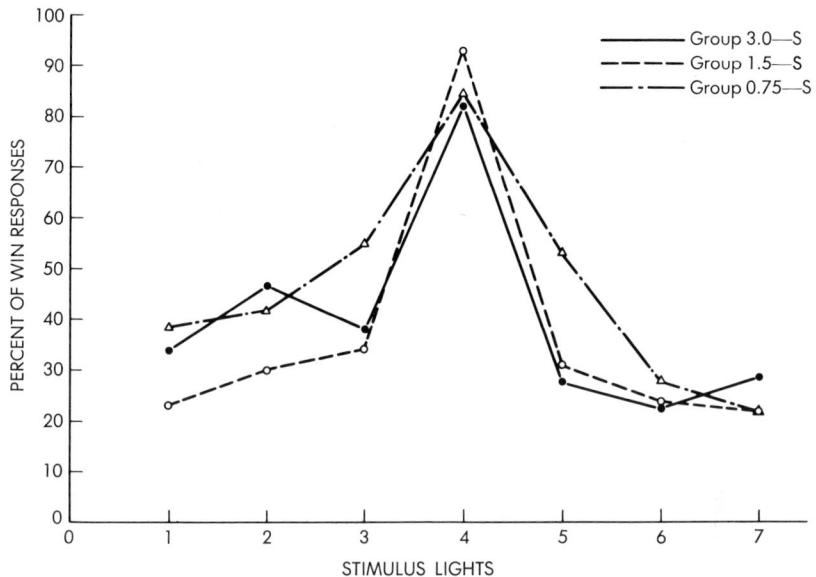

FIGURE 23-2. Comparison of groups 3.0-S, 1.5-S, and .75-S (Experiment II).

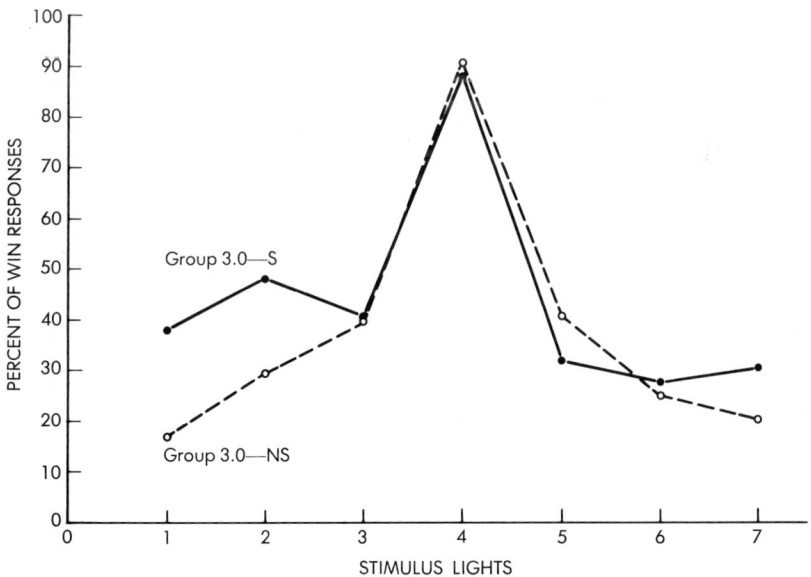

FIGURE 23-3. Comparison of groups 3.0-S and 3.0-NS (Experiment II).

From these results it is clear that at wide stimulus intervals the presence of a screen which prevents the subject from seeing more than one stimulus at a time does destroy the generalization gradient. This supports the conclusion that the gradient obtained at wide stimulus separations in Experiment I was, indeed, a relational gradient based on relative stimulus positions, and not on absolute spatial intervals between stimuli. When the interval between the lights is very small, however, a gradient appears. It seems likely that this gradient is of a different type based on the subject's inability to identify the elements. In group .75-S less than 25 percent of the subjects could even guess the number of stimulus lights which had been presented. In group 3.0-S all subjects guessed the correct number of stimulus lights.

The results of Experiments I and II indicate that depending upon the details of experimental procedure, either a relational or an absolute dimension may serve as the basis for stimulus generalization. There are, however, important differences in the processes involved. The absolute gradient results when the subject confuses stimuli. The relational gradient occurs under the circumstances which make such confusion most unlikely.

Experiment III

The previous experiments in this study seem to have established that a gradient may be formed upon a relational dimension. But there remains one possibility which has been examined in this experiment. This possibility is that the generalization gradients obtained in Experiment I were actually based on a connotative dimension provided by an implicit numbering of the stimuli. If the subjects had been implicitly numbering the stimulus lights, these numbers could have served as the dimension for the generalization. To investigate this alternative explanation it seems appropriate to perform an experiment in which position is held constant and numbering is encouraged. If a gradient is formed under these conditions, we will not be able to say that the relational positions of the stimuli are the basis for the generalization gradients previously obtained.

METHOD. The apparatus was modified so that only the middle six inches of the translucent screen could be seen by the subject. Rather than using the lights for stimuli, transparent plastic slides were inserted behind the screen always in the same position. These seven slides contained identical silhouettes of a race horse. Above each horse was a one-inch high number from 1 to 7. The general procedure and instructions were the same as in Experiment I. One group of ten subjects was used. This group is designated CP for the constant position of the stimuli. The entire procedure is very similar to that used by Bass (1958) to establish generali-

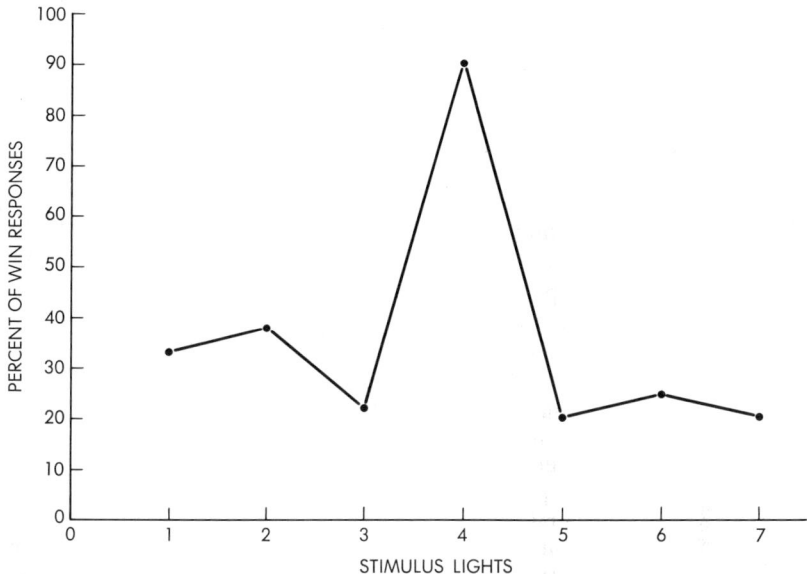

FIGURE 23-4. Curve of responses with stimuli in a constant position (Experiment III).

zation gradients for a series of horses with shades of gray as the dimension of generalization.

RESULTS AND DISCUSSION. Figure 23-4 presents the generalization gradient in terms of mean percentage of "win" responses to each stimulus horse. This figure suggests that there were no differences among numbers of win response to the lights flanking the most heavily reinforced light. Statistical tests support this interpretation. The F value for slope was 1.39 ($p < .05$).

These data suggest that the results of the previous experiments are probably not due to an implicit numbering of the stimuli. No generalization was found when the numbers of the stimuli differed but the position of the stimuli was the same. It is therefore concluded that the gradients obtained in Experiment I were not based on a connotative dimension.

Experiment IV

Thus far we have seen that a gradient may be formed to the stimulus lights under two different conditions. First, if the lights are very close together, and if a comparison of location is impossible, the subject may form a gradient based on difficulties of discriminating among stimuli. Second, when the stimuli are far apart and comparison is possible another type of gradient may appear apparently based on the subject's perception of the relationships among the stimulus lights. This second type of gradient brings to mind the explanation of stimulus generalization proposed by Lashley and Wade (1946). These authors believed that a gradient was the result of the organism's having learned a dimension by comparisons of the stimuli. If this view is correct, then an initial training on the gradient during which the subject is allowed to compare the stimuli might allow him to continue to show a gradient even when comparison of stimuli is prevented. In short, it may be that the comparison of the stimuli is only necessary to allow the subject to learn about the stimulus dimension. After such learning, the comparison might no longer be necessary in order for the subject to continue to respond in terms of the relational dimension. The purpose of this experiment is to test this hypothesis.

METHOD. The apparatus and procedures were the same as in Experiment I except for the conditions of training. In this experiment there was one group of ten subjects run under conditions which made comparisons with previous groups possible. This group, group 3.0-PS (PS = part screen), received the first 84 trials without the screen and with the stimulus lights 3.0 inches apart. For the second 84 trials the screen was present. This second half of the trials was comparable to the conditions under which group 3.0-S in Experiment II had previously shown not to produce a gradient. Group 3.0-NS has been shown to form a relational type gradient. We thus have in group 3.0-PS a situation in which the subjects are allowed to learn the dimension initially but are prevented from comparing the stimuli during the period to be used for the test of the hypothesis.

RESULTS AND DISCUSSION. Figure 23-5 shows a comparison of the first 84 trials of groups 3.0-PS and 3.0-NS from Experiment I. Obviously there are no important differences in performance between the two groups, a fact supported by appropriate statistical analysis.

Figure 23-6 presents a comparison of the last 84 trials of groups 3.0-PS and 3.0-NS. It can be seen that the addition of a screen actually facilitated the formation of the gradient. The F value for between group slopes for the data plotted in this figure was 9.00 and that for between group means is 34.43. Both of these values are significant at the .005 level of confidence. We should also note that in the second half of the trials, group 3.0-PS was run under conditions comparable to those for group 3.0-S of Experiment II where no gradient was obtained.

The results obtained support Lashley and Wade's (1946) emphasis upon learning the stimulus dimension by comparison of the stimuli. Apparently the subjects only need a small amount of training in comparing the stimulus elements to continue to produce a gradient even when the comparison is no longer possible.

The Dimensional Bases of Stimulus Generalization 333

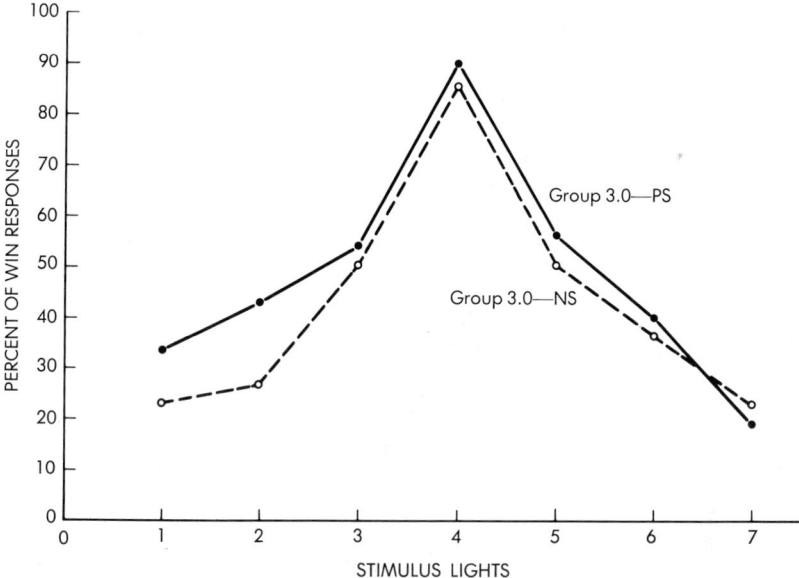

FIGURE 23-5. Comparison of groups 3.0-PS and 3.0-NS for the first half of the trials (Experiment IV).

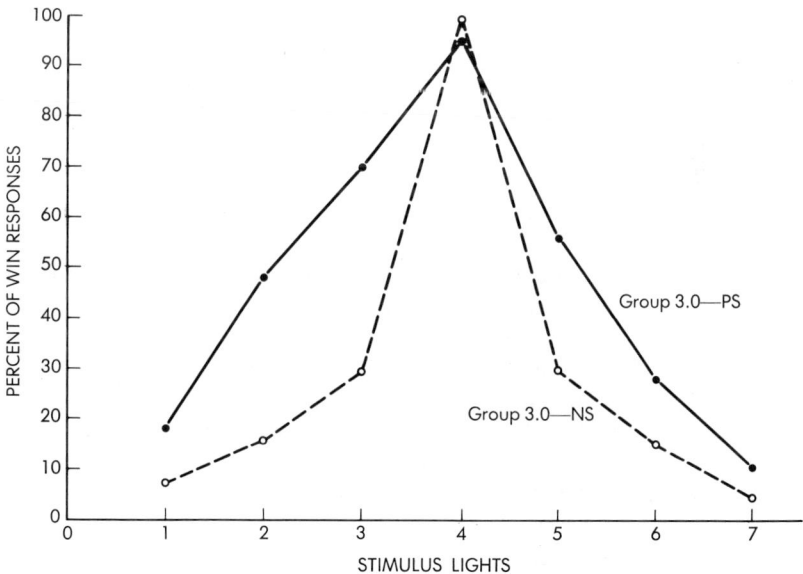

FIGURE 23-6. Comparison of groups 3.0-NS and 3.0-PS for the second half of the trials (Experiment IV).

The most surprising result was that the gradient produced by initially training without the screen and then testing with the screen in place led to a more pronounced gradient than was produced by allowing the subjects to compare the stimuli on all trials. This result was unexpected and the explanation does not seem obvious. Perhaps the slight degree of ambiguity added by the screen produced a confusion in the subject which contributed to the formation of the gradient. If so, this is one of the cases referred to previously, in which the two types of generalization occur together.

GENERAL DISCUSSION

The results of these experiments have tended to suggest that either the absolute physical properties or the relational properties of the stimuli may serve as the dimension of stimulus similarity upon which a subject may produce a stimulus generalization gradient. One of the conditions found to be necessary for the formation of a gradient based upon a relational dimension is the presentation of the stimuli in a way that allows the subject to compare them. This finding supports the position of Lashley and Wade (1946). The relational gradient was found not to depend upon the discriminability of the individual stimulus elements.

The importance of the relational gradient of stimulus generalization is probably very great. Modern S-R theory of transfer of training usually makes the assumption of stimulus generalization as a basic postulate. In most transfer experiments, however, it is very difficult to believe that the transfer occurs only because the learner confuses the test situation with the training situation. The existence of dimensions of similarity based upon relationships among the stimuli seems absolutely necessary to account for the transfer of training in most of the usual situations employed to study this process.

Even many situations which have previously been explained using absolute physical dimensions may be interpreted much more easily using the concept of relational cues rather than absolute physical cues as the basis of the transfer. An example of such a situation is provided by the classical study on spatial generalization by Bass and Hull (1934). It seems improbable that the subjects in these experiments were confused as to the stimulus locations, and much more likely that they were responding to the relational order of the stimuli along the body. A similar set of examples are found, of course, in previous experiments using the methods employed in the present study. Another, rather important, example of the possible use of relational dimensions might be found in the studies which utilize the concept of the goal gradient (Brown, 1942). In most life situations organisms do not approach their goals through homogeneous environments such as the all gray straight-a-way alley provides. In many cases it will probably be much more profitable to look upon the goal gradients of organisms as ordinal relationships between distinctive stimuli along the path to the goal object. Notions such as this seem to lie behind Miller's (1959) liberalization of S-R theory to include relational cues as determinants of behavior.

Another important result of the present study has been to clarify the relationship between the generalization gradient produced utilizing an absolute dimension and discrimination. The evidence indicates that the procedures for studying stimulus generalization and discrimination could be placed at extremes of a continuum representing the amount of information the organism possesses at the beginning of the experiment. This is the position taken by Brown, Bilodeau, and Baron (1951) who have stated, "The relation of psychophysical studies to generalization experiments might be clarified if they were treated as the two extremes of a series of experiments arranged according to the degree to which their procedures permit the appearance of empirical generalization."

With two bases for stimulus generalization reasonably well established by this study, it seems important, as a final comment, to repeat that it may be necessary to consider many types of dimensions in the analysis of stimulus generalization and transfer. The results of this study indicate that any general theory of stimulus generalization must include absolute and relational dimensions; other evidence (e.g., semantic generalization) points strongly to a connotative dimension. It does not seem impossible that many situations give rise to all these and probably other types of dimension at the same time with various weights assigned to each. It may also be that different people use the various dimensions to different degrees in the same situation. All in all, it is easy to see that we have barely scratched the surface of the question of stimulus generalization and the transfer of training.

SUMMARY

The main purposes of this study were, first, to demonstrate the existence of both relational and absolute dimensions of stimulus similarity as bases of stimulus generalization, and, second, to investigate the conditions under which each type of gradient appears.

The general method used in this study was similar to that used by Brown, Clark, and Stein (1958) of spatial generalization with human subjects. This procedure involved the reinforcement of the center light in a row of seven lights. The resulting gradient of generalization was then measured in terms of percentage of responses to the other lights in the row.

The present study consisted of four experiments. In Experiment I the stimulus lights were placed at different spatial intervals for different groups. The center light was reinforced 80 percent of the time and all other lights were reinforced twenty percent of the time. Since the resulting generalization gradients for the groups with different spatial intervals between the stimuli were the same, it was concluded that the dimension upon which the generalization took place was not one of physical distance.

In Experiment II the same procedure was used; but a translucent screen was placed in front of the stimuli, preventing the subject from seeing all of the stimuli simultaneously. In this case no gradients were found at stimulus intervals adequate to produce gradients when the screen was not in front of the lights. A gradient was produced, however, when the lights were closer together. From these facts it was inferred that the gradient demonstrated in the first experiment was relational and depended upon the subject's ability to see all of the stimuli simultaneously. It was also shown that the gradient produced when the screen is in place is based upon the dimension of absolute physical space and is related to the discriminability of the individual stimulus elements.

Experiment III presented evidence that the gradient produced in Experiment I was not based upon an implicit numbering of the stimuli and the resulting connotative dimension. This was shown by presenting a series of numbered silhouettes in a constant position behind the translucent screen. In this case the numbered stimuli did not produce a gradient of generalization.

In Experiment IV the hypothesis of Lashley and Wade (1946) was tested. These authors proposed that stimulus generalization is always relational and occurs only after the organism has become familiar with the dimension. This hypothesis was confirmed for relational dimensions by allowing the subjects to see the stimuli simultaneously for a series of trials and then covering them with the translucent screen. With this condition, the subjects produced generalization gradients with the translucent screen in place at stimulus intervals which had in Experiment II produced no gradients.

The results of these experiments were discussed in terms of the need for a general theory of stimulus generalization which could take into account the fact that different types of dimensions probably subserve stimulus generalization depending upon the particulars of the experimental situation.

24

The Generalization of an Instrumental Response to Stimuli Varying in the Size Dimension

G. ROBERT GRICE

ELI SALTZ

One of the most important concepts in modern learning theory is that of stimulus generalization. Hull (1943) has made extensive use of the concept in his behavior theory, and it is the concept by means of which Spence (1937, 1941, 1942a) was able to predict several of the transposition phenomena in visual discrimination learning. The importance of generalization is widely accepted. Yet in spite of the theoretical significance of the problem, relatively few experimental studies have been directly concerned with it. While the existence of generalization gradients has been adequately demonstrated, there is relatively little evidence concerning the precise nature of the functional relationships between the amount of generalization and various stimulus dimensions.

The most frequently cited studies are those of Hovland (1937a, 1937b), employing auditory stimuli and the conditioned galvanic skin response. Hovland found generalized response strength to be a negatively accelerated decreasing function of the number of j.n.d.'s difference in pitch or loudness between the test stimulus and the training stimulus. The gradient for intensity was much flatter than the pitch gradient. Humphreys (1939), using the same response, and frequency of tones as the stimulus dimension, also found the negatively accelerated gradient, but found a very flat or possibly a positively accelerated gradient if conditioning occurred under conditions of partial reinforcement. Until recently, there was very little data involving the generalization of instrumental responses. Brown (1942) demonstrated generalization of a running response in the rat to three degrees of brightness. Schlosberg and Solomon (1943), studying latency in a jumping stand choice situation, report data from four rats

[1] Reprinted from the *Journal of Experimental Psychology*, 1950, 40, 702–708 by permission of the American Psychological Association and the authors.

in which log latency was a linear function of difference in brightness from the initial positive stimulus. Their brightness scale was an equal appearing intervals scale based on human judgments. Recently, studies by Frick (1948) and Raben (1949) have demonstrated generalization of instrumental resposes to different levels of illumination, but yield no evidence as to the form of the primary gradient, since both studies involve discrimination training from the beginning of practice. Differential reinforcement, i.e., reinforcement of the positive stimulus and non-reinforcement of the negative, results in the narrowing of the range of empirical generalization gradients. Thus the form of such response gradients becomes a function of the number of non-reinforced trials to the generalized stimuli. This was especially well demonstrated by Raben. However, gradients obtained in this way do not reflect the primary generalization of habit strength in any simple way, but may best be interpreted as a joint function of generalized habit strength and inhibitory factors. In order to obtain a function which may be regarded as indicating the nature of primary stimulus generalization, it is necessary to build up habit strength to one stimulus and *then* to test for generalization to other stimuli on the dimension. For this purpose, no extinction of responses to the test stimuli should be introduced prior to the generalization test.

On the theoretical level, Hull (1943) has assumed, on the basis of Hovland's data, that the generalization gradient of habit strength is symmetrical and negatively accelerated when plotted on a j.n.d. scale. With respect to intensity dimensions, he has recently predicted (1949) that response gradients to stimuli of higher intensity will be convex, while those to stimuli of less intensity will be concave. (This is predicted because response strength is a function not only of habit strength, but of stimulus intensity per se.) Spence (1942), in his transposition theory, has assumed that the generalization gradients for the visual size dimension are convex when plotted on a logarithmic scale of area. The only evidence to support this assumption is the success of the theory in predicting transposition phenomena. No studies directly concerned with the generalization of instrumental responses to stimuli varying in the size dimension have been performed. The obtaining of such data seems desirable, both in relation to the problem of generalization as a whole, and in relation to the more specific discrimination learning theory. If empirical functions could be obtained for both generalization of habit strength and inhibition, rather precise predictions of transposition and related phenomena should be possible if the general principles of the theory are valid.

The present study is an attempt to determine the form of the stimulus generalization gradient for the visual size dimension in the white rat. Animals were trained to make a simple instrumental response to white circles of a particular size, and then separate groups were tested for amount of generalization to circles of differing sizes.

Experimental procedure

SUBJECTS. The subjects were 135 experimentally naive albino rats from the colony maintained by the Department of Psychology at the University of Illinois. There were 70 males and 65 females, the sexes being approximately evenly distributed among the experimental groups. The ages of the subjects ranged from 70 to 110 days at the beginning of the experiment. The animals' diet during the experiment consisted of seven grams of Purina Laboratory Chow administered in individual feeding cages after each daily experimental session. They were adapted to this schedule for a period of one week prior to the beginning of the experiment.

APPARATUS. The size stimuli employed in this experiment were white circles which have been previously described (Grice, 1948a). Briefly, they were white disks cut from sheet metal, with a small square door in the center. The door, which was flush with the surface of the disk, could be pushed open by the rat's nose. Attached to the back of the disk, just below the door, was the food dish, and the rat could easily obtain the food by pushing its nose through the door. The incentive used was pellets made of a mixture of Purina Chow and flour, which averaged 0.15 gm. in weight. The circles used in the experiment were 79, 63, 50, 32, and 20 sq. cm. in area. These represent equal logarithmic steps in area with the exception of 63, which is a half step between 79 and 50.

The apparatus in which the stimuli were presented has also been previously described (Grice, 1949). In brief, they were presented at the end of a 24-inch runway. The runway contained vertically sliding doors at each end and in the middle. It was mounted on a pivot at the center so that each half could become in turn the starting end and the reaction end. By rotating the alley after each trial, it was unnecessary to handle the

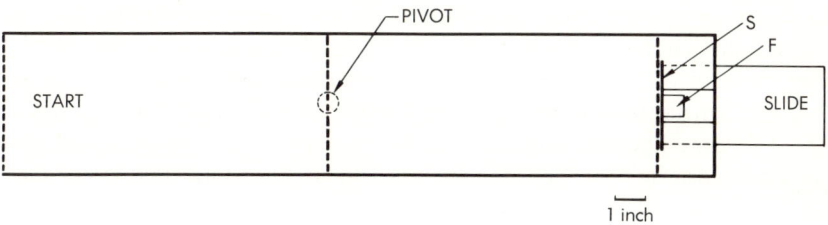

FIGURE 24-1. Floor plan of the apparatus. Heavy dotted lines indicate vertical sliding doors. The dotted circle indicates the point at which the 24-inch alley was pivoted. S indicates the stimulus circle, and F, the food dish. The 2-inch section of alley containing the circle could be moved back on the slide block to permit turning the long alley.

animal except at the beginning and end of the experimental session. Figure 24-1 is a schematic floor plan of the apparatus. The circle was housed at the front of a two-inch continuation of the alley which could be slid back to permit rotation of the alley. All of the circles were mounted with their centers equally distant from the floor. Thus, irrespective of the size of the circle, the small door was the same distance above the floor and the response to be made to each circle was the same.

PRELIMINARY TRAINING. The first step was to train the animals to open the small door in the circle and obtain food. On the first day the animal was placed in the reaction compartment with the door in the circle open, and was allowed to eat 10 pellets from the food dish. Then the alley was rotated and the rat ate 10 more pellets with the other end of the alley as the reaction compartment.

On the second day, the rat was placed in the starting compartment and was allowed to enter the reaction compartment and eat one pellet with the stimulus door wide open. Then the alley was rotated and the second trial was run with the door closed slightly. In all, 10 such trials were run with the door being more nearly closed on each trial. By the ninth and tenth trials the door was completely closed. Five animals which did not learn to open the door with this training procedure were eliminated.

The circle used in preliminary training was the one to be used in further reinforcement training. Animals to be tested for generalization to larger stimuli were trained on the 20 sq. cm. circle, and those to be tested for generalization to smaller stimuli were trained on the 79 sq. cm. circle.

REINFORCEMENT TRAINING. On each of the next three days the rats were given 20 trials of opening the door to obtain food. The alley was rotated between trials, and the trials were run in immediate succession—allowing only time for the rat to eat and for a new pellet to be placed in the food dish. Latencies were recorded from the time the door from the starting compartment was opened until the rat's nose moved the door in the stimulus circle. As soon as the food was obtained, the vertical sliding door in front of the stimulus circle was lowered, and the animal was allowed to eat the food before rotating the alley for the next trial.

The experimental work was conducted between the hours of one and five in the afternoon. Each animal was run at the same time every day.

GENERALIZATION TESTS. The tests of generalization consisted of a series of 25 extinction trials to the stimulus being tested. Animals being tested for generalization to larger stimuli were trained on the 20 sq. cm. circle and groups of 15 subjects each were then tested on circles of 20, 32, 50, and 79 sq. cm. Animals being tested for generalization to smaller stimuli were trained on the 79 sq. cm. circle and groups of 15 were extinguished on circles of 79, 63, 50, 32, and 20 sq. cm. The 63 sq. cm. circle (one-half of a log step between 79 and 50) was added after an inspection of preliminary data indicated the desirability of further information concerning the function in that area.

On the extinction day, the animals were first given five additional reinforced trials to the original stimulus. Then extinction trials to the test stimulus were begun without a break and were run one immediately following the other. On these trials, the door in the circle was locked so that it would open only $\frac{1}{8}$ inch and there was no food in the food dish. All of the circles were identical except for size, and were mounted so that their centers were all the same distance from the floor. For animals tested on a circle of the same size as that during initial training, a new circle of the same size was substituted. The criterion of a response was sufficient contact of the animal's nose with the door in the circle to move it. Latencies were recorded, and if the animal failed to respond in 60 seconds, the trial was scored as a failure of response. The measure of generalization employed was the number of responses made during the series of 25 extinction trials.

Results

The number of responses made by each animal during the extinction series and the mean for each group are given in Table 24-1. The generalization functions obtained are presented graphically in Figure 24-2. Mean number of responses during the test series is plotted as a function of area of the test stimuli in logarithmic units. The solid line represents generalization to stimuli of larger size and the broken line represents generalization to smaller stimuli. It may be seen that responses were made to all stimuli tested. In other words, generalization did occur; it extended in both directions; and all of the stimuli used fell within its range. Both gradients show a decreasing amount of generalization as a function of the difference in size from the training stimuli. This decrease was statistically significant. Analyses of variance were applied to each gradient to test the hypothesis that the means were equal. The F-values were 8.61 for generalization to larger stimuli and 9.59 for generalization to smaller stimuli, which, for the appropriate degrees of freedom, were both significant at the .001 level of confidence. Thus the null hypothesis may confidently be rejected in both cases.

With respect to the forms of the functions, it is first apparent that the two gradients are different. The gradient for generalization to smaller areas is concave or negatively accelerated, while the gradient for generalization to larger stimuli is first convex or positively accelerated and then becomes negatively accelerated. An analysis was performed to test the hypothesis that the two functions are of the same form. For this purpose

TABLE 24-1

Number of responses in 25 extinction trials*

TRAINING STIMULUS	79 sq. cm.					20 sq. cm.			
TEST STIMULUS	79	63	50	32	20	20	32	50	79
	15	16	5	9	7	9	22	8	12
	18	8	10	8	7	19	13	11	4
	9	12	10	8	0	10	17	2	1
	11	5	7	14	8	21	20	3	8
	13	9	17	5	11	10	8	4	14
	20	10	17	11	7	18	22	6	14
	9	12	11	9	9	11	12	10	5
	13	8	7	16	9	18	8	13	8
	5	11	7	7	2	23	14	15	4
	10	18	6	4	6	10	9	10	11
	22	12	6	9	8	10	8	4	3
	18	8	5	8	3	10	14	10	5
	17	11	7	8	1	9	13	4	5
	10	10	4	8	0	10	16	8	4
	12	12	9	10	0	8	4	1	0
MEAN	13.5	10.8	8.5	8.9	5.2	13.1	13.3	7.3	6.5

* Each value in the body of the table is the result of a single animal.

one function was reversed, both being plotted as functions merely of the number of log steps between the training and test stimuli. (The 63 sq. cm. point was omitted for this purpose since there was no corresponding point on the other curve.) The test employed was Case 9 suggested by Lindquist (1947). Specifically the hypothesis tested was that the means of successive differences between the points on the two curves was equal to zero. The analysis yielded an F of 6.73 which was significant at the five percent level of confidence, and approached significance at the one percent level. ($F = 6.87$ required for significance at the one percent level.) In other words, the test indicated the probability that the populations from which the two curves were drawn do not coincide and that the apparent difference in the functions is probably genuine.

Discussion

Probably the first point which should be mentioned in connection with the present data is that again the existence of generalization gradients has

The Generalization of an Instrumental Response

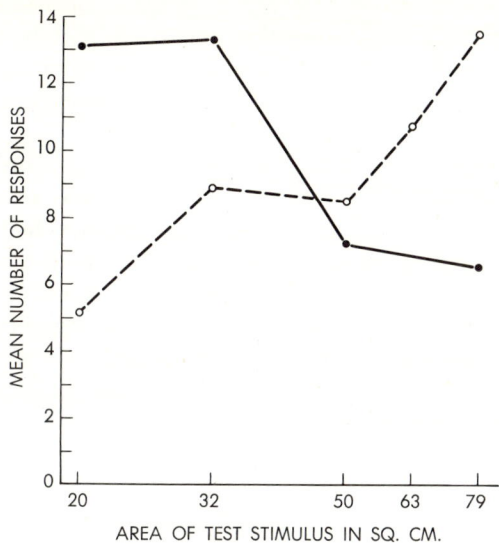

FIGURE 24.2. Generalization functions showing mean number of extinction responses for each test group.

been experimentally verified. This comes as no great surprise, but is of interest in relation to the contention of Lashley and Wade (1946) that such gradients, when obtained, are experimental artifacts due to training and testing under conditions which involve poor opportunity for discrimination. They argued that when stimuli are presented successively, allowing no opportunity for direct comparison, such gradients result merely from failure of the animal to discriminate. The present experiment was conducted in a situation where it has been experimentally demonstrated that discrimination learning proceeds equally well whether there is opportunity for direct comparison or not (Grice, 1949). Consequently, the Lashley and Wade explanation is invalid for the present experiment, and cannot legitimately be raised as an argument against the theory which assumes a spread of habit strength to other stimuli in the dimension.

The fact that the two functions obtained are different in form is contrary to the assumptions of Spence (1937) and Hull (1943) who have assumed the functions to be symmetrical. (It will be pointed out later, however, how Hull's assumption does not necessarily lead to the prediction of symmetrical *response* gradients for intensity dimensions.) The function for generalization to smaller stimuli which is negatively accelerated is similar to that assumed by Hull and found by Hovland for pitch. The function for generalization in the larger direction, which involves positive acceleration and an inflection, closely resembles that assumed by Spence in his most recent formulation (1942). In so far as Spence's theory deals with transposition in the larger direction, this result may be regarded as a tentative verification. At least the basic principle of assuming the existence of decreasing gradients to account for transposition phenomena appears to be sound.

A point of further interest in connection with the present study is its possible relation to Hull's recent discussion (1949) of the "stimulus intensity dynamism." In this discussion Hull assumes that the primary generalization gradient for reaction potential ($_sE_R$) is of the simple negatively accelerated type. He further assumes that reaction potential is also an increasing function of stimulus intensity. *Empirical* generalization functions are then assumed to be a multiplicative function of generalized reaction potential and the stimulus intensity factor. This theorizing leads Hull to five predictions regarding the nature of generalization functions for intensity dimensions. A discussion of the present experiment in this connection would, of course, be contingent on the assumption that the visual size dimension may properly be regarded as an intensity dimension. Since white stimuli were employed, the total amount of reflected light would be a function of stimulus area. This suggests that at least a tentative examination of the data with respect to Hull's predictions would be worthwhile.

The design employed here is the type of design to which Hull's predictions apply. A particular part of the dimension was selected, and generalization to larger sizes was studied from the lower extreme, and generalization to smaller sizes was studied from the upper extreme. Thus, both gradients fall within the same range of stimulus values. Hull's predictions together with the present findings concerning them are as follows:

1. The effective gradient for generalization toward more intense stimuli will be convex. This prediction is partially fulfilled since the obtained gradient does show convexity before its inflection. The inflection, however, was not predicted.

2. The effective gradient for generalization toward weaker stimuli will be concave. This prediction was fulfilled.

3. "The origin of the gradient originating at the stronger stimulus extreme will have a stronger reaction potential than that originating at the weaker stimulus extreme." The obtained means were 13.5 and 13.1 with the difference in the direction predicted, but the difference is definitely insignificant. This prediction cannot be regarded as clearly substantiated.

4. The gradient for generalization to weaker stimuli will show a greater drop than that for generalization to stronger stimuli. The drop between the point of origin and the extreme test point was slightly greater for the generalization to smaller sizes, but an analysis of variance revealed that this difference was not statistically significant.

5. "The two gradients intersect at their mid-point." This prediction was essentially verified.

In general, the correspondence between the obtained gradients and Hull's predictions is quite striking. This is especially true of the predicted asymmetry of the two curves, which was essentially verified except for the inflection in one curve. In this connection it is perhaps of interest to note that the experiment was designed and completed prior to the publication of Hull's paper, and that Hull was unaware of the present data when the theory was formulated. The reasons for the failure to verify all of the predictions is not at once apparent. The possibility that the discrepancies may be due to sampling error cannot be rejected. There is also the question as to whether size may be properly regarded as an intensity dimension. And, of course, future data may reveal the need for further refinements or modifications of the theory.

SUMMARY

1. One group of 60 white rats was trained to open a door in the center of a white circle 20 sq. cm. in area. Sub-groups of 15 were then tested by means of 25 extinction trials on circles of 20, 32, 50, and 79 sq. cm. A second group of 75 rats were trained to respond to the 79 sq. cm. circle and sub-groups were tested on circles of 79, 63, 50, 32, and 20 sq. cm.

2. Functions were obtained showing generalization to stimuli both larger and smaller than the training stimulus. Both gradients showed a significant decrease in response strength as a function of increasing difference in size from the training stimulus. Response strength to smaller stimuli was a negatively accelerated decreasing function of log area. The function relating log area and response strength to larger stimuli was inflected, showing initial positive acceleration.

3. The results are interpreted as supporting the validity of the concept of stimulus generalization as employed by such theorists as Hull and Spence. They lend further support to the use of the concept in the interpretation of visual size discrimination learning phenomena.

4. The data are further interpreted as being in essential but not complete agreement with recent predictions made by Hull on the basis of a stimulus intensity factor.

25

A Study of the Transposition Gradient[1]

DAVID EHRENFREUND

Despite the mass of data collected on the white rat, a recent study by Kendler (1950) represents the only report to date in which the transposition phenomenon has been systematically investigated with this [species]. . . .

[Moreover, most previous studies] have restricted themselves almost exclusively to the transposition experiment which limits its test to but one step removed from the training pair, e.g., subjects are first trained on medium gray positive versus light gray negative and then tested on a medium gray opposed to a dark gray. Under certain conditions, the responses on such a test are to the dark gray. Since the subjects were originally trained on the "darker than" and respond likewise in the test situation one might assume that the original discrimination was learned on the basis of responding to a relationship or configuration rather than to the absolute properties of each cue. Such assumptions, however, are neither logically demanded nor necessarily the most appropriate ones.

In their well-developed gestalt theory, Gulliksen and Wolfle (1938) discuss the illegitimacy of the relational assumption.

"*Transfer* on a relational basis is . . . interpreted as evidence that *learning* was on a relational basis. It has now been demonstrated that relative transfer can be predicted from a theory based on a directional definition of the response. Since this prediction is possible, it is not legitimate to use the fact of relational transfer to support the assumption that the animal's original learning was relational in nature" (p. 240).

Their formulation, however, does not account for instances of either choice scores or reversals in the test (transfer) situation.

A theory more capable in this respect is that proposed by Spence (1936, 1937, 1941, 1942a). [Spence] does not assume that the animal is responding to some abstract relational property, or to a primitive structure-process. He holds, on the contrary, that the positive member in the stim-

[1] Reprinted from the *Journal of Experimental Psychology*, 1952, 43, 81-87, by permission of the American Psychological Association and the author.

A Study of the Transportation Gradient

ulus-series acquires excitatory properties as a result of training to the response of approaching it and, furthermore, that there is a gradient of generalization of this excitation to other members of the stimulus-series, including the negative stimulus-object. With failure of re-enforcement of response to the latter, however, an inhibitory tendency develops which, in turn, is assumed to generalize to adjoining members of the stimulus-series.

The theoretical picture presented by Spence has successfully predicted not only the success or failure of transposition when tests are conducted on logarithmically equal whole-step stimulus pairs but also generates testable hypotheses concerning probability of transposition when the tests are not so restricted. In other words, the theory does not demand that the difference between the members of the test pair be equal to the difference employed in the original discrimination. Nor are the tests necessarily limited to such pairs as are whole-step units removed from the training pair. Employing a stimulus series that varies in a single dimension, the theory should predict the relative amount of transposition on any pair after training on any other pair. . . .

In the present investigation [such predictions were tested] by first training a large group of subjects on a brightness discrimination in which the difference between the members was fairly large. Upon reaching the criterion of learning each subject was tested on one of four new pairs of stimuli differing along a brightness dimension at various partial steps distant from the original.

Method

SUBJECTS. The subjects were 80 albino male rats from the colony maintained by the psychology department of the State College of Washington.

APPARATUS. The apparatus was a simple T-maze design, the stem of which was walled and covered with hardware cloth. The arms were open as in an elevated maze. The floor consisted of a grid of $\frac{1}{8}$-inch wire spaced $\frac{1}{2}$ inch apart. Each arm, from the center of the choice point, could accommodate a 4 x 10-inch stimulus card. At the end of each runway, a glass food cup (furniture coaster) could be fastened to a two-pronged wire holder in such a way as to be invisible from the choice point. A T-shaped aluminum door at the choice point prevented both retracing and correction. The sole illumination was provided by a 20-watt fluorescent lamp shielded by two thicknesses of transluscent tracing paper. The stimuli for the brightness continuum consisted of eight 4- by 10-inch sheets of 060-gauge cellulose acetate plastic. These were purchased from the Container Corporation of America and are identical to the brightness series employed in the second edition of the Color Harmony Manual. The main advantages of this material lie in its rigidity, homogeneous matt surface, and ability to withstand repeated use and washing. The stimuli were calibrated by the Container Corporation as having the following diffuse reflection factors on their matt (painted) side: .91, .57, .34, .22, .13, .09, .05, .035. In the present discussion these stimuli will be referred to simply by number from 1 (white) to 8 (black).

PROCEDURE. After the subjects were tamed and had experienced at least a week of being fed an 8-gram daily ration of laboratory chow, they were introduced to the apparatus. On the first two days, each subject was allowed to consume ten pellets of calf manna on each arm of the maze. During this time, the door was closed. On the next two days, each subject was allowed ten runs from the starting box to the food cup where it consumed one pellet of food. These runs were forced left and right in a balanced random order. Learning of the original discrimination was then instituted. The appropriate stimulus cards were introduced for the first time and each subject was given ten noncorrection trials per day until the criterion of 18 out of 20 errorless trials, with the last ten errorless, was attained. During the training series, the food cup was placed only on the rewarded side. In Experiment I, subjects were trained on Stimulus 1 (—) vs. Stimulus 4 (+). In Experiment II, they were trained on Stimulus 8 (—) vs. Stimulus 5 (+). Each subject was then tested for two days (20 trials) on a new pair A, B, C, or D as indicated in Table 25-1.

On the test trials all responses were rewarded. Thus, in Experiment I, the subjects were trained to the darker stimulus and transposed down the scale. In Experiment II, subjects were trained to the lighter stimulus and transposed up the scale. All transposition (test) scores are in terms

TABLE 25-1

Training pairs and various test pairs (A to D) used in both experiments

Stimulus pairs Exp. I	Stimulus cards Diffuse reflection factors				Ratio	Stimulus pairs Exp. II
Training pair	(4)*	.22	(1)	.91	4.1:1	D
A	(5)	.13	(2)	.57	4.4:1	C
B	(6)	.09	(3)	.34	3.8:1	B
C	(7)	.05	(4)	.22	4.4:1	A
D	(8)	.035	(5)	.13	3.7:1	Training pair

* These numbers refer to stimulus cards.

A Study of the Transportation Gradient

of whether the subject responded in a manner consistent with the direction employed in training, i.e., to the darker or to the lighter. Ten subjects were tested on each condition of each experiment.

Results

Trial and error scores for the original discrimination were fairly low. In Experiment I, in which the subjects were trained to discriminate Stimulus 1 (nonrewarded) from Stimulus 4 (rewarded), the mean trials and errors were 86.9 and 42.6. In Experiment II (Stimulus 8 nonrewarded, Stimulus 5 rewarded), the mean trials and errors were 75.5, and 34.2.

The test trials for each test pair in both experiments were subdivided into successive five-trial blocks. The mean transposition scores obtained on these blocks of trials, as well as the total for all 20 trials, are presented in Table 25-2. The trends revealed in this table can be analyzed in terms of both columns and rows. Inspection of the rows, i.e., the subdivided test scores for any one test pair, reveals no consistent trend that will describe all of the tests. The scores for Test Pair A of Experiment 1 rise steadily from 86 to 94. On the other hand, the scores for Test Pair D of the same experiment fall steadily from 66 to 54. Scores for other test pairs show various fluctuations. Apparently any block of trials is as appropriate as

TABLE 25-2

Percent of transposition by five-trial blocks

TESTS	\multicolumn{5}{c}{TRIALS}				
	1-5	6-10	11-15	16-20	1-20
Exp. I. Ss trained on Stimulus 1 (−) vs. Stimulus 4 (+)					
A (2-5)	86	88	92	94	90
B (3-6)	82	86	78	74	80
C (4-7)	48	42	46	40	44
D (5-8)	66	58	54	54	58
Exp. II. Ss trained on Stimulus 8 (−) vs. Stimulus 5 (+)					
A (7-4)	84	84	84	80	83
B (6-3)	78	90	92	86	86.5
C (5-2)	28	26	20	28	25.5
D (4-1)	40	34	44	50	42

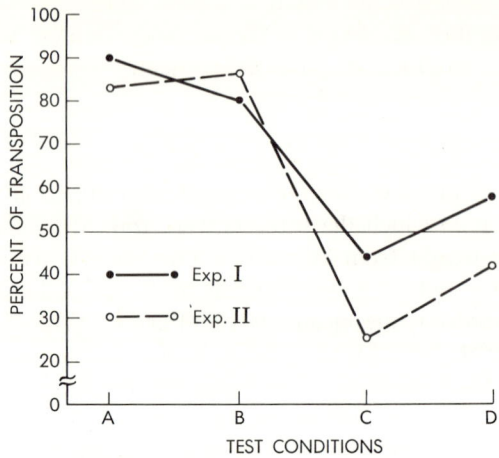

FIGURE 25-1. Transposition gradients for subjects transposed down the brightness scale (Experiment I), and for subjects transposed up the brightness scale (Experiment II).

any other as a measure of transposition. The various columns within each experiment, however, all reveal similar tendencies.

The percents of transposition, based on all 20 trials, are presented in Figure 25-1. It will be recalled that in Experiment I, the subjects were trained with the darker positive and tested on still darker pairs. Transposition is high on the near test and falls in an S-shaped fashion to a value below the 50 percent point and then rises above the 50 percent point. In Experiment II, subjects were trained on the lighter and tested on still lighter pairs. The data for Experiment II show the same general trends just described for Experiment I. A similar S-shaped tendency is evident except that the scores fall farther below the 50 percent point on Test Pair C (significant at the 1 percent level), and Test Pair D is still below 50 percent.

Discussion

A recent study by T. S. Kendler (1950) posed some interesting problems both in respect to the nature of the transposition function and the adequacy of Spence's theory. The nature of the function was difficult to determine in the Kendler study due to the fact that on any one test pair, the later test trials produced consistently higher scores than the earlier test trials. Therefore, the data were plotted using three response measures: Test Trials 1–5, 6–10, and 1–10. . . . Inspection of these curves reveals that not only are they different, but no matter which curve is employed

A Study of the Transportation Gradient

as the more appropriate function, it only partially corroborates the expectations from Spence's theory. Thus, although the amount of transposition decreased as a function of the difference between training and test stimuli, the test scores did not reach or go below the chance level as theoretically expected. According to the analysis made above for the present set of data, no such consistent trends between the subdivided test scores for the same test stimuli were discovered. This finding, coupled with the fact that the transposition function is essentially similar no matter which block of test trials is employed, justifies acceptance of the curves in Figure 25-1 as at least close approximations to the empirical law relating amount of transposition to the distance between training and test stimuli along a brightness dimension.

Although the Kendler study was similar in many respects to the present one, she used direct lighting, and several complications attendant upon the use of direct rather than reflected light could easily account for the differences between the findings of her study and the present one. Some, such as the problem of dark adaptation and the changing efficiency of the rat's eye as trials continue, were discussed by Kendler. The possible necessity for positing "other factors in the present [Kendler] training or test situations in addition to those posited by Spence to determine the final results" (p. 561) was suggested in a footnote but was not elaborated. These "other factors," which seem to the present author to be pertinent and peculiar to the direct illumination situation as employed by Kendler, include:

1. The change in extra-maze cues when the subject is shifted from the training to the test pair of stimuli. The use of direct illumination in an otherwise nonilluminated room results in a change in room cues from few to many or vice versa depending on the direction of training and testing. This change would, of course, be greatest for those groups tested on the farthest pair and least for those tested on the nearest pair.

2. Employing stimulus cues having drive value. The level of illumination employed on Test Pair 5 for Kendler's Condition 1, or for training in Condition 2, was of a magnitude comparable to that employed in other studies as noxious stimuli.

Thus, although the use of a situation employing direct illumination may not be the most appropriate one with which to test the specific assumptions posited by Spence to account for transposition, the Kendler study suggests a degree of complexity perhaps not heretofore appreciated and which merits further study, particularly in relation to attempts at more elaborate theoretical formulations. Furthermore, as Kendler points out, her results can be described within the framework of S-R reinforcement theory by employing, in addition to Spence's postulates, Hull's concepts of patterning of stimulus compounds and his recently formulated stimulus dynamism (Hull, 1943, 1949).

Turning now to the implications of the present set of data for Spence's theory, we find a close approximation between prediction and results. Particular note should be made of the fact that the low point on each curve occurred on Test Pair C which is only one step removed from the training pair. In Experiment I, Test Pair C was composed of Stimulus 4, the positive stimulus employed in the training situation, and a new Stimulus 7. Instead of responding to Stimulus 7, as predicted by some form of relational theory, 56 percent of the responses were to the absolute stimulus, i.e., Stimulus 4. One might say that since the response was about chance, neither theoretical viewpoint was supported. According to CR theory, however, the amount of transposition will reach a chance level at some point, and under certain conditions will fail to occur, i.e., the response will be to the absolute stimulus (Spence, 1941, 1942). Apparently this is what happened in Experiment II, where Test Pair C was composed of Stimulus 5, the reinforced stimulus of the training situation, and a new Stimulus 2. In this instance, 75 percent of the responses were to the absolute stimulus. Furthermore, nine of the ten subjects responded better than 50 percent and three subjects responded 100 percent to the absolute stimulus.

Although both transposition curves are in line with the general prediction from the theory, the difference between them may be important in terms of certain theoretical refinements. The generalization gradients of excitation and inhibition posited by Spence (1942) to account for transposition are symmetrical for both directions of the stimulus continuum. A recent study by Grice and Saltz (1950) indicates that for size, at least, such may not be the case. He found that the generalization gradient to the "larger" end of the continuum was of the same general shape as posited by Spence. However, toward the "smaller" end of the continuum, the gradient was discovered to be an exponential type not unlike that posited by Hull (1943). There is also the question whether the generalization gradients for inhibition may be asymmetrical. Spence (1941) has suggested that ". . . the shape of the generalization curve [of inhibition] in the direction of larger stimulus-areas differs from that of the smaller" (p. 229).

If asymmetrical generalization gradients may be expected for the brightness dimension, as well as the size dimension, then the difference between the two transposition gradients of the present study conforms to that expectation. In Experiment II there was a greater failure of transposition than in Experiment I. In fact, these data are almost exactly as predicted.

That is, according to this schema, the percent of responses consistent with the direction of the original training should at first decrease until they drop to well below the 50 percent level (i.e., lead to a reversal of the originally learned preference) and subsequently rise and level off at a response value, presumably 50 percent, where the difference between the theoretical effective excitatory strengths becomes zero (Kendler, 1950, pp. 560–561).

Thus, it appears, from the present set of data, that Spence's theoretical generalization gradients are more appropriate for predicting transposition up the brightness scale than down. In Kendler's (1950) study, the form of the curve was also more in line with the theory when subjects were transposed up the brightness scale rather than down.

SUMMARY

Two transposition experiments employing reflected light were conducted. In Experiment I, 40 albino rats were trained to respond to the darker of two bright stimuli and tested at various partial steps down the brightness scale. In Experiment II, 40 albino rats were trained to respond to the brighter of two dark stimuli and tested at various partial steps up the brightness scale. In each experiment, four tests were carried out at points increasingly distant from the training pair. Both transposition curves confirmed the general prediction from Spence's theory to the effect that transposition is less perfect as the difference between training and test pairs is increased.

The low points on each transposition gradient, which was either chance (Experiment I) or below chance (Experiment II), occurred on Test C which was only one step removed from the training pair. Thus, the data from Experiment II are more in line with the theory, being almost exactly as predicted. The differences between the two sets of data were discussed in terms of the possible need for positing asymmetrical generalization gradients.

26

Prediction of Preference, Transposition, and Transposition-Reversal from the Generalization Gradients[1]

WERNER K. HONIG

The present study concerns the prediction of responding in a two-stimulus operant situation from response rates obtained with the same stimuli in single presentation. Generalization gradients on the spectral continuum were used to provide different response rates. Various studies with pigeons have shown that orderly, reliable gradients can be obtained in this situation after different kinds of training (e.g., Guttman & Kalish, 1956; Hanson, 1959; Honig, Thomas & Guttman, 1959; Kalish & Guttman, 1957); in all of these, the tests were conducted with the presentation of single stimuli. In the present research, such single-stimulus (SS) tests were administered concurrently with double-stimulus (DS) tests, in which two stimuli lying on the gradient were presented simultaneously. In a general sense, these studies represent an attempt to predict choice behavior when the responsiveness to each single stimulus is known. More specifically, they comprise a test of the power of the generalization gradient in the determination of behavior in situations more complex than the single-stimulus condition in which it is usually assessed.

The desired relationships were first studied after simple acquisition with one stimulus value. In Experiment 1, the pairs of stimuli presented on the DS tests were comprised of adjacent values in the stimulus series used to obtain the generalization gradient. In Experiment 2, the values comprising test pairs were nonadjacent, and were chosen to lie on opposite sides of the generalization gradient. In Experiments 3 and 4, generaliza-

---

[1] This paper is adapted from a doctoral dissertation submitted to the Department of Psychology, Graduate School of Arts and Sciences, Duke University, in 1958. A previous version (Honig, 1962) has been published. The research was supported by Grant MH-1002 from the National Institute of Mental Health to Norman Guttman. The author is much indebted to Norman Guttman for advice and guidance throughout the research. The preparation of this version was supported by Grant M-2414 to the author from the National Institute of Mental Health.

tion gradients and preference measures were obtained from some of the subjects used in Experiment 1 after successive (Experiment 3) or simultaneous (Experiment 4) discrimination[2] training. The latter are particularly relevant to Spence's (1937) explanation of transposition of a discrimination along a stimulus dimension. According to this view, the mode of the post-discrimination gradient (PDG) is not at the positive stimulus (S+) but is shifted away from S— on the continuum, due to the algebraic summation of gradients of excitation and inhibition generated around these two respective stimuli. On a transposition test, the subject should tend to choose the stimulus that is higher on the PDG. If suitably chosen pairs of stimuli are presented, transposition should occur between S+ and the new mode, and transposition-reversal should be obtained with values lying beyond that mode.

Using a technique very similar to the successive discrimination of the present study, Hanson (1959) obtained a displacement of the mode of the PDG in the direction predicted by Spence. This makes it possible to predict the occurrence of transposition and transposition-reversal in terms of specific stimulus values. In previous studies of transposition (e.g., Alberts and Ehrenfreund, 1951; Baker and Lawrence, 1951; Ehrenfreund, 1952; Kendler, 1950) the transposition tests have not been accompanied by determinations of the PDG with single-stimulus presentation. Clear-cut transposition-reversal has not generally been obtained, and sometimes even transposition has failed; it cannot be determined from these studies whether such failures were due to the form of the PDG's, or to a lack of correspondence between the PDG and stimulus preferences on the transposition tests. The methods used in the present study permitted concurrent evaluation of the shape of the PDG and of the choice behavior which defines transposition and transposition-reversal.

EXPERIMENTS 1 AND 2

Method

APPARATUS. The automatic key-pecking apparatus used in the present investigation was similar to that employed in other spectral generalization studies (e.g., Guttman and Kalish, 1956) except that it included two separately illuminated keys 7½ inches from the floor with 2 inches between centers. Bausch and Lomb monochromatic interference filters, with

---

[2] A *successive discrimination* refers in this paper to the case where only the positive or the negative stimulus value is presented at one time to the subject, or the "go, no-go" discrimination. The term has been used in this sense by Grice (1949) and Baker and Lawrence (1951). Other authors (Bitterman, Spence) have more recently used *successive discrimination* to refer to a conditional left-right discrimination, but this usage is not intended here.

band widths at half height of 7–9 mμ provided the different spectral values. In the text, stimuli will be referred to by the nominal value of the filters, but the spacing of points on the abscissae of the figures corresponds to the actual transmission peaks which differ slightly from the nominal values in some cases.

The monochromatic filters transmitted a secondary peak at $\frac{2}{3}$ the value of the primary peak. This fell into the visible range for primary values between 570 and 610 mμ, and a yellow (Wratten K-2) filter was inserted in series with these values in order to prevent contamination of the monochromatic colors.

The various spectral values were equated for apparent brightness by a human observer with the aid of a Macbeth illuminometer. This appears justified by the work of Blough (1957), which indicates that the spectral luminosity function of the pigeon is similar to that of man. No illumination was provided in the box other than the light falling on the keys, except during the presentation of grain, when a magazine light went on.

SUBJECTS. The subjects were 28 white Carneau pigeons reduced to 75% of their free-feeding weight. Twenty-two experimentally naive animals were used in Experiment 1. The 6 subjects used in Experiment 2 had served in a previous experiment in which 10 sessions of pecking at a 550-mμ stimulus on a variable interval schedule were followed by a generalization test in which the values used in the present study were presented. The previous experiment was run in a different apparatus which had one key.

PROCEDURE. *Preliminary training and conditioning.* Over a period of several daily sessions, the subject was adapted to the experimental box and trained to eat during the 4-second magazine cycle. After at least 25 cycles with reliable eating, the subject was trained by the method of successive approximations to peck at one key illuminated by a 550-mμ light. The subject was then permitted to obtain 30 consecutive reinforcements. This initial training was carried out on the left key for half the subjects and on the right key for half the subjects. On the day following initial conditioning, the subject received six blocks of five continuous reinforcements for pecking at a single illuminated key. The position of the illuminated key was alternated between the six blocks.

Variable interval (VI) training. Following conditioning, the subject received ten daily sessions of training on a VI schedule with a mean interreinforcement interval of about one minute. Each session consisted of 30 one-minute periods separated by ten seconds of blackout. During half of the periods, one key was illuminated by 550 mμ. During the remaining periods, both keys were illuminated by 550 mμ. The single stimulus appeared for half the time on the right and for half the time on the left key. With two stimuli, the reinforcement was contingent on pecking at the left key for half the periods and at the right key for the other half. The order of these stimulating and reinforcing conditions was randomized, and reinforcements on the VI schedule fell randomly within the different training conditions. It was assumed that over ten sessions the total number of reinforcements received under all conditions would be about the same.

VI training was discontinued after ten sessions if the subject reached a criterion of 900 responses by that time. Otherwise, the subject received further sessions until it did reach the criterion. Of the 22 subjects in Experiment 1, five had one extra session, one had two, one had three, and one had six extra sessions.

This training procedure was abbreviated for the subjects in Experiment 2, as they had been trained in a previous study. Magazine training and conditioning of key-pecking were omitted. After ten continuous reinforcements, VI training began immediately in the manner described above. All subjects received seven rather than ten sessions of VI training, and easily reached 900 responses per session by the seventh session.

Generalization testing. On the two days following the last session of VI training, the subject received a generalization test under extinction, consisting of 189 30-second periods of stimulus presentation alternating with 10 seconds of blackout. These periods were divided into nine blocks of 21 each with six blocks given on the first day of testing and three on the second. A single stimulus value was presented on 11 of the 21 periods within each block and a pair of stimulus values on the remaining ten periods. The single stimulus values ranged from 490 to 610 mμ in 10 mμ steps, with the omission of 500 and 600 mμ. The stimulus pairs were also composed of these values, and the manner in which the values were paired provided the principal difference between Experiments 1 and 2, as shown in Table 26-1. It can be seen that in Experiment 1, the pairs were composed of adjacent stimuli in the series. In Experiment 2, they were so chosen that the differences in mμ between the test values and the CS correspond to those for Experiment 1, but they have opposite signs. In other words, in Experiment 1 the stimuli in each pair lie on the same side of the CS, while in Experiment 2 they lie on opposite sides.

The 21 stimulus conditions were randomized within each block of presentations. Within a given block, 490, 520, 540, 560, 580 and 610 mμ were presented on one key and 510, 530, 550, 570 and 590 mμ were presented on the other key. This arrangement alternated on successive blocks.

By means of this testing procedure, it was possible to present a generalization test consisting of singly presented stimulus values in the same session with a test consisting of stimulus pairs. These will be distinguished

TABLE 26-1

Composition of stimulus pairs on the generalization tests in experiments 1 and 2

EXPERIMENT 1		EXPERIMENT 2	
Absolute value ($m\mu$)	Difference from CS ($m\mu$)	Absolute value ($m\mu$)	Difference from CS ($m\mu$)
490, 510	−60, −40	490, 590	−60, +40
510, 520	−40, −30	590, 520	+40, −30
520, 530	−30, −20	520, 570	−30, +20
530, 540	−20, −10	570, 540	+20, −10
540, 550	−10, 0	540, 550	−10, 0
550, 560	0, +10	550, 560	0, +10
560, 570	+10, +20	560, 530	+10, −20
570, 580	+20, +30	530, 580	−20, +30
580, 590	+30, +40	580, 510	+30, −40
590, 610	+40, +60	510, 610	−40, +60

as single-stimulus (SS) and double-stimulus (DS) generalization tests, even though they were presented concurrently in the same session. The testing procedure thus provided a control for differences between animals and for the effects of extinction in the course of testing.

Results

Experiment 1. The last day of VI training for each subject was analyzed with respect to the number of responses given in the single- and double-stimulus conditions and the distribution between the two keys in the latter situation. When both keys were illuminated, mean responses were 23.7 per minute to the left and 22.2 per minute to the right. A t test for paired scores failed to reveal a significant difference ($t = .51$). The mean total rate with both keys illuminated was 45.9/minute which was 10 percent greater than the rate of 41.6 per minute with one key illuminated. This difference is significant ($t = 2.9$, 21 df, $p < .01$.)

The generalization tests provided three measures, which are all presented in Figure 26-1. The mean total responses obtained in the SS test for each stimulus value comprise the single-stimulus gradient (SSG). The mean total response to each stimulus value of each pair in the DS test are shown by the filled and unfilled bars, with adjacent bars representing each stimulus pair. The bars are located between the appropriate stimulus values on the abscissa, with the filled bar representing the value that is

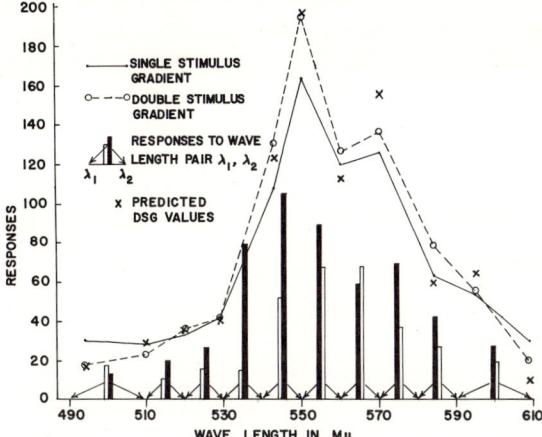

FIGURE 26-1. Single-stimulus and double-stimulus gradients and responses to wavelength pairs (Experiment 1).

closer to the CS (550 mμ). Finally, the total responses to each stimulus *value* in the DS test have been obtained from the two pairs in which that value appears. In this manner a double-stimulus gradient (DSG) is generated. It should be kept in mind that each point on the DSG is not yielded by a single testing situation, but is derived from two testing situations involving different stimulus pairs (except for 490 and 610 mμ, which each appeared in only one test pair).

The SSG has its peak at 550 mμ and decreases to both sides of the CS. There are inversions between 490 and 510 mμ and between 560 and 570 mμ. The former inversion is small and may be due to random error, as the gradient is almost flat in that region. The latter inversion is sometimes found when stimuli in this region are equated for brightness (Honig, Thomas, & Guttman, 1959).

The direction of preference within each stimulus pair is in agreement with the difference between the number of responses given to the members of that pair in the SS test. Accordingly, the stimulus nearer 550 mμ received more responses in all pairs except 490, 510 mμ and 560, 570 mμ which reflect the inversions between the corresponding stimuli on the single-stimulus gradient. Furthermore, it appears that the degree of preference, or the difference in height between the two bars from each pair, is systematically related to the slope between corresponding points on the SSG.

The DSG is very similar to the SSG except that the central values are somewhat higher. This may reflect the difference in response level between the SS and DS conditions that was manifested at the end of VI training. In fact, the 10 percent difference in response levels of the two gradients is identical to the training difference. On the other hand, the higher values obtained on the DSG can also be derived from a method of predicting response totals in the DS situation that will be presented later in this paper, and from which the "predicted DSG values" on the figures are obtained.

Experiment 2. (see Figures 26-2 and 26-3) The SSG is similar to that obtained in Experiment 1, except that the response level is generally

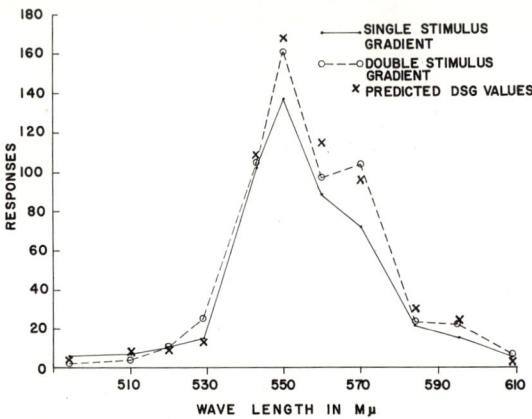

FIGURE 26-2. Single-stimulus and double-stimulus gradients (Experiment 2).

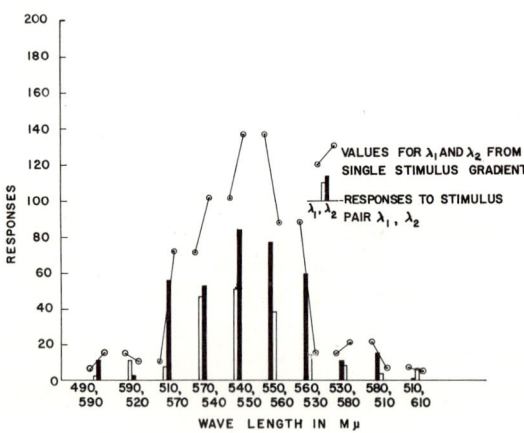

FIGURE 26-3. Responses to wavelength pairs with corresponding single-stimulus values (Experiment 2).

lower by 20 to 30 responses, and there is no inversion between 560 and 570 mμ. The overall difference in the rate of responding may be attributable to the fact that the subjects had previously undergone a generalization test and therefore extinguished more rapidly in the present one.

The bar graph of the responses within wavelength pairs is presented separately from the single-stimulus gradient in Figure 26-3, as the stimulus pairs do not generally consist of adjacent values. In order to afford a comparison between the responses to the members of each pair and the responses to the corresponding stimuli on the SS test, the latter values are plotted over the appropriate bars in Figure 26-3. The direction of preference within each stimulus pair is in agreement with SS values in all but two cases: the pairs 530, 580 mμ and 510, 610 mμ. The stimuli comprising these pairs lie near the ends of the gradient, where the general response level is quite low, and the differences in the number of responses are quite small.

The SSG and DSG (Fig. 26-2) are quite similar except that the central values are again somewhat higher in the DSG, and the DSG has an inversion between 560 and 570 mμ. The considerations mentioned with regard to a similar difference in Experiment 1 apply here also.

EXPERIMENTS 3 AND 4

Method

Experiments 3 and 4 provide data on the effects of successive and simultaneous discrimination training on the SSG and DSG and on the distribution of responses between pairs of stimulus values. Aside from the introduction of discrimination training, the method in these experiments was similar to that for Experiment 1. The same apparatus and 14 of the same subjects were used.

PROCEDURE. On the day following the completion of the generalization test in Experiment 1, the subject received 10 continuous reinforcements with one key illuminated in order to reinstate the conditioned operant. Discrimination training then began immediately. Each session consisted of 30 1-minute periods of stimulus presentation alternating with 10 seconds of blackout. Responding to 550 mμ (S+) was reinforced on the VI schedule used previously. Responding to 560 mμ (S—) was never reinforced, and the reinforcement programmer was interrupted when it was presented in Experiment 3.

In the *successive* discrimination training of Experiment 3, both keys were illuminated either by S+ or S— during each period. S+ and S— were each presented for 15 periods in a session. The order was randomized but excluded the presentation of the same condition for more than three consecutive periods. Reinforcement was available for responding to the left key for half of the S+ periods and for responding to the right key for the other half.

The criterion for discrimination was reached when a block of 10 consecutive 1-minute periods was completed under the following conditions. (1) The block contained five positive and five negative periods. (2) At least two of the negative periods were consecutive. (3) The subject gave no responses to S—. (4) The subject gave 10 or more responses during each presentation of S+. All except one subject reached this criterion within 10 sessions. A second generalization test (see below) was administered to this subject under the considerations that on Training Sessions 7 through 10, less than 2 percent of its total responses were to S—, with no responses to S— on as many as four successive S— periods.

In the simultaneous discrimination training of Experiment 4, one key was illuminated by S+ and the other by S— during each period. The side on which these appeared was randomized, with the exclusion of more than three successive periods with the same arrangement. The criterion for discrimination was reached when a block of five consecutive 1-minute periods was completed under the following conditions: (1) S— appeared on one key for two periods and on the other key for three periods. (2) The subject gave no responses to S—. (3) The subject gave at least 10 responses each period to S+. Of the 8 subjects in Experiment 4, 6 reached criterion within five sessions or less. The other 2 subjects stabilized at about 20 percent responding to S—. They apparently developed a chained response of pecking at S— and then S+ in rapid succession. This could be reinforced, since no delay of reinforcement was contingent on responding to S—. These 2 subjects were therefore discarded.

GENERALIZATION TESTING. When the subject reached the criterion for discrimination, the training session was discontinued. On the two following days, the subject was given a generalization test identical to the one it received after VI training in Experiment 1.

Results

A full description of the course of discrimination training in these two experiments is beyond the scope of this paper, but a comparison of the two groups reveals several differences which indicate that the simultaneous discrimination was much easier. (1) The successive discrimination group made seven times as many responses to S— as did the simultaneous group before reaching the criterion. (2) The number of periods required to reach criterion was twice as great for the successive discrimination group, but since S+ and S— were each available only half the

Predictions from the Generalization Gradient

time in the successive procedure, the training time in terms of total minutes of exposure to each stimulus was about the same. But since the birds learning the simultaneous discrimination spent most of their time responding to S+, the "functional" exposure time to S— was probably much less for that group. (3) The proportion of responses to S— out of the total responses was consistently less for the simultaneous discrimination group throughout comparable portions of the discrimination training process. (4) Rate of responding to S+ was much *higher* in the successive discrimination group. This is a "behavioral contrast" phenomon often found when periods of extinction are alternated with periods of reinforcement in operant situations (Reynolds, 1961); Hanson (1959) obtained a similar effect when he introduced a successive discrimination between 550 and 560 mμ. No such increase occurred with rate to S+ in the simultaneous discrimination, even when responding to the concurrently presented S— declined to a negligible level.

Single-stimulus gradients. The SSG's following the two training procedures were quite different; this is apparent from a comparison of Figure 26-4 and 26-5. The gradient obtained after the successive discrimination in Experiment 3 is very similar to that obtained by Hanson (1959), in that (a) responding to wavelength values above 550 mμ is virtually zero; (b) the mode of the gradient is not at 550 mμ, but has shifted to 540 mμ; (c) the slope of the gradient is steeper on both sides of the mode than after simple acquisition.

The SSG obtained in Experiment 4 does not appear to differ radically in form from the gradient obtained after simple acquisition in Ex-

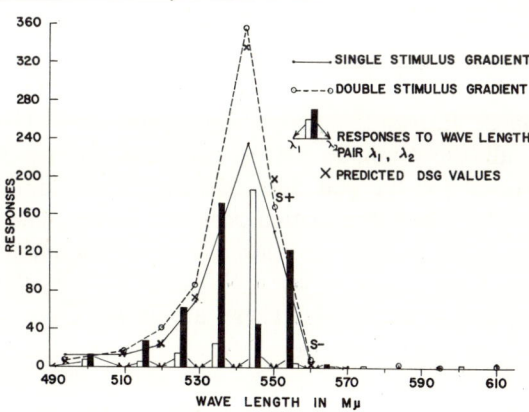

FIGURE 26-4. Single-stimulus and double-stimulus gradients and responses to wavelength pairs (Experiment 3).

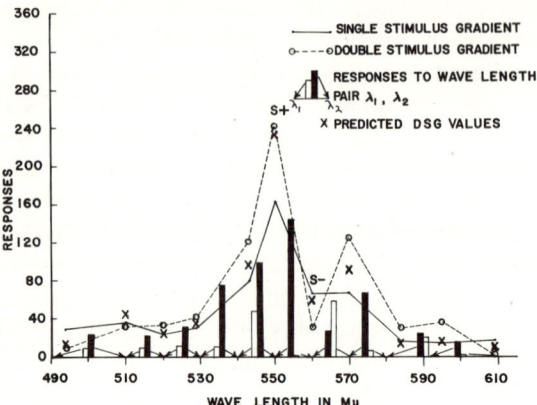

FIGURE 26-5. Single-stimulus and double-stimulus gradients and responses to wavelength pairs (Experiment 4).

periment 1. The mode remains at 550 mμ, and there is considerable responding to values between 560 and 610 mμ, with a small inversion between 560 and 570 mμ. It does appear, however, that the level of responding between 560 and 590 mμ is reduced, particularly in view of the fact that the modal value at 550 mμ is almost identical for the two gradients. The number of responses obtained on the SS test is 32 percent less than that obtained for the same six subjects in Experiment 1 for the values below 550 mμ, and 57 percent less for the values above 550 mμ. The largest reduction (a mean of 75 responses, or 54 percent was at 560 mμ, and the reductions (in terms of absolute amount) decreased with only one inversion between 560 and 610 mμ. All animals showed more reduction at the values above 550 mμ than below.

Experiment 3: *Responding within wavelength pairs.* The direction of preference for all the stimulus values conforms to the SSG. This is especially significant for the pair 540, 550 mμ, as the direction of preference is toward the postdiscrimination peak of 540 mμ. The preference of 540 mμ over S+ is an instance of *transposition of discrimination.* For the pairs comprised of the values between 490 and 540 mμ, the direction of preference is clearly toward S+. These are instances of *transposition-reversal.*

Experiment 4. The direction of preference conforms to the SSG in all but two pairs: 510, 520 mμ and 590, 610 mμ. Both of these pairs are comprised of values near the ends of the gradient, where the slope is essentially zero. It is of greater significance that transposition was not obtained between 540 and 550 mμ, nor for any other pairs, quite in accordance with the absence of a peak shift in the SSG.

One discrepancy between the shape of the SSG and responding to DS values can be seen for the pair 550, 560 mμ in Figure 26-5. There is virtually no responding to 560 mμ when paired with 550, in accordance with the simultaneous training discrimination training carried out before the test, but there is considerable responding to 560 mμ presented alone. The simultaneous discrimination did not transfer completely to the successively presented stimuli. Very good transfer did take place in the opposite direction, as one can see from Figure 26-4, where there is virtually no responding to 560 mμ presented singly or together with 550 mμ in the 550, 560 mμ pair.

Double-stimulus gradients. The DSG's are in both experiments quite similar to the SSG's, though on the average somewhat higher, following the pattern set in Experiments 1 and 2. At the modes of the gradients the DSG points are considerably higher, and there are also large differences for Experiment 4 and 560 and 570 mμ. These differences can be understood on the basis of the analysis of double-stimulus rates to be presented in the next section.

PREDICTION OF DOUBLE STIMULUS RESPONSE TOTALS

Consideration of responding within DS pairs has so far been restricted to the *direction* of preference. If a general empirical relationship can be established between the response totals on the SSG and response totals for the DS pairs, the *degree* of preference can also be predicted from the generalization gradient. Such a relationship can indeed be demonstrated, and it can be derived from some basic assumptions about the behavior of the subject in the DS situation.

The following symbols will be adopted: For any stimulus pair, λ_1, λ_2, the stimulus value that evokes the greater number of responses during the SS test is represented as λ_1; in other words, λ_1 is the "stronger" stimulus when the members of the pair are presented independently. Likewise, λ_2 represents the "weaker" stimulus.

$R_1 =$ the number of responses emitted to λ_1 in the SS test.
$R_2 =$ the number of responses emitted to λ_2 on the SS test.
$r_1 =$ the number of responses emitted to λ_1 in the DS test.
$r_2 =$ the number of responses emitted to λ_2 is the DS test.

The general problem is to predict r_1 and r_2 when R_1 and R_2 are known;

in other words, to predict DS response totals from SS response totals. The form that this prediction takes is based upon a rather straightforward behavioral analysis.

First, let us make a distinction between the *rate* of responding to λ_1 or to λ_2, and the time (or *duration*)[3] in which that rate is applied. The product of these quantities results in the response totals actually obtained in the generalization test. Second, let us assume that the *rate* of responding to λ_1 is independent of the presence of λ_2; in other words, when the pigeon responds to λ_1, it does so at a characteristic rate whether this value is presented in the SS or DS situation. A similar assumption holds for the independence of the rate of responding to λ_2. Third, let us assume that the simultaneous presentation of stimuli affects the *duration* for which the appropriate rate is applied to either of them, and that the time spent responding to λ_1 and to λ_2 is proportional to the rates that these stimuli characteristically evoke. In other words, when λ_1 and λ_2 are presented together, the pigeon responds to each of these at a characteristic rate, which is the same as the rate evoked in single presentation, but he divides the time spent responding in the proportion of these characteristic rates.

To illustrate the way in which these assumptions can predict response totals, let us consider a case where response rate to λ_1 is appreciable, but where the rate to λ_2 is close to zero. This is found for the pair 550, 560 mμ in Experiment 3. These are the stimuli for which successive discrimination with 550 mμ as S+ was carried out before the generalization test. The implications of these assumptions are as follows: The rate of responding to 550 mμ is not affected by the presence of 560 mμ, nor is the response rate (which is virtually zero) to 560 mμ affected by the presence of 550 mμ. Since the pigeon divides his time between these two stimuli in accordance with the proportion of the response rates, he responds almost exclusively to 550 mμ at the appropriate rate; he does not sit in front of 560 mμ doing nothing. We can therefore expect that r_1 for 550 mμ will be very close to R_1, since equal numbers of SS and DS trials were presented in the generalization test, while the r_2 and R_2 should both be close to zero. This is confirmed in Figure 4; the SSG value for 550 mμ is very similar to the DS value in the appropriate pair, and the SS and DS totals for 560 mμ are both close to zero.

With these assumptions we would also predict that where the SSG is flat—that is, where R_1 and R_2 are about equal—the pigeon should respond with equal rates to the two stimuli when they are presented together, and should divide his time about equally between them. As a result, r_1 and r_2 should be about equal, and each of these values should

---

[3] Gilbert (1958) has provided empirical support for a distinction between *tempo* and *perseverance*, which correspond roughly to *rate* and *duration* as used in this paper.

Predictions from the Generalization Gradient

be about ½ of R_1 and R_2, since the total exposure of the two stimuli separately is twice as long as their exposure together. This case is illustrated for the pair 560, 570 mμ in Figure 1, where there is a slight inversion in the SSG. Here, R_1 and R_2 are each close to 120, while r_1 and r_2 are close to 60, or about ½ of the SSG values.

The prediction of r_1 and r_2 is not as obvious for most of the other stimulus pairs, where there is appreciable responding to both members of the pair presented separately, but where R_1 and R_2 are unequal. For these cases, the behavioral assumptions lead to a rather straightforward arithmetic formulation. As we saw above, r_1 and R_1 would be equal if λ_2 were ineffective in evoking responses. But λ_2 generally is not ineffective, and responding to λ_1 is reduced by the amount of time spent in responding to λ_2. What we need, therefore, is an expression representing the amount of time left for responding to λ_1, and this can be derived from the assumption that the total response duration is divided between the stimuli in the proportion of the rates to each stimulus. Since these rates are proportional to the total response output to each stimulus in the SS situation, the proportion of time spent responding to each stimulus would be

$$\frac{R_1}{R_1 + R_2} \text{ for } \lambda_1 \quad \text{and} \quad \frac{R_2}{R_1 + R_2} \text{ for } \lambda_2.$$

The DS values will therefore be predicted from the SS totals according to these expressions:

$$r_1 = R_1 \left(\frac{R_1}{R_1 + R_2} \right)$$

$$r_2 = R_2 \left(\frac{R_2}{R_1 + R_2} \right)$$

Predictions have been carried out with these functions for each subject for each DS value in each of the four experiments in order to obtain predicted values for r_1, r_2, and $r_1 + r_2$, as well as predicted DSG values. The mean predicted values are plotted against the mean obtained values for Experiment 1 and 2 in Figure 26-6 and for Experiment 3 and 4 in Figure 26-7. The three groups of predicted values, r_1, r_2, and $r_1 + r_2$ are separated along the vertical axes for the sake of clarity. Within each group, each point represents the mean responses (predicted and obtained) to a given stimulus value, or in the case of $r_1 + r_2$, to a pair of values. The stimulus values are not indicated except where they represent S+ and S— from a discrimination pair. In general, the higher values come from the middle of the gradients, where response rates are higher, while the lower values come from the ends of the gradients.

In these figures, the diagonal lines represent perfect prediction (x = y); deviations from this are indicated by the vertical distance be-

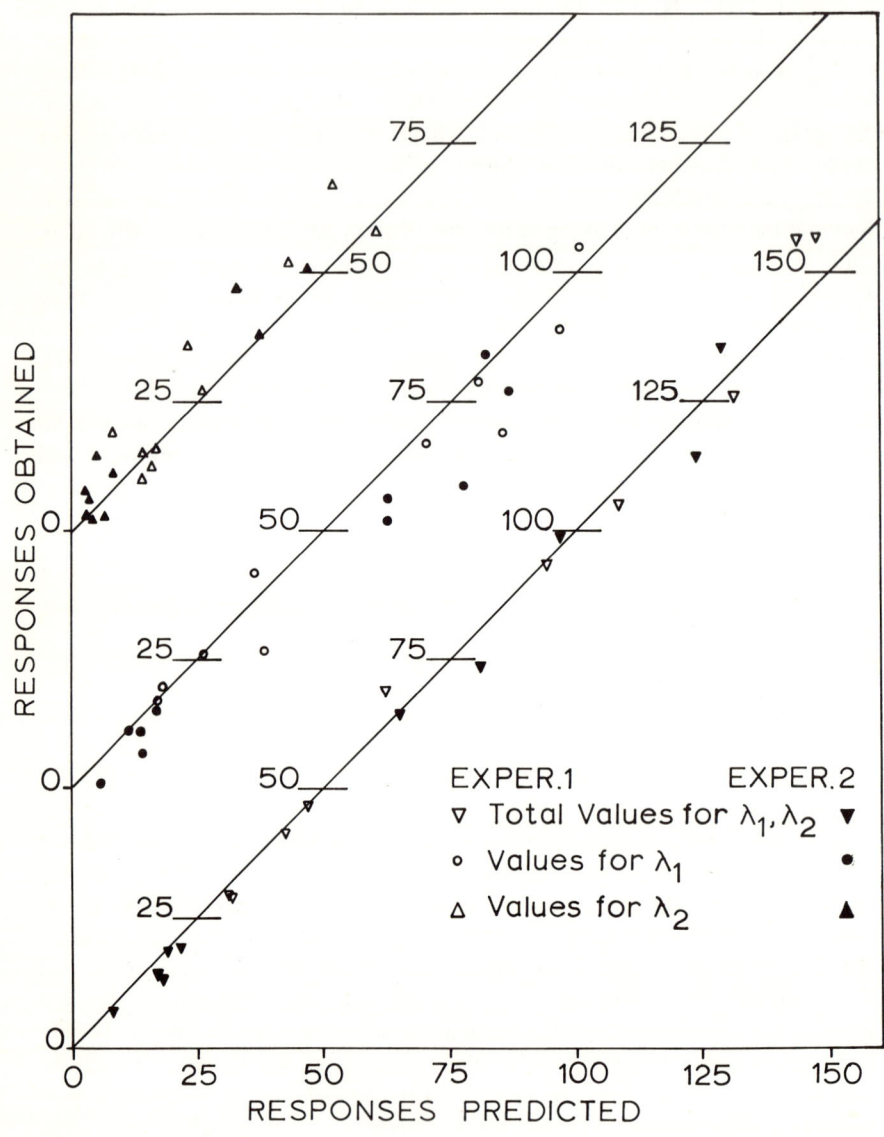

FIGURE 26-6. Predicted and obtained double-stimulus values (Experiments 1 and 2).

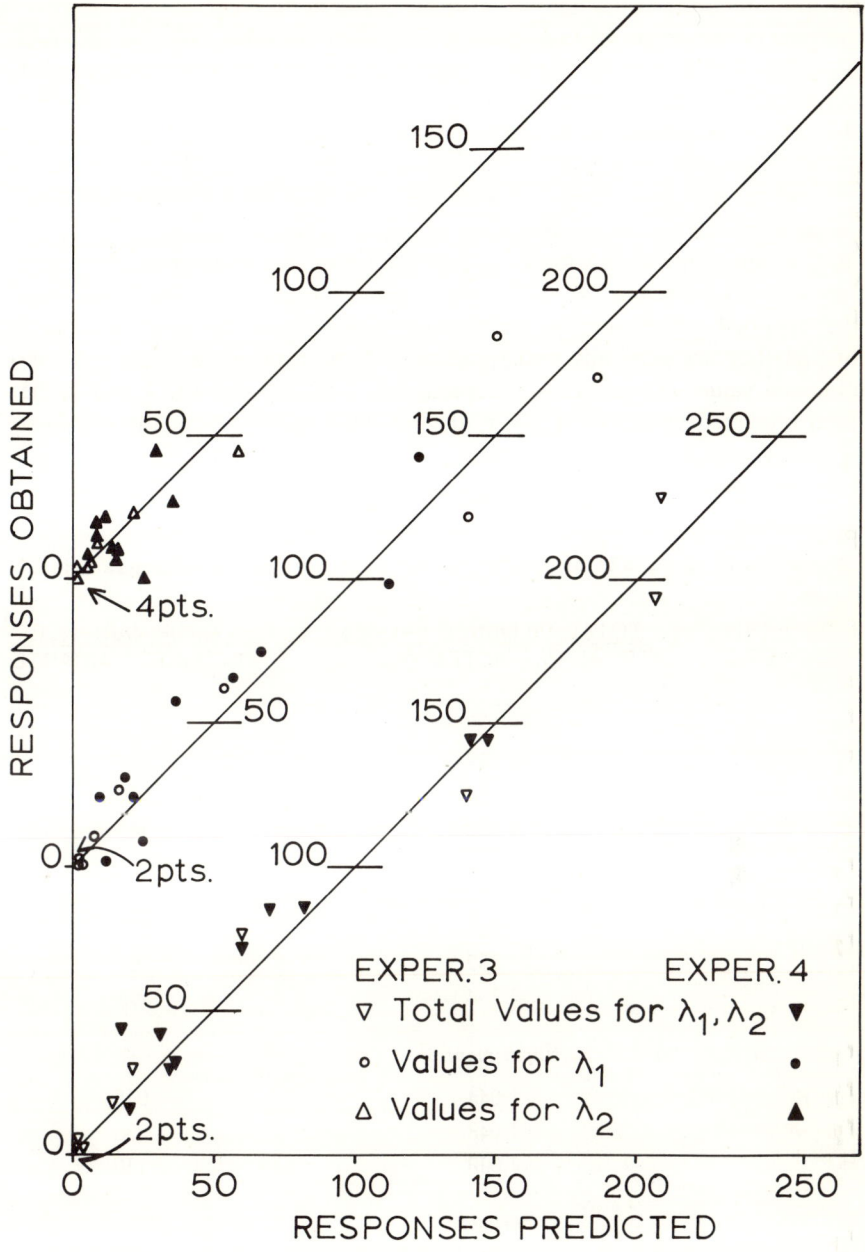

FIGURE 26-7. Predicted and obtained double-stimulus values (Experiments 3 and 4).

tween each point and the appropriate diagonal line. In general, the agreement between predicted and obtained values is quite satisfactory, but some analysis of the errors of prediction would seem desirable. We can ask two questions in this regard: (1) Are there systematic error tendencies toward overprediction or underprediction of the obtained values? (2) What is the actual "goodness of fit" between the predicted and obtained values?

Mean direction of error. Systematic error tendencies can be seen from an analysis of the mean direction of error. This is presented in Table 26-2 as the ratio of the total obtained value to the total predicted value for each set of points. If this ratio is greater than 1.0, it indicates that the obtained values are on the average higher than the predicted ones, or that they are generally underpredicted; if the ratio is less than 1.0, the obtained values are generally overpredicted. For Experiments 1 and 2, the total predicted values for $r_1 + r_2$ do not differ greatly from the obtained

TABLE 26-2

Measures of goodness of prediction for double-stimulus response totals

PREDICTED VALUES	TOTAL OBTAINED VALUES / TOTAL PREDICTED VALUES	ERROR VARIANCE / OBTAINED VARIANCE
	Experiment 1	
$r_1 + r_2$	1.019	.015
r_1	.955	.050
r_1	1.130	.145
	Experiment 2	
$r_1 + r_2$	.963	.010
r_1	.852	.064
r_2	1.194	.105
	Experiment 3	
$r_1 + r_2$	1.044	.015
r_1	1.048	.036
r_2	1.018	.110
	Experiment 4	
$r_1 + r_2$	1.090	.064
r_1	1.107	.101
r_2	1.038	.772
r_2 corrected		.427

values. While r_1 is to some degree overpredicted, r_2 is generally underpredicted. Since r_1 is the value obtained from the stronger stimulus in each pair, this indicates that the model predicts a sharper discrimination or preference between the simultaneously presented values than was actually obtained.

In Experiments 3 and 4, all values are somewhat underpredicted. The values for r_1 are more underpredicted than those for r_2, which is a reversal of the pattern obtained in Experiments 1 and 2. Thus, after discrimination training, the preferences between stimuli are slightly greater relative to predicted values than before such training. This may well reflect an increase in the sensitivity of the subjects to the various stimulus values as a result of the discrimination training procedure.

Goodness of prediction. Any measure of systematic error tendency must be supplemented by a measure of goodness of fit, which takes the total error variance into account. Even if the mean error is close to zero, the scatter of obtained points around a predicted function can be considerable. A frequent measure of goodness of fit around a fitted function is the proportion of the total variance of the obtained values that can be attributed to the predicted values. In such a case, the error variance and the variance of predicted values add up to the total obtained variance. Since the present line of "perfect prediction" is not a fitted function, but is derived from independent considerations, this additive principle does not hold exactly, but since the accuracy of prediction is generally high, the ratio of the error variance to the obtained variance will still provide a comparable measure of the goodness of prediction. This ratio is presented for each set of predicted values in Table 26-2; the lower the value, the smaller the error, and the better the fit.

This ratio is generally quite small, indicating a high degree of correlation between the predicted and obtained values. In each experiment, the prediction is best for $r_1 + r_2$, next for r_1, and poorest for r_2. This is due not so much to differences in the size of the error variance (though such do exist) as it is to large differences in the obtained variance by which the error variance is divided. It would be misleading to think that the absolute amount of error increases as the predicted values decrease.

The one case in which predictions were not satisfactory, as indicated from Figure 26-7 and from Table 26-2, is for r_2 in Experiment 4. This is partly due to the fact that the simultaneous discrimination did not transfer to the SS situation. Therefore, substantial values were predicted for 560 mμ on the DS test, while the actual responses obtained to this value when presented with 550 mμ were very close to zero in accordance with the trained discrimination. For this reason, it seems justified to omit the values for predicted and obtained 560 mμ (from the 550, 560 mμ pair) in the calculations of r_2 errors. The corrected error values are presented in Table 26-2, and show a marked decrease.

Statistical tests. One method of testing goodness of fit of empirical data to theoretically predicted points suggested by Lindquist (1953, pp. 344 ff.). This was used to test the hypothesis that the obtained values do not differ significantly from predicted values. In this method, the error can be divided into two components, "vertical placement," or differences between predicted and obtained means, and "departure from pattern," or the error remaining after these means have been equated. Each of these components provides a mean square which can be divided by the residual error variance of the obtained data after the data have been corrected for systematic effects, in our case wavelength and subjects. The resulting F ratio provides a test of significance similar to those obtained in analyses of variance. If the F ratio reaches significance, this means that it is unlikely that the difference between the expected and obtained values can be attributed to sampling error alone. This analysis was carried out for all the r_1 and r_2 values for the four experiments. The only errors reaching significance are for r_2 in Experiment 1, where both vertical placement and departure from pattern are significant at the .001 level. This one obtained significant departure from prediction does indicate that by the present method, r_2 is systematically underestimated following simple acquisition.

Since this method of testing significance depends for its error term on the obtained scores of the subjects, it is subject to the vagaries of sample size and residual variability. In Experiment 2 the percent mean error for r_2 was larger than in Experiment 1, but the vertical placement component only approached significance at the .05 level. This could well be due to the fact that only six subjects were used in that study. In Experiment 4, the departure from pattern of r_2 was clearly greater than in Experiment 1, but again is not significant, perhaps due to a large residual error term. Such a "goodness of fit" test puts one into the position of trying to support a hypothesis of no difference between obtained and predicted values, and this always leaves open the possibility that with a larger sample or smaller residual variability, the null hypothesis would have to be rejected.

Prediction of DSG values. Consider the three stimulus values λ_1, λ_2, and λ_3, providing the SS response totals R_1, R_2, and R_3. A DSG value for λ_2 is obtained when the predicted or obtained values to λ_2 are summed across the two pairs λ_1, λ_2, λ_3. The two DS response values to λ_2 (r_{2a} and r_{2b}) are predicted by the DS function as follows:

$$r_{2a} = R_2 \left(\frac{R_2}{R_1 + R_2}\right) \quad r_{2a} = R_2 \left(\frac{R_2}{R_2 + R_3}\right)$$

Adding these and collecting terms:

$$r_{2DSG} = R_2 \left(\frac{R_2}{R_1 + R_2}\right) + \left(\frac{R_2}{R_2 + R_3}\right)$$

Predictions from the Generalization Gradient

These predictions were carried out for the DSG gradients and are entered as crosses in Figures 26-1, 26-2, 26-4, and 26-5, where they can be compared with the obtained DSG's. In general, it is clear that predicting the DSG's in this fashion is more satisfactory than predicting the DSG from the SSG alone; in other words, the suggested method of prediction will account for a large portion of the differences between the DSG and the SSG. The following considerations will amplify this point.

Each of the fractions in the equation for predicting r_{2DSG} can range from 0 to 1. Therefore, the multiplier for R_2 can run from 0 to 2, and thus $0 \leq r_{2DSG} \leq 2R_2$. The relative sizes of r_{2DSG} and R_2 (the obtained SSG value) depend on the sum of the two fractions, and this in turn depends on the shape of the gradient at λ_1, λ_2, and λ_3. In the case, for example, where λ_2 is a peak, each of the fractions must be greater than .5 since R_2 is greater than R_1 and R_3; the predicted DSG value must therefore be higher than the SSG value. The size of this difference will be correlated with the difference between the peak value and its neighbors. It can be seen that particularly after discrimination training, where rather sharp peaks are obtained, the DSG values at the 550 or 540 mμ peak are very high, and are quite accurately predicted. In general, the two fractions in the equation for R_{2DSG} will add up to 1 (thus providing equal SSG and DSG values) only if the points on the gradient form a geometric series. Thus if the gradient is flat (where the multiplier for the series is 1), the DSG and the SSG points coincide, but if it is rising in linear fashion (arithmetic series) the DSG points will lie above the SSG values. Near the center of the gradients the slope is generally linear, and the expected difference in height is seen to occur.

The mean error of prediction for the DSG's is the same as for $r_1 + r_2$, since each group of values when summated represents the total of the predicted responses. Referring again to Table 26-2, it can be seen that the DSG in Experiment 1 was overpredicted by 3.7 percent in Experiment 1 and underpredicted by 1.9 percent in Experiment 2. In contrast, note that if the SSG were used as the predictor, the DSG's would be underpredicted by 10 and 18 percent, respectively. It was suggested earlier that this difference could be attributed to differences in the VI training rates obtained from the DS and SS presentations of 550 mμ. Now it is clear that this assumption is not necessary—predicting the DSG's from the proposed formulae, rather than from the SSG, will provide the proper DSG response levels.

DISCUSSION

The foregoing analysis indicates that the direction and degree of preference between stimuli lying on a generalization gradient can be predicted from the independent response strengths of the stimuli in accordance with some very general principles regarding their interaction. The occurrence of transposition and transposition-reversal in conjunction with a shift in the mode of the gradient follows from these principles directly. In this respect, Spence's analysis of transposition and his prediction of transposition-reversal have been supported. On the other hand, the obtained correspondence between the PDG and choice behavior does not necessarily confirm the theoretical derivation of the PDG from the simple summation of excitatory and inhibitory gradients generated around S+ and S—, respectively. Hanson (1959) has already discussed the difficulties encountered in such a derivation for a very similar set of data involving a successive discrimination between 550 mμ (S+) and 560 mμ (S—). The PDG should be lower at all points than a comparable control gradient obtained after simple acquisition because of the subtractive effect of the negative gradient around S—. But in Hanson's study, the PDG was higher between 510 and 540 mμ (inclusive) than the gradient obtained after simple acquisition. Since the discrimination training procedure may have raised the positive gradient in a manner not reflected by the control gradients, Hanson constructed hypothetical positive gradients which were at all points higher than the obtained PDG. Then he constructed hypothetical negative gradients which, when subtracted from these, would provide the obtained PDG, and concluded that the negative gradients would have their minima (i.e., the greatest amount of inhibition) at S+ rather than S—, which is certainly contrary to Spence's theory.

The present data involve many of the same features. The SS PDG following successive discrimination training (Exp. 3) exceeds the postacquisition gradient of Experiment 1 at 530 and 540 mμ. Since the birds in Experiment 3 received additional reinforcement in the course of discrimination training, some increases in the positive gradient can be expected. An adequate control group is not available, but it is of interest to compare the PDG from Experiment 3 with that obtained in Experiment 4, where the subjects received about as many exposures to S+—and thus an equal number of additional reinforcements on S+—as they did in the successive discrimination. Again, the gradient from Experiment 3 is higher at 530 and 540 mμ, since the PDG from Experiment 4 is rather similar to that obtained after simple acquisition. It appears, then, that the effects of successive discrimination training cannot be accounted for by a simple algebraic interaction of excitatory and inhibitory gradients generated around S+ and S—.

The obtained differences in results after successive simultaneous discrimination training are not expected from the "absolute" theory of discrimination learning proposed by Spence, or from "configurational" accounts of discrimination learning and transposition. According to Spence's theory, the development of excitation and inhibition is essentially independent of the manner of stimulus presentation, and the speed of learning should be about equal for the two kinds of discrimination training. Furthermore, equal amounts of transposition should be obtained after discrimination is achieved. According to configurational theory, discrimination learning is facilitated by the opportunity to compare discriminanda, and since transposition is based on the perception of the relationship between two stimuli, it should be greater after simultaneous discrimination training. The present results are at variance with these theories, since (a) the simultaneous problem (Exp. 4) is clearly easier by a number of criteria, and (b) in spite of this, transposition was obtained only after the successive training procedure (Exp. 3).

In general terms, the problem is that the difference in the opportunity to compare stimuli in the two training procedures is confounded with a number of other procedural differences which probably do not affect the "perceptual" aspects of the training situation, but may well influence the course of learning. In simultaneous discrimination training, S+ was available on every trial, and reinforcement could always be obtained within the restrictions imposed by the VI schedule and the changeover delay contingency for errors. Since the mean error rate never exceeded 20 percent in the training phase of Experiment 4, there was little disruption of the VI reinforcement schedule available in simple acquisition. In the successive discrimination, however, reinforcement was available only on half the trials, no matter how good the discrimination performance. In the terms of the analysis presented above, it was possible for the subjects in Experiment 4 to maintain reinforcement on the acquisition schedule by shifting the total duration of responding to S+; a change in rate was not required. Once S— came to serve as a cue for shifting, the discrimination was learned. In the successive situation, S— had to serve as a cue for not responding, and a genuine decrease in response rate developed in the presence of S—, with an accompanying increase (behavioral contrast) to S+. Thus, while in both experiments equivalent discrimination criteria were achieved in terms of zero responding to S— over an equivalent number of trials, the learning processes were probably quite different. The "extinction" resulting from a shift in response duration is not equivalent to extinction resulting from a decrease in rate; this is demonstrated by the fact that while the successive discrimination transferred perfectly to simultaneous presentation, the reverse was not the case. A shift in the mode of the gradient, and concomitant transposition, may well depend on the development of "genuine" extinction involving a change in response rate in the presence of S—. If this is the case, the "perceptual" aspects of simultaneous and successive presentation may be incidental to the true cause of the difference in the effects of the two training procedures. A proper assessment of the perceptual aspects must await the development of techniques where other features of the learning situation, such as the frequency of reinforcement, are not confounded in the two conditions.

Most other studies involving comparisons between successive and simultaneous learning procedures have also suffered from the confounding of training variables, although the results have usually differed from those presented here. Grice (1949) found that the acquisition of successive and simultaneous discriminations in rate was equally rapid in a runway, and he obtained equal amounts of transfer between the two conditions. The frequency of reinforcement available on each trial varied between the training conditions in a manner similar to the present study, except that he used a discrete-trial procedure. For his discrimination criterion, Grice considered relative running times in the successive situation to be equivalent to stimulus preference. His rats met the successive criterion when they achieved a nonoverlapping distribution of running times to S+ and S— in the course of ten trials; in the simultaneous situation they had to choose S+ consistently in ten trials. It is quite likely that Grice's results depended on the measures he considered equivalent; he did not apply an extinction criterion in the usual sense to the successive situation by requiring that running time exceed some absolute value over a number of trials. Had he done so, successive discrimination training would presumably have taken longer. Conversely, if the criterion for the successive discrimination in the present study had been no more than nonoverlapping distributions response rates to S+ and S—, the discrimination would have been "learned" much faster and transposition might have been much less.

Baker and Lawrence (1951) compared transposition after simultaneous and successive training and obtained better transposition with the former procedure. They adopted the general methods and criteria developed by Grice, and the considerations mentioned above certainly apply to their study also. With a criterion of nonoverlapping response speeds in the successive procedure, and a noncorrection method in the simultaneous procedure, it is quite possible that "true" extinction to S— was greater in the simultaneous case, leading to more of a shift in the mode of the PDG and to more transposition. This cannot be directly assessed, since they did not obtain any generalization gradients. Furthermore, they did not run a group that shifted from the successive to the simultaneous procedure on the original training stimuli. Since transposition trials are necessarily conducted with simultaneous presentation of stimuli after either kind of training, such a control is necessary to assure that poorer transposition is not due merely to a shift in procedure.[4]

In other studies, attempts have been made to overcome these problems by having S+ and S— available on each trial, while manipulating

---

[4] This control was provided in Experiment 3 of the present series by the DS trials on which 550 and 560 mμ were presented together.

the opportunity to compare them. Thompson (1955) taught rats two concurrent discrimination problems, one involving a reflectance difference, and the other a size difference. The comparison group had the size discriminanda paired on half the trials and the reflectance discriminanda on the other half. For the noncomparison group, the negative reflectance stimulus was always paired with the positive size stimulus, and vice versa. Learning speed was equal for the two groups. Initial transposition was somewhat better for the noncomparison group on the size discrimination, but Thompson says that this difference did not reach significance. When Thompson trained both of his groups on the transposition problem in the comparison situation, he found that the group originally trained in that situation learned more rapidly and with fewer errors. But since initial transposition did not differ significantly, it is likely that the difference in the speed of learning reflected a general transfer effect. Again, there was no control for this in the form of a group switched from the noncomparison to the comparison situation with the original training stimuli.

Riley, Ring, and Thomas (1960) approached the problem somewhat differently. Rats were trained on a brightness discrimination where the discriminanda were both presented on all trials to each group. The difference between comparison and noncomparison procedures consisted only of a barrier which prevented the noncomparison group from seeing both stimuli at once. Training was carried out with a difficult discrimination in the first study, and with an easy discrimination in a second study. The second experiment included an important control group, lacking in the research up to this point, in which the subjects were shifted from the noncomparison to the comparison procedures with the original training stimuli.

The authors found, first, that learning was considerably easier with the comparison procedure both on easy and on difficult discriminations. Furthermore, there was significantly more transposition following comparison training; in fact, the amount of transposition following noncomparison training on the difficult problem was not much above chance. When the noncomparison control group was shifted from noncomparison to comparison training conditions, the subjects demonstrated a somewhat higher level of transfer than the amount of transposition obtained from the main noncomparison group, but this difference only approached significance. It is still possible, therefore, that the difference in transposition can be accounted for by imperfect transfer from one learning situation to the other, and that the perceptual differences in the training situations do not selectively influence the occurrence of transposition per se.

In summary, it seems clear that both the speed of learning and the amount of transposition will be affected by a number of procedural variables in the learning situation, of which the manner of stimulus presentation is only one, and which can easily be confounded with the manner of stimulus presentation. The manner in which responding to S— is eliminated is particularly important, since this will affect the form of the PDG and thus the amount of transposition. Under appropriate conditions, it may be possible to reverse the effects of simultaneous and successive training found in this study, by using a noncorrection procedure in the simultaneous problem, for example, and reinforcing failure to respond in the successive problem. When all other variables are held constant, it does appear from the experiments by Thompson (1955) and Riley, Ring, and Thomas (1960) that the opportunity to compare stimuli on a given dimension produces faster learning, but it still needs to be demonstrated conclusively that this will result in greater transposition when general transfer effects between simultaneous and successive procedures are controlled for. Even if the comparison situation does result in more transposition, this effect may be restricted to continua in which differences between stimuli are quantitative, such as size or reflectance, rather than qualitative, such as spectral value.

SUMMARY

The relationship between stimulus preference and the response strength of singly presented stimuli was investigated with the use of a generalization gradient to provide stimuli of different response strengths. After being trained to peck at a 550-mμ stimulus on a VI schedule, pigeons were given two concurrent generalization tests: one consisted of single stimulus values ranging from 490 to 610 mμ, and the other consisted of pairs of values chosen from this range. The direction of preference within each pair was found to be in direct accordance with the number of responses obtained with single stimulus values during the generalization test. This relationship was not affected by the size of the difference between the stimuli that comprised a test pair.

Two groups of birds then received discrimination training between 550 mμ as S+ and 560 mμ as S—, one with successive stimulus presentation, and one with simultaneous. After this, generalization and preference tests were administered a second time. The successive discrimination produced a shift in the mode of the gradient away from S— and a concurrent transposition of the discrimination between S+ and the new mode, with transposition-reversal beyond that mode. The simultaneous discrimination produced little change in the gradient and no concurrent transposition.

An arithmetic model is proposed for the prediction of responses to members of stimulus pairs from the rates obtained with single-stimulus values. The determination of stimulus preference by the generalization gradient follows directly, and transposition is no more than a special case.

The operant situation is analyzed in terms of some simple response dimensions (momentary rate and duration of responding) to provide a basis for the arithmetic model. The differential results obtained from successive and simultaneous discriminations are discussed with reference to the nature of the extinction to S— produced with these different procedures, and the results are related to previous studies of transposition obtained after these training procedures.

V

MOTIVATION AND REWARD

27

The Effects of Training and Motivation on the Components of a Learned Instrumental Response[1]

RICHARD AUSTIN KING

The response which acts upon the environment to produce a change is the dependent variable in studies of instrumental learning. For different purposes this response has been considered at two levels.

1. At the level of the observation of behavior, S-R theorists who have been interested in instrumental learning have not, with a few exceptions, been concerned with the exact form of the response being measured. Any gross, observable, molar response will do, so long as it produces a specified environmental effect. Thus, Thorndike (1898, 1913) speaks of the stamping in of correct responses and the stamping out of incorrect ones. No attention is given to the details of the correct and incorrect responses. Hull (1943, 1951, 1952) and Spence (1956) use response measures, time, number of responses to extinction, and probability of a correct response, which may mask important details of the response. Guthrie (1952) and Logan (1956) are exceptions. Both are impressed with the importance of movements, patterns of movements, and stereotyped responses (Guthrie & Horton, 1946).

2. At a theoretical level all the above theories have made use of the components of response. Thorndike's (1913) account of transfer of training in terms of similar elements implies an analysis of behavior into its details. Skinner's (1938, 1953) use of the concepts of response differentiation, successive approximations and chaining relies on the partitioning of responses. Hull (1930, 1943, 1951, 1952) and Spence (1956) use miniature responses (r_G) to help account for such things as expectancy, the goal gradient and incentive motivation. Guthrie (1952) speaks of stimuli becoming conditioned to movements. A movement may be as small a fraction of the total goal response as the contraction of a single fiber. These are the basic units of learning for Guthrie.

[1] Based on the author's Ph.D. dissertation completed at Duke University in 1959. With the author's permission I have revised and shortened the article. [Ed.]

Thus, a consideration of the components of a response has proved to be of importance at the theoretical level. It seems possible that similar considerations at the empirical, observable level may prove fruitful. Logan (1956) and Gilbert (1958) have started the trend toward such an analysis, of which this study may be regarded as a part.

In this paper the response of running down a straight-alley-runway is divided two ways. First it is divided spatially; running-time measures are taken in alley segments close to the goal, far from the goal, and in the middle of the alley. Second, running time is measured two ways. (a) One measure is total running time which includes time spent running toward the goal plus time spent making interfering responses (responses which are incompatible with running). (b) The other measure is running time with these interfering responses excluded. The following problems of learning have been considered with this type of analysis:

1. It is generally agreed that running time will decrease as a function of trials under the conditions of this experiment. The question is whether this change in performance of an instrumental response consists of the strengthening of the running response, or simply the elimination of other, interfering, reactions.

2. It has been shown in numerous investigations that increases in drive level increase the vigor of performance of an instrumental act. The question is whether drive level affects performance in this way by strengthening a given response, or whether the effect is due to the selection of qualitatively different responses associated with each drive level. The experiment most directly relevant to this question is that of Cotton (1953), whose analysis involved the same two response classes as are used here. He found that performance improved with increases in drive, even when all the trials on which there were interfering responses were excluded from analysis, although the magnitude of the drive effect was considerably reduced. This experiment provides an opportunity to test the validity of Cotton's results in a slightly different way.

3. Most learning-type behavioral theories state or imply that the observable behavior of an organism is the result of the action of more or less temporary energizing agents (motives, drives, etc.) on more or less permanent learned elements (habits, etc.). While there is agreement with regard to the effect of drive on performance, there is considerable disagreement over the question of whether the level of drive at the time of acquisition affects learning. Considered from the point of view of the response analysis described above, the question is whether drive level affects learning, if it does, by strengthening a given response, or whether the effect is due to the learning of different responses under different drive levels, a possibility suggested by Campbell and Kraeling (1954).

4. The spatial classification of the running response is the same as

that which was done by Hull (1934) in his analysis of the goal gradient. There are two questions with regard to the spatial components of this instrumental response. The first of these is whether the goal gradient is the result of the strengthening of a given response in different parts of the alley, or whether it is due to the fact that qualitatively different responses are made in different parts of the alley.

The second question is whether drive level influences the slope of the goal gradient, and if it does, whether this comes about as a result of an influence on the running response or through an effect upon interfering behavior.

These problems provide an indication of the possibilities of the analysis of the components of the observable response in instrumental learning. Extensions of such an analysis may make it less necessary to postulate unobservable components. It should be specifically mentioned, however, that the description of possible outcomes above has been presented in terms of dichotomous alternatives. It is, of course, conceivable that the results of experimentation will suggest an influence of practice, drive and spatial distance from a goal which affects both classes of behavior.

Method

SUBJECTS. The subjects were 80 male rats of the Wistar strain which were obtained from a commercial supplier. They were approximately 90–150 days old at the beginning of the experiment. The subjects lived in individual cages during the experiment.

APPARATUS. A straight-alley-runway was used. It was 5 feet long, $2\frac{1}{2}$ inches wide and 3 inches high, painted black, covered with a hinged Plexiglas lid, and floored with hardware cloth. A starting-box and a goal-box of the same construction as the runway were attached to either end. These were both 1 foot in length. Guillotine doors separated both the starting- and goal-boxes from the alley. These were operated by strings by the experimenter.

For purposes of excluding external stimuli, the whole apparatus was enclosed in a larger black wooden box and was illuminated by nine $7\frac{1}{2}$-watt light bulbs which were placed so that the runway was uniformly lighted. The experimenter was able to watch the subjects through small Plexiglas covered openings in the hinged lid of the enclosing box. A masking noise was provided by a small fan which was located near the goal end of the alley.

The door between the starting-box and the alley activated a switch when it was raised. Seven photoelectric cells (Knight Kit, model 83Y702) were arranged along the alley. The first of these was 6 inches down the alley from the starting-box door. Activation of this cell made it possible to measure the time that it took the subject to leave the starting-box and move 6 inches down the alley (latency). The other six cells were then spaced at intervals of 8 inches down the alley. Therefore, the last photoelectric cell was 6 inches in front of the goal-box door. Running times were recorded from a point 6 inches in front of the starting-box door to a point 6 inches in front of the goal-box door. The light which activated the photoelectric cells passed through bottles of iodine, which acted as filters and effectively reduced visibility of the light beam. The switch on the starting-box door and the photoelectric cell relays were wired to work the pens of a 10-pen Esterline-Angus operations recorder. There were almost no failures with this system. From these records the running time in each 8-inch segment of the alley could be obtained. One pen of the recorder was attached to a switch which the experimenter activated for the time that the subject was making an interfering response (to be defined below). Thus, the length of time spent by the subject in making interfering responses in each segment of the alley could be determined.

METHOD. The experiment was done in three stages for 40 subjects and in four stages for the other 40 subjects. The first two stages, habituation and pretraining, were the same for all subjects. The third stage, training, differed for the two sets of 40 subjects. One set, the 2-, 24-, 48-, and 72-hour training deprivation groups of 10 subjects each, received 50 reinforced trials, while the other set, the 12- and 60-hour training deprivation groups of 20 subjects each, received 20 reinforced trials. These latter groups were then subjected to a fourth stage, 30 extinction trials.

The experiment was done in five replications for the 2-, 24-, 48-, and 72-hour groups and in 10 replications for the 12- and 60-hour groups.

1. *Habituation.* After receipt from the supplier, the subjects were fed ad lib. for three days. Then they were moved to another room and placed on the deprivation schedule which was used throughout the experiment. This consisted of five-day cycles of 72 hours deprivation followed by 48 hours ad lib. feeding. Subjects were run after they had been deprived the appropriate number of hours within the 72-hour period. Four such cycles (20 days) were completed before the subjects were put in the alley for pretraining. During this period approximately 10% of the subjects, having been weakened somewhat by this treatment, died of various diseases. Extra animals which had been subjected to the same habituation treatment as the subjects which died were substituted for them. The subjects were handled every day at the time of the experiment (7:00 P.M. to 1:00 A.M.). This handling continued throughout all stages. In the second cycle, the subjects were fed a dry form of the food later used as reinforcement (Gaines dog food pellets). Starting with the third cycle,

and continuing for the rest of the experiment, the subjects were fed wet food which was the same as the reinforcement food during the last half hour of the eating period. During this half-hour period they were also fed by hand until they refused to eat for at least one 30-second period.

2. *Pretraining.* At the end of the 20-day habituation period the subjects were placed in the goal-box, under the experimental deprivation conditions, with about four times as much food as would later be used for reinforcement. The deprivation conditions were 2, 12, 24, 48, 60, and 72 hours. The subjects were left in the goal-box until they had consumed this food. They were then taken out, and, after an interval which varied from about 2 to 30 minutes, were placed again in the goal-box a second time. Ten pretraining trials of this sort were given, the amount of food decreasing gradually until it was the same amount, a round pellet about $\frac{1}{8}$ inch in diameter, as that used in training.

3. *Training.* At the appropriate time in the next cycle (the 6th cycle) after pretraining the subjects were given training trials at the rate of 10 per day. A subject was placed in the starting-box and the experimenter waited 10 seconds. At this time the starting-box door was opened regardless of the orientation of the subject. The subject then ran down the alley while the experimenter recorded the time of interfering responses. The subject could retrace and re-enter the starting-box, although few did because of the difficulty of turning around in the narrow alley. When the subject had entered the goal-box the door to the goal-box was lowered. The subject was removed from the goal-box as soon as possible after eating. All subjects ate almost immediately upon entering the goal-box. The subject was then confined in his home cage for approximately 5 minutes between trials while other subjects were run. The total time of running was thus approximately one hour. Five days later, at the appropriate time in the next cycle, all subjects were given 10 more training trials. Thus, each subject had 5 days between each block of 10 trials. Since all subjects except the 72-hour ones continued to be deprived for variable periods after running, care was taken to wait for a few minutes before feeding the 72-hour subjects after their runs. The 2-, 24-, 48-, and 72-hour groups were given 50 training trials, while the 12- and 60-hour groups were given 20 training trials followed by 30 extinction trials.

4. *Extinction.* The conditions in extinction were exactly the same as those in training except for the omission of reinforcement and the following changes in deprivation schedules. The 12-hour training group was divided into two groups, a group which was under 12 hours deprivation during both training and extinction (12–12 group) and a group which was under 12 hours deprivation during training and 60 hours deprivation

during extinction (12–60 group). The switch in deprivation time was accomplished by simply waiting for a different length of time in the deprivation part of the 5-day cycle, a consideration which eliminates problems deriving from changes in overall schedule. Similarly, the 60-hour training group was divided into two groups, a group which was under 60 hours deprivation during both training and extinction (60–60 group) and a group which was under 60 hours' deprivation during training and 12 hours' deprivation during extinction (60–12 group). These four groups formed the groups in the following 2 × 2 factorial design.

	TRAINING	
	12	60
EXTINCTION 12		
EXTINCTION 60		

It is possible, by using extinction measures, to evaluate the effects of training and extinction separately with such a design.

TREATMENT OF RESULTS. There are six points to be made here.

1. The times for two classes of response are treated. Class I responses are those which include both the running response and interfering responses. These are the responses usually measured in experiments using straight-alley-runways. Class II responses are running responses only, without interfering responses. Interfering responses were defined as any response which did not advance the subject toward the goal. Thus, retracing, stopping, grooming, sniffing, etc., were counted as interfering responses and their times were recorded. Response times for Class II responses were obtained by subtracting interfering response times from the total running time (Class I responses).

2. Since there were 20 subjects in the 12-hour and 60-hour groups, ten were selected at random for comparison with the other groups of 10 subjects (2-, 24-, 48-, and 72-hour groups), a procedure necessitated by the analyses of variance employed.

3. The analyses of results are based on the logarithms of response times in order to convert the skewed distributions of the data into distributions on which analyses of variance could be done.

4. Latencies were also recorded. These data are not included here because they show essentially the same things as the running-time data. Also, no analysis of interfering responses is possible with the latency data.

The Effects of Training and Motivation

5. A criterion of extinction of two consecutive trials with Class I response times over 5 seconds was used for purposes of computing number of trials to extinction. All but three subjects (one in the 60–12 group and two in the 60–60 group) met this criterion. Since there were 30 extinction trials, these subjects were given scores of 30.

6. In order to simplify the analysis, the data for adjacent maze segments were combined. This gives records on three alley segments rather than six.

Results

The overall performance curves for the 50 acquisition trials of the 2-, 24-, 48-, and 72-hour groups and for the 20 acquisition trials of the 12- and 60-hour groups are presented in Figure 27-1. Each point is the

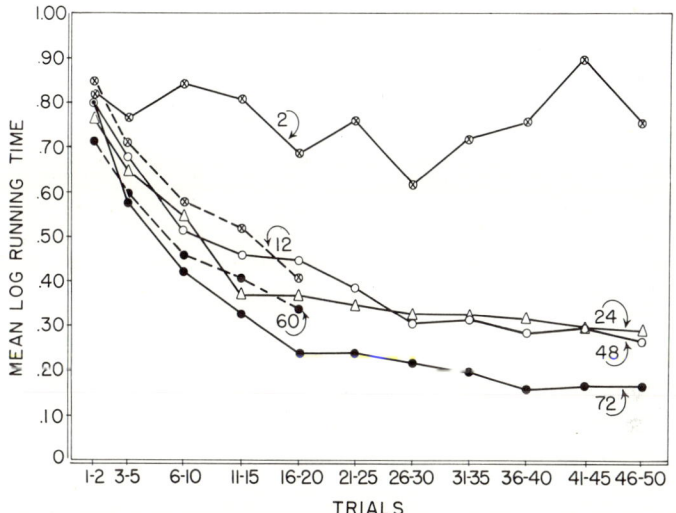

FIGURE 27-1. Overall performance curves of the 2-, 12-, 24-, 48-, 60- and 72-hour groups in acquisition (Class I responses).

mean of the logarithm of time for responses of Class I (running time plus interfering response class) for all the subjects of a group over five-trial blocks. These overall results must be considered in greater detail in order to answer the four questions raised in the introduction.

1. *Are changes in performance as a function of trials due to increases in the strength of a single response class or to the selection of qualitatively different responses?*

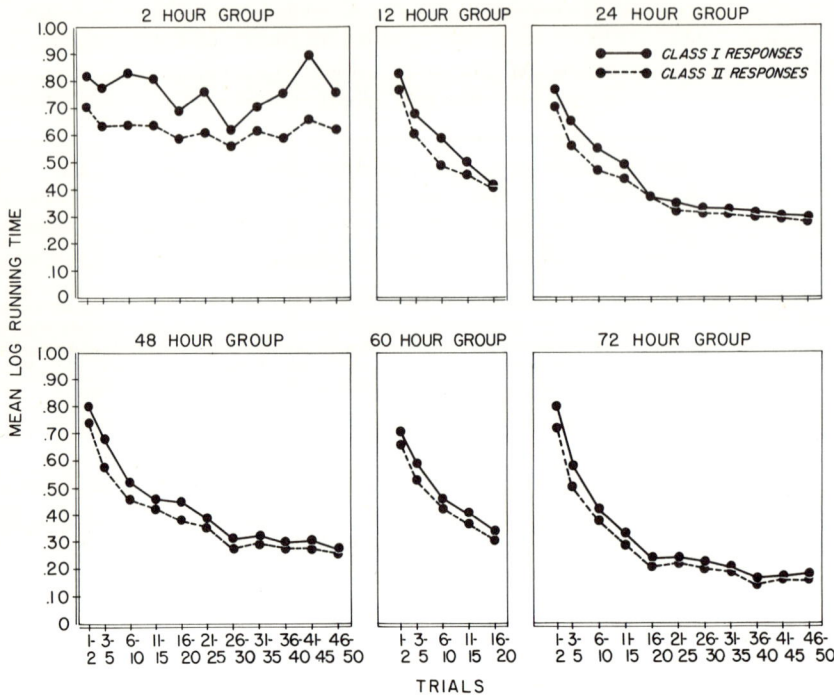

FIGURE 27-2. Class I and Class II response times as a function of trials for the 2-, 12-, 24-, 48-, 60- and 72-hour groups.

Results bearing on this question are shown in Figure 27-2, where, for each group, the means of the logarithms of time for Class I responses and Class II responses (running time only) are plotted against trials. These curves clearly indicate that, for all groups that improved with training (all except the 2-hour group), the improvement is largely due to increases in the strength of the running response and not to the elimination of competing reactions.

2. *Does drive level affect performance by strengthening a given response or by the selection of qualitatively different responses associated with each drive level?*

Results bearing on this question are shown in Figure 27-3. The means of the logarithms of time for the two response classes are plotted as a function of drive for trials 16–20 and 46–50. For both classes of response, the mean logarithm of time decreases rapidly from 2 to 12 hours. From 12 to 72 hours, the decrease is much more gradual. In fact, there is no significant effect of drive in the 12- to 72-hour range under the

The Effects of Training and Motivation

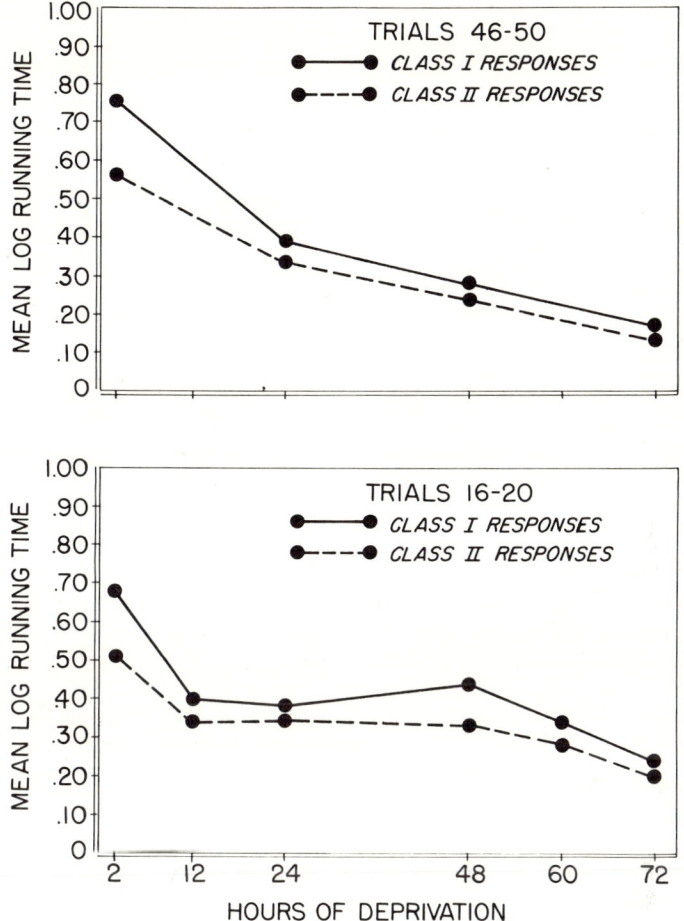

FIGURE 27-3. Class I and Class II response times as a function of drive level for Trials 16-20 and 46-50.

conditions of this experiment. But, the 2-hour group is significantly different from the others in both classes of response ($p < .005$ in all of several analyses).

3. The question here is twofold. (a) *Does drive level affect learning as well as performance?* (b) *Is the effect of drive on learning, if any, due to the acquisition of qualitatively different responses under different drive levels?*

Results which bear on the first of these questions are shown in Figure 27-4. When drive during extinction (performance) is equated and the groups are compared on the basis of drive during learning, as in the sec-

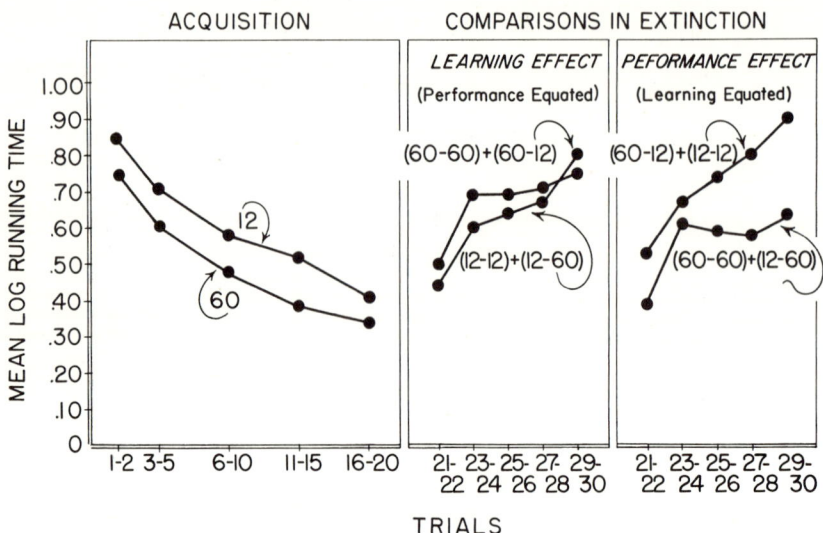

FIGURE 27-4. Class I response time for the 12- and 60-hour groups in acquisition and for the 12-12, 12-60, 60-60 and 60-12 hour groups in extinction.

ond segment of the graph in Figure 4, any difference must be due to the level of the learning drive. If this difference is significant, drive during learning has affected performance. In Figure 27-4 the groups trained under high drive seem to be slightly faster during the first six trials of extinction, but the difference is not significant. The results of an analysis of variance which shows the significance of effects due to treatments and their interaction are shown in Table 27-1. This analysis was done on the

TABLE 27-1

Results of an analysis of variance of logarithm of response time (response Class I) on trials 21-26

Source of variation	df	MS	F
Learning (L)	1	.0366	2.09
Performance (P)	1	.1199	6.85*
L × P	1	.0007	< 1.00
Error	36	.0175	
Total	39		

*p < .025.

mean logarithm of running time (Class I response) on these first six extinction trials. The difference shown in the second segment of Figure 27-4 is evaluated by the "learning" effect and is not significant. The difference shown in the third panel is evaluated by the "performance" effect and is significant. Similar analyses done on number of trials to extinction and on logarithms of running time (Class I response) for the 1st, 11th, and 21st trials of extinction (the first trials of each daily session) produced essentially the same results: a significant effect of "performance" drive, but no effect of "learning" drive.

Since there was no learning effect, the part of the question which seeks to account for this effect is not applicable.

4. A second way of analyzing the straight-alley running response is spatially. There are two questions here. (a) *Is the goal gradient due to the strengthening of a given response in different parts of the alley or is it due to the fact that qualitatively different responses are made in different parts of the alley?* (b) *Is the slope of the goal gradient a function of drive?*

Results which bear on the first question are presented in Table 27-2. The typical form of the goal gradient is present. In every case, running time (Class I response) is slowest in the first segment, fastest in the middle segment, with at least some deceleration in the final segment (Hull, 1934, 1952).

Analyses of variance were done to show the significance of effects with response time in the first two segments as one dimension and drive level as the second dimension. These analyses were done for both response classes on trials 1–10, 11–20 and 41–50. These gradients are considerably flattened when response Class II (running time only) is analyzed. In spite of this, the goal gradient effect is still present ($p < .001$) in all three 10-trial blocks.

Findings bearing on the second question, that of a change in slope of the goal gradient with increases in drive level, are also shown in Table 27-2. The slope of the line which would connect the first two segments is about the same for all levels of drive on trials 11–20. This slope does not seem to be the same for all levels of drive on trials 1–10 and 41–50. Appropriate statistical analyses reveal that this slope is significantly different for the several drive groups, for Class I responses, on trials 1–10 and 41–50. It is not significantly different, for Class I responses, on trials 11–20. The slope never varies significantly for Class II responses.

Discussion

The meaning of the results can now be considered in terms of each of the four questions about which this investigation has been organized.

TABLE 27-2

Mean logarithms of 10 × response time for both response classes in the three alley segments on trials 1-10, 11-20 and 41-50

2-HOUR GROUP

Trials	Segments					
	1		2		3	
	Class I	Class II	Class I	Class II	Class I	Class II
1-10	1.49	1.25	1.10	1.08	1.20	1.16
11-20	1.38	1.21	1.06	1.04	1.18	1.13
41-50	1.56	1.27	1.15	1.10	1.16	1.12

12-HOUR GROUP

Trials	Segments					
	1		2		3	
	Class I	Class II	Class I	Class II	Class I	Class II
1-10	1.29	1.18	1.05	1.03	1.11	1.08
11-20	1.10	1.04	.86	.86	.87	.87

24-HOUR GROUP

Trials	Segments					
	1		2		3	
	Class I	Class II	Class I	Class II	Class I	Class II
1-10	1.24	1.13	1.01	.99	1.07	1.05
11-20	1.07	1.03	.82	.82	.88	.87
41-50	.94	.92	.72	.71	.74	.74

1. *Are changes in performance as a function of trials due to increases in the strength of a single response class or to the selection of qualitatively different responses?*

From Figure 27-2 it is apparent that most of the improvement in performance for the 12-, 24-, 48-, 60-, and 72-hour groups, in which improvement occurs, results from the strengthening of the running response rather than the dropping out of interfering behavior. Since the difference between Class I and Class II responses gets smaller with trials, it is also apparent that some of the effect is the result of the dropping out of interfering tendencies.

The fact that the major part of the decrease in running time in acquisition is due to increases in the strength of a single response class, running response only, suggests a comparison with amplitude measures in classical conditioning. For the straight-alley, Spence (1956) has proposed a theory which states that improvement in performance with practice is the result of the increase in amplitude of responses which are classically conditioned to alley stimuli. Improvement in performance with practice is not accounted for on the basis of the fact that less time is spent making interfering responses. They are not involved in the explanation.

If we assume that response Class II (running response only) reflects such classically conditioned responses, the results of this experiment confirm Spence's theory. As is shown in Figure 27-2, most of the improvement in performance is the result of changes in vigor within this class. The forms of these response Class II curves are also predicted by Spence. Further work with this type of analysis of instrumental responses into components may make it possible to test Spence's assumptions that running time is an amplitude measure, and that the mean of the superthreshold values of $_sE_R$ is directly proportional to the running time.

2. *Does drive level affect performance by strengthening a given response or by the selection of qualitatively different responses associated with each drive level?*

With respect to this question, it is plausible to postulate that one way in which drive might influence behavior is through its ability to restrict the range of responses. Cotton's (1953) results are highly suggestive of such an interpretation in that, when the response measure employed was strictly limited to running, the effect of drive was also markedly reduced. There are also certain obvious affinities between such a position and Tolman's (1948) view of drive as a narrower of cognitive maps. On the other hand, a more conventional idea is Hull's (1943) conception that the vigor of some one response system is enhanced by drive.

Thus, two things may happen as a result of increases in drive. First, the range of responses may be decreased and more time spent in running than in doing other things. Second, the vigor of the running response itself may increase. Figure 27-3 seems to show that both of these results have been obtained. That the time spent in doing things other than running decreases as a function of drive is shown by the decreasing difference between Class I and Class II responses. That the speed of the more restricted Class II responses increases as a function of drive is shown by the significance of the "drive" effect in the analyses of variance. These results are thus in accord with the findings of Cotton, but they also support the general energy view of motivation.

One further implication of these data needs to be mentioned. Eisman (1956) has proposed that there are two parameters which affect the strength of hunger drive, number of hours of food deprivation and total number of hours of food deprivation within some fixed period of time. Thus, the subjects of this experiment were deprived for different amounts of time, 2, 12, 24, 48, 60, and 72 hours, before running, but all subjects were starved for 72 hours out of a five-day period. Eisman has proposed that response measures will vary with all deprivation times if the total time of deprivation within some fixed time is not constant. If the total time of food deprivation in some fixed time is constant, however, only those response measures for subjects deprived for about 4 hours or less will differ from the others. Eisman obtained results which were in line with this prediction, using a discrimination task and probability of a correct response as the response measure. The present results, with vigor measures, confirm Eisman's hypotheses: There was no significant difference between Class I or II response times for the 12-, 24-, 48-, 60-, and 72-hour groups, but there was a significant difference when the 2-hour subjects are compared with the subjects of the other groups on Class I and II responses.

3. (a) *Does drive level affect learning as well as performance?* (b) *Is the effect of drive on learning, if any, due to the learning of qualitatively different responses under different drive levels?*

The conclusions to be drawn from the results of the analyses of variance are clear. The performance effect of drive is significant for all three measures, while the learning effect is never significant. With regard to performance, these results are in accord with almost all experiments on drive level. The finding is simply that drive level does have an effect on performance. With regard to learning [question (a)], these results indicate that, under the conditions of this experiment, drive has no effect on learning.

Campbell and Kraeling (1954), who obtained an effect of drive on learning, have proposed that their subjects learned different things under high and low drives during acquisition. Specifically, they suggested, on the basis of informal observation that the high-drive subjects acquired, among other things, a marked readiness to leave the starting-box, which the low drive subjects did not. In the terms of this study, this may mean that the latter subjects may make more interfering responses and be reinforced for them, while the high drive subjects make few interfering responses. Thus, drive or any other variable which influences the time spent making interfering responses will have an effect on learning, which could be understood only in terms of a detailed analysis of the responses being learned. According to this view, drive will have an effect on learning if response Class I, which includes interfering responses, is used as the measure. If response Class II, which excludes interfering responses, is used, drive will have no effect on learning. An attempt to test these hypotheses was made here. It failed because there was no effect due to drive during acquisition when Class I responses were used. According to the above proposal, failure to demonstrate the effect of drive on learning would be expected if the time spent making interfering responses was about the same for the high and low drive groups. An examination of the curves for the 12-hour and 60-hour groups in Figure 27-2 shows that this was the case.

The evidence on this point from this experiment, thus, does not contradict the argument for interfering responses as the crucial elements in the determination of the effect of drive on learning. It does not support the argument, either. To be sure of this type of explanation, it would be necessary to show that, in cases where drive during learning did have an effect, the low and high drive groups differed, during learning, in the time spent making interfering responses. The data presented in Figure 27-2 show that only the 2-hour group differs markedly from the other groups in this regard. Thus one way of obtaining differences in the amount of time spent making interfering responses may be to use very low drive levels (4 hours or less in the case of hunger).

4. (a) *Is the goal gradient due to the strengthening of a given response in different parts of the alley or is it due to the fact that qualitatively different responses are made in different parts of the alley?* (b) *Is the slope of the goal gradient a function of drive for both response classes?*

The hypothesis that the goal gradient is entirely the result of interfering responses would hold that the time spent making interfering responses is greater farther from the goal than closer to it, and that this difference in interfering response time accounts for the goal gradient completely. The results of this study, however, show that the goal gradient is still present when Class II responses (running time only) are considered. The above hypothesis must thus be rejected.

The answer to question (b) is implied by the observation that the effect of drive, when significant, was only significant for response Class I and is never significant for response Class II. This result points to interfering responses as the chief factors influencing slope.

The goal gradient obtained in this study here is similar to the approach gradient of Miller (1948) and others which is widely used to predict behavior in a number of situations. Some of the predictions which are made involve assumptions about the effect of drive on the approach gradient. The effect is assumed to be one of a simple upward displacement of the gradient as a whole. The results presented here do not support this idea.

Since the goal gradient (approach gradient) may be derived from the generalization gradient which exists along the spatial continuum of maze stimuli (Spence, 1947), the present study may be compared with studies which have investigated the effect of drive on the generalization gradient. The results of this study agree with those obtained by Jenkins, Pascal and Walker (1958) and by Thomas and King (1958). Both of these studies show that the generalization gradient is flattened as drive increases.

SUMMARY

Four groups of ten albino rats were run for 50 acquisition trials under conditions of 2, 24, 48, and 72 hours of food deprivation. Two additional groups of 20 rats were run for 20 acquisition trials under conditions of 12 hours and 60 hours of food deprivation. These groups were then divided into four groups and run for 30 extinction trials. The four groups formed during extinction were a 12–12-hour group, a 12–60-hour group, a 60–60-hour group, and a 60–12-hour group. The first number in the above group designations represents drive under acquisition conditions, while the second number represents drive under extinction conditions. This design made it possible to separate the effects of drive on learning and on performance.

The response in this experiment was running time in a 4-foot straight-alley-runway. Running times were taken for two classes of response. The first class consisted of total time taken by the subject to traverse the alley (running response plus interfering responses). The second class consisted of the time of the running response only. Running times in three different segments of the alley were also obtained.

The results were as follows: (1) Learning in this situation is due largely to an increase in the strength of the running response alone and not to the dropping out of interfering responses. (2) Drive level affects both classes of response. (3) Drive, at the levels used here, and with a situation which minimizes extra-maze stimulation, affects performance but not learning. (4) The goal gradient is the result of the joint action of both response classes. The goal gradient (approach gradient) flattens as drive increases. This is a function of the elimination of interfering responses.

An attempt was made to relate each of these findings to the results of other experiments. Generally, the study of the components of an instrumental response should lead to an increase in our ability to specify the conditions necessary for a variable to be effective.

28

The Effectiveness of Drives as Cues[1]

CLARK J. BAILEY

In learning theories such as those of Hull (1943), Miller and Dollard (1941), and Guthrie (1935), drives are classed as stimuli. Kendler (1946) accepts this drive-stimulus concept with the qualification that only cues produced by drives that are reduced can be associated with the response. But other theorists, such as Skinner (1938, p. 376), reject the drive-stimulus concept. Still others, like Campbell and Sheffield (1953), assume that drives lower thresholds of response but do not serve as cues.

Experiments by Hull (1933) and Leeper (1935) produced evidence that apparently confirmed the drive-stimulus hypothesis. But their experiments, in which rats were rewarded with food or water which reduced the same drive that was assumed to provide the cue, do not prove that hunger and thirst are stimuli which function as cues. A sign-gestalt theory of learning might predict that an animal learns the location of goal objects, and that when the demand for such an object is great enough, the animal can easily find its way to it. Theories which assume that drives lower response thresholds might predict that the rat, when it is hungry, has a lower threshold for habits involving food than for those involving some other reward, but that it does not perceive hunger as a stimulus.

The most direct attack on the problem of whether drives may serve as cues is found in those experiments involving discrimination learning in which the cues are provided by one set of drives (irrelevant drives) and in which the performance is motivated by another set (relevant drives). For example, Amsel (1949) found in an experiment using fear as the relevant drive that after 450 trials only 2 of 10 rats learned to discriminate hunger and thirst. More convincing evidence that drives produce cues is furnished by an experiment by Levine (1953). After 450 trials, 10 of 11 rats learned to turn out a light by pressing one panel if they were hungry and another panel if thirsty.

---

[1] Reprinted by permission of the American Psychological Association and the author from the *Journal of Comparative and Physiological Psychology*, 1955, 48, 183-187.

Considering the evidence from the studies of Amsel and Levine, it seems reasonable to assume that internal drive states like hunger and thirst do have the properties of cues. The present experiment was designed to gather further evidence to test this assumption. It is not yet clear whether *both* hunger and thirst are cues. In the experiments which have yielded positive results, the animals could have been discriminating on the basis of hunger and its absence, or thirst and its absence. Therefore, another purpose of this experiment was to find out if both hunger and thirst serve as cues.

Amsel and Levine both emphasize that internal stimuli, at least those arising from irrelevant drives, acquire associations only after considerable practice. The fact that considerable practice is necessary fits Hull's principle of the dynamic state of stimuli (1943, p. 207), which asserts that unchanging stimuli acquire habit strength slowly. In contrast to a buzzer or light, the cues produced by the hunger and thirst drives can certainly be considered static. But since the Amsel and Levine experiments used no animals that had to discriminate exteroceptive cues, it is not clear whether this considerable practice results from the ineffectiveness of the drive cues or of some other aspect of the learning situation. Accordingly, two further purposes of this experiment were: (a) to see if drives are inefficient cues as compared to an exteroceptive cue (e.g., a tone of short duration) in the same learning situation and (b) to evaluate the effect of the static-dynamic variable by a comparison of a long and a short tone.

Method

APPARATUS. The apparatus was essentially the same as the one used by Levine (1953). The animals were trained in a wooden box containing two metal panels. The interior of the box was gray; one panel was white and the other black. The front of the box was a piece of Plexiglas through which the animals could be observed; the lid was a sheet of Plexiglas scratched to diffuse light entering the box. A 150-watt lamp suspended 6 inches above the lid furnished the relevant drive. This lamp was shaded so that the small, dark, sound-shielded room containing the apparatus was not illuminated. A $7\frac{1}{2}$-watt bulb was used for reading instruments and recording.

For some parts of the experiment a 10,000-cycle tone was used. A 4-inch speaker mounted on the back of the box filled the box with sound but allowed little to escape into the room. An 8-inch speaker mounted on the wall of the room near the ceiling filled the room with sound.

When the lid of the box was closed, two electric timers started. Five seconds later the drive light automatically turned on, and, if it was desired, the tone automatically sounded. If the subject pressed the incorrect panel, one of the timers stopped; when the subject pressed the correct panel, the other timer stopped, and the light turned off. The tone, when it was used, was turned off manually 15 seconds after a correct response.

SUBJECTS. Fifty naive male albino rats from the Albino Farms, Red Bank, N. J., were used throughout the experiment. They were between 80 and 100 days old at the start of the experiment. Levine's rats were from the same strain (Wistar) and of the same age.

PROCEDURE. After five trials given to each rat to eliminate those least motivated by light, the 50 survivors of the original group of 70 were randomly divided into experimental groups of 10 each. The first three groups had to learn to discriminate between certain internal stimuli arising from irrelevant drives. The first group, hunger versus thirst (HT), virtually a repetition of Levine's experiment, was hungry but not thirsty on some days, and thirsty but not hungry on others. The second group (H) was satiated with water every day but was hungry on some days and not hungry on others. The third group (T) was satiated with food every day but was thirsty on some days and not thirsty on others. The fourth and fifth groups had to learn to discriminate between the presence and absence of a tone. This tone was turned on at the end of a day's trials and presented to all groups overnight (about 18 hours). For the rats in the HT, H, T, and short-sound (SS) groups the tone was always turned off at least 1¼ hour before a day's trials. For the rats in the SS group the tone was suddenly produced on some days 5 seconds after the rat entered the box, and was turned off 15 seconds after the correct response; other days were silent. For the animals in the long-sound (LS) group the tone was turned off some days 1¼ hours before training and remained off throughout the day's trials. On other days it was continually present and not turned off until the end of the day's training for this group. So there would be no chance that the continual tone would disturb the animals in the other groups, the LS group completed their day's trials before any other animals were run. The order of running the animals in the other groups was randomized within each replication.

The maintenance schedule consisted of depriving all rats of both food and water except for two feeding and/or watering periods a day. If an animal was to be hungry during its trials, it was given water, but no food, for a period of 1 hour starting 1¼ hours before running, and both food and water for a period of 1 hour ending 1¼ hours after running. If an animal was to be thirsty during its trials, it was given food, but no water, before running, and both food and water after running. If the rat was to be satiated, it was given both food and water before running. The H animals were given food after satiation trials; T animals were given water after satiation trials. Half the animals in each of the SS and LS groups were always run satiated and the other half always hungry, as a check on the effect of an irrelevant drive which could not serve as a cue. Those animals of the SS and LS groups which were always run satiated were given either food or water on alternate days after running. Rats were weighed once a week, and large differences in body weight were reduced by adjusting the length of the satiation periods.

At first the procedure duplicated Levine's; the animals were given five trials a day and were left in the box until they made a correct response. After this response each animal was left in the dark box for 15 seconds before being put into its home cage. The sequence of cues was randomized with the restriction that no more than three successive days of the same cue were permitted.

After a period in which there was no apparent learning, some of the conditions were changed. Because the relevant drive seemed too low, a 300-watt lamp was substituted for the 150-watt lamp. An incorrect response was slightly punished by installing a photoflood lamp that lighted when the incorrect panel was pushed and stayed on as long as the panel was held back. In order to maximize any reward which might follow escape from the box, the subject was removed from the box immediately after making the correct response. In order to correct the strong position habits which some of the rats had developed, the number of trials per day was varied. The correction method which was used at first had insured that every trial ended with a correct response; this method was modified so that every day ended with a correct trial. On the days when the position habit coincided with the correct response, an animal might run only one trial; on days when the position habit was incorrect, an animal might run many incorrect trials before running a correct one. This procedure gave the subject more practice in the habit opposing its position habit and less practice in the one agreeing with its position habit.

All animals were run under these conditions for at least 50 days. Not all replications were started training on the same day, but any change was made on the same day for all rats. Hence, various replications were given different amounts of training, ranging from 119 days for replications 1 to 3 to 93 for replication 10.

Results

All results are presented in terms of the day's first trial for any rat. Figure 28-1 shows that during the early training there was little difference between the groups; no group was very different from chance. After the changes were made, four groups showed learning: HT, H, T, and SS. The LS group remained slightly below chance. Therefore, we shall discuss only the first-trial correct responses during the last 50 days of training.

Table 28-1 presents a summary of the analysis of variance among the five groups; Table 28-2 shows the five means and the t tests between

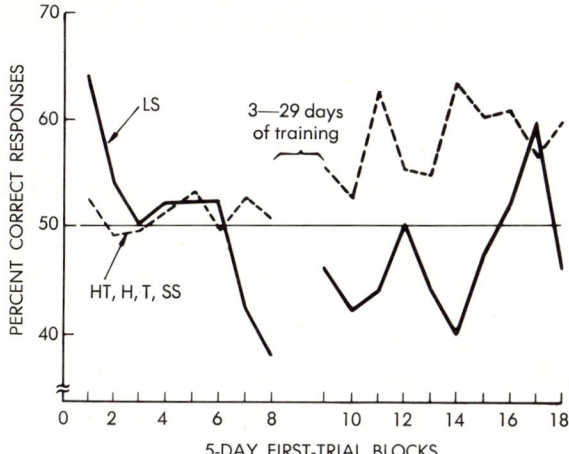

FIGURE 28-1. Learning of the panel-pushing response. All changes of procedure took place between blocks 8 and 9.

pairs of group means. The analysis of variance indicates that there are real differences in the five groups. The means for the total correct responses of all groups except the LS group are shown by t tests to be significantly greater than chance (25 correct responses in the 50-day period); the significance varied from the .04 to the .001 level. It was predicted before the experiment that the LS group would not learn, or at least would learn significantly slower than the other four groups. The mean for this group is below chance but not significantly so. Since a restriction was placed on the randomization of cues (no more than 3 successive days of the same cue were given), it can be argued that the difference of a mean from the mean of the LS group is a more sensitive indication of learning than the difference of the mean from chance. If there is any tendency for a rat to learn to go to the panel where it turned off the light on the previous day, the subject is more likely, other things being equal, to per-

TABLE 28-1

Analysis of variance of total correct responses in last 50 days of training

SOURCE	df	VARIANCE	F	p
Between groups	4	80.68	4.84	.005
Within groups	45	16.67		
Total	49			

TABLE 28-2

Differences from chance and between groups in terms of total correct responses in last 50 days*

	Long sound	Short sound	Hunger thirst	Hunger	Thirst
MEANS	23.3	28.1	29.1	31.0	27.7
DIFFERENCES					
From change (25)					
t	−1.317	2.401	3.176	4.648	2.091
p	>.10	.02	.004	<.001	.04
From LS					
t		2.629	3.176	4.217	2.410
p		.01	.004	<.001	.02
From SS					
t			.548	1.588	−.219
p			>.10	>.10	>.10
From HT					
t				1.040	−.767
p				>.10	>.10
From H					
t					−1.807
p					.08

* The within-groups variance was used as the estimate of the population variance in all t tests. The degrees of freedom in these tests, therefore, are 45. All p values are based on two-tailed tests.
N = 10 in each group.

form below chance than above it, for the cue changes more often than it remains the same. The LS group would be expected to do at least as well as a group which had no discriminable cue at all. The p's of the differences between each of the groups and the LS group vary from the .02 to the .001 level. There are no statistically significant differences between the means for the HT, H, T, and SS groups.

An analysis of variance of the total correct responses during the last 50 days of training of the always-hungry and always-satiated subgroups of the LS and SS groups was performed. The LS-SS difference ($F = 5.236$) is significant beyond the .05 level; the hungry-satiation difference ($F = 1.100$) and the interaction ($F = 0.582$) are not significant. Tests for heterogeneity of variance in the analysis in Table 1 and in the analysis of the LS and SS subgroups yielded chi squares of 8.270 and 1.819, respectively; the null hypotheses of homogeneity of variance cannot be rejected.

Discussion

It is possible to draw the following conclusions from the results: (1) the hunger and thirst drives both produce cues to which overt responses can be attached, (2) the cues of the hunger and thirst drives seem to be as effective as a brief tone which functions as a "dynamic stimulus," and (3) the hunger and thirst drives are more effective cues than a tone that is present for about as long before the response as the drives.

The level of learning in this experiment is somewhat lower than that reported by Levine (1953), whose single group of rats discriminating hunger and thirst is comparable to the HT group in this experiment. Levine's rats were correct about 75 percent of the time; the HT group in this experiment was correct about 60 percent of the time. Levine trained all his rats longer than any rat was trained in this experiment. He used a complex maintenance procedure, feeding limited amounts of food and watering for varying periods of time. Since a greater number of animals were used in this experiment, a simpler maintenance schedule was used. It cannot be determined which, if either, of these differences in procedure accounts for the difference in learning between Levine's experiment and this one.

The relatively poor learning of the SS group is probably the most surprising element in the results. It was expected that this group would show the most rapid and complete learning of any group. Perhaps a partial answer can be found in an experiment reported by Eninger (1951) who trained rats in a tone–no-tone discrimination on a T maze. The animals were delayed in the stem of the T while the tone was sounded. It required 500 trials for animals with a 15-second delay to reach a 90 percent criterion. The SS rats in the present experiment made the response in 16.73 seconds, on an average, after the onset of the tone. It is possible that the drive was too weak to result in a response soon enough to make the tone distinctive.

There are other factors which may explain the relatively low level of learning found in the SS and in the other groups: (1) It is possible that the restriction to either one cue or the other throughout the trials in one day, and the consequent loss of any immediate contrast effect, deterred learning. (2) Besides its effect of delaying the SS group, the low drive strength may have resulted in inefficient learning in all groups. (3) There was no strong penalty for an incorrect response. (4) The whole situation, including the panel-pushing response, may have been a poor one for discrimination learning. Any one or combination of these factors may account for the incomplete learning found in the HT, H, T, and SS groups.

Nevertheless, the SS animals did learn the discrimination, and the LS animals did not. These facts show that with this method and apparatus, a 10,000-cycle tone–no-tone discrimination is possible, but that a long delay between the onset of the stimulus and the opportunity for the response makes the task very difficult. Because of possible differences in the intensities of the stimuli and because of the completely different receptor systems involved, it is perhaps not quite correct to make comparisons between any two of the five groups. However, insofar as such comparisons are possible, it can be said that cues resulting from the drives of hunger and thirst are about as discriminable as a brief external stimulus and more discriminable than an external stimulus of long duration. This statement raises the intriguing speculation that, if hunger and thirst could be as suddenly produced as a tone, they would function as better cues.

These results are consistent with any theory which assumes drives to be stimuli which produce cues, but the results are not consistent either with the selective principle of association (Kendler, 1946) or with a theory based solely on differential lowering of response thresholds (Campbell & Sheffield, 1953). However, the results of an experiment by Jenkins and Hanratty (1946) indicate that rats can discriminate two intensities of the hunger drive. It is possible that the three hunger and/or thirst groups in this experiment actually discriminated two levels of a general motivational intensity rather than the qualitative drive itself. The HT group may have had a strong hunger and a weak thirst or vice versa. However, if the animals discriminated levels of general motivational intensity, one would expect the HT group to be significantly poorer than either the H group or the T group, if not both groups. The HT group is poorer than H but better than T and significantly different from neither. Further evidence which tends to refute the assumption of discrimination of levels of general motivational intensity is furnished by an experiment on cats involving a hunger-thirst discrimination (Bailey & Porter, 1955). The thirst drive, originally weaker than the hunger drive, was made stronger during tests; the cats generalized correctly. It seems reasonable, therefore, to conclude that the rats in the present experiment were responding to the cues of the drives themselves, whatever these cues may be.

SUMMARY

This experiment had two purposes: (a) to see if both the hunger and the thirst drives can function as cues, and (b) to compare the effec-

The Effectiveness of Drives as Cues

tiveness of drive cues and of exteroceptive cues (tones of short and of long duration).

Fifty male albino rats were required to press one of two panels to turn off a light. Which panel was correct varied randomly from day to day and depended upon which cue (either of two drive states, or the presence or absence of a tone) was presented to the animal.

That both the hunger and the thirst drives produce cues is shown by the discrimination learning of three groups: (a) hunger versus thirst, (b) hunger versus satiation, and (c) thirst versus satiation. The means of these three groups were all significantly greater than chance; the significance varied from the .04 to the .001 levels in terms of total correct responses.

A group which discriminated the presence or absence of a tone sounded suddenly just before the response learned the discrimination, whereas a group which discriminated the tone's presence or absence when it was sounded about as long before the response as the drive-produced cues, did not learn. The mean of the short-sound group was significantly greater than chance at the .02 level. It was significantly greater than that of the long-sound group at the .01 level.

Since there were no significant differences between any of the four groups that learned, it may be said that in this situation hunger or thirst, the presence or absence of hunger, and the presence or absence of thirst are about as effective as cues as is the presence or absence of a short sound. Since each of these four groups is significantly superior to the long-sound group at or beyond the .02 level, it may be said that in this situation the cues produced by the hunger and thirst drives are more effective as cues than is a normally effective sound when the sound is present about as long as the drives are.

29

A Quantitative Comparison of the Discriminative and Reinforcing Functions of a Stimulus[1]

JAMES A. DINSMOOR

INTRODUCTION

Among the functional relationships which must presumably be included in a systematic description of behavior are those between the stimuli which are present in a situation and the strength or probability of a given response. In *The Behavior of Organisms* (1938), Skinner uses the rate of bar-pressing by the white rat as a measure of these functions. If the cumulation of responses is recorded as a function of time, variations in rate are described by variations in the slope of the curve in a graphic representation or by the first derivative of the equation for this curve. It may be added that this derivative in turn represents the probability density of the response as a function of time.

The key concept in the conditioning of such operant or instrumental responses as bar-pressing is that of reinforcement. The defining observations for a reinforcing stimulus are that (1) responses which produce the stimulus in question increase in their rate of emission, and that (2) when the stimulus is later withheld, the rate of responding approaches but does not fall below the unreinforced or operant rate previously observed; that is, a "reserve" of responses is established.

The possible roles of a stimulus are classified by Skinner in four categories: eliciting, reinforcing, discriminative, and emotional. The two roles which are to be compared in the present study are those of discrimination and what is known as conditioned or secondary reinforcement.

Discriminative stimuli. The operations for the establishment of a pair of discriminative stimuli are the reinforcement of responding in one stimu-

[1] Reprinted from the *Journal of Experimental Psychology*, 1950, *40*, 458–472, by permission of the American Psychological Association and the author.

lus situation and the withholding of reinforcement in a differing stimulus situation. Since these two general situations must differ in one or more physical dimensions, two points on such a dimension may be abstracted and defined in terms of their selective relationship to the occurrence of reinforcement. The specific stimulus which has set the occasion for the reinforcement of a response may be labelled the S^D and that which has set the occasion for non-reinforcement of this response may be labelled the S^Δ.

The concrete training procedure followed by Skinner in the establishment of a discrimination involved the presentation of the S^D at a constant temporal interval (i.e., every five minutes). The first depression of the bar which occurred in its presence produced the reinforcing stimulus and terminated the S^D. The alternative condition S^Δ continued until the next presentation of S^D; during this time, no further responses were reinforced.

The discriminative effects of a stimulus pair established in this fashion may be diminished or abolished by either of two techniques: responding may be reinforced in S^Δ or reinforcement may be withheld for all responses emitted in the presence of the S^D.

Two measures have been used for the difference in behavior which corresponds to the distinction between S^D and S^Δ. As in other functions, the standard measure is the rate of responding, which may be used for S^Δ during the training period or for either stimulus during a test period of continuous extinction. When only one response is made, however, as under the S^D in the standard training, or when the rate is contaminated by behavior incidental to the reinforcing operation (i.e., eating of pellets), this measure is no longer useful. In such cases, the period of time between the presentation of the stimulus and the occurrence of the first response, commonly known as the *latency,* is sometimes substituted, although this procedure does not yield stable values. . . . However, the total number of responses obtained during a prolonged period of extinction is not a suitable measure in Skinner's opinion. Indeed, he is inclined to believe that the two stimuli act in a manner analogous to a filter, that they control the initial rate of emission without affecting the asymptote which the cumulative curve of responses will approach under either stimulus condition (Skinner, 1938, p. 225).

Secondary reinforcing stimuli. The concept of secondary reinforcement arises from the observation that an initial member may be added to a chain of responses which is now or was once followed ultimately by primary or unconditioned reinforcement. This initial member increases temporarily in its rate of emission, even though the total chain may no longer be followed by the original reinforcing stimulus. Such an effect is attributed to the action of a stimulus produced by the response in question, a stimulus which had no reinforcing power prior to the original training. For this stimulus, discrimination training is a sufficient establishing operation . . . and may be a necessary establishing operation. . . .

The operation which exhausts or extinguishes the reinforcing effect of such a stimulus is at least similar to that for the abolition of an S^D. It is the use of the stimulus, without further primary reinforcement, as itself a reinforcing agent for some response in the usual operant or instrumental procedure. That is, the stimulus is repeatedly produced by the response.

The effect of a stimulus, so utilized, on the response in question, is said to be reinforcing. In a test situation, the rate of emission is observed to increase, whether the response has previously produced primary reinforcement (Bugelski, 1938) or not (Skinner, 1938, pp. 82 ff.), and the term *reinforcing* implies that the total number of responses to be expected over an indefinitely prolonged period of extinction (the "reserve") is likewise increased.

PRESENT STUDY

The present study is designed to determine whether the two stimulus functions are equal or unequal in their effect on the rate of response when the governing variables are manipulated in the same fashion. All animals are first given extended discrimination training on the bar-pressing response, as an establishing operation. They are then divided into three groups, which are extinguished under corresponding stimulus schedules: (1) continuous presentation of the S^D until the response is emitted; (2) production of the S^D by the response; (3) complete absence of the S^D. The first procedure is considered a test of the discriminative function, the second a test of the secondary reinforcing function and the third an experimental control. Following three daily sessions of this extinction, the discriminative and secondary reinforcing groups are further sub-divided, and half of each group is transferred to the alternative stimulus schedule for the three remaining sessions.

If the cumulative curves of responding are recorded for the first three days of extinction, their height and shape may be compared. This comparison shows whether a difference in effect is obtained between the two main stimulus schedules, following identical training and during equal periods of unreinforced responding. Another comparison is obtained from the last three sessions of extinction, following the reversal of half of each experimental group. The rate obtained under either schedule of stimulus administration is tested following an equal period of extinction under the same usage or under the alternative usage. This shows whether the dis-

The Discriminative and Reinforcing Functions

criminative use of the stimulus subtracts to an equal degree from the consequent rate of responding under a reinforcing schedule, and whether the reinforcing use of the stimulus subtracts to an equal degree from the consequent rate of responding under a discriminative schedule.

Subjects and apparatus

The organisms used in the present experiment were 36 male rats of albino Wistar stock, ranging in age from 90 to 100 days on arrival. Throughout the course of the investigation they were housed under environmental conditions which were permitted to vary as little as possible. The housing and experimental room was insulated from external sources of sound by a double door, and an electric fan was kept in continuous operation as an auditory masking device. Illumination was low, consisting of daylight coming through and around a blackout curtain and reflected light from a 25-watt lamp, which was shielded by a metal shade and a wooden partition from the table on which the living cages were kept. Temperature, with but occasional exceptions due to outside variation, was maintained from 78 to 80 degrees Fahrenheit.

Cages. The living and experimental cages in which the animals were continuously housed throughout the period of experimentation were of galvanized iron, $10\frac{1}{2}$ by 8 inches in floor space and 8 inches in height. They differed only in minor details from those described by Frick, Schoenfeld, and Keller (1948). One end included an attached water bottle, which was removed only for replenishment of the supply, and an opening for the insertion of a tray of powdered food. The other end included an H-shaped opening, with a horizontal slot $3\frac{1}{2}$ inches above the floor of the cage for the insertion of the bar. This end also bore a square food tube which opened above a small metal tray or cup on the inside.

Experimental chamber. During the experimental sessions, these living cages were placed inside a chamber constructed of $\frac{3}{4}$-inch board and lined with a $\frac{1}{2}$-inch layer of sound-absorbing celotex. The internal dimensions were 24 by 24 inches in floor space, 20 inches in height. This chamber was sound resistant and light proof except during S^D periods during the discrimination training, when it was necessary to open a 12 by 12 inch door in the front in order to permit the manual delivery of food pellets.

Pellets. The food pellets used as the unconditioned or primary reinforcement were molded from wet Purina chow and dried. They were cylindrical in form and averaged .07 gram in weight. These were dropped manually from a constant height of approximately $5\frac{1}{2}$ inches through a plastic extension of the metal tube.

Bar. The bar was a modified version of that in standard use in the Columbia laboratories. A cross-bar of $\frac{1}{8}$ inch hardened aluminum rod extended 4 inches horizontally, parallel to the cage front and approximately $\frac{7}{8}$ inch inside. On this cross-bar and its supporting shafts was folded a thin sheet of zinc 4 by $\frac{5}{8}$ inch. This envelopment was largely successful in eliminating such responses as gnawing and shaking of the bar with the teeth. The height of the bar was $3\frac{1}{2}$ inches; when depressed $\frac{1}{4}$ inch, which required a force between 5 and 6 grams, it actuated a microswitch and completed the recording circuit.

Stimuli. Two levels of illumination were used inside of the experimental chamber. One condition consisted ordinarily of total darkness, slightly modified when the door in the front of the chamber was opened to permit reinforcement. The alternative condition was the illumination furnished by two 40-watt bulbs, laterally centered about 4 inches from the side of the cage and operated on 60 volts A.C. The indirect illumination through openings in the front, back and top of the cage averaged about 3 foot-candles and the illumination on an internal test-plate approximated .15 foot-candle. The change of illumination was controlled by the experimenter during discrimination training, by means of a hand switch, and by an automatic timing apparatus during extinction.

Measurements of the temperature inside the closed chamber revealed that in the course of prolonged light stimulation there was a rise to a maximum of about 90 degrees.

Records. The occurrence and duration of all stimulus changes and all bar-pressing responses were recorded automatically on a waxed tape which moved at a constant rate of 1 mm. per second. . . . This recording device, together with a mechanical counter for tallying responses and apparatus for the control of stimulation during extinction, was kept outside of the experimental room. The only sounding apparatus inside the room was a solenoid in circuit with the bar, which served to set back a timing arm during discrimination training.

Procedure

Daily schedule. For three days before the conditioning session, and thereafter throughout the experiment, each animal was placed on a daily schedule of 23 hours of deprivation and 1 hour in which dry powdered food was available. All experimental sessions were conducted in the preceding hour. It was also the practice to remove each animal from the cage for two or three minutes of fondling or gentling at some time later in the day.

Conditioning. On the day preceding conditioning, a supply of pellets such as were to be used for reinforcement was placed on top of the powdered food. At the beginning of the conditioning session itself, five pellets were first delivered simultaneously through the tube and their consumption observed. Ten pellets were then delivered in discrete succession, each arriving after the last previous was consumed, in order to further condition the approach to the tray and to reduce the latency of this approach following the auditory and visual stimuli which signalled the arrival of the pellet. Finally, the bar was inserted and 10 depressions were reinforced. Reinforcement was judged to have occurred when the animal was observed to find and commence eating the pellet within a few seconds after releasing the bar. There were relatively few occasions on which animals pressed without meeting this criterion.

Discrimination training. The training procedure which was used to establish a stimulus control over responding was a modification of the original schedule followed by Skinner (1938). The first response made in the presence of the S^D, which was light for one half of the animals and darkness for the other half, was reinforced by the delivery of a pellet of food. The criterion for termination of the S^D was made the seizure of the pellet and the beginning of eating, in order to avoid the possibility that the S^Δ for bar-pressing might become an S^D for approaching the tray. After the first 20 or 30 trials, however, the animal's reaction became faster than the experimenter's.

The duration of the alternative stimulus condition, S^Δ, was not determined by a constant interval, as in Skinner's work, but by the animal's behavior. The criterion for the termination of S^Δ was the lapse of a period of 30 seconds without a response. This criterion had two purposes: (1) to prevent secondary reinforcement or delayed primary reinforcement of responses in S^Δ due to occasional appearance of the S^D immediately following a response; in no case was a response in S^Δ followed either by the S^D or by a pellet within 30 seconds; (2) to provide more time for the extinction of S^Δ responding to those animals characterized by relatively high rates, thus tending to reduce the variability in the later test period of extinction.

Ten cycles of discrimination training, involving 10 reinforcements, were given immediately after conditioning, as a part of the first experimental session. On the six succeeding days of experimentation, the following number of cycles were given: 10, 15, 25, 30, 50, and 60. Thus, each animal received a total of 200 presentations of S^D and S^Δ. This schedule was based upon exploratory data and was intended to limit the experimental session to no more than 50 minutes.

Extinction. Six daily 50-minute sessions of extinction were given to each rat. Two stimulus schedules were utilized for the experimental groups: (1) during most of the session, the stimulus condition (which may be termed *prevailing* stimulus) was light, but each response was followed by 3 seconds of darkness; (2) the prevailing stimulus was darkness, but each response was followed by 3 seconds of light. This 3-second period was timed automatically from the beginning of each bar-depression and was reset by release of the bar. Thus, a further response during the 3-second period led to its extension. Since this dichotomy of schedules bisected the dichotomy formed by the use of light or darkness as the S^D in training, in a factorial design, two of the sub-groups thus formed were presented with the S^D until the occurrence of the response—a test of the discriminative role of the stimulus—and the other two sub-groups produced the S^D by responding—a test of the secondary reinforcing role. It should be noted that the stimulus conditions under which these two roles were tested are matched by this design.

Following the first three daily sessions of extinction, each 50 minutes in duration, half of the animals on each schedule were transferred to the alternative schedule, and extinction was continued for three more daily sessions of the same duration. This additional dichotomy bisected the experimental groups once again. The 32 experimental animals were thus divided and sub-divided by three orthogonal criteria of classification into eight sub-groups.

For control purposes, four additional animals were extinguished in the absence of the S^D. In two cases, the stimulus condition was light, in two cases darkness. The complete design is summarized in Table 29-1.

Statistical treatment

The statistical techniques used for the evaluation of the null hypothesis in the present experiment were analysis of variance and analysis of covariance. The factorial design permitted the segregation of several variables contributing to the experimental effects. For example, such effects as those due to the prevalence of light or of darkness during extinction should not be included in the estimate of random variation derived from the variance among individual animals within their respective groups. This might lead to an exaggeration of the estimate and a consequent diminution in the sensitivity of the test. The data show that this treatment was well advised in the present instance.

The use of analysis of covariance is roughly equivalent to the procedure of preliminary matching of the animals in the experimental groups on a measure believed to be related to the dependent variable. Four difficulties in matching, however, were surmounted by this technique. First, the best predictor or set of predictors for the extinction totals was not known in advance. Second, the predicting variables actually used could not have been obtained prior to the assignment of animals to their

TABLE 29-1

A summary of the experimental design*

GROUP	TRAINING		FIRST 3 DAYS EXTINCTION		LAST 3 DAYS EXTINCTION		SEQUENCE
	Prevailing stimulus	S^D	Prevailing stimulus	Procedure	Prevailing stimulus	Procedure	
A	dark	light	light	S^D	light	S^D	same
B	light	dark	dark	S^D	dark	S^D	same
C	light	dark	light	S^r	light	S^r	same
D	dark	light	dark	S^r	dark	S^r	same
E	dark	light	light	S^D	dark	S^r	reversed
F	light	dark	dark	S^D	light	S^r	reversed
G	light	dark	light	S^r	dark	S^D	reversed
H	dark	light	dark	S^r	light	S^D	reversed
J			same	S^Δ	same	S^Δ	

* For each sub-group of four rats the prevailing stimulus condition is listed for each stage in the procedure, the stimulus role which is tested, and the sequence from the first to the second half of extinction.

respective groups. Third, matching could not be made as accurate as adjustment of the original values by means of a regression equation. And finally, no appropriate statistical treatment is at present available.

The choice of predictive variables for the analyses of covariance was made after the examination of a number of rank-difference correlations. In view of the small size of the coefficient in each case and the small variance between group means, it seemed unlikely that a substantial change in the F-ratios would be produced. . . . In the light of negative findings, however, a failure to disprove the null hypothesis, it seemed desirable to make the test as sensitive as possible. The calculations followed the routine outlined by Fisher. Determination of the intraclass correlations incident to these analyses also make possible slight adjustments in the more important group means.

A characteristic difficulty encountered in the statistical treatment of operant responding is that the distributions of latencies, rates and extinction totals are limited at the lower end by the numerical value of zero but are not effectively limited at the upper end. Such a circumstance tends to produce skewed distributions, and this tendency was actually observed both in the training and the extinction data, although moderate in the latter case. Furthermore, occasional extreme values were obtained which seemed, by subjective observation, to be associated with behavioral artifacts. In the training period, for example, long latencies of response to the discriminative stimulus were produced by the emission of abortive responses, inadequate in force to close the recording circuit, and by drinking from the water bottle at the opposite end of the cage. In extinction, similarly, high rates were produced by the intervention of such responses as gnawing, shaking the bar, jumping, climbing, poking the nose through the slot in the cage, and a "trotting" motion of the forepaws across the width of the bar. In the absence of complete experimental control, it seemed desirable to minimize the contribution of these possibly spurious responses to measures of central tendency and scatter. For this reason, and to correct the mild positive skewing of the distribution, all analyses of variance and covariance were based upon the logarithms of the original cumulative response totals, and geometric means were used to express the relative performance of the several groups. An exception was necessary in the treatment of the latency and number of responses in S^Δ during discrimination training, due to the presence of zero readings; here medians were substituted for the respective geometric means.

Results and discussion

Training. The first seven days of experimentation were devoted to conditioning and discrimination training. The animals received 200 presentations of the S^D, with consequent reinforcement in each case, and 200 presentations of S^Δ, under which reinforcement was withheld. As indicated in Table 29-2 the number of responses declined in successive cycles

TABLE 29-2

Separation in strength of reflexes during discrimination training*

CYCLE NO.	10	20	30	40	50	60	70	80	90	100
Responses	0.3	11.5	7.5	3.5	2.5	2.0	1.3	1.4	1.0	1.1
Latency	17.0	8.5	4.3	4.5	4.7	5.5	2.7	2.5	2.0	2.9
CYCLE NO.	110	120	130	140	150	160	170	180	190	200
Responses	1.0	0.9	0.9	0.9	1.3	0.6	0.8	0.8	0.8	0.8
Latency	2.5	2.5	3.2	2.8	1.5	2.0	1.7	2.8	1.9	2.0

* The median latency in seconds of the first response is S^D and the median number of responses emitted in S^Δ are presented for each tenth cycle.

The Discriminative and Reinforcing Functions

of S^Δ, and the period of time between the onset of S^D and the occurrence of the response, often termed the *latency*, became progressively shorter. The data indicate that the decrement in each case was most rapid in the early stages of training and that little further change took place in the later stages. This suggests that the difference in effect between the two stimulus conditions was close to the maximum which could be achieved by the present procedure.

An interesting phenomenon, which may be peculiar to some specific aspect of the present training procedure, was that in the last series of cycles the typical behavior consisted of the emission of a single response in the first few seconds of the S^Δ period.

In order to avoid confusion in discussion between the use of a stimulus as an S^D in training and the test of a discriminative schedule in extinction, the stimulus which functioned as S^D in training will hereafter be termed *positive* or *effective*.

First three days of extinction. The initial test period consisted of three 50-minute sessions on three successive days. This period served to compare the rate of bar-pressing and the changes in rate when the effective stimulus was, first, presented prior to the response, as a discriminative stimulus, or, alternatively, was produced by the response, as a secondary reinforcer. The mean number of bar-pressings for these two groups, and for the control group, which did not receive the effective stimulus at any time, are cumulated and plotted in Figure 29-1 at five-

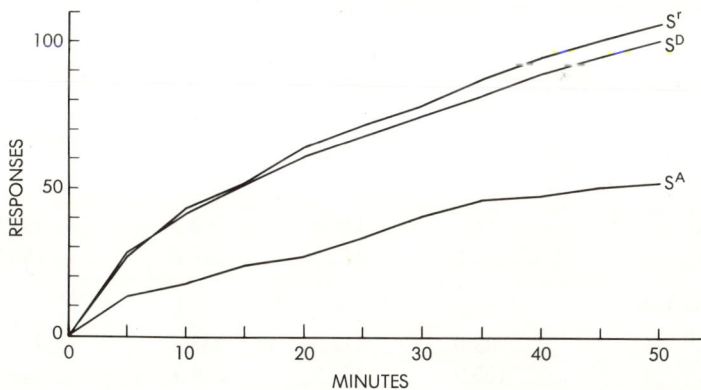

FIGURE 29-1. The mean number of responses emitted by three groups of rats, cumulated at 5-minute intervals during the first session of extinction. The first group extinguished in the presence of the stimulus which had previously set the occasion for reinforcement (S^D), the second received this stimulus for three seconds after each response (S^r), and the third or S^Δ group was extinguished in the absence of the stimulus, as an experimental control.

minute intervals for the first day of extinction. It will be noted that the curves for the two experimental groups attain their maximum separation toward the end of this session.

The total responses cumulated for days one, two and three are represented by geometric means, and the final set of means is corrected by the use of a regression coefficient derived from the duration of the last 50 cycles of training for each animal. These are presented in Table 29-3, along with the means of those animals which were extinguished in the light as a prevailing stimulus and those which were extinguished in the dark. Comparison of these means indicates that: (a) a substantial and progressive difference in totals is associated with the prevailing condition of illumination; (b) the rate of response is quite low, relatively, in the continued absence of the effective stimulus; and (c) the groups performing on discriminative and secondary reinforcing schedules achieve almost identical totals at the end of the second and third days.

The statistical significance of these differences in cumulative totals for days one and three was evaluated by analysis of covariance, utilizing the duration of the last 50 cycles of training as the correlated variable (.12 and .14). These analyses concurred in showing that the difference due to the prevalence of light or darkness was significant, the chance

TABLE 29-3

Geometric means for first half of extinction*

CLASSIFICATION	GEOMETRIC MEANS			
	1	2	3	3 (corrected)
Prevailing stimulus				
Light	77.4	138.8	192.3	195.0
Darkness	121.2	213.2	287.8	283.9
Stimulus role				
S^D	93.0	172.2	235.6	233.8
S^r	100.9	171.9	234.9	236.7
Control				
S^Δ	48.4	84.1	128.5	

* Geometric means of the cumulative totals of responses at the ends of days one, two, and three of extinction, classified by prevailing stimulus condition and the role of the stimulus. The corrected value for day three is based upon the regression of the original totals with the duration of the last 50 cycles of training.

probability in each case being less than one in a hundred. Whether this effect can be attributed to the photic or the thermal aspects of the stimulus, however, cannot be determined, for the two aspects have been confounded. On the other hand, the difference between the two stimulus functions, S^D and S^r, yields an F-ratio of less than one; the data afford no basis for rejection of the null hypothesis.

Contamination of the tests. It may be objected that neither the test procedure for a discriminative role nor the test procedure for a reinforcing role is completely distinct operationally from the other. Each time that the positive or effective stimulus is produced by the response (reinforcing operation), it is possible for a subsequent bar-pressing response to follow in the presence of the stimulus (discriminative operation). And each time that the positive stimulus reappears following the response in its presence (discriminative operation), it may serve as a delayed secondary reinforcement for this response.

It is extremely improbable that the correspondence in height and shape of the cumulative response curves produced under either test schedule is a coincidence resulting from the chance balancing of two stimulus functions in each case. There are three systematic ways in which such a quantitative result could be produced, and each of these must be evaluated:

1. The correspondence of the curves might be produced by completely pure and distinct tests of two stimulus functions which were equal in their effects on responding. In the light of the foregoing discussion, however, such an assumption seems to be untenable.

2. The correspondence of the curves might be produced by the summation in each test of the two stimulus functions, if the discriminative effect of the stimulus were equally strong in both cases at all times during the test and if the reinforcing effect of the stimulus were equally strong in both cases at all times during the test. Neither of these equalities appears to be possible: a delayed reinforcement (during the discriminative test) does not maintain as high a rate of responding as an immediate reinforcement; a discriminative stimulus which is limited to 3 seconds in duration (test of secondary reinforcement) cannot be as effective in the production of a consequent response as a discriminative stimulus which is maintained until the occurrence of the response.

Furthermore, if the contamination is assumed to be complete in the tests used in the present study, operational separation of the two stimulus roles for measurement purposes would seem to be impossible. For example, if the bar were removed after each reinforcement with the positive stimulus, in order to preclude a response due to its discriminative role, rate of responding would no longer be available as a measure, and previous data show that other measures such as latency and magnitude are not satisfactory. . . . Also, the removal of the bar would itself involve the removal of one of the stimuli which was present during the original establishment of the strength or effectiveness of the stimulus.

Similarly, if the discriminative stimulus were removed for a substantial period of time following each response, say, 30 seconds, rate of responding would again be lost as a measure, and the same difficulty follows.

Thus, the assumption of total contamination seems to be untenable. In any case, such an assumption would cast serious doubt on the possibility of operational separation of the two stimulus roles.

3. The assumption which is tenable is that some responses are produced discriminatively in the reinforcement test and that some responses are produced by secondary reinforcement in the discriminative test. This assumption is tenable if a second assumption be granted, that the discriminative use of the stimulus to produce a response exerts an equal weakening influence on the reinforcing function of the stimulus, and that the reinforcing use of the stimulus exerts an equal weakening influence on the discriminative production of responses. According to these assumptions, there is a common "reserve" of responses or resistance to extinction under the control of the positive stimulus, and this rate and total may be discharged either by presenting the stimulus discriminatively (prior to the response), by presenting it as a reinforcement (following the response), or by combining both methods of presentation. Supporting evidence for this contention is presented in the following section.

A rough indication of the actual degree to which the record of S^r responding is contaminated in the present study by the discriminative influence of the secondary reinforcing stimulus may be gained from a comparison of the temporal distribution of responding in the two experimental groups. Under the secondary reinforcing schedule, the effective stimulus is presented for 3 seconds following each response; the next succeeding response will often occur before the end of this period of stimulation. Similarly, under the discriminative schedule, the effective stimulus is removed for 3 seconds following each response; again, the next succeeding response may occur before the 3 seconds have elapsed. In the secondary reinforcing case, however, where the stimulus condition is positive, 41.4 percent of all responses during the first session of extinction are emitted under these circumstances, but in the discriminative case, where the stimulus condition is negative, only 28.8 percent of all responses are emitted during the same period. The difference of 12.6 percent, therefore, may presumably be attributed to the discriminative action of the positive stimulus under the secondary reinforcing procedure.

Last three days of extinction. Following the initial test period, half of the discriminative animals were placed on a secondary reinforcing schedule and half of the secondarily reinforced animals were placed on a discriminative schedule. Extinction was then continued for three more daily sessions for all animals. The geometric means of the group performances on this test are presented in Table 29-4. The differences have been evaluated by an analysis of covariance, utilizing the cumulative response totals for the first three days of extinction as the correlated variable (.18). The difference in illumination is probably still a factor in the rate of response, since there is a sharp "break" or discontinuity in the individual curves (not shown) and since the difference in means would be produced by chance less than five times in a hundred. The reversal of stimulus schedule, however, is not itself a significant factor; indeed, the animals which were reversed show somewhat less responding, on the average, than those which remained on the same schedule.

It may be concluded that unreinforced use of a stimulus for discriminative purposes produces an equal loss in its effectiveness for secondary reinforcing purposes and that unreinforced use of a stimulus for secondary reinforcing purposes produces an equal loss in its effectiveness for dis-

TABLE 29-4

Geometric means for last half of extinction*

CLASSIFICATION	GEOMETRIC MEANS			
	4	5	6	6 (corrected)
Prevailing stimulus				
Light	53.3	83.4	115.1	113.6
Darkness	71.7	135.4	184.6	187.0
Sequence				
Same	70.9	112.4	157.5	157.8
Reversed	53.9	100.5	134.9	134.6
Control				
S^Δ	24.9	49.0	67.8	

* Geometric means of the cumulative totals of responses from the beginning of day four to the ends of days four, five, and six of extinction, classified by prevailing stimulus condition and by the sequence in procedure from the first to the second half of extinction. The corrected value for day six is based upon the regression of the original totals with the total of responses during the first three days.

criminative purposes. In short, the two stimulus uses may be interchanged as operations for diminishing or abolishing the effectiveness of the stimulus.

THEORETICAL IMPLICATIONS

The strength of members of a chain. The present study constitutes an attempt to segregate so far as is operationally possible two stimulus-response sequences ($R \rightarrow S^r$ and $S^D \cdot R$) which would normally be observed as successive, or indeed overlapping, segments of a more extensive stimulus-response chain ($\ldots R \rightarrow S^{r,D} \cdot R \ldots$). The original observations of chaining made by Skinner (1938) were based upon a chain which included such items as bar-pressing, magazine sound, approach to the food tray, sight of pellet, seizure and so on. These were formulated in terms of the "reflex" ($S^D \cdot R$), which he considered the element of the chain. Two basic relationships in strength between successive reflexes in such a chain were noted:

First, it was found that an S^D which had set the occasion for the reinforcement of one response could be used as a reinforcing agent to add a prior member to the chain. That is, a response occurring at an operant or extinction rate could be increased in emission, both in terms of rate itself and in terms of resistance to extinction. Furthermore, "The number of responses due to the reinforcing effect of the sound of the magazine is again of the same order as in the initial extinction curve itself. It is tempting to suggest the following law: a discriminative stimulus (such as the sound of the magazine) used as a reinforcement in the absence of ultimate reinforcement creates in another reflex a reserve just equal to that of the reflex to which it belongs" (Skinner, 1938, p. 105). The logic of such a deduction from the data given is difficult to follow, but credit should be given for the formulation of a statement which is verified by the present study.

Skinner's second observation was that a chain of reflexes could be "broken" at any arbitrary point by withholding one of the reinforcing stimuli in the sequence. For example, when the food pellet was withheld, both bar-pressing and approaches to the tray appeared to extinguish; or, when the sound of the food magazine was withheld, only the bar-pressing extinguished. This finding was formulated as the Law of Extinction of Chained Reflexes: "In a chain of reflexes not ultimately reinforced only the members actually elicited undergo extinction" (Skinner, 1938, p. 105).

One amendment of this law seems to be necessary on the basis of previous data and one extension is indicated by the present findings. First, the correction stems from the observation that when one response (i.e., bar-pressing of a certain force or duration) is strengthened by reinforcement or weakened by non-reinforced emission, similar responses (i.e., of greater force or duration or of differing topography) seem to be strengthened or weakened simultaneously. . . . "A dynamic change in the strength of a reflex may be accompanied by a similar but not so extensive change in a related reflex, where the relation is due to the possession of common properties of stimulus or response" (Skinner, 1938, p. 32). No position will here be taken as to whether so-called *response induction* is a direct consequence of the similarity of the responses themselves or a result of the similarity in the proprioceptive stimulation which they produce; indeed, the distinction would be difficult to test. However, it is suggested that such a relationship must hold between successive members of a chain, and this factor must be kept in mind in any consideration of the extinction of chained reflexes.

Second, it will be noted that Skinner's law deals only with the intact reflex ($S^D \cdot R$), possibly due to a realization of the difficulty of using a stimulus as a secondary reinforcer without at the same time causing the emission of the next response in the chain on a discriminative basis. An extension seems to be warranted by the findings of the present experiment. This extension would summarize the effects of extinction of the preceding sequence $R_2 \rightarrow S^r$, insofar as it may be distinguished operationally for test purposes, on the strength of the sequence $S^D \cdot R_1$, when the stimuli in each sequence are identical.

The relationship between identical response members of a reflex chain may be formulated in the following terms: when both are governed by the same stimulus ($S^{r,D}$), their rates and totals will be equally increased by the continued availability of the stimulus, but when either is produced by the stimulus without completion of the chain and ultimate reinforcement, the amount of additional responding remaining under the control of the stimulus becomes smaller and smaller. When the responses differ in some respect, a similar interdependence may be predicted, although the rate and number of each may differ as a function of several variables associated with the difference in definition or specification.

It should be possible to obtain a further substantiation and generalization of the latter formulation by the study of an intact chain which includes at least two differing but recorded responses. Let the initial member of the chain produce the S^D for the next response; in the presence of this S^D, let the next response be reinforced periodically, at a fixed interval. The rate, then, or the extinction ratio (number of unreinforced responses emitted per reinforcement) serves as a measure of the strength of this later response. The rate of the response under these conditions can then be compared with the rate of the same response when its S^D is presented arbitrarily by the experimenter rather than as a consequence of an initial member of a chain.

Filter versus reserve. When a response is increased in its rate of emission by being allowed to produce a stimulus which has previously set the occasion for the reinforcement of another response, Skinner speaks of "secondary reinforcement." This implies an increment in his hypothetical variable, the "reserve." Precisely defined, this reserve consists of the total number of unreinforced responses which will thenceforth be emitted; since a test period cannot be extended to an infinite duration, this is not measurable. However, Skinner further suggests that this reserve is diminished by each successive unreinforced response and that the rate of emission is a function of the size of the remaining reserve. Thus, the rate approaches the unconditioned or operant level of emission as an asymptote; when this asymptote is very nearly reached, the total number of responses which have been emitted serves as a fairly accurate measure of the reserve, although the criterion itself is not completely determinate. Such a measure has frequently been termed *resistance to extinction.*

In the case of the discriminative use of a stimulus during extinction, Skinner is inclined to believe that it acts as a "filter." That is, it affects the initial rate of emission independently of the reserve. If this is granted as an assumption, the rate is no longer a lawful function of the remaining reserve, and the approach of this rate to an asymptote is no longer so satisfactory a criterion for the duration of a test period designed to measure the reserve. Once more the reserve seems to be removed from the realm of exact measurement.

There remains, however, the possibility of using resistance to extinction as an important dependent variable in its own right. The question then becomes whether the presentation of the stimulus, either discriminatively or as a secondary reinforcer, merely influences the initial rate of responding (acts as a "filter") or whether it adds to the number of responses occurring prior to the approach of the rate to the operant level (resistance to extinction).

It may first be pointed out that the extinction curves produced in the present study by the discriminative or reinforcing use of the stimulus are the same. It would be contradictory, therefore, to maintain separate formulations of the two stimulus effects. A choice must be made.

The operant or unconditioned rates of responding of the individual rats used in the present experiment have not been obtained. However, it has generally been assumed that when there is no known distortion of the results due to such factors as changes in drive or in emotional state resistance to extinction can be adequately predicted from the total number of responses emitted during an extended period; most experimenters have accepted a duration considerably shorter than that of the present study. Since the data demonstrate a substantial and progressive difference between the total responses accompanying the presentation of the effective stimulus either as S^D or as S^r and the total responses emitted in the

The Discriminative and Reinforcing Functions 425

absence of the stimulus, it may be concluded: resistance to extinction is increased, and to the same degree, by the use of either schedule of stimulus administration. Consequently, the filter analogy is rejected.

Theoretical distinction. Within the theoretical framework developed by Skinner, it has been customary to treat the discriminative stimulus (S^D) and the secondary reinforcing stimulus (S^r) as two distinct and largely independent functional categories. Yet it has long been recognized that there are certain establishing operations, at least, which are common to both uses of the stimulus. Indeed, a survey of the experimental literature at the present time reveals no concrete evidence of a difference in the variables which govern the acquisition of these properties by a stimulus.

The present study further indicates that when the stimulus is continuously available the effectiveness of the two schedules of stimulus administration will be equal and will remain equal during the process of extinction; that is, they vary together in effectiveness as a function of at least one of the governing variables. It is conceivable that this correspondence is an accidental occurrence and that a change in other parameters such as size or quality of reinforcement, number of reinforcements, duration of cycle, physical characteristics of the stimulus, etc., would destroy it. It seems more probable, however, that the correspondence is a general one, which will be maintained under a variety of circumstances, provided that the temporal schedule of administration is not itself manipulated.

This conclusion permits a considerable simplification in the theoretical treatment of discriminative and reinforcing stimuli. It is no longer necessary to assume that the two uses of the stimulus are differentially affected by variations in the training procedure whereby they acquire control over behavior. That is, it is no longer necessary to provide two separate theoretical accounts of the manner in which a stimulus acquires the power to raise the rate of response. Moreover, the expenditure of the influence of the stimulus under either schedule brings about an equal reduction in the effectiveness of the other. The previous distinction between two types of stimulus is reduced to a distinction between two categories of temporal schedule for the administration of the stimulus: in the case known as secondary reinforcement, the presentation of the stimulus follows a specified response and is dependent upon the occurrence of the response; in the discriminative case, the stimulus is presented independently by the experimenter, without any necessary temporal relationship to a given response.

It is to be expected, of course, that differing schedules of stimulus administration will sometimes have different effects on the amount of responding. For example, the stimulus might be presented at fixed intervals of time, rather than continuously. The duration of presentation might be varied. The production of the stimulus might be made dependent upon a fixed number of responses. Just as variations in the temporal schedule for the administration of a food pellet affect the rate of responding and resistance to extinction, so may variations in the administration of this conditioned type of stimulus produce quantitative variations in behavior. A distinction may here be drawn between procedures in which the production of the stimulus is dependent in some way on the emission of responses (S^r) and procedures in which the onset of the stimulus is in no way affected by the animal's behavior but is independently determined by the experimenter (S^D). It should be realized, however, that such a distinction is by no means exhaustive and that it is not always relevant to the number of responses which will be emitted. In the present study, for example, the rate and total are not affected. Thus, the distinction seems to be no more important in quantitative terms than many another distinction in administrative schedule.

Another aspect of the administration of the stimulus is the selective effect which it may exercise over the various responses in the organism's repertoire. When the presentation of the stimulus is made dependent upon instances of a certain class of responses, e.g., bar-pressing, it may be said to be selectively correlated with this response. Occasions when it closely follows or precedes instances of some other response category will be coincidental. On the other hand, when the presentation of the stimulus is not dependent upon the occurrence of a specified response, no temporal correlation is imposed and no independent selection is exercised by the experimenter. Its temporal contiguity to any response which may be emitted is determined by the animal's own behavior.

A problem which demands further investigation in this case is the prediction of which response will be strengthened, or, more precisely, what factors determine the relative strengthening of a variety of response categories. The occurrence of relatively fixed sequences of responding in chaining situations makes it evident that the response which has actually been reinforced in the presence of a particular S^D is the one which is most affected by this stimulus, but experiments by Estes (1943, 1948) and Walker (1942) demonstrate that this is not the only response which may thus be strengthened. Among the possible factors which may determine the relative effects of an S^D on a variety of responses are: (1) the degree of induction between each response and the specific response used in training; (2) the number and quality of previous reinforcements directly produced by each response; (3) the operant rate of each response; or (4) a combination of these variables.

SUMMARY AND CONCLUSIONS

Thirty-six rats were given 200 cycles of discrimination training on the bar-pressing response, half with light as the S^D, half with darkness.

Following this training, the bar-pressing response was extinguished under three schedules for the administration of the S^D: (1) 16 rats were extinguished in the presence of the S^D, but each response was followed by 3 seconds of S^Δ; (2) 16 rats were extinguished in S^Δ, but each response was followed by 3 seconds of S^D; (3) 4 rats were extinguished without the presentation of S^D at any time. These procedures were considered tests of (a) the discriminative role of the stimulus, (b) the reinforcing role of the stimulus, and (c) rate of responding in the absence of the stimulus (control). The cumulative curves of the first two groups could not be reliably distinguished, although they differed substantially from that of the control group.

Half of each of the experimental groups was transferred after the third daily session to the alternative test procedure and extinction was continued for three more days for all animals. Again, the rats which had undergone a change of procedure responded at the same rate as those rats which had remained on the same procedure.

These results indicated that the efficacies of the discriminative and reinforcing roles of a stimulus covary under the establishing and abolishing operations which were utilized. Three further generalizations are indicated by these findings:

1. Skinner's Law of the Extinction of Chained Reflexes should be amplified to include the observation that the extinction of a sequence $R \rightarrow S^r$ may reduce the strength of the following sequence $S^D \cdot R$.

2. The suggestion that an S^D acts only as a "filter" during extinction governing the initial rate of emission but not the total number of responses emitted, conflicts with the implication that an S^r can be used to create a "reserve" of responses. The data suggest that both usages affect total responding (resistance to extinction).

3. It no longer seems necessary to provide separate theoretical accounts of the manner in which a discriminative or reinforcing stimulus gains or loses the power to raise the rate of response. The previous distinction between the two types of stimulus appears to be reduced to a distinction between two categories of temporal schedule for the administration of the stimulus. This distinction is relevant chiefly to the determination of the distribution of the stimulus effects among the variety of responses in the organism's repertoire.

30

Strength of Fear as a Function of the Number of Acquisition and Extinction Trials[1]

HARRY I. KALISH

Fear is usually defined as an anticipatory conditioned response to cues preceding pain (Miller, 1951b; Mowrer, 1939). It is assumed that fear functions as a cue (May, 1948) and as a drive (Miller, 1948a). A number of studies (Brown & Jacobs, 1949; Brown, Kalish, & Farber, 1951; Gwinn, 1951; May, 1948; Miller, 1948) have indicated that fear can motivate behavior and when reduced in strength can reinforce the immediately preceding responses.

In a recent survey of acquired drives, Miller (1951b) has indicated that if fear has the characteristics of a response, then its intensity, the probability of its occurrence, and its resistance to extinction should vary with those factors which affect the acquisition and extinction of other responses. On this basis, it is reasonable to expect fear to increase as a monotonic function of the number of conditioning trials and to weaken progressively with successive extinction trials.

The available data bearing on this expectation are fragmentary and inconclusive. In a study by Miller and Lawrence (cited in Miller, 1951b) no significant difference was observed between two groups of animals given 4 and 24 trials of fear conditioning. This failure to demonstrate the anticipated superiority of the 24-trial group was attributed, in part, to the fact that subjects in both groups received a large number of shocks during their preliminary trials. It was also suggested that fear may have reached a maximum in only four trials because the fear-arousing cues were very distinctive. The results of a study by Brown, Kalish, and Farber (1951) support this latter suggestion since strongly conditioned fear reactions were noted after only three paired presentations of a CS and shock. It is conceivable, therefore, that although strength of fear may indeed be an in-

---

[1] Reprinted from the *Journal of Experimental Psychology,* 1954, 47, 1–9, by permission of the American Psychological Association and the author.

creasing function of number of reinforcements, it may reach a maximum in substantially fewer trials than is commonly the case with conditioned skeletal responses.

In an investigation by Gwinn (1951) designed in part to determine the relationship between number of reinforcements and strength of fear, one group of rats was given 4 and another 16 trials on each of which they were placed in a box and shocked. Intensity of shock was also varied in the same design. The results, measured in terms of persistence of escape from the box, indicated that resistance to extinction in the weak-shock group was greater for those animals given 16 fear-conditioning trials than for those given 4. The group given 16 strong shocks, however, showed less resistance to extinction than the group given 4 strong shocks.

The only available study with animals in which values have been obtained for more than two points on the function relating fear to number of trials is that of Brown, Kalish, and Farber (1951). In this experiment tests for fear were interpolated during the course of fear acquisition, i.e., after varying numbers of acquisition trials. But, since shock was omitted from each test trial on which fear was measured, the procedure was essentially one of partial reinforcement. The function reflecting growth of fear under these circumstances may thus have suffered some distortion. One purpose of the present investigation, therefore, was *to determine the relation between strength of fear and number of acquisition trials independent of non-reinforced test trials.*

With respect to extinction of fear in animals, no studies exist in which fear has been measured after varying numbers of extinction trials, and in which an extinction trial is defined, in accordance with the classical conditioning paradigm, as the presentation of the fear-arousing CS in the absence of the UCS. In most of the aforementioned studies the CS was presented without shock and extinction did occur. But the duration of the CS could not be controlled because it depended on the animal's response. Thus, although fear may have been undergoing some extinction on each escape trial, the response being measured typically showed an initial increase in strength because of the reinforcement provided by fear reduction. The fact that new responses were learned may be said to indicate the presence of fear, but the magnitude of the response at any moment cannot be said to reflect degree of fear. Brown, Kalish, and Farber have provided some systematic data relevant to the extinction of fear under conditions in which the duration of the CS is controlled and no new response is learned. However, the introduction of a startle stimulus (used as an index of fear) during the shockless trials may have had a disruptive effect upon the course of extinction. The second purpose of the present experiment, therefore, was *to investigate extinction of fear as a function of number of nonreinforced trials under conditions in which no overt response was reinforced.*

Method

APPARATUS. Two sets of apparatus were used: one for acquisition and extinction, and the other for the hurdle-jumping phase of the experiment.

In general, the acquisition procedure involved paired presentations of the CS and the UCS while extinction consisted of the presentation of the CS in the absence of the UCS. The acquisition and extinction phases of the experiment were conducted in the same apparatus which consisted of four boxes each constructed of $\frac{3}{4}$-inch pine, 11 inches long, 6 inches wide, and 5 inches deep (outside dimensions). These boxes were arranged in a row; four boxes were used to permit the running of four subjects simultaneously. Since most subjects had been used in studies involving black-white discrimination, the boxes were painted gray to obviate the necessity of equating for color preference. All the boxes were fitted with lids constructed by tacking hardware cloth to a wooden frame. The grid floors of the boxes were $\frac{3}{32}$-inch brass rods mounted in bakelite strips at intervals of $\frac{7}{16}$ inch. Simulated guillotine doors were constructed at one end to increase the similarity between these boxes and the box used during hurdle jumping. A buzzer and light, which served as the compound CS, were attached to the other ends of the four boxes. The buzzers, 24-volt D.C. relays modified to produce the sound of a buzzer, were fastened to the lids and were energized by 24-volt A.C. Measurements obtained using a General Radio Sound Level Meter Type 756 indicated a sound level of 73 decibels inside one of the boxes with all four buzzers energized stimultaneously. The lights, 115-volt, 7.5-watt frosted bulbs, were mounted in holes drilled into the end panels directly below the buzzers and protruded $\frac{5}{16}$ inch into the boxes. The illumination in these boxes, provided by a shaded overhead light in the center of the room, was .9 foot-candle as measured by a Macbeth illuminometer. When these lights were on, the illumination was increased to 5 foot-candles. The light and buzzer were presented simultaneously and were interrupted three times per second in an effort to increase their distinctiveness. The UCS for the fear reaction consisted of a 60–70-volt, 60-cycle shock delivered directly to the grids from a Variac connected to the 110-volt, A.C. line. No current-limiting resistor was used since it was necessary to shock four subjects simultaneously and since a commutator device, similar to that used by Skinner (1947), was incorporated into the circuit to reduce the shorting effect of feces. The presentation of the CS and UCS was automatically controlled by electronic timers.

The hurdle-jumping phase of the experiment was conducted in a separate apparatus. Here the CS was presented without the UCS and subjects were permitted to escape. The hurdle-jumping apparatus consisted of a box 22 inches long, 6 inches wide, and 5 inches deep (outside dimensions) of $\frac{3}{4}$-inch pine. The box was painted gray and divided into two equal compartments by a guillotine-type door which extended down through the top at the center and rested directly on the upper edge of a 2-inch partition. The two compartments formed by the guillotine door were fitted with lids. One of them contained a grid floor and a buzzer and light, and was identical with the boxes previously described. The other compartment was similar, but was without a buzzer and light and contained a smooth floor. The sound level in the hurdle-jumping box was approximately the same as that in the acquisition-extinction boxes. The latency of each hurdle-jumping response was measured to the nearest .01 second by means of a Standard Electric Timer. The timer started automatically when the door was raised (leaving a 2-inch barrier over which the subject had to cross) and stopped when the door was lowered by the experimenter following a response.

SUBJECTS. The subjects were 138 female, hooded rats from the colony maintained by the psychology department of the State University of Iowa. They ranged in age from 130–226 days at the beginning of the experiment. All subjects had been used previously in studies involving form and color discrimination, but none had been exposed to shock. Prior to the experiment, they were fed 10 grams of Purina Laboratory Chow per day for 10–15 days and were provided with a constant supply of water. Four days before the experiment proper, and during the course of the experiment, food and water were available in the living cages at all times.

EXPERIMENTAL DESIGN. A 4×4 factorial design was employed in which the four columns consisted of the number of extinction trials: 0, 3, 9, and 27. The four rows of the design comprised the number of acquisition trials: 1, 3, 9, and 27. One group of 16 subjects (one subject assigned to each cell) constituted a replication and the entire experiment contained eight replications. A control group, consisting of 10 subjects who received backward conditioning, was also incorporated into the design.

Acquisition of fear. A single fear-acquisition trial consisted of the paired presentation of the compound CS and shock. A group of four subjects, all receiving the same number of acquisition trials, was selected and its members placed in the individual acquisition-extinction boxes. In accordance with the experimental design, different numbers of trials, from 1 to 27, were given the separate groups. On each acquisition trial the duration of the CS was 5 seconds, and 4 seconds after its onset the shock was presented for 1 second.

In an attempt to extinguish the fear aroused by such cues as the box and grid equally for all groups, it was necessary to equate the amount of time each group was exposed to these cues. Accordingly, all subjects were kept in the boxes for the same period of time (81 minutes) and received the designated number of acquisition trials during this interim. At the end of the 81-minute period, one group of subjects was returned to its living cages and another group obtained. The intertrial interval during acquisition and extinction was 3 minutes.

Extinction of fear. Extinction was administered on the day following acquisition. During these trials the procedure was identical with that followed during acquisition except that no shock was presented. The subjects were again run in groups of four.

Those subjects assigned to the zero extinction group were placed in the boxes for 81 minutes, but were not presented with the CS.

The order in which the different groups of subjects in one replication received treatment during acquisition and extinction was randomized throughout the eight replications.

Acquisition of hurdle jumping. During the acquisition of hurdle jumping each subject was run individually. Twenty seconds after having been placed in the grid side of the hurdle box, the subject was presented with the CS and the sliding door raised. This enabled the subject to cross the hurdle and enter the second compartment after which the CS was terminated by the experimenter. The subject remained in the compartment for a period of 10 seconds and was then removed to a carrying case in an adjoining room to await its next trial 4 to 5 minutes later. During this interval three other subjects were given one trial each. If the subject did not cross the hurdle within 60 seconds, the door separating the two compartments was closed and a latency of 60 seconds was recorded for the trial.

All subjects received 12 trials in the hurdle-jumping apparatus immediately following extinction. A minimum amount of time was allowed to elapse between extinction and hurdle jumping in an attempt to reduce spontaneous recovery of fear and its subsequent influence on the first-trial latencies. On the day following extinction and hurdle jumping, all subjects received an additional 12 trials in the hurdle-jumping apparatus.

The acquisition and extinction treatments were evaluated in terms of their effect upon hurdle-jumping performance. The latency of the first trial in the hurdle-jumping apparatus was used as an index of level of fear following varying numbers of extinction trials for each level of acquisition. Since the first-trial latency is unaffected by the reinforcement provided by fear reduction, it should represent a relatively pure measure of the growth and decay of fear attributable to the acquisition and extinction trials. This is based on the assumption that the motivation due to fear will directly affect the subjects' latencies.

The latency of the subsequent trials in the hurdle-jumping situation should continue to reflect residual fear persisting from the acquisition and extinction trials. A decrease in these latencies would indicate the effect of fear reduction on the acquisition of hurdle jumping; increasing latencies obtained near the end of these trials would denote further extinction of fear.

Control group. The ten subjects in the control group were treated in the same way as those given 27 acquisition and 0 extinction trials except that a backward conditioning procedure was employed in which the 1-second shock was followed after 15 seconds by the 5-second CS. This group was introduced for two purposes: (1) to ascertain whether performance in hurdle jumping was due to any inherently noxious characteristics of the CS; (2) to determine whether the cues of the fear-conditioning box were eliminated by keeping subjects in the box for an 81-minute period following acquisition.

Results

First-trial latencies. The latencies obtained from the first hurdle-jumping trials for the 16 groups were transformed to logarithms (plus a constant of 2.0 to avoid negative values) and summed over all extinction conditions for each level of acquisition. The resultant means for 1, 3, 9, and 27 fear-acquisition trials confirmed the theoretical expectation in showing a slight progressive decrease in latency as a function of increasing numbers of acquisition trials. Since the differences between these means were small and the variances large, an F test showed no reliable difference.

Latencies for Trials 1–24, Days 1 and 2. The response latencies for each animal on Trials 1–24, Days 1 and 2, were summed over blocks of three trials and the means transformed as above to increase the stability of the measures and satisfy the assumptions involved in the statistical analyses. The results, organized in this manner, were treated by an analysis of variance in which the four levels of acquisition, four levels of extinction, and eight replications constituted the between-subjects comparisons, and the four blocks of three trials comprised the within-subjects comparisons (Lindquist, 1953). This analysis (Table 30-1) made it possible to examine simultaneously the performance curves of all 16 experimental groups and to test the hypothesis that these curves are parallel to each other, i.e., that their trends do not differ.

The obtained F for the triple interaction (Acquisition $\times$ Extinction $\times$ Trials) failed to exceed unity and the hypothesis of parallel curves could not be rejected. In view of this, the double interactions, Acquisi-

TABLE 30-1

Summary of analysis of variance: Day 1

SOURCE	df	MEAN SQUARE	F
Between subjects	127	.57	
Acquisition	3	4.62	15.00*
Extinction	3	4.45	14.44*
Replications	7	.55	
A × E	9	.66	2.13
A × R	21	.26	0.84
E × R	21	.57	1.87
A × E × R	63	.31	
Within subjects	384	.07	
Trials	3	2.74	
A × T	9	.19	4.34*
E × T	9	.22	5.07*
R × T	21	.04	0.79
A × E × T	27	.03	0.80
A × R × T	63	.05	1.05
E × R × T	63	.05	1.05
A × E × R × T	189	.04	
Total	511		

* Significant at the 1 percent level.

tion × Trials and Extinction × Trials were examined. The mean values for the curves are plotted in Figures 30-1 and 30-2.

An examination of Figure 30-1 reveals that the theoretical expectations were supported. The curves for Day 1 show that an increase in the number of fear-conditioning trials produced an increase in the slope and a decrease in the overall mean latency. Further evidence for this is revealed in the tests for interaction and vertical displacement (Table 30-1) which were significant beyond the 1 percent level of confidence. A further analysis of the trends for the individual curves discloses a decrease in latency for every level of fear acquisition since the F in each case was significant beyond the 1 percent level.

The results for Day 2, as plotted at the right of Figure 30-1, were also analyzed in the above manner and show a continued, marked superiority of the 27-trial group, no apparent extinction for any group, and a shift in the relative position of the 9-trial group. The test of interaction

Strength of Fear as a Function

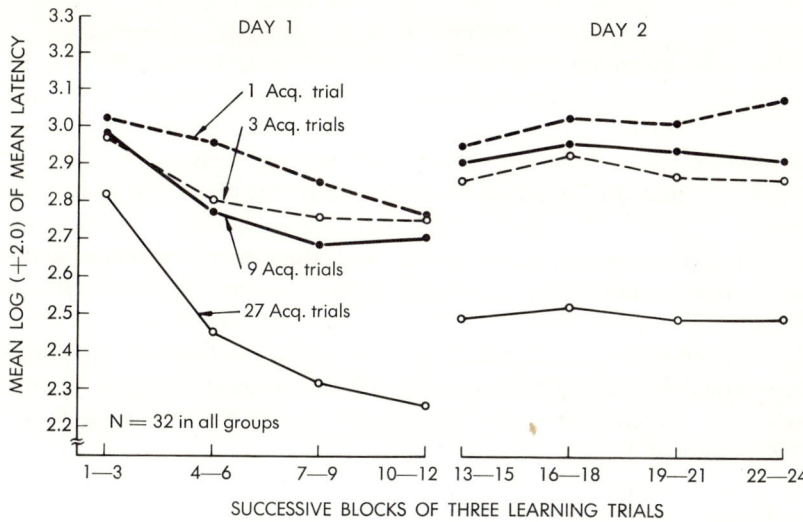

FIGURE 30-1. Response latency as a function of successive hurdle-jumping trials for groups given varying numbers of fear-acquisition trials. All levels of extinction pooled for each level of acquisition.

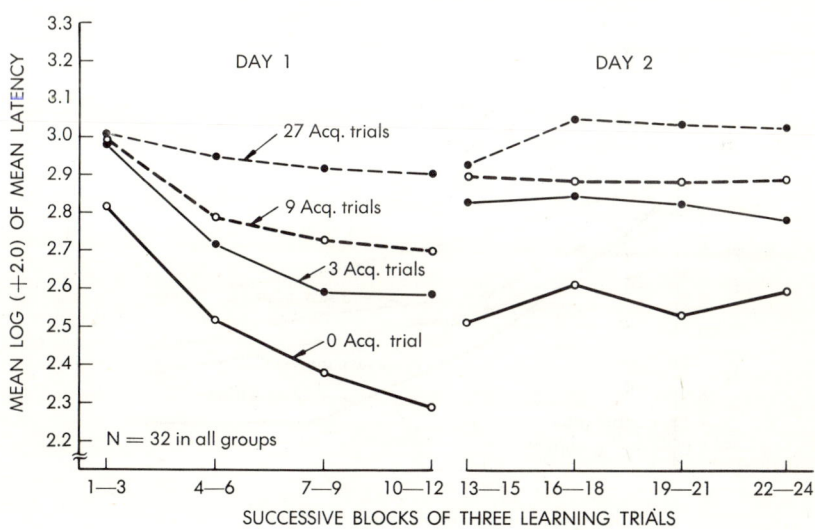

FIGURE 30-2. Response latency as a function of successive hurdle-jumping trials for groups given varying numbers of fear-extinction trials. All levels of acquisition pooled for each level of extinction.

failed to attain significance at the 5 percent level. The test for vertical displacement was significant beyond the 1 percent level of confidence.

The data illustrated in Figure 30-2 (Day 1) indicate that performance in hurdle jumping is inversely related to the number of fear-extinction trials and suggest that the extinction conditions of the present experiment were successful in diminishing differentially the fear aroused by the CS. This is substantiated by the tests for the main effects of extinction and the Extinction $\times$ Trials interaction which were both significant beyond the 1 percent level. Tests of trend for the individual curves revealed a decrease in latency which was significant at the 1 percent level for Groups 0, 3, and 9. The F for Group 27, however, was not significant. A similar analysis of the curves for Day 2 (Fig. 30-2) revealed that the hypothesis of no-interaction could not be rejected with any significant degree of confidence. The overall F for vertical displacement, however, was significant at the 1 percent level.

Analysis of simple trends for zero extinction level. The values plotted in Figure 30-3 were obtained from the groups given four levels of acquisition, but no extinction trials. The curve for the zero extinction group in Figure 30-2 (Day 1) is a composite of these four curves. The control group was also included in this analysis since this group received 27 shock trials (backward conditioning) and no extinction trials. The extremely large interaction found for these curves ($F = 8.58$, $p < .01$) is due solely

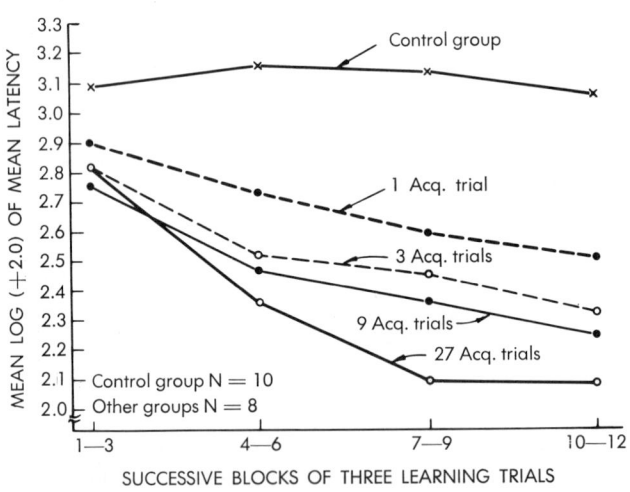

FIGURE 30-3. Response latency as a function of successive hurdle-jumping trials for fear-acquisition groups 1, 3, 9, 27, and 27 (control) at the zero extinction level (Day 1).

to the presence of the control group since no significant interaction was found in a separate analysis for the other groups.

The failure of the control group to evince any decrease in latency with successive trials, as indicated by a test of trend, suggests that the CS was neither inherently noxious nor had acquired fear-arousing properties for this group. The performance of the control group also indicates that the procedure introduced to reduce the effectiveness of the box and grid as potential fear cues was successful, and that the significant (beyond 1 percent level) decrease in latency for the other groups can be ascribed to the acquired drive characteristics of the CS. The t tests for the separate means indicate that the control group differed significantly from the other groups beyond the 1 percent level. Of the remaining groups, the largest difference, between 1–0 and 27–0, was found to be significant at the 2 percent level for a single-tailed hypothesis.

Discussion

The results of the present experiment provide additional support for the supposition that fear increases as a monotonic function of the number of fear-conditioning trials and weakens progressively with successive extinction trials. These conclusions are based primarily on the rewarding aspects of fear reduction rather than upon its motivating properties as revealed by latencies of the first hurdle-jumping trials. Although the reaction latencies of the four fear-acquisition groups ordered themselves in the anticipated manner on the first trial, these measures proved to be unsatisfactory as an index of level of fear because of their extreme variability.

Since, in the present instance, no crouching behavior was observed, this variability was due to the fact that the subjects differed widely in length of time taken to orient toward the guillotine door after being placed in the hurdle-jumping box. If controls were instituted so that all subjects oriented more uniformly toward the second compartment, the measures obtained on the first trial might be more adequate indicators of level of fear.

The latencies of the subsequent trials in the hurdle-jumping box indicate that different numbers of acquisition and extinction trials resulted in significantly different levels of performance for the various groups (cf. Figs. 30-1 and 30-2). Within the framework of Hull's theory, there are two alternative explanations for these dissimilar performance rates and the resulting dissimilar asymptotic values reached by the various acquisition and extinction groups. Both of these alternatives are based on the assumption that performance is directly determined by reaction potential ($_sE_r$) which, in turn, is a function of the multiplicative combination of habit strength ($_sH_r$) and drive (D).

The first interpretation involves the assumption that the habit strength for hurdle jumping increased at the same rate for all groups as a function of successive reinforcements provided by fear reduction during the hurdle-jumping trials. The differences in performance reflected in the divergent curves would then be due to the unequal multiplicative effects of the different levels of fear-produced drive in the several groups. Thus, at the beginning of hurdle jumping the habit strength is low and generally equal for all groups. Therefore, the multiplicative combination of $_sH_r$ and D would result in relatively small differences between the groups. If $_sH_r$ increased at the same rate for all groups, however, the habit strength at the end of the hurdle-jumping series would be high, but still very nearly equal for all groups. In this case multiplying $_sH_r$ and the differing D values would produce large differences between groups.

The second possibility is that the habits for hurdle jumping increase most rapidly for the groups having the greatest fear. According to this assumption the increments in $_sH_r$ per reinforcement would vary directly with the magnitude of the drive whose reduction provided the reinforcement. Although this does not seem to be a tenable assumption in the case of the effects of appetitive drives on habits, a recent eyelid-conditioning study by Spence (1953) suggests that it may operate in the case where the drive is provided by noxious stimulation. In the present instance the increasing divergence of the curves in Figures 30-1 and 30-2 would be attributable to both the differential rates of growth of $_sH_r$ and the multiplicative effects of the different drive levels.

It is interesting to compare the results of the present study with those obtained by Miller and Lawrence (see Miller, 1951b). These experimenters found that, although two groups of animals learned a wheel-turning response to escape fear-arousing cues after one group had been given 4 and the other 24 trials of fear conditioning, the difference between their levels of performance was not significant. In the present experiment, the two groups most nearly comparable to those in the Miller-Lawrence study were the groups given 3 and 27 fear-conditioning trials. Both of these groups showed a significant decrease in latency with successive hurdle-jumping trials, but the performance of the 27-trial group was significantly superior to that of the 3-trial group. Since strength of fear is also a function of the intensity of the UCS, it is conceivable that the failure of Miller and Lawrence to obtain a difference was due to the use of a more intense shock. The amount of shocking voltage was not mentioned, however, in a report of the study.

The findings of the present study tend to substantiate that part of Gwinn's experiment (1951) in which it was found that 16 fear-conditioning trials produced greater resistance to extinction than did 4 trials. Although Gwinn's and the present study agree that fear increases beyond four acquisition trials, it is, nevertheless, apparent that substantial amounts of fear can be acquired in a very few trials. . . .

The failure of the control group to manifest any decrease in latency during hurdle jumping suggests that the CS was not in itself noxious and that the cues associated with the fear-conditioning box had not acquired any drive-producing characteristics. These findings support the notion that the performance of the other groups was due primarily to the acquired-drive characteristics of the CS.

SUMMARY

The present experiment was designed to (a) determine the relation between strength of fear and varying numbers of acquisition trials, and (b) investigate the extinction of fear under conditions in which no new response is learned during extinction.

A total of 138 hooded, female rats, and a control group of 10 subjects were run in a factorial study in which the experimental variables were (a) number of fear-acquisition trials (1, 3, 9, and 27), and (b) number of fear-extinction trials (0, 3, 9, and 27).

All subjects went through experimental phases which involved acquisition of fear (paired presentations of CS and shock), extinction of fear (CS without shock), and acquisition of hurdle jumping. During the hurdle-jumping trials the CS was presented without shock and subjects were permitted to jump a hurdle and enter a second compartment. After this response was completed the CS was terminated by the experimenter. The latency of hurdle-jumping response was measured. A backward conditioning procedure was employed for the control group to control for possible sensitization effects.

The results indicated that the experimental variables had a significant effect upon the acquisition of hurdle jumping. It was concluded that fear increases as a monotonic function of number of fear-conditioning trials and weakens progressively with successive extinction trials.

Two alternative interpretations within Hull's learning theory were proposed to explain the results.

31

Experiments on Motivation:[1] Studies Combining Psychological, Physiological, and Pharmacological Techniques[2]

NEAL E. MILLER[3]

The importance of motivation in both normal and abnormal behavior is generally recognized. For example, the proper regulation of hunger is vital if the extremes of either malnutrition or obesity are to be avoided; psychotherapists have found that it is much more effective to deal with the underlying motivation in a psychogenic disorder than to treat a specific symptom.

This article describes experiments from our laboratory in which a combination of behavioral, physiological, and pharmacological techniques is used to study motivation. The experiments deal with hunger, thirst, sex, aggression, and a centrally aroused pain-fear-like response. These drives are induced or reduced in a variety of unusual ways, such as by direct electrical or chemical stimulation of the brain.

Our main reason for manipulating drives in unusual ways is to learn more about the mechanisms of the drives themselves and more about the roles of drives in learning and performance.

A subsidiary reason is to test a specific hypothesis, the drive-reduction hypothesis of reinforcement. It is well known that turning off a strong motivational stimulus, such as an electric shock, will serve as a reward to reinforce whatever response the animal was making just before it escaped

---

[1] Reprinted with permission of the author and publisher from *Science*, 1957, 126, 1271–1278.

[2] This article is the report of the work of a group at our laboratory. In addition to the students and coworkers cited, Arlo K. Myers made many ingenious contributions to the apparatus involved, Judith B. Levine performed the histology, Burton S. Rosner served as an expert consultant on histology, Ruth Bartlett implanted electrodes in the brains of rats, and colleagues in other departments gave useful advice.

[3] In order that the students working on the experiments should be given maximum credit, their names are cited in the article, but in some cases the reference . . . given may be that of the article in which the results are summarized and hence may have a different author. More complete reports are planned in a forthcoming book.

from the shock. It is also known that food will serve as a reward for a hungry animal and that this same food will reduce the strength of the hunger drive. The drive-reduction hypothesis attempts to abstract a common element from such observations. In its weak form, it states that the sudden reduction in the strength of any strong motivational stimulus always serves as a reward, or, in other words, is a sufficient condition for reinforcement. In its strong form, it states that all reward is produced in this way, or, in other words, that drive reduction is the necessary and sufficient condition for reinforcement.

Although I believe that the strong form of this hypothesis has much less than a 50 percent chance of being correct, I have been interested in subjecting it to rigorous tests. Actually, the correlation between reward and satiation does not tell us anything about the causal relationship; it could be a spurious correlation built into the organism by conditions of natural selection which have eliminated animals that were not pleasantly rewarded by conditions that reduced their drives. But if this correlation is such a spurious one, it might disappear when drives are manipulated in unusual ways not involved in natural selection.

Finally, the results of these studies show the value of using a diversity of rigorous behavioral tests to determine, point by point, whether the effects of the unusual interventions, such as electrical stimulation of the brain or administration of drugs, have all the functional properties of normal increases or reductions in drive. It is on this methodological point that we begin.

Some studies of hunger

Most studies of hunger have used but a single technique, measuring the amount of food consumed. If one is interested only in problems of energy exchange, the caloric intake obviously is the relevant measure. But if one is interested in the broader aspects of hunger as a drive to motivate the learning and performance of foodseeking behavior, it is not safe to rely solely on this measure.

In an early study, Miller, Bailey and Stevenson (1950) studied the motivational effect of a bilaterial lesion in the region of the ventromedial nuclei of the hypothalamus, which studies summarized by Brobeck (1946) had shown would cause rats to overeat until they became very fat, like the one shown in Figure 31-1. Because this lesion produces such a large increase in food intake, one might assume that it also has the more general effect of increasing hunger. We tested this assumption by using a behavioral measure—the rate at which the rats will work at the task of pressing a bar to secure food when they are rewarded on a variable-interval schedule. In this test, which was developed by Skinner (1938) at Harvard, hungry animals are first trained to press a bar actuating a

FIGURE 31-1. Effects of excessive eating caused by lesions in the hypothalamus of the rat. [*Photo by J. A. F. Stevenson.*]

device which automatically delivers tiny pellets of food. Then the device is set so that pressing the bar pays off only at unpredictable intervals, although the average frequency of pay-off remains constant. Under these conditions, the rate of bar pressing is quite constant at a given level of food deprivation but changes when the level of food deprivation is changed. Hence, the rate of working for food on these terms seems to be a relevant measure of hunger. But to our surprise, the animals with lesions, which were eating reliably *more* than the controls, worked reliably *less* at the bar to secure food.

The two measures—volume of food consumption (consummatory response) and rate of bar pressing—yielded opposite results. To resolve this dilemma, we devised a variety of other tests. One of these involved putting simple lids on the food dishes. When the lids were not weighted, the test animals ate more than the normal controls did, but when 75-gram weights were put on, the difference was reversed. In order to control for factors such as motor dexterity and fatigue, we imposed an entirely different type of deterrent to eating: the food was made progressively more bitter by adulteration with quinine. This quite different type of deterrent also caused consumption on the part of the test animals to fall below that of the controls. Similarly, it was found that the test rats ran more slowly down an alley to food than the controls did, pulled less hard when temporarily restrained by a harness, and were stopped by lower levels of electric shock at the goal. These results prove that, under the conditions of our experiment, the lesions did not have the same general motivational effects as a normal increase in hunger had.

Further thought stimulated by these results makes it clear that the amount of food consumed ad lib. is not determined by how hungry the animal gets after moderate or extreme periods of deprivation but rather by the low levels of hunger that keep the subject nibbling before it is completely satiated.

Some techniques used

The next experiments involved a small plastic fistula sewn into the stomach of the rat, threaded under the skin up its back, and emerging immediately behind its ears. Figure 31-2 shows an x-ray picture of a

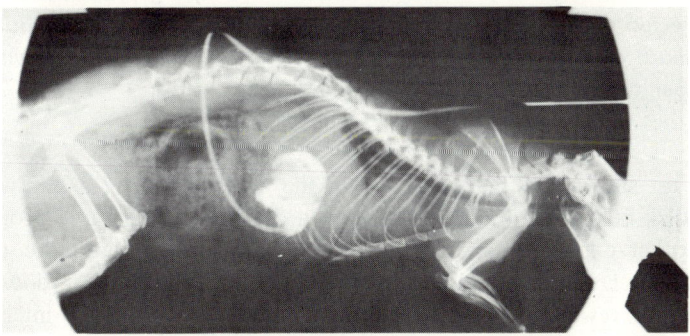

FIGURE 31-2. X-ray picture of rat with fistula chronically implanted into the stomach. A barium solution is being injected.

barium solution being injected into a rat's stomach through such a fistula. Figure 31-3 shows a picture of a rat with two such fistulae. One ends in a rubber balloon, which can be used to distend the stomach or to record stomach contractions; through the other an enriched milk solution is being injected directly into the stomach. (For purposes of photography, black rubber tubes were slipped over the smaller translucent plastic tubes of the projecting fistulae.)

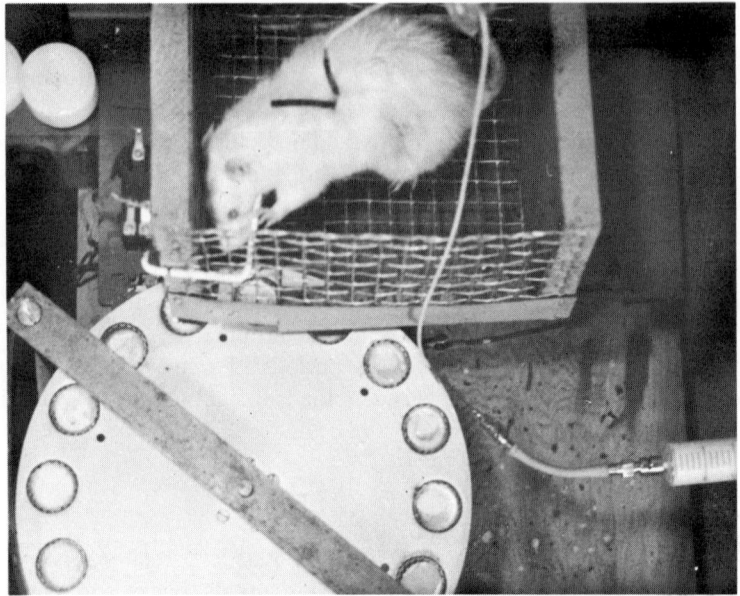

FIGURE 31-3. Hungry rat pressing bar to secure reward of three drops of enriched milk. Through one fistula connected to a syringe, additional milk can be injected directly into the stomach; through the other fistula, a balloon in the stomach can be inflated. To make the small transparent fistulae visible, black rubber tubes have been slipped over them.

The rat shown in Figure 31-3 is in the act of pressing a bar which causes a disk below to rotate and bring it a cup containing three drops of milk. In other experiments, pellets of food or drops of water are used. During the later stages of training and testing, pressing the bar does not always deliver reward; it works only at variable, unpredictable intervals.

The same apparatus is used for the quinine test. The bar is removed, and a different cup is rotated into place automatically once every 30 seconds. Each cup contains three drops of liquid adulterated with quinine hydrochloride in amounts that increase progressively from concentrations of 0, 0.004 percent, 0.008 percent, and 0.016 percent up to 1 percent. For each cup that it cleans up, the rat receives 2 points; for each one that it starts without finishing, 1 point; and for cups that it does not touch, 0.

Comparison of four measures of hunger

In one study preformed with this apparatus, Miller and Marion Kessen (Miller, 1956) compared the effects of hours of food deprivation on four different measures of hunger. The results are shown in Figure 31-4. It can be seen that, under the conditions of these experiments, the volume of food (in this case, an enriched milk solution) drunk in a given period—a figure which presumably would have been at a very low level initially had we had the wit to give tests immediately after satiation—had approximated its maximum after 6 hours of deprivation and did not increase appreciably thereafter. Although the reduction in eating observed after 30 hours is not statistically reliable, other work in our laboratory and elsewhere has demonstrated a similar reduction at longer intervals in animals habituated to a 24-hour feeding cycle. As shown in Figure 31-4, the curve for stomach contractions seems to parallel that for volume of milk drunk. But the other two measures, rate of bar pressing and amount of quinine required to stop the animal from drinking, follow a different course, continuing to increase throughout the test period. From these results it seems reasonable to conclude that hunger continues to mount for at least 54 hours but that the volume of food consumed in a limited time reaches a ceiling determined by the volume of the stomach or by the ability of the body to handle the food.

The results of these two experiments clearly show that it is desirable to supplement the measure of amount of food consumed with other behavioral tests.

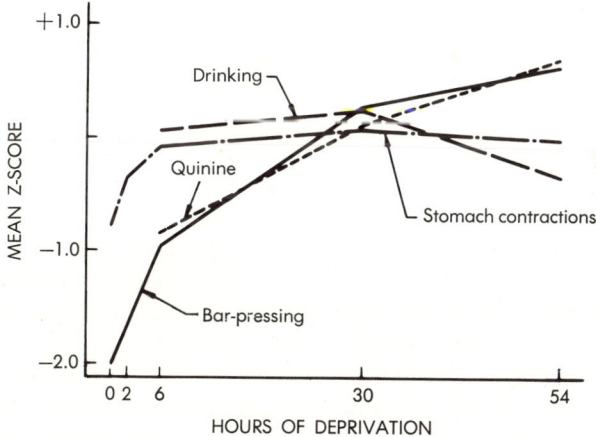

FIGURE 31-4. Comparison of four measures of hunger: (1) drinking—the volume of enriched milk required to satiate the rats; (2) the amount of adulteration with quinine required to prevent eating; (3) the rate of bar pressing reinforced by food on a variable-interval schedule; and (4) sum of excursions of the record of stomach contractions measured from a balloon permanently implanted on the end of a plastic fistula. [From Miller, 1956.]

Oral versus gastric factors

If hunger were not reduced until tissue needs were restored, the long delay between eating and drive reduction would make drive reduction by eating ineffective as a reward; the animal would also be motivated to continue after it had eaten enough. Therefore, satiation probably is controlled, at least in part, by other mechanisms. These logical considerations are backed up by the subjective reports of patients with fistulae and by the results of certain animal experiments, which have been limited, however, to the single measure of food consumed (Hollander, 1955). The following experiments in our laboratory were designed to secure more comprehensive information on such mechanisms.

Kohn (1951) compared the effects of 14 milliliters of enriched milk drunk normally by mouth with those of 14 milliliters of milk injected via fistula directly into the stomach or of 14 milliliters of isotonic saline injected directly into the stomach as a control. He measured hunger by an instrumental response—the rate of bar pressing reinforced on a fixed-interval schedule. Berkun, Kessen, and Miller (1952) ran a parallel experiment comparing the effects of the same three treatments—14 milliliters of milk drunk normally by mouth, 14 milliliters of milk injected directly into the stomach, and 14 milliliters of isotonic saline injected directly into the stomach. They measured hunger by the consummatory response—the volume of enriched milk the rat would drink to satiation immediately after a given treatment.

Figure 31-5 shows that both measures produce similar results; milk injected directly into the stomach produces a prompt reduction in hunger, but milk drunk normally by mouth produces an even greater reduction. Furthermore, when Kohn's results are analyzed for successive 3-minute intervals, it is evident that the effects appear immediately and that there is no tendency for them to get progressively greater during the 30-minute test, as would be expected if digestion and absorption into the blood and tissues were an appreciable factor. These results suggest that there are at least two means of producing immediate reductions in hunger, one involving the mouth and throat and the other, the stomach.

As a different means of investigating the role of the oral factor, we used a sweet-tasting but nonnutritive substance, saccharin. Previous experiments by Sheffield and Roby (1950) have shown that saccharin serves as a reward for hungry animals. Therefore, the strong form of the drive-reduction hypothesis demands that saccharin should also be found to reduce hunger.

A series of experiments by Miller, Roberts, and Murray (Miller, 1955) confirmed the deduction by showing that prefeeding with saccharin solution reduces both the subsequent consumption of that solution and the rate of bar pressing reinforced by saccharin. It also reduces the im-

Experiments on Motivation

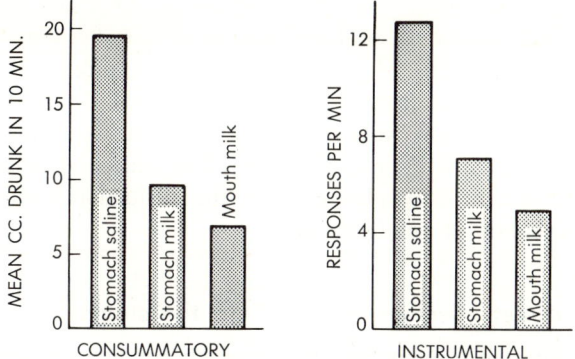

FIGURE 31-5. An injection of 14 milliliters of enriched milk directly into the stomach reduces hunger more than does the same volume of isotonic saline, but milk drunk normally by mouth produces still greater reduction. The same pattern of results is shown by both measures: the volume of milk consumed and the rate of performing an instrumental response (bar pressing) rewarded by food on a fixed-interval schedule. [Data from Kohn (1951), and Berkun, Kessen, & Miller (1952).]

mediately succeeding consumption of dextrose, milk, lab chow, or fat. But the effects of saccharin are less than those of an equally "preferred" solution of dextrose. Perhaps the most interesting result is that shown in Figure 31-6. It can be seen that saccharin, when drunk normally by mouth, has a definite effect, but that when it is injected via fistula directly into

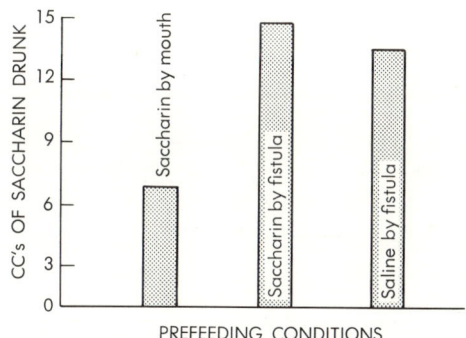

FIGURE 31-6. Saccharin injected directly into the stomach by fistula has approximately the same effects as a control injection of a saline solution with the same osmotic pressure, but saccharin drunk normally by mouth greatly reduces the subsequent consumption of saccharin.

the stomach it has no effect. This is in contrast to our results with nutritive substances, which have both oral and gastric effects. Perhaps the absence of a gastric effect explains why saccharin seems to produce less of a reduction than equally "preferred" dextrose.

The results of these experiments with saccharin provide additional evidence of a separate oral drive-reducing effect independent of the restoration-of-tissue needs; they also confirm the deduction from the drive-reduction hypothesis of reinforcement.

Reward by direct injection of food into the stomach

If food injected directly into the stomach produces a prompt reduction in the strength of hunger, the drive-reduction hypothesis of reinforcement demands that such injection should serve as a reward to produce learning. But since food taken normally by mouth produces a greater reduction, it should serve as a stronger reward. In order to test this deduction, Miller and Kessen (1952) performed an experiment in a simple T-maze. One group of hungry test animals found a dish of isotonic saline if they turned to the left and a dish of milk if they turned to the right. Another group received an injection of isotonic saline via fistula directly into the stomach if they turned to the left and an injection of milk if they turned to the right. (For half of each group the positions of the milk and the saline were reversed. All animals were given a second trial each day, during which they were forced to the side of the maze opposite to that selected on their first, free-choice trial.)

As Figure 31-7 shows, both groups learn to choose the correct side

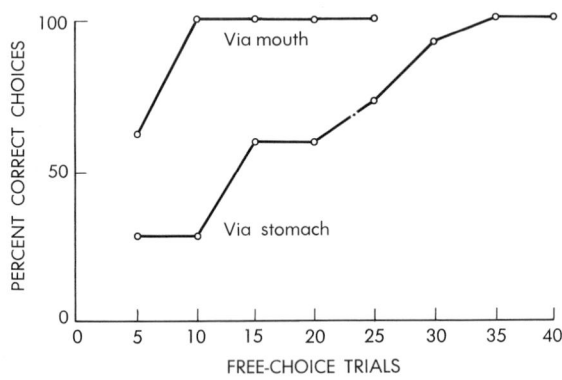

FIGURE 31-7. Hungry rats rewarded by milk injected directly into their stomachs learn to choose the correct side of a T-maze, but other rats, drinking milk normally by mouth, learn more rapidly.

Experiments on Motivation

100 percent of the time on free-choice trials, but the group getting milk by mouth learns much more rapidly. Similar learning curves are also shown by the time scores.

These results support the drive-reduction hypothesis by showing that milk injected directly into the stomach can serve as a reward. They run counter to other hypotheses which would make either the performance of the consummatory response or the taste of the food the sole source or reward, although they do not rule out these factors as additional sources of reward. Furthermore, these results serve as a control to eliminate the possibility that the reductions in the rate of bar pressing and in the amount of food consumed observed in the previous experiments were produced solely by a conflicting drive, such as nausea induced by the unnatural injections via fistula, rather than by a genuine reduction in hunger.

Effects of stomach distension

The preceding studies controlled for volume of fluid injected into the stomach. But since saline solution may easily leave the stomach, they did not necessarily control for stomach distension. In order to study the effects of distension, Miller and Kessen (Miller, 1955) prepared animals with two fistulae, one of the normal kind and the other ending in a small thin rubber balloon in the stomach. The rat in Figure 31-3 has two such fistulae. Figure 31-8 shows that distension of the stomach by inflating

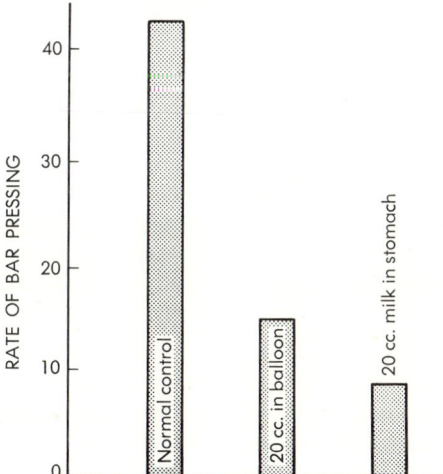

FIGURE 31-8. Distention of the hungry rat's stomach by inflating a balloon with 20 milliliters of fluid reduces the rate of working for food, but distension by 20 milliliters of milk injected directly into the stomach produces a slightly greater reduction.

the balloon with 20 milliliters of fluid markedly reduces the rate of bar pressing and that distension by injection of 20 milliliters of milk directly into the stomach reduces the rate slightly more. The greater effectiveness of the milk, though slight, was statistically highly reliable.

Stomach distension by milk and by balloon have markedly similar effects on rate of bar pressing. Do both types of distension produce similar reductions in the hunger drive? If the hunger drive is reduced by inflation of the balloon, the drive-reduction hypothesis would lead one to expect that such distension would serve as a reward for the hungry rat. To test this deduction, hungry rats were run in the simple T-maze with the balloon inflated when they went in the goal box at one side but not when they went in the goal box at the other side. As Figure 31-9 shows, instead of

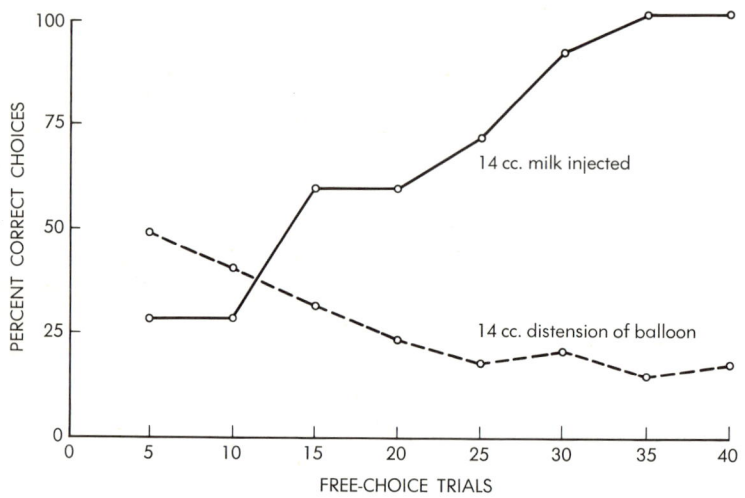

FIGURE 31-9. One group of hungry rats learns to choose the side of a T-maze where their stomachs are distended by milk injected via fistula; another group learns to avoid the side where their stomachs are distended by inflation of a balloon.

learning to go to the side where the balloon was inflated, the animals learned to avoid it. Although stomach distension by milk and by balloon have similar effects on the rate of bar pressing, this new learning test shows that these two types of distension produce qualitatively different effects. There is some mechanism in the stomach which reacts differentially to the food and to the balloon.

One interpretation of this result is that, while the milk reduces the rate of bar pressing by reducing hunger, the balloon reduces it by in-

Experiments on Motivation

ducing a conflicting motivation, such as nausea. A *post hoc* assumption of this kind is not satisfying, however, unless it can be supported by additional evidence. If distension of the balloon induces some other motivation, such as nausea, we should be able to use the reduction in this motivation, when the balloon is deflated, as a reward to reinforce new learning. We are in the process of trying to confirm this prediction, but our preliminary results so far have been negative. We also have preliminary results suggesting that inflation of the balloon may produce a much greater reduction in the rate of bar pressing than in other measures of motivation. These two results, though still tentative, cause us to be cautious; we may be forced to some different interpretation.

In any event, it is clear that it was worth while to use the additional test, which differentiated the rewarding effects of distension by milk from the aversive ones of distension by the balloon.

Hunger-motivated habits elicited by stimulating brain

In his monumental, pioneering work on stimulation by means of electrodes chronically implanted in the brains of cats, Hess (1954) reports that eating, and even the gnawing of inedible objects, can be elicited by stimulating certain points in the hypothalamus. Recently, Smith (1956) has reported similar results with rats. In our laboratory, Edgar Coons and I are studying this phenomenon to see whether it has some of the more general motivating properties of hunger. The possibility that it is merely a reflexlike gnawing response is raised by the fact that stimulated animals will frequently bite off and chew inedible objects such as pieces of wood.

Our tests have involved determining whether or not the electrical stimulation of the brain which elicits eating in the satiated animal will also elicit various habits that have been rewarded by food when the animal was hungry. In one experiment hungry rats were trained to press a bar which delivered the reward of food on a variable-interval schedule. Next, the rats were thoroughly satiated, first in the home cage and then in the bar-pressing apparatus. Finally, the satiated rats were tested with alternate 2-minute periods of stimulation by means of the electrode that would elicit eating and of nonstimulation. Each time the rat pressed the bar, a recording pen moved up a small distance. Whenever the bar delivered a tiny pellet of food, the pen drew a spike below the curve.

Figure 31-10 shows the photograph of a record of the results. The almost horizontal lines of the record during the 2-minute periods of nonstimulation show that the rat pressed the bar very infrequently during these control periods. The upward steps, starting relatively soon after the onset of stimulation and ending relatively soon after its termination, show that electrical stimulation of this point in the brain motivated bar pressing.

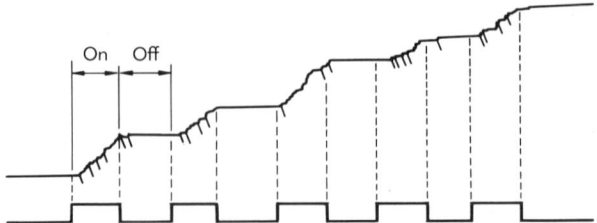

FIGURE 31-10. A cumulative record of a satiated rat repeatedly performing the learned habit of pressing a bar for food when the brain stimulation is on, and seldom performing it when the brain stimulation is off. The downward spikes on the record indicate the times when pressing the bar on the variable-interval schedule actually paid off with a pellet of food.

The median rate without stimulation was 0.5, and with stimulation 8.5, responses per minute.

In another apparatus we have trained rats to run, when thirsty, to the nozzle of a water bottle and drink and to go, when hungry, to a different place and push back a small hinged door to secure pellets of food hidden in a little trough behind it. When thoroughly satiated, these rats were relatively inactive until electrical stimulation was delivered to the critical area in their brains, at which time they soon ran to the proper place and repeatedly pushed back the hinged door to get and eat pellets. Thus, the electrical stimulation of the specific area in the rat's brain seems to have had at least some of the general properties of normal hunger in that it will elicit not only eating but also the performance of learned, food-seeking responses.

Coons is now investigating whether stimulation in this area has another of the properties of hunger: Will turning off such stimulation serve as a reward?

Studies of thirst

Oral versus gastric factors in thirst have been investigated by Miller, Sampliner, and Woodrow (1957). The results are similar to those found with hunger: water injected directly into the stomach of rats produces a prompt reduction in thirst, measured either by the rate of working at pressing a bar to get water or by the amount of water consumed; water taken normally by mouth produces a still greater reduction in thirst, measured in either of these ways.

Other experiments are in progress on the effects on thirst of stomach distension produced by a balloon on the end of a plastic fistula and on the effects of injecting saline or water directly into the blood stream by

Experiments on Motivation

means of a catheter permanently implanted into a vein. Working with the latter technique, Donald Novin is especially interested in trying to determine whether the sudden increases in thirst induced by hypertonic injections via the catheter into a vein can be a means of conditioning to produce a learned drive and whether the reduction in thirst produced by injections of water into the vein can serve as a reward in a simple learning situation.

Minute injections into ventricles of the brain

Andersson (1953) in Stockholm found that minute injections of hypertonic saline into the region of the third ventricle of goats would cause them to drink, presumably by stimulating osmoreceptors in the brain. In order to see whether this result would be repeated with cats and whether injections of water would have the opposite effect, Miller, Richter, Bailey, and Southwick (Miller, 1961b) permanently implanted hypodermic-needle devices in the third and lateral ventricles of the brains of cats. Tests were made on cats which were moderately thirsty so that we could note either increases or decreases in drinking.

The results are shown in Figure 31-11. It can be seen that the amount consumed after a minute injection (0.15 milliliter) of isotonic saline is no different from that after a mock procedure in which nothing is injected. Apparently this volume of fluid has no effect per se. But when the injection is slightly hypertonic (2 percent of sodium chloride), the volume

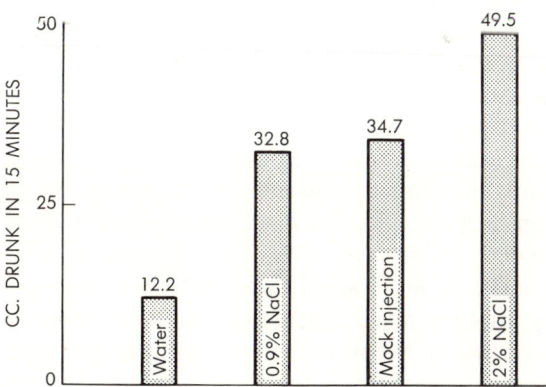

FIGURE 31-11. Effects on thirst of minute injections into the ventricles of the cat's brain. The two controls, 0.15 milliliters of isotonic saline and a mock injection, produced similar effects. An injection of 0.15 milliliters of water reduces subsequent drinking, while injection of the same amount of slightly hypertonic saline increases subsequent drinking.

consumed is increased. This result confirms Andersson's results with goats.

Conversely, it can be seen that an injection of 0.15 milliliters of distilled water decreases consumption. This new finding shows that minute injections of hyper- and hypotonic solutions have opposite effects.

A second experiment, by Miller, Richter, Lacy, and Jensen (Miller, 1961b), showed that the effects demonstrated in the experiment just described are not limited to the response of drinking but include some of the more general motivational effects produced by normally-induced thirst. In order to secure water, cats were trained to pull in spoons mounted radially on a disk. During the later stages of training and throughout testing, the water was placed in the spoons on a variable-interval schedule. In extensive tests, different doses of either a 2 percent sodium chloride solution of pure water were administered in a balanced order between mock injections. The injections of hypertonic saline reliably increased the rate of performing the learned response rewarded by water, while the injections of water reduced it.

These results, together with those of the afore-mentioned experiments, show that the regulation of thirst can be effected by mechanisms located in at least three places: mouth-throat, stomach-intestine, and brain.

Are certain drives heterogeneous clusters?

Most of us are accustomed to thinking of a given drive, such as thirst, as a single unitary variable. If a drive really is a single unitary variable—representing the activity of a single substance in the blood, a central state, a center or an integrated system in the brain—it is obvious that all pure measures of the drive should be perfectly correlated.

On the qualitative level, our experiments on oral versus gastric factors show the type of agreement which would be expected if drives are unitary factors. The measures of amount consumed and rate of bar pressing both agree in showing that normal consumption, by mouth, produces more drive reduction than does an injection made directly into the stomach but that the latter produces some reduction. Such agreement is shown for both hunger and thirst. In the case of thirst, these measures agree in showing that a minute injection made directly into the third ventricle, if hypotonic, decreases drive and, if hypertonic, increases it. In the case of hunger, an additional measure, learning in the T-maze, shows the reward effects to be predicted from the other two measures—namely, more rapid learning when food is administered by mouth than when it is administered by stomach, but some learning under the latter condition. Furthermore, electrical stimulation of the brain has similar effects on two different measures: it elicits the consummatory response of eating and also the performance of learned instrumental responses rewarded by food.

When the stomach is distended by a balloon, however, there is disagreement; distension reduces the rate of bar pressing but acts as a punishment rather than as a reward. This result cannot be accounted for by a single unitary factor, and it forces us to assume a second factor, such as nausea induced by distension.

Although the experiments just reviewed show an impressive amount of agreement among measures, it should be recalled that the first experiments described in this article show some disagreement. We found that the lesion in the hypothalamus increases one presumptive measure of hunger—the amount of *food consumed—while it decreases other measures such as the rate of bar pressing and the amount of quinine required to stop the animals from eating.* In the second experiment, we saw that the volume of food consumed fails to increase with more than 24 hours of deprivation, while other measures, such as bar pressing and quinine scores, continue to increase. Other studies from our laboratory, summarized elsewhere (Miller, 1956), have yielded additional discrepant results. For example, Miller and Levine find that a certain dose of amphetamine increases the rate of bar pressing which has been reinforced by food but decreases both the quinine score and the amount of food consumed. Similarly, Choy finds that a strong saline solution, administered by stomach tube to animals which have just eaten dry food, decreases the rate of bar pressing for water but increases the amount of quinine required to stop the animals from drinking and increases the amount of water consumed.

Such discrepant results can be explained in two ways: (1) by assuming that the drive is not a single unitary intervening variable but rather a cluster of interrelated variables such as might be expected if a number of neural centers are involved which are differentially affected by various regulators and have differential effects on various response systems; or (2) by assuming that the drive is a unitary variable, perhaps integrated by a single neural mechanism, but that the measures are impure and hence can be affected by factors other than the drive. For example, the rate of bar pressing might be susceptible to a stimulating side-effect of amphetamine, which might more than compensate for that drug's interference with hunger.

The possibilities we have been discussing open up new problems for research which will require experimental designs that have seldom been used by behavioral scientists. As has been pointed out elsewhere (Miller, 1959), the type of experimental design required (but almost never used) to make intervening variables, such as drives, meaningful is one in which it is possible to compare the effects of a number of different experimental operations on a number of different measures of the variable. The concepts of physical science are convincing and useful because their functional unity and generality is confirmed by tests of this general design. Thus, electricity produced by a variety of different experimental operations—by an electrostatic machine, a chemical reaction in a battery, or the wires of a generator cutting magnetic lines of force—has the same effects on a variety of means of measuring electricity—repelling like charges on an electrometer, depositing silver in an electroplating bath, and creating magnetic lines of force which deflect the needle of a meter. Similarly, on a highly quantified level, electrons from diverse sources all have exactly the same charge, which can be measured by a variety of independent techniques.

The fact that there is a word in the English language to describe a phenomenon does not guarantee that it has generality and functional unity of the type we have just illustrated. Perhaps, as we are forced to modify some of our concepts because they do not have this type of unity, we may eventually "carve nature better to the joint" and achieve more powerful concepts which do have such generality and unity.

Learning motivated by electrical stimulation of the brain

The first experiments to demonstrate instrumental learning motivated by electrical stimulation of the brain were designed to use a number of different techniques to show whether a pain-fear-like "alarm" reaction to central stimulation had all of the functional properties of normally aroused pain and fear. Normally aroused pain and fear have the following properties: (1) their evocation can motivate and their termination can reinforce the learning and performance of instrumental responses; (2) they can be used to establish a conditioned response; (3) they can be used to condition, in the test subject, an emotional disturbance to new stimuli which will provide motivation for the learning and performance of new responses; (4) they can serve as a punishment to establish an approach-avoidance conflict, so that a hungry animal will avoid food. Delgado, Roberts, and Miller (1954) performed the experiments described below to show, point by point, that electrical stimulation of certain places in the diencephalon has all of the foregoing properties.[4]

In the first experiment, cats were placed in an apparatus one end of which contained a little paddle-wheel device, rotation of which turned off the stimulation. When critical points in their brains were stimulated, the cats, which had previously been trained to escape electric shock in the same apparatus, became active, until by chance, aided by transfer from their previous training, they rotated the wheel and turned off the stimulation. After a number of such trials they learned to rotate the wheel immediately when the stimulation was turned on. Figure 31-12 shows suc-

---

[4] To date, "alarm" reactions eliciting avoidance learning have been obtained by stimulating cats in the vicinity of the recognized pain system (medial lemniscus and thalamic nucleus ventralis posterior), the hippocampal gyrus, or the intralaminar nuclei.

Experiments on Motivation

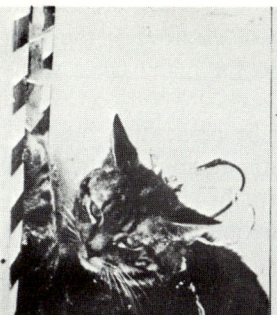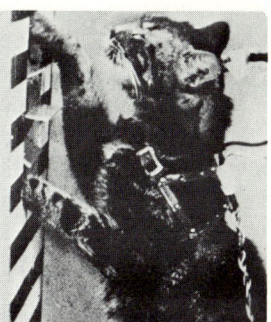

FIGURE 31-12. The learned instrumental response of rotating a paddle wheel to avoid shock to the feet is elicited by direct electrical stimulation of specific points in the brain. The stimulus was turned on between taking of the first and second pictures. [*Selected frames from a motion picture shown by me at the meetings of the American Psychological Association, September, 1953.*]

cessive frames from a motion picture of a cat performing this response when its brain is stimulated.

In the second experiment, a tone was used as a conditioned stimulus. This tone preceded the centrally aroused emotional disturbance. The cat had to rotate the wheel to turn off the central stimulation, but if it rotated the wheel in time, it turned off the tone and avoided the central stimulation. At first, the tone elicited no response, but after a number of avoidance-conditioning trials, the cats learned to respond promptly to the tone and thus to avoid the central stimulation.

In the third experiment, the cats were placed in an apparatus consisting of two distinctive compartments separated by a partition, in the upper front corner of which was a hole just large enough to allow them to climb through. During initial tests they showed no marked preference. On training trials, they were locked into one of the compartments and stimulated there. After a number of such trials, they showed obvious signs of fear of that compartment. Then, on test trials, without any further central stimulation, the hole between the two compartments was opened. During these trials the cats rapidly learned the new response of escaping by climbing up through the narrow hole to the other compartment. Control cats, stimulated in a sensorimotor area with a higher voltage which produced an apparently more violent motor response, did not learn to be disturbed in the compartment or to avoid it.

In the final experiment in this series, hungry cats were trained to eat fish from a dish and were then stimulated just as they started to eat. Test cats, stimulated at the critical point, learned in one or two trials to stay completely away from the food. Control cats were stimulated in the sensorimotor cortex with a higher voltage, which produced a more violent lurch back from the food. With proper placement of electrodes, the cats could be made to pull violently back from the food for many trials without learning any avoidance of the food.

The foregoing experiments have shown, point by point, that the particular emotional reaction elicited by electrical stimulation of the cat's brain has all of the functional properties of externally elicited pain and fear: (1) its evocation can motivate and its termination can reinforce the learning and performance of an instrumental response; (2) it can be used to establish a conditioned response; (3) it can be used to condition an emotional disturbance to a distinctive test compartment, after which, during trials in which there is no further stimulation, the cat learns to escape from that compartment; and (4) it can act as a punishment to teach hungry cats to avoid food.

Some unexpected effects

Figure 31-13 shows a response of extreme activation which Roberts and I observed in a cat stimulated in the vicinity of the posterior hypothalamic nucleus. Following Hess (1954), we called this a "flight" reaction. In spite of all of the superficial indications of strong motivation, we discovered to our surprise that large numbers of trials failed to produce any obvious sign of emotional conditioning in the two-compartment apparatus. Therefore, we tentatively concluded that it did not produce any learning.

Fortunately, we decided to give additional tests to prove the obvious. Again we were surprised. We found that if the cat was stimulated for 5 seconds before it was placed in the start of a T-maze and if the stimulus was turned off only after the cat had run to the correct arm of the maze, it learned within a few trials to dash to the correct side as soon as the stimulus was turned on; the cat demonstrated rapid escape learning. But even after 200 additional trials, the cat still failed to show any avoidance learning; it sat calmly waiting until the stimulus was turned on.

In a subsequent rigorously controlled study, Roberts (1958a) has shown that cats motivated by centrally elicited "alarm" or peripheral "pain" will rapidly learn to avoid the stimulus by leaving the starting box before the stimulus is turned on. Cats stimulated at "flight" points will learn as rapidly to run to the correct side after the stimulus is turned on but will not learn to avoid the stimulus by starting during the 5 seconds before it is turned on. In these experiments, a level of "flight" stimulation was selected which appeared to be stronger than that of "alarm" or of peripheral pain in that it would cause the animals to run faster and to pull harder against a temporary restraint than did the other two types of stimulus.

FIGURE 31-13. "Flight" response elicited by stimulation in the vicinity of the posterior hypothalamic nucleus. To our surprise, the stimulation eliciting this response was also rewarding.

While further investigating the "flight" response, Roberts (1958b) made another unexpected discovery. He found that, although cats would learn to run to the correct arm of a T-maze in order to escape "flight" stimulation, paradoxically they would learn to press a bar in order to get stimulation of the same voltage at the same point. In other words, they would show not only a rewarding effect from the *termination* of presumably aversive stimulation, as originally demonstrated in the hypothalamus by Delgado, Roberts, and Miller (1954), but also a rewarding effect from the *onset* of stimulation analogous to that found in the septal area by Olds and Milner (1954). Previously, these two effects had been observed only from different places, and it is indeed surprising that they should both be elicited from stimulation at the same point in the brain. Furthermore, looking back at Figure 31-13, I believe it is clear that, from observation alone, one would not suspect that stimulation at the point where such a response is aroused could function as a reward. Again, the need for rigorous behavioral tests is demonstrated.

Subsequently, Gordon Bower and I have secured the same paradoxical rewarding and aversive effects by stimulating in the hypothalamus of rats along the medial forebrain bundle near the fornix. Figure 31-14 shows a picture of a rat exhibiting these paradoxical dual effects of reward and punishment. It can be seen that this rat has learned to run to a bar and press it in order to turn on electrical stimulation of his brain. Once the bar has been pressed, the stimulation continues until it is turned off by rotation of a wheel. Having worked at the bar to turn on the stimulation, the rat then runs to the wheel to turn it off and after that, returns to the bar to turn it on, repeating the sequence over and over.

The *simultaneous* elicitation of rewarding and punishing effects would be clearly contrary to the drive-reduction hypothesis, since rewards should involve reductions, and punishments should involve increases, in drive. But such a phenomenon would also run counter to all other current notions of reward and punishment, since these two concepts seem to be mutually exclusive, by definition. While we should not hesitate to reexamine radically our time-honored definitions, there are at least three other possibilities here, involving successive effects: (1) that we are stimulating a single system that responds with pleasant sensations at first, which continue to increase until they become unbearable; (2) that we are stimulating a single system but that the stimulation has first an inhibiting, drive-reducing, rewarding effect followed by a drive-inducing, punishing effect; or (3) that we are stimulating two different adjacent systems which have different temporal characteristics, so that the reward is predominant first and the aversion thereafter. The first of these possibilities would be contrary to the drive-reduction hypothesis; the second two, which must be considered also in other tests of this hypothesis, would be congruent with it. Furthermore, it is possible that an initial reward effect is what prevented Roberts' cat from showing avoidance learning.

However the theoretical problems may be resolved, these paradoxical effects show the practical need for systematically submitting each logical, and illogical, possibility to rigorous behavioral test.

Effect of drugs on rewarding and punishing functions in the brain

The paradoxical dual effects of stimulation in the medial forebrain bundle near the fornix may give us a technique for discovering drugs that accentuate the positive, rewarding functions of the brain or minimize the negative, punishing ones. Similarly, drugs with differential effects may help us to analyze the functions of motivational systems in the brain.

A promising start has been made, and described in an unpublished paper, by Robert Kirschner, who used an apparatus which consisted of two bars, one black and one white, but otherwise similar, placed diagonally across from each other in the corners of a square box. Pressing one of the bars turned the stimulation on; pressing the other bar turned it off. Both the rate of bar pressing and the total time of stimulation were recorded.

After exploring a number of drugs, he selected methamphetamine and chlorpromazine. When the cycle for pressing of both bars was recorded, he found that both drugs produced marked and similar depressions in the over-all rate: methamphetamine reduced the rate to 16 percent of that recorded after a control injection of isotonic saline, and chlorpromazine, to 12 percent. But when the positive and negative components were measured separately, there was a striking difference. Methamphetamine *increased* the speed with which the stimulus was turned on to 270 percent of the control rate and *reduced* the speed with which it was turned off to 11 percent of the control rate. By contrast, chlorpromazine reduced the speed of turning on the stimulus to 5 percent of the control rate and that of turning off the stimulus to 56 percent of the control rate.

The fact that methamphetamine appeared to potentiate the rewarding, and reduce the punishing, effect seems to fit in with the clinical observation that it tends to produce euphoria. The fact that chlorpromazine seems to produce its greatest reduction in the rewarding effect may explain why it sometimes causes patients to be depressed. It is conceivable that the patients who are helped are the ones who have far too strong a striving for certain unrealistic or tabooed rewarding goals.

The striking differences in the patterns produced by these two drugs show that the technique has discriminating power. We hope that it will be useful in analysis of the effects of drugs on different motivational systems in the brain and in the search for new drugs which have therapeutic effects in certain kinds of mental illness. Additional techniques for studying the effects of drugs on motivation are described elsewhere (Miller, 1956, 1959).

Aggression and sex

As originally reported by Hess (1954), stimulation in certain regions of the hypothalamus of cats can produce a spectacular attack response which often is not stereotyped but is flexibly directed at suitable targets. Figure 31-15 shows an attack response we obtained when stimulating a cat. Prior to such stimulation the cat had ignored the toy dog thrust into the apparatus. When the appearance of the dog was paired with elec-

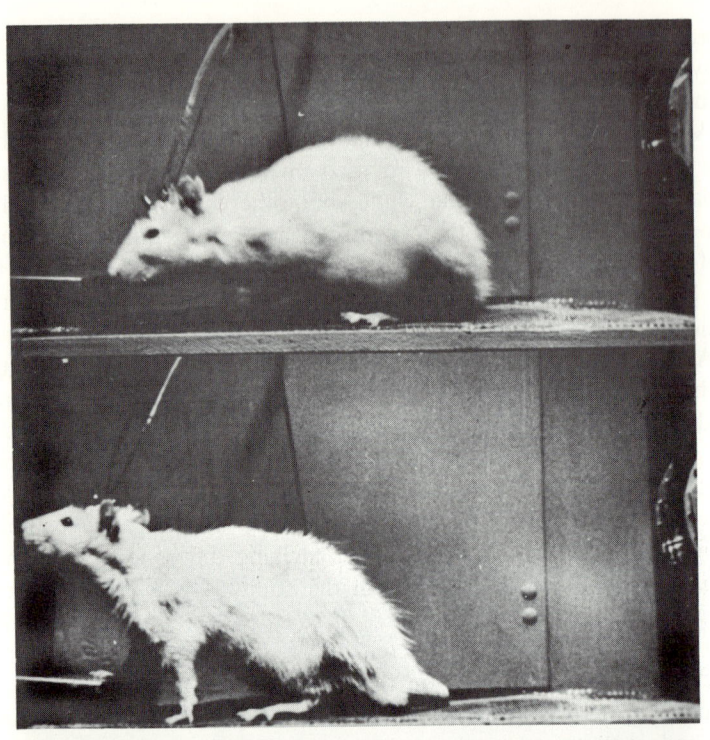

FIGURE 31-14. A rat presses a bar to turn on electrical stimulation of his brain, rotates a wheel to turn it off, and continues to repeat this sequence. [*Pictures taken by Martin Iger in our laboratory for Harcourt, Brace and Company.*]

trical stimulation, the cat attacked the dog. After a number of such trials, a similar conditioned attack was elicited without electrical stimulation.

This beautiful experiment has one flaw, however—subsequent histology showed that the electrode was completely outside the brain, so that the rage must have been elicited by peripheral pain from stimulation of tissues below the brain. Nevertheless, the cat serves as a control to show that aggression elicited by peripheral pain can be conditioned. To date, Roberts has failed to condition a number of cats showing similar attack patterns elicited by stimulation of the hypothalamus. This negative result confirms earlier reports by Masserman (1941). We are continuing to search, nevertheless, for new areas and techniques which may elicit rage responses that are more like the normal motivation in that they can be conditioned.

Finally, we have observed ejaculations elicited by repetitive stimulation at a number of points in the rat's brain, especially from a point in the medial forebrain bundle near the fornix, which also produces the para-

FIGURE 31-15. An attack response elicited by stimulating a cat. This particular response was conditionable but probably was elicited by pain produced by stimulating beneath the base of the brain. In other cats we have not been able to condition apparently similar rage responses elicited by stimulation in the hypothalamus.

doxical combination of rewarding and punishing effects. Milton Trapold is studying the relationship of these reactions to normal sexual behavior. For example, will electrically induced ejaculation have the same effect on subsequent sexual behavior as would complete satiation by normal means? Such studies may help to tell us whether sexual motivation is relatively unitary in character or is made up of a number of components which can be independently elicited and satiated by electrical stimulation of different parts of the brain.

32

Some Psychophysiological Studies of Motivation and of the Behavioral Effects of Illness[1]

NEAL E. MILLER

[In this report, I shall] summarize some of the recent work from my laboratory, much of it done by my students. Since we are working on a variety of things, it will be heterogeneous, and will include earlier studies when these are necessary to supply the rationale for the present work.

When is a reward reinforcing?

The first problem [concerns] the point at which a reward occurs in the temporal sequence of finding food—putting it in the mouth, swallowing it and digesting it.

Figure 32-1 shows some results from an experiment which Mrs. Kessen and I (1952) did a number of years ago. If hungry rats in a T-maze turned to the correct side, milk was injected directly into their stomachs through a chronic fistula; if they turned to the incorrect side, isotonic saline was injected. As can be seen from the solid curve, these rats learned to go to the correct side when the food was injected directly into their stomachs. In another experiment each rat had a balloon chronically implanted in his stomach. This balloon was inflated with the same amount of liquid that had been injected as a reward in the first experiment. As [can be seen] from the dashed line, these rats learned to avoid the side of the maze on which the balloon was inflated. So apparently the stomach discriminates between being distended by food and being distended in some other way, and the sensory feedback from food in the stomach can serve as a reward to a hungry animal.

About the same time another of my students, Nagaty (1951), did an experiment to determine whether food administered immediately before a

---

[1] Address to the Annual Conference of the British Psychological Society, Reading, 1963. Reprinted with permission from the *Bulletin of the British Psychological Society*, 1964, 17, 1–20.

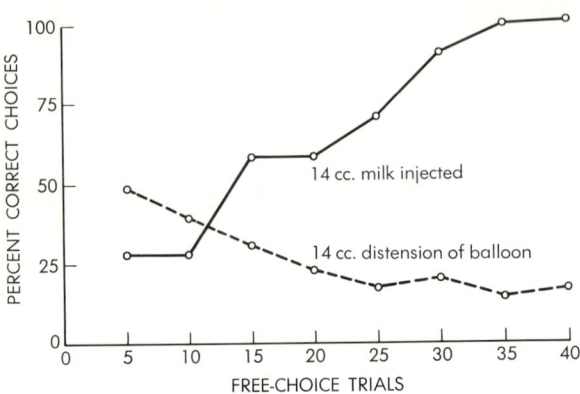

FIGURE 32-1. One group of hungry rats learns to choose the side of a T-maze where their stomachs are distended by milk injected directly via fistula. Another group learns to avoid the side where their stomachs are distended by the inflation of a balloon. [*From Miller, 1957.*]

response rewarded it. He trained rats to press a bar as soon as it was inserted into the apparatus. In this way he had control over the timing of the response; the rats learned to press the bar as soon as it was inserted. He habituated them sometimes to receive a pellet of food before the bar was inserted, as well as after they had pressed it, so that this procedure would not change the stimulus situation and disturb them during a subsequent test. He then extinguished the rats by leaving the food out after they had pressed the bar. The question was whether or not receiving food immediately *before* pressing the bar would serve as a reward.

Figure 32-2 shows the results. The top curve shows the effect of reward after bar pressing. For each animal the delivery of food was delayed for an interval which was equal to that elapsing in the other group between the delivery of food before the bar was inserted, and the bar press by the rat. As is to be expected, the results show that the rats rewarded two seconds after pressing the bar did not extinguish at all. But the rats rewarded two seconds before pressing the bar did extinguish. There are various control groups which do not concern us here; the point is that the reward before did not serve to strengthen the response at all. On the other hand, it did not serve to hasten the extinction. The food delivered before the bar was pressed probably was still being chewed and tasted, or was still going down the esophagus, and certainly was in the stomach and being digested after the rat pressed the bar. Why did the food in the stomach fail to be rewarding in this experiment, while it was rewarding in the first one?

Some Psychophysiological Studies of Motivation

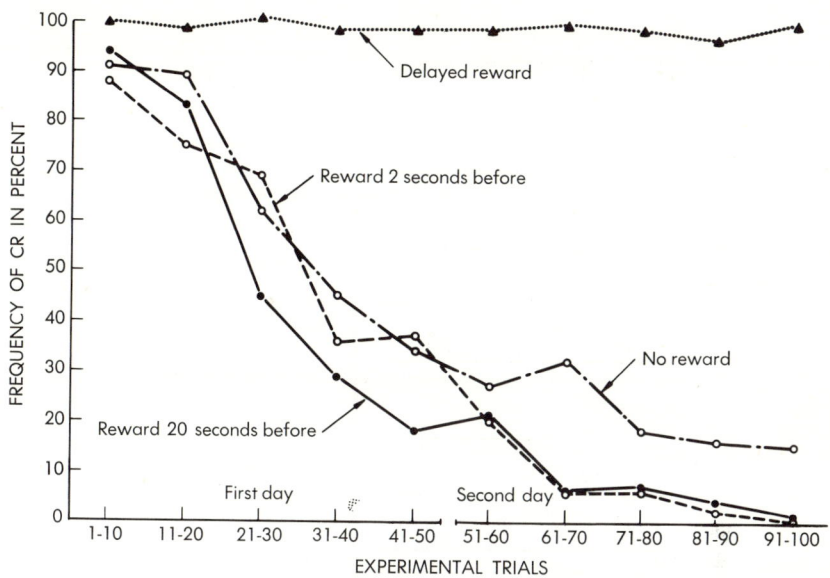

FIGURE 32-2. Reward delayed two seconds after the occurrence of a CR prevents its extinction; reward presented two seconds before the CR does not affect extinction. [From Nagaty, 1951.]

After puzzling over this, another student, David Egger, and I (1962, 1963) got the idea that since food in the mouth ordinarily is always followed by food in the stomach, the arrival of food in the stomach does not give any new information. Perhaps the reward occurs primarily at the point at which new information about food occurs. In testing this suggestion, we used the procedure of secondary reinforcement in which a neutral stimulus acquires the ability to act as a reward after it has been paired with food. We used this procedure because we could control more precisely the stimuli which we administered than the bar presses which the rat performed.

In order to test for the secondary reinforcing value of the stimulus that had been associated with food we used rats which had been trained to press a bar for food (without this stimulus) and then extinguished by nondelivery of food until they would press it only infrequently. Then with the feeder still disconnected, we made the bar deliver the stimulus, a tone or a light, that was being tested for secondary reinforcement and measured the ability of this stimulus to restore the habit. This procedure had the advantage of greater sensitivity since it is easier to restore an extinguished habit than to learn a new one; and we also got rid of the variability which is involved when the rats are first learning the skill of how to press a bar.

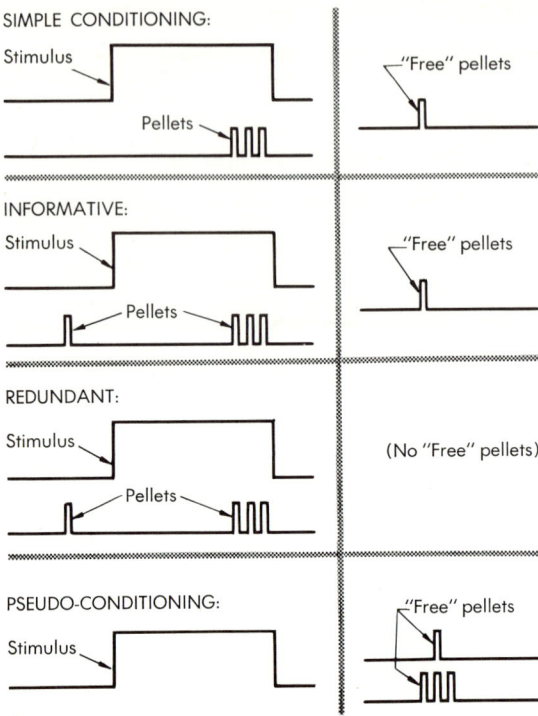

FIGURE 32-3. Schematic representation of the training procedure of the four groups used to test the information hypothesis of reinforcement. [*From Egger & Miller, 1963.*]

Figure 32-3 illustrates the design of the experiment. Let us start with the condition labelled "Redundant." To that group of hungry rats we gave one pellet first, followed by the stimulus, and then three pellets. This sequence was invariant. Thus the pellet reliably predicted the occurrence of the subsequent three pellets and the stimulus was redundant since it did not supply any new information.

How can we preserve the details of the foregoing situation and still make the stimulus informative? The way in which this was done is shown in the part of the figure labelled "informative." Here we used exactly the same sequence of one pellet, the stimulus and three pellets, but we gave occasional "free" single pellets between trials. Thus the single pellet did not reliably predict the subsequent occurrence of three pellets; these come only after the stimulus. Hence the stimulus did provide new information, namely that the first pellet was going to be followed by three additional pellets.

For purposes of comparison we used the conventional procedure for establishing secondary reinforcement which is represented in Figure 32-3 as "simple conditioning." We left out the pellet before the stimulus and merely had the stimulus predict the occurrence of three pellets. Between trials we gave the same "free" pellets that we gave in the other situation. Finally we had a control for pseudoconditioning in which both the stimulus and the pellets (sometimes single "free" and sometimes "three") were presented the same number of times as under the other conditions, but there was never any association between the stimulus and the delivery of pellets.

The results are shown in Figure 32-4. [The] rats were extinguished

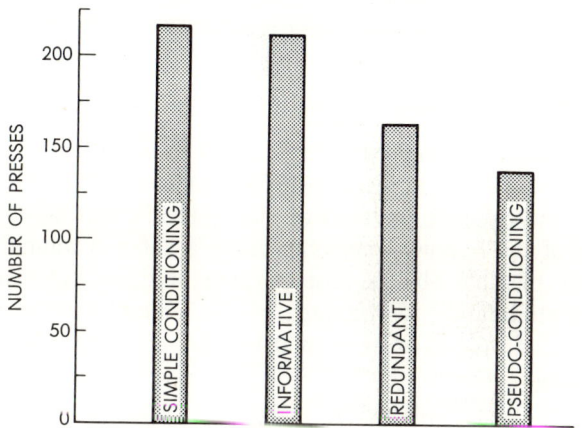

FIGURE 32-4. Food administered immediately before a CS does not interfere with the acquisition of secondary reinforcement, provided the stimulus remains an informative predictor of additional food, but does produce a substantial reduction, to a level not reliably different from the base line of pseudoconditioning, if it makes the CS redundant. [From Miller, 1961c.]

so that a certain amount of spontaneous recovery of bar pressing should occur while they were retrained under secondary reinforcement. Therefore, the proper base line is the number of presses of the pseudoconditioning group. . . . [The] conventional "simple conditioning" procedure and the informative procedure gave virtually the same results. In other words, the single pellet coming before the stimulus had no appreciable inhibiting effect on acquisition of secondary reward value when the stimulus was informative. . . . [When] the stimulus was redundant there was a considerable reduction in its reinforcement value as measured by the number of presses ($p < .01$). It is hard to say whether redundancy reduced the reinforcement to zero; in fact the difference from pseudoconditioning is not statistically reliable.

From this experiment, and another somewhat similar one which yielded similar results (Egger & Miller, 1962), we can conclude that the secondary reinforcement value of the stimulus is dependent on its informative value, which in turn, confirms our notion that perhaps the point at which reward occurs in a sequence is the point at which new information occurs concerning the delivery of food.

Finally, . . . the stimulus is not entirely redundant in the experiment just described. Although the single pellet predicts the trio of pellets for the redundant group, the stimulus does yield a little additional information, namely, that the three pellets will be delivered right now. So we can suppose that if we stretch out the time interval between the single pellet and the "redundant" stimulus, it will acquire secondary reinforcing value.

Hunger elicited by electrical stimulation of the brain

A somewhat different line of research has been carried on primarily in collaboration with E. E. Coons (1963), (Miller, 1957; 1960a, 1963b). It has been known since the days of Hess (1954) that stimulation in the lateral area of the hypothalamus can cause a satiated animal to eat, and also to gnaw inedible objects. The purpose of these experiments was to see whether stimulation in this area of the lateral hypothalamus has all of the functional properties of normal hunger, or whether it merely elicits reflex gnawing.

One reason for starting this line of work was that I had been singularly unsuccessful in establishing a learned drive based on hunger or thirst (Myers & Miller, 1954; Novin & Miller, 1962). The difficulties in these published, and yet other unpublished, attempts contrast with the ease of demonstrating that fear can be learned and then have all the functions of a normal drive (Miller, 1951). Immediately after the animal is exposed to the previously neutral cues, however, fear can be elicited rapidly by pain, while hunger and thirst build up more slowly. Perhaps this unfavourable practical condition, rather than any innate absence of a mechanism for a learned drive, is the source of difficulty with hunger. It seemed to me that, if the reaction to electrical stimulation of the brain did have the properties of normal hunger, eliciting it quickly by such stimulation might be a way of circumventing the unfavourable condition for learning that drive, if indeed that condition was the real source of the difficulty.

Furthermore, if the lateral "feeding area" of the hypothalamus could be demonstrated to be involved in normal hunger, perhaps recording from this area might yield a more direct measure of hunger. This measure might allow one to determine whether a stimulus with secondary reinforcing

Some Psychophysiological Studies of Motivation

value based on food elicits a decrease, an increase, or a decrease followed by an increase in hunger. This, and similar information on the immediate effects of a small nibble of food would allow the drive-reduction hypothesis of reinforcement (Miller, 1963a) to be tested more rigorously.

Finally, an obvious reason for using behavioural techniques to determine the functional properties of such electrical stimulation was to learn more about the mechanism of hunger.

How can we differentiate between reflex gnawing and a motivation such as hunger? If electrical stimulation of the lateral hypothalamus (ESLH) elicits the innate reflex of gnawing, we would not expect it to elicit a learned food-seeking response; if it elicits hunger we would expect it to motivate such a response. The first experiment tested whether ESLH resembles hunger in being able to elicit a habit previously learned on the basis of hunger and reinforced by food. Figure 32-5 shows the record

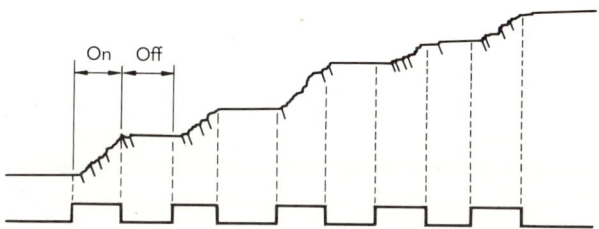

FIGURE 32-5. Food-seeking habit elicited by stimulating satiated rat in lateral hypothalamus. Rat had previously learned when hungry to press bar which occasionally delivers food. Each bar press moves pen up a small step. The downward spikes indicate when pressing the bar paid off with a pellet of food. The signal marker at the bottom indicates electrical stimulation of the brain. [From Miller, 1957.]

of a rat which had been trained when hungry to press a bar that delivers food on an average of once every thirty seconds. He is completely satiated at the beginning of this test; the flat initial portion of the record shows that he is not pressing the bar. Shortly after the current is turned on, stimulating the lateral feeding area of the hypothalamus with approximately 15 microamperes, he starts pressing the bar. Each press causes the pen to step up a small distance; every time food is delivered, the pen makes a downward pip. Shortly after the current is turned off, he stops pressing the bar, but when it is turned on again, he resumes pressing. It is quite clear that the ESLH will cause this thoroughly satiated rat to work at his learned habit of pressing the bar for food.

Similar experiments show that a stronger amount of current will elicit faster rates of bar pressing, exactly as one would expect if stimulation of this area has all of the properties of normal hunger. This relationship holds only within certain limits, however, because too strong a current induces motor side-effects and eventually convulsions that interfere with bar pressing.

But perhaps the ESLH only has a general activating effect, arousing the somnolent satiated rat, instead of eliciting a specific drive of hunger. How can we test for this possibility?

If the electrodes are properly placed, the stimulation will cause satiated rats to gnaw solid food but not to drink pure water. If such rats are tested when they are drinking water because they have been deprived of it for forty-eight hours, activation should cause them to drink more vigorously, but a strong enough hunger should cause them to leave the water to go to food. Our tests showed that ESLH has the latter effect.

But if the rats with these electrodes are tested with sugar water instead of pure water, the stimulation will cause them to drink it even though they have been thoroughly satiated on it. Furthermore, the sweeter the water is, the faster they will drink it in response to a given level of electrical stimulation; similarly, for a given sweetness, the stronger the stimulation, the faster they will drink it, within limits. As with normal hunger, these faster rates of drinking are caused by fewer and shorter pauses, rather than by faster rates during a given burst of licking.

Since the current elicits gnawing of solid foods, and lapping of liquid foods, the response to stimulation in this area of the brain is not defined in terms of a specific set of motor movements, biting or lapping, but in terms of a specific kind of sensory feedback, namely, that from the taste of food. I think that many more motor responses than we realize probably are determined by sensory feedback, rather than by an impulse for a specific muscle contraction (Miller, 1959, p. 251).

How strong is the hunger elicited by ESLH? Recently, Tenen and I (1964) have balanced hunger against the amount of quinine required to stop rats from drinking milk. In line with previous results (Miller, 1957; 1961c) we found that the more food-deprived rats are, the more quinine is required to stop them from drinking milk. We also found that, if they are completely satiated, the more current with which you stimulate the hypothalamus, the more quinine it takes to stop the rat from drinking the milk. Again, the effects of normal hunger and of ESLH are similar. Furthermore, the effects of ESLH are at least as strong as those of eighty-four hours of food deprivation.

The effects of food deprivation and ESLH are similar, but how do they summate? It could be that these two treatments would interfere with each other, or that only the stronger of the two would determine the amount of resistance to quinine. Actually, the effects of these two treatments do summate, as might be expected if they both involved the same mechanism. Higher concentrations of quinine are required to stop rats with specific amounts of both food deprivation and ESLH than with either treatment given separately.

As another indication of the strength of ESLH and its functional similarities to normal hunger Eric Steinbaum and I recently found that, if you give rats sufficient stimulation, you can cause them to overeat so that they become abnormally obese. But if rats are not forced to eat more than their daily ration in this way, they will compensate by reducing their ad lib eating and maintain approximately normal body weight.

Having demonstrated that ESLH can produce strong effects which have the properties of normal hunger, Coons and I have tried to condition eating suddenly elicited in this way immediately after the presentation of a neutral stimulus. While it would be unwise to conclude that such conditioning is completely impossible under all imaginable circumstances, I believe we can safely conclude that, even when the hunger is elicited suddenly by ESLH, it is much more difficult to condition it (if indeed such conditioning is possible at all) than to condition fear.

Finally, as Coons and I (Miller, 1960a) have shown, turning off ESLH serves as a reward, exactly as would be demanded by the drive-reduction hypothesis of reinforcement, but, paradoxically, turning on such stimulation also seems to act as a reward, a fact that is embarrassing for the drive-reduction hypothesis. While there are various ways in which this last embarrassing result might be accounted for without abandoning the drive-reduction hypothesis, this and other evidence has caused me to consider also a completely different hypothesis of reinforcement (Miller, 1963a).

Variety of effects from ventromedial nucleus of hypothalamus

A somewhat different line of research deals with the role of the ventromedial nucleus of the hypothalamus, a region which seems in some ways to be antagonistic to the lateral area which we have just been considering. It has been known for some time that bilateral lesions of the ventromedial nucleus will cause rats to overeat greatly and become obese. From this fact one might think that this lesion releases hunger from inhibition and makes it stronger. But Bailey, Stevenson and I (1950) showed that rats with such lesions would not work as hard at pressing a bar to get food and required less quinine to stop them from eating. Therefore, it seems reasonable to conclude that this lesion interferes with the complete satiation of hunger instead of releasing it from inhibition.

Finally, Teitelbaum and Epstein (1962) found that stimulation in the ventromedial nucleus of the hypothalamus will cause rats to stop eating, which is exactly what one might expect if it has an inhibitory effect on the lateral hypothalamus. We have found the same thing in our laboratory. One of my students, Franklin B. Krasne (1962), has observed the matter further and found that stimulation of this nucleus is aversive, so that rats will learn to press a bar to turn it off. Perhaps it is this aversive property which causes the rat to stop eating.

As might be expected if this were the case, Krasne also found that such stimulation would stop animals from drinking. Figure 32-6 summarises data on separate threshold tests for aversiveness as measured by pressing a bar to turn off the stimulation, stopping eating with only food and no bar present, and stopping drinking with only water present. For the different rats you can see that there is a high correlation among these thresholds. These results strongly suggest that the ventromedial nucleus may have other functions besides inhibiting the eating of rats when they are satiated.

As further evidence for such more general functioning, Krasne has studied the effects of lesions in the ventromedial nucleus on thirst. In order to control for the indirect effect mediated via food consumption, he gave all animals an amount of food adequate to maintain their weight, but restricted enough so that all rats would eat everything offered. As Figure 32-7 shows, he found that under these conditions, they all drank the same amount of tap water. However, putting quinine in the water stopped the lesioned animals more quickly than the normal controls. At the end of the experiment, all animals were given food ad lib: under these conditions the lesioned animals ate more food than the controls, showing that the lesions were in the right place.

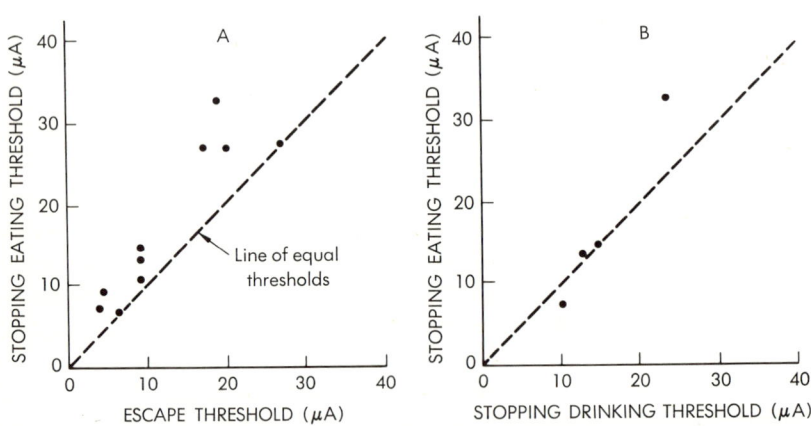

FIGURE 32-6. Correlation between strength of stimulation of the ventromedial nucleus of the hypothalamus required to inhibit eating for different rats and that required to motivate escape behavior or to stop drinking. [*From Krasne, 1962.*]

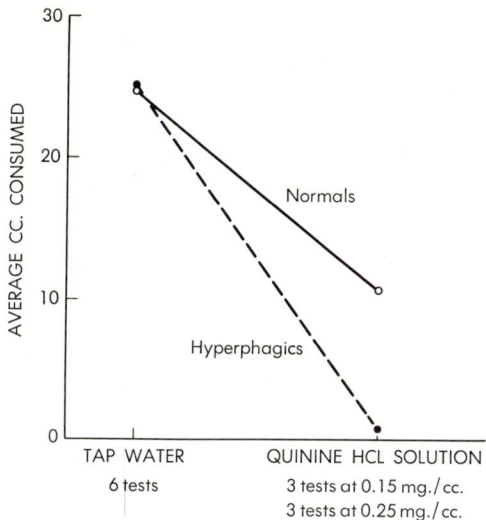

FIGURE 32-7. Rats with lesions in the ventromedial nucleus of the hypothalamus drink the same amount of tap water as normals, but have their drinking reduced much more than do normals when the water is lightly adulterated with quinine. [*Unpublished data by Franklin B. Krasne from the author's laboratory.*]

Chemical coding in the brain

Now let us turn to a slightly different but related topic, chemostimulation, which is giving us a more discriminative way than electrical stimulation to study the brain. One of my students, Grossman (1960; 1962a; 1962b), has used a double cannula which is implanted under anesthesia through the skull and later used to introduce liquids or crystals into a limited area of the brain. He aimed his first cannulas at the "feeding-drinking" area of the lateral hypothalamus of rats. He found that if he stimulated the rat's brain via the same cannula by acetylcholine or by carbachol, he caused satiated rats to drink in one experiment, or in another one, to perform a learned response of pressing a bar that delivered water. But if he stimulated exactly the same point in exactly the same way with epinephrine or norepinephrine, he caused satiated rats to eat or to press a different bar that delivered food. This result suggests that there is a chemical specificity for the eating and drinking elicited in this area of the brain.

Norepinephrine and acetylcholine are known to be involved in the peripheral transmission of neural impulses. But perhaps the effects which Grossman secured by injecting these substances into the brain are some sort of an artifact and are not really involved in normal hunger or thirst. How can we tell? A number of controls were run for factors such as osmotic pressure, pH, vasoconstriction, or vasodilation. But perhaps the most convincing evidence comes from the differential effects of certain blocking agents. From experiments on the peripheral nervous system it is known that atropine sulfate blocks the effect of acetylcholine and carbachol, while ethoxybutamoxane blocks those of epinephrine and norepinephrine. The first experiments showed that intraperitoneal injections of these two substances had similar differential blocking effects on the drinking and eating elicited respectively by putting crystals of carbachol or norepinephrine into the rat's brain. Furthermore, these two blocking agents had similar differential effects on normally induced hunger and thirst. This led us to believe that chemically different mechanisms are indeed involved in these two drives.

It is known that thirsty animals will not eat dry food. Is this merely because their dry mouth makes it unpleasant to swallow such food, which in turn further dehydrates them, or is there, in addition, some central mechanism, analogous to reciprocal inhibition, whereby the brain centres involved in thirst tend to inhibit those involved in hunger? Similarly, food-deprivation causes animals to drink less water. Is this merely because they do not need the water to process the dry food, or does it reflect a central incompatibility between the mechanisms involved in hunger and thirst?

The technique of chemostimulation seems to provide a way to answer these questions. The left-hand side of Figure 32-8 shows the results of an experiment on rats which had been deprived of food for twenty-four hours. You can see that administering norepinephrine to the lateral hypothalamus caused them to eat more than the normal control level, but administering carbachol caused them to eat markedly less. The other side of the figure shows symetrically opposite results: carbachol increased the water intake of normally thirsty rats, while norepinephrine decreased it. These results suggest that the antagonism between hunger and thirst may be partly central in origin.

Recently [Miller, Gottesman, and Emery (1964)] have been interested in two additional problems: (a) the dose-response effects of this type of chemostimulation of the brain, and (b) determining whether the effects of such stimulation have the more general properties of hunger and thirst, rather than eliciting specific gnawing or lapping reflexes. We ruled out any possible effect of gnawing versus lapping reflexes by using a liquid food which is lapped from a drinking tube in exactly the same way that water is. This liquid food was a commercially available balanced diet, Metrecal, to which enough salt had been added so that water-deprived animals would not drink it, whereas food-deprived animals would.

Figure 32-9 shows the results. The left-hand side shows the effects of increasing doses of carbachol. From the bottom curve we see that they

Some Psychophysiological Studies of Motivation

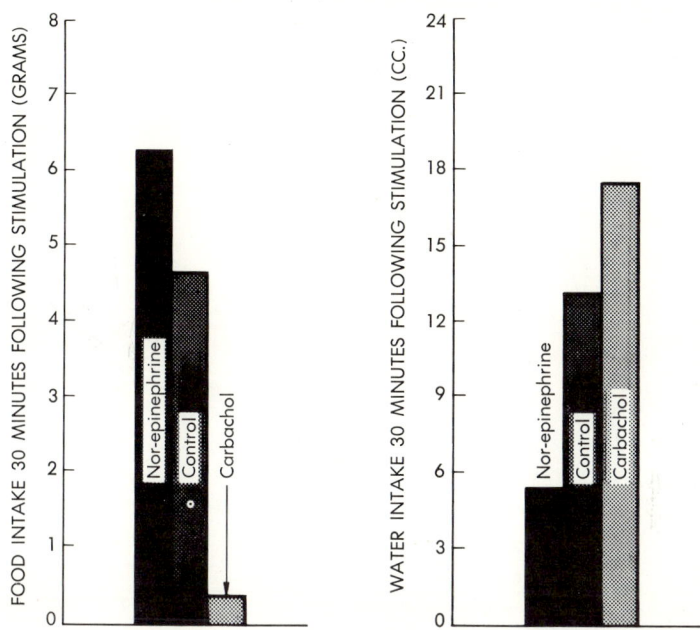

FIGURE 32-8. When introduced into the lateral hypothalamus, minute amounts of norepinephrine increased food intake of rats deprived of food for twenty-four hours, while similar stimulation by carbachol reduces food intake. The same substances via the same cannula have opposite effects in similar tests for water intake. [From Grossman, 1962a.]

produce very little increase in the amount of Metrecal drunk, and from the top curve, that they produce a much greater increase in the amount of water drunk. On the right-hand side, we see that norepinephrine produces the opposite result; increasing doses produce little effect on the amount of water drunk, and a great increase in the amount of Metrecal drunk. In both cases, the effects tend to drop off when the doses become too high (illustrated in Figure 32-9 only for norepinephrine), because such doses produce lethargy or convulsions that interfere with eating or drinking.

It is interesting to note that 2.7×10^{-10} moles, or, in other words, five one hundred millionths of a gram of carbachol, will elicit drinking. Somewhat more norepinephrine is required to elicit eating. But in both cases, it is not unreasonable to assume that the concentrations in brain tissue as a result of these injections are in the same order of magnitude as those occurring at the active sites of synapses that are firing.

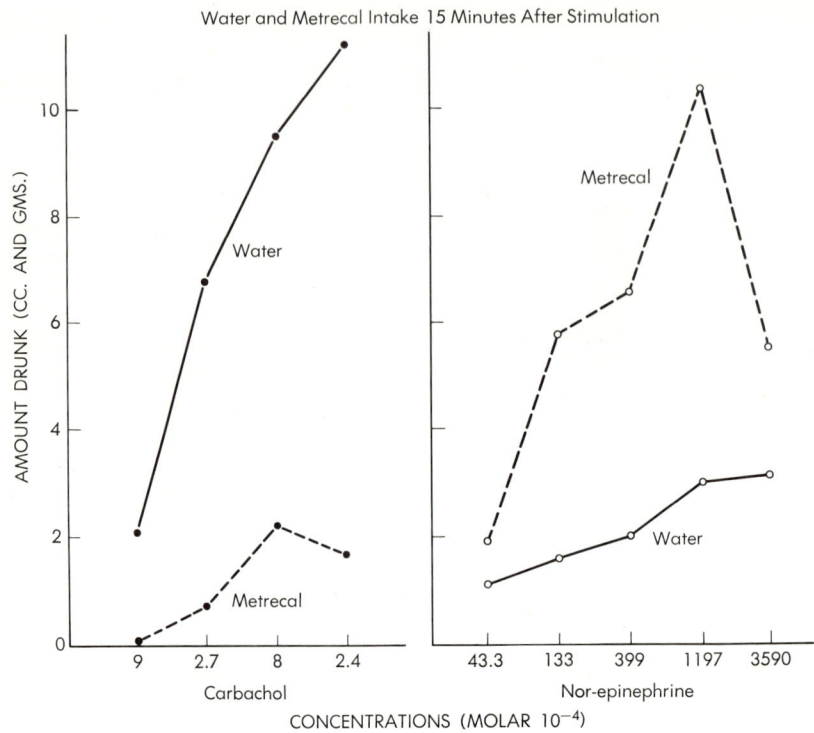

FIGURE 32-9. Dose-response curves for effects of carbachol and of norepinephrine in the lateral hypothalamus on consumption of liquid food and of water. [Data from Miller, Gottesman and Emery, 1964.]

Exploratory results show that the administration of carbachol to the motor cortex does not produce drinking. The first effect is convulsions when injected into the hypothalamus, which was roughly 100 times higher than the minimal dose required to elicit drinking there.

At the same time, another student, George Wolf, and I (1964) have been using a combination of the techniques of chemostimulation and electrolytic lesions to try to track down the neural systems involved in drinking elicited by stimulation of cholinergic neurons. We find that carbachol will elicit drinking when injected into the preoptic area, which is anterior to the "feeding-drinking" area of the hypothalamus, and that it will also elicit drinking if injected into the posterior hypothalamus. Lesions in these anterior or posterior areas do not eliminate either normal drinking or drinking elicited by carbachol in the lateral hypothalamus. On the other hand, the immediate effect of bilateral lesions in the lateral hypothalamus is virtually to eliminate both normal drinking and drinking elicited by carbachol injected either anterior or posterior to this area. After a few weeks, normal drinking is largely recovered. But drinking in response to carbachol in these two other areas showed little, if any, such recovery. Our tentative conclusion from these results is that the "feeding-drinking" area of the lateral hypothalamus plays a primary role in thirst elicited centrally by chemostimulation of these two other areas.

Coons, Fonberg and I (1964) have been using a similar combination of the lesioning and electrical stimulation techniques to begin to track down the neuromechanisms involved in the self-rewarding effect originally reported by Olds and Milner (1954). We find that lesions in the hypothalamus virtually abolish the self-rewarding effect elicited by stimulation in the cingulate area, while lesions in the cingulate area leave the self-rewarding effect of hypothalamic stimulation relatively unaffected. The next question to be asked is whether various differential blocking agents will produce temporary biochemical lesions with effects similar to those of the physical ones. Such tests could throw light on the possible chemical coding of the reward and aversion systems which can be activated by direct electrical stimulation of the brain.

A method for studying behavioral effects of illness

In the final studies which I want to report, Holmes and I (1963) started out trying to manipulate hunger and thirst in a different way, namely, by a bacterial endotoxin. Dubos and Schaedler (1961) had found that a bacterial endotoxin from E. coli inhibited the consumption of water by mice. We thought that this might be a selective tool for investigating further the mechanism of thirst. Our original aim was to see if this effect could be duplicated in rats, and if so, whether it was specific to thirst or also affected hunger. If it was specific, we thought we might go on to see whether thirst could be inhibited by administering minute amounts directly into specific sites in the brain as well as by administering larger amounts intraperitoneally.

Exploratory work showed that about 75 milligrams per kilo administered intraperitoneally (which was about one-fourth of the dose that would kill 50 percent of the rats) would reduce the daily water intake below 50 percent of normal. Next we went on to more exact studies, one of which determined the time of onset of the effect. In order to do this we trained rats to press a bar, again on a variable interval schedule, so they got a drop of water on the average of once every 30 seconds. Figure 32-10 is a photograph of a typical record of performance. The top of the figure shows that after an injection of isotonic saline, the rat keeps working away at a steady rate for water. The lower half of the figure shows that after the injection of the toxin, the rat works steadily for the water until between thirty and forty-five minutes later, when suddenly it practically stops working. We have similar records for a total of fourteen rats.

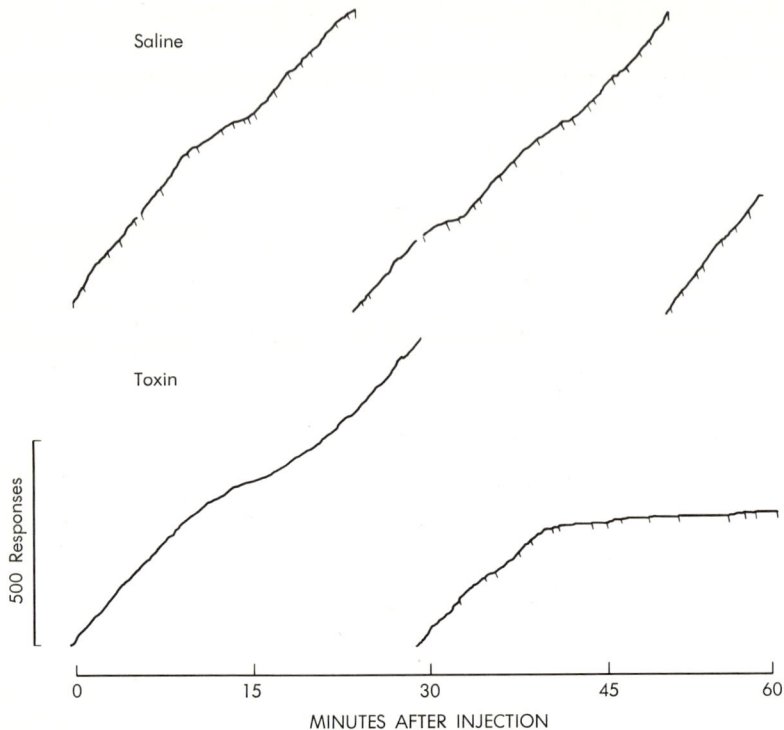

FIGURE 32-10. Effects of injection of isotonic saline (upper record) or bacterial toxin (lower record) on the rate at which thirsty rats will press a bar to get water. Injections given at beginning of one-hour test. Each bar press raises the pen a small step; downward spikes indicate when water was delivered. When pen reaches top of paper, it automatically starts over again at bottom.

It is interesting that these rats will virtually stop bar pressing. If they are given water after such a period of not working, they will drink at least 5 milliliters. This demonstrates that the bar-pressing response is more sensitive than the consummatory one, although the volume consumed is also reduced.

The next test investigated the duration of the effect. Rats on ad lib food were given water for thirty minutes at a certain time each day. Different groups were given injections of the toxin at various intervals before the drinking test. For each rat the effect was calculated as a percentage of his normal intake. Figure 32-11 shows the results. . . . [There] was a considerable reduction when they were tested one hour after the toxin, at least as much when they were tested three hours after the toxin, and that the effect gradually wore off so that those tested forty-eight hours later drank the normal amount.

We also gave two other groups of rats analogous tests in which we measured the amount of food eaten. As Figure 32-11 shows, food consumption was reduced greatly twenty-four hours after the toxin and was still considerably reduced forty-eight hours afterwards.

At first we thought that this reduction in eating might be an indirect effect of the fact that the toxin stopped the rats from drinking since thirst is known to reduce the consumption of food. We tested this in two ways. First, we let water-deprived rats drink one hour before injection and tested them three hours later, so that they did not have a chance to get very thirsty. Their food consumption was found to be reduced to 30 percent of normal. The second test involved rats which were given the toxin and then fed water through a stomach tube. We had previously determined that tube feeding with water would not appreciably interfere with eating. But, if the rats had received the toxin, they cut down their eating

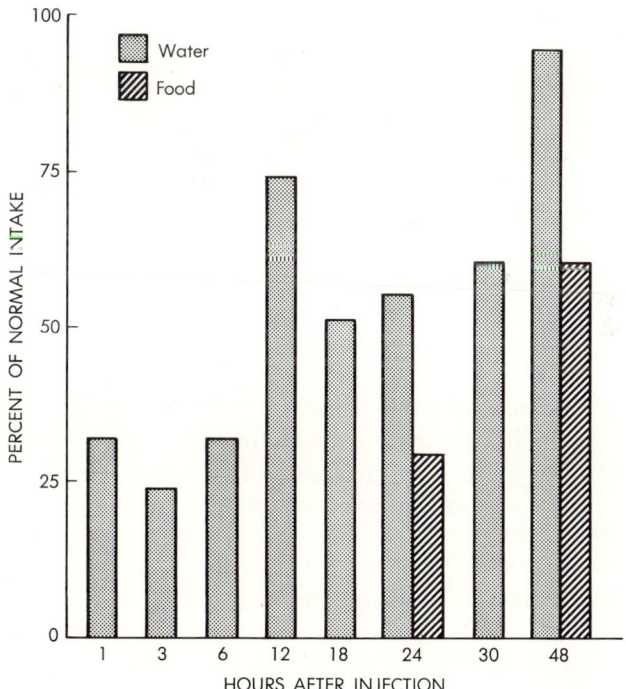

FIGURE 32-11. Effects of bacterial endotoxin injection on subsequent water or food intake. Each bar represents the average intake of a different group of six rats tested at the specified time after injection.

even though their stomachs had just been loaded with 10 milliliters of water. We concluded that the inhibition of eating was not a secondary effect of dehydration.

The foregoing results spoiled our prospects of using this toxin as an agent to affect differentially thirst and hunger. After a certain amount of disappointment, however, we decided that we might be able to capitalize on this generalized effect; perhaps it provided a way of studying the behavioural effects of feeling ill. One of the things we did to study the generality of the effect of the toxin was to use rats which had been trained to press a bar for the rewarding effects of electrical stimulation in the lateral hypothalamus.

This work was started by Holmes and continued by Edward E. Stricker. They found that the toxin would virtually eliminate bar pressing for such a reward. But rats will also work to turn off electrical stimulation in this area. The toxin reduces the rate of turning off such stimulation, but the tentative results that we have to date suggest that it does not come as close to eliminating it. Finally, Mrs. Eleanor R. Adair is testing the effects of the toxin in a situation in which rats have to press a bar to cause a motor-driven activity wheel in which they must walk to be temporarily stopped. The toxin does not seem to produce any obvious decrement in this task; in fact, preliminary results suggest that it may possibly even increase the rate of such bar pressing, much as the toxins of other diseases may cause me to be more likely to call out: "Turn off that confounded ratio!"

What is the mechanism of the toxin's effects? Other people have speculated that the cessation of drinking which was originally observed, occurred because the toxin poisons the brain. But Holmes and I (1963) found that injections directly into the eating-drinking area of the lateral hypothalamus did not affect pressing a bar for water if the dose was somewhat below that which, when injected intraperitoneally, would stop bar pressing. This occurred in spite of the fact that the concentration in this area of the brain must have been enormously higher than that when the same dose was given intraperitoneally. In order to check on whether we were in the eating-drinking area, we injected a little bit of the local anesthetic, lidocaine, and found that this would stop the animals from pressing the bar for food. One rat had the cannula in the wrong area, as discovered by subsequent histology; fortunately this rat was the only one of five which did not respond to an injection of lidocaine by stopping pressing the bar. Therefore, I think it is fairly clear that this toxin, if it acts directly on the brain, does not act directly on the eating-drinking area of the lateral hypothalamus.

You will remember that there is a thirty to forty-five minute interval between the injection of the toxin and its behavioural effects. This seems more than enough time for the toxin to get through the blood stream and into the brain. So we wondered what happens during that latent period. It is possible that the toxin does not act directly on the brain, but that it sets off a series of changes in the body which after thirty or forty-five minutes produce an end product, perhaps a factor X in the blood, which is what affects the brain and makes the animal feel sick. In an attempt to locate such a factor, we extracted the serum from blood drawn from a rat at the height of the toxin effect. But an injection of such serum into the eating-drinking area of the hypothalamus did not stop the rat from eating. This could mean that there is no "factor X" in the serum, that this "factor X" was destroyed very rapidly while we were handling the blood, or that we injected into the wrong area of the brain. A great deal more work remains to be done.

The general notion behind this work is that, if we could localize the region in the brain that is involved in this general reaction of feeling sick, we might learn more about the mechanism of feeling sick and could provide a rational basis for devising steps to control the behavioral effects of illness. As a more modest goal, our methods might provide a good way to test certain drugs. For example, it is hard to get any animal test which is sensitive to the psychological benefits of aspirin, although aspirin seems to be quite effective in making ill people feel better. Perhaps our procedures could be used as screening tests to discover a drug which would be superior to aspirin.

Whatever the results of such work may be, I believe it would be highly desirable to study in more detail the psychological effects of physical illness. One of my children, for example, is ordinarily very good and pleasant, but sometimes becomes a little devil, and we almost always find that shortly afterwards this child comes down with a cold or other illness, that is, the child has really been getting sick, but the physical symptoms do not show up until after the psychological ones. I find that if I have been ill with certain types of grippe or flu, I can recover to a point where I am perfectly able to do a task provided that I must, for example, prepare and deliver a lecture for a class which meets on that day. But, if I have a choice about doing something, I suffer a "paralysis of initiative" so that, for example, I will not prepare a lecture for the next week or work effectively on writing a paper for publication. Perhaps you have observed such effects of certain kinds of illness on yourselves and others.

People who have had infectious hepatitis are almost universally observed to go into what is usually described as a reasonably severe depression for a considerable time afterwards. Even after they seem to have recovered physically, as indicated by medical tests, they still have this psychological depression. I believe it would be quite interesting to study the psychological effects of various forms of illness. To begin with, one could select people who were suffering from different kinds of illness, test them, even with something as simple as an adjective check list

(Nowlis and Nowlis, 1956), to see if different patterns of psychological effects are associated with different types of illness. The same patients could be retested after thorough recovery. I think such work could conceivably provide a clue to some of the mechanisms involved in personality changes, or even in mental illness, because I am convinced that people undergo personality changes when they are suffering from different kinds of illness. For example some children suffer hallucinatory nightmares as a relatively specific reaction to a strep throat. . . .

VI

EXTINCTION AND THE VARIETIES OF INHIBITION

33

"Inhibition of Reinforcement" and Phenomena of Experimental Extinction[1]

CARL IVER HOVLAND

In the literature on conditioned reflexes, two contrasted varieties of curves of experimental extinction have been described. The first type, illustrated in the experiments of Pavlov (1927), Kleitman and Crisler (1927), Switzer (1930) and others, is characterized by a continuous decline in the magnitude of the conditioned response on successive unreinforced elicitations. The decline is rapid at first, then more and more gradual. The second type, reported by Switzer (1933), Scott (1930), Hudgins (1933) and Hilgard and Marquis (1935), shows a larger response on the second or third extinction trial than on the first, demonstrating the initial rise characteristic of these curves. Hull (1934), in his summary of studies of conditioned reflexes, points out that "as yet the experimental conditions which bring about these two types of curve have not been determined" (p. 438).

The initial rise in the extinction curves of the second variety has been attributed to a "practice effect" or "improvement through use." This fails to explain why the rise is not uniformly observed. Research by the writer on the irradiation of conditioned responses has suggested an explanation based upon the experimental conditions of the reinforcement process. There appears to be a negative adaptation to continuous reinforcement, an effect which may be labeled, for descriptive purposes, the *inhibition of reinforcement*. Following protracted reinforcement the omission of the unconditioned stimulus might be expected to produce *disinhibition,* resulting in an augmentation of response on the second or third extinction trial. This explanation for the rise in their extinction curves has been recently proposed by Hilgard and Marquis: "The first extinction trial is followed by altered conditions. . . . This unexpected omission may act as a disinhibitor, and result in a larger response . . . on the second trial" (1935, p. 48).

[1] Reprinted with permission from the *Proceedings of the National Academy of Sciences,* 1936, 22, 430–433.

The proposed hypothesis of inhibition of reinforcement, in conjunction with other recognized conditioned response principles, would lead to the following deductions: (1) Inhibition of reinforcement should increase with an increase in the number of massed reinforcements. An initial rise in the curve of extinction should consequently be expected only when a considerable number of massed reinforcements have produced "inhibition" in sufficient quantity to make possible "disinhibition." Some experimental evidence for the validity of this deduction is afforded by Wenger's observations that more inhibition is manifested after twenty-five than after twenty reinforcements. (2) When reinforcements are distributed over a long period of time the inhibition of reinforcement should be dissipated between successive reinforcements, and hence no initial rise in the extinction curve due to disinhibition should be produced. This deduction is in accord with the statement of Pavlov that "one and the same stimulus which is constantly reinforced and repeated many times at long intervals of time loses only little of its effect: the same stimulus when applied at short intervals of time quickly diminishes in its effect" (1927, p. 248). (3) Similarly, if a period of time is allowed to elapse between conditioning and extinction, the "inhibitory" process, declining more rapidly than the "excitatory" [cf. Pavlov (1928), ". . . the process of internal inhibition is more labile (unstable) than that of stimulation" (p. 138); Pavlov (1927, pp. 58 ff. and 99); and Hull (1935, p. 503)], should be dissipated; consequently no disinhibition, producing an initial rise in the curve of extinction, should be anticipated.

The experimental procedure used to test the above deductions was the following: the response conditioned was the galvanic skin reaction. The Burr-Lane vacuum-tube electrometer was employed for measuring potential changes independently of resistance variations. An electric shock produced by an inductorium was the unconditioned stimulus. The conditioned stimulus was a tone of 1000 cycles, 40 decibels above the threshold, produced by a beat-frequency oscillator. The stimuli were presented automatically; the tone was sounded for 400 msc. and was followed, after a pause of 100 msc., by the shock.

Four groups, of twenty subjects each, were equated on the basis of galvanic response to the unconditioned stimulus before conditioning. Group I was given 8 reinforcements. Extinction was started immediately after conditioning. The subjects in Group II were given three times as many reinforcements; extinction was likewise begun immediately after reinforcement. Group III was given the same number of reinforcements as Group II but 30 minutes were allowed to elapse between reinforcements and extinction. Twenty-four reinforcements were likewise given to Group IV, but they were divided into three groups of eight reinforcements each, separated by 30-minute intervals. Extinction was begun immediately after

"Inhibition of Reinforcement"

the termination of the last group of reinforcements. In all cases the reinforcements and extinction trials were given at approximately one-minute intervals, varied slightly to prevent temporal conditioning.

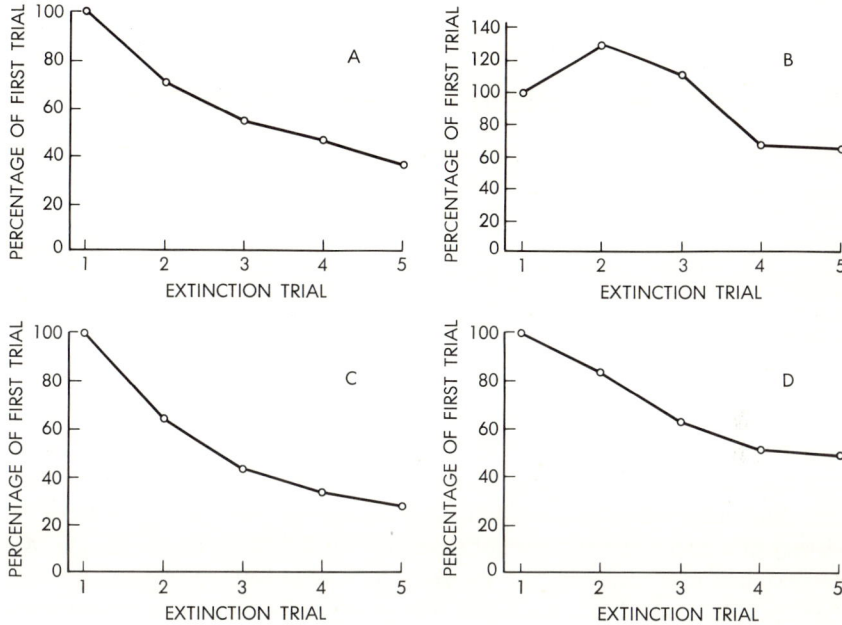

FIGURE 33-1. Extinction curves following various conditions of reinforcement. Results plotted in terms of ratios (in percent) of responses on successive extinction trials to response on first extinction trial. (A) 8 reinforcements. Extinction immediately. (B) 24 reinforcements. Extinction immediately. (C) 24 reinforcements, distributed into 3 groups of 8 each. Rest period of 30 minutes between groups. Extinction immediately after last group of reinforcements. (D) 24 reinforcements. Extinction 30 minutes after last reinforcement.

The results, presented in the accompanying figure, are in accord with the deductions, and thus constitute confirmatory evidence for the hypothesis of inhibition of reinforcement. When few reinforcements are given, a continuous fall in the extinction curve results (A). With a much larger number of reinforcements, however, the curve manifests an initial rise (B), in harmony with the theoretical expectation. When the reinforcements are distributed (C), or when time is allowed to elapse between reinforcements and extinction (D), no initial rise is obtained. Statistical procedures show the results to be reliable, and over 90 percent of the individual curves follow the pattern of the group average for the particular experimental procedure employed.

34

Quantitative Studies of the Interaction of Simple Habits: Recovery from Specific and Generalized Effects of Extinction[1]

DOUGLAS G. ELLSON

This study was designed to obtain a preliminary quantification of two behavior principles used by Hull (1937) in his derivation of more complex behavior. They are: (a) the rate of recovery of habit strength as a function of time interval following extinction, and (b) the rate of recovery of a habit as a function of time interval following the extinction of a second habit. These will be referred to respectively as recovery from (a) specific, and (b) generalized, effects of extinction. Two bar-pressing habits similar to those described by Skinner (1932) and Youtz (1938a) were used in the experiment.

Youtz found with a horizontal-bar-pressing habit that after extinction to a point where no responses were made for twenty minutes, a second extinction twenty-four hours later showed approximately 55 percent recovery. Miller and Stevenson (1936) found negative acceleration in the rate of recovery of speed of running a straight alley. One part of the present experiment is designed to plot the amount of recovery of the bar-pressing response from *specific* extinction effects as a function of time following extinction. A second part is intended to plot the amount of recovery of the bar-pressing habit from *generalized* extinction effects, under conditions as similar as possible to the first. Youtz (1939) has shown convincingly that the extinction of one bar-pressing habit reduces the strength of another similar habit. If extinction is a state of relaxation, as suggested by Wenger (1937), then presumably the curves of recovery from the specific effects and from generalized effects of extinction should be parallel. Although this experiment does not offer a direct test of Wenger's hypothesis, the data obtained should have a bearing upon it.

[1] Reprinted from the *Journal of Experimental Psychology*, 1938, 23, 339–358, with permission from the American Psychological Association and the author.

The Interaction of Simple Habits

Subjects and apparatus

Two hundred albino rats from sixty to one hundred days of age were used as subjects. All except eight were male. The females were distributed among the eight experimental groups. Twenty-nine additional animals were discarded in the course of the experiment, fourteen for failure to learn, and fifteen because of extreme measures on one of the balancing criteria. Eight of the animals, distributed equally among the experimental groups, had been used previously in a maze experiment. The remainder had had no training of any kind.

The apparatus consisted of four separate double-walled boxes, similar to those used by Skinner and Youtz, and a constant-speed polygraph having eight markers. The experimental boxes were insulated with three inches of rock wool. The rat's compartment of each box, 12 by 12 by 12 inches, was lighted by means of a 7.5-watt bulb resting on a double-paned observation window in the top of the box. The laboratory vacuum system supplied ventilation. One end of the rat's compartment was formed by a panel through which a vertical and a horizontal bar (see Fig. 34-1) could be introduced by means of levers outside the box. When either bar was retracted behind the panel, a shutter automatically closed the slot in the panel through which the bar had been extended.

When the bars were in the position where they were operated by the rat, they projected one-half inch from the panel. A downward pressure of fifteen grams and a sidewise pressure to the left of eight grams were required to move the horizontal (H) and the vertical (V) bars respectively. The movement of each bar was recorded by a separate marker on the polygraph. The mercury-cup switches operated by the bars were designed to record movements of $\frac{3}{16}$ inch or more, the maximum movement being $\frac{3}{8}$ inch. Slight jiggling movements not involving a definite pressure response did not activate the markers.

A knife switch on the outside of each box could be set so that a recorded pressure on either bar would operate an electromagnetic food mechanism which delivered a small pellet of food to the tray below the bar. The accompanying click of the mechanism was heard as a thud inside the box. The pellets of food were made from a calf-meal mash rolled into $\frac{1}{8}$-inch cylinders and cut into $\frac{1}{4}$-inch sections, each pellet weighing .05 gram when dry.

Procedure

For two or more weeks the subjects were housed in the laboratory and fed at the usual time of beginning experimentation in order to establish a feeding and activity rhythm. Three days before being used in the

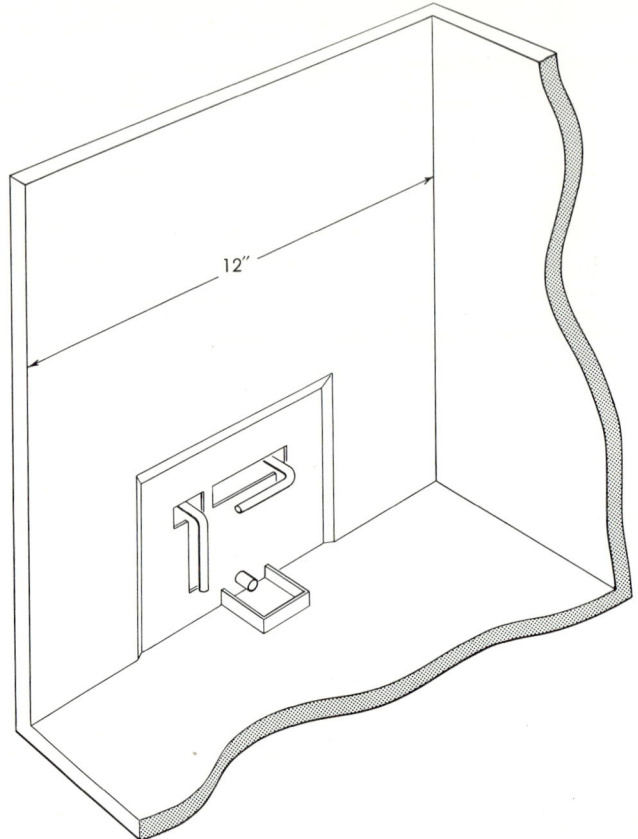

FIGURE 34-1. View of panel end of rat's compartment in the experimental boxes. Both bars are shown in position to be operated. During the experiment, only one bar was presented at a time. When either bar was withdrawn, a metal shutter automatically closed the opening in the panel.

experiment the animals were placed in individual cages and each day fed all they would eat in a one-hour period. During the experiment proper they received only the 120 pellets incidental to habituation and training.

The two problems involved in this study, (a) the rate of spontaneous recovery from the primary effects of extinction and (b) the rate of recovery from the generalized effects of extinction, were approached by separate experiments, each having four subgroups. The use of four experimental boxes made it possible to run four rats at a time, one in each subgroup. In alternate three-day periods (the time required to complete the procedure with four animals in one experiment) four rats were run in

The Interaction of Simple Habits

each experiment. Habituation and training procedures were the same in both experiments. In Experiment I, on the third day the horizontal-bar habit was extinguished and its recovery measured after four different intervals, using a separate group of twenty-five animals for each interval. In Experiment II, the vertical-bar habit was first extinguished and the recovery of the horizontal-bar habit tested after the same four intervals. A detailed account of the daily procedure is given below.

DAY 1. *Habituation to box and to the click of the food mechanism.* The four animals were placed in the experimental boxes late in the evening and left overnight. In the morning they were returned to their living cages for ten minutes, during which time ten pellets of food were placed in the food tray of each box. The animals were then returned to their respective boxes and allowed to eat the food and explore for thirty minutes. Two more similar ½-hour habituation periods were given, each followed by the ten-minute intermission. After the intermission following the last period, the animals were again placed in the boxes, this time with no food in the tray. During this period thirty pellets were given one at a time by the experimenter, who operated the food mechanism by means of a switch outside the box. Each pellet was delivered only after the preceding one had been eaten. By this procedure the animals learned to respond at once to the sound of the mechanism by obtaining the food. This was done with the expectation that they would secure the reward quickly after they had pressed the bar during the training on the following day, and thus learning would be facilitated. After thirty pellets had been given in this way the animals were returned to their living cages.

DAY 2. *Training of the vertical and horizontal bar habits.* The animals were placed in their respective boxes, the food mechanism circuit connected so as to deliver food when the bar was depressed, and the *H*-bar introduced. A piece of moist food was placed behind the panel so that the food odor was drawn through the slot behind the bar by the ventilating system. In investigating this odor, the animals sooner or later incidentally pressed the bar and a pellet was automatically delivered to the tray. The bar was withdrawn after fifteen such reinforced trials, and the animals returned to their living cages for thirty minutes. Then fifteen more reinforced trials were given, these with the odor stimulus removed. A similar training of the *V*-bar habit was begun thirty minutes later, again with the odor stimulus for the first fifteen trials only. Thus thirty reinforcements were given on each habit.

Not all the animals learned immediately. In cases when ten or fifteen minutes elapsed without a response on the bar, the back of the experimental box was opened and one or both of two expedients employed. An electric fan was turned on to increase the current of odor-laden air passing through the slot behind the bar, or a screw-driver with a small amount of moist food smeared on it was pushed through the slot and rattled gently. If still no response occurred within ten minutes or so, the animal was discarded.

DAY 3. *Extinction and tests of recovery.* Habituation and training days were the same for all animals. A different procedure was used for the animals in Experiment I and Experiment II on the third day.

PROCEDURE OF EXPERIMENT I. *Recovery from the specific effects of extinction.* The four animals were placed in their respective boxes and the H-bar introduced immediately, with the switches set to record responses but not to operate the food mechanism. Each animal was permitted to press the bar until a period of five minutes elapsed in which it had made no response. At the end of this period the bar was retracted behind the panel and the rat returned to its living cage for the remainder of the recovery interval assigned to that particular animal. The recovery intervals used were 5.5, 25, 65, and 185 minutes, measured from the time of the last response preceding the 5-minute criterion period. At the end of the interval each rat was again placed in its experimental box and given a second period of extinction on the H-bar habit to the same 5-minute criterion, to test recovery.[2]

PROCEDURE OF EXPERIMENT II. *Recovery from the generalized effects of extinction.* The procedure was the same as that for Experiment I except that the first period of nonreward was given on the V-bar habit. Recovery was measured by test of the H-bar habit as before.

Twenty-five animals were used in each of the eight groups. The four subgroups in Experiment I and the four in Experiment II were balanced by selection of group members on the basis of recorded performance on days 2 and 3 with respect to (a) learning time for both habits and (b) number of responses made during the first extinction. This selection resulted in a random distribution of the four groups in each experiment among the four experimental boxes. The large number of animals employed and the alternation in the running of Experiments I and II were relied upon to make the two experiments comparable. Table 34-1 gives measures by which the success of balancing may be judged. Because of the difficulty of equalizing extreme cases with only twenty-five animals in each

---

[2] The animal in the 5.5-minute-interval group was carried to its living cage and placed inside; the cover of the cage was closed and opened, and the animal immediately returned to the box for the test of recovery. This procedure occupied 30 seconds which, added to the 5-minute criterion period, accounts for 5.5 minutes of recovery in this group. The additional recovery time with the remaining groups was spent in the living cages.

TABLE 34-1

Equivalence of experimental groups*

EXPERIMENT I. FIRST EXTINCTION ON H-BAR HABIT

Measure	Group (recovery interval used)				Mean of all 100 cases
	5.5 min.	25 min.	65 min.	185 min.	
H-bar learning time in minutes	10.9	11.0	10.9	10.3	10.8
V-bar learning time in minutes	13.2	11.5	8.9	10.4	11.0
No. responses, first extinction	49.9	50.0	48.9	50.1	49.7
Time for extinction, in minutes	15.0	16.3	15.7	17.3	16.0
Rate (mean interval between responses in minutes)	.31	.39	.33	.37	.35

EXPERIMENT II. FIRST EXTINCTION ON V-BAR HABIT

Measure	Group (recovery interval used)				Mean of all 100 cases
	5.5 min.	25 min.	65 min.	185 min.	
H-bar learning time in minutes	11.0	11.4	11.1	11.0	11.2
V-bar learning time in minutes	13.6	12.0	9.9	12.5	12.0
No. responses, first extinction	42.4	42.2	41.0	42.1	42.0
Time for extinction in minutes	12.7	11.0	10.7	12.8	11.9
Rate (mean interval between responses in minutes)	.32	.27	.22	.42	.31

* Measures of learning time and extinction. Experiments I and II can be compared only for learning time, since the first extinction was on the H-bar habit in Experiment I and on the V-bar habit in Experiment II.

group, rats giving more than 125 responses during the first nonreward period on either habit were excluded from the regular groups. The figure 125 was selected arbitrarily early in the experiment as being approximately twice the mean number of responses made during the first extinction. This caused the elimination of eleven animals in Experiment I, and four animals in Experiment II.

Results and discussion

Relationship between learning and extinction. The correlation (r) between total time required to make thirty reinforced responses during the learning and the number of responses made before the 5-minute criterion was reached during the first extinction on the following day was — .14 ± .06 for both the horizontal and vertical bar habits. These correlations are based on 111 and 104 cases respectively, the animals making more than 125 responses being included here although excluded from the experiment proper. These figures differ radically from those found by Youtz (1938a, 1938b) who obtained a rho of + .69 ± .18 (based on ten rats for the corresponding measures with twenty-four hours between learning and extinction, and — .77 ± .14 (based on nine rats) when the extinction occurred immediately at the conclusion of learning. Youtz trained only the horizontal-bar habit, giving forty reinforcements, ten per day for four days, and used a 20-minute criterion of extinction. The complete reversal in Youtz's results, together with his small number of cases, makes it seem likely that the small negative correlation found in the present experiment more nearly represents the true figure, at least when extinction occurs on the day following learning.

Recovery from the specific effects of extinction. Youtz (1938a) has demonstrated spontaneous recovery of the bar-pressing habit following its weakening by nonreward (extinction). In a later paper (1939) he also showed that the extinction of one bar-pressing habit weakened a second similar habit. The present experiment extends this work to plot the curve of recovery in both stiuations under comparable conditions. This section presents spontaneous recovery in terms of three measures: (1) number of responses made before the 5-minute criterion was reached, (2) time from first to last response, and (3) rate of response, i.e., the mean interval between responses. This last measure is obtained by dividing time by the number of responses, separate scores being calculated for each rat. The means σ_m's, and medians for these three measures are presented in Table 34-2 for each of the four recovery intervals. The reliability of difference between means for the four recovery interval groups is given in Table 34-3. Figure 34-2 shows the distributions of one of these measures (number of responses), together with the mean and median curves. These distributions are fairly typical of those for the other measures.

Figure 34-3 presents the recovery in terms of mean number of responses, together with the empirical equation describing the function. It can be seen from Figure 34-2 that the distribution for the 5.5-minute-interval group is decidedly skewed, causing the mean to fall considerably above the median in this group. For this reason the equations for the medians were also calculated, and are presented [in the description of] Figure 34-3. However, the mathematical expressions show only slight differences.

The generality of these mathematical statements of recovery can be determined only by further experimentation of two kinds. Recovery as

TABLE 34-2

Data for Experiment I. Measures of recovery from the specific effects of extinction*

MEASURE OF RECOVERY	FIRST PERIOD OF EXTINCTION ON H-BAR HABIT (N = 100)	RECOVERY INTERVAL GROUP			
		5.5 min.	25 min.	65 min.	185 min.
(a) *No. responses*					
Mean	49.7	7.6	14.4	19.5	24.4
σm	2.6	1.7	1.8	3.9	4.5
Median	43.3	3.0	13.5	18.0	21.0
(b) *Time to reach criterion (min.)*					
Mean	16.0	2.6	5.0	8.4	11.6
σm	.97	.64	.92	1.24	1.76
Median	15.5	1.2	4.1	7.4	9.0
(c) *Time (mean interval between responses)(min.)*					
Mean	.35	.42	.36	.54	.66
σm	.02	.07	.05	.07	.14
Median	.33	.42	.34	.34	.50
No. cases	100	17	22	23	25

*Means for recovery groups are based on 25 animals with the exception of those for (c) rate of response. Since this measure (mean interval between responses) was obtained by dividing the total time from first to last response by (N − 1) responses, it does not include cases where less than two responses were made.

such may be plotted under different conditions, or deductions based on these equations in combination with other principles may be tested experimentally. The former type of experiment is represented by the work of Miller and Stevenson (1936), who measured recovery of running speed following nine extinction runs in a straight alley maze. Their curves of recovery differ from [those] of Figure 34-3 in that almost 100 percent recovery occurs in 55 minutes, and initial recovery is relatively much faster, causing a sharp break in the curve at the shortest interval. Miller and Stevenson attribute the break in their curve to an artifact of their experimental procedure, so the shape of their curve cannot be compared with the curve presented in Figure 34-3. However, the percentage of re-

TABLE 34-3

Reliabilities of measures of recovery from specific effects of extinction*

PAIRED RECOVERY-INTERVAL GROUPS	MEASURES OF RECOVERY		
	No. of responses	Time required to reach criterion	Rate of response
5.5 min. vs. 25 min.	C.R. =2.75	C.R. =2.14	C.R. =0.70
5.5 min. vs. 65 min.	=2.80	=4.16	=1.21
5.5 min. vs. 185 min.	=3.49	=4.81	=1.53
25 min. vs. 65 min.	=1.19	=2.20	=2.09
25 min. vs. 185 min.	=2.06	=3.32	=2.73
65 min. vs. 185 min.	=0.82	=1.49	=0.76

* Critical ratios (diff./σdiff.) of the means for the four recovery-interval groups. The first column shows the pairs of groups for which C.R.'s are given.

covery is clearly different in the two experiments, which indicates that the equations obtained in the present experiment can only be considered as representative of the rate of recovery and not as a general statement of a law.

Figure 34-4 presents recovery in terms of mean time required for extinction. This measure shows negative acceleration similar to that of number of responses. However, using time as a measure, there was 72.5 percent recovery in 185 minutes, while measured by number of responses there is only 49.1 percent recovery in that period. This difference, it should be noted, was obtained when two measures were taken on the same group of animals at the same time. Both might be used as measures of "habit strength," or "excitatory tendency." One conclusion which may be reached is that such terms as "habit strength," "excitatory tendency," etc., should always be qualified by the phrase, "as measured by. . . ."

A third measure of recovery (rate of response) is shown graphically in Figure 34-5. This measure, which would seem to correspond most closely to that of Miller and Stevenson (1936) (running speed), differs from it even more than the measures discussed above. None of the differences between groups was acceptably reliable for this measure (see Table 34-3. However, it should be noted that the difference between the 25-minute and the 185-minute groups, which has a probability of 99.7 in 100 of being real, is in a direction counter to expectation. According to number or responses and time measures, the habit was stronger in the 185-minute group, yet the animals responded at a much slower rate. Since

The Interaction of Simple Habits

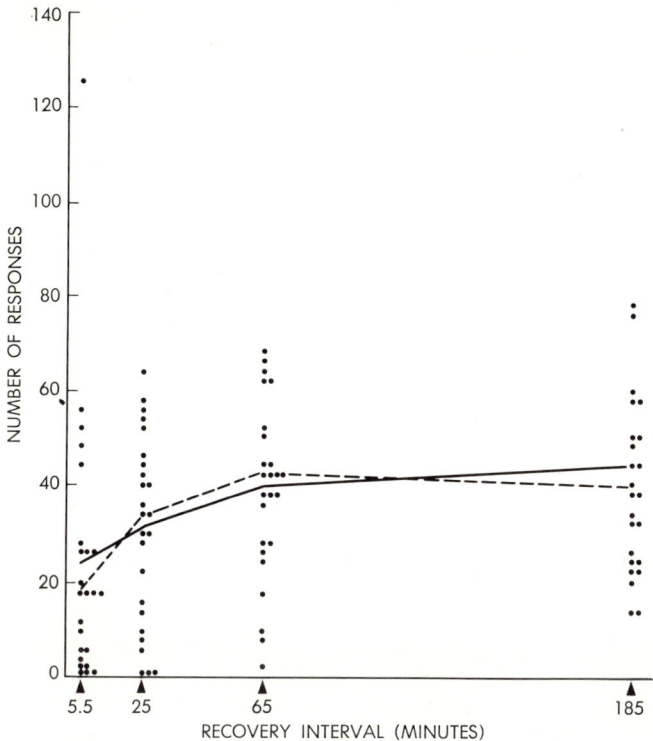

FIGURE 34-2. Distribution of number of extinction responses made by the four groups in Experiment I during tests of recovery from the effects of extinction. Means are graphed by the solid line, and medians by the broken line.

the reliability of the rate measure was comparatively low, no theoretical explanation is attempted here. If a similar relationship were found in other experiments, however, the phenomenon would demand more study, since it is the reverse of the somewhat analogous relationships of frequency and latency with other measures of conditioned-response strength.

Recovery from the generalized effects of extinction. As was mentioned above, Youtz (1939) showed that the extinction of one bar habit reduces the number of responses made during the immediately following extinction of a second habit. This section of the present paper demonstrates the recovery from these "generalized effects of extinction." Again three measures of recovery are used. These measures were obtained in the extinction of the horizontal-bar habit beginning 5.5, 25, 65, and 185 minutes after the last response of the vertical-bar-habit extinction. Means, σ_m's, and medians for number of responses, time, and rate of response

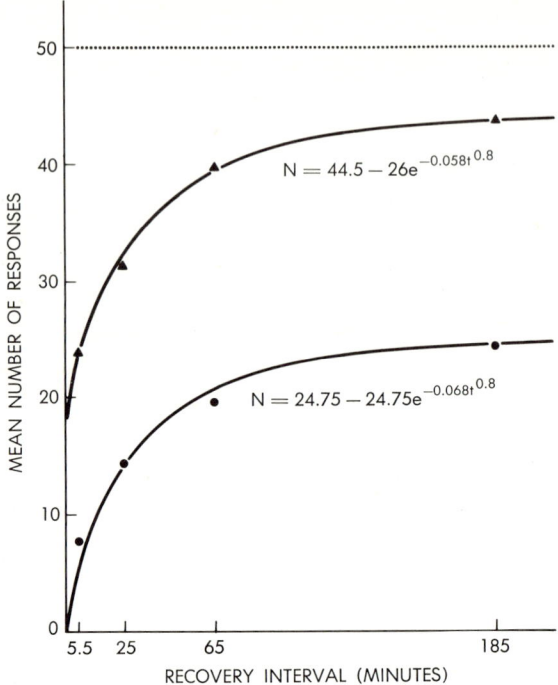

FIGURE 34-3. Recovery as measured by mean number of responses. Recovery from the specific effects of extinction is shown by the small circles and recovery from generalized effects, by the small triangles. The smooth curves in both cases are obtained by plotting the empirical equations which have been fitted to the data shown. The horizontal dotted line shows the mean number of responses made during the first extinction of the H-bar habit by the Experiment I animals. Equations fitted to the median numbers of responses, corresponding to the means shown here, are as follows (N = median No. responses and t = recovery interval in minutes):

Experiment I. $N = 21.5 - 21.5\ e^{-.075t^{.8}}$
Experiment II. $N = 42.0 - 32.0\ e^{-.093t^{.8}}$

are given in Table 34-4. The distributions of number of responses are plotted for the four groups in Figure 34-6. In Figures 34-3, 34-4, and 34-5 the mean values for the three measures are plotted together with the empirical equations for recovery in terms of responses and time. Recovery measured by number of responses and time appears again to be fairly regular and negatively accelerated, while rate measures show reversals.

The critical ratios of the differences between the means (Table 34-5)

The Interaction of Simple Habits

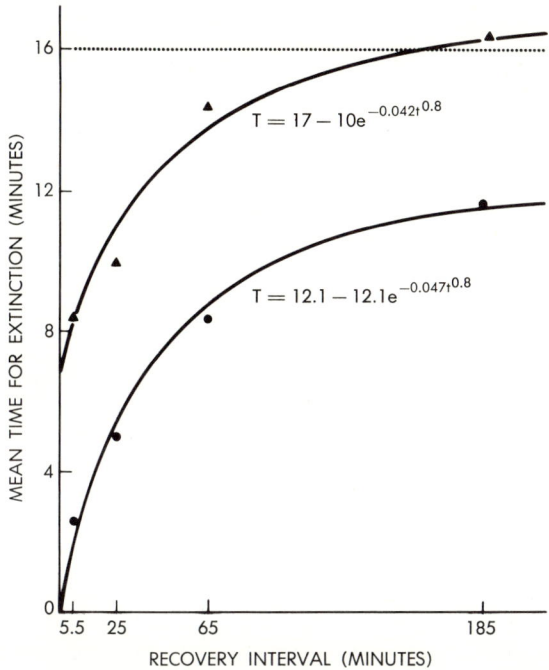

FIGURE 34-4. Recovery from specific and generalized effects of extinction as measured by the time required to reach the 5-minute criterion in the tests of recovery. Means for recovery from specific effects of extinction are given by the small circles and those for recovery from generalized effects by the small triangles. The smooth curves in both cases are obtained by plotting the empirical equations which have been fitted to the data shown. The horizontal dotted line shows the time required for the first extinction of the H-bar habit by Experiment I animals.

are with few exceptions smaller than the corresponding ones for Experiment 1. Given in order from greatest to least reliability, the measures are time, number of responses, and rate of response. This was true also for recovery from the specific effects of nonreward (Table 34-3), which disagrees with Youtz's finding that the number of responses was a more reliable measure than the time required to make these responses.

The differences between corresponding measures of mean recovery from specific and generalized effects of extinction are approximately equal for number of responses and time measures. In other words, the effect of lapse of time following the extinction has approximately the same effect upon the absolute amount of recovery from specific and generalized extinction. This point can be better appreciated by subtracting

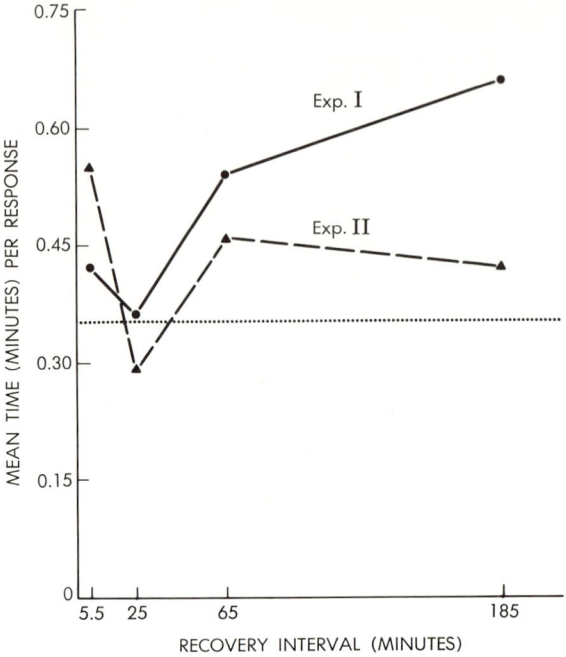

FIGURE 34-5. Mean interval between responses during tests of recovery. Means for Experiment I are given by the small circles, and those for Experiment II by the small triangles. The horizontal dotted line shows the mean interval between responses during the first extinction of the H-bar habit in Experiment I.

mean or median values in Table 34-2 from the corresponding values in Table 34-4. The results of these subtractions, representing differences in the absolute measures of recovery from specific and generalized effects of extinction, are almost constant for the four recovery intervals. This is supporting evidence for the dissipation of a general state of the organism which had resulted from the initial extinction. Wenger (1937) suggests that this state may be identified as generalized relaxation. However, the evidence from the present experiment can be merely suggestive for two reasons: (1) only one set of conditions was tested and therefore the parallel effect may be just a coincidence; and (2) there is no assurance that the units of recovery are constant for different absolute values.

Rate of response during the course of extinction. The data were further analyzed to find the rate of response (mean interval between responses) for successive fifths of the total number of responses made by each animal during extinction. All groups were averaged for the first horizontal-bar-habit extinction and figured separately for the second

TABLE 34-4

Data for Experiment II. Measures of recovery from the generalized effects of extinction*

MEASURE OF RECOVERY	FIRST PERIOD OF EXTINCTION ON H-BAR HABIT (N = 100)	RECOVERY INTERVAL GROUP			
		5.5 min.	25 min.	65 min.	185 min.
(a) *No. responses*					
Mean	49.7	23.9	31.2	39.6	43.9
m	2.6	5.5	3.9	3.6	5.2
Median	43.3	18.5	34.0	42.5	39.5
(b) *Time to reach criterion (min.)*					
Mean	16.0	8.5	10.0	14.6	16.4
m	.97	1.85	0.87	1.45	1.92
Median	15.5	6.5	9.5	13.5	17.2
(c) *Rate (mean interval between responses)(min.)*					
Mean	.35	.55	.29	.46	.42
m	.02	.10	.03	.08	.05
Median	.33	.33	.28	.36	.38
No. cases	100	21	22	25	25

* The figures in the second column are taken from the first extinction of the *H*-bar habit in Experiment I. Means for recovery groups are based on 25 animals with the exception of those for (c) rate of response. Since this measure (mean interval between responses) was obtained by dividing the total time from first to last response by $(N-1)$ responses it does not include cases where less than two responses were made.

(recovery test) extinction of each group. These data are presented in Table 34-6. It was noted that all four of the Experiment I groups showed a "warming up" phenomenon, that is, an increase in rate of response during the second fifth of the total responses, while this phenomenon was seen in only one of the Experiment II groups. However, further analysis seems to indicate that this difference did not represent a qualitative dissimilarity in the effects of specific and generalized extinction. The presence or absence of the initial increase in rate of response is apparently determined by the strength of the response tendency being extinguished. When the animals are separated into two groups (those making 20 or

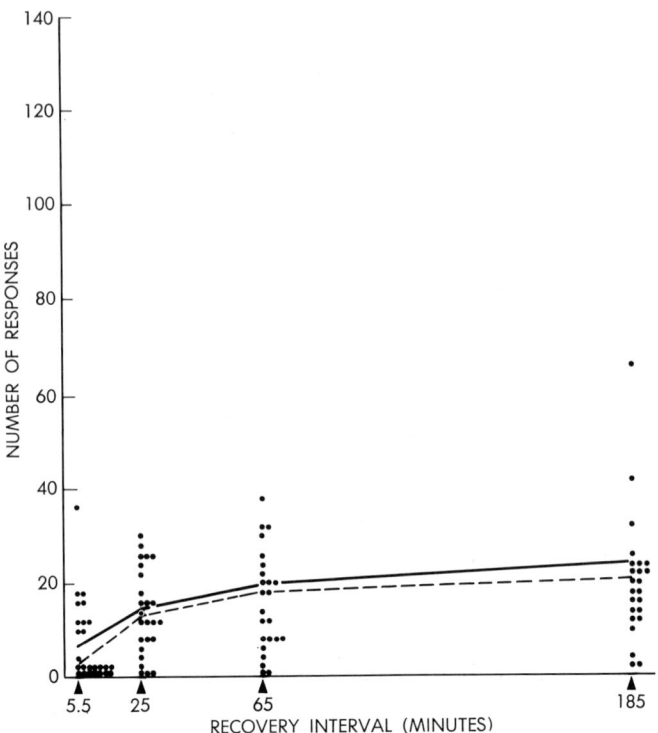

FIGURE 34-6. Distributions of number of responses made by the animals in the four groups of Experiment II, recovering from the generalized effects of extinction. Means are shown by the solid line, and medians by the broken line.

less responses during extinction and those making 21 or more), the warming up phenomenon is found only for those making fewer responses (see Table 34-7). This was true for the first H-bar extinction and for the recovery test extinction of the Experiment II animals.

It might be supposed that dividing the total responses into fifths obscured an initial increase in rate for the group making 21 or more responses because of the larger average number of responses included in each fifth. That this was not the case may be seen by reference to Table 34-8. The records for the Experiment I animals which made 21 or more responses during the first extinction of the H-bar habit were remeasured. The mean intervals between responses for the first five successive groups of three responses did not show any indication of a warm-up. The evidence as a whole seems to show that an increase in rate of response early in the course of extinction is found only when the response tendency is relatively weak.

TABLE 34-5

Reliabilities of measures of recovery from generalized effects of extinction*

PAIRED RECOVERY-INTERVAL GROUPS	MEASURES OF RECOVERY		
	No. of responses	Time required to reach criterion	Rate of response
5.5 min. vs. 25 min.	C.R. =1.07	C.R. =0.73	C.R. =2.50
5.5 min. vs. 65 min.	=2.39	=2.59	=0.70
5.5 min. vs. 185 min.	=2.64	=2.96	=1.16
25 min. vs. 65 min.	=1.58	=2.72	=2.00
25 min. vs. 185 min.	=1.95	=3.04	=2.24
65 min. vs. 185 min.	=0.68	=0.78	=0.43

* Critical ratios (diff./σdiff.) of the means for the four recovery interval groups. The first column shows the pairs of groups for which C.R.'s are given.

Switzer (1933), Scott (1930), Hudgins (1933), and Hilgard and Marquis (1935) found an initial rise in extinction curves. Hovland (1936), investigating the conditions under which this rise occurred, found that it was favored by a large number of reinforcements, massed practice, and extinction immediately following training. In contrast, the phenomenon was found in this experiment where the habit was relatively weak and when nonreward occurred twenty-four hours after training. This would indicate that the inhibition-of-reinforcement hypothesis, by which Hovland explains his data, is not the factor involved here.

An hypothesis which accounts for the warming up phenomenon very nicely is that suggested by Guthrie's (1935) approach. According to his analysis the conditioned stimuli for any response would include internal stimuli resulting from posture. Since during learning one response follows another, the postures involved in making one response furnish stimuli to which the response itself is conditioned—circular conditioning. During extinction or nonreward, stimuli from the first few responses facilitate the occurrence of those following so that they should occur with greater frequency (until the weakening effects of nonreward overcome this trend).

If the previous conditioning had been very strong the external stimuli alone would cause a maximum rate of response at the beginning of extinction, so that no further increase in rate could occur. This last assumption would require that the initial rate for those animals making a large number of responses should be faster than for those giving few responses. Reference to Table 34-5 shows this to be the case.

TABLE 34-6

Mean interval between responses for successive fifths of the total responses*

CONDITIONS OF EXTINCTION	NO. CASES	FIFTHS OF TOTAL RESPONSES				
		1	2	3	4	5
Exp. I. First extinction of H-bar habit	99	.15	.20	.33	.39	.63
Exp. I. Recovery test, second extinction of H-bar habit						
5.5-min. interval	10	.31	.24	.44	.69	.21
25-min. interval	20	.18	.14	.33	.46	.67
65-min. interval	22	.31	.30	.39	.67	.59
185-min. interval	22	.50	.38	.39	.52	.56
Exp. II. Recovery test on H-bar habit following extinction on V-bar habit						
5.5-min. interval	18	.24	.30	.40	.57	.56
25-min. interval	22	.11	.18	.22	.41	.52
65-min. interval	24	.24	.18	.36	.59	.55
185-min. interval	25	.15	.30	.34	.64	.72

* The number of cases is usually less than 25 since only those animals making more than five responses are included.

In addition to Guthrie's concept of specific (circular) facilitation there is the possibility of a general facilitatory effect. Emotion or excitement is commonly associated with nonreward (frustration), and this is assumed to have an energizing effect upon any response which may occur. If this hypothesis were applied to the data, the difference in the measurable effect of this factor upon a strong or a weak tendency would, presumably, again be accounted for in terms of the initial maximal or submaximal rate.

SUMMARY AND CONCLUSIONS

Two hundred albino rats were given thirty food-rewarded training trials on a horizontal-bar-pressing habit and thirty on a vertical-bar habit. Half of these animals were later allowed to perform the *H*-bar habit unrewarded until they reached a criterion of no responses in a period of

TABLE 34-7

Interval between responses for successive fifths of the total number of responses made during extinction*

TOTAL RESPONSES	NO. CASES	FIFTHS OF TOTAL NO. RESPONSES				
		1	2	3	4	5
Exp. I. First extinction of H-bar habit						
20 or less responses	13	.22	.23	.21	.36	.49
21 or more responses	86	.14	.20	.34	.39	.65
Exp. II. Test of recovery from generalized extinction effects						
20 or less responses	20	.29	.27	.33	.51	.63
21 or more responses	69	.15	.22	.31	.43	.58

* The data are given separately for those animals given less than 20 and more than 21 responses. Only those animals giving more than 5 responses are included.

TABLE 34-8

Mean interval between responses for the first five successive groups of three responses during the first extinction of the H-bar habit in Experiment I

TOTAL RESPONSES	NO. CASES	SUCCESSIVE GROUPS OF 3 RESPONSES				
		1	2	3	4	5
21 or more	86	.11	.14	.20	.19	.19

five minutes. Recovery of the H-bar habit was measured by a second extinction test performed 5.5, 25, 65, or 185 minutes after the last response, a separate group of twenty-five animals being used for each interval. With the remaining 100 animals, following extinction of the V-bar habit, the recovery of the H-bar habit was measured, using the same recovery intervals (recovery from the generalized effects of extinction). The criterion of no responses in five minutes was used for original extinction period and for all tests of recovery.

Measured by number of responses and time to reach the 5-minute criterion, recovery from the specific effects of extinction was negatively accelerated, showing approximately 50 percent and 75 percent recovery respectively in 185 minutes. The curves of recovery from generalized effects were approximately parallel to the curves of recovery from specific effects of extinction, but showed 85 percent and 100+ percent recovery in terms of number of responses and time measures respectively. Measured by mean rate of response, there was no recovery in the ordinary meaning of the term. The curves of recovery from both specific and generalized effects of extinction found by this measure showed marked reversals.

A finding which is implicit in the above results is the operation of generalization of extinction to weaken a habit which has not itself been extinguished. A somewhat analogous phenomenon has been demonstrated (Pavlov, 1937, p. 152, and Bass and Hull, 1934) with conditioned reflexes, but its operation in other forms of learning has been questioned (Thorndike, 1931, p. 110). The present experiment confirms the results of Youtz (1939) in showing that the nonrewarded performance of one motor habit has a weakening effect upon a second habit for some time thereafter.

It should be remembered that Pavlov's (1927) "irradiation of inhibition" involves but one response conditioned to several stimuli: extinction of the response to one stimulus reduces the amount of secretion when another conditioned stimulus is presented soon after. The present experiment and that of Youtz employ two responses, so that the two situations are clearly not identical. However, Thorndike has assumed them to be essentially similar (1931, pp. 110–111), and it is the writer's opinion that the two phenomena are probably closely related. The frequency with which functional similarities are found between conditioned reflex and other phenomena supports the belief that there are certain basic "principles of behavior" which underlie both.

Extinction curves were plotted as the rate of response in successive fifths of the total responses made during the extinction. Pooled curves or animals making twenty or less extinction responses gave evidence of a warming up phenomenon—an initial increase in rate of response. This was not found in the pooled results for animals making more than twenty responses.

35

A Comparison of Two Methods of Producing Experimental Extinction[1]

GREGORY A. KIMBLE
JOHN W. KENDALL, JR.

The experiment reported in this paper compares two methods of producing experimental extinction. One method is that which Guthrie (1935) calls the "toleration" method and recommends for the breaking of undesirable avoidance habits. In this method the signal for the avoidance reaction is introduced gradually by increasing its intensity slowly. Under optimal conditions, according to Guthrie, it should be possible to extinguish a response by this technique without the overt occurrence of the response. The other method is the conventional one of presenting the conditioned stimulus (CS) several times without reinforcement. Guthrie sometimes calls this the "exhaustion" method, and predicts that the extinction of a response in this way will require many more extinction responses than the toleration procedure.

As Sheffield (1949) has pointed out, the most obvious deduction from Hull's (1943) theory would predict the *same* number of responses to extinction under the two procedures. For this reason, he feels that the present experiment is a critical test of Hull's and Guthrie's theories of extinction. Although we do not believe that a single, critical test of the two theories is possible, we agree with Sheffield that an empirical attack on the problem is long overdue, and that results favoring Guthrie's position would necessitate a reconsideration of Hull's explanation of extinction.

Method

APPARATUS. The apparatus used in this investigation is the same as that described by Kessen (1953). It consists of a training box with an electrifiable grid as the floor. One side of the box is of transparent

[1] Reprinted from *Journal of Experimental Psychology*, 1953, 45, 87–90 with the permission of The American Psychological Association.

Plexiglas through which diffuse illumination can be introduced as a CS. Into one end of the box is inserted a movable wheel which can be rotated to turn off the shock used as the unconditioned stimulus (UCS).

For this experiment, the CS was provided by a 7-watt bulb which was operated on 70 volts, and gave a training intensity of 20 foot-candles. The light circuit was wired through a variable transformer so that the intensity of the CS could be raised from zero to the training intensity by manipulating voltage. Operating the light on 70 volts rather than 110 volts made this procedure somewhat easier and also minimized color changes when the CS was presented as several intensities.

The shock used as the UCS was of 90 volts with a fixed resistance of 250,000 ohms in series with the rat.

SUBJECTS. Twenty male albino rats of the Sprague-Dawley strain, 100–150 days old, were subjects in the experiment. They were housed in the experimental room, kept on an ad lib supply of food and water and were tamed by being handled.

PROCEDURE. Pretraining, training, and extinction were completed in a single session. Each subject was placed in the training box for a 2-minute adaptation period and then given a pretraining series of five 15-second presentations of the CS without reinforcement. Following pretraining, each subject was given 60 trials of avoidance training separated by a minimum of 40 seconds. On each such trial the CS and UCS were turned on in succession with a 5.8-second interstimulus interval. By rotating the wheel, the subject could turn off the shock, or avoid it by making the same response during the 5.8-second interstimulus interval. The CS was turned off about 5 seconds after the subject's response, whether shock was avoided or not. Finally, subjects were extinguished by either the toleration method or the exhaustion method. The assignment of rats to extinction condition was done at random before beginning the experiment.

The subjects in the first condition were given seven toleration "trials" immediately. On each such "trial," the CS intensity was raised in 5-volt steps from some lower value to the training level of 20 foot-candles. Each step lasted 15 seconds and a response was recorded if it occurred in any of these 15-second periods. Successive "trials" started at progressively higher voltages, in order to adapt the subject to the sudden onset of stimulation in case this variable was more important than intensity per se. The first toleration "trial" started at an intensity of zero; the second started at 10 volts, the third at 20 volts, the fourth at 30 volts, and so on, until on the eighth trial the CS was turned on at the training intensity. Counting from this eighth trial, the subject was then given 30 exhaustion trials.

The subjects in the exhaustion group rested in the apparatus for 16 minutes (the time required for the toleration procedure in the other group) and then received 30 ordinary extinction trials, in which the CS was presented without shock for 15 seconds on each trial and a response counted if it occurred in this period.

A third group of 32 subjects from the same population, conditioned by Kessen (1953) in the same apparatus and extinguished *immediately*, provided data in terms of which the effect of the 16-minute rest may be assessed.

Results

The data most directly pertinent to a comparison of extinction by the toleration and exhaustion methods are mean numbers of extinction responses. For the toleration method this value is 6.5; for the exhaustion method it is 14.4 ($p = .01$). The average of 6.5 responses obtained in the toleration group is made up of 5.4 responses which occurred in the toleration procedure and 1.1 responses which occurred in the subsequent exhaustion series. But only two subjects in the toleration group gave *any* responses in the exhaustion test. One subject gave nine responses; the other gave two. It is quite clear that, as Guthrie predicts, the toleration procedure results in very efficient elimination of an avoidance reaction.

To make this point as convincingly as possible, the following facts are cited. (1) During training the two groups were similar. Mean number of CR's during training were 36.0 for the toleration group, and 38.6 for the exhaustion group ($p = .40$). (2) The introduction of the 16-minute rest for the exhaustion group had no significant effect on their extinction behavior. Kessen's 32 animals, which were given 42 trials in the same apparatus, gave an average of 14.7 responses in 30 extinction trials. This value is not significantly different from the measure reported above for our exhaustion group. (3) This difference in number of extinction responses occurs in spite of the fact that our procedure gave the subjects in the toleration group 92 chances to respond as against 30 in the exhaustion group. (4) Such CR's as occurred in the toleration procedure were, on the average, separated in time by a greater amount than those which occurred in the exhaustion procedure. This difference in the degree of massing favors a result opposite to the one obtained. (5) The few responses obtained from our toleration group in the exhaustion series all occurred in the first 15 extinction trials. It seems unlikely that the toleration procedure merely produced a temporary suppression of the response.

Discussion

This demonstration of the effectiveness of the toleration procedure in producing experimental extinction calls into question the mechanism proposed by Hull (1943) to account for extinction. According to Hull, extinction results from the accumulation of an inhibitory potential (I_R) which is subtracted from reaction potential and eventually leads to the elimination of the response. Furthermore, according to Hull, the development of I_R requires the occurrence of the response. This theory leads to the prediction that our two groups should have produced the same number of responses in the extinction series. Our results, therefore, disprove this portion of Hull's theory.

This does not mean that we believe that Hull's position cannot handle the results of this experiment. An explanation of them which uses ideas implicit in *Principles of Behavior* is developed briefly in the paragraphs which follow.

While it never seems to have been recognized by Hull, his theory contains an alternative account of extinction in which the phenomenon is explained as a reduction of habit strength ($_SH_R$). The equations which relate habit strength to the amount of reinforcement are such that a change in the amount of reinforcement will result in a change in the maximum of $_SH_R$. Although Hull demonstrates that an increase in the amount of reward will lead to an increase in the maximum of $_SH_R$, he apparently did not see that a *decrease* in the amount of reward would produce a decrease in habit, or that, in the special case of the reduction of amount of reward to zero (extinction), $_SH_R$ would gradually reduce to zero. The concept of inhibition, by this argument, is expendable, except for the explanation of the effects of massed practice and the phenomenon of spontaneous recovery. But the position still seems to demand the occurrence of a response for extinction to occur. This latter consideration brings up the next point in our explanation.

Avoidance reactions in avoidance training experiments are mediated responses. That is, they depend for their elicitation upon an acquired drive of fear. Assuming that fear is an internal *response,* it becomes obvious that, if this response can be extinguished, behavior depending on it will automatically be extinguished. We believe that this is what happens in extinction by the toleration method. To describe the process as we think it occurs, we shall need two further concepts from Hull's theory: generalization decrement and the generalization of extinction.

In extinction by the toleration procedure, the stimulus for a fear reaction is presented first in a highly generalized form. This stimulus presumably tends to call out the conditioned fear, but to so small a degree that the instrumental response does not occur. Not because of the accumulation of inhibition, but simply because it is not reinforced, the fear reaction is partially extinguished and this extinction generalizes to adjacent stimulus intensities. Thus, when the intensity of the CS is raised slightly, the fear reaction will occur again, but still in a weak form, and the process described above is repeated. Successive application of the fear stimulus at intensities too weak to produce the avoidance reaction may then finally eliminate it by extinguishing its acquired motivational basis.

SUMMARY

Two groups of male albino rats were trained in a wheel-turning situation to avoid a shock and were then extinguished by two different procedures. One group was subjected to extinction by a toleration method which the conditioned stimulus is introduced gradually. The other group was extinguished by the conventional procedure of presenting the conditioned stimulus at full intensity without the shock. Mean numbers of responses in the extinction series were 6.5 for the toleration group, and 14.4 for the other group ($p = .01$). This result confirms one of Guthrie's theoretical ideas and necessitates a reformulation of Hull's theory of extinction. Such a reformation, based on the idea that the toleration procedure extinguishes a mediating fear reaction, was attempted.

36

The Effect of Random Alternation of Reinforcement on the Acquisition and Extinction of Conditioned Eyelid Reactions[1]

LLOYD G. HUMPHREYS

The fundamental concept in conditioning theory is that the conditioned response develops with repeated reinforcement and diminishes (extinguishes) with continued non-reinforcement. The extent of either acquisition or extinction has been supposed to depend on the number of reinforcements or non-reinforcement, respectively. Hull and Spence, for example, have explicitly assumed that specific increments of strength of conditioned responses result from each reinforcement, specific decrements from each non-reinforcement. Rational learning curves have been constructed by others (Gulliksen, 1934; Gulliksen & Wolfle, 1937; Thurstone, 1919; Wiley & Wiley, 1937) upon the similar assumption that repeated rewards or frustrations produce corresponding increments or decrements.

Since it is customary to reinforce every trial during acquisition of conditioned responses, and to omit reinforcement entirely during extinction, the increases appear to correspond directly to the frequency of reinforcement, the decreases to the frequency of non-reinforcement. There are a few fragmentary data, however, which suggest that the relationship of acquisition and extinction to the frequency of reinforcement or non-reinforcement is not so simple. Pavlov, for example, reports experiments on one dog (1927, p. 384) in which a conditioned reflex was first developed by the "20th application," which is stated to be about average (p. 385). Using a new conditioned stimulus and reinforcing only one-third of the trials, the response developed by the "7th application," but the animal became "extremely excited." The norm for subsequent reflexes after the first has been established is from "3 to 5" (p. 375).

Skinner (1938) has made considerable use of a technique which he calls "periodic reconditioning" in which reinforcement occurs only at regular time intervals, intervening responses being non-reinforced. He

[1] Reprinted from the *Journal of Experimental Psychology*, 1939, 25, 141–158, by permission of the American Psychological Association and the author.

The Effect of Random Alternation of Reinforcement 515

states that, except at very short intervals, the rate of responding is inversely proportional to the length of the interval. Periodic reconditioning builds up a greater "reserve" than continuous reconditioning.

By use of another technique, "reinforcement at a fixed ratio," Skinner has obtained as many as 192 responses in rapid succession for one reinforcement. Here the relationship between frequency of reinforcement and rate of response breaks down. Presumably a large reserve is again created.

Razran (1934) makes the statement that continuous reinforcement may decrease the frequency of conditioned responses developed to shock and that optimum distributions are needed. Such distributions are supposedly especially important after some training, i.e., after the reflex has been "established." In support of this conclusion he states that Israelson and Platonov have given many trials without reinforcement after the conditioned reflex was once established.

Evidence pertinent to Razran's conclusion has recently been reported by Brogden (1939). After establishing three different responses by continuous reinforcement, "frequency" of reinforcement was varied. No significant decrements were observed when only one-fifth of the trials were reinforced.

The use of the test-trial procedure in conditioning experiments results in occasional non-reinforcement. Wolfle (1932), in a minor part of her study, omitted the 30 test-trials from the 600 acquisition trials in the first 3 practice periods for one group of subjects and compared their acquisition results with those from her usual procedure where the test-trials were always included. Differences were in favor of the no-test-trial group, but they were not significant statistically.

Experimental procedure

In order to test the effect upon acquisition and extinction of reinforcing only one half of the trials, it was necessary to choose a standardized conditioning situation. The eyelid reaction was chosen as being eminently suitable and convenient. Three experimental groups were found to be necessary. The main experimental group received reinforcement on only half of the trials during acquisition, an arrangement to be described as 50 percent reinforcement. Acquisition (and subsequent extinction) could then be compared with the results from control groups receiving reinforcement each time the conditioned stimulus was presented, i.e., 100 percent reinforcement. One of these control groups was given as many total trials as the experimental group, each trial being reinforced; the other was given as many reinforced trials as the experimental group, rest intervals being substituted for the non-reinforced presentations of the conditioned stimulus.

The essential features of the apparatus have been described by Dodge (1926) and by Hilgard and Campbell (1936) except for one modification: lever-recording of eyelid movement is used in place of the earlier artificial-eyelash-recording. The eyelid is attached to a light wooden lever by a thread. A small mirror mounted on the fulcrum of the lever reflects light onto the film. Several advantages result from this arrangement: the distracting bright light shining across the line of vision, necessary in the other method of recording, is now absent; complete closures are recorded; magnification of response is constant at 1.75 throughout the entire range of movement, amplitude being read to the nearest millimeter.

The conditioned stimulus, an increase in illumination of approximately 15 foot-candles behind a panel of flash glass, was followed at an interval of approximately 400 msc. by the unconditioned stimulus, a puff of air to one cornea. After 12 reflex adaptation trials had been given, 6 to the puff alone and 6 to the light alone, in that order, the three groups of subjects were given the conditions of 100 percent reinforcement-massed, 50 percent reinforcement, and 100 percent reinforcement-spaced previously described.

Group I—100 percent reinforcement-massed. Twelve reflex adaptation trials, 96 paired stimulations of the light and puff, and 24 extinction trials.

Group II—50 percent reinforcement. Twelve reflex adaptation trials, 48 paired stimulations interspersed at random[2] intervals by 48 non-reinforced trials, and 24 extinction trials. Otherwise the conditions for this group were exactly the same as for Group I.

Group III—100 percent reinforcement-spaced. Twelve reflex adaptation trials, 48 paired stimulations interspersed by rest periods at exactly the same intervals as in Group II (in place of non-reinforced trials), and 24 extinction trials. Otherwise the conditions for this group were identical with those for Groups I and II.

Trials were given every 30 seconds, with a 1-minute rest interval between groups of 12 trials (6 trials and 6 rest intervals for Group III), each subject serving for an experimental session on each of two successive days. Subjects were male and female psychology students from elementary classes at Stanford University during the winter and spring quarters of 1937–1938. Nine men and 13 women were obtained for each group. Standard preliminary instructions were read to all, and introspections were obtained at the close of the experiment to routine questions.

---

[2] The order deviated slightly from a random one in that no more than two trials of any one kind were given in succession, and there were 6 reinforced and 6 non-reinforced trials in each group of 12.

TABLE 36-1

Acquisition scores for two measures of conditioning (22 subjects in each group)

	Probability of occurrence: Number of responses over total trials		Magnitude: Millimeters on record, including zero responses	
	M	σ	M	σ
Group I (100 percent reinforcement-massed)	.65	.19	5.97	4.41
Group II (50 percent reinforcement)	.59	.25	5.82	4.50
Group III (100 percent reinforcement-spaced)	.64	.25	6.68	5.28
	σdiff.	t	σdiff.	t
I and II	.06	1.00	1.28	.11
I and III	.06	.17	1.10	.65
II and III	.08	.63	1.48	.58

Results

Initial comparability of groups. Since comparisons depend throughout on the assumption that the three groups would have yielded comparable results if they had been treated alike, it is important to secure some measure of their initial comparability. [It is known] that there is a significant relationship between reflex sensitivity, as measured by the reflexes originally present to the experimental stimuli, and the strength of conditioned responses which develop. The range of the 6t's obtained when each group is compared with every other for reflex responses to the light and to the puff within the initial adaptation trials is from .16 to 1.28, and the median is .60. It may thus be inferred that the groups were essentially alike in sensitivity, and if treated alike would have yielded similar conditioned responses.

Acquisition. Table 36-1 presents data indicating the extent and significance of the differences between the three groups of subjects in [probability of occurrence] and magnitude[3] of conditioned responses

---
[3] Trials of zero amplitude are included in magnitude. Although highly correlated with frequency, more of the variance of magnitude is attributable to amplitude of responses than to their frequency.

during acquisition.[4] [The first of these measures] shows that Groups I and III are most alike and that Groups I and II are least alike, but all of the differences could easily have arisen through the operation of chance alone. Magnitude indicates that Groups I and II are most alike, the differences with Group III being somewhat larger, but they are again easily within the range of chance expectancy.

As would be expected from the negligible total score differences, the performance curves indicating the course of acquisition over the two-day period are strikingly comparable. This is exemplified by the curve for frequency presented in Figure 36-1. All of the acquisition trials are divided into 8 groups for facility in presentation. Thus each point represents 12 reinforced trials for Group I, 6 reinforced and 6 non-reinforced trials for Group II, and 6 reinforced trials plus 6 one-half-minute rest intervals for Group III. The break between trials 48–60 and 1–12 indicates the 24-hour interval between the first and second days. Reflex adaptation trials 1–12 on the first day are, of course, omitted.

The performance of Group II in frequency is somewhat lower on the first day than that of either of the other groups. By the second day differences are smaller. At no point do they approach significance.

The preceding, presumably chance differences are in striking contrast to the differing conditions of reinforcement in the three groups; i.e., 96 reinforced trials in Group I, 48 reinforced and 48 non-reinforced trials in Group II, and 48 reinforced, but spaced, trials in Group III. In view of the rapidity of extinction of the eyelid reflex in man, present lack of effect from non-reinforcement in Group II is indeed paradoxical.[5] It is evident that the results are not sufficiently accounted for by an algebraic summation of reinforcements and non-reinforcements.

Extinction. Table 36-2 presents total score differences in extinction for [probability of occurrence] and magnitude. Conditions during extinction were identical in all groups so that differences in scores are to be attributed to the conditions of reinforcement during acquisition.

The group receiving 50 percent reinforcement is strikingly more resistant to extinction than either of the control groups (I and III), which are essentially alike. While the differences between Groups I and III are minimal, the *t* values for the differences in both frequency and magnitude between Group II and the other groups suffice to indicate the probability of genuine differences.

---

[4] In making these computations subjects were first matched on the basis of reflex sensitivity to light and to puff. The mean of the distribution of differences between matched individuals was then tested for the significance of its departure from zero.

[5] Subsequent research suggests that this paradoxical effect resulted from the use of a short CS-US interval [Ed.].

The Effect of Random Alternation of Reinforcement

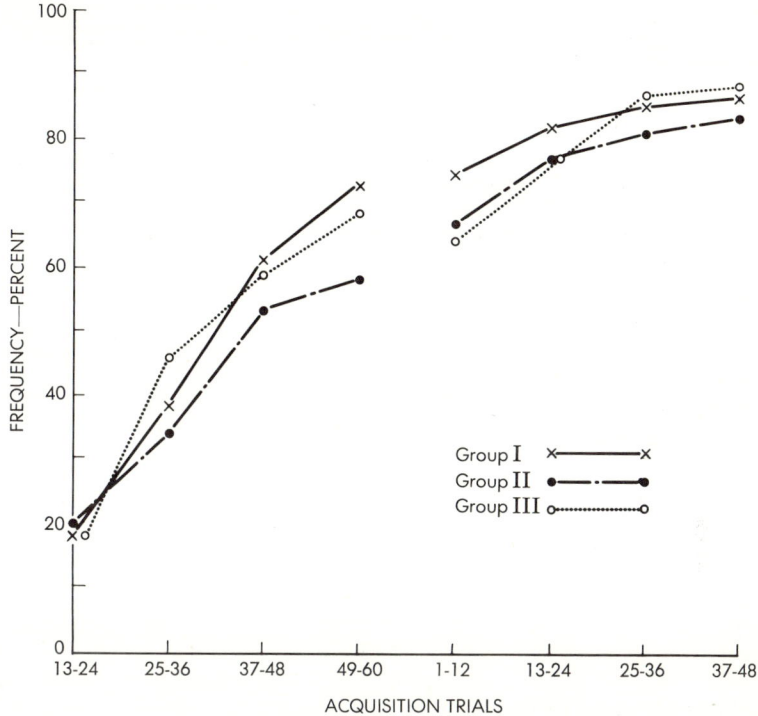

FIGURE 36-1. Course of acquisition-frequency. The acquisition trials are divided into 8 groups for facility in presentation. Thus each point represents 12 reinforced trials for Group I (100 percent reinforcement-massed), 6 reinforced and 6 non-reinforced trials for Group II (50 percent reinforcement), and 6 reinforced trials plus 6 one-half-minute rest intervals for Group III (100 percent reinforcement-spaced). The break between trials 48–60 and 1–12 indicates a 24-hour interval between two days of experimentation. Reflex adaptation trials 1–12 on the first day are omitted. The essential comparability of the three groups is easily apparent.

Figure 36-2 presents the performance curves in extinction for frequency. The 24 extinction trials are divided into 4 groups of 6 trials each. An average for the preceding 24 acquisition trials is plotted to serve as a reference point for the extinction results. The essential comparability of Groups I and III is easily apparent, while Group II responds at a consistently higher level throughout than either of the others. A statistical comparison of the points plotted indicates that the differences are relatively larger early in the extinction series.

It is obvious that comparable performance during acquisition does

TABLE 36-2

Extinction scores for 24 non-reinforced trials (22 subjects in each group)

	Probability of occurrence: Number of responses over total trials		Magnitude: Millimeters on record, including zero responses	
	M	σ	M	σ
Group I (100 percent reinforcement-massed)	.31	.24	1.69	1.16
Group II (50 percent reinforcement)	.60	.33	5.35	5.37
Group III (100 percent reinforcement-spaced)	.34	.27	2.50	2.06
	σdiff.	t	σdiff.	t
I and II	.08	3.61	1.06	3.45
I and III	.08	.38	.43	1.90
II and III	.08	3.25	1.00	2.84

not lead in all cases to comparable performance in extinction. Group II, given 50 percent reinforcement in acquisition, was somehow enabled to respond at a significantly higher frequency and magnitude during extinction than groups given 100 percent reinforcement. This differential effect of 50 percent reinforcement as contrasted to 100 percent reinforcement for extinction, in spite of similarities in the course of acquisition, requires interpretation.

Discussion

The results just presented are definitely contradictory to a conditioning theory which posits specific increments of excitatory strength for each reinforcement and specific decrements for each non-reinforcement. From the theory one would predict that Group I should show the greatest amount of acquisition; Group III, receiving only one-half the reinforcement, should follow at a slower rate; and Group II, also receiving only one-half the reinforcement plus an equal number of non-reinforced trials, should show little if any acquisition. Contrary to expectations, acquisition is essentially alike for all groups. According to conventional theories, one of two results might be expected to extinguish most slowly. Or, since all groups were essentially alike at the end of the reinforcement session, they might all be expected to extinguish equally. Both of these expecta-

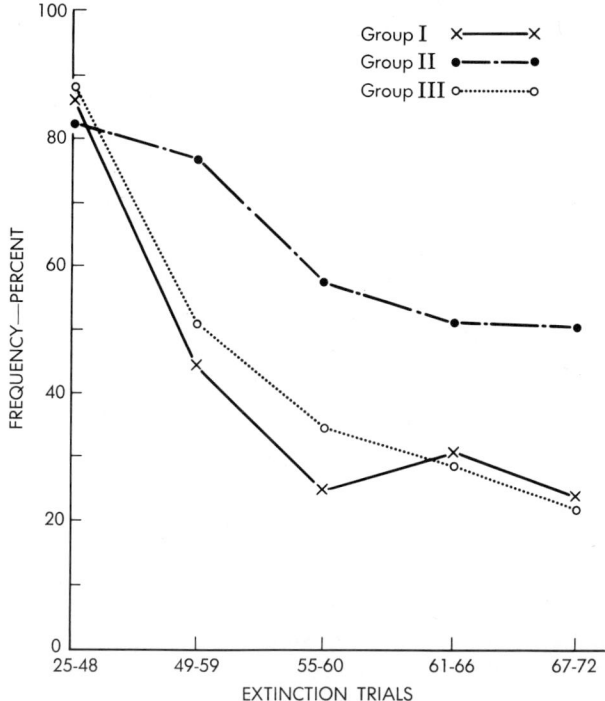

FIGURE 36-2. Course of extinction-frequency. The 24 extinction trials are divided into 4 groups of 6 trials each. An average for the preceding 24 acquisition trials is plotted to serve as a reference point for the extinction results. The essential comparability of groups I and III (100 percent reinforcement) is easily apparent, while Group II (50 percent reinforcement) responds at a consistently higher level throughout than either of the others.

tions are contradicted, since Group II, with 48 reinforcements and 48 non-reinforcements, and not superior at the end of the acquisition period, extinguished by far the slowest.

The results are likewise inconsistent with the concept of "excitatory-potential" recently made explicit by Hull.[6] He states that "an excitatory-potential is a central condition or state of an organism which, given appropriate circumstances, will result in a specified form of action." The magnitude of the potential is dependent upon numerous factors in the conditioning situation and in the situation in which the potential later becomes actual. Among these are the number of reinforcements, the num-

[6] The reference is to an unpublished manuscript. Similar statements appear in *Principles of Behavior* (Hull, 1943) and the comment applies to this work as well [Ed.].

ber of responses in extinction, the drive during reinforcement and during extinction, etc. The excitatory-potential is then manifested in several ways. Among these are amplitude, latency, number of frustrations undergone, and time for extinction. Potentials of equal strength will always be manifested in *exactly the same way*. When it can be shown, however, that three groups of subjects have excitatory-potentials of approximately equal strength for the period of acquisition (no significant differences in frequency and magnitude of responses), but that one of these (Group II) has an apparently stronger potential for extinction, sufficient evidence is available to deny the general validity of the hypothesis.

Skinner (1938) differentiates between the "reserve" and the "strength" of a reflex, the two including the characteristics of Hull's excitatory-potential. Depending on the conditions of the experiment, equal strengths may result from unequal reserves. The results from the present experiment might thus be described in those terms; i.e., conditioned responses in the three groups are of equal strength at the end of acquisition, but a greater reserve has been built up in Group II through 50 percent reinforcement. Skinner, however, makes the traditional assumptions concerning the effects of frequency of reinforcement and non-reinforcement, so he would be unable to explain the development of the greater reserve in Group II. He would be at a loss, similarly, to explain the results from his own technique of "periodic reconditioning" which was discussed in the introductory paragraphs of this paper.

An alternative theory. Since the conventional theory of conditioning is inadequate to the experimental data, some alternative is required to harmonize the results. A satisfactory alternative theory requires a new interpretation of the roles of reinforcement and of non-reinforcement. One such alternative is that conditioned responses are a consequence of anticipated reinforcement, extinction of anticipated non-reinforcement, and that the role of frequency in the repetition of reinforcement or non-reinforcement is by way of its influence on the subject's expectations of the stimuli which are to appear. Hilgard (1936) and his co-workers (Hilgard, Campbell and Sears, 1937, 1938) have interpreted conditioned discrimination in this way, following the writings of Tolman and Brunswik (1935) and Krechevsky (1932, 1938).

Acquisition depends on the probability that the light will be followed by the air-puff. In the cases of Groups I and III the light is uniformly followed by the air-puff, so that the more trials the higher the probability that the air-puff will follow. That the increase in rate within both groups is similar, even though one has twice the reinforcements of the other, must be attributed to whatever factors cause the advantage in spaced over massed practice. . . . To account for the results in Group II a suggestion from Tolman and Brunswik is in order. They suggest that a cue to a noxious stimulus, even though it is "ambiguous," is reacted to as "dangerous." Thus the light is reacted to as though it may be followed by the air-puff, even though the subject knows very well that it may not be so followed. This accounts for the development of the conditioned responses at normal rate in spite of the interspersed non-reinforced trials.

Extinction, correspondingly, must depend on the expectancy of non-reinforcement. The rapid extinction in Groups I and III must be explained as a shift from the expectation of uniform reinforcement to that of uniform non-reinforcement. A single non-reinforced trial is a much more impressive experience after uniform reinforcement than after many previous non-reinforced trials as in Group II. In fact, even after several non-reinforced trials, the subjects of Group II may continue to expect reinforcement, since reinforcement has often previously followed non-reinforcement. Hence the resistance to extinction is explained.

These conjectures satisfactorily account for the data, provided, of course, that the conjectures may be substantiated. Two sets of evidence are available from within the reported experiments, first, certain individual trials in extinction, and, second, the introspective comments of the subjects.

Individual trials in extinction. The most significant trials for the "expectancy" interpretation lie within the first 6 trials and those immediately preceding and following the 1-minute rest period in the middle of the extinction series. Data for frequency are quite representative of other measures and are presented here in Figure 36-3. The first point plotted is again the mean from the immediately preceding 24 acquisition trials to serve as a reference point for the extinction results. Very striking are the rapid drops for both Groups I and III and the slight rise on the third trial for Group II. Both facts fit perfectly the "expectancy" hypothesis. That there is also a great deal of uncertainty in Group II even after the third trial is indicated by the slowness of the drop thereafter (no more than two non-reinforced trials had ever occurred together previously). The uniform rise between the last trial before the rest period and the first trial thereafter is also congruent—at the start of a new series "anything can happen." It is interesting to observe that his phenomenon is equivalent to that of spontaneous recovery, the recovery in this case taking place during a single minute.

Introspections. The introspective comments took the form of answers to three questions: (1) Did you notice the change in the last two groups of trials? (2) When did you become sure of the change? (3) What difference did it make to you? The importance of such introspections was not realized until after the first few subjects had been used, but all were questioned thereafter.

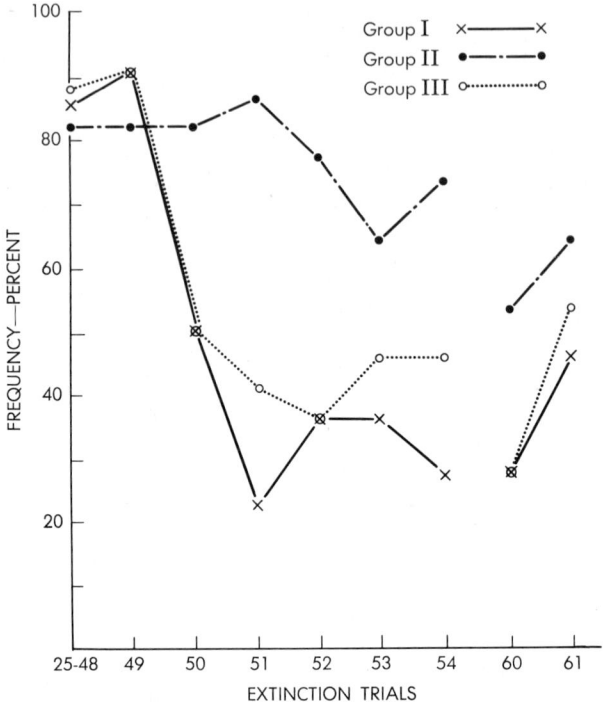

FIGURE 36-3. Individual trials in extinction-frequency. The first 6 trials in extinction and the trials immediately preceding and following the 1-minute rest interval in the middle of the series are plotted here for the three groups of subjects. The first point plotted is again the mean from the preceding 24 acquisition trials to serve as a reference point. Very striking are the rapid drops for both groups I and III (100 percent reinforcement) and the slight rise on the third trial for Group II (50 percent reinforcement).

When the answers to these questions were analyzed, it was found that subjects could be roughly classified into 3 categories: (1) those who kept on expecting the air-puff throughout the 24 extinction trials; (2) those who changed their hypothesis more or less rapidly and decided that there would not be any more air-puffs; and (3) those who said that they were not thinking about the experiment and thus were not able to answer the last two questions. This analysis is presented in Table 36-3, including the number of those not questioned, the number and percentage of the total introspections that were placed in each of the categories, and the performance in acquisition and extinction of those in the categories as measured by percentage-frequency of response.

Although there are individual exceptions, average frequency scores

TABLE 36-3

Analysis of introspections

	N	PERCENT OF INTROSPECTIONS	PERCENTAGE-FREQUENCY	
			Acquisition	Extinction
Group I (100 percent reinforcement-massed)				
No introspections	5			
Expected puff for 24 extinction trials	3	17.7	44	42
Changed hypothesis during extinction	12	70.6	65	28
Didn't think about experiment	2	11.7	67	58
Group II (50 percent reinforcement)				
No introspections	4			
Expected puff for 24 extinction trials	8	44.4	62	66
Changed hypothesis during extinction	5	27.8	50	35
Didn't think about experiment	5	27.8	57	73
Group III (100 percent reinforcement-spaced)				
No introspections	3			
Expected puff for 24 extinction trials	6	31.6	66	55
Changed hypothesis during extinction	12	63.1	65	24
Didn't think about experiment	1	5.3	68	8

indicate that those who kept on expecting the air-puff, no matter in which group they are found, tended to give more conditioned responses than those who changed their hypothesis concerning the air-puff. That this is not a function of acquisition level is evident from a comparison of the respective percentage-frequencies. It should also be noted that there were more who kept expecting the air-puff in Group II than in either of the other groups.

There are, however, two possible anomalous findings in the introspection results. Firstly, although there is the difference between those who expect the puff and those who do not, irrespective of group, Group II still responds at higher levels in each of the categories than do the other groups. This may be merely a "chance" difference, or it may be due to differing degrees of expectancy not taken into account in the broad categories used. Secondly, with the exception of the single case in Group III, those who "didn't think" performed much more like those who kept on expecting the puff than those who didn't. More information is needed to clarify this relationship.

Is expectancy purely verbal? It might be supposed that the results reported for conditioned eyelid reactions merely reflect the verbalizing ability of human subjects, so that, in fact, eyelid reactions are unsuitable for conditioning experiments. While verbal abilities undoubtedly influence the results, they are not the sole explanation. It has also been shown that expectancy of stimulating situations is not the same as preparation for specific acts (Hilgard & Humphreys, 1938), i.e., conditioned eyelid reactions in human subjects are not under full voluntary control.

Parallel results may be anticipated from experiments with lower animals. The results of Pavlov and Brogden, previously mentioned, are similar to those presented here. Skinner's results from periodic reconditioning and reinforcement at a fixed ratio can best be understood in accordance with expectancy. A phenomenon comparable to the verbal conditioning of the psycho-galvanic response (e.g., Cook & Harris, 1937) has been observed in lower animals, e.g., the conditioning without paired stimulation of Grether (1938) and Sears (1934). It is suggested that generalization is not a radically different phenomenon, the criterion of differentiation being merely the presence or absence of previous pairing of stimuli. This is strikingly evident in the cases of extremely wide generalization, e.g., from buzzer to light or vice-versa as in Schlosberg's results (1934). Hence it cannot be assumed, without proof, that the results as reported here would not also apply to non-verbalizing animals.

SUMMARY AND CONCLUSIONS

In order to test the effects of random alternation of reinforcement on the acquisition and extinction of conditioned eyelid reactions, 66 college students were conditioned to a light followed by a puff of air to the cornea. This training occurred under three differing conditions, subjects being grouped according to the procedure used. Group I was given 100 percent reinforcement for 96 trials, the light always being followed by

The Effect of Random Alternation of Reinforcement 527

the puff, followed by 24 extinction trials. Group II was given 50 percent reinforcement for 96 trials, the light being followed by the puff on only one-half of the trials, followed by 24 extinction trials. Group III was given 100 percent reinforcement for 48 trials, with 48 interspersed rest intervals where non-reinforced trials occurred in Group II, followed by 24 extinction trials. The findings justify the following conclusions:

1. There are no significant differences in the acquisition of conditioned responses, measured by frequency and magnitude, under the three experimental procedures. This is clear evidence that non-reinforced trials do not always result in significant decrements (Group II). It also points to an advantage of spaced trials over an equivalent number of massed trials (compare Groups I and III).

2. There are significant differences in the extinction of the conditioned responses, measured by frequency and magnitude, between Group II (50 percent reinforcement) and Groups I and III (100 percent reinforcement). Group II responds at a significantly higher level over the 24 extinction trials than Groups I and III.

3. Neither the acquisition nor the extinction results are in harmony with classical conditioning theory which stresses merely the frequency with which reinforcement or non-reinforcement occurs. An alternative interpretation, provisionally designated the expectancy hypothesis, is coherent with all of the data within the reported experiment.

37

External Inhibition of the Conditioned Eyelid Reflex[1]

HENRY S. PENNYPACKER

One of the most basic phenomena studied by Pavlov in his pioneering and definitive researches on conditioned reflexes is that of indirect or external inhibition: the process by which perception of a new or unusual stimulus disrupts or suppresses ongoing reflex activity. In almost all cases, this disruption is thought to be occasioned by the evocation of a competing investigatory reflex by the novel stimulus. In order to serve as an external inhibitor, therefore, it seems very probable that a stimulus must have the capacity of evoking an extraneous or orienting reflex.

Pavlov went on to specify in some detail the variety of effects produced by the presentation of an external inhibitor and discussed the conditions under which such effects were found to occur. He found, for example, that the extent of inhibition of a well established conditioned reflex varied directly with the intensity of the external inhibitor. He further showed that if the intensity of the external inhibitor was held constant, then the degree to which a conditioned reflex was inhibited varied inversely with the strength of the reflex as inferred from the number of times its elicitation had been reinforced.

Undoubtedly of greater theoretical significance was Pavlov's discovery that the presentation of an external inhibitor did not always lead to inhibition of an existing conditioned reflex, but that in some cases the reflex was strengthened. He found this to be the case when the reflex in question was being subjected to some other form of inhibition at the time the external inhibitor was presented. Thus, for example, in the case of a well established reflex, presenting a novel stimulus early in the interval of delay often elicited the reflex which ordinarily should not have occurred until a point in time more nearly coincident with the unconditioned stimulus. Pavlov suggested that such an elicitation of the conditioned reflex was due to inhibition by the external inhibitor of internal inhibition

---

[1] Based on the author's Ph.D. dissertation completed at Duke University in 1962. A briefer description of this study has been published (Pennypacker, 1964).

of delay, the term used to describe the withholding of a conditioned response until reinforcement is imminent. Such inhibition of inhibition Pavlov called *disinhibition*. He went on to show that this too depends for its effect upon the intensity of the external inhibitor and the amount of inhibition present to be disinhibited which in turn depends again upon such things as the number of previous reinforcements.

These relationships are clearly exemplified in the following experiment conducted in Pavlov's laboratory. A conditioned salivary reflex had been established in a dog using tactual stimulation of the skin as a CS and acid as a UCS. After a considerable number of reinforcements the CR displayed the typical pattern of failing to occur until toward the end of the CS-UCS interval. In Pavlovian terms, this meant that early in the interval the response was held in check by inhibition of delay. Presenting a weak odor of camphor together with the CS had no effect on the course of the CR; it was initially inhibited, then evoked. Presenting thermal stimulation at 50°C, again in conjunction with the CS, interrupted the primary inhibitory phase of the reflex and the animal salivated throughout the presentation of the two stimuli. Both the inhibitory phase and the later excitatory phase were disrupted when a whistle was blown during the presentation of the CS; the animal salivated early in the interval but the flow decreased as the UCS approached. Finally, when a loud whistle was blown, no conditioned response at all was made during the interval of delay.

Other types of internal inhibition can similarly be disinhibited by the presentation of an external inhibitor. Moreover, it follows that the same external inhibitor can on one occasion in an experiment inhibit a conditioned reflex though it facilitates the occurrence of the reflex on another occasion. Thus, Pavlov writes, "We have seen that the very same extra stimuli, which, when they evoke strong extraneous reflexes, produce, when their effect is weak from the start or weakened by repetition, disinhibition of the conditioned reflexes which were made to undergo extinction" (Pavlov, 1927, p. 67).

The foregoing statement has, to the author's knowledge, been verified only once in the American conditioning literature. M. A. Wenger, in 1936, conditioned the GSRs of human subjects to a red light, using a shock to the sole of the right foot as reinforcement. Twice during acquisition, he presented tactual vibration to the subject's left hand; he then recorded the amplitude of the GSR made to the next presentation of the light CS and found in each case that it was smaller than the reponse made to a nonreinforced CS presented immediately prior to the inhibitor. After extinguishing the response to its level prior to reinforcement, he again administered the tactual vibration and observed an increment in the GSR made to the immediately succeeding presentation of the CS. Wenger had divided his subjects into two groups which differed according to the intensity of the tactual vibration presented and found, as Pavlov would have predicted, an increase in both the inhibitory and disinhibitory effects associated with the more intense external inhibitor.

Effects like those of external inhibition can be found elsewhere in the American conditioning literature. Dufort and Kimble (1958) compared eyelid conditioning with and without a ready signal, the latter being a buzzer of 1.0 second duration, terminating 2, 3, or 4 seconds prior to the onset of the CS. They found acquisition impaired in the presence of the ready signal. McAllister and McAllister (1960) were able to replicate these findings using the word "ready" instead of a buzzer and Chapman (1962) has extended both sets of results by showing that the degree of impairment of conditioning varies inversely with the proximity of the ready signal to the onset of the CS. A reasonable interpretation of these findings would suggest simply that the orienting reflex, or traces of it, made to the ready signal is, at the onset of the CS, activating parts of the subject's nervous system necessary to conditioning; as this activation is given time to die away, the resulting interference is diminished. In addition, Dufort and Kimble present evidence which would suggest that the orienting reflex to the ready signal diminishes in intensity, and hence in inhibitory capacity, with repeated elicitations; the greatest differences in performance among their groups occur early in training.

It will be noticed that both the Wenger experiment and those just discussed differ from the Pavlovian experiments cited earlier in one important theoretical detail: Pavlov applied his external inhibitors during the presentation of the CS and therefore, according to him, at a time when excitatory or inhibitory states under the control of the CS were in effect. The other investigators mentioned applied external inhibitors at times when the CS was not present, though it is possible, particularly in the case of the Wenger experiment, to assert that lingering excitatory and inhibitory effects, developed in the presence of the CS, were effected by the extra stimuli.

A few American investigators have actually presented external inhibitors during the operation of the CS (Rodnick, 1937; Spence & Runquist, 1958), but these investigations have invariably been concerned with the nature of the response made to the external inhibitor, usually a very weak stimulus used as a probe, rather than with the effect of the extra stimulus upon the primary reflex.

With respect to disinhibition, Kimble (1961) has recently reported observing such a phenomenon under conditions where some form of internal inhibition associated with the CS may have been assumed to be operating. In this instance, however, the primary inhibition was observed as a diminution of the unconditioned reflex; presenting an external inhibitor during the interval of delay served in some cases to restore the amplitude of the unconditioned reflex. Since most investigators of the phenomenon of CS-controlled inhibition of the unconditioned reflex feel that it is a result of inhibition of delay (Kupalov, 1960; Kimble & Ost, 1961; Pennypacker & Kimmel, 1961), Kimble's data may well represent the first American demonstration of disinhibition of inhibition of delay, at least where human subjects are involved.

Finally, in a preliminary study in this laboratory, it was found that a novel visual stimulus, presented instead of the usual visual CS after 15, 30, and 60 reinforcements, inhibited the conditioned eyeblink and that the degree of inhibition varied inversely with the number of prior reinforcements. In contrast to Wenger's findings, however, was the suggestion that the presentation of the novel stimulus during acquisition was followed by a period of heightened excitation, a phenomenon labeled *induction* by Pavlov. Unfortunately, all subjects in this experiment were administered the three trials involving the novel stimulus hence no controls were available against which to assess the presence and amount of such an inductive effect.

The present study was designed in an effort to correct this failing as well as to verify the inhibiting properties of a novel stimulus presented with, rather than instead of, the conditioned stimulus. Since the primary interest was in an inhibitory rather than disinhibitory effect, it was decided that the external inhibitor should be presented during the second, usually excitatory, phase of the interval of delay rather than throughout the interval as Pavlov had done. This procedure was also adopted with the expectation that as a result of inhibiting the excitatory phase in this manner, inhibition of the UCR might also be observed. Finally, to substantiate Pavlov's and Wenger's assertion that the same extra stimulus which serves as an inhibitor during acquisition will, in the presence of inhibition acquired as a result of experimental extinction, act as a disinhibitor, a series of post-extinction trials was administered with the extra stimulus added as it had been during acquisition.

Method

SUBJECTS. The subjects were Duke University undergraduate students who participated voluntarily in order to fulfill a part of the laboratory requirement of an introductory psychology course in which they were enrolled. None had had previous experience in an eyelid conditioning situation.

Usable data were collected from 60 of the 77 subjects who participated. Nine of the remaining subjects were discarded as voluntary responders, 6 failed to produce at least 5 conditioned responses during the acquisition period, and an exceedingly high resting blink rate made the records of the remaining two unreadable.

The subjects were assigned serially in order of their apearance at the laboratory to one of three groups, differing only with respect to the number of acquisition trials administered with the external inhibitor present. The assignment of subjects to groups was partially restricted in order that each group of 20 subjects would finally be composed of 14 males and 6 females, approximately the ratio of the sexes in the parent population.

APPARATUS. The subject was comfortably seated alone in a well-lighted, sound-deadened cubicle whose internal dimensions were 84 by 36 by 84 inches. Immediately in front of the subject was a table-like shelf upon which he could rest his hands and forearms. Communication between the subject and the experimenter was available, when needed, through an intercommunication system.

Throughout the procedure, the subject wore a headpiece to which was attached the air delivery tube and a microtorque potentiometer. The arm of the latter was connected by means of a light cotton thread to a false aluminum eyelash which was taped to the subject's right eyelid; movements of the eyelid were thus mechanically transformed into movements of the potentiometer arm. These movements were relayed to a Grass Model 5E D.C. Driver Amplifier through a $22\frac{1}{2}$ volt balanced connecting circuit designed and supplied by the Grass Instrument Company. The output of the Driver Amplifier was ink-recorded on one channel of a Grass Model 5 polygraph at a paper speed of 30 mm. per second. Two event-marking pens were employed; one recorded the onset of the conditioned stimulus and the cessation of the unconditioned stimulus while the other marked the onset and cessation only of the unconditioned stimulus. The chart drive was started manually approximately 3 seconds before the onset of the conditioned stimulus and allowed to run until approximately 3 seconds after the delivery of the unconditioned stimulus.

The unconditioned stimulus, a puff of air, was delivered through a $\frac{3}{64}$-inch aperture to the temporal corner of the subject's right eye from a distance of about one-half inch. The intensity of the air puff was maintained at the equivalent of 180 mm. of mercury as measured by a gauge and was controlled by a system of valves leading from a tank of dry compressed air. The duration of the air puff was .10 second and was controlled by the action of a solenoid valve.

The conditioned stimulus was a circular red light, $1\frac{1}{4}$ inches in diameter, produced by a Grason-Stadler Model E 4580 multiple stimulus projector and mounted equidistant from either side at a height of 70 inches in the cubicle wall facing the subject. The extra stimulus, or external inhibitor, was a 1000 cps tone delivered at an intensity of approximately 70 decibels (re: .0002 dynes/cm.^{2}) by an RCA Beat Frequency Oscillator Model 154 through a $3\frac{1}{2}$-inch speaker mounted in the wall of the cubicle to the subject's left.

All stimulus durations and interstimulus intervals were controlled by Grason-Stadler electronic interval timers. Trials were presented in a repeating sequence of 25, 15, 20, 28, 12, 23, and 17 seconds by means of a Gerbrands tape programmer whose action after the appropriate interval automatically initiated the sequence of events defining a trial.

PROCEDURE. When the subject arrived at the laboratory, he was led into the cubicle and seated in a cushioned, reclining office-type chair with a padded headrest. He was told to lean back as far as he could in the chair and use the footrest provided for his feet. The experimenter then began reading aloud the instructions, pausing at the appropriate point to affix the headpiece and false eyelash and adjust the air delivery tube. The intent of the instructions was twofold: to acquaint the subject with the general procedure without revealing to him its purpose, and second, to inhibit the production of voluntary responses by introducing a set to "respond naturally." After eliciting and answering any questions, the experimenter left the cubicle and closed the door.

All subjects first received two trials with the conditioned stimulus alone followed by three trials with the unconditioned stimulus alone. This was done to familiarize the subject with the stimuli he was to encounter and to provide a measure of responsivity to these stimuli prior to conditioning. Paired conditioning trials were then presented with the onset of the conditioned stimulus (CS) preceding the onset of the unconditioned stimulus (UCS) by 1.0 second; the duration of the CS was 1.0 second so that its termination was coincident with the onset of the UCS. On trials involving the tone as an extra stimulus, the onset of the CS preceded that of the tone by .5 second, both stimuli terminating together. All such trials were reinforced during acquisition to prevent the development of discrimination and to permit observation of the effects, if any, of the external inhibitor upon the UCR.

Depending upon the experimental condition to which he was assigned, the subject received 15, 30, or 60 such trials before receiving his first trial with the external inhibitor present. Group I received 60 CS-UCS trials, one trial with the external inhibitor, and five more CS-UCS trials. Group II received 30 CS-UCS trials, an external inhibitor trial, 30 more CS-UCS trials, then another external inhibitor trial followed by five CS-UCS trials. Group III subjects received their first external inhibitor trial after 15 CS-UCS trials, their second after the 30th CS-UCS trial, and a third after the 60th CS-UCS trial, again followed by five final CS-UCS trials. Thus, provision was made to compare subjects' performance following presentation of the external inhibitor after 15 and/or 30 reinforcements with the performance of subjects who had not yet experienced the external inhibitor.

All subjects were treated alike in extinction. Three extinction trials involving only the CS were administered, followed by five nonreinforced trials in which the tone was added to the CS as it had been in acquisition. This procedure was carried out with 57 subjects, 19 from each group. The first subject run in each condition was administered 10 straight extinction trials; subsequent addition of the tone produced no change in what was typical extinction behavior. This suggested that fewer nonreinforced presentations of the CS would be necessary to prevent the development of so much extinctive inhibition that no effects of the external inhibitor could be observed.

Results

All data were derived from measurements and judgments made from the ink-written records. The records were evaluated with the aid of a transparent template; decisions concerning questionable voluntary responses were made with the assistance of another experimenter who was experienced in reading these records.

Definition of the dependent variable. A conditioned response was defined as any deflection from a stable baseline in the direction of closure that (1) was greater than or equal to 1 mm., (2) occurred at least 600 msc. after the onset of the CS, and (3) did not return to the baseline prior to the onset of the UCS. The first two of these specifications are, with minor variations, in rather widespread use. The third, however, requires special justification.

It is well known that the presentation of virtually any suprathreshold novel stimulus will evoke an orienting reflex on the part of a human subject and that one component of this reflex is an eyeblink. Since, as Grant and Norris (1946) and others have shown, the latency of such a reflex blink may be as much as 110 msc., it was entirely possible in the present study for reflex (or alpha) blinks to the onset of the tone to be mistaken for conditioned responses on those trials in which the tone was intended to serve as an external inhibitor. By requiring that a conditioned response blend with the unconditioned response, the likelihood of inadvertently including alpha responses on these trials was greatly reduced since the duration of an alpha reflex is not apt to be more than 100 msc. As a check on the efficacy of this procedure, the data were tabulated with and without using the blending criterion. On the reinforced trials that included the tone, the blending criterion eliminated 39.4 percent of the responses that would otherwise have been classified as CRs; it eliminated only 10.6 percent of such responses on the other acquisition trials. It is assumed that this difference reflects the presence of alpha reflexes to the onset of the tone which were appropriately omitted from the analysis. In order to insure statistical comparability,

External Inhibition of the Conditioned Eyelid Reflex

however, the blending criterion was applied to all reinforced responses, thus making any statistical demonstration of external inhibition due to the presence of the tone somewhat more difficult than it would have been had the blending criterion only been applied to those responses made in the presence of the tone. The blending criterion was not used in the case of responses observed during extinction.

With the definition of the dependent variable established, it is proper to proceed to a consideration of the results of the experiment. For each group, Figure 37-1 shows the mean percentage of conditioned responses

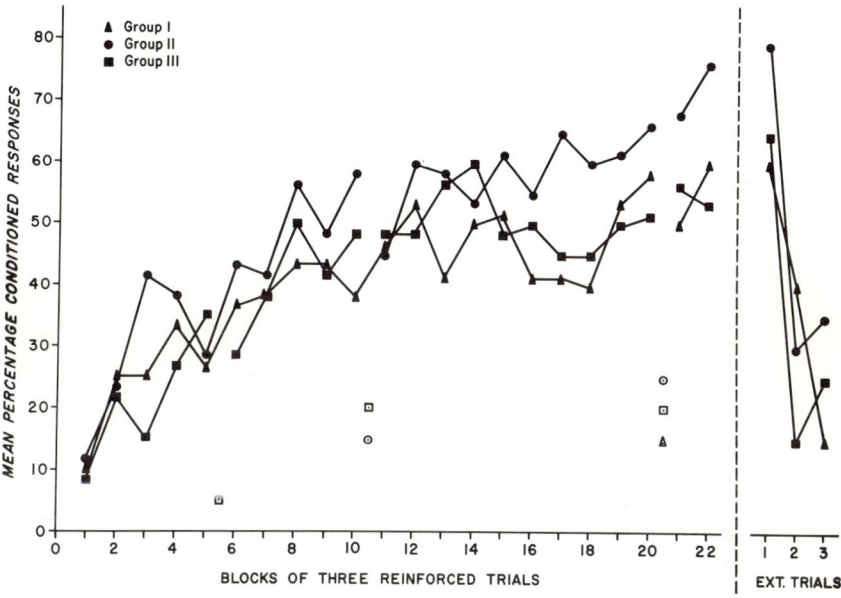

FIGURE 37-1. Mean percentage of conditioned responses for the three groups presented by blocks of three trials in acquisition and trial by trial in extinction.

in acquisition (including the first extinction trial) plotted as a function of blocks of three trials. Performance in extinction is similarly plotted trial by trial for the three trials during which only the CS was presented. The open symbols in Figure 37-1 represent performance of the various groups on the trials which included the external inhibitor. Inspection of the figure clearly indicates that a large decrement in performance resulted from presentation of the external inhibitor, but that the amount of decrement is not greatly affected either by the number of prior reinforcements or by the number of prior presentations of the external inhibitor itself. Statistical tests of all possible differences among these points confirm the latter impression.

The decrement which occurred in the presence of the external inhibitor was evaluated for each group separately by means of the Cochran Q test (Siegel, 1956); this technique simultaneously compared each subject's performance on the external inhibitor trial with his performance on each of the three immediately preceding trials. Similar analyses were performed on the pooled data of Groups II and III following 30 CS-UCS trials and on the data of all three groups following 60 CS-UCS trials. The results of these analyses, presented in Table 37-1,

TABLE 37-1

Cochran Q tests of effect of tone on conditioning

	After 15 reinforcements	After 30 reinforcements	After 60 reinforcements
Group I			$Q = 14.445^*$ $.001 < p < .01$
Group II		$Q = 15.000$ $.001 < p < .01$	$Q = 16.200$ $.001 < p < .01$
Group III	$Q = 9.900$ $.01 < p < .02$	$Q = 12.382$ $.001 < p < .01$	$Q = 8.581$ $.02 < p < .05$
Pooled		Groups II and III: $Q = 22.963$ $p < .001$	All groups: $Q = 11.473$ $.001 < p < .01$

* $df = 3$ in all cases.

demonstrate that the decrement in performance due to the presentation of the external inhibitor is statistically reliable in every case.

Although analysis of the groups' performance on the external inhibitor trials reveals no differences which can be reliably attributed to differential habit strength as inferred from the number of prior reinforcements, examination of the data for individual subjects provides evidence of a strong inverse relationship between the effectiveness of the tone as an inhibitor and the level of conditioning. The distribution of total number of conditioned responses produced in acquisition was dichotomized at the median; a 2 by 2 frequency table relating this index of response strength to whether or not a conditioned response was made on any of the external inhibitor trials is presented in Table 37-2. The degree of association ex-

TABLE 37-2

Relationship between total conditioned responses and effect of the inhibitor

	Did not respond in presence of tone	Did respond in presence of tone
Below median number of total CRs	26	4
Above median number of total CRs	19	11

hibited by this table was evaluated by means of Fisher's exact test which yielded a probability value of .0358. Thus, support is provided for the Pavlovian contention that the effect of an extra stimulus presented during the interval of delay will be a function of the strength of the conditioned response being delayed, specifically that a strong CR is harder to disrupt in this way than a weak one.

Figure 37-2 is a series of tracings showing the variety of effects produced by the introduction of the tone at the midpoint of the interval of delay. Although total inhibition of the CR occurred in 83.3 percent of the trials in which the tone was presented, it is of interest to examine some of the characteristics of the responses made on the remaining 16.7 percent. It might be, for example, that, even if the tone were not completely effective as an inhibitor, partial effectiveness would serve to lengthen the latency of the conditioned response as shown in the top panel of Figure 37-2. One might also suppose that in a few cases the tone would operate as a disinhibitor, removing the inhibition of delay thereby decreasing the latency of the conditioned response. Such an effect is shown in the bottom panel of Figure 37-2.

In order to see if either or both of these effects occurred with any regularity in those cases where the tone failed to block completely the production of a conditioned response, response latencies were recorded for each subject on the last trial on which the external inhibitor produced a CR. These, together with the latencies of the two immediately prior and two immediately subsequent conditioned responses, are presented in Table 37-3.

It can be seen from Table 37-3 that introduction of the tone has no particular effect on the mean latency of either the responses made to the tone or those made immediately after its presentation. There is, however, a significant increase in variability of these latencies; F-ratios were formed between the variance of the latencies obtained on the trials

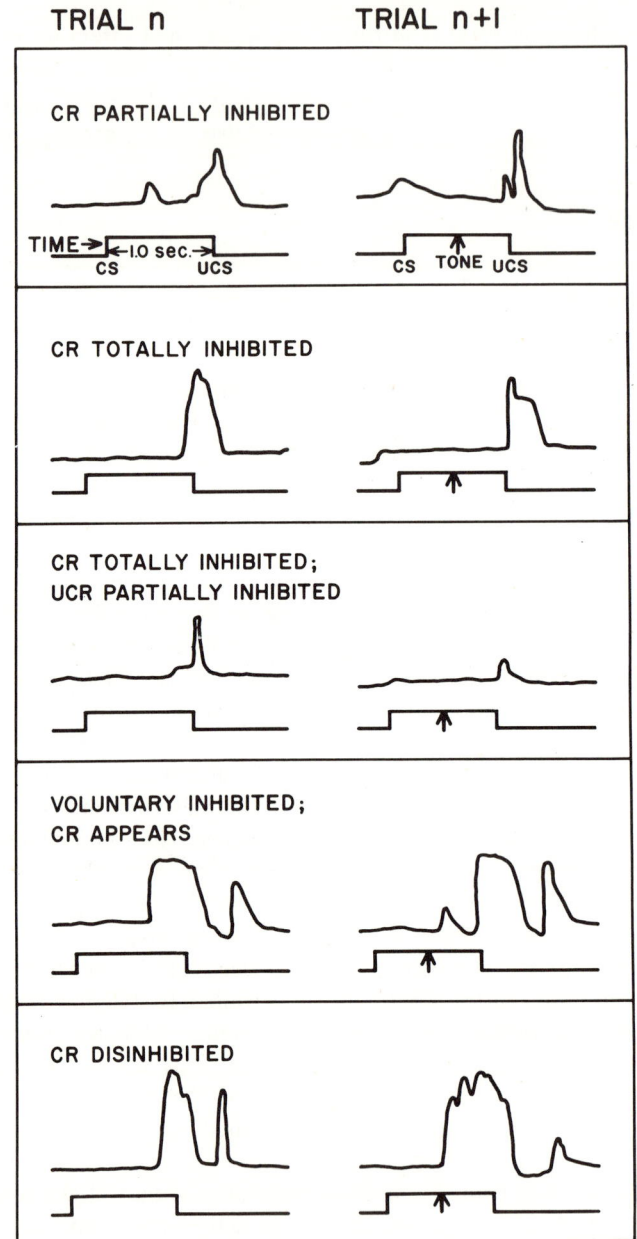

FIGURE 37-2. Tracings of actual records showing the effects of the tone on various eyelid reflexes.

TABLE 37-3

Latencies in seconds of conditioned responses prior to tone, in the presence of tone, and following tone

No. of S	2nd CR prior to tone	1st CR prior to tone	CR during tone	1st CR after tone	2nd CR after tone
24	.92	.92	.83	.63	.66
33	.79	.86	.92	.92	.69
41	.79	.76	1.02	.86	.73
43	.96	1.02	.63	.86	1.02
48	.92	1.06	1.00	.59	.69
20	.89	.89	1.02	1.00	.63
35	.73	.73	.66	.63	1.00
39	.76	.83	.69	.73	.96
40	.76	.83	.83	.76	1.06
44	.79	.79	.83	.76	.79
50	.89	.89	.59	.76	.79
53	.86	.96	.79	.79	1.02
19	1.02	.83	1.06	.89	1.06
32	.86	1.02	.89	.66	.59
42	.86	.63	1.06	.89	.63
Mean	.85	.87	.85	.78	.82
σ^2	.006	.013	.023	.014	.029

with the external inhibitor and the pooled variance of the latencies of the two previous conditioned responses ($F = 2.467$, $df = 29/14$, $p < .025$) and between the pooled variance of the two subsequent conditioned responses and the pooled variance of the two previous conditioned responses ($F = 2.253$, $df = 29/29$, $p < .05$). The comparison involving the latencies of the CRs obtained in the presence of the external inhibitor and those of the two subsequent conditioned responses failed to reach significance ($F < 1.00$). Thus we have evidence that, in these subjects at least, if the external inhibitor fails to produce total inhibition of the CR, it may alter the latency not only of the conditioned response produced in its immediate presence, but of subsequent conditioned responses as well.

Extinction data. Table 37-4 presents the number of conditioned responses made by each of the three groups on the eight extinction trials. It will be recalled that the data in the last 5 columns are based on 57 subjects since the first subject run in each group was administered 10 straight extinction trials. For the 57 subjects who received three nonreinforced presentations of the CS followed by five nonreinforced presenta-

TABLE 37-4

Performance in extinction by trials for the three groups

	CS ALONE (n = 60)			CS PLUS TONE (n = 57)				
Extinction trial	1	2	3	4	5	6	7	8
Group I	12	8	3	5	3	2	2	6
Group II	16	6	7	4	5	5	5	5
Group III	13	3	5	6	3	5	6	8

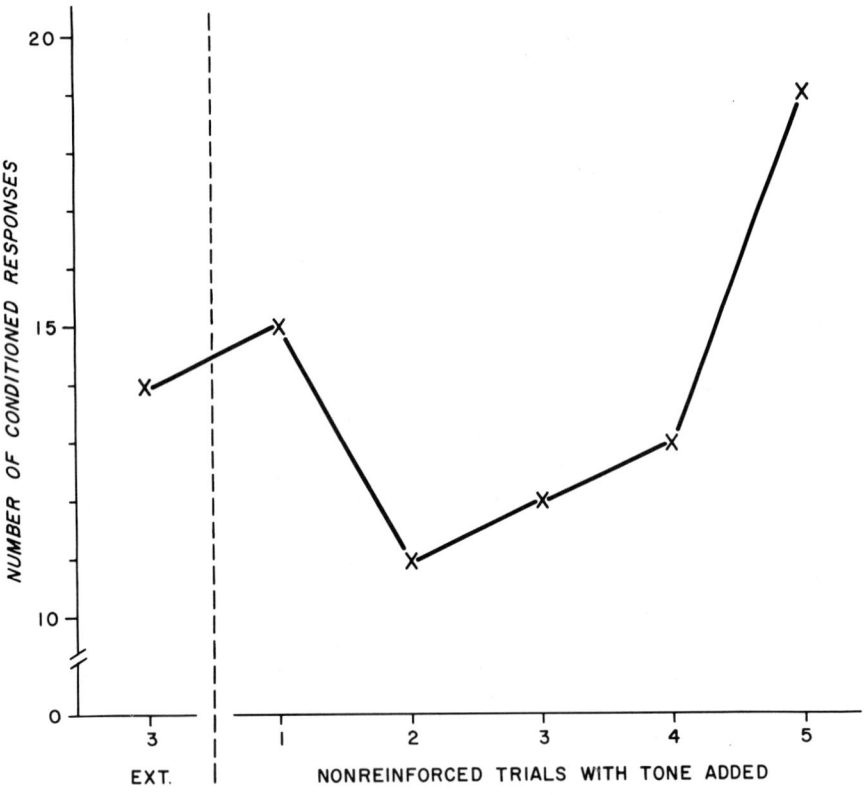

FIGURE 37-3. Number of conditioned responses presented trial by trial for the last six extinction trials.

TABLE 37-5

Analysis of variance of conditioned responses made to tone in extinction

SOURCE OF VARIATION	df	SUMS OF SQUARES	MEAN SQUARES	F
Groups	2	10.133	5.067	2.924*
Trials	4	13.333	3.333	1.923
Linear	(1)	3.333	3.333	1.923
Quadratic	(1)	9.524	9.524	5.496†
Groups × Trials	8	13.867	1.733	
Total	14	37.333		

* p .10.
† $.025 < p < .05$.

tions of the CS plus the tone, performance in the last straight extinction trial is, for comparative purposes, presented with performance on the 5 CS plus tone trials in Figure 37-3. A groups × trials analysis of variance of performance on these final five trials appears in Table 37-5.

One notes in examining Table 37-5 that a nearly significant difference in performance occurred as a function of the number of times the tone had been presented and reinforced during acquisition; the mean number of CRs per subject in Groups I, II, and III was .95, 1.26, and 1.47, respectively. This trend suggests that attempting to avoid the formation of discrimination during acquisition by reinforcing all presentations of the tone may have led to somewhat different levels of conditioning to the tone for the three groups: indirect evidence that a discrimination might indeed have been formed had the tone not been reinforced though it was presented at most only three times.

The most interesting feature of Table 37-5, however, is evidence for the reliability of the quadratic relationship depicted in Figure 37-3. The upward extension of the curve over the last three trials appears to confirm Wenger's finding that an external inhibitor in acquisition will, if presented during extinction, assume disinhibitory capacities. It must be added, however, that these results are only suggestive because of the absence of necessary controls against which to assess the effect of further ordinary extinction trials and the extent to which there are UCRs to the tone alone.

DISCUSSION

The principal result of this study was its confirmation in human eyeblink conditioning of the existence of a phenomenon of basic importance in classical conditioning: external inhibition. Specifically, it has been shown that the introduction of an extra stimulus during that portion of the interval of delay which is commonly thought to be excitatory will inhibit the production of a conditioned response.

The Pavlovian explanation for external inhibition is that a novel stimulus evokes an orienting reaction and that this reaction obliterates the conditioned response. The data support such an interpretation indirectly. It will be recalled that 39.4 percent of the responses made in the presence of the tone during acquisition were not considered in the analysis because they did not blend with the UCR whereas only 10.6 percent of the responses made in the absence of the tone were similarly eliminated. Inspection of the records indicates that the vast majority of the former were probably orienting reflexes; they occurred with appropriate latency and were usually of brief duration. In considering cases in which the tone failed to elicit an orienting blink but did inhibit the production of a conditioned response, it should be recognized that the blink reflex is probably only a part of the orienting reflex and perhaps not the essential part for the occurrence of external inhibition. Therefore, failure of the reflex blink to occur to all presentations of the tone cannot be taken as evidence that the orienting reaction also failed to occur.

The present demonstration of the susceptibility of the conditioned human eyeblink to external inhibition and, tentatively, disinhibition, affords us the opportunity to verify at the human level the Pavlovian implications of these phenomena. An obvious next step, for example, would involve manipulating the intensity of the external inhibitor to see if the amount of external inhibition produced does vary directly with the intensity of the extra stimulus; the results of our preliminary study compared with those of the main study predict such an outcome since less inhibition was observed in the presence of a visual stimulus than in the presence of a more novel auditory one.

The Pavlovian investigators often used variations in the amount of external inhibition produced by a standard extra stimulus to make inferences about the amount of excitation present at the time of application of the external inhibitor. We should now be able similarly to investigate the hypothesized growth of excitation during the interval of delay by presenting tones at various points in such an interval and noting the amount of inhibition produced. This procedure might also shed light on the role of the orienting reflex to the onset of the extra stimulus in the production of external inhibition; if external inhibition is nothing more than a result of the orienting reflex and its refractory period, extra stimuli presented early in the delay interval should have less of an inhibitory effect than those presented later. The possibility exists, moreover, that an extra stimulus presented at a point in the interval too late to effect the anticipatory CR would have an inhibitory effect on the UCR, but the effect was observed in isolated instances (see Figure 37-3, third panel).

The results of the present study failed to confirm the expected presence of an induction effect in trials immediately following the presentation of the external inhibitor (see Fig. 37-1).[2] Since the preliminary study which suggested the likelihood of an inductive effect differed from the present one in that the external inhibitor was (a) visual and (b) presented *instead of* the CS rather than in conjunction with it, it seems likely that one or both of these differences is responsible for the disparity of results. We would assume, with Pavlov, that induction varies with the amount of inhibition produced, yet the observation that external inhibition varied inversely with the number of prior reinforcements in the preliminary study would suggest that that procedure generated less inhibition than the present one. A resolution of this paradox must await further research, including replication of the preliminary study with proper controls such as were incorporated in the present design. It may turn out that reinforcement delivered in the presence of a totally novel stimulus temporarily sensitizes the subject so that in the preliminary experiment, we observed a pseudo-induction effect that was not, in fact, preceded by a great amount of internal inhibition. By contrast, in the present experiment, the external inhibitor apparently was not of sufficient intensity to produce an inductive effect, but since it was presented in the presence of the CS, subsequent reinforcement was probably not as sensitizing. Thus, it would appear that the demonstration of an induction effect following the presentation of an external inhibitor during the interval of delay must await the use of a more intense inhibiting stimulus.

Finally, it is advisable to reiterate and enlarge upon the cautions mentioned earlier attendant to interpretation of the extinction results. Although there is in these results the strong suggestion that the same novel stimulus which serves as an external inhibitor during acquisition acts as a disinhibitor after a certain amount of extinction has been permitted to occur, it is possible that what is being considered as evidence for disinhibition may only be the recovery of the orienting reflex. This would be interesting if it were true for it would imply that the extinction process not only involves the development of inhibition of conditioned responses,

---

[2] A *t* test comparing the performance of Group II on trial blocks 10 and 11 (separated by their first experience with the tone) yielded a ratio less than unity. Since this difference is one of the largest to be found in Figure 37-1, either within or between groups on comparable or adjacent trial blocks, no effort was made to procure statistical support for either an induction effect or a locally perseverative inhibitory effect among the other points.

but of other types of responses as well. To check this possibility, it would have been necessary to introduce trials involving only the tone immediately after acquisition and compare the incidence of short latency blinks in that situation with that in the present procedure where the tone was introduced in the company of the CS after three extinction trials.

Just as in the case of external inhibition in acquisition, we do not know the role played in disinhibition of extinctive inhibition by the variables of stimulus intensity and the point in the delay interval at which the extra stimulus is presented. Moreover, in the research reported here, the number of extinction trials prior to the presentation of the disinhibitor was held constant at three. If the number of such trials were manipulated, we might expect the amount of disinhibition to vary directly with the intensity of the disinhibitor but inversely with the number of prior extinction trials. It is difficult to suggest the manner in which varying the point in the delay interval at which the disinhibitor is presented would interact with these two variables. Presumably, extinctive inhibition should develop most readily where inhibition is already assumed to be present, early in the delay interval. Weak external stimuli should therefore be successful as disinhibitors later in the internal where some residual excitation may yet exist after a series of extinction trials.

38

External Inhibition of the Conditioned Eyelid Reflex as a Function of the Temporal Locus of the External Inhibitor

HENRY S. PENNYPACKER
WILLIAM R. FOWLER

In an earlier report (Pennypacker, 1964) it was demonstrated that an extraneous auditory stimulus presented at the midpoint of the CS-UCS interval generally inhibits the blink reflex conditioned to a light. Interpretation of this result centered on the role of the orienting reflex to the extraneous stimulus in the disruption of the conditioned response. Thus, an extraneous stimulus presented early in the interval of delay should have little effect on the subsequent CR, particularly if the latter is well established. Presenting an extraneous stimulus late in the delay interval on the other hand, might be expected to leave the CR unaffected while exerting its inhibitory influence upon the UCR. The present experiment is an attempt to further substantiate this competing response interpretation of external inhibition by examining the foregoing implications.

Method

APPARATUS. The conditioning laboratory and apparatus were identical in all respects to those used in the earlier study. Briefly, eyelid responses were recorded by means of a microtorque potentiometer attached mechanically to the subject's right eyelid. The output of the potentiometer was amplified and recorded on a moving paper record; separate channels monitored the occurrence of the conditioning and novel stimuli. The US was a puff of dry compressed air of .10 second duration delivered to a point about $\frac{1}{2}$ inch from the temporal corner of the subject's right eye at an intensity sufficient to support the 180 mm. column of mercury.

The CS was a circular red light $1\frac{1}{4}$ inches in diameter mounted at eye level in the wall of the conditioning chamber facing the subject. The extra stimulus, or external inhibitor, was a 1000 cps tone delivered at an intensity of approximately 70 db (re: .0002 dynes/cm^2) through a speaker mounted in the cubicle wall to the subject's left.

The CS-US interval was 1.0 second, offset of the CS coincided with onset of the UCS. All stimulus durations and interstimulus intervals were controlled by a Grason-Stadler Electronic Interval Timer. Intertrial intervals ranged from 12 to 28 seconds with mean of 20 seconds, and were controlled by a Gerbrands Tape Programmer whose action after the appropriate interval automatically initiated the sequence of events defining a trial.

PROCEDURE. After the subject was comfortably seated in the cubicle and recording equipment attached, a set of standard eyelid conditioning instructions, designed to inhibit the production of voluntary responses by introducing a set to "respond naturally," were read to him. All subjects then received two nonreinforced CS presentations, three presentations of the UCS alone, and 69 paired presentations of the CS and US. On trials 16, 32, and 63, the tone was introduced at the point in the CS-UCS interval appropriate to the experimental condition. For Group I, the tone occurred .05 second after the onset of the CS; for Group II, it occurred .50 second after the onset of the CS; and .75 second after CS onset for Group III. In all cases, the tone terminated with the offset of the CS and the onset of the UCS.

SUBJECTS. Usable data were collected from 76 Duke University undergraduates who participated voluntarily as part of the requirements of the Introductory Psychology course. Groups I and III each contained 25 subjects; an additional subject was inadvertently included in Group II increasing the size of that group to 26. The assignment of subjects to groups was random with the exception that an effort was made to keep the ratio of the sexes approximately the same in all three groups.

Results and discussion

Definition of the dependent variable. A conditioned response was defined as any deflection from a stable baseline in the direction of closure that: (a) was greater than or equal to 1 mm.; and (b) occurred at least 600 msc. after the onset of the CS. The blending criterion employed in the earlier study was used only on trials involving the tone (test trials). In order to insure statistical comparability, the blending criterion was used on the test trial data of all three groups although its effectiveness in eliminating alpha blinks to the onset of the tone that might otherwise be included as CRs is undoubtedly limited to the data of Group II.

Figure 38-1 presents the acquisition performance of the three groups as a function of blocks of three reinforced trials together with their test

External Inhibition as a Function of the Temporal Locus

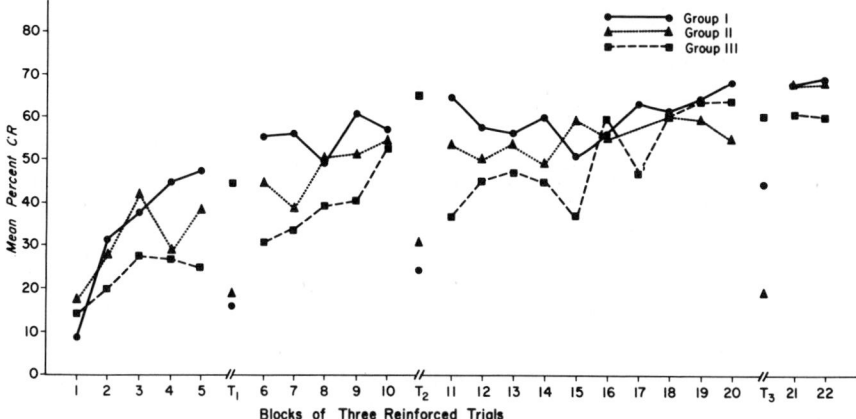

FIGURE 38.1. Mean percentage of conditioned responses for the three groups presented as functions of blocks of three CS-US trials and the three test trials individually.

trial performance plotted for the three test trials individually. All possible comparisons among the three groups on each test trial were made using the difference test for independent proportions (McNemar, 1956). The results of these comparisons, expressed as z-scores, are presented in Table 38-1. Inspection of the figure and the table reveals two important outcomes of the experiment. First, as was predicted from the competing response hypothesis of the mechanism of external inhibition, the amount of external inhibition generated by presentation of the novel stimulus early in the delay interval (Group I) decreases as the strength of the CR increases. Since this is not the case when the extra-stimulus is presented midway in the interval of delay (Group II), support is provided for the view that the period of effectiveness of the extra-stimulus as an external

TABLE 38-1

Z-Score contrasts of the three groups' test trial performance

CONTRASTED GROUPS	TEST TRIAL		
	1	2	3
I vs. II	<1.0	<1.0	1.91
I vs. III	2.16	2.85	1.13
II vs. III	1.90	2.37	2.98

inhibitor gradually becomes isolated to, say, the 300 msc. immediately following its onset. This view is, of course, consistent with the notion that the temporal limits of action by an external inhibitor are congruent with the temporal limits of the orienting response made to the external inhibitor.

The second striking feature of Figure 38-1 concerns the test trials performance of Group III. Presentation of the extra-stimulus late in the delay interval not only failed to produce external inhibition, but, early in training, appears to have produced a small amount of disinhibition. This result is somewhat at variance with the expectations of Pavlovian theory; according to that view, any disinhibition which might occur as a result of presentation of the novel stimulus late in the interval of delay should occur *late* in training as a result of interference with the gradually acquired process of inhibition of delay (Kimmel & Greene, 1964).

A more parsimonious explanation of the present data emerges with recognition of the fact that the majority of the responses made by Group III on test trials may well have been alpha blinks which the blending criterion failed to eliminate. In this context, it was noteworthy that Group I made a total of 48 alpha responses (latency range: 50–150 msc.) on the test trials while the total number of CRs (blending or not) made by Group III on the same trials was only 52. Thus it would appear that if the orienting responses could be removed from the test trial data of Group III, there might remain evidence that external inhibition is maximal when the extra-stimulus is presented late in the interval. Further information concerning the nature of the responses made by Group III on test trials should be obtained by comparing their data with those of a control group which received a comparable number of presentations of the CS and US in an unpaired, random order. If their behavior in the presence of the tone resembled that of the present Group III further support would accrue to the view that Group III's performance is heavily contaminated with alpha blinks.

The effect of presentation of a novel stimulus late in the CS-US interval upon the UR is typified by the portion of a sample record presented in Figure 38-2. Evidence for the generality of this effect was obtained by comparing (for Group III only) the UCR amplitude on those test trials on which no CR occurred with the amplitudes of the UCRs on the two immediately preceding CS-UCS trials during which CRs failed to occur. The mean amplitudes of the two preceding URs were, respectively, 30.83 mm. and 3069 mm. The mean test trial UR amplitude was 27.92; this reduction in amplitude is statistically reliable, $F(2.70) = 3.27$. It would seem that this result bears indirectly on the interpretation of Group III's test trial performance suggested above. Since this comparison involves only test trials on which no scoreable response occurred, it is obvious that whatever the nature of the reaction to the novel stimulus

External Inhibition as a Function of the Temporal Locus

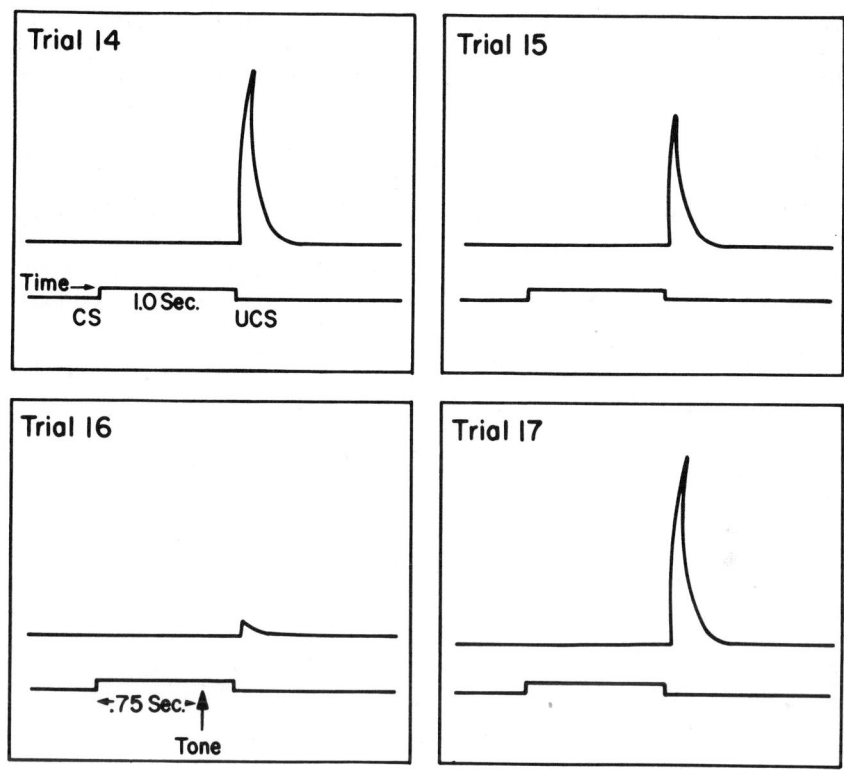

FIGURE 38-2. Tracing of an actual record showing the effect upon the UCR of introducing the novel stimulus late in the interval of delay.

on those trials, it did not involve an eyelid closure. As was pointed out in the earlier paper, the orienting reaction to a suprathreshold novel stimulus need not include a reflex blink; indeed, since the source of the novel stimulus was located to the subject's left and since the cubicle was well lighted throughout the experimental procedure, an equally adaptive response to the novel stimulus might be a sudden shift of gaze and head orientation in the direction of the sound followed immediately by visual search, an activity incompatible with a lid closure. Under these conditions, the effectiveness of the UCS in producing a lid closure would be attenuated by the subject's need to keep his eyes open. Reducing the intensity of the extra-stimulus to a level where it is no longer likely to evoke a startle reaction (and hence an eyeblink) should, if this interpretation is correct, produce (a) fewer ambiguous responses prior to the onset of the UCS, and (b) more frequent instances of diminution of the UCR as a consequence of a "what-is-it" reaction.

In summary, the results of this experiment tentatively indicate that the amount of external inhibition produced by the introduction of a novel stimulus in the interval of delay depends upon the temporal relation of that stimulus to the conditioning stimuli. Specifically, the closer the onset of the novel stimulus is to the expected time of occurrence of the CR, the less likely is the CR to occur. It is suggested that external inhibition may be viewed most profitably as a natural consequence of whatever incompatibilities exist between the orienting reaction to the novel stimulus and the conditioned response. Future investigations in which the relative strengths of the CR and orienting reaction are controlled would be of great value in eliminating alternative, less parsimonious, explanations.

39

Does the Interval of Delay of Conditioned Responses Possess Inhibitory Properties?[1]

ELIOT H. RODNICK

The recent publication of Lepley's (1932, 1934) hypothesis concerning the relationship between the remote excitatory tendencies in rote learning and trace conditioned responses, and the incorporation of this hypothesis by Hull (1935) as a postulate in a deductive system accounting for many of the phenomena of rote series learning, have called attention to the probable importance of trace conditioned responses in human learning. The extensive use of this postulate makes particularly urgent the confirmation on human subjects and under controlled conditions of Pavlov's (1927) contention that the interval of delay of delayed and trace conditioned responses possesses inhibitory properties capable of being generalized to other reactions which might occur during this interval.

The present investigation was specifically designed to determine whether the "inhibition of delay" is actually a genuine phenomenon with human beings. This inhibition should be observable as a decrement in the amplitude of a reaction inserted in the interval of delay.

The general procedure for the investigation of this problem requires first the establishment of a delayed conditioned response, which under the conditions of the present experiment occurs about 8 to 10 seconds after the onset of the conditioned stimulus. This is shown diagrammatically in Figure 1, where the two lines immediately below the time line represent an established delayed conditioned response (e.g., galvanic skin response) to a persisting stimulus (light). The interval AB is the "interval of delay."

Now, if the interval of delay actually possesses inhibitory properties which are generalized to other reactions, another conditioned response such as an eyelid reaction occurring in the interval of delay (AB) should be weakened below its normal magnitude. In the two lower lines of Figure 39-1 are represented the stimulus for the lid reaction (V, a vibratory

---

[1] Reprinted from the *Journal of Experimental Psychology*, 1937, Vol. 20, with the permission of the author.

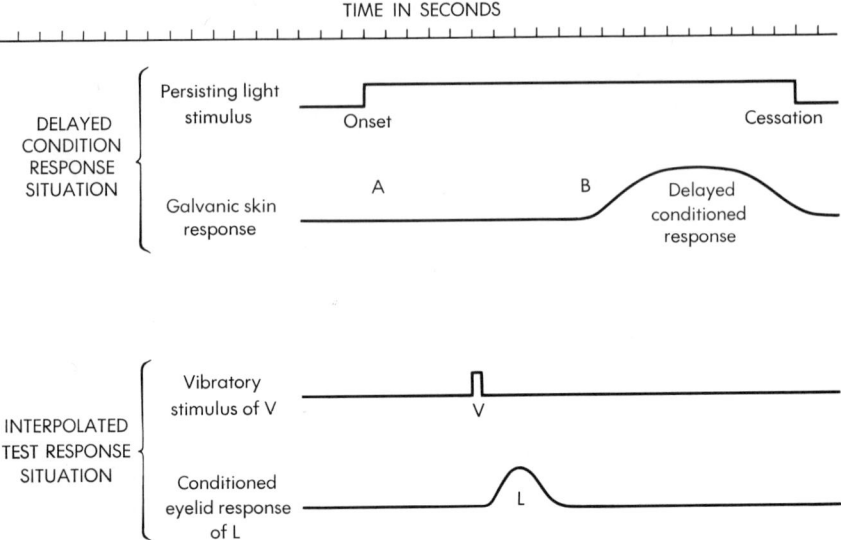

FIGURE 39-1. Diagrammatic representation of the method of testing for the "inhibition of delay."

stimulation of the skin) and its conditioned response (L), both occurring midway in the interval of delay, AB.

Since the lid response in this situation is designed to serve as an indicator of the presence of a generalized inhibition, it may be termed the *test* conditioned response. In order to determine whether the interval of delay really depresses this test response, the magnitude of the reaction when occurring during the period of delay (AB) of a delayed conditioned response must be compared with its magnitude under normal conditions. The normal magnitude of the test response can be found by presenting the stimulus for the lid response a few minutes before or after the interval of delay of the delayed conditioned response. The presentation of the stimulus for this lid response when it precedes the testing (period of delay) situation may be termed the pre-test control; when it follows it may be called the post-test control. A test cycle thus comprises the successive presentations of the pre-test, test, and post-test situations. If there is actually an inhibition of delay, the amplitude of the test conditioned response should be smaller in magnitude than the mean of the pre-test and post-test responses.

Apparatus

. . . The subject sat in a comfortable Morris chair, completely enclosed in a darkened cabinet. A 60-cycle A.C. current through headphones furnished a hum which effectively masked possible extraneous noises and cues.

Galvanic skin response. The conditioned stimulus for the galvanic skin response (delayed conditioned response) was a patch of faint light from a 6-volt flashlight bulb mounted in the front panel of the cabinet. This stimulus, dimmed by a layer of black sateen, had a duration of 21.3 seconds.

A moderate tetanizing shock delivered to the right wrist served as the unconditioned stimulus. The current was derived from a 6-volt lead storage battery and passed through a Cambridge inductorium. The shock had a duration of .625 second and was presented 20.1 seconds after the onset of the light in such a way that the latter continued for about .6 second beyond the termination of the shock. This is illustrated in Figure 39-2 (light and shock stimuli only), which is a transcript of part of a typical record.

The Tarchanoff phenomenon of the galvanic skin response was recorded. Two silver electrodes the size of quarter-dollars were strapped about one fourth inch apart against the palm of the left hand and were connected to the D'Aronval galvanometer. The tracing of the galvanometer movement was recorded upon the moving waxed paper of the polygraph at a reduction of 4 to 1.

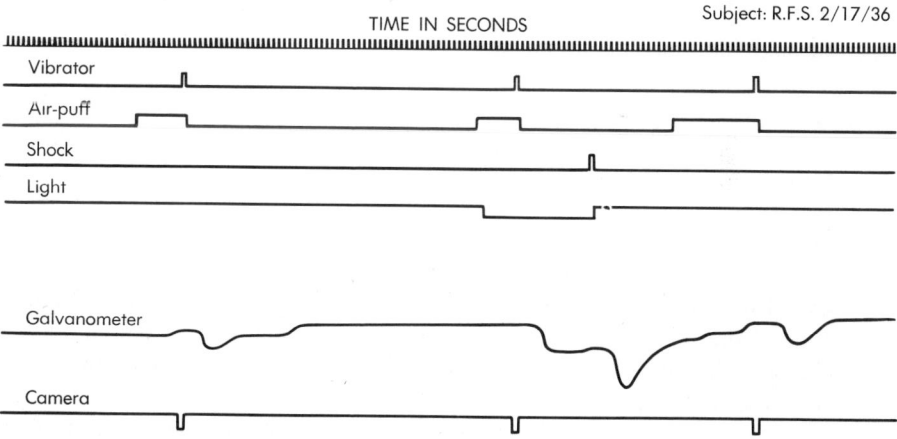

FIGURE 39-2. Tracing of a section of a typical stylographic record showing a complete test cycle: the vibrator-puff combination at the extreme left (pre-test control), the vibrator-puff in the delay period of the delayed conditioned response evoked by the light stimulus (test), and the vibrator-puff at the extreme right (post-test control). The air-puff valve was released at the down stroke of the notch.

Eyelid response. Photographic recording of the eyelid response was used. A weak tactual-vibratory sensation having a duration of .24 second served as the conditioned stimulus for the eyelid response (interpolated test response). This was delivered to the right forearm by an electrical stimulator, described by Bass and Hull (1934). The stimulator was actuated by a 4-volt 60-cycle A.C. current and delivered 120 pressures per second.

Reflex eyelid closure was obtained by directing a stream of air against the lateral margin of the left cornea. . . . An air pressure equivalent to 55 mm. of mercury in a closed-tube manometer was built up behind an electrically operated valve by means of a rubber bulb. Upon release of the valve, a stream of air passed through a rubber tube at the end of which was a rubber-tipped glass nozzle placed about 1 cm. from the cornea. The intensity of the stimulation was sufficient to evoke complete closure of the eyelid. The stimulus was recorded simultaneously with its presentation by diverting one half of the airstream against a paper marker in front of the camera aperture.

For most subjects, the air-puff was presented 500 milliseconds after the onset of the vibrator. In a few cases, however, when the conditioned response did not reach its maximum amplitude within this period, the interval between the stimuli was lengthened to 640 milliseconds.

Shadow recording of the winks was accomplished by means of a very slender bamboo rod supported at one end by a flat celluloid spring. A human hair cemented to the subject's eyelid passed straight upward through an opening in the roof of the cabinet to the bamboo marker. Tension of the hair was regulated by vertical adjustment of the bamboo rod. Photographic calibration of this recording system showed that the bamboo recorder followed the motion of the eyelid with no observable distortion, inertia, or overthrow. The subjects reported that the resistance of the recorder to the lid movement could not be felt. Amplification of the eyelid movement was about two to one.

A camera of special construction was employed to photograph the eyelid movement only during a stimulation. . . . The latency and amplitude of the conditioned response can thus be accurately measured without the omission of the reinforcing stimulus. This anticipation of the eyelid response is shown in Figure 39-3.

The timing of the stimuli and operation of the camera were controlled by the combined action of a synchronous motor timer and a heavy pendulum. The stimuli for the eyelid response and the period during which the camera was operating were recorded stylographically. . . . The photographic and the stylographic records supplemented each other synchronously in such a way that it was always possible to tell to what point in the continuous polygraph record each individual photographic exposure referred—a matter indispensable for the interpretation of the results. Immediately after their development the photographic records were keyed up with the polygraphic accompaniments by appropriate notations in pencil.

Procedure

The general procedure adopted to investigate the alleged inhibition of delay consisted of the following three steps:
1. The eyelid response was conditioned.
2. A satisfactory delayed conditioned response was established.
3. Tests of the inhibition of delay were made by presenting the stimulus for the conditioned eyelid response in the interval of delay. The magnitude of this led response was compared with those of the pre-test and post-test control lid responses completing the test cycle. Typical records of such a test cycle are shown in Figures 39-2 and 39-3.

Twenty male university students, paid by the hour, were employed on two successive days in the main experimental group. Two other groups of twenty subjects each served in the control experiments. The subjects were directed to look in the general direction of the light throughout the experiment, and to be sure to gaze at the visual stimulus during each presentation.

Session I. One hour. On this session, which was the same for both the experimental and the control groups, the conditioned lid response was established. Vibrator-puff combinations were presented until the subject showed a fairly consistent conditioned eyelid response for about 10 successive trials. Thirty-five trials were usually necessary to reach this criterion (range 16 to 50 trials).

Twenty-six subjects were dismissed because the conditioned responses did not meet the consistency criterion within 50 trials. To prevent distortion of the photographic records, eight subjects were rejected for winking faster than a rate of 20 winks per minute. Eight additional subjects were dismissed because of maximal responses, since slight inhibitory or facilitative effects could hardly be apparent if the lid responses were full closure. For this reason, only enough training trials were given to establish a consistent conditioned response without overtraining.

Session II. Two and one half hours. The second session was divided into two parts. The control series was designed to determine to what extent the persisting light stimulus, before any conditioning to the shock had occurred, would influence the conditioned lid reaction. The experimental series, which followed immediately, comprised the training trials for the delayed conditioned response and the tests to determine whether the interval of delay was actually inhibitory. On all test trials the vibrator-puff

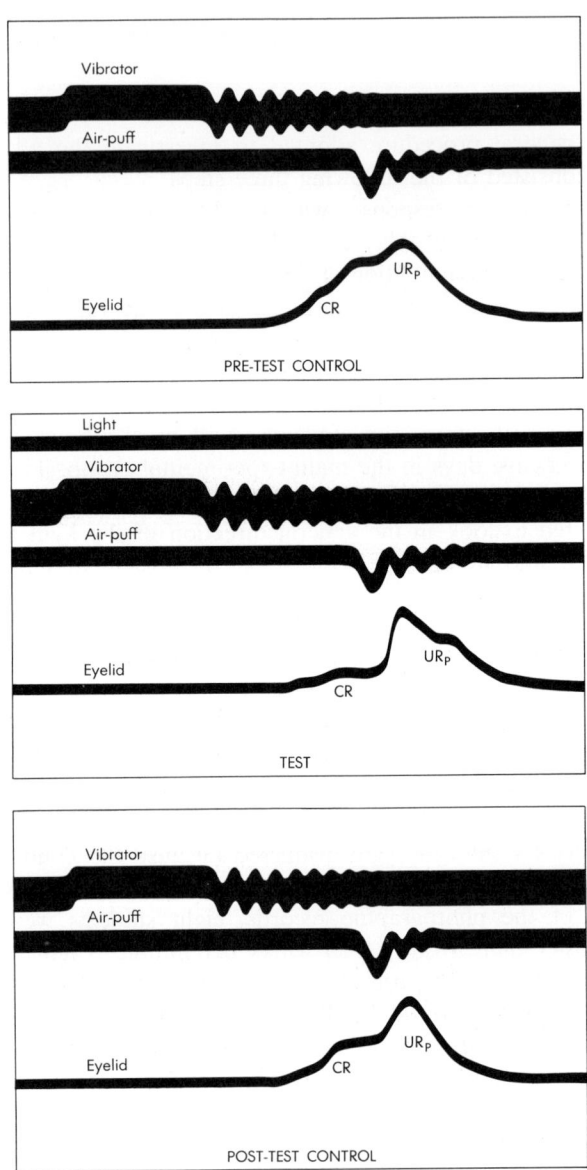

FIGURE 39-3. Specimen photographic records of a complete test cycle. The test record shown in the center was taken during the interval of delay of a delayed

The Interval of Delay of Conditioned Responses

combination was presented 5 seconds after the onset of the light. Vibrator-puff combinations both preceded and followed each test trial (pre-test and post-test controls), and were scattered among the presentations of the light. In this way the subject was unable to identify the test trials prior to actual stimulation.

A formal description of the procedure is as follows:

A. Control series.
   (1) 3 presentations of vibrator-puff combination. (10 presentations if the conditioned eyelid response was quite weak.)
   (2) 10 presentations of the unreinforced 21.3-second light. (Presentations 1, 5, and 10 were test trials.)
B. Experimental series.
   (3) 3 presentations of simultaneous light-shock combinations.
   (4) 20 presentations of 21-second light-shock combinations. (Presentation 16 of the 21-second light-shock combination was a test trial.)
   (5) 15-minute rest interval (subject allowed to exercise).
   (6) 28 presentations of 21-second light-shock combination. (Presentations 36, 40, 45, and 48 were test trials.)

Development of the conditioned eyelid response

Photographic records of the development of the conditioned eyelid response during Session I were taken on alternate stimulations with 39 of the 60 subjects used in this investigation. The records of the other 21 subjects were not measured, since they were taken at irregular intervals and served merely to inform the experimenter of the general progress of the development of the conditioned eyelid reaction.

Some of the subjects showed a maximal response after the first few reinforcements. If, upon being questioned, these subjects replied that they

---

conditioned response, 5 seconds after the onset of the light stimulus. The pre-test control was taken 85 seconds prior to and the post-test record 45 seconds following this testing situation. It is seen that the conditioned response (CR) occurs before the unconditioned response (UR_P) and is considerably smaller in magnitude. Horizontal lines measure amplitude in mm. The fine vertical time lines are 20 msc. and the heavy lines 100 msc. apart.

By comparing the test conditioned lid response with the mean of the controls the effect of the interval of delay may be determined. In this figure, the persisting light stimulus depresses the amplitude of the test response to an extent of 71 percent. The increment in latency is 9 percent.

were deliberately anticipating the air-puff, they were instructed not to do so; if the eyelid response to the conditioned stimulus then reappeared as a less than maximal response the subjects were retained for the main part of the experiment on the second session. As has already been pointed out, this method of selection was necessary in order to avoid using subjects who were responding maximally. With 13 subjects who admitted closing their eyes deliberately to avoid the air-puff, this wink dropped out and later reappeared as a less than maximal response. The upper curve in Figure 39-4, based on the data from 10 of these subjects, shows that the instructions to the subjects eliminated the "deliberate," large-amplitude, initial responses which would otherwise have been included with the smaller, more involuntary conditioned responses. This is evidenced by the initial rapid rise and subsequent fall of the curve.

The development of the conditioned response itself is shown by the lower curve, from which the data of the ten subjects who responded deliberately were excluded. This curve has a positive acceleration in the earlier stages of the conditioning process similar to other curves of the

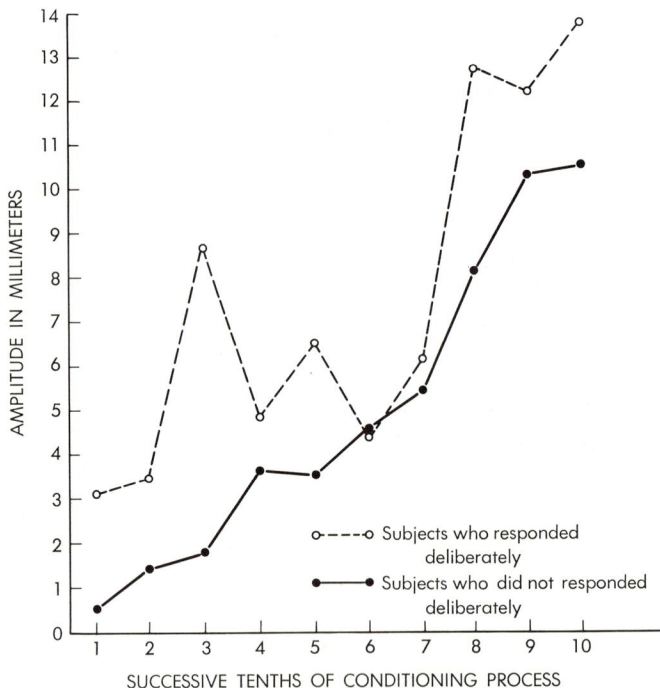

FIGURE 39-4. Composite Vincent curves showing the increase in the amplitude of the eyelid response during conditioning.

acquisition of a conditioned response. Note that the lower curve does not begin to level out until the very end of the session. This can be readily explained by the small number of training trials given to prevent maximal conditioning of the eyelid reaction; with further training the curve would have completed its S-shape.

The steeper rise of the second half of the upper curve indicates that the development of the conditioned response for those subjects who responded deliberately at first was facilitated by their earlier "deliberate" responses. As an association between the conditioned stimulus and the eyelid response had already been established, conditioning proceeded more rapidly.

Tests of the inhibition of delay

The development of the delayed conditioned response during the training has been discussed elsewhere (Rodnick, 1937). There it was reported that the latency of the conditioned galvanic skin response increased from a mean of 4.8 seconds to a mean of 10.1 seconds during the experimental session. In 74 out of 80 tests of the inhibition of delay (last four test cycles only), the test stimuli for the conditioned lid response fell within the period of delay.

The summary of the mean amplitudes of the conditioned eyelid responses for the last four test cycles is presented in Table 39-1. It may be seen that there is a weighted mean[2] decrement in the eyelid reaction of 19 percent on test trials occurring in the interval of delay. This decrement is quite reliable in view of the high critical ratio of 4.4 for the arithmetical mean of −24 percent and the fact that 17 out of 20 subjects show this tendency. Of the three subjects who manifest no decrement, one does not show any change, and the other two show only small differences in the opposite direction.

The mean latencies presented in Table 39-2[3] indicate a similar tendency in the expected direction. The conditioned wink occurring in the delay period shows a mean increment in latency of 15 percent over the

[2] The mean values used in this discussion are weighted means based on the variable number of satisfactory test records obtained for each subject. Although each subject was given the same number of tests, some of the records of the conditioned lid reaction had to be discarded because of faulty registration, interference by spontaneous winks, or failure of the recording mechanism. If one of the records constituting a particular test cycle was faulty for any of these reasons, the whole cycle was discarded. However, the standard errors and the critical ratios are based upon straight arithmetical means.

[3] In a few cases no conditioned eyelid response occurred on test trials. These were included in the amplitude measures as zero amplitude. The latency values for these cases were taken arbitrarily as the length of time between the onset of the vibratory and the air-puff.

pre-test and post-test controls. This difference is 4.1 times its standard error. Only three subjects show a small reversal in the opposite direction.

The similarity of the amplitude and the latency values indicates a significant though not too high negative correlation between the two sets of measures. The product moment correlation between the mean amplitude and the mean latency measures of the several pre-test, test, and post-test conditioned responses for each of the twenty subjects of one of the control experiments was found to be $-.49 \pm .09$. This compares favorably with the correlation of $-.39$ based on mean values found with conditioned responses in dogs by Hilgard and Marquis (1935). However, the correlation between individual measures should be much lower, since the use of means obscures some of the variability. For example, the correlation of the measures of one subject who gave 23 conditioned responses was found to be only $-.06$.

In view of the high reliability of both the amplitude and the latency differences, this tendency of the test conditioned response to be partially inhibited when it occurs in the delay period of the delayed conditioned response may in all probability be regarded as genuine.

The results from the control series, however, indicated that the persisting light stimulus tended to inhibit the test response even before any conditioning had occurred, although this tendency was considerably less marked than that observed after the delayed conditioned response had been established. The decrement in amplitude of the test response was 10 percent; the increment in latency, 13 percent. The critical ratios for these values, based on the standard error, are 1.2 and 3.4 respectively. There was, however, a rapid drop in this inhibitory effect from the first to the third test cycle of the control series, which indicated an adaptation of the subject to the persisting visual stimulus.

The possibility then arose that the inhibitory effect obtained in the experimental series was largely a result of the continuation and intensification of that observed in the control series. The greater inhibitory influence of the period of delay might be due not to the conditioning process but to the shock per se through the arousal of interfering sensitized responses to the light. The presentation of the shocks alone might conceivably arouse a general apprehension in the subject which would increase the inhibitory effect obtained in the control series. To investigate this possibility, two control experiments with twenty subjects each were performed.

The first group of control subjects was treated exactly the same as the Experimental Group, with the single exception that no shocks whatever were given. The object was to measure the effect of continued adaptation to the light alone upon the test conditioned lid response. The difference between the results of this group and those of the Experimental Group

TABLE 39-1

Summary of the mean amplitude in millimeters of conditioned lid closure at each of the three stimulations of the test cycle*

Subject	Total no. test cycles	Pre-test trials	Test trials (T)	Post-test trials	Mean of pre-test and post-test (Mpp)	T − Mpp	$\frac{T - M_{pp}}{M_{pp}} \times 100\%$
1	4	12.3	14.0	17.3	15.2	−1.2	− 8%
2	4	14.4	11.3	13.1	13.7	−2.4	−18%
3	4	3.3	4.6	7.2	6.3	−1.7	−27%
4	4	15.1	14.0	14.7	14.9	−0.9	− 6%
5	4	14.8	12.1	17.4	16.0	−3.9	−24%
6	4	14.3	13.9	14.6	14.4	−0.5	− 3%
7	4	17.1	17.0	17.0	17.0	0.0	0%
8	4	14.3	11.0	18.3	16.3	−5.3	−33%
9	2	3.4	0.0	9.1	6.3	−6.3	−100%
10	4	20.3	17.3	21.0	20.7	−3.4	−16%
11	3	7.6	8.1	10.2	8.9	−0.8	− 9%
12	4	14.0	10.0	12.7	13.4	−3.4	−25%
13	4	25.1	24.9	25.5	25.3	−0.4	− 2%
14	4	6.3	0.7	9.2	7.7	−7.0	−91%
15	4	16.7	16.0	16.9	16.8	−0.8	− 5%
16	?	13.9	13.9	15.6	14.8	−0.9	− 6%
17	2	16.0	17.8	15.9	16.0	+1.8	+11%
18	2	16.2	15.9	14.7	15.5	+0.4	+ 3%
19	4	13.4	12.6	14.7	14.0	−1.4	−10%
20	4	12.7	10.3	14.7	13.7	−3.4	−25%
Total	71						
Weighted mean		13.9	12.4	15.2	14.6	−2.2	−19%
Mean							−24%
σm							5.4%
$\frac{M}{\sigma m}$							4.4%

* On test trials the test vibrator-puff stimulation was presented during trials 36, 40, 45, and 48 of the persisting light-shock combination, 5 seconds within the period of delay. Pre-test and post-test trials completing each test cycle consisted of conditioned lid reactions to the vibrator-puff combination when it was presented alone at variable intervals before and after the test trials. Negative values signify a decrement of the test conditioned lid reaction.

should be due to the presence of the shock in the latter, which would permit a determination of the effect of the shock upon the test response.

The second group of control subjects was also put through the same procedure as the Experimental Group, except that the light and shock stimuli were never presented in a combination which would set up a conditioned reaction. The stimuli were scrambled systematically in such a manner that if any conditioning did occur, the response would be promptly extinguished. The difference between the Experimental Group and this Control Group should permit an estimation of the effect of the shock when unassociated with the visual stimulus.

Comparison of the experimental group with the control groups

The comparison of the three groups of subjects for both the control and experimental series is shown in Table 39-3. All the groups were treated identically during the control series, the procedure varying only during the experimental series.

It may be seen in column 2 of Table 39-3 that while the Experimental Group manifests a decrement of 19 percent in the amplitude of the eyelid response in the tests of the experimental series, the two control groups register either no change (Shock Group) or an actual increment of 9 percent (No-Shock Group). Thus the amplitude of the conditioned wink showed an 18-percent greater decrement in the tests of the Experimental Group than in those of the Shock Group. The difference between the arithmetical means of these two groups is 3.10 times the standard error of the difference, which is quite significant. The difference between the Experimental Group and the No-Shock Group is 28 percent. The relative differences in the latency increments of the test responses may be seen to follow a similar trend. . . .

Inasmuch as the only difference in procedure between the two control groups is the presence of the shock, the greater inhibitory effect obtained with the Shock Group must be a result of the influence of the faradic stimulation, when it is unassociated with the visual stimulus.

Since the three groups of subjects did not manifest the same amount of change in the test responses during the control series (column 1, Table 39-3) even though the procedures were identical, the groups may have been unevenly balanced as to the number of subjects exhibiting a marked inhibitory effect. This would account for the inequality of the means of the inhibitory effect in the control series of the three groups of subjects. Unless these groups were balanced in some way, this same constant error would be operative in a direct comparison of the results of the experimental series. To avoid this possibility, the amount of the inhibitory effect obtained in the test cycles of the control series was de-

TABLE 39-2

Summary of the mean latency in milliseconds of the conditioned lid response at each of the three stimulations of the test cycle*

Subject	Total no. test cycles	Pre-test trials	Test trials (T)	Post-test trials	Mean of pre-test and post-test (Mpp)	T − Mpp	$\frac{T - M_{pp}}{M_{pp}} \times 100\%$
1	4	461	439	383	422	+17	+ 4%
2	4	363	471	411	387	+84	+22%
3	4	261	275	240	251	+24	+10%
4	4	334	408	353	343	+65	+19%
5	4	250	251	190	220	+31	+14%
6	4	293	290	275	284	+ 6	+ 2%
7	4	351	321	285	318	+ 3	+ 1%
8	4	259	299	220	239	+60	+25%
9	2	300	500	293	297	+203	+68%
10	4	263	294	243	253	+41	+16%
11	4	331	343	366	349	− 6	− 2%
12	4	276	330	256	266	+64	+24%
13	4	263	281	259	261	+20	+ 8%
14	4	341	473	330	337	+136	+40%
15	4	469	429	453	461	−32	− 7%
16	2	433	453	265	349	+104	+30%
17	2	395	415	380	388	+27	+ 7%
18	3	347	375	422	384	− 9	− 2%
19	4	303	389	285	294	+95	+32%
20	4	311	361	320	316	+45	+14%
Total	73						
Weighted mean		326	364	310	318	+46	+15%
Mean							+16%
σm							3.9%
$\frac{M}{\sigma m}$							4.1%

* These values correspond to the mean amplitude measures given in Table 39-1.

TABLE 39-3

Showing the mean percent difference in amplitude and in latency between the mean of the test and the mean of the pre-test and the post-test conditioned eyelid responses for each series of each group of 20 subjects*

GROUP		CONTROL SERIES		EXPERIMENTAL SERIES		DIFFERENCE BETWEEN EXPER. AND CONTROL SERIES	DIFFERENCE BETWEEN EXPER. GROUP AND CONTROL GROUP
		Weighted mean	$\overline{\sigma m}$	Weighted mean	$\overline{\sigma m}$		
		(1)		(2)		(3)	(4)
Experi-	Amplitude	−10%	1.2	−19%	4.4	− 9%	
mental	Latency	+13%	3.4	+15%	4.1	+ 2%	
Shock	Amplitude	−16%	1.9	− 1%	0.4	+15%	−24%
control	Latency	+13%	5.0	+ 7%	2.1	− 6%	+ 8%
No-shock	Amplitude	−13%	1.1	+ 9%	1.5	+22%	−31%
control	Latency	+ 9%	3.7	+ 3%	1.6	− 6%	+ 8%

*Negative values signify a decrement of response on test trials. The critical ratios are based upon arithmetical means.

ducted from the results of the experimental series. This procedure is equivalent to making the inhibitory effect obtained in the control series of each group of subjects the baseline, from which the results of the experimental series deviate.

The values obtained in this way are given in column 3 of Table 39-3. It may be seen that the Experimental Group manifests a 9 percent greater decrement in the amplitude of the test lid response in the experimental series than in the control series, whereas the No-Shock and the Shock groups show 22 percent and 15 percent less decrement respectively. As shown in the last column of this table, the Experimental Group exhibits 31 percent more decrement in the amplitude of the test response during the experimental series than does the No-Shock Group, and 24 percent more than the Shock Group.

The latency values corresponding to the amplitude differences discussed above indicate that the increment in the latency of the test response is 2 percent greater in the experimental series than in the control series. On the other hand, both control groups show a decline of 6 percent from the increment of the test response latencies of the control series, making a net difference of 8 percent between the Experimental Group and the Control Groups.

Since the presence of the shock when it is not associated with the light only slightly retards the subject's adaptation to the light alone (cf. experimental series of both control groups), it seems safe to assume that the inhibitory phenomenon observed with the Experimental Group is somehow a result of the association of the shock with the light. . . .

There remains the further possibility that the inhibition of the test lid response in the Experimental Group was produced by a refractory phase or interference effect of some unrecorded response after the onset of the light, such as an eyelid reaction, resulting from either conditioning or sensitization by the shock. This reaction may not have been present in the control subjects. Unfortunately, with the Experimental Group no records were taken of the lid movement during the first few seconds of the light, although 20 records taken with the Shock Control Group disclosed no signs of an eyelid reaction to the light. The answer to this question was found, however, in the results of another experiment with long delayed conditioned reactions, in which by a series of five progressively lengthened steps over a period of seven experimental sessions the interval between the onset of the persisting light stimulus and the shock was increased to 60 seconds. At the end of this period the conditioned lid response was established and tests of the inhibition of delay were made by presenting the stimuli for the lid response 15 seconds after the onset of the light. The data of 11 tests given to 3 subjects indicated that the amplitude of the lid response was inhibited to an extent of 24 percent when it occurred 15 seconds within the period of delay. This had a critical ratio of 4.0 based upon the standard error. The corresponding latency increment was 13 percent.

It thus appears that the inhibitory effect obtained with the Experimental Group is not confined to the onset of the conditioned stimulus, but may persist for a considerable period of time. The indication is therefore that the interval of delay of a delayed conditioned response possesses inhibitory characteristics which may depress another conditioned reaction occurring during that interval. . . .

Pavlov (1927, p. 103) has suggested that this behavioral phenomenon may be reduced to the generalized inhibition supposedly operative in experimental extinction. The development of the delay may be accounted for by the fact that the responses near the onset of the conditioned stimulus are extinguished because they are remote from the point of reinforcement. Pavlov's explanation of the inhibition of conditioned responses in terms of cortical processes is, however, much less convincing. The underlying mechanism may eventually be found to be more in line with other psychological and physiological processes operative in the facilitation and inhibition of reaction systems.

SUMMARY

1. Twenty subjects were employed in an experiment to test for the inhibition of delay in delayed conditioned responses (i.e., to determine whether the interval of delay possesses inhibitory characteristics which may be generalized to other conditioned responses). On the first session of one hour, a conditioned lid response was established to a tactual-vibratory stimulus followed by a puff of air to the cornea. On the second session of two and a half hour's duration, a delayed conditioned galvanic skin response was set up to a light reinforced after a 20-second interval by an electric shock. On certain trials, the stimuli for the lid response were presented 5 seconds within the interval of delay. The amount of change in the amplitude and latency of the conditioned lid response on these test trials as compared with the magnitude of this same response under normal conditions constituted a measure of the inhibitory characteristics of the interval of delay.

2. The visual stimulus alone produced a mean decrement of 13 percent in the amplitude and a mean increment of 13 percent in the latency of the test conditioned lid response before any reinforcement of the light by the shock had occurred. There was a rapid decrease of this inhibitory tendency with continued nonreinforcement of the visual stimulus.

3. After a delayed conditioned response had been established, the conditioned lid reaction suffered a reliable decrement of 19 percent in amplitude when it occurred in the interval of delay. There was a corresponding increment of 15 percent in the latency of the response.

4. Two other groups of 20 subjects each were employed in control experiments. The first control group was treated exactly the same as the Experimental Group with the exception that no shocks were ever given. The second control experiment differed only in the respect that the visual and shock stimuli were never presented in a combined order. Neither of these groups showed any decrement in the amplitude of the conditioned wink on test trials. Only a slight increment occurred. Less inhibitory effect was obtained with the first control group than with the second. Thus the inhibition of the eyelid response in the main experiment was definitely a result of the associated order of the visual and shock stimuli.

5. Three subjects were employed in another experiment on long delayed conditioned responses in which the interval between the onset of the visual stimulus and the shock was extended to 60 seconds. A 24 percent decrement in amplitude and a 13 percent increment in latency was obtained when the test lid response occurred 15 seconds within the interval of delay.

40

Conditioned Diminution of the Unconditioned Eyelid Reflex[1]

GREGORY A. KIMBLE[2]

Recently I have become interested in a phenomenon of eyelid conditioning that appears to resemble what Kupalov calls the pathological irradiation of inhibition. This phenomenon consists of the marked diminution of the unconditioned eye-blink when it is elicited in the presence of the conditioned stimulus. Figure 40-1 presents tracings of a series of eye-blink records taken from a human subject in an eyelid-conditioning experiment run according to the following plan. After the usual pretests with conditioned and unconditioned stimuli alone, there was a series of 20 trials in which the CS (a dim light) and the US (corneal air puff) were paired. Trials 21 to 25 consisted of stimulations with the US alone. Trials 26 to 30 again consisted of paired presentations of CS and US. The panels in Figure 40-1 are representative of the responses obtained in the various parts of this procedure.

Note that, beginning with the initial test trial and proceeding through Trial 20, there is a progressive diminution in the amplitude of the UR. This reduction might be regarded as reflex habituation were it not for the evidence to the contrary obtained on Trials 21 to 25, two of which are shown in Figure 40-1. Note that on Trial 21, without the CS, the reflex regains full strength and maintains it on all trials with the US alone. On Trial 26, when the CS is presented again, there is a reduction in response strength to a small fraction of its value on Trial 25. The records taken from Trials 26 and 30 are typical. In no case did the unconditioned reflex attain its original strength on trials when the CS was presented.

The implication here is that, whatever the process involved, it is under the control of the CS. The experimental work of my co-workers and

---

[1] A peculiar and interesting variety of inhibition has been observed informally in numerous investigations and has been the object of a few full scale investigations (e.g., Kimble & Ost, 1961). This consists of a stimulus-controlled inhibition of the unconditioned reflex. The nature of the phenomenon is presented in this brief chapter. [Ed.]

[2] Reprinted with permission from *Annals of the New York Academy of Sciences*, 1961, 92, 1189–1192.

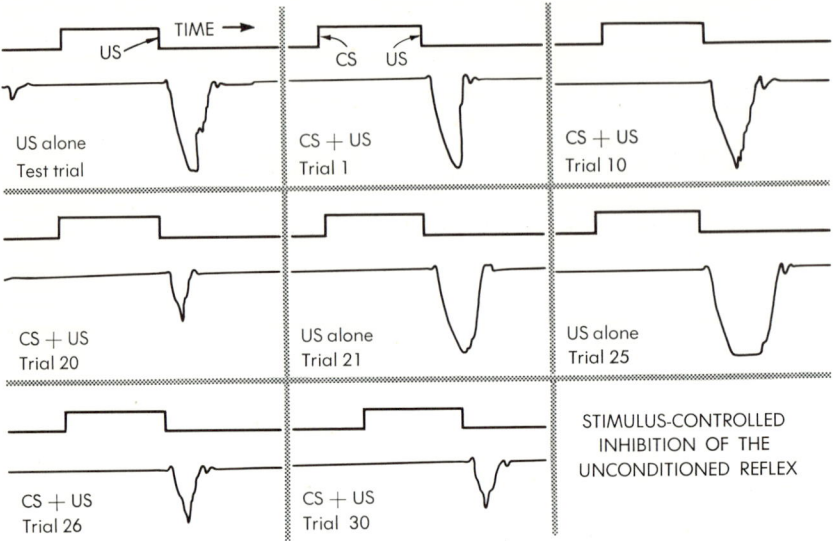

FIGURE 40-1. The upper line records onset of light (CS) and air puff (US). For purposes of making essential measurements the signals for these events occur on all trials, even if the stimulus was not presented. Note the decrease in amplitude of the UR that appears most markedly on Trials 20, 26, and 30. On Trials 21 to 25, without the CS, the reflex regained its normal strength.

myself has been devoted to finding out more about this phenomenon. In the first of our experiments we studied the relationship of this inhibitory process to the interstimulus interval. In this study there was a total of 64 subjects divided into four groups. Each group was conditioned at a different interstimulus interval: 0.25 second; 0.50 second; 1.0 second; and 2.0 seconds. Each subject was run for one session and received the following trials: (a) five test trials with the CS; (b) five trials with the US, to determine the initial amplitude of the reflex; (c) 50 conditioning trials with the CS and US paired at the appropriate interval; and (d) 10 trials with the US alone again. Our chief interest was in a comparison of the amplitude of the URs at the end of conditioning and during subsequent trials without the CS. Somewhat to our surprise, the function emerging from this study was one that exactly paralleled the usual function for the relationship between conditioning and the interstimulus interval; that is, the magnitude of the inhibitory process was greatest when conditioning occurred at a CS-US interval of 0.5 second, and less at either shorter or longer intervals. Later we found out that the effect occurs in the records of individual subjects. Figure 40-2 is a record taken from a single subject who was tested at all of these intervals. The reduction in the amplitude of

Conditioned Diminution of the Unconditioned Eyelid Reflex

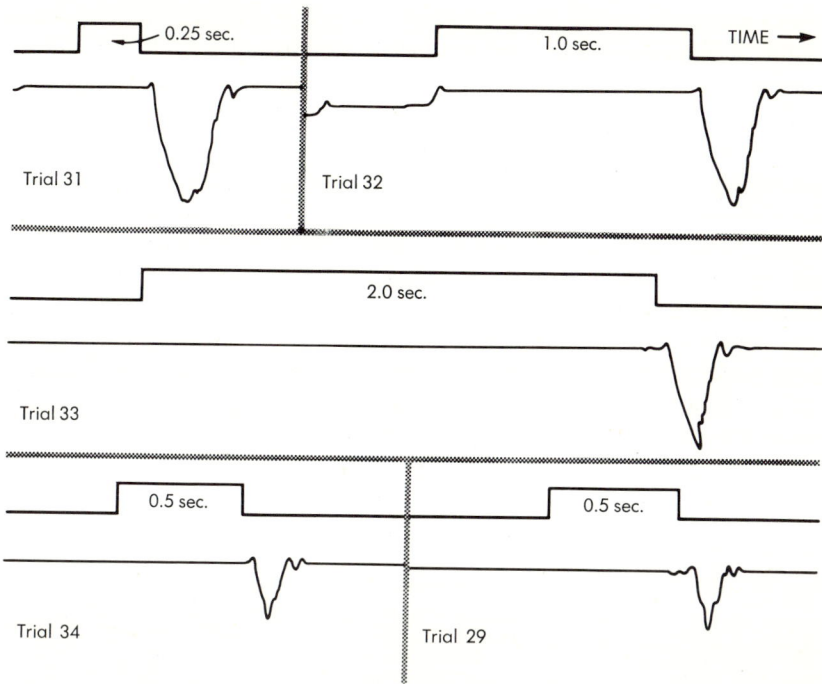

FIGURE 40-2. Trials 31 to 34 were selected because the four test intervals occurred in sequence in these four trials. Thus no bias is introduced by the selection of records. Trial 29 was the next to the last in a series of 30 trials with a 0.5-second interval. The record on Trial 30 was not used because it was marred by random blinks.

the UR on trials with 0.5 second between the CS and US is quite obvious. This means that the inhibitory effect is strongest at the very same temporal point as the (excitatory) tendency to make a conditioned response.

Pursuing our inquiry into the nature of this inhibitory process somewhat further, we have found that it is related to individual differences. In brief, some subjects show the effect rather markedly, while other subjects show the opposite effect; that is, in the absence of the conditioned stimulus some subjects' unconditioned reflexes are somewhat weaker than in the presence of the conditioned stimulus. On the basis of evidence such as this we have been led to wonder whether we may not have discovered in human subjects a difference that parallels that originally noted by Pavlov in dogs. It looks very much as if at the human level, too, there are excitable and inhibitable organisms. Subjects who show the inhibitory effect in very great strength typically do not develop conditioned responses. Such facts have led us to speculate whether the inhibition involved might not be the same as the Pavlovian inhibition of delay, extending forward in time to the point at which it inhibits not only the conditioned reflex but also the unconditioned reflex as well, much as Kupalov describes it in his paper. If this were the case, one might expect two phenomena to appear. In the first place, one might anticipate that a subject who shows this inhibitory phenomenon in great proportions, while giving no conditioned responses at usual optimal interval of one-half second, might display conditioned responses at a longer interval. A second expectation is that an extra (disinhibiting) stimulus might lead to the appearance of conditioned responses in the interstimulus interval.

Thus far we have not examined these possibilities systematically. We have, however, tried the indicated experimental operations informally on a few subjects with results that are encouraging. Figure 40-3 presents a series of typical records taken from a subject who did not condition well at 0.5 second, although he did not develop a substantial amount of stimu-

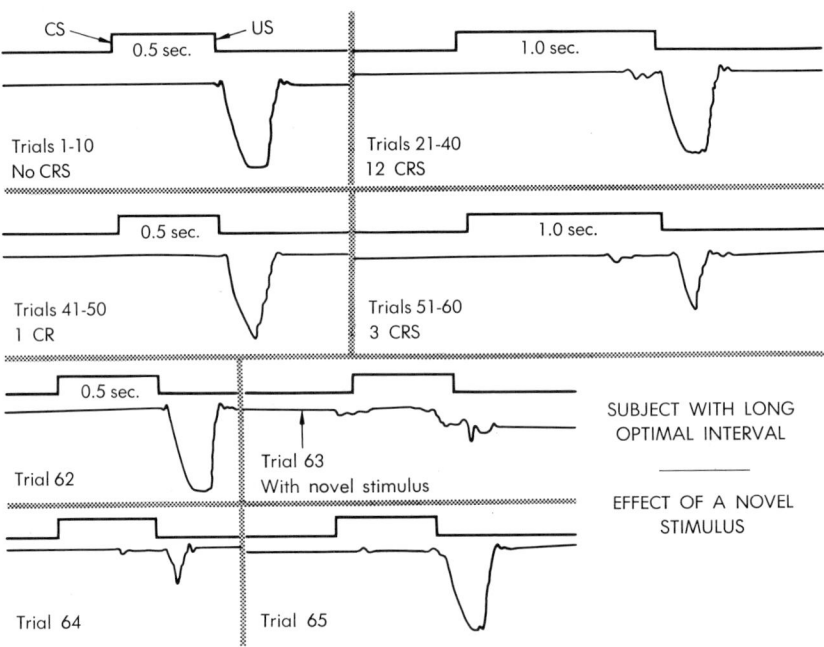

FIGURE 40-3. The records are typical of the blocks of trials in question. Those with 0.5-second intervals have only unconditioned responses. Conditioned responses appear on the records for the 1.0-second trials. The disinhibiting stimulus was presented only on Trial 63. Its effect, however, persisted on Trial 64 and, perhaps, on Trial 65.

lus-controlled inhibition either. Examination of the series of records presented in Figure 40-3 will show that our two expectations were realized: (1) extending the interstimulus interval to a full second produced a good many more conditioned responses than occurred at half a second; and (2) adding a disinhibiting stimulus (produced by raking a plastic ruler across the face of the intercommunication system between the experimenter and the subject) produced a disinhibiting effect which persisted for a number of trials. Unfortunately this subject was not one of those who showed a marked diminution in the amplitude of the UR. Only further work will make it possible to tell whether the preliminary results presented in Figure 40-3 and the inhibitory mechanism are related.

41

Pathological Diminution of the Eyelid UR in the Squirrel Monkey: Some Anecdotal Observations[1]

HENRY S. PENNYPACKER
WILLIAM A. COOK

In the course of our efforts to extend the techniques of eyelid conditioning to lower primates, we have noted that with extended training the unconditioned response to a 5.0 PSI air-puff seems, in some animals, to disappear entirely. A typical example, occurring in this case during the 5th daily 100-trial conditioning session, is presented in Figure 1 which contrasts the UR of the first trial of the session with the UCR of the 50th trial.[1]

Although Figure 41-1 portrays the chief behavioral characteristics of the phenomenon under consideration, there are several additional aspects of the behavior which are worthy of note.

1. Extreme diminution of the blink response is not limited to the conditioning stimuli or the conditioning situation; it is possible to remove the monkey from the conditioning chamber and manually stimulate the cornea of the affected eye without eliciting an observable blink.

2. In all cases the phenomenon has been restricted to the eye which has been receiving the air-puff. Observation of the opposite eyelid during conditioning trials indicates that it engages in the normal variety of responses, including alpha blinks, conditioned anticipatory blinks and unconditioned blinks.

3. Once established, the phenomenon persists for periods up to 24 hours. Several hours after the recordings presented in Figure 41-1 were

[1] In all instances reported here, the values of the conditioning parameters were: CS, 3000 cps tone delivered at 75 db.; US, 5.0 psi of .10 second duration; CS-US interval, 2.0 seconds; and mean intertrial interval, 30 seconds. For a complete description of the apparatus and general procedure, see Pennypacker *et al.*, in press.

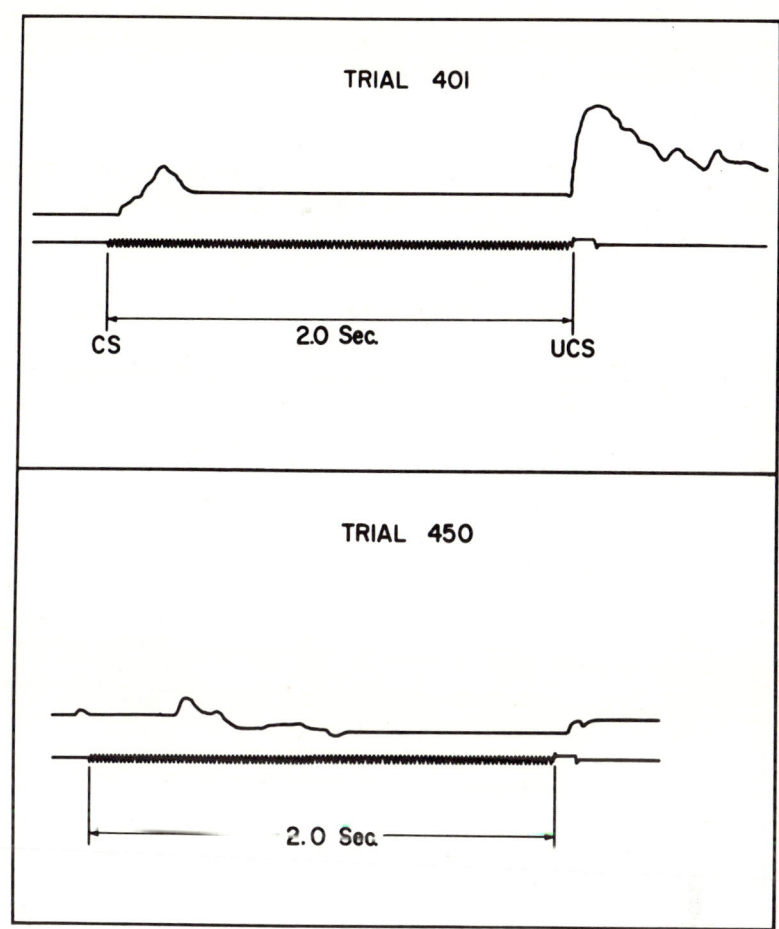

FIGURE 41-1. Actual tracing showing extent of UR diminution observable in monkeys.

made, the animal was observed in his living quarters making random blinks with only his left (non-puffed) eye.

4. The oculomotor component of the blink reflex appears to be undisturbed. Presentation of the air-puff results in rather vigorous vertical eye movements, thus insuring lubrication of the cornea in the absence of any lid closure.

Since, to date, we have been unable to produce this phenomenon deliberately in our animals, experimental attempts to investigate its nature have been limited to somewhat hastily contrived manipulations which were carried out as the phenomenon appeared. For example, in order to examine the possibility that we are observing the product of a centrally mediated inhibitory state, a 1 mg/kg dosage of thorazine was injected intraperitoneally into an animal which we believed was just beginning to exhibit the behavior. It was our expectation that a mild dose of a tranquilizing agent might be effective in disrupting such inhibition if it was administered before the inhibition became profound. The results of this manipulation are presented in Table 41-1, which, indeed, would appear to support our contention. The entries in Table 41-1 are the amplitudes of

TABLE 41-1

UCR amplitudes before and after administration of thorazine

BEFORE		AFTER	
Trial No.	UR Amplitude	Trial No.	UR Amplitude
5	6mm.	5	16mm.
10	11mm.	10	16mm.
15	4mm.	15	16mm.
20	7mm.	20	16mm.
25	2mm.	25	16mm.
30	5mm.	32	16mm.
35	9mm.	36	16mm.
41	12mm.	40	16mm.
45	13mm.	45	12mm.
50	12mm.	50	11mm.

every 5th UCR (provided a CR did not occur on that trial in which case the nearest eligible UCR in either direction was substituted) for the 50-trial periods before and after the administration of the thorazine. Unfortunately, attempts to replicate this procedure using a graded series of thorazine dosages were impossible since we were unable to produce a substantial UR reduction thereafter in that particular animal. Administration of similar dosages of thorazine to animals undergoing states of greater UCR diminution than that presented in Table 41-1 have failed to produce any noticeable recovery of the UR. Thus we are left with a shred of evidence suggesting the operation of a central inhibitory mechanism; this evidence can be systematically evaluated if a reliable method for controlled production of UR diminution can be found.

We also examined the alternative possibility that the inability of these animals to close one eye might be the result of a spasm or cramp in the *levator principalis*, the muscle whose function is to raise the upper eyelid. Gathering evidence in support of this hypothesis would involve demon-

Pathological Diminution of the Eyelid UR

strating that the activity of the *obicularis oculi* (the sphincter muscle which closes the eye) was essentially the same in both the affected and unaffected eyes. An experiment testing this idea was carried out on a different animal who had received 400 conditioning trials as previously described. Following the administration of an additional 60 paired presentations of the tone and air-puff, pairs of EMG electrodes were implanted subdermally in the sphincter muscles of both eyes and a reference electrode attached to the animal's ear. Since only one EMG preamplifier was available, blocks of 10 trials were recorded from each eye in a *b b a* order. Figure 41-2 presents the records obtained of the 30th and 31st trials of this procedure, these trials being separated by the second shift in record-

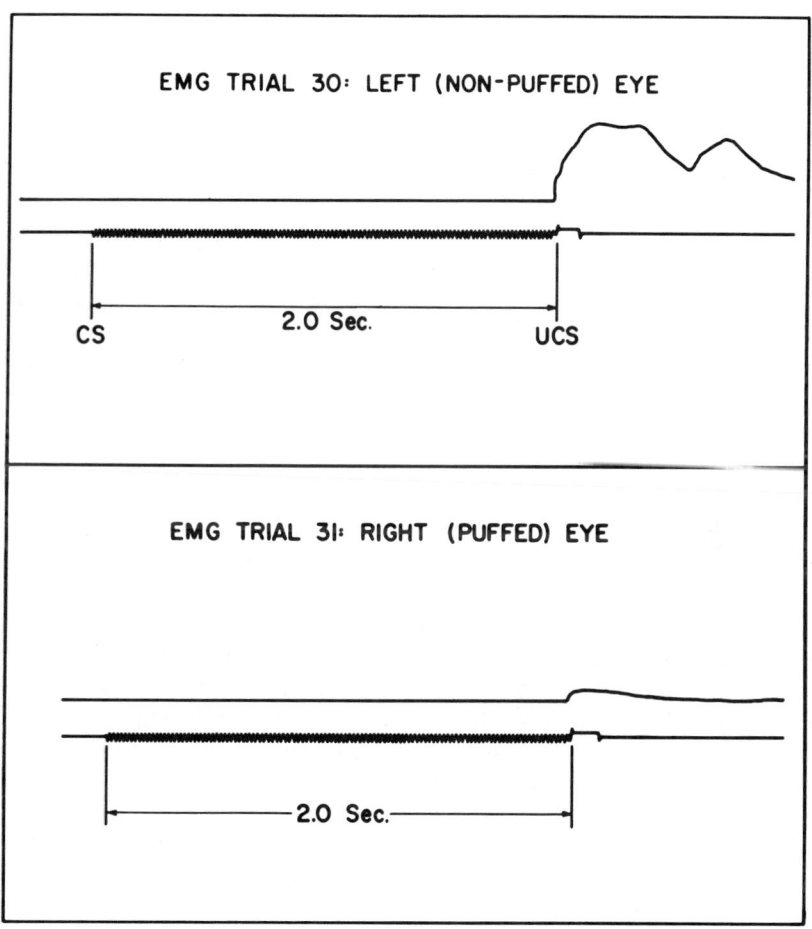

FIGURE 41-2. Comparison of EMG tracings from the sphincters of the puffed and nonpuffed eyelids.

ing site. It is evident from Figure 41-2 that whatever the nature of the inhibitory process responsible for the unilateral reduction in blinking behavior, its influence is exerted upon the *obicularis oculi*. This, however, does not entirely rule out the possibility that the disorder is focused upon the *levator principalis;* in all probability the two muscles are enervated in a reciprocal manner so that excessive contraction of the levator would be expected to result in a complimentary relaxation of the sphincter.

Two general hypotheses are, at this writing, being entertained to account for the phenomenon in question. First, it is remotely possible that the conditioning apparatus, which includes two pieces of plexiglass pressed tightly against the sides of the animal's head to position it, is somehow damaging the facial nerve, producing a syndrome similar to Bell's Palsy in humans (Peele, 1954). In addition to being rather uninteresting from a psychological point of view, this hypothesis is questionable in view of the relatively rapid recovery of seventh nerve function shown by our animals. Peele states that regeneration of the seventh nerve, when it occurs in humans suffering from Bell's Palsy, often requires several months, a far different order of magnitude from the few hours required by our monkeys.

The second, and by far the more engaging, hypothesis is that we are dealing with an extreme form of the behavior identified in humans by Kimble and Ost (1961). If this is the case, it is conceivable that we have experimentally produced, through the process of classical conditioning, a behavior state analagous to that described in the clinical literature as hysterical paralysis. This would not be surprising in view of the demonstrated susceptibility of monkeys to the development of psychosomatic disorders in the conditioning situation (Brady, 1962).

Under the assumption that the latter of these two hypotheses is the more tenable, research is currently underway involving manipulation of both type and intensity of the US while recording the activity of both eyelids simultaneously. It is hoped that this procedure, which permits continual comparison of reflex strength between the stimulated and nonstimulated eyelids, will enable us to detect the onset of the phenomenon at an earlier stage of conditioning as well as to identify the experimental conditions under which the probability of its occurrence is maximized.

We are also experimenting with techniques for the artificial creation of profound UR diminution by temporary anesthetization of the seventh nerve.[2] Injection of small does of xylocaine into the area immediately anterior to the auditory foramen has produced the desired result: complete immobility of the ipsilateral side of the face (including the eyelid) without sacrificing the sensory consequences of the US (Martino, 1939)—

---

[2] We are indebted to Dr. F. A. King for his advice and technical assistance with this procedure.

stimulating the cornea on the paralyzed side produces vigorous lid movements on the contralateral side in addition to some oculomotor movements of the stimulated eye. In addition to its obvious usefulness in studies centering on the nature of reinforcement in classical conditioning, we expect that this technique, when perfected, will permit us to observe what, if any, adaptive function is promoted by development of profound UR inhibition in the natural state. We may then be better able to evaluate its place within the larger domain of classical conditioning.

VII

RELATIONS TO COMPLEX PROCESSES

42

Thomas M. French on the Relationship Between Psychoanalysis and the Experimental Work of Pavlov

GREGORY A. KIMBLE

Freud's theory of psychoanalysis and Pavlov's studies of conditioned reflexes were developed at about the same time and it is not surprising that many psychologists sought to demonstrate relationships between the two lines of work. The next chapter presents a recent effort of this type (Bridger, 1964). One of the earliest attempts of a similar kind was the extremely insightful paper of Thomas M. French (1933), "The Relationship Between Psychoanalysis and the Experimental Work of Pavlov," read at the eighty-eighth meeting of the American Psychiatric Association in 1932. In many ways the most interesting aspect of the paper is his analysis of learning which he arrived at by playing Freudian and Pavlovian ideas off against each other. A summary of the main points made by French thus seems very much in order and I have attempted to provide one here. In the presentation I have assumed what I believe to be the position of French.

Although they are derived from different traditions, there are similarities between psychoanalysis and the work of Pavlov. At the simplest level, the Pavlovian concept of conditioning and the Freudian concept of association of ideas essential to psychoanalytic thought and therapeutic practice appear to be identical. Somewhat less obvious is the parallel between inhibition in the Pavlovian theory and the concept of repression in psychoanalysis. Both are mechanisms that interfere with the occurrence of a response and both entail the assumption that the absent reaction still remains available if repression or inhibition can be removed.

In attempting to draw the parallel between inhibition and repression, the first question to arise is whether the appropriate analogy is to external or to internal inhibition. Since repression, in Freudian theory, is typically produced by a tendency other than that subjected to repression, the most obvious suggestion is that repression corresponds to *ex-*

ternal inhibition in which a conditioned reflex is inhibited by an unconditioned orienting reflex. On the other hand, some of the most convincing evidence favoring the more general conclusion that the two processes are related comes from the properties of *internal* inhibition. For example, the facts of disinhibition and spontaneous recovery (both associated with internal inhibition) indicate that the inhibited conditioned reflex is not destroyed but, as is true of repressed tendencies, is merely prevented from being expressed. Similarly, the processes of irradiation of inhibition and positive induction (also associated with internal inhibition) supply a possible explanation for the fact that repressed tendencies so often find expression in substitute gratifications. For the time being we must rest content with the observation that repression and inhibition are not so absolutely unrelated as superficial appearances suggest. The decision as to whether external inhibition, internal inhibition (or both) provides the closer parallel to repression will have to wait upon the further development of the various concepts involved.

Turning now to somewhat less obvious matters, the Pavlovian mechanism for the establishment of a differentiation has suggestive similarities to a number of processes recognized in psychoanalysis. To illustrate: Freudian theory holds that, at the time of puberty, the adolescent boy possesses strong, but successfully repressed, sexual wishes directed toward his mother. Moreover, these wishes, or urges, as well as the repression of them have been generalized to include all women. The increasing intensity of sexual desires at puberty breaks through this repression and the boy is forced, if he is to manage his new urges, to differentiate between appropriate objects and inappropriate objects (e.g., the mother) of sexual expression. The problems of resolving this Oedipal conflict suggest a surprisingly straightforward translation into Pavlovian terms.

In terms of Pavlovian concepts, the preadolescent boy has a set of widely generalized sexual tendencies, all of them subject to a level of inhibition sufficient to prevent their expression. With puberty, however, the sexual drive undergoes a marked increase. Pavlov specifically holds that increased motivation has the effect of broadening the generalization gradient. As a result of this, many of the boy's sexual tendencies break through their inhibitory restraints. What is required is the development of a set of differentiations (just as Freud maintained) between appropriate and inappropriate sexual goal objects. Pavlov's work on "experimental neurosis," however, suggests that this differentiation will be difficult partly because the appropriate and inappropriate objects are not easy to tell apart and partly because the high sexual drive requires a high level of inhibition to curb it. Under circumstances involving difficult discriminations and strong excitation and inhibition, behavioral maladjustment (experimental neurosis) often appeared in Pavlov's subjects. It is not surprising, on this ground, to find that adolescence, too, is a time of precarious adjustment and difficult relationships.

Pursuing these ideas further, a case can be made for the argument that differentiations of the type demanded by the Oedipal situation also have a more general significance. The problem posed by the Oedipus conflict is one of adjusting to external reality, but this particular problem is only one of a whole range of such problems with which the individual must deal in the course of his lifetime. In psychoanalysis, this dealing with reality is attributed to an insightful activity of the ego. Thus, we are led to ask whether the Pavlovian analysis can contribute anything to the understanding of the function of the ego.

On the way to an answer to this question, it is important to keep in mind the Pavlovian conception that the establishment of a differentiation occurs under circumstances where excitatory and inhibitory tendencies exist simultaneously. This state of affairs defines a type of conflict. Thus, the first point suggested by the Pavlovian analysis is that the external reality function of the ego derives from conflict. We know from Pavlov's work on experimental neurosis, however, that as the conflict becomes too strong, differentiation cannot be established and the animal may react to all stimuli in ways that are exclusively excitatory or exclusively inhibitory. No differentiation (in the psychoanalytic vocabulary, no external reality function) develops. Jointly, then, the concepts of the two disciplines appear to suggest that the reality function of the ego depends upon conflict, but conflict that is not so strong as to preclude the development of differentiations.

At this point, the suggestion also arises of a possible relation to the origin of neurosis and psychotherapeutic strategy. Psychoanalysis assumes that neurosis results from a series of traumata; Pavlovian analysis suggests that trauma may be an experience calling forth a conflict between excitation and inhibition so intense as to preclude the establishment of necessary differentiations. On this ground it can be argued that the task of the therapist is to aid the patient in achieving adequate differentiations. In order to do so, he must reawaken these conflicts but in an intensity low enough to allow differentiation to proceed.

Before proceeding further, we should call attention to a major deficiency in Pavlovian theory, its failure adequately to consider the role of drive in the control of behavior. Although Pavlov regarded an adequate level of drive to be essential for the formation of conditioned responses and, as we have seen, recognized a relationship between drive and generalization, the concept needs further development if we are to deal with certain problems. There is good evidence, for example, that drive states, perhaps through a mechanism of drive stimulation, can provide conditioned stimuli. If we are to pursue the parallels between Freudian and Pavlovian theory much further, it will be necessary to rely heavily on such conditioning. It seems very likely that what psychoanalysis calls the unconscious may be understood in these terms.

We use a simple example. A hungry man dreams of food. This may mean that, when hungry before, the sight of food had been followed by food itself and that hunger now evokes a conditioned image of food. In psychoanalytic theory, what has just been described is the mechanism called *primary process*. The Freudians go a step further and hold that these conditioned images have a reward value much like that of the imagined object. But the work of Pavlov leads us to recognize that conditioned images of this type would be subject to the laws of differentiation. Not being followed by satisfaction in the form of real food, they would be extinguished. Thus, the distinction between wish and reality that is characteristic of the conscious begins to develop. The development of this differentiation is a part of what the Freudian means by *secondary process*.

Wherever this discrimination is difficult, a segment of the organism's adjustment to the world would remain which tends to blur the distinctions between the real and the unreal. Such reactions exist in that part of the personality referred to in psychoanalysis as the unconscious. Thus, there are suggestive parallels between certain aspects of Freudian thinking and certain elements of Pavlovian theory to the effect that something as complex as the conscious-unconscious dimension may be understandable in terms of Pavlovian concepts. In brief, the suggested analysis is the following: (1) The unconscious may be understood in Pavlovian terms as originating in the conditioning of responses to drive states. (2) This conditioning may lead to a state of affairs where the drive state calls up the image of a satisfying goal object (primary process). (3) Normally, differentiation leads to the accurate discrimination between such images and reality (secondary process). But (4) Pavlov has demonstrated that some discriminations involving high levels of excitation and inhibition may be difficult or even impossible. In these cases, the individual is left with a poorly developed distinction between wish and reality. These mechanisms may potentially explain the wish-fulfilling activities of the unconscious and describe the differentiation between conscious and unconscious.

These ideas lead in some directions that have a basic importance for the psychology of learning. We have already seen that a psychoanalytic interpretation of Pavlovian theory suggests that classical conditioning may lead to the establishment of wish-fulfilling fantasy (conditioned image), the stimuli for which are drive stimuli. Once learned, however, these fantasies serve a wider function. The organism in a state of need now has a mechanism that allows him to know (have a conditioned image of) the objects that will satisfy his need. Somehow these conditioned images obviously serve to initiate goal-seeking activity. A possible explanation for this is the problem to which we turn now. In this connection, it is important to keep two points in mind: (1) The fact that goal-seeking activity exists at all implies the distinction between image and reality. Lacking this distinction, there would be no reason for seeking the imagined object which, for all practical behavioral purposes, would already be present in the form of the image. (2) The responses involved in goal-seeking behavior are almost always quite different from those involved in Pavlovian conditioning. In the latter situation, conditioned and unconditioned responses are grossly similar. But in the type of (instrumental) learning now under examination, they are characteristically not the same.

It is important to note in this connection that more than mere salivation occurs in the behavior of the animal in the Pavlovian conditioning situation. Such additional behavior includes approaching and seizing food and a posture of motor "attentiveness" or "expectancy" (Zener, 1937). It is particularly interesting to note next that the effect of food used as a reinforcer is not the same for motor behavior as it is for salivation. Whereas the US *excites* or produces salivation, the same operation *inhibits* the motor acts and brings them to a halt. Thus, it appears that the mechanism of reinforcement may be an excitatory one in the case of the classical CR and an inhibitory one in case of the motor response.

Recall now (1) that taking our lead from psychoanalysis, we have proposed that classical conditioning involves the formation of a learned image or fantasy of the object that will satisfy a state of need, (2) that initially there is no distinction between image and reality, (3) that the satisfying object (and since no distinction exists, the image of such an object) inhibits motor behavior, (4) that, although initially no distinction between image and object exists, the laws of discrimination learning lead to the establishment of one, (5) that the establishment of such a discrimination entails the inhibition of the conditioned image and (6) that the inhibition of motor behavior is essential to the reinforcement of such behavior. These ideas make it possible to construct an hypothesis to account for the effects of incentives on motor acts. A possible account is as follows:

Through the mechanism of drive stimulation, the organism in a state of need tends to have an image of the object that will satisfy that need. The effect of this image is to inhibit or restrain motor behavior because, as we have just seen, the presentation of the US inhibits the motor activity that occurs in the conditioning situation. Once elicited, however, the conditioned image tends to be inhibited because, as we have also seen, the organism has learned to discriminate between image and reality. Presumably the inhibition of the image involves its suppression and effective absence. But the absence of the US (and, by extension, the image of the US) is the very condition that leads to the release or occurrence of instrumental behavior. Thus, the mechanism of incentive seems to involve two processes that occur in quick succession: (1) The occurrence of a conditioned image provides the organism with a knowledge of the object that will satisfy its need. (2) The inhibition of this image releases appropriate motor behavior.

In Freudian terminology we say that the activating effect of a wish upon goal-seeking behavior carried out in the service of that wish is a direct consequence of the inhibition of its reality value.

43

Contributions of Conditioning Principles to Psychiatry[1]

WAGNER H. BRIDGER

In this paper I will outline an approach to some problems of psychopathology and therapy based on conditioning principles. This theoretical approach derives from the Pavlovian concept of signalling systems with some contributions from American learning theory. I will first describe some of the experimental data that gave rise to the basic theory and then discuss certain psychiatric symptoms and other psychological phenomena, such as dreams and hypnosis, in order to show how this theory can generate hypotheses about explanatory mechanisms.

The Pavlovian Model

In Pavlov's original experiment the dog salivated as he ate meat, but did not salivate when a neutral tone was presented. However, when the tone preceded the food for several presentations, the tone itself elicited salivation in the dog, i.e., the conditioned stimulus (the tone) evoked the same response as the unconditioned stimulus (food). This is the classical conditioning paradigm—unconditioned stimulus (food) elicits unconditioned response (salivation); conditioned stimulus (tone) originally does not elicit the response, but having been paired with the unconditioned stimulus several times, does produce the unconditioned response. The major concern of conditioning theory has been the understanding of the nature of the connections being made; the substitution of one stimulus for another, or, as it has been called, the signalling process.

In Pavlov's original experiment the tone became the signal for food; in other experiments the buzzer signals or stands for shock. We know that conditioning has occurred when an originally neutral stimulus becomes a signal for an unconditioned stimulus. However, on both logical and empirical grounds it is obvious that although the conditioned stimulus

[1] Reprinted from *Pavlovian Conditioning and American Psychiatry* Symposium No. 9, copyright 1964, Group for the Advancement of Psychiatry.

may be the signal for the unconditioned stimulus, it is never *identical* with it. The lack of identity is most clearly demonstrated in the second major phenomenon of conditioning: extinction. If the conditioning process consisted only of the pairing of stimuli, then once two stimuli were paired, either one independently would continue to evoke the same response in the organism throughout its life. The dog would forever salivate to a tone years after the initial conditioning. However, when many trials occur in which the dog no longer receives food after the tone, he stops salivating to the tone; the rat who no longer receives shock after the buzzer stops jumping to the buzzer; the human being who no longer receives shock after a buzzer stops giving a Galvanic Skin Response (GSR) to the buzzer. Thus extinction takes place: a conditioned stimulus that is no longer paired with an unconditioned stimulus after a number of trials no longer elicits a response. Clearly, the signal does not assume all of the properties of the event being signalized, or there would be no extinction.

Our basic assumption is that conditioning (the making and breaking of stimulus connections) may be a fundamental process of human thought and behavior as well as psychopathological phenomena. It might be best to clarify this formulation by describing some of the experiments that led to it.

Experimental evidence

As early as 1913 Pavlov found that disturbed, maladaptive behavior could be experimentally produced in animals. Since then, these so-called experimental neuroses have been produced by many investigators through the use of conflicting and excessive stimulation. One drawback in extrapolating the findings of these experiments to human clinical psychiatry is that the methods described have not been used to induce neuroses in human beings. In order to draw a more fruitful analogy between human and animal psychopathology it would be necessary to use the same method in producing experimental behavioral disturbances in both species.

In 1952, while I was working at the Pavlovian Laboratory at the Johns Hopkins University, there was a revived interest in the use of hallucinogenic drugs to experimentally induce disturbed states of consciousness in human subjects. I thought that hallucinogenic drugs could be useful in bridging the gap between human and animal experimental psychopathology. The specific drug I chose was mescaline, which had been widely used to produce disturbances in consciousness in normal human subjects. These disturbances included forms of behavior, such as hallucinations and delusions, which at times were analogous to those seen in schizophrenic patients. Mescaline, I thought, could be used to produce disturbed behavior in both animals and humans.

My first study (Bridger & Gantt, 1956) dealt with the effects of mescaline on classical defense responses of dogs. Normally, the dogs would lift a paw at the onset of the conditioned stimulus (tone) that had been previously paired with the unconditioned stimulus (shock). They would howl and bark when they received the shock itself. Under the influence of mescaline, the specific motor act of lifting the paw was inhibited. However, they howled and barked to the conditioned stimulus tone, even though no shock was applied. This behavior had previously been seen only in response to the presentation of the unconditioned stimulus (electric shock) during the non-drug control period.

Other workers have reported similar observations. Sivadjian (1934), working with rats, paired a buzzer with electric shock. He found that under mescaline, the rats squealed in response to the buzzer alone as if they were being shocked. Courvoisier (1956) reported a similar experiment and found the same phenomenon which she described as a veritable hallucinatory crisis. Under mescaline, in response to each presentation of the conditioned stimulus (a bell), the rats squealed and jumped up and down "as if they were being shocked," an event that never occurred in the unmescalinized state. From this phenomenon (the animal responding to the signal for shock as if it were the shock) I concluded that under the effects of mescaline the usual relationship between the conditioned stimulus and the unconditioned response was disturbed. The conditioned stimulus began to have an effect on the animal as if it were the unconditioned stimulus, or, as then postulated, the signal for imminent reality appeared to have the attributes of current actuality. I further predicted that under mescaline the conditioned response would take longer to extinguish. The prediction was made under the assumption that the conditioned stimulus had assumed some of the functional properties of the unconditioned stimulus and thus the response could not be extinguished. Normally, a conditioned response is extinguished after the presentation of a number of non-reinforced (no shock) trials. When an animal is conditioned to respond to a buzzer followed by shock, and the buzzer (the conditioned stimulus) is then presented alone without shock reinforcement for a number of trials, he stops responding to the buzzer. However, if the buzzer acquires the attributes of the electric shock, the animal should be responding to the buzzer not as a signal for the shock, but as if it were the shock itself.

Conditioned versus unconditioned responses

I tested this hypothesis with rats, using two different types of conditioned responses: the conditioned emotional response and the conditioned avoidance response (Bridger, 1960). In the conditioned emotional response the animal is shocked on every trial and shows a great deal of emotional reactivity in terms of crouching, defecation, and other fear behavior in response to the conditioned stimulus. In the conditioned avoidance response the animal quickly learns to avoid the shock and shows very little fear behavior in response to the conditioned stimulus. When extinction was carried out under mescaline, the conditioned emotional response was not extinguished while the avoidance response was rapidly extinguished. This abolition of the extinction of the emotional response supported my hypothesis that under mescaline the conditioned stimulus assumes the attributes of the unconditioned stimulus. The animal reacted to the signal in the same manner as he did to what was being signalized.

In order to understand how mescaline produced this disturbance of conditioned stimulus-unconditioned stimulus relationships, I surveyed data relevant to both the electrophysiological correlates of conditioning and the neuropharmacological effects of mescaline. Both Gastaut (1958) and Rowland (1957) in their descriptions of the electrophysiological correlates of conditioning, showed that the conditioned stimulus and the unconditioned stimulus were accompanied by different bioelectrical responses in the neocortex. Gastaut said that the unconditioned stimulus produced a primary evoked response in the neocortex. The conditioned stimulus, however, produced only a local desynchronization and a secondary evoked response in this same somato-sensory area. Malcolm (1958) found that during conditioning there was no difference between the responses evoked in the hippocampal region by the conditioned stimulus and the unconditioned stimulus. It would seem from these experiments that the conditioned stimulus produces a different electrical response in the neocortex from that produced by the unconditioned stimulus. However, in the hippocampus and other subcortical structures, both conditioned and unconditioned stimuli produce the same electrical response. It has also been reported (John, 1958) that when avoidance conditioning is well established, and the animal is no longer showing evidence of fear, the hippocampal-evoked responses lessen and disappear. Therefore, it seems that the more emotion associated with the stimulus, the greater the hippocampal activity. This is consistent with the behavioral observation of the differential effect of mescaline on emotional vs. avoidance behavior.

Experiments by the Killams (1956), Marrazzi (1955), and Purpura (1956) on the neuropharmacological effect of hallucinogenic drugs suggest that both LSD and mescaline inhibit neocortical synapses with the simultaneous activation of limbic structures.

When the data from behavioral, neuropharmacological, and electrophysiological levels are integrated, it would seem that there is evidence at the neocortical level of differentiated responses to the conditioned and unconditioned stimuli. At the level of the more primitive limbic system the evidence does not indicate such a differentiation. In an emotional learning situation which produces hippocampal activity, mescaline will increase this activity while simultaneously inhibiting the neocortex. I therefore suggest that any condition which would inhibit the neocortex and simultaneously activate the limbic system will produce a confusion between the conditioned stimulus and the unconditioned stimulus; between the signal and what is being signaled. This lack of differentiation between signifier and what is being signified occurs primarily in strong emotional situations when hippocampal activity is present.

This hypothesis, however, is based on an analysis of the simple conditioning paradigm. The relevance to human behavior of this conditioned stimulus-unconditioned stimulus relationship must be amplified. This relationship is characterized by the fact that through experience one stimulus, the conditioned stimulus, comes to stand for, signalize, or signify the other stimulus, the unconditioned stimulus. In the typical Pavlovian experiment the bell is a signal for the object (food) or the action (eating); it is a signal in that it stands for, but is not identical with, the food or eating. A similar signal-object relationship holds true for human thinking. Our ideas or verbal designations are the signals of objects or of actions. However, they are not identical to these objects or actions. Thus the conditioned stimulus-unconditioned stimulus relationship is analogous to, but far less complex than, the symbol-object relationship of human thinking. Normally, the dog does not confuse the buzzer with the electric shock and man does not confuse his ideas with his percepts of reality.

The Pavlovian signal systems

Before proceeding further I would like to describe Pavlov's concepts of signal systems. Pavlov divided human thought into two systems. He said: "If our sensations, perceptions and direct impressions of the surrounding world are for us the primary signals of reality, the concrete signals, then words are secondary signals. They represent themselves as abstractions of reality and permit generalizations. Thus the human brain is composed of the animal brain, first signalling system, and the purely human part related to speech, second signalling system" (Pavlov, 1955, p. 590).

This, by the way, is similar to Freud's statement that ". . . the conscious idea comprises the concrete idea plus the verbal idea corresponding to it, whilst the unconscious idea is that of the thing alone" (Freud, 1956, p. 134).

Piaget (1951) has stated that the child develops the symbolic function by gradually differentiating the signifier from the signified. The child transforms the signal into the symbol; words are treated more and more by second signalling system processes and less and less by first signalling system processes. This gradual differentiation of the symbol from what is being symbolized is very similar to the relationship between the signal and what is being signalized. Going back to what I stated before, it is the neocortex which manifests differential responses to the signal as compared to what is being signalized while the subcortical structures and the limbic system do not show such differential responses. I therefore propose that the distinction between the symbol and the object symbolized will be determined by the balance between neocortical and limbic system activity. The more affectively charged an experience is the greater will be the limbic system activity and the closer will be the bond between the symbol and the object symbolized. Neocortical inhibition will also decrease the distinction between the symbol and the object symbolized.

As a general approach to cognition, I would postulate that words and thoughts can have different properties, varying from the abstract, logical categorization to the hallucinatory image of the particular object itself. The word "chair" can mean a general category of all chairs; it can also mean a particular chair. It can even conjure up the hallucinatory image of the chair itself. When a word or idea is used in the general abstract categorical sense, it is called a symbol and follows the rules of second signalling system activity, logical rules. When a thought is dealt with as a particular concrete thing, it is called an image, signal, or sign, and the rules of thinking at this sensory level of cognition are those of the first signalling system. Strong emotional experience would tend to shift the cognitive process from the rational toward the perceptual and sensory. If one has recently sat on a chair on which a tack has been placed, the word "chair" would probably not be thought of as a symbol for the general category of chairs. The word "chair" would produce a tendency to think of, or imagine, the particular chair associated with the trauma. In addition, any condition which inhibits the neocortex would also shift the cognitive process toward first signalling system activity, i.e., lessen the gap between the signifier and the signified.

First signal system activity

My basic hypothesis is that as the level of human mental functioning becomes more primitive and less symbolic, it corresponds more closely to the phenomena of animal conditioning, first signal system activity. The following processes describe the kinds of associations or stimulus substitution seen in first signal system activity.

1. *Primary stimulus generalization.* Things become associated be-because of physical similarity, i.e., if a square paired with shock produces a fear response, a rectangle will also produce the same fear response.

2. *Generalization based upon temporal or spatial contiguity.* Wickens (1959) has shown that if a light is followed by a buzzer which in turn is followed by shock, the light and buzzer come to signalize not only shock but each other.

3. *Stimulus generalization based upon identity of affect or activity.* If a light is paired with shock and produces both fear and avoidance behavior and a buzzer paired with shock produces only fear, the buzzer alone will later produce avoidance behavior similar to that elicited by the light. The avoidance response is generalized from the light to the buzzer because of the identity of the affect, fear.

4. *Generalization based upon identity of function.* Animals know objects only in terms of their direct experience. A dog repeatedly fed on a chair responds to the chair only as a place to be fed, not as an object independent of this experience. This is analogous to Von Domarus' principle of equivalence of objects through identity of predicate. Objects are then associated according to the function they serve.

In the animal world of first signalling system activity, signals or objects in reality are associated because of physical similarity, contiguity, similarity of function or use, and similarity of biological need or affect.

Interaction of first and second signal systems

I will now postulate two basic psychophysiological mechanisms. First, any condition which produces neocortical inhibition will shift the level of thinking from abstract symbols toward concrete signals; from second toward first signalling system activity. The second mechanism concerns the affective experience of the individual. The more affect there is in a situation, the more likely will be the shift from second toward first signalling system activity, from secondary toward primary process functioning. As a corollary to this, it is suggested that the phenomena seen in so-called primary process thinking can be explained by the above-mentioned principles of animal learning, the laws of stimulus generalization. I should mention at this time that inhibition and excitation are considered to be active molar physiological processes closely related to behavior and that they are not necessarily indicated by the number or frequency of neuronal firings. Bioelectrical potentials should not be thought of as identical with the specific physiological process itself.

Having outlined this basic Pavlovian signalling system hypothesis, I will describe some animal experiments in support of it. Solomon and Wynne (1954) produced what they termed traumatic avoidance conditioning in dogs. After the dog had been conditioned to avoid a very painful electric shock by jumping a hurdle, this response was found to be remarkably resistant to extinction. A further attempt to extinguish the response was made by presenting the conditioned stimulus when the hurdle was absent and the animal could not avoid the anxiety-producing situation. However, when the hurdle was replaced, the conditioned stimulus again elicited the hurdle jumping response. Solomon concluded that normal learning theory could not explain this so-called fixated pathological phenomenon and hypothesized the partial irreversibility of the traumatic classical emotional response. As I described previously, if the limbic system is markedly activated in a conditioning situation, the organism would have great difficulty distinguishing the conditioned stimulus from the unconditioned stimulus. In Solomon's experiment perhaps the dog was not able to distinguish the conditioned stimulus from the electric shock, which was also true in my mescaline experiment. This suggests a mechanism for the so-called partial irreversibility of the pathological conditioned response.

Certain neurophysiological experiments shed further light on the role of the neocortex in reality testing. Zeleny and Kadykov (1938) described an experiment in which they dealt with learning in decorticate dogs. Despite 300 presentations of the conditioned stimulus without reinforcement, extinction failed to occur. Wing and Smith (1942) found that extinction of the conditioned response to light proceeded much more slowly after the removal of the striate cortex. Marquis and Hilgard (1937) found that the conditioned eyelid response to light failed to extinguish in monkeys whose occipital lobes had been removed.

There are a few other observations which also support the hypothesis that neocortical inhibition produces a shift from second to first signalling system activity. Both sleep deprivation (Armington & Mitnick, 1959) and sensory deprivation (Heron, et al., 1956) have been shown to produce disturbances in thinking similar to those seen in schizophrenia. These experimental conditions also show EEG correlates of sleep, and thus one would assume that they are accompanied by some amount of neocortical inhibition. Of course dreams are a prime example of this shift from second to first signalling system activity during neocortical inhibition. The hallucinatory character of the dream may be due to the individual's inability to distinguish the signifier from the signified; the idea from the percept. Jouvet (1960) has shown that the EEG desynchronization present during dreaming is probably not due to neocortical activation but mediated by subcortical and limbic system excitation. As previously stated, at the level of the limbic system there seems to be no differentiation between the signifier and the signified, the idea and the percept, the symbol and the object. The primary process character of dreams may be explained by the principles of stimulus generalization of animal conditioning. These conditioning principles are formulated as experimentally verifiable hypotheses, and are at a nodal point of transition between physiology and psychology.

The use of words as conditioned stimuli is a convenient technique in studying the interaction of the first and second signalling systems. In this procedure a conditioned response is established to a word, e.g., "cat." Then generalization to related words is studied. If the subject responds to phonetically related words like "hat" and "tack," we assume that first signalling system activity predominates. If the subject responds to semantically related words such as "animal" or "dog," then second signalling system activity predominates.

In a series of studies of verbal conditioning, Luria and Vinogravoda (1959) and Schwartz (1960) have shown that chloral hydrate, hypnosis and fatigue all produce a shift in generalization from semantically to phonetically related words, i.e., a shift from second toward first signalling system functioning.

Conditioning and psychopathology

Thus far I have presented some conditioning principles and data that I feel may contribute toward our understanding of certain aspects of human behavior. I would now like to apply these concepts to psychopathology and therapy without in any way implying that they deal with all or even the most significant aspects of abnormal behavior and its alteration. The theoretical approach described is appropriate to the formal properties of psychopathology and contributes less in respect to etiology and symptom specificity. Nevertheless, I believe that conditioning theory can provide a fruitful framework for the investigation of some of the complex problems confronting psychiatry.

This approach is based upon the previously discussed Pavlovian concepts of signal systems and upon the contributions of the learning theorists, Shoben (1949), Dollard and Miller (1951), and Wolpe (1958). Central to the learning theory approach to neurosis is the concept that neurotic symptoms can be interpreted as the conditioning of anxiety and the subsequent development of behaviors that lead to the reduction or avoidance of this anxiety. The point of view presented in this paper is that the meaning or context of symptoms can be explained by learning theory and that the formal properties of symptoms can be explained by shifts in signal-system functions. In addition, it is likely that certain aspects of the symptoms are also need-gratifying. In either case, the meaning of the symptom in relation to the original significant experiences are explained by the psychoanalytic concept of symbolic transformation. I propose that the Pavlovian concept of the first signalling system with its laws of stimulus generalization supplies an explanatory mechanism for the phenomena classified by psychoanalysts as symbolic transformation. There is generalization due to physical similarity, contiguity, identity of function, and identity of affect. This occurs when there is a shift from second toward first signalling system activity, either due to the non-verbal nature of the experience, increased emotionality or because the verbal cues are anxiety-provoking and are thus avoided. The latter resembles the psychodynamic mechanism of repression. The increased emotionality may reflect the reactivation of early significant experiences.

Symptomatology

I would now like to deal with the formal aspects of the symptomatology. The first symptoms to be discussed are hallucinations. The normal individual usually differentiates his ideas from real percepts, his daydreams from reality. However, because of the total life experience of an individual, if an idea becomes highly emotionally charged, subcortical structures including the limbic system are activated. Perhaps as a necessary requirement, the neocortex is also under a state of partical inhibition. With the disturbed balance between neocortical and limbic system activity the individual cannot distinguish his ideas from reality and accepts them as percepts, and thus undergoes an hallucinatory experience.

The next symptoms are delusions. The normal person usually has explanations for his feeling states and behavior. However, when testing these explanations against reality he is able to revise his ideas in accord with the real situation, i.e., he can extinguish one idea and replace it by another as he undergoes various experiences. However, if his ideas are accompanied by strong emotions, they shift from second to first signalling system functioning and are treated not as ideas but as reality. The signifier merges with the signified and becomes a delusion. If the signifier is identical with the signified, it is an hallucination.

Hysterical conversion symptoms are similar to the increased suggestibility seen in the hypnotic state. Platonov (1959) stated that under hypnosis the verbal suggestion "you are drinking water" can produce a diuresis. The words act on the subject as real objects—the subject does not differentiate the signal from what it stands for. In hysteria, autosuggestion allows the thought of paralysis to produce a real paralysis. There is heightened first signal activity and decreased second signalling system functioning. The anxiety-reducing thought is transformed into its equivalent physical symptom. It is thereby avoided or repressed through decreased second signal functioning. The symbolic meaning of the symptom can be explained by the laws of stimulus generalization.

Phobias are similar to repressions except that the phobic avoids external anxiety-provoking cues while repression concerns the avoidance of internally produced cues (thought and ideas). While the content of the phobia is explained by stimulus generalization, its marked persistence is perhaps related to the fact that there is a lack of distinction between the phobic stimulus and the original fear stimulus. The normal laws of extinction do not apply, and one gets something akin to the partial irreversibility described by Solomon and Wynne (1954).

According to Pavlovian concepts, the obsessive-compulsive patient is just the opposite of the hysteric. The latter shows a predominance of first signal system activity, while the former shows second signalling system predominance. Normally, there is a certain balance between first and second signalling system functioning. Symbols are related to the objects they represent but do not become merged or identical with them. The obsessive-compulsive has completely separated the second from the first signalling system and uses words not as signifiers but as independent anxiety-reducing devices. The fixated animal repeatedly presses a lever to avoid anxiety, while the patient repeatedly thinks certain thoughts to reduce his anxiety.

Obviously the application of Pavlovian signal systems to explain psychopathology is in a preliminary state of development and only partially successful. The specific differences between hysteria, schizophrenia, and obsessive-compulsive neurosis are not clearly differentiated by the "signal-signalized" concept.

Pavlovian basis for therapy

In regard to therapy there are two possibilities. The first considers that the symptomatology is in part determined by a disturbed relationship of the neocortex and the limbic system; e.g., it is postulated that in schizophrenia, the limbic system is undergoing increased activation and simultaneously the neocortex is under state of partial inhibition. Since physiological treatment should be related to the presumed physiological disturbance, the treatment of schizophrenia should be directed toward increasing neocortical activity and inhibiting subcortical and limbic structures. This would include the effects of pharmacological agents.

The second method is that of psychotherapy. Since a conditioning approach assumes that these symptoms can be explained by certain laws of learning, their removal may also be influenced by the application of learning principles. I would suggest that the fixed nature of neurotic symptoms is caused by the individual's inability to differentiate symbols from what is being symbolized, which in turn produces the apparent irreversibility of the maladaptive behavior. In other words, the neurotic reacts to the symbol as if it was the unconditioned stimulus. Since his pathological behavior has properties similar to those of unconditioned responses, the question for therapy is: How does one inhibit unconditioned responses? It has been shown by Pavlov that electric shock, which is an unconditioned stimulus for a defense response, can become the conditioned stimulus for food and thereby lose many of its noxious properties. As the shock becomes a signal for something else, the unconditioned response to the shock undergoes inhibition. This is what may occur during successful psychotherapy. The patient links his anxiety signals with new reinforcement or reality situations, and thus inhibits or extinguishes his previous neurotic responses. When the psychotherapeutic aspects of the doctor-patient relationship are effective, this relationship acts as an unconditioned stimulus eliciting confidence, acceptance, and security.

Since most neurotic symptoms are handled at the first signalling system level, it may be necessary initially to allow these experiences to enter consciousness through the use of drugs, hypnosis, and free association which promote first signalling system activity. However, as we all know, just labelling or giving verbal designations to feelings or experiences is not enough; this so-called intellectual insight does not produce the appropriate change in behavior. The lack of change may be due to the fact that since the neurotic symptom is produced by activity in the first signalling system, therapy must involve not only words but direct experience.

I have recently performed an experiment that gives evidence in support of this kind of approach. In this study normal volunteer college students were told that they would receive an electric shock after a specific conditioned stimulus, a light. They were given 20 trials with the stimulus and received the shock on every trial. They developed a conditioned GSR to the stimulus. They were then informed they would no longer receive shocks, the shock electrodes were removed, and the conditioned stimulus was again applied. The subjects continued to show physiological responses even though they stated they were convinced that they would not and could not be shocked. They had to go through the experience of not getting shocked after the light before they stopped showing physiological responses.

Another group of subjects were threatened with one very powerful shock after the specific conditioned stimulus. The conditioned stimulus was repeatedly applied and the subjects showed large physiological responses to the conditioned stimulus even though they did not receive the shock. They just expected it. These responses were just as large as those found in subjects who actually received shock reinforcement. The electrodes were then removed and the subjects were informed that they were not shocked because we were just testing their fear responses. The conditioned stimulus was again applied to test for resistance to extinction. The previously conditioned fear response was not present even on the first presentation of the conditioned stimulus. There was immediate extinction of the conditioned response. Seemingly, what these subjects learned through second signalling subjective expectancy could be removed through the experimenter's second signalling instructions. The subjects who had first signalling direct experience had to undergo new first signalling direct experiences in order to extinguish their responses. This would support the concept that corrective emotional direct experiences are necessary in order to change maladaptive behavior patterns (Bridger and Mandel, 1964).

SUMMARY

To summarize, I have presented a theoretical approach to psychiatry based on conditioning principles. Briefly, I hypothesized that when the neocortex is inhibited and the limbic system is excited, signals of a stressful experience tend to assume some of the functional properties of the real experience itself. Thus abstract ideas are responded to as if they were concrete signals or images. It was suggested that principles of animal learning provide a mechanism to explain the irrational fluidity of the primary process thinking that accompanies this regression or primitivization of cognitive functioning. Specifically, stimulus generalization through physical similarity and contiguity, and identity of affect or function explain the phenomena of condensation, displacement, and symbolic transformation. It was also suggested that the conditioning of anxiety and the subsequent avoidance of external and internal anxiety-provoking cues contribute to an understanding of certain aspects of psychopathology. Psychotherapy was viewed as the inhibition of maladaptive behavior through corrective emotional experiences.

In conclusion, I would propose that maladaptive behavior is more influenced by the affects of the first signal system than by rational thought. These affects, in turn, are determined by direct experiences. Alterations in maladaptive behavior can be achieved through new practical activities. However, intellectual insight may be useful in guiding the patient to these new experiences.

44

Pain-Aggression[1]

ROGER E. ULRICH

Aggression occurs in a great variety of complex forms, both in man and in lower animals. Generally defined, it refers to fighting and means the act of initiating an attack. We are all aware of the existence of aggression at various levels and both scientists and laymen have long been interested in its causes and control.

As in the initial study of many behavioral phenomena, the early studies of aggression were of animals fighting in their natural habitat. An observer hidden by a blind or some other obstruction would watch from afar and attempt to determine the variables which related to the particular behavior in question. In the case of aggression it was noted that territorial encroachment, limited space, and direct attack from predators were environmental factors related to fighting (Scott, 1958). It was found among the horned ruminants such as deer, buffalo, and mountain sheep, that fierce fighting between the males always occurred during the rutting season (Scott, 1958).

Certainly naturalistic observations such as these are of great importance in providing information which relates to causes and control of aggression. Nevertheless, the large number of uncontrolled variables existing in a natural setting often make definite statements of causality impossible. These difficulties no doubt explain the more recent trend toward a more exact laboratory analysis of aggression and those factors which produce it. For example, experimental studies have shown heredity to be an important variable, often manifested in the widespread tendency among wild strains of rats to show greater aggressiveness than their domestic counterparts (Covain, 1949; Richter, 1950). It has further been shown that heredity has an important physiological effect on fighting, act-

---

[1] The majority of the research reported in this paper has been conducted in collaboration with N. H. Azrin of the Behavior Research Laboratory, Anna State Hospital, Anna, Illinois. Other investigators closely associated with the Pain-aggression research and from whom I have received valuable assistance in the preparation of this paper are: R. R. Hutchinson, P. C. Wolff, T. J. Stachnik, and John H. Mabry. Some of the materials in this chapter appeared in the January 1965 issue of the *Psychological Record*.

ing through the male hormone (Beeman, 1947; Collias, 1944; Bevan, Davis, & Levy, 1960). Bard (1950) found that the surgical removal of a large part of the hypothalamus would cause cats to display less aggression. Some other factors which have been manipulated experimentally and found to relate to aggression are the level of food deprivation, the age of the animal (Seward, 1945), and the amount of fighting experience (Scott, 1958).

Another variable frequently cited as a probable cause of aggression is that of pain. Little children are admonished not to hurt their pets so as not to make them bite. Wounded animals suffering pain are known to be more apt to attack than they would under more normal circumstances. In the case of the common house mouse, pain is one of the primary sources of stimulation for fighting (Scott & Fredericson, 1951). As soon as a young mouse has its teeth, it will turn around and try and bite anything which pinches its tail. The same type of behavior has been observed to occur in rats whose tails have been accidentally pinched when closing the door of the experimental chamber. The tactile stimulation of one mouse's rough grooming of another is often enough to start a fight. Another common stimulus for producing fighting among adult mice is a painful attack by another mouse.

Indeed several investigators (Daniel, 1943; O'Kelly, & Steckle, 1939; Richter, 1950) have noted the relation of pain to aggression while pursuing other studies. In the study by O'Kelly and Steckle (1939), six rats were placed in an experimental chamber where periodic electric shocks were delivered through a floor grid. Although the rats had been docile prior to the delivery of shock, they immediately stood up, faced one another and struck vigorously once it was presented. Other investigators have shown that shock elicits fighting behavior in wild rats (Covain, 1949) and domestic mice (Tedeschi, et al., 1959) as well as in domestic rats. In each of these studies, however, the relation of pain to aggression was in the main an incidental observation. For these reasons, Dr. N. H. Azrin and I decided to explore some of these earlier observations systematically through a strict experimental analysis of the phenomena.

General method

As is true in any scientific analysis of behavior, the first step is to describe accurately the behavioral phenomena to be investigated. In the case of aggression the definition of the response varies from species to species; but, as was stated earlier, it generally refers to fighting and means the act of initiating an attack. Pain, as it is used in the present series of experiments, is synonymous with aversive stimulation and incorporates those variables which organisms have been observed in the past to escape, or avoid.

A good example of the pain-aggression phenomenon is contained in one of the initial studies (Ulrich, 1961). In it, paired rats were placed in an experimental chamber and observations were made of their behavior prior to the delivery of shock presented to the feet of the animals. At no time during this period did any aggression appear. Soon after shock was delivered, however, a drastic change took place in the rats' behavior. They would suddenly face each other in an upright position, and with mouths open they would strike out at one another, assuming the stereotyped posture shown in Figure 44-1. To date the majority of the fighting research has employed human observers to record the aggressive behavior of this type. Fighting responses are recorded by an observer depressing a microswitch for any striking or biting movement of either of the animals toward the other. Reliability checks, run by having different observers simultaneously record the fighting behavior, have shown that the charac-

FIGURE 44-1. Example of a pair of rats assuming the stereotyped fighting posture immediately after the onset of shock. (Ulrich & Craine, 1964.)

Pain-Aggression

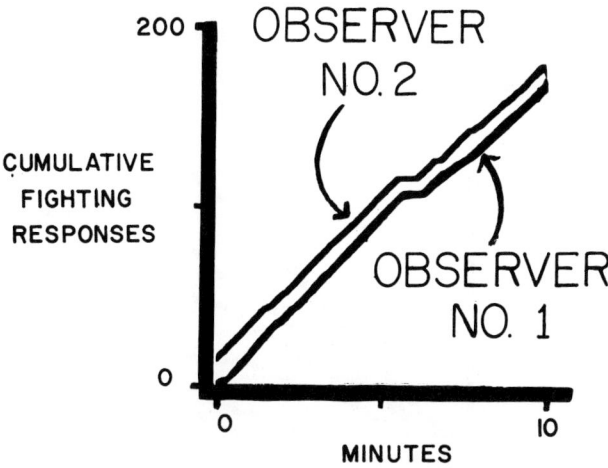

FIGURE 44-2. Agreement between observers in the simultaneous recording of fighting responses.

teristic pattern of the fighting response is sufficiently clear to allow for accurate recording (Ulrich and Azrin, 1962) (Fig. 44-2).

More recent experiments have sometimes employed automatic techniques for the recording of pain-elicited aggression. For example, Azrin, Hutchinson and Sallery (1964) found that monkeys placed in a loosely restraining chair would attack a cloth ball following the onset of shock. The string suspending the ball was attached to a switch which closed when the ball was pulled. The results obtained by this automatic method of recording fighting behavior were found to agree closely with those produced by a human observer closing a microswitch to record the same reactions.

Shock-elicited aggression

In early studies the primary stimulus used to elicit fighting was electric shock to the feet and most of this research was concerned with the effects of the important parameters of shock. For example, it was found that certain aspects of fighting between rats occurred as a nonmonotonic function of shock intensity (Ulrich & Azrin, 1962) (Fig. 44-3). Increasing the shock intensity from 0 to 2 ma. produced an increased frequency of fighting, but at higher intensities (3–5 ma.) the rate of fighting decreased. The decrease in fighting behavior at higher intensity appeared to be partly a consequence of the debilitating effects of shock and partly the consequence of competing behavior. At lower intensities (below about 2.0 ma.) the shock did not seem to be sufficiently aversive, while at

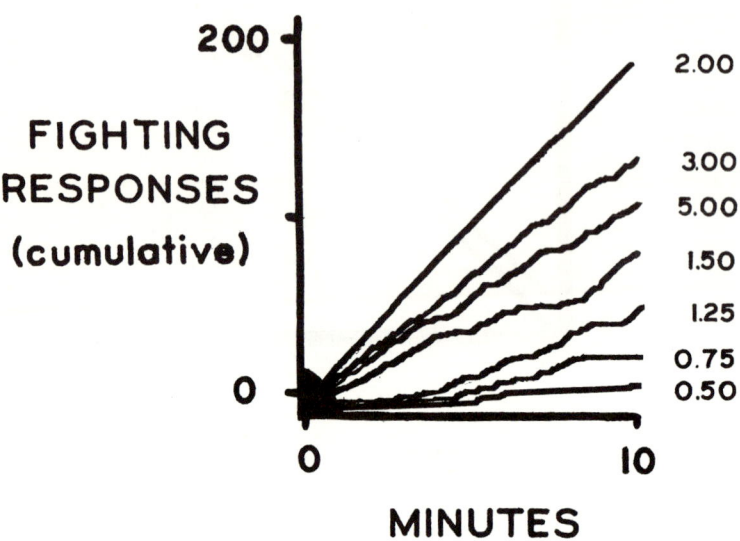

FIGURE 44-3. Typical cumulative records of the fighting responses that were elicited from one pair of rats at various intensities of foot-shock.

higher intensities, the shock appeared to be debilitating and to elicit competing behavior.

In addition to its relationship to shock intensity, the elicitation of the fighting reflex was also found to occur as a direct function of the frequency of shock presentations (Fig. 44-4). The more often the shock was presented, the more often the subjects fought. When shock was made so frequent as to be continuous, however, the fighting decreased and much of the rat's behavior appeared to be directed toward escape from the experimental chamber, behavior that obviously would interfere with the usual fighting. The lower rate of fighting at the lower frequencies of shock presentation again seemed to be related to the existence of competing responses. For example, during the longer interval between shocks, the rats frequently assumed positions incompatible with the stereotyped fighting posture. The optimum frequency of shock presentation for eliciting fighting between rats thus appears to be approximately 30 to 40 shocks per minute (Ulrich and Azrin, 1962), but this frequency may be specific to rats. Lower frequencies have been found to be equally effective in species whose fighting tends to persist long after the shock has been presented (Azrin, Hutchinson, & Hake, 1963).

Fighting has also been found to be a direct function of the duration of the shocks (Fig. 44-5), the longer the duration of shock, the

Pain-Aggression

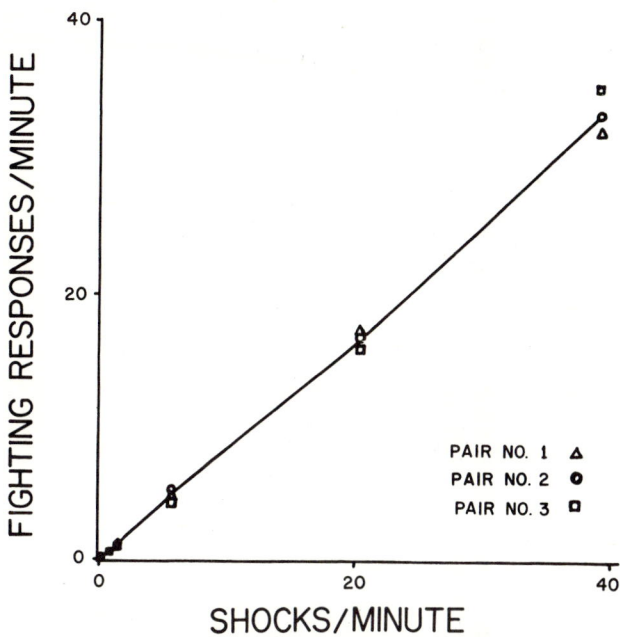

FIGURE 44-4. The elicitation of fighting responses as a function of the frequency of presentation of foot-shock for each of three pairs of rats.

greater the probability of fighting. As we have seen however, continual delivery of shock partially reversed this relation. Beyond this the parameter of duration interacts with the amount of training: very brief shock durations become progressively more effective during continued shock presentation; and longer durations become less effective as a session progresses (Azrin, Ulrich, Hutchinson and Norman, 1964). In these studies gross observation of the rats indicated that the longer shock durations gave ample opportunity for the rats to acquire postures and movements such as jumping, which reduced the receipt of shock. These escape attempts appeared to compete with the fighting reaction. The shorter shock durations did not appear to produce such attempts to escape. It was also observed that the longer shock durations may have indirectly reduced the likelihood of fighting by physically weakening the rats.

In other studies the method of shock presentation has been found to be critical. Failure to scramble the polarity of the electrified grids produced inconsistency in fighting (Fig. 44-6). Many early investigations of shock-produced fighting used a type of shock circuit in which alternative bars of the floor grid were wired in parallel. Such a design permits the animal to avoid shocks by standing on bars of the same polarity and

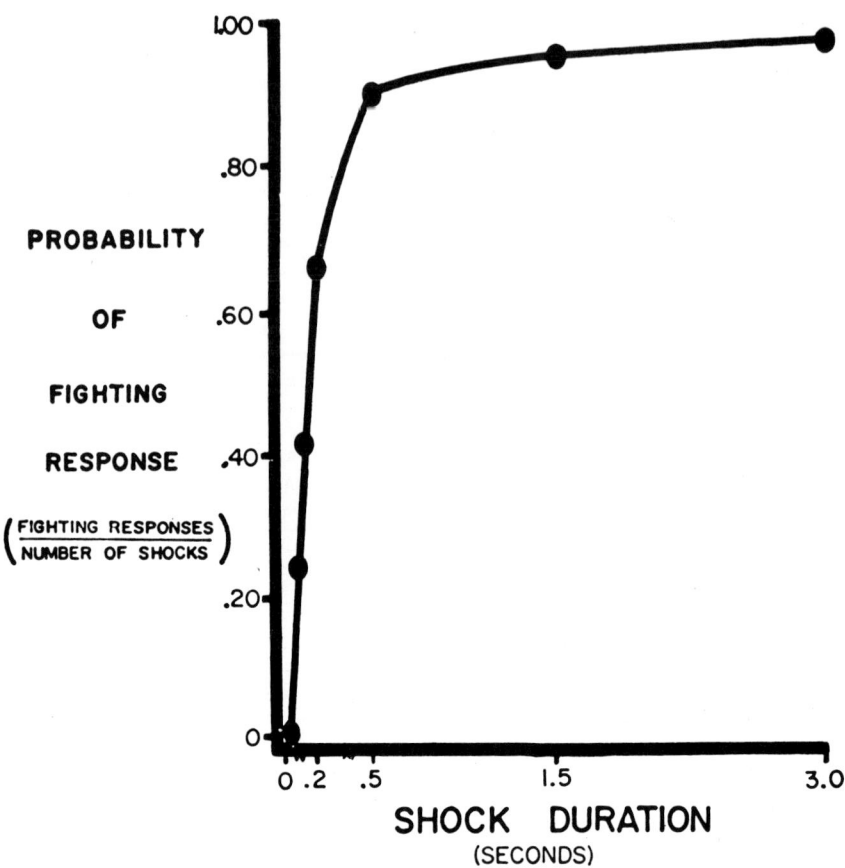

FIGURE 44-5. Probability of obtaining a fighting response between a pair of rats following the delivery of foot-shocks of different durations. The curve is for the first 20 shocks delivered during each session and is an average for 6 pairs of rats.

may account for the frequent failure of shock to elicit fighting behavior reported by other investigators (Miller, 1948; Richter, 1950).

Other conditions that elicit aggression

Fighting in response to aversive heat delivered to the paws was obtained in one investigation when paired rats were placed in an experimental chamber with a pre-heated thin metal floor. The heated floor appeared to elicit fighting in much the same manner as a continuously electrified floor grid.

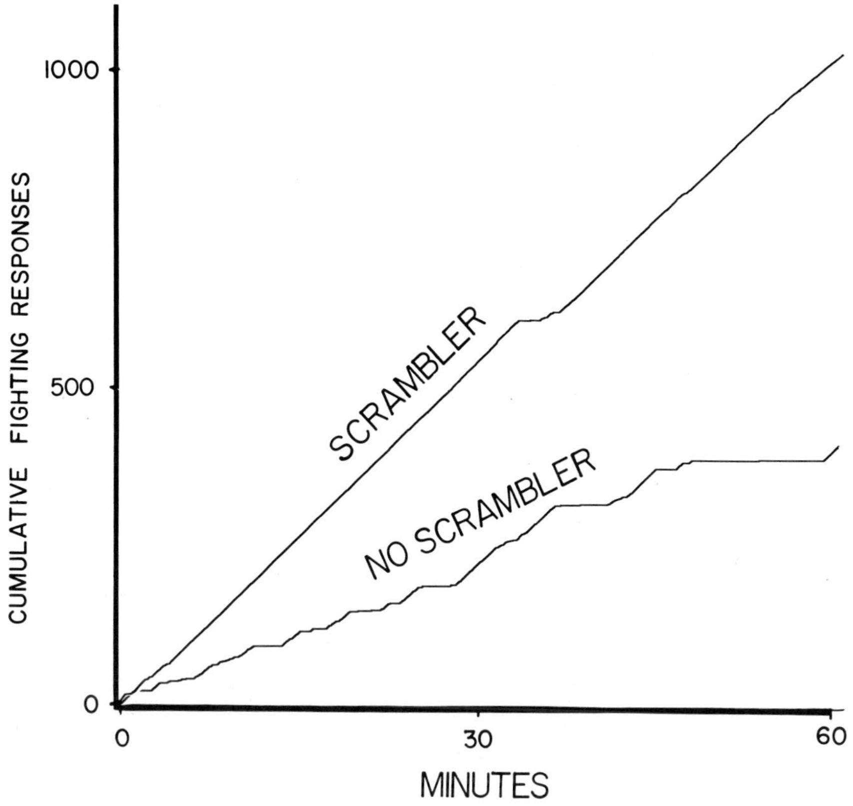

FIGURE 44-6. The elicitation of fighting responses by foot-shocks that were delivered with and without a polarity scrambler for the floor grids. (Ulrich & Azrin, 1962.)

Another form of aversive stimulation which has proven an effective elicitor of fighting is electrode shock. In one study (Ulrich & Azrin, 1962) electrodes were implanted beneath a fold of skin on the back of a single rat. A harness and swivel arrangement allowed the animal complete freedom of movement. When a shock was delivered only a spasmodic movement of the rat resulted if no other rat was present. When the shock was delivered in the presence of a second rat, however, the stimulated animal usually assumed the stereotyped fighting posture and attacked the unstimulated rat. Upon being attacked, the unstimulated rat in turn often assumed the stereotyped posture and returned the attack.

In a more recent study by Azrin, Hake and Hutchinson (1964), the delivery of a painful physical blow was also demonstrated to be effective in eliciting unconditioned attack behavior. Monkeys held tightly in restraining chairs were subjected to a blow on the tail. It was found that attack against a ball hanging just in front of the monkey occurred as a direct consequence of the blow.

Another recent study by Azrin (1964) obtained aggression in the extinction of an operant response. In this study, a pigeon was conditioned to peck at a key by making food available immediately after the peck. After the response was well established, the food-deprived bird was placed on a schedule in which food reinforcement was given after each of 20 pecks (continuous reinforcement). Following the 20 reinforced pecks the bird was placed on an extinction schedule in which none of the pecks resulted in food delivery. When no other animal was present in the chamber, the bird emitted a flurry of responses, which is typical following the initiation of extinction. However, when another pigeon was located nearby, the behavior changed and the hungry bird would instead rush over to the other pigeon and begin attacking its head in a manner previously observed by Levi (1959) and Smith and Hosking (1955). It thus appears that situations which involve no physically painful stimulation will produce aggression upon the termination of a favorable schedule of continuous reinforcement.

Other variables relating to pain-elicited aggression

Several variables that play a part in the elicitation of pain-aggression as well as some that do not have been discovered in several studies of the phenomenon. Two variables in the latter category are sex of the subject and whether more than two animals are subject to painful stimulation. Fighting elicited by painful shock to the feet occurs in and between rats of both sexes. Moreover, sexual behavior tends to be completely displaced by fighting under these circumstances (Ulrich & Azrin, 1962). Similarly, shock-evoked fighting occurs when more than two rats are shocked. When three, four, six, or eight rats were shocked simultaneously (Ulrich & Azrin, 1962; Antal & Kemeny, 1964), the usual stereotyped fighting response occurred although two or more rats sometimes attacked a single rat.

A somewhat more surprising outcome of this same general sort obtained by Ulrich and Azrin (1962) was that increasing numbers of aversive stimuli have little or no effect upon the rate of fighting. In this study frequent shocks were delivered to pairs of rats for an uninterrupted period of 7.5 hours. The results are shown in Figure 44-7 where it is clear that the fighting reflex was extremely resistant to fatigue. Over 10,000 fighting responses occurred without a noticeable reduction in rate.

Among the variables that make a greater difference are the following:

1. *Available area.* The amount of fighting between rats in response to shock was found to depend in a critical way upon the amount of floor

Pain-Aggression

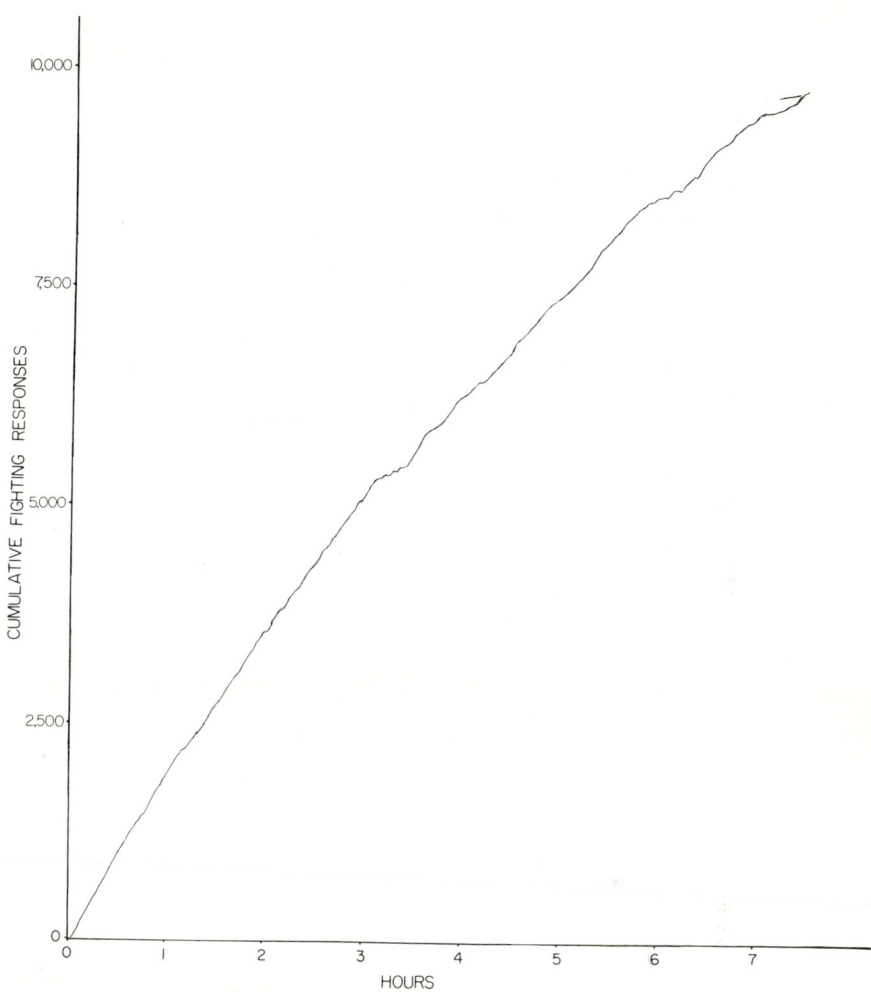

FIGURE 44-7. Cumulative record of the fighting responses that were elicited from a pair of rats during a long period (7.5 hours) of frequent (every 1.5 seconds) shock presentation. (Ulrich & Azrin, 1962).

space available (Ulrich & Azrin, 1962). As is shown in Figure 44-8, the amount of fighting decreases to a very low level when the available space is greater than about 2.0 square feet.

2. *The availability of visual stimulation.* In order to study the role played by visual stimuli in this behavior, animals were blinded and shocked. Although blinding decreased the amount of fighting, it did not eliminate it completely, as the results in Figure 44-9 show. On the other

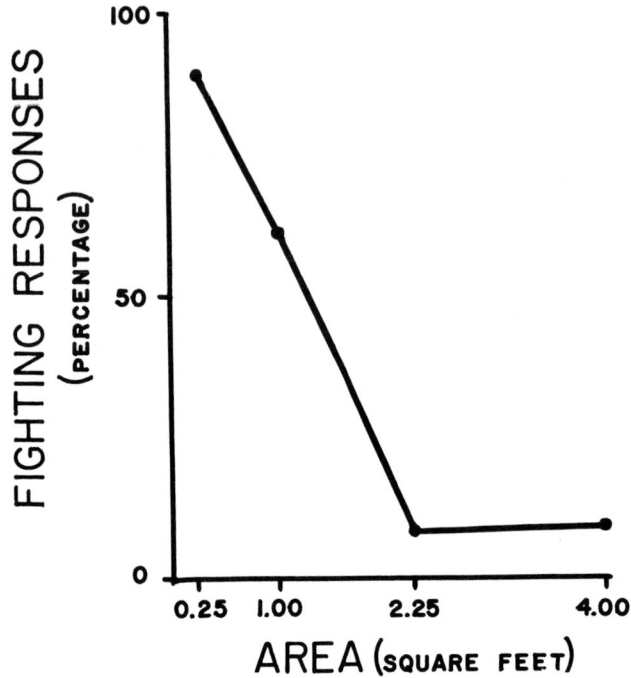

FIGURE 44-8. Elicitation of fighting responses from two rats by foot-shock in a square chamber of constant height and variable floor area.

hand, rats whose eyes were removed fought more than rats who were simply hooded. The reason for this probably is that the hoods covered the rat's whiskers, thereby eliminating another source of sensory reception which appears to be related to fighting (Flory, Ulrich, & Wolff, 1964).

3. *Initial orientation.* Another factor affecting the probability of fighting is the subjects' orientation toward each other at the moment of the shock. It has been noted in several experiments (Ulrich & Azrin, 1962; Brierton, Stachnik, & Ulrich, 1964) that the subjects will occasionally slip out of the fighting posture and assume other positions. On other occasions the animals may not be facing each other when the shock comes on. From the results of the experiments referred to above it is clear that fighting in response to shock is more likely to occur if the animals are facing each other at the moment of shock delivery and if they are in the fighting posture.

4. *Time since shock.* The temporal course of a given aggressive display was determined in a study by Azrin, Hutchinson, and Sallery (1964). In this study, it was shown that the probability of attack gradually

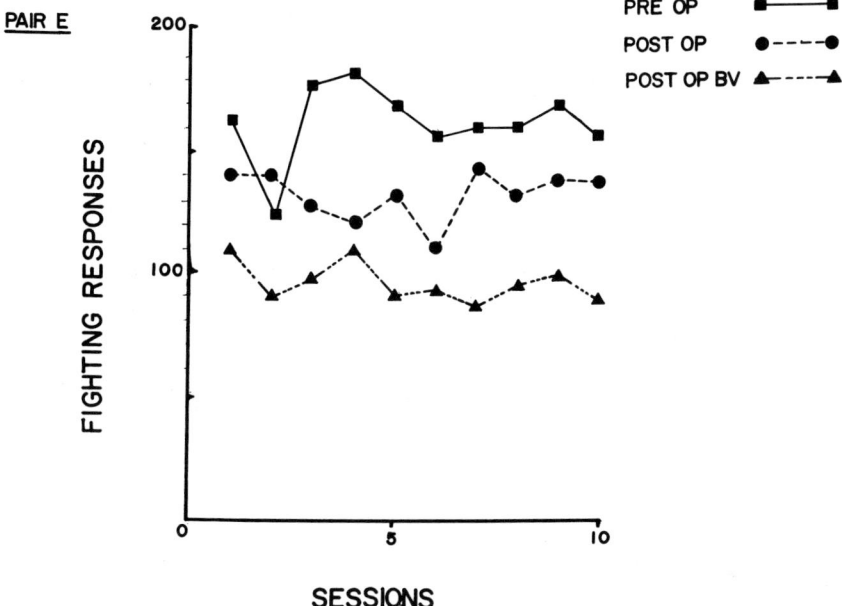

FIGURE 44-9. Subjects run for ten sessions under conditions of normal vision (Pre op), under conditions of permanent-visual impairment (Post op), and under conditions of blindness, plus vibrissae removed (Post op BV). (Flory, Ulrich, & Wolff, in press.)

diminished immediately after shock until it reached zero some moments later. Thus, it was determined that there is an inverse relationship between the time elapsed following the painful stimulus and the probability of an attack response.

5. *Age.* Hutchinson, Ulrich and Azrin (1965) have recently completed a series of experiments aimed at discovering some of the variables which control the development of the reflexive aggression response. In one experiment, naive rats of various ages were tested for aggressive behavior. The study demonstrated that reflexive aggression in response to pain-shock developed as a direct function of the subject's age, from weaning to maturity. Thus, physical maturation is an important consideration in the prediction of aggressive behavior.

Generality of pain-elicited aggression

In addition to rats, paired snakes, turtles, chickens, and hamsters (Ulrich & Azrin, 1962) have all been found to react to electric shock with sudden attack movements that might be called aggressive. Azrin and

Hutchinson (unpublished) found that placing two snakes of different species together without shock resulted in exploratory behavior with neither snake paying any attention to the other. Once shock was delivered, however, both snakes immediately responded by striking at each other with mouths wide open. Such striking movements frequently resulted in one of the snakes' being bitten.

Although the turtles' reactions to shock are much slower, they do eventually result in attacks toward each other. The general reaction of paired chickens to shock is also attack. However, as with monkeys, there is a greater tendency for one subject to become the dominant partner. Delivery of shock to a pair of hamsters produced a type of stereotyped fighting posture and attack similar to rats. The only differences were that these fighting responses could be consistently elicited at lower intensities of shock than that required for rats. Also the hamsters persisted longer in their fighting, often biting and rolling over each other on the grids. This persistence in fighting beyond the moment of shock presentation was again observed in cats (Ulrich, Wolff, & Azrin, 1964) and in squirrel monkeys (Azrin, Hutchinson, & Hake, 1963). Furthermore, both cats and monkeys often fought until forcibly separated; unless precautions were taken they frequently inflicted serious physical injury.

Pain-elicited aggression has also been found between members of different species. Snakes, raccoons, opossums, monkeys (Azrin & Hutchinson, 1963), rats, hamsters (Ulrich & Azrin, 1962), and cats (Ulrich, Wolff, & Azrin, 1964) have all been observed to attack members of different species as a function of aversive stimulation. In most instances the topography of the inter-species fighting response is the same as that observed between members of like species. What differences do appear seem to be a function of such variables as the relative size of the two subjects and the amount of reciprocal fighting. For example, rats when shocked will consistently show aggression toward hamsters, as will the hamster toward the rat (Ulrich & Azrin, 1962), whereas reciprocal attacks by the rat toward snakes, opossums, cats and monkeys are infrequent. A possible reason for this lack of return of aggression in the case of the snake is the fact that the snake strikes so swiftly. Although rats have occasionally been observed to assume the stereotyped shock-induced fighting posture in the presence of cats (Ulrich, Wolff, & Azrin, 1964), such behavior has at best been short-lived and thus difficult to investigate further.

Another example of a modification in the attack response when fighting a member of a different species was observed when rats were paired with guinea pigs. In this case, all the attacking was done by the rat, and it attacked only the head of the guinea pig. The guinea pig reacted by withdrawing from the rat's biting attacks. During the attack, the rat assumed a semi-crouching position with forepaws raised slightly, a posture which differed from the upright position assumed by rats fighting each other. Since the guinea pig never stood upright, the crouching position of the rat brought its head to the level of the guinea pig's head. In this case, the otherwise inflexible and stereotyped fighting position of the rat appeared to be modified by the position of the guinea pig.

A final aspect of pain-elicited aggression which has received considerable study is the extent to which aversive stimulation will produce attack toward inanimate objects. Casual observation has indicated that animals, from rats to men, will occasionally strike out against the inanimate objects such as a stuffed doll or a round ball. This attack is not a random thrashing-out at the environment; selective attacks were made upon a cloth-covered object to the exclusion of a metal box when both inanimate objects were simultaneously available (Azrin, Hutchinson, & Sallery, 1964).

Other species such as raccoons and opossums have also been observed to attack inanimate objects as a function of aversive stimulation (Azrin, 1964). And our own experience with rats on a Sidman avoidance schedule (Sidman, 1953) has been that rats will often bite the projecting response bar shortly after the delivery of a shock. Again, the object of attack is probably not random. When an insulated doll was placed with a rat while shock was being delivered, no attack toward the doll occurred. Similarly, no attacks were made toward either a conducting doll or a recently deceased rat. Dolls moved rapidly about the chamber also failed to produce fighting. Fighting responses were elicited only when the dead rat was moved about the chamber on a stick. The fact that certain stimulus objects and not others will be attacked in the presence of shock indicates that additional research is necessary in the elicitation of pain-agression.

Conditioned aggression

So far we have discussed the effects of aversive stimulation as an elicitor of aggression prior to any specific conditioning. It now seems very likely, however, that pain-aggression can be conditioned according to Pavlovian principles. In an experiment conducted by Ulrich (1962) it was found that fighting which was originally elicited by the unconditioned stimulus alone eventually appeared in its absence, although in a somewhat modified form. The procedure was as follows: two animals, both of whom lived separately since 18 days of age and had been isolated except for daily sessions in the experimental chamber, were given a series of daily sessions involving 200 shocks. In this situation they became aggressive. Following this experience, these animals were placed in another chamber with two other animals. In this latter situation their behavior toward the unfamiliar animals was very dramatic. Any slight movement or noise by any other animal would immediately elicit the fighting posture and occasional striking responses. This continued for two days in a manner very similar to that reported by O'Kelly and Steckle (1939) in their article, "A Note on Long Enduring Emotional Responses in the Rat."

The occurrence of this behavior can best be explained by the principles of classical conditioning. The only time these animals had been together since 18 days was in a situation where shock was presented every 3 seconds. Always associated with the shock was the other animal whose shock-elicited fighting and other varied movements inevitably preceded another shock. The other animals who originally were simply neutral stimuli later became, through consistent pairing with shock, a conditioned stimulus capable of producing the long enduring conditioned fighting behavior observed in the second chamber.

Other studies concerned with classically conditioning the fighting response have paired a buzzer with the shock and observed the number of fighting responses eventually made to the buzzer alone. Azrin (1964) found that both monkeys and chickens will occasionally attack following the onset of the buzzer. Similar research with paired rats has shown that the fighting posture can be more readily elicited by the conditioned stimulus than the actual striking motions, although the striking movements do sometimes occur (Brierton, Ulrich, & Wolff, 1964; Ulrich, 1962). On several occasions rats have been removed from the chamber in which they were conditioned and placed in another chamber nearby. Following their placement in the second chamber, the conditioned stimulus was presented and they immediately assumed the stereotyped posture. Although these findings show that fighting can be elicited not only by the aversive unconditioned stimulus, but also by conditioned stimuli, it is felt that the inconsistency of such elicitation necessitates further research into the question of classically conditioned aggression.

Pain-elicited aggression and reinforcement theory

A study often referred to as an illustration of the dependence of aggression upon drive-reduction was that of Miller (1948). In this study paired rats were placed in a chamber and shocked. When the subjects happened to approach each other in a sparring position similar to that used by rats when fighting, the shock was abruptly turned off. After a minute without shock the current was again turned on, and the animals were given another trial. Thus, the act of sparring was said to be rewarded by escape from shock, and it was reported that this technique proved very effective for producing aggressive behavior.

If we consider the well-documented fact of pain-elicited aggression, however, this interpretation seems unnecessary. It is obvious that simply presenting an aversive unconditioned stimulus will produce aggressive attacks, whether or not this response terminates the painful stimulus. Such findings suggest that the "conditioned" fighting found by Miller would have occurred even if no reinforcement through shock termination had been given. Thus, we see that the effect of shock removal on fighting is clouded by our knowledge of the fact that aversive stimulation alone produced fighting.

On the other hand, a factor which quite probably affects the aggression manifested by any given animal is the degree to which the animal has been reinforced for such behavior. We know that the probability of a response's occurrence can be increased by following that response with a positive reinforcer and numerous examples exist of conditioning rather bizarre responses on this basis. With the exception of a handful of investigations (Reynolds, Catania, & Skinner, 1963; Ulrich, Johnston, Richardson, & Wolff, 1963), however, the operant conditioning of aggression has received little attention. The attempts made to investigate this area, however, have provided some interesting findings.

In the study by Ulrich et al. (1963), rats were individually trained to go to the water magazine at the simultaneous onset of a buzzer and light. Following this, fighting behavior was conditioned by making the buzzer, light, and water contingent upon aggressive responses. First striking the control animal in the area of the head and then contact of two or three seconds were successively reinforced. No fighting responses were observed when the rats were first placed together in the experimental chamber. Through the method of successive approximations, however, responses typical of attack and fighting were eventually conditioned. The experimental animals would make striking movements toward the head of the control animals, shove the control animals about the chamber, and frequently knock them down. During this period the control animals remained submissive, only occasionally squeaking, often moving away (Fig. 44-10). Finally the experimental animals were placed in the chamber together. Visual observation showed that when the experimental animals were paired, both the magnitude and the duration of the attack responses were greater than had been observed for an experimental and a control animal. The experimental animals would often grapple with each other and continue to fight and did not respond immediately to the buzzer by drinking (Fig. 44-11). It appeared that the attack movements initially conditioned through operant reinforcement eventually resulted in the elicitation of apparent "innate" aggressive reactions. It was also observed that a pattern of dominance occurred after many pairings of the experimental subjects. This relationship finally became similar to that observed between the experimental and the control rats. When both experimental subjects no longer received reinforcement following a fighting response, there was at first a slight increase in fighting, following which all aggressive behavior ceased.

FIGURE 44-10. Example of the experimental rat striking the head of a passive control rat. (Ulrich, Johnston, Richardson, & Wolff, 1963.)

These results showed that fighting behavior can be operantly conditioned in rats through the use of water reinforcement. Furthermore, it appeared that such behavior became more than simply an operant response strengthened by the procurement of a reinforcement. Instead, fighting eventually occurred which had many of the qualities typical of unconditioned aggression (Ulrich & Azrin, 1962; Ulrich, Wolff, & Azrin, 1964). These findings are similar to those of Reynolds *et al.* (1963), who reported that in pigeons, aggression through food reinforcement may be complicated by aggressive behavior from other sources, generated by the mere presence of another bird. The fighting observed in the present investigation, however, appeared to be primarily a function of operant reinforcement since extinction occurred when the water contingency was removed. The presence of the other rat in and of itself was not sufficient to maintain the aggressive behavior. On the other hand, the fact that a slight burst of fighting occurred at the beginning of extinction suggests that the removal of positive reinforcement contains aversive aspects capable of temporarily eliciting increased aggression.

Another example of the operant reinforcement of aggression can be seen in the results of a study presently being conducted in this laboratory.

Pain-Aggression

FIGURE 44-11. Example of the fighting behavior of paired experimental rats. (Ulrich, Johnston, Richardson, & Wolff, 1963.)

In it rats have been conditioned to attack other rats by making hypothalamic stimulation contingent upon the successive approximation of aggression. Using this technique the stimulated animals have been conditioned to display vigorous fighting which frequently elicits return attacks from the nonstimulated animals. In summary, the results of these various studies show quite clearly that aggression can be shaped as an operant and that such instrumentally conditioned aggression eventually takes on some of the characteristics of elicited aggression.

The fact of this interaction between operant and respondent aggression, together with the fact that aggression can be elicited by pain, raises some interesting questions. For example, "Can animals be kept from fighting in a situation where they are together and are both receiving a painful stimulus?" In order to answer this question, Ulrich and Craine (1964) conducted an experiment to determine if paired rats could be conditioned not to fight when presented with electric shock by reinforcing nonaggressive responses with shock removal and allowing all aggressive responses to procure further shock. Pairs of rats were placed in an experimental chamber, and after 60 seconds had elapsed, continuous shock was presented until a non-fighting response occurred, whereupon the shock was immediately terminated for another 60 seconds. Following this 60-second period, the shocks were again presented and the same procedure was repeated. A record was kept of the amount of time the subjects spent fighting. It was found that the amount of time spent fighting during the later sessions was actually greater than that observed at the beginning (Fig. 44-12). This increase in fighting occurred in spite of the fact that shock was terminated following non-aggressive responses and continued following aggressive responses.

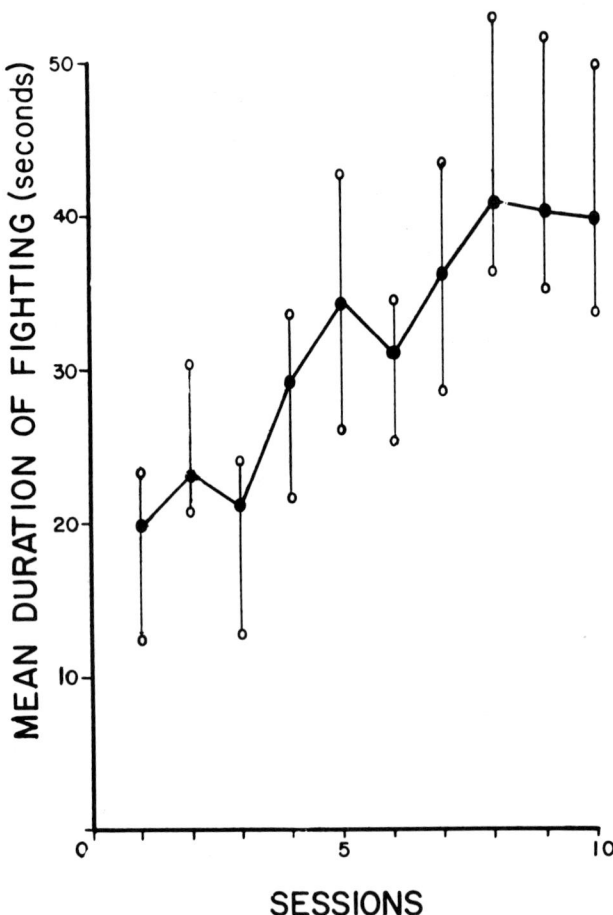

FIGURE 44-12. Mean number of seconds (dark circles) spent fighting by four paired rats during ten sessions. Open circles represent the range. (Ulrich & Craine, 1964.)

Such findings imply that pain-elicited aggression cannot be suppressed by the mechanism of reinforcing other behavior. Other studies have proven, however, that environmental experiences can alter innate response patterns (Beach & Jaynes, 1954; Farris, 1963), suggesting that this conclusion should be accepted with great caution. Indeed, further study by Ulrich and Craine (1964) did show that under certain circumstances fighting between paired rats in response to shock could be suppressed. Recall that in the initial procedure used to eliminate pain-elicited aggression, the continuation of shock was solely contingent upon aggression, although its termination was related to a number of different responses. The animals, for example, could move away from each other in several directions. One animal might simply drop to the floor as the other jumped back toward an opposite wall, or both might fall away from each other on their backs. In short, the escape, i.e., nonaggressive response, was not specific. In order to assess the significance of this fact, Ulrich and Craine used a procedure incorporating a specific escape response.

Two rats with a long history of stable performance in a discriminated avoidance situation were used along with one naive rat and one small rat-sized rubber dummy. Using the Sidman avoidance procedure the animals had been trained to press a bar which produced a period of 20 seconds of no shock. If the bar was not pressed, brief (0.5 sec.) shocks (1 ma.) occurred every 5 seconds. A signal was always presented 2 seconds prior to the shock. During the test procedure considered now, each animal was run as usual for 4 hours. For 3.5 hours the situation was exactly that just described; but during the final 30 minutes either the naive rat or the dummy was placed in the chamber. The results were as follows. No major change in avoidance behavior took place when the dummy was in the chamber. When the live naive rat was placed with the previously trained animal, however, there was a sharp reduction in the number of avoidance responses. Direct observation indicated that, in this latter situation, bar-pressing had been replaced by fighting behavior. During the first two sessions, the subjects fought after almost every shock. In the subsequent sessions, the frequency of fighting fell off rapidly to an average of 10 responses per session. It is interesting, however, that the escape-avoidance response did not return to the single subject rate (Fig. 44-13). It appeared that the reason for this lack of recovery in bar-pressing was related again to the fighting phenomenon. In the single subject situation the avoidance animals tended to remain near the bar and only occasionally following a response did they move away. After a bar-press in the presence of another live subject, by contrast, the avoidance animal would frequently return to the naive animal and reassume the stereotyped fighting posture. This posture was maintained until the pre-shock stimulus appeared, whereupon the avoidance animal would return to the bar and press it, then return again to the naive animal, thus apparently lowering

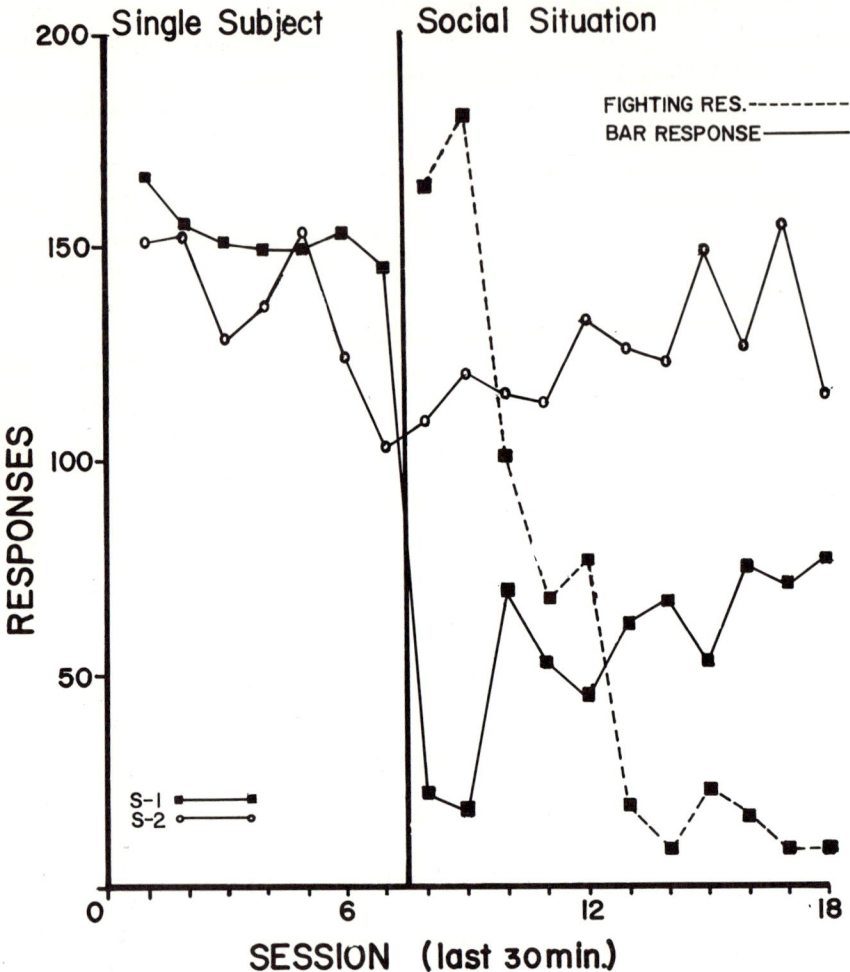

FIGURE 44-13. Fighting and bar press responses in a social situation as compared to a situation where only one animal was present. S-1 (black squares) was paired with a naive rat, S-2 (open circles) was paired with a small rat-sized rubber dummy. Fighting responses are depicted by the dotted line and occurred only toward a line, second subject. (Ulrich & Craine, 1964.)

the probability of bar-pressing. This preoccupation with the naive animal appeared to be one of the factors responsible for the lower frequency of avoidance responding.

Further studies investigating the interaction between fighting and avoidance have shown that simply placing naive subjects in a chamber and allowing their shock-induced random movements to produce a bar-press, which in turn terminates shock, will eventually bring about avoidance behavior in both paired and single subjects. Single subjects, however, performed consistently better in such a situation than did the paired subjects. Single subjects received fewer shocks, responded at higher rates, and learned the bar-pressing response quickly, whereas the paired subjects received more shocks and responded at lower rates. It was apparent in these studies that the poor avoidance behavior which occurred in the social setting was related to the high incidence of shock-elicited aggression (Ulrich, Stachnik, Brierton, & Mabry, 1965).

Possible relations to human aggression

The fact that pain-aggression has been found to exist in several species, particularly monkeys, suggests the possibility of generalizing the findings to humans. Obviously the use of painful stimuli as a technique of control is a common practice in our culture. Since physical punishment is by definition the delivery of aversive stimulation, one might expect from the results described in this chapter that a side-effect of punishment would be aggression. Anecdotal records and casual observations indicate that this expectation is sound. When a child is spanked, it is not uncommon to see him strike back at the person doing the spanking or perhaps soon thereafter attack a brother or sister or the family pet. Similarly, we bump our heads and strike out at the beam, when hitting the beam clearly does nothing to relieve the pain.

Much more research obviously needs to be done concerning the effects of aversive stimulation as it related to human aggressiveness. Nevertheless it does appear, that with human beings, like animals, when painful circumstances exist, there is a high probability of attack against other nearby people. The implications of this for the use of punishment are far-reaching. First, the main objective of eliminating a response by punishing that response may have the completely unexpected side-effect of eliciting aggressive behavior from the punished individual. And it is to be expected that this aggression will take the form of an attack against other persons, even when they have not delivered the punishing stimulus. Moreover, the evidence that the aggressive response is classically conditionable suggests that primary aversive stimulation itself is not always necessary to elicit an attack: the mere presentation of stimuli that have in the past been paired with aversive stimuli will later be capable alone of producing attack.

SUMMARY AND CONCLUSION

Although certain studies have shown that the probability of aggression will increase if the aggression is positively reinforced [for example with food (Skinner, 1959; Ulrich, Johnston, Richardson, & Wolff, 1963; Reynolds, Catania, & Skinner, 1963), a decrease in painful stimulation (Miller, 1948), access to a female by a male (Tinbergen, 1951), or maintenance of territorial privileges (Tinbergen, 1951, 1953)], the form of aggression discussed in this chapter does not originate from such operant reinforcement since no positive consequences follow such aggression. The condition required for the elicitation of such aggression is the mere presentation of an aversive stimulus. Moreover the evidence continues to accumulate that physically painful stimuli are not required for the evocation of aggressive behavior. Shifts from favorable to unfavorable schedules of reinforcement tend to produce aggressive behavior (Azrin, 1964), and it seems virtually certain that other psychologically unpleasant events will have the same effect.

Perhaps the most important fact about the aggression elicited by aversive stimuli is its generality. It is a form of behavior appearing, not only in a variety of stimulating conditions, but also in a wide range of species. With such generality established, an obvious first step in investigation is to attempt to isolate the variables that control the phenomenon and to discover the laws that regulate it. Our progress so far in this direction has been reported in this chapter.

These studies have also yielded two important by-products which suggest interesting lines of new research. The first of these is the discovery mentioned above, that aggression appears in situations that are not *physically* aversive. A further specification of the conditions of this type that produce aggressive behavior appears to be a matter of first importance.

The second interesting by-product derives from studies of instrumentally conditioned aggression as, for example, when a pigeon is reinforced with food for pecking another pigeon. Under these conditions, an interesting change appears in the animal's behavior with continued training. At first the "aggressive" responses seem to be routine, "emotionless" operant reactions, not unlike the pigeons reactions to the key in the key-pecking apparatus. Later on, however, signs of emotional arousal appear. The feathers of the pigeon become ruffled and the pecking takes on the vigor of "real" aggression. It is as if the respondent aspects of aggression "ride in" (Skinner's expression) on the instrumental act of aggression. If this apparently unlearned dependence of aggressive emotion upon aggressive behavior is general, it is a phenomenon of great interest and far-reaching significance. In particular the question arises whether aggression can ever be eliminated from a world in which there is pain. Obviously our research has not yet brought us to a point where we can grapple with questions of this magnitude, but it does seem to have taken an important step in that direction.

45

The Goal-Gradient Hypothesis Applied to Some "Field-Force" Problems in the Behavior of Young Children[1]

CLARK L. HULL

The hypothesis of the goal-excitatory gradient,[2] as well as that of the habit-family hierarchy,[3] was originally expounded in connection with a consideration of the behavior of albino rats in the ordinary enclosed maze. In such mazes the possible pathways of approach to the goal as well as the range of vision are greatly limited. Indeed, in former papers the sense of vision as a distance receptor was almost entirely neglected. The present paper, on the other hand, is concerned with some of the implications of the two hypotheses and a number of closely related principles when behavior, chiefly locomotor, is taking place in situations such that the field of vision is practically unobstructed. And, while certain limitations will be placed on the opportunities for locomotion in the situations to be considered, freedom in this respect will be comparatively unrestricted. Lastly, the phenomenon to be studied will be mainly the naive striving behavior of organisms such as young children who are only slightly sophisticated regarding obstacles at distances greater than the arm's length. A number of the problems to be examined have already been subjected to a Gestalt analysis by Lewin.

---

[1] Reprinted from the *Psychological Review*, 1938, 45.

[2] The hypothesis, as originally stated (Hull, 1932) is, "that the goal reaction gets conditioned the most strongly to the stimuli preceding it, and the other reactions of the behavior sequence get conditioned to their stimuli progressively weaker as they are more remote (in time or space) from the goal reaction." The "goal" is the point of reinforcement. Because of the somewhat anthropomorphic connotation of the term *goal*, it would, perhaps, be better if this principle could be known as the *gradient of reinforcement,* as suggested by Miller and Miles (1935).

[3] A habit-family hierarchy consists of a number of habitual alternative behavior sequences having in common the initial stimulus situation and the final reinforcing state of affairs (Hull, 1934a).

I

We shall begin by considering the influence of the subject's being able to see clearly, though usually at some distance, the lure or goal (G) from the starting point of his sequence of locomotion (S), together with numerous discriminable aspects of the intervening space. It is clear that the visual stimulation changes constantly, particularly as to the size of the image on the retina, as the subject approaches the lure, i.e., the point of reinforcement. According to the goal excitatory gradient hypothesis, the several phases of the flux of this stimulus complex will become conditioned to the accompanying movements leading to the point of reinforcement with a strength increasing with proximity to the goal. Thus, after a certain amount of training the organism should advance more vigorously the closer it is to the goal. Yoshioka's (1929) experiment involving the power of rats to discriminate short from long paths indicates that this increase in excitatory tendency follows rather closely the logarithmic principle.

A convenient presentation of such a logarithmic function is shown in Table 45-1. By means of this table it will be easy to see in a clear and precise manner the quantitative implications of the goal-gradient hypothesis as bearing on the locomotor excitatory tendencies of a considerable variety of situations. Let us take as our first example one in which the visual stimulus of the lure (G) is placed at two distances from the subject, the second distance being three times as great as the first (Fig. 45-1). Suppose that the first starting point (S) is 5 units distant from the goal, and that the second is 15 units distant. By Table 45-1, the excitatory potentiality of the visual image encountered at 5 units distant has a value of 6.000 points, whereas its strength at 15 units is only 3.27 points, a difference of 2.73. This fundamental relationship may be represented graphically as in Figure 45-2.

It follows from the preceding that if an experimental situation should be so arranged that two distinct alternative paths of these respective lengths *both* lead from S to G, path A would be chosen in preference to path B because the stimulus at the point of choice would have an excitatory tendency leading to the acts constituting A nearly twice as great as to those constituting B. A situation of this kind is, of course, the limiting case of a habit-family hierarchy: the fact that two paths begin and end at the same points makes them a family; the fact that one is preferred above the other constitutes them a hierarchy (Hull, 1934a).

By a simple extension of the above reasoning, certain corollaries may be derived. It may be shown, for example, that the difference in excitatory

TABLE 45-1

The hypothetical strength of the conditioning of stimuli received at different distances from the goal to reactions occurring simultaneously*

Units distant from goal (D)	Strength of excitatory tendency (E)	Units distant from goal (D)	Strength of excitatory tendency (E)
1	10.000	26	1.903
2	8.277	27	1.809
3	7.270	28	1.718
4	6.554	29	1.631
5	6.000	30	1.547
6	5.547	31	1.465
7	5.164	32	1.386
8	4.831	33	1.310
9	4.539	34	1.236
10	4.277	35	1.164
11	4.040	36	1.094
12	3.824	37	1.026
13	3.625	38	.959
14	3.441	39	.895
15	3.270	40	.832
16	3.109	41	.771
17	2.958	42	.711
18	2.816	43	.652
19	2.682	44	.595
20	2.554	45	.539
21	2.433	46	.484
22	2.317	47	.431
23	2.207	48	.379
24	2.101	49	.327
25	2.000	50	.277

*It is assumed that the excitatory tendency one unit from the goal acquires a strength of ten units and that the strength of the excitatory tendency acquired at each of the remaining distances diminishes with their remoteness according to the equation $E = a - b \log D$, where a has a value of 10, b has a value of 4, and the logarithms are taken with a base of 5.

FIGURE 45-1. Two pulls to the same goal; S, starting point of one path and S', of the other. Path A is represented as being 5 units in length and path B as 15 units in length. The dynamics of the two situations are represented in Figure 2. It is to be observed that if Path S' → G' were suitably curved and shifted about in a manner such that point S' would coincide with point S, and point G' would coincide with point G, the combination of paths thus resulting would constitute a habit-family hierarchy.

tendency leading to the locomotor action of traversing pairs of paths differing in length by a constant amount grows less and less as the paths jointly become longer and longer. Suppose, for example, that the shorter path in the above example increases from 5 to 20 units in length and the longer one from 15 to 30. The difference in excitatory strength produced by the difference of 10 units in length would (Table 45-1) shrink from 2.73 points to 1.00 point. When the shorter path is further increased to 40 units in length, a second path 10 units longer makes a difference in excitatory tendency of only .56 of a point, and so on. Conversely, by shortening both paths a constant difference in their lengths will give rise to greater and greater differences in their excitatory potentialities. This principle has important implications which will be taken up below. So far as the author is aware, these corollaries have not been subjected to experimental test; they offer a ready means of further testing the hypothesis.

II

At this point we may conveniently consider the bearing of the present system of hypotheses on the interesting problem of the allegedly deleterious influence of increasing the excitatory strength of the lure upon the solution of certain types of problems (Kohler, 1925). Let us assume once more that a naive organism has two distinct habit sequences corresponding to paths *A* and *B* of Figure 45-1, each leading to the same goal or point of reinforcement. In this case, however, there is supposed to be an effective physical barrier at the beginning of the shorter path (*A*) so that solution of the problem consists in traversing the longer path (*B*). Let us assume, further, that in one situation the excitatory potentialities of the goal one unit distant have been doubled, say, by increasing the quantity of the reward. Presumably the remainder of the gradient would

The Goal-Gradient Hypothesis

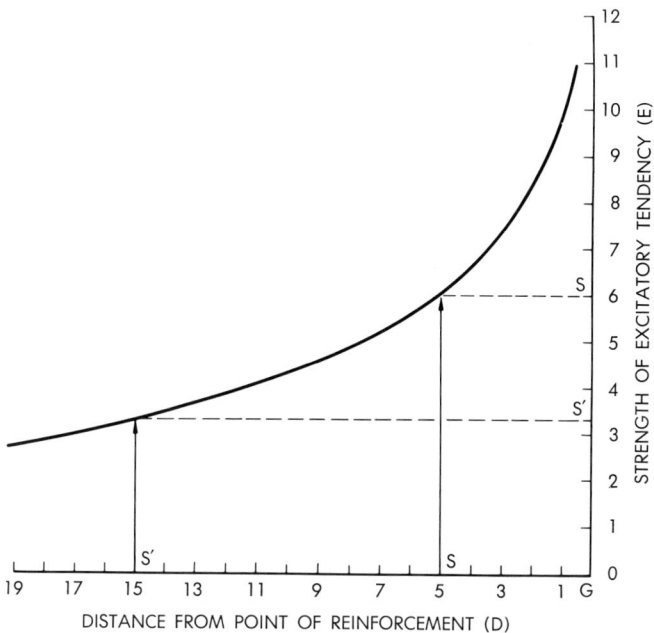

FIGURE 45-2. Diagrammatic representation of the hypothetical dynamics of the two paths to goal G shown in Figure 45-1. The curve represents the excitatory potentialities of the visual stimulus of the goal complex at all distances from 1 to 19 units according to the equation, $E = a - b \log D$. The strengths at 5 and 15 units distant have been projected upon the scale at the right. It is evident to inspection that S has nearly twice as great excitatory potentiality as has S'.

rise proportionately. On this assumption the resulting situation may be represented with precision by plotting the values of Table 45-1 on two different ordinate scales, one twice as great as the other. Graphs produced in this manner are presented in Figure 45-3. An inspection of this figure shows that the difference between the excitatory tendency to take the respective paths under the weak lure is only 2.73 units (6 — 3.27), whereas this difference rises to 5.46 units (12 — 6.54) in the presence of the strong lure.

Here it becomes necessary to introduce a second hypothesis, which is that a strong excitatory tendency diminishes the same number of units in excitatory strength from a given amount of frustration as does a weak excitatory tendency. Applying this principle to the supposititious case before us, it follows that it would take as long (or as many futile attempts

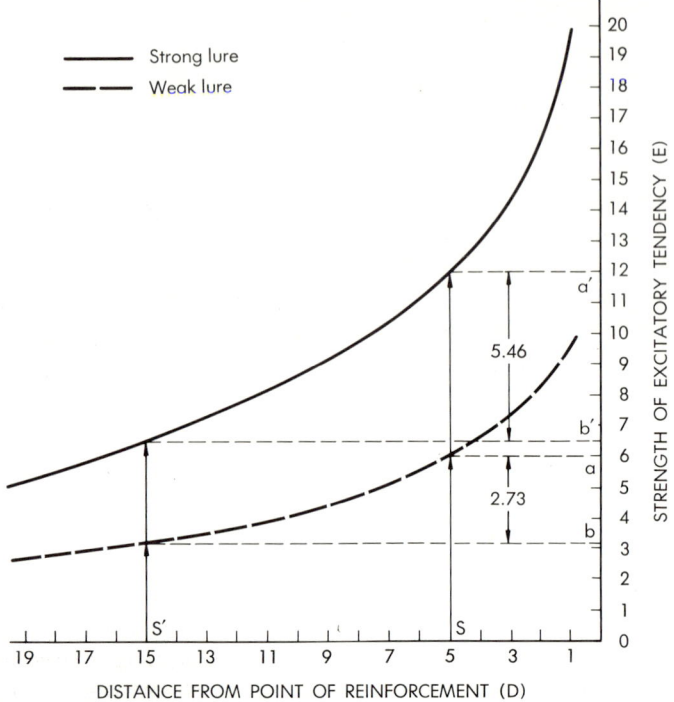

FIGURE 45-3. Diagrammatic representation of the dynamics of doubling the strength of the lure at 1 unit from G, Figure 45-1. The two curves represent the hypothetical strength of exictatory tendency of the optical image of the respective lures for all distances between 1 and 19 units of remoteness from G. The equation for the weak lure (lower curve) is $E_w = 10 - 4 \log_5 D$, whereas that for the strong lure (upper curve) is $E_s = 20 - 8 \log_5 D$. The excitatory potentialities (E) at S and S' are projected upon the scale at the right. It is evident to inspection that the difference between S and S' is greatly increased by adding to the strength of the lure.

on the part of the organism) for the presence of the barrier to path A to diminish by 4 units an excitatory tendency initially with a strength of 12 units (strong lure) as one initially with a strength of only 6 units (weak lure). In the former case the problem would not have been solved in this length of time, since the obstructed path would still have a strength of 8 units (12—4) which would be well above the strength of the long but unobstructed path (6.54). In the case of the weak lure, on the other hand, the obstructed path would have, after the same period (or amount) of frustration, a strength of only 2 units (6—4). Since this is well below

The Goal-Gradient Hypothesis

the strength of the long path (3.27) the latter would presumably have been chosen some time before the end of the period in question, solving the problem of the organism. Thus the paradox of an increased lure interfering with, rather than facilitating, the solution of certain problems apparently finds an explanation.

In this same general category probably will be found to fall phenomena resulting from increasing the craving of the organism. If the lure is food, general observation as well as experimental results (Hull, 1934b) indicates that increased hunger (food privation) heightens the excitatory gradient very much as does increasing the quantity of the lure. By the same reasoning as that of the immediately preceding paragraph, increasing hunger with a constant food lure should impede the solution of this type of problem very much as would increasing the lure with constant craving or drive.

Another situation closely paralleling the influence of increasing the excitatory value of the lure while leaving the lure itself objectively unchanged ought, according to the present set of hypotheses, to result from progressively shortening both paths at the same time keeping the absolute difference between them the same. A special case of this kind studied by Lewin (1933, 1935) is presented by the two situations shown in Figure 45-4. Suppose that direct path A is approximately 5 units long. Then in-

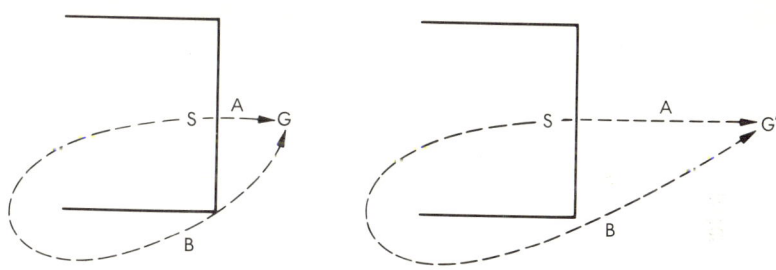

FIGURE 45-4. The figures represent an organism located at S and observing a lure G and G' respectively. There are two potential paths to G, A and B, and two to G', A' and B'. The problem is which goal will be more easily attained, and why. The present system of hypotheses favor G', providing no other lures complicate the situation by leading the organism around the barrier.

direct path B will be about 29 units long. By Table 45-1 (leaving out of consideration for the moment the directional factor), the excitatory tendency at point S to take these respective paths should be 6.00 units and 1.63 units respectively; this leaves a difference of 4.37 points of excitatory potentiality to be extinguished by the barrier in path A before path B

can become active. In the case of the right-hand figure, direct path A' has a length of 12 units and indirect path B' has a length of approximately 35 units. By Table 1, the excitatory tendency at choice point S to take paths A' and B' to G' should be 3.82 units and 1.16 units respectively, with a difference of only 2.66 units to be worn down by the barrier frustration before path B' can become active. Assuming, again, something like a constant rate of extinction from the frustration produced by the barriers to the direct paths, goal G' should be easier of attainment than goal G', in some inverse function of the proportion of 4.37 to 2.66.

To sum up, then, we arrive at the tentative conclusion that three different changes in a problem situation are substantially equivalent in their supposed paradoxical tendency to impede the solution of problems involving alternative paths to a goal where the shorter, or preferred, path has a barrier: increasing the strength of the lure, increasing the strength of the drive or craving, and decreasing the remoteness of the lure. The last two of the three cases are capable of general demonstration by the ordinary mathematical procedures analogous to those applied to the first. This analysis serves to raise not only the experimental question as to the postulates involved, such as the shape of the goal excitatory gradient and the rate of weakening of excitatory tendency under frustration, but, quite as insistently, the question of the reality in detail of the three supposed paradoxical tendencies themselves. It is highly doubtful whether either set of phenomena is as simple as the above treatment would imply.

III

Consider once more the situation represented in Figures 45-1, 45-2, 45-3, and 45-4, on the former assumption that the short path A has a barrier near its beginning. In the preceding sections we have proceeded on the tacit assumption that the only thing necessary before path B will be chosen is that the strength of the tendency to take path A shall be weakened from s (Fig. 45-2) to a value somewhat below s'. It now becomes necessary to point out in the competitional situations considered, the operation of a factor—temporarily ignored—which is variously called the irradiation of inhibition or the generalization of extinction (frustration). From the present point of view this principle is that every extinguished reaction has a tendency to inhibit (weaken) all other reaction tendencies, the stimuli of which impinge on the organism closely following the extinction process. It follows from this principle that when A is being extinguished from s to s', B has been undergoing a secondary extinction which will depress its excitatory potentiality appreciably below s', say to s''. But by this time path B will have suffered further secondary weakening.

The Goal-Gradient Hypothesis

This raises the question as to how far the extinction of A must go before it will actually reach a level beneath that of B. So far as the present writer is aware, this problem has not yet been investigated experimentally, though it should be a relatively straightforward matter on the conditioned-reflex level. In advance of the possession of actual knowledge of this relationship, however, it is easy to tell roughly what should result under various suppositions. It is clear, for example, that, other things equal, the shorter the distance between s and s', the less inhibition there will be to irradiate and the shorter the distance below s' at which reaction B will take place. Secondly, the smaller the proportion of inhibition which irradiates, the shorter will be the distance below s' at which B will take place.

There remains to be considered the special case of the possibility that A could be extinguished to a functional zero, yet reaction B never take place at all. It seems inevitable that this would occur under certain conditions: Suppose that 50 percent of the inhibition of A irradiates to B and that at the outset A stands at 6.00 and B at 2.00. When A has reached zero, B would have suffered 3 units of inhibition; this would place it at -1.00, i.e., one unit below zero. In this case striving for this particular goal (reinforcing state of affairs) would cease altogether, at least for a time. If the time available for solution is limited it follows that the organism may completely fail to solve its problem.

IV

At this point we must return to the consideration of a principle which was latent in the situation considered in Section II above, especially as represented in Figure 45-4. This is the influence (in the case of very naive subjects) of the angle which any path except the one leading directly to the goal makes with the latter. The consideration of this problem may be facilitated by referring to the diagram shown as Figure 45-5. The question is: What bearing does the size of the angles of paths B, C, D, E, and F with path A at point S have on the relative strengths of excitatory tendency of the paths in question?

The hypothesis here tentatively put forward is that in the random locomotion, and even hand movements, of the organism throughout its previous existence, a movement terminating at G but initiated in the direction of path B at point S will, *on the average*, require the traversing of a distance something like that of path B. The same is assumed of the initial angles of paths C, D, E, and F. As a result, the principle of the goal excitatory gradient demands that the greater the angle of the path at point S, the weaker will be the tendency to take the particular path. Thus path

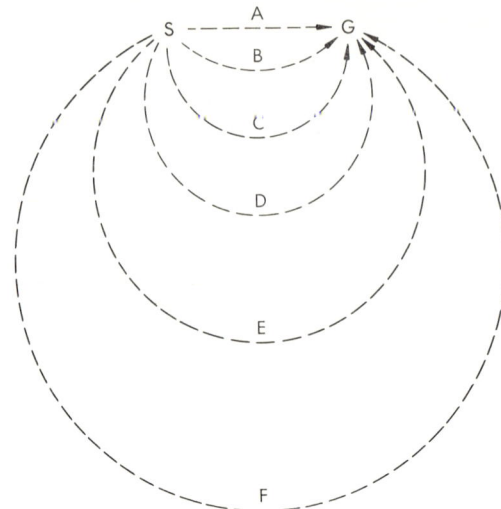

FIGURE 45-5. Diagrammatic representation of what are conceived to be approximations to typical *mean* pathways by which the organism has passed by means of random locomotion in its previous history from one point (S) to another point (G). It will be noted that the angle which each path makes with path A at point S is a direct function of the length of the path—the larger the angle, the longer the path. It is understood that a substantially similar family of potential circular paths lies on the other side of direct path A.

F as represented in Figure 45-5 is about eight times as long as path A. Assuming path A to be 5 units in length, and path F to be 40, the respective excitatory tendencies will be, according to Table 45-1, in the proportion of 6.00 to .83; i.e., the strength of the tendency to start for G in the initial direction of path A would be over seven times as great as the tendency to set out in the initial direction of path F. This hierarchy of excitatory tendencies based on the initial angles of locomotion toward a goal thus appears to be a special case of the habit-family hierarchy.

It follows at once from these considerations that in certain situations the difference between the excitatory tendencies of a naive organism to take the initial steps of two paths may be considerably greater than the difference between the actual lengths of the two paths would warrant. This may be illustrated by the situation represented in Figure 45-6. Let us suppose that the organism at S has the choice of paths B and C around the barrier to G. Path C is 26 units long, whereas path B is only 22 units long. Nevertheless, a naive organism might be expected to choose path C because the initial angle of path C has presumably in its past history represented, on the average, a path something like C', of only 8 units,

The Goal-Gradient Hypothesis

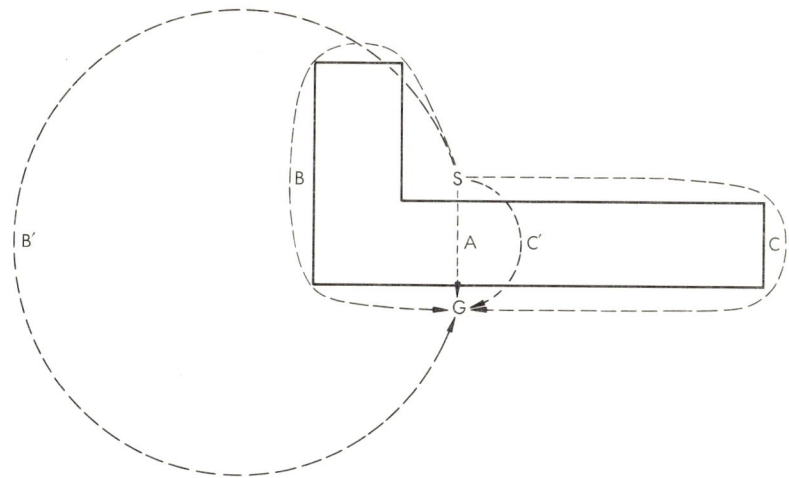

FIGURE 45-6. Diagrammatic representation of an experimental situation designed to show the influence of the angle of the initial portion of a path upon the strength of its tendency. S is the organism, G is the lure. The right-angled figure in bold outline represents a barrier. Path B is actually shorter than path C, yet it is assumed that the naive organism will choose C rather than B because at the outset C is the beginning of paths which, on the average, in the past have been approximately of the length of path C', and path B at the outset is the same as paths which in the past have averaged in length something like that of B'.

whereas the initial angle of path B has, on the average, represented a path something like that of B', which has a length of 42 units. By Table 45-1, the angles therefore represent naive excitatory tendencies in the proportion of 4.8 to .7 in favor of path C, i.e., from the point of view of the initial angle of the pathway the excitatory tendency to take path C should be something like seven times as great as that to take path B, even though path B is actually the shorter of the two.

It is to be expected, of course, that the principle of the goal gradient operating directly (e.g., under conditions such that the organism would be forced to take the two paths of Figure 45-6, say, in alternation each being followed by reinforcement) would ultimately lead to the giving up of path C and to the preferential choice of path B, because the beginning of path B is actually much nearer the point of reinforcement than is that of path C. Such training accordingly leads to a form of sophistication distinct from the individual use of speech as pure-symbolic acts. Thus we arrive at a kind of operational definition of the term "sophistication" as here employed.

V

With admirable perspicacity, Lewin has called attention to a very important series of problems involving conflicting tendencies to action, i.e., situations which involve simultaneous impulses both to approach and to retreat. Such conflicts of excitatory tendency he has aptly termed *tensions*. One supposititious case illustrating this point is that of a child on the shore looking at a toy swan floating in the water. The swan as a stimulus object tends to evoke in the child movements of approach, whereas the water as a stimulus object tends to evoke movements of flight. In this connection Lewin remarks (1933, p. 607), "It is important that here, as frequently in such cases, the *strength* of the field forces which correspond to the negative valence diminishes much more rapidly with increasing spatial *distance* than do the field forces corresponding to the positive valence. From the direction and strength of the field forces at the various points of the field it can be deduced that the child must move to the point P where *equilibrium* occurs. (At all other points there exists a resultant which finally leads to P.)"

A still more striking and dramatic form of this general problem is found where the positive and negative stimulus objects are both small and occupy substantially the same point in space. It is assumed, further, that the negative gradient at one unit distant from the object, say, has a greater excitatory potentiality than the positive excitatory gradient at the same distance but, owing to its steeper slope, the negative gradient soon diminishes to a strength of excitation below that of the positive gradient, thereafter remaining permanently in an inferior position. As pointed out above, there is evidence indicating that the positive excitatory gradient possesses a roughly logarithmic shape. Corresponding study of negative excitatory tendencies has not yet been made. Analogy, however, suggests that negative excitatory tendencies may show at least a negative acceleration.

A situation based on these assumptions is represented diagrammatically in Figure 45-7. The positive gradient JJ' represents the excitatory potentialities of G as a stimulus to distance receptors leading to locomotor reactions of approach, whereas the negative gradient KK' represents the excitatory potentialities of G at the various distances to evoke movements of retreat or flight. It may be seen in the figure that at a distance of 17 units the positive gradient dominates; accordingly the organism should move forward with a force corresponding to the difference in excitatory tendency between J and K. However, as locomotion continues it should diminish in speed progressively until point O is reached,

The Goal-Gradient Hypothesis

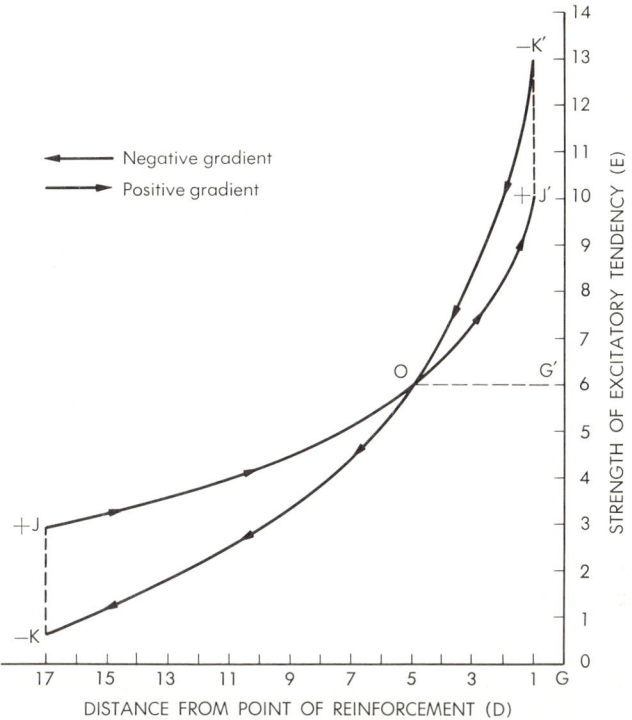

FIGURE 45-7. Diagrammatic representation of the functional relationships of two gradients of different sign and different slope. The positive gradient is represented by the equation, $E_+ = 10 - 4 \log D$, and the negative gradient is drawn according to the equation, $E_- = 13 - 7 \log D$. The two gradients intersect at $D = 5$ with a common E value of 6.

at which forward locomotion should cease altogether except for momentum effects. If, on the other hand, the organism should find itself at a distance of one unit from G, locomotion would take place in an opposite direction. The rate of locomotion in this case, as in the one just considered, would presumably correspond to the difference in excitatory tendency existing between K' and J'. This should diminish progressively as point O is approached, at which it should cease just as when the movement was in a forward direction.

As a corollary from the above deduction it is evident that, assuming radial symmetry of the positive and negative gradients about point G, distance OG must be constant in all directions. It follows from this that the locus of tensional equilibrium about point G must be a circle (Fig. 45-8). Assuming the presence in the situation of stimuli leading to action

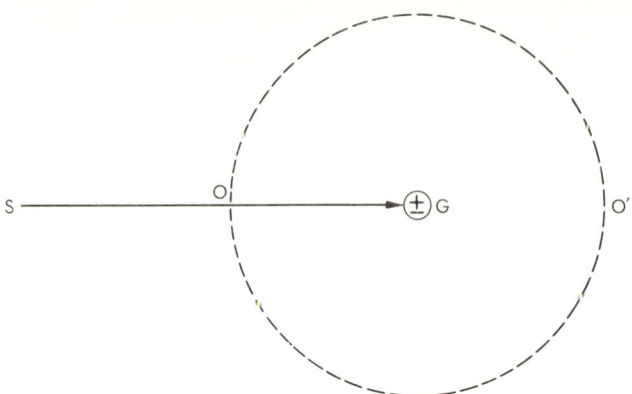

FIGURE 45-8. Diagrammatic representation of the locus of the point of equilibrium when the critical stimulus giving rise to two gradients of opposite sign such as those represented in Figure 45-7, emanates from a single point G. So long as the gradients remain constant, distance OG must remain constant, which necessarily makes the locus of equilibrium circular, as shown by the fine dotted line.

in the direction of numerous minor goals located according to chance, it is to be expected that there will occur irregular oscillations not only toward and away from point G, but laterally as well. In the former case it is to be expected that such oscillatory tendencies will be opposed by the summation gradient tending to the locus O, whereas those tangent to this locus will meet with no such opposition. It follows that the lateral movements will display a greater amplitude than those perpendicular to locus O. Accordingly the naive organism if given time enough may be expected to make completely circular movements about point G, though these will be complicated by approaches, retreats, and much retracting.

As a second corollary it should be pointed out that even without the presence of distracting stimuli the organism at point O (Fig. 45-8) probably will not remain absolutely passive, i.e., in a state indistinguishable from mere idleness characteristic of no effective stimulation whatever. On the contrary, it is reasonable to expect that, since there is a great deal more stimulation of a dynamic sort present in conflict situations than in a case where inaction is due to the lack of effective stimulation, the muscles of the organism should show a conspicuous excess of tonicity in the former case as contrasted with the latter. Muscular tonicity may accordingly offer a convenient supplementary means for gauging the extent of this type of conflict.

The deductions of the preceding paragraph tacitly assume a constancy of both the positive and the negative gradients while the organism remains suspended, as it were, between the antagonistic difference gradients to action which the situation evokes within him. There is strong reason to doubt such a constancy. In addition to the very general empirical principle that in organisms tendencies to action are always in a state of flux, there is in this case the specific expectation that, assuming an objectively constant G as a stimulus object, both gradients should diminish in height, presumably throughout their whole effective length. This follows from the frustration hypothesis already considered.

A test of the above hypothesis which immediately suggests itself could be arranged as follows. Place two objects, one with a negative value and the other with a positive value, one above the other so as to produce the conflicting gradients shown in Figure 45-7. Determine the initial potentialities of each object separately at the outset by measuring the speed-of-locomotion of given organisms in a positive or negative direction at representative distances from G. Then place both objects together and let the organism remain at point O (Figs. 45-7 and 45-8) in the state of tensional equilibrium for about as long as this will persist. At once repeat, with separate subgroups, the test of the excitatory potentiality of each object singly, as at the beginning of the experiment. The frustration hypothesis demands that in this latter case the rate of locomotion toward the positive object and that away from the negative object shall both be diminished.

Two corollaries flow from this deduction. The first, based on the principle of spontaneous recovery, is that after a lapse of time (possibly within the range of one or two hours) the speed of locomotion in both cases should have increased to a very considerable extent, though the recovery should not be perfect. A second corollary, again based on principles derived from conditioned-reflex experiments, is that an organism placed in the state of tensional equilibrium a second time will show both a more rapid inhibition of the respective excitatory tendencies than it did on the first occasion and also a slower and more imperfect spontaneous recovery.

One of the most obvious questions which arise from the consideration of conflict situation when the latter is viewed in the light of the frustration hypothesis, is the effect of the continuation of the state of tensional equilibrium upon the distance (OG) from the goal objects (G), which the organism at first maintains. It is obvious, of course, that if both gradients should decline simultaneously and at a certain relative rate the distance OG would remain constant. When we consider the number of other possibilities of variation, however, the chance that this particular set of changes should take place is exceedingly improbable. It accordingly seems almost certain that the distance OG will undergo a progressive change in length with the duration of the conflict or tension.

Whether, upon the whole, the change will be to diminish or to increase distance OG can only be predicted when we know more concerning the resistance of positive and negative, steep and gentle, gradients. It is evident that here is a rich and almost virgin field for investigation, both with animals and with young children. One apparently relevant principle we have, however, thanks to the work on conditioned reactions. Other things equal, that gradient which is the oldest should resist frustration the best. This factor should tend to lengthen or shorten distance OG according to whether the older gradient is the negative or positive one respectively.

In this connection there should also be considered the matter of progressive changes in the drive. As already pointed out above, an increase in a drive such as hunger presumably increases both the height and the slope of the positive gradient. This increase should obviously diminish the distance OG and reduce the radius of the circular locus of tensional equilibrium.

Finally, the significance of this whole psychology of conflicting excitatory gradients as a challenge to experimental psychology should be emphasized. Its importance for psychopathology, particularly the conflicts of the positive sexual gradient and the specific negative gradient based on social tabus and prudential considerations, has been emphasized in the clinical field by the psychiatrists for many years. Coitus interruptus and what, in current slang, is called "petting," are cases in point. The bad repute of these practices in mental hygiene emphasizes the possible significance of conflicting gradients in either time or space. In this connection it is to be noted that the mutual checking of two impulses as represented in Figure 45-7 might be expected to produce something like twice as great an amount of internal inhibition as would be the case where one tendency was completely over-ridden by the other because in the one case two excitatory tendencies are frustrated, whereas in the other, only one is thwarted. It would not be surprising if this mechanism should be found to play an important role in the so-called psychogenic disorders.

SUMMARY

The preceding analysis of certain problems in the behavior dynamics of naive organisms has proceeded mainly on the following assumptions:

1. That simultaneously occurring stimuli and reactions (both of approach and flight) tend to be associated more strongly the closer they are to a reinforcing state of affairs, the diminution in excitatory tendency with remoteness from the point of reinforcement proceeding with a negative acceleration.

2. That situations may arise where stimuli originating in sub-

The Goal-Gradient Hypothesis

stantially the same point in space will give rise in a given organism to incompatible excitatory tendencies, notably the opposing tendencies to acts of approach and of flight.

3. That the flight gradient may, at least under certain circumstances, be both steeper and higher near the stimulus object.

4. That an organism in which positive and negative excitatory tendencies are active behaves at any given instant according to the algebraic sum of such tendencies.

5. That the positive gradient of excitation grows both higher and steeper with the increase in the drive, e.g., food privation.

6. That, other things equal, this gradient of excitation grows higher and steeper with the increase in the amount of reward.

7. That a strong functional excitatory tendency is weakened after a given amount of frustration by a smaller proportion of its original strength than is a weak functional excitatory tendency.

8. That spontaneous recovery from extinction effects will occur but this will not be complete.

9. That a second extinction will occur more rapidly than the first and its spontaneous recovery will be less complete.

10. That in the history of organisms it is a fact that upon the whole the larger the angle the beginning of a pathway makes with the straight line leading to the object, the longer the path to the object.

11. That the prevention by any circumstance of the reaction normally evokable by any stimulus or stimulus component results, other things equal, in weakening (extinguishing) the particular excitatory potentiality of such stimulus or stimulus component.

12. That the older an excitatory tendency, the more resistant to the extinction from frustration.

13. That a considerable weakening of a given excitatory tendency appears at once following the extinction of another excitatory tendency.

From these assumptions in the main the following conclusions have been drawn concerning the behavior of naive organisms, unmentioned factors being assumed as equal:

1. In a problem situation such as shown in Figure 45-4, a naive organism will have more difficulty in solving the problem where the lure is large than where it is small.

2. There will be more difficulty where the lure is close to the barrier than where it is farther away.

3. There will be more difficulty where the drive is strong than where it is weak.

4. The functional excitatory tendency of weak alternatives in a habit-family hierarchy may be depressed to "below zero" by generalized extinction effects from the frustration of a stronger member of the hierarchy.

5. This depression below zero is the more likely to occur, the greater

the percentage of the extinction effects in the strong tendency which are generalized to the weak tendency.

6. The depression below zero is the more likely to occur the weaker the absolute strength of the weak tendency.

7. The depression below zero is more likely to occur the greater the difference between the competing excitatory tendencies.

8. For a naive organism, the larger the angle which the beginning of a pathway to a point makes with the straight line to the point, the weaker the excitatory tendency to execute the acts which constitute taking the divergent path.

9. Naive organisms through the misleading action of the angular hierarchy will, under certain circumstances, choose the longer of two paths.

10. With sophistication of the organism consisting of actually traversing both of such paths as considered in (9), the tendency to take the longer path will gradually give place to a degree of preference to be expected on the basis of the uncomplicated goal excitatory gradient hypothesis.

11. Under the conditions of assumptions 2 and 3, there will be a distance (D) from the ambivalent stimulus object at which the two opposed excitatory tendencies of a tensional situation will be equal.

12. Under the conditions of (11), the organism will tend to move toward this point of equal excitatory tendency.

13. Under the conditions of (11), assuming an unchanging stimulus object and the presence of minor lures of appreciable potentiality distributed in a chance manner throughout the neighborhood, the organism will tend to take a roughly circular course around the ambivalent stimulus object.

14. These circular movements will be very irregular in rate and extent, and be characterized by much retracing.

15. There will be some irregular oscillation toward and away from the ambivalent stimulus.

16. The movements of (15) will, upon the whole, be less in extent than will those of (14).

17. Where cases of tensional equilibrium persist for an appreciable period, both excitatory tendencies arising from an ambivalent stimulus object will be weakened progressively.

18. With the passage of time there will be a progressive recovery from this weakening.

19. Recovery from this frustrational weakening will never be complete.

20. A second period of tensional equilibrium will produce an extinctive weakening more rapid than the first.

21. The second recovery will be less rapid than the first.

22. The second recovery will be less complete than the first.

23. As the state of tensional equilibrium continues there will usually

The Goal-Gradient Hypothesis

occur a progressive shift in the distance the organism maintains from the stimulus object.

24. This shift will tend to be in the direction of the older of the two opposed excitatory tendencies.

25. The secondary frustration effects will be greater in cases of tensional equilibrium than in cases where one tendency is strong enough to over-ride the other.

Of the forty or so propositions assembled above from the preceding theoretical analysis, scarcely one is yet established on a secure quantitative experimental basis. Perhaps the chief outcome of the analysis is the sharp realization of our profound ignorance concerning the essential principles operative in such relatively simple dynamical situations. However, admissions of ignorance, while momentarily depressing, are likely to be wholesome. Each recognized item of basic ignorance constitutes a challenge to a critical experimental determination. Thus a resolute attempt at theoretical integration naturally leads the way to a systematically coordinated program of investigation. In the present case, such an integrated program of research appears to fall into three portions or phases.

The first phase consists of the direct experimental determination of the principles or laws, now almost entirely in the state of hypothesis or guesswork, which are suggested by the first of the above lists of propositions. These determinations should be quantitive in nature and so designed as to yield functional curves of basic relationships. Equations fitted to such data become the postulates of the system.

The second phase is logical and mathematical. It consists of deriving by means of mathematics, and perhaps of symbolic logic, the behavioral implications of the postulates yielded by the first movement when acting in the greatest possible variety of conditions. The substance of note 12 gives an indication of the general nature of this theoretical portion of the program.

The third phase consists of the systematic experimental verification of the behavioral expectations resulting from the mathematical activities of the second movement. Whenever this systematic verifying procedure reveals disagreements, work on the first movement is resumed in an effort to rectify presumptive defects in the postulate determinations. Following such new postulate determinations, new implications are drawn, new verification experiments are set up, and so on in continuously recurring cycles until disagreements fail to manifest themselves, if such a time ever comes.

Such a self-conscious scientific procedure may with some propriety be called "logical empiricism." It begins with an empirical determination of its postulates and ends with an empirical check on the validity of its theorems; between the two lies the integrating symbolic structure of logic and mathematics.

46

Attitudinal Factors in Eyelid Conditioning[1]

GREGORY A. KIMBLE

The procedural simplicity of the eyelid conditioning experiment has the unfortunate consequence of suggesting that the learning which takes place there is also simple. It is difficult to avoid reaching the erroneous conclusion that the conditioned eyeblink measured in these studies represents the total modification of the subject. Of course, those of us who have done a few experiments in this field know that this conclusion is wrong and, informally, confess that there is more to such conditioning than meets the eye. In our more formal, published expressions, however, the implication that eyelid conditioning is eyelid conditioning, pure and simple, is almost universally present.

The chief exceptions to this generalization appear in the studies of the Iowa investigators. Spence and his colleagues, in recent years, have paid a great deal of attention to various aspects of the subjects' motivation and set and have shown, in a series of experiments, that these influences contribute in important ways to the progress of conditioning and extinction. In this paper I wish to describe four experiments in the same general tradition, but employing a somewhat different type of approach.

Method

In all of these experiments, the important elements of apparatus and procedure were as follows. The conditioned stimulus was a reddish circle of light, about 1¼ inches in diameter provided by a Grason-Stadler multiple stimulus presenter. The unconditioned stimulus was a 50-millisecond puff of air directed at the right cornea, delivered at a pressure sufficient to support a 180-mm. column of mercury. The time between conditioned and unconditioned stimuli has most often been either ½ second or 1.0 second. In our experience the level of conditioning at these two intervals is high and about equal. Timing of stimuli and trials has been accom-

---

[1] This chapter is a revised version of the author's presidential address delivered to the Division of Experimental Psychology, American Psychological Association, in 1964.

plished by a sacrilegious application of conventional operant conditioning equipment to the experimental study of this particular respondent.

The eyeblink was measured in the conventional way. The subject wore a headpiece which carried a microtorque potentiometer and the nozzle through which the airpuff was released. A false eyelash attached to the right lid was linked to the arm of the potentiometer by a light silk or nylon thread. Ink-written records of eyelid movement were made on a Grass polygraph. These records were of the type shown in Figure 46-1. The onset of conditioned and unconditioned stimuli are indicated by upward and downward deflections of the pen. The eyelid reaction appears on the lower line. These particular records show conditioned and unconditioned responses obtained from the same subjects on adjacent trials. The comparison has no significance for this paper.

The effect of instructions

The first of the studies I wish to report, by Nicholls and Kimble (1964) has been published. I describe it here mainly to call attention to

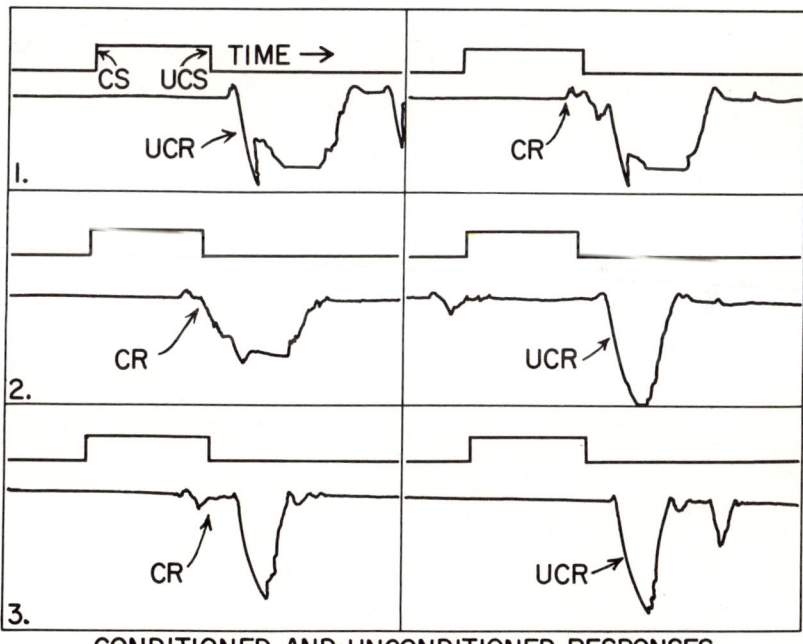

FIGURE 46-1. Conditioned and unconditioned responses on adjacent trials in the same subjects.

one feature of the results that hindsight endows with greater importance than it had when we wrote the article and sent it in for publication. The study dealt with the effects of instructions upon eyelid conditioning. There were two groups of 16 subjects in the experiment, conditioned with fairly standard versions of facilitatory and inhibitory instructions. Conditioning curves for these groups appear in Figure 46-2 where percentages of CRs are plotted against trials in blocks of five. It is apparent that the subjects in the group with facilitative instructions ("Let your reactions take care of themselves") performed much better than those conditioned with inhibitory instructions ("Concentrate on not blinking until you feel the puff of air"). There is no news in this outcome, of course. The same result has been obtained by several investigators previously. Two items of new information did come from the experiment, however. First, the group

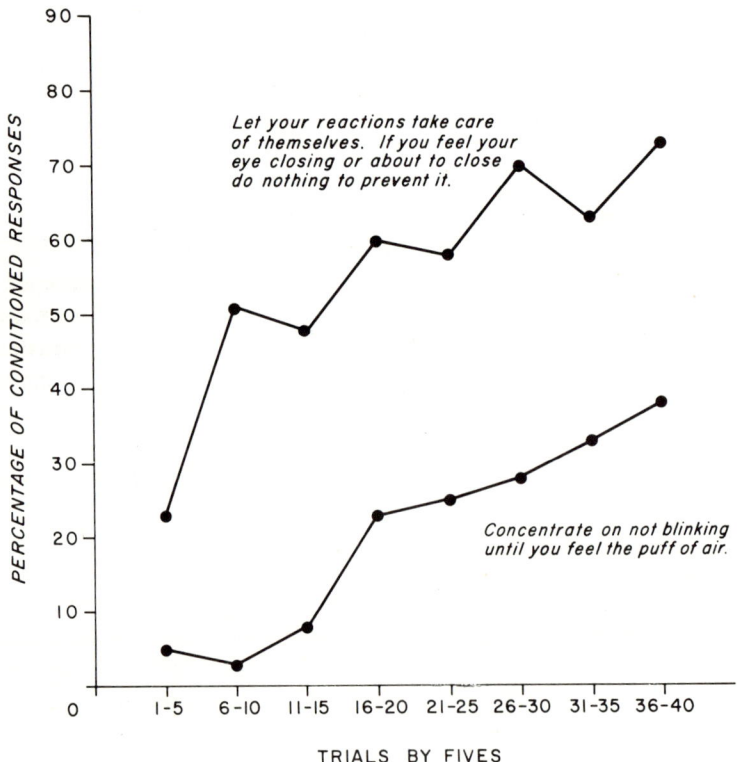

FIGURE 46-2. Percentage of conditioned responses as a function of trials by fives for subjects conditioned with facilitatory and inhibitory instructions. Except for sentences on the two curves, instructions were the same for both groups. (Nicholls & Kimble, 1964.)

conditioned with the inhibitory set showed a decrement, not only in the level of conditioning, but also in the amplitude of the unconditioned reflex. We shall deal with this fact later. Second, and more important, the speed with which the two curves separate (then becoming parallel) suggests the operation of two interacting processes. The first is a facilitatory or inhibitory set which has achieved its full strength in something less than 10 trials. The second is the conditioned eyelid reflex that requires much longer to establish. The fact that the curves remain separated by an approximately constant amount after this initial quick separation suggests that the first of these factors, once established, exercises a relatively constant influence on the progress of conditioning. Furthermore, it seems possible that the relationships appearing in this figure reveal the characteristic operation of a variable whose influence is mainly on the subject's set or attitude. That is, this set may develop very early in learning and have a fairly constant effect on performance from then on. More abstractly, this suggestion is that these variables may have an effect that is additive. The influence of inhibitory instructions, for example, might be treated theoretically as subtracting from an excitatory tendency in a manner essentially identical to the relationship between $_sE_R$ and I_R proposed many years ago by Hull.

The next question is whether there are other variables that affect eyelid conditioning in the same way. In an attempt to answer this question, last fall, at the University of California, I read through a few papers on eyelid conditioning. Armed with proportional dividers, I measured the differences, trial-by-trial, between pairs of acquisition functions produced by the manipulation of a number of different variables, and transferred these differences to another graph. For each of these pairs of curves I was interested in the question of whether the difference between them remained constant after a small number of trials, or whether the curves showed a tendency toward steady divergence. The latter relationship might result from an underlying multiplicative interaction of influences rather than the additive one which appears to apply to the effect of instructions.

As could have been anticipated, certain complexities emerged during the course of this survey, many of them reflecting ceiling effects. Often, for example, a variable produced a large difference in performance early in conditioning but, later, the curves came together resulting in a decrease in the size of the difference. On the other hand, certain rough regularities appeared in the 14 papers and 20 variables examined. In brief, the manipulation of certain variables did appear to produce steadily diverging curves of conditioning. Another group of variables seemed to produce a much more rapid separation of the functions but this difference might be followed by a continuing relatively constant effect or by a tendency toward convergence. Interestingly, the variables that produced divergence seemed in every case to be motivational variables; for example, intensity of the UCS, threat of an increased UCS and level of anxiety. Those which seemed to have their maximal effect earlier were more of a mixed bag, including the effect of a ready signal, sex of the subjects, prior adaptation to the UCS, massing of practice and schedule of reinforcement. More recently, in connection with preparing this paper, I have examined a dozen or so additional sets of data with some care and have noted only one type of finding that suggests a modification of my original conclusion. Some results look very much as if a high level of anxiety has an effect which appears very quickly and may belong in part, or under certain circumstances, to the second collection of variables.

Whatever the ultimate value of this way of assessing the theoretical point of impact of a variable, such considerations figured prominently in the planning and interpretation of the studies to which I shall turn now. The first has to do with the effect of a ready signal upon eyelid conditioning.

Ready signals and conditioning

Previous work on the influence of this variable has been entirely consistent in showing that the effect of a ready signal is inhibitory. Beyond this, however, little or nothing is known. We do not know, for example, whether the effect is upon learning or performance, or whether the length of time separating the ready signal and the conditioning trial has an effect. Barbara Turner (1963) undertook to obtain answers to these questions in the work for her doctoral dissertation. There were four groups of 20 subjects each in this experiment. The design of the experiment was a factorial one and two of these groups were conditioned initially with a ready signal and two were conditioned without a ready signal. For the former two groups, the ready signal preceded the CS by 1.0, 2.0, 3.0, 5.0 or 7.5 seconds, these values having been suggested in a large-scale preliminary study. Shorter intervals were not sampled because two stimuli separated by less than 1.0 second would surely function as a compound CS, and longer intervals seemed too likely to be confounded by the effects of the intertrial interval. The intervals employed were randomized trial-by-trial with the constraint that each block of 15 trials contain 3 trials with intervals of each of the five durations.

A within-groups breakdown of performance at each of these intervals appears in Figure 46-3. It is important to be clear on the point that the five curves in this figure are all for the same 40 subjects, the points plotted representing performance at each RS-CS interval, using this abbreviation to refer to the interval between ready signal (RS) and conditioned stimulus (CS). It appears that, after 30 trials or so, performance

Attitudinal Factors in Eyelid Conditioning

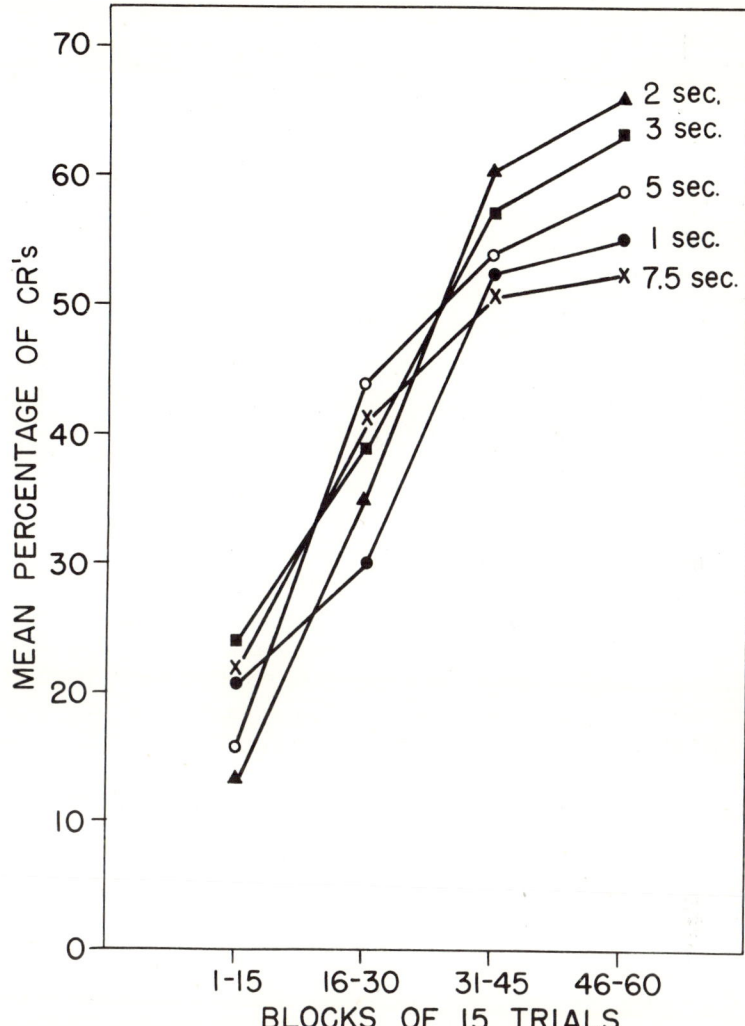

FIGURE 46-3. Percentage of conditioned responses as a function of trials by fifteens obtained at five different RS-CS intervals. (Turner, 1963.)

is dependably related to the RS-CS interval, with the best performance occurring at the 2.0-second interval.

The type of function represented by this result is clearer in Figure 46-4 where mean percentage of CRs on Trials 30-60 has been plotted against the duration of the RS-CS interval. There is an obvious peak of the function at 2.0 seconds, for which two explanations suggest themselves. The first is that 2.0 seconds may provide for a state of optimal "readiness."

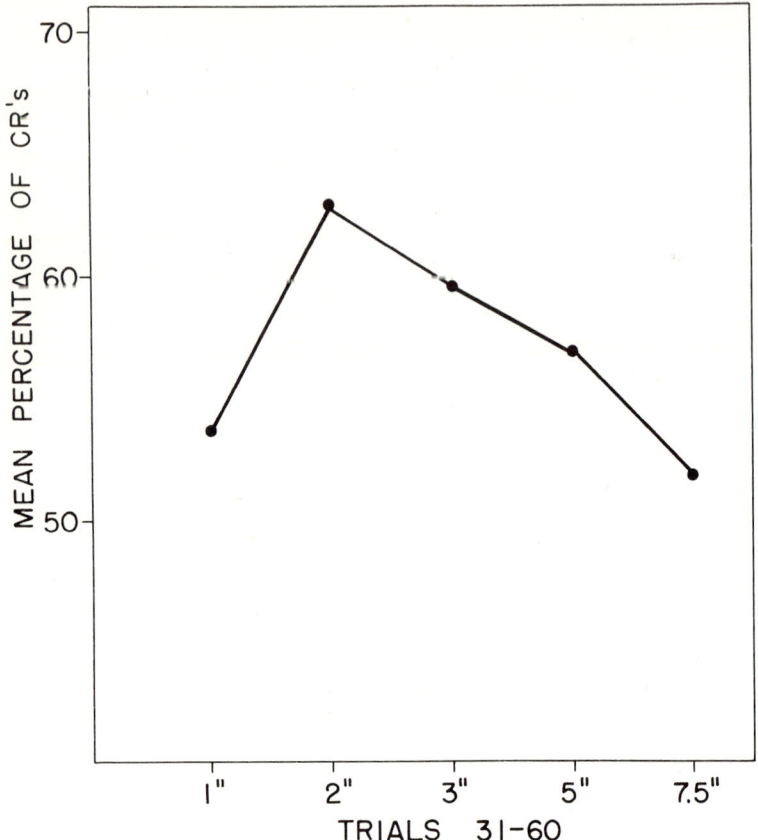

FIGURE 46-4. Percentage of conditioned responses on Trials 31-60 as a function of the length of the RS-CS interval. (Turner, 1963.)

Two seconds is an interval in the range of those found to be optimal in some studies of simple reaction time where the effect of the length of the foreperiod has been investigated. It is possible that the RS-CS interval in conditioning and the foreperiod in simple reaction time have the same psychological significance as Hartmann, Grant and Ross (1960) have noted. The other suggested explanation is that the 2.0-second interval may be associated with a maximal level of arousal which occurs as a CR to the ready signal. This process might then function as an acquired drive and energize the eyelid CR maximally at about 2.0 seconds. Obviously the ready signal does occupy the position of a CS on any conditioning trial and, in my opinion, the evidence is beginning to accumulate that something of the order of 2.0 seconds may be the optimal CS-UCS

Attitudinal Factors in Eyelid Conditioning

interval for conditioning certain emotional reactions. I prefer this latter explanation, partly because of one difficulty with the readiness hypothesis. As we shall see in more concrete terms in a moment, conditioning without a ready signal is probably superior to any point on this function. It is even somewhat (but not reliably) superior without a ready signal than at the optimal 2.0-second interval. The readiness hypothesis, thus, leads to an awkward paradox in that it suggests that conditioning is best with an optimal readiness at a 2.0-second interval, but even better with no readiness at all.

All of this indicates, of course, that it is now time to look at the comparison of conditioning with and without a ready signal obtained by Turner in this study. Recall that there were four groups in the experiment, two conditioned with a ready signal and two without. These ready-signal and no-ready-signal groups were treated identically for 60 trials, but beginning with Trial 61, a ready signal was introduced for one group previously conditioned without one. Similarly, the ready signal was omitted, from Trial 61 on, for one of the ready-signal groups. The reason for using this before-and-after factorial design, obviously, was to see whether the effect of the ready signal was on learning or performance.

The results of the experiment are presented in Figure 46-5 in which conditioning curves are presented for all four groups. In this figure the abbreviations, RS and NRS, stand for "ready signal" and "no ready signal." The two abbreviations on each curve identify the conditions that were obtained on Trials 1–60 and 61–90, respectively. Thus, Group RS-NRS had a ready signal on Trials 1–60 but not on Trials 61–90.

The first point about these curves is that the difference on Trials 31–60 between Groups NRS-RS and NRS-NRS must be the result of sampling error since, up to Trial 60, the subjects in the groups were treated the same and had been assigned to conditions without bias. Beyond this, we note the following points. (1) During Trials 1–60 the performance of these groups is like that observed in previous studies. Subjects conditioned without a ready signal perform at a higher level than those conditioned with a ready signal. (2) As the results of factorially designed studies are usually interpreted, the effect of the ready signal is upon learning rather than performance, an outcome which I believe is unique in studies of this type. We arrive at the conclusion that the effect is on learning because the introduction or omission of the ready signal on Trials 61–90 has no effect at all upon performance. (3) What I regard to be the most important outcome of the experiment requires a very special form of the interpretation just suggested. Note that the difference in performance between the combined RS groups and the combined NRS group is at least as large on Trials 1–15 as it is on Trials 76–90. Thus, although we may want to attribute the influence obtained in this experiment to learning, we probably cannot assign it to an effect directly on

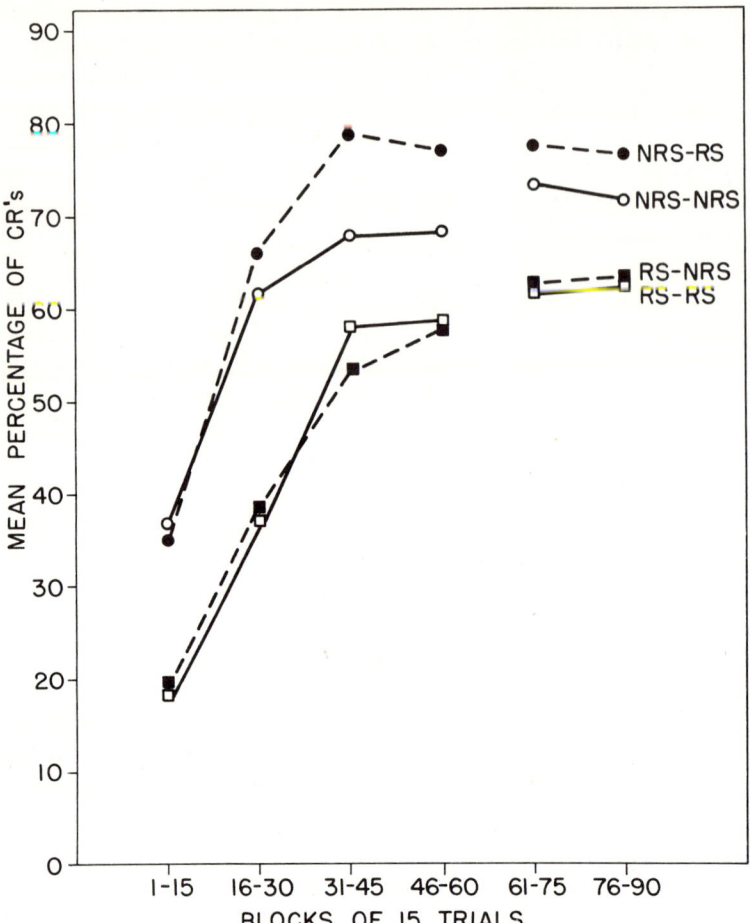

FIGURE 46-5. Conditioning curves showing the effect of introducing or omitting a ready signal from Trial 61 on. (Turner, 1963.)

the conditioned eyeblink. Obviously the effect, which resists the manipulation of introducing or removing the ready signal, is already established in just 15 conditioning trials whereas the strength of conditioning appears to increase for at least 60 trials.

Appropriate statistical analyses confirm and strengthen the foregoing interpretation. The interaction between trials and experimental condition is not significant when this analysis covers the first 60 trials in blocks of 15. The curves do not diverge. Analysis of performance during the first 15 trials, when these are broken down into blocks of 3 trials, by contrast, yields quite a different picture. There is a significant interaction in this analysis. Moreover, detailed inspection of the data reveals that this interaction is caused by the fact that the curves begin together and then diverge rapidly. After 6 trials, the functions differ by about 20 percent, a separation which persists for some 85 trials and survives a manipulation which under other circumstances would have a powerful effect.

This outcome has already been seen in this presentation. The use of a ready signal in eyelid conditioning appears to have exactly the same consequences as the use of inhibitory instructions. The similarity of these results makes it difficult to avoid the conclusion that similar processes are involved and, beginning with the most commonly offered explanation for the effect of instructions, one suspects that, in both cases, the experimental manipulation has altered the subjects' attitude or set.

Attitudinal factors and schedule of reinforcement

Before proceeding further, one or two points should be made about the attitudinal process, and the term itself should be explained. First, by the subject's attitude, I am referring to a general reaction to the experiment and the manipulations it involves. As I have said, I believe it is important to separate this general reaction to the experimental situation from the more specific eyelid CR also established there. Second, the attitudinal reaction is unfortunately complicated. It includes the cognitive element emphasized in some of Spence's recent writings and, in addition, an emotional and a motivational component. To put it less elegantly than attitude theorists would probably like, the subject learns certain facts about the procedures of the experiment, such as the nature of the CS and UCS, the fact that they come together, that they occur without warning or following a ready signal, that they always come together or that sometimes the CS occurs alone and so on. This is what I mean by a cognitive component. The subject then learns that the procedures are either harmless or noxious (the emotional component). Finally he decides how to react to the situation, whether to resist the manipulations or become passive and comply (the motivational component). At the present time, I see no necessity, in this context, to distinguish between the concept of attitude and that of set, although for me the connotations of the term *set* are somewhat narrower than those of *attitude*, and suggest the motivational component more than they suggest the cognitive or emotional reactions.

As I mentioned earlier, one of the variables which seems to produce a quick and relatively constant decrease in performance in eyelid conditioning is a schedule of partial reinforcement. This mainpulation, too, may have its direct effect on the subject's attitudes and only indirectly upon conditioning. With only one or two exceptions, relevant investigations have shown that partial reinforcement seriously interferes with the progress of eyelid conditioning. In this respect, such learning appears to differ from instrumental learning where we now know that except on early trials a partial schedule certainly does not retard performance and often has a positive effect.

With our suspicions aroused, by the similarity of the influence of partial reinforcement to the influence of instructions and the effect of a ready signal, that the effect might reflect the operation of an inhibitory set, we were led to speculate about the details of the operation of this negative set. One idea that suggested itself almost immediately was that, if this inhibitory attitude occurs as a reaction to the conditioned stimulus, its arousal would take time. Suppose, to be utterly sophomoric about it (a stance that does not seem inappropriate given the population from which our subjects were drawn), that the situation is as simple as this. After a few trials in the conditioning situation involving a partial schedule, the naive and trusting subject discovers that he is the object of an annoying hoax. Specifically, having developed a tendency to blink at the light before the arrival of the airpuff, it, now and then, happens that the subject blinks but there is no puff. In short, he has been tricked. Now most college students I know would dislike being made a party to such shenanigans and, after about two nonreinforcements, would probably react at least implicitly with something like the following: "If that smart SOB thinks he is going to fool me again, he's got another think coming." And when this subject perceives the CS the next time, he steels himself to resist its effect and, to reverse a more familiar conception, becomes a "voluntary nonresponder." It does not seem out of line with this general idea to suspect further that the dirtier the trick appears to the subject (for example, if the UCS is extremely unpleasant), the more likely he is to react in this way. In support of this latter interpretation, we were able to uncover the following promising fact. Most studies of the effect of the intensity of the UCS in eyelid conditioning have shown the influence to be positive; the stronger the UCS, the higher the level of conditioning. A curious exception to this outcome sometimes occurs when the manipulation of UCS intensity occurs in the context of a partial reinforcement experiment. Under these circumstances a strong UCS may lead to poorer conditioning than a weak one. It seemed to us that this could mean that if a partial schedule of reinforcement leads a subject to adopt an inhibitory set, for the reasons we just developed, the use of a strong UCS might deepen this set and interfere with performance still further.

What has now been stated is the theoretical basis for our study of partial reinforcement. The essential idea in this study was that the negative set produced by a partial schedule would take time to mobilize, even in fractional form. Thus, we reasoned a partial schedule of reinforcement should have a much more seriously detrimental effect in an experiment where the interval between CS and UCS is long than when it is short.

Attitudinal Factors in Eyelid Conditioning

To test the validity of this deduction, William Fowler (1964) has just completed the obvious experiment for his doctoral dissertation. Four groups of 18 subjects each were conditioned. The experimental design was a 2 × 2 factorial with 50 percent and 100 percent schedules of reinforcement defining one marginal and interstimulus intervals of .4 seconds and 1.1 seconds defining the other. These intervals were chosen because, though widely different, previous work in our laboratory indicates that they produce high and about equal levels of conditioning under a continuous schedule of reinforcement. Our hypothesis involving the concept of attitude, however, led us to anticipate a conspicuous difference in favor of the subjects conditioned with the shorter interval under partial reinforcement. The subjects in the four groups received identical numbers of reinforced trials.

The results of the study are presented in Figure 46-6 where the number on each curve is the interstimulus interval in seconds and C and P stand for "continuous" and "partial," respectively. As this figure shows, our theory predicted the outcome of the study very well. Condi-

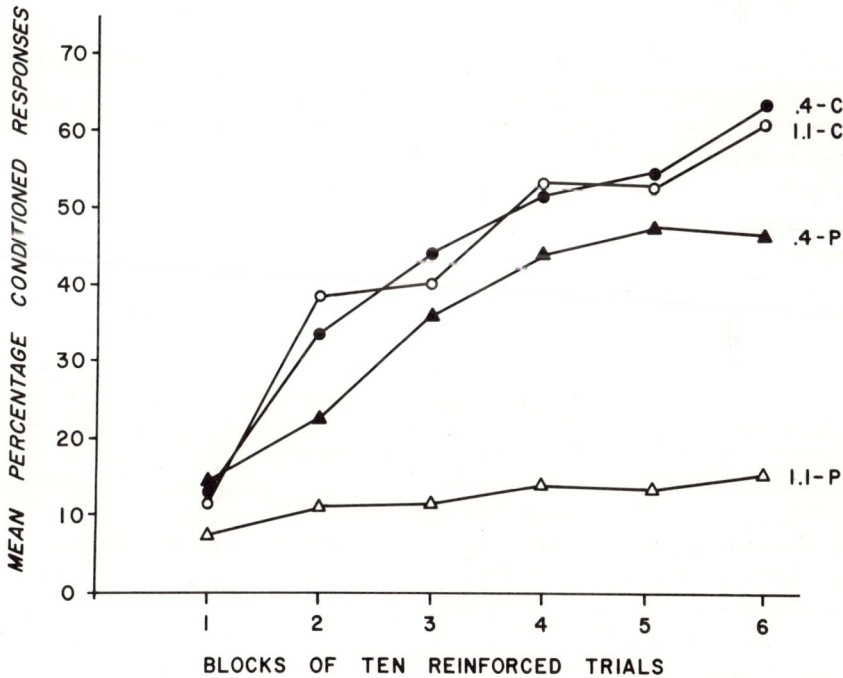

FIGURE 46-6. Conditioning curves plotted for blocks of ten reinforced trials for groups conditioned with continuous (C) or partial (P) reinforcement and with interstimulus intervals of .4 second and 1.1 seconds (Fowler, 1964.)

tioning is not noticeably affected by schedule of reinforcement when the interstimulus interval is short but is markedly influenced at the 1.1-second interval. It thus appears that student subjects probably do have unflattering names they covertly apply to experimenters who trick them and attitudes of noncooperativeness to go along with these epithets.

In addition to their influence upon the progress of conditioning, the attitudinal influences I have just described have related consequences that are of some importance. In the Nicholls and Kimble study, we found that inhibitory instructions produced a greater decrement in the amplitude of the UCR than was associated with facilitatory instructions. A common observation in studies of eyelid conditioning is a progressive diminution in the amplitude of the unconditioned blink of the type illustrated in Figure 46-7. In the Nicholls and Kimble study, the amount of this decrement under inhibitory instructions was about three times as great as under facilitatory instructions, although the amplitudes of the unconditioned blinks of the two groups of subjects were indistinguishable on the early conditioning trials.

A similar result appeared in Fowler's study of partial reinforcement. The amount of diminution of the UCR was much greater in the group

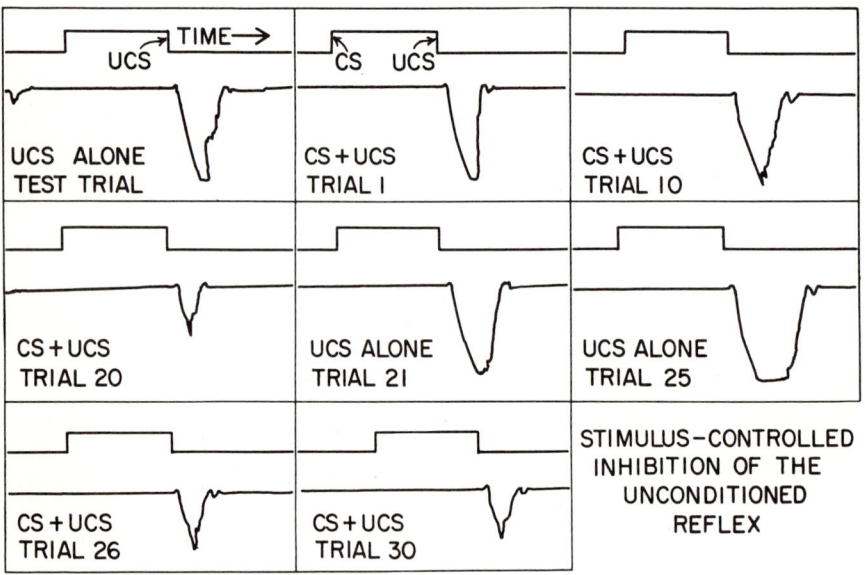

FIGURE 46-7. A series of records showing a decrease in amplitude of the UCR for 20 trials. As the gain in amplitude on Trials 21-25 with UCS alone indicates, this diminution occurs as a reaction to the CS and can be reinstated (Trials 26-30) by reintroducing the CS.

conditioned with a partial schedule and a long interval than the average for the other three groups. In terms of our measurements, the decrease in amplitude was about 3.5 mm. on the average in the other groups and 8.4 mm. for the partial group with the long interstimulus interval. In the Nicholls and Kimble study of instructions, the corresponding values were 2.7 mm. decrease with facilitatory instructions and 8.3 with inhibitory instructions. These values are obviously quite similar to those obtained by Fowler.

Beyond this, in Fowler's study there was a comparable effect on the magnitude of the conditioned response. Again in terms of the measurements we make on our records, mean CR amplitude for the partial, long interval, group was approximately 10.4 mm. as compared with an average of 19.8 mm. for the other three groups. In making these measures we did *not* count a trial without a CR as a trial on which a CR of zero amplitude occurred. The measurements were all on responses counted as CRs by other criteria. A possible importance of these demonstrations of an attitudinal influence on response amplitudes is that they may provide a badly needed criterion for identifying the subjects whom Spence has referred to as "inhibitors" and are a source of difficulty in numerous experiments.

Development of attitudinal questionnaire

The next bit of information we have obtained about attitudinal effects on eyelid conditioning will answer a question which surely must have occurred long ago to any social psychologists in the audience and by now may even have suggested itself to a few of the less pure experimentalists: "If you are so all-fired interested in attitudinal factors and their effect on conditioning, why don't you quit all this manipulative and measuring hocus pocus and just study the subjects' attitudes toward your experiments and find out whether they have anything to do with your results?" This seems a sensible query, although somewhat impolitely put, and as it happens, we have begun to do some work along these lines.

What we have done is to prepare an 18-item questionnaire entitled "subject's evaluation of the experiment" which each participant completes at the end of the experiment. The subject makes a series of judgments by encircling one of the 11 values which represent the 11 decile steps between 0 and 100.

To illustrate the procedure with some of the items which will figure in later discussion, here are three examples.

1. One of my chief initial reactions to this experiment was a feeling of nervousness or anxiety. Circle 0 for no nervousness or anxiety at all; 100 for great fear or apprehension.
   0   10   20   30   40   50   60   70   80   90   100
   no anxiety   great fear

2. One of the points which bothers me about psychological experiments is that they involve the manipulation of a person's behavior without his consent. Circle 0 if the point is of no concern to you; 100 if it troubles you greatly.

    0   10   20   30   40   50   60   70   80   90   100
    no concern   troubles greatly

3. In this experiment, I found myself resisting an apparent attempt to manipulate my behavior. Circle 0 if you noticed no such attempt *or* did not resist; 100 if you noticed and resisted vigorously.

    0   10   20   30   40   50   60   70   80   90   100
    no resistance   vigorous resistance

At the present time this questionnaire is entering its third revision, having been modified twice as a result of experience. What I have to report here are data obtained from the second edition of the questionnaire, specifically from the subjects in Fowler's dissertation and those in a comparison of high- and low-anxiety subjects recently completed by Mark Ominsky.

There are several points of view from which these data may be examined. Perhaps the most obvious is to ask about the correlation of performance on the questionnaire with conditioning. To obtain an estimate of the degree of this relationship, we have resorted to computer analysis and have obtained multiple correlations in which each item is treated as a test and assigned an appropriate weight in the computation. At least in terms of what I had hoped for, the correlations are almost unbelievably high, approximately .70 for an overall analysis. When the computer selects, for each subgroup, the five items accounting for the most variance and computes separate correlations for each condition, these range from about .75 to over .90. I am convinced that the size of these correlations depends on the fact that the questionnaire was administered following the conditioning session. It is important to sample attitudes developed in the experiment as well as tendencies the subject brings to the experiment ready made.

We come finally to the relationship between anxiety and conditioning to which I have already alluded once or twice. As many of you know, the Kings, John Gorman and I (1961) have published one of the few studies of eyelid conditioning in which level of anxiety did not relate positively to level of conditioning. In one pair of groups the relationship was actually negative. Beyond this, until recently, an examination of the performances of high- and low-anxiety subjects in experiments concerned with other matters never revealed a difference in favor of the high-anxiety subjects. Obviously there is a discrepancy between the results obtained in our laboratory and those obtained elsewhere that needs explanation.

In recent months we have acquired a new laboratory at Duke. Our conditioning chambers are now IAC soundproof rooms which resemble a bank vault, or perhaps a built-in refrigerator, and they are equipped with dental chairs rather than the office-type seats we originally used in our conditioning set-up. These features lend the whole experiment a somewhat more frightening air than was the case with our previous apparatus. The first experiment to be performed with this equipment was a comparison of conditioning in high- and low-anxiety subjects. The outcome, as is shown in Figure 46-8, was in the typical direction. It is quite apparent that now our results are like those obtained in other laboratories.

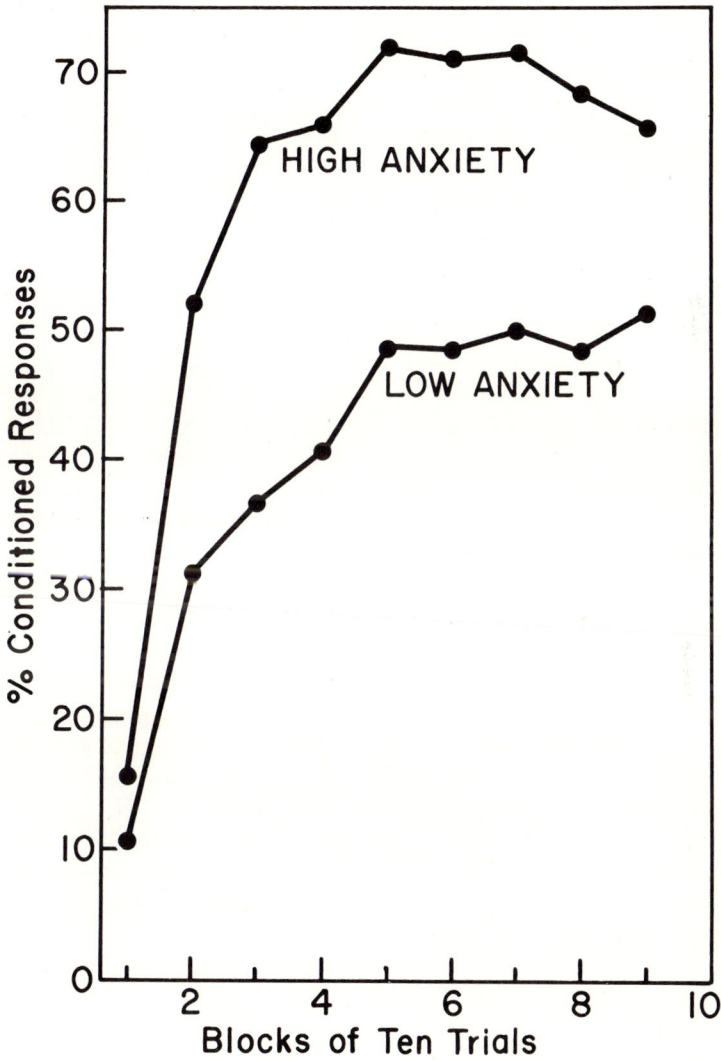

FIGURE 46-8. Conditioning curves for subjects with high and low anxiety. (Ominsky & Kimble, 1965.)

The obvious implication is that the general features of the situation are important in determining whether or not anxiety has an effect upon conditioning. In addition, an analysis of the details of our subjects' responses to the questionnaire, leads to some suggestions as to the nature of the process. Considering all of our data of this type and subjecting them to a factor analysis which is partly intuitive and partly real, it is clear (as others have pointed out) that there is more to the personalities of our subjects than a level of chronic anxiety or a penchant for experiencing that emotion episodically. Although I am not on firm ground here, I will suggest that three clusters of reactions to the eyelid conditioning experiment summarize the most important of our subjects' attitudes. The first of these I can only call the power of positive thinking. It correlates positively with conditioning and involves a pattern of willingness to participate in psychological experiments, approval of the procedures employed, and a readiness to yield to the effects of these procedures. The second cluster also correlates positively with conditioning. It is emotional, and other, arousal and includes such components as anxiety, feelings of discomfort and a tendency to consider oneself an active participant in the experiment. The third factor might be called resistance. It correlates negatively with conditioning and appears to entail reactions of hostility, suspicion, and resistance to being manipulated.

Does this analysis contain any suggestion as to why a variable such as anxiety might have a particular effect in one experiment and none or the opposite effect in another? There is at least a hint of a mechanism in our data. In Ominsky's experiment we found that anxious subjects express a greater worry about being manipulated in a psychological experiment than low-anxiety subjects and also report that they resist such manipulation more. As we have just seen, this last reaction is related to a low level of conditioning. Now suppose that an anxious subject fails to have his anxiety aroused in a conditioning experiment, because the procedures are too benign, but that these procedures do succeed in eliciting a reaction of resistance to being manipulated to which the high-anxiety subject is also predisposed. This latter influence interferes with conditioning so that, if it is the main reaction of the high-anxiety subject, this could lead to a reversal of the usual effect of anxiety. It seems probable that something of the sort happened in one replication in the King, Kimble, Gorman and King experiments where low-anxiety subjects conditioned better than high-anxiety subjects.

CONCLUSION

To me the one most impressive outcome of our recent studies has been to underline the importance and to stress the complexity of the attitudinal influences on eyelid conditioning. It seems to me that those of us who are interested in such learning are forced, at this juncture, to face up to the individual differences that exist in conditioning and to deal with them as something more than just annoying sources of statistical error. As a concluding statement, I would like to make one or two additional comments in this vein.

There is no doubt that experimental psychology has benefited greatly from its long-standing allegiance to whatever is plainly objective, operationally solvent and securely quantitative. It has, in fact, benefited to the point where we no longer need to maintain our traditional nervousness when dealing with some of the more complex aspects of our field. It seems to me that, if the materials I have presented have any general significance, it is that they reveal that the phenomena associated with such conceptions as attitude, set, resistance to being manipulated, and even volition may not be as unapproachable by the methods of objective psychology as most of us have thought. These concepts now seem to me to figure in laws which differ from those with which we are accustomed to deal only in being more complex. These concepts can be treated as straightforward intervening variables which arise (in the present context) as the consequence of such experimental manipulations as introducing a ready signal or varying the schedule of reinforcement. Their influence is then detectable through their effect on performance in the conditioning situation. They are involved in an ordinary, but complicated, example of an S-R law.

Another approach to an understanding of these influences is through the correlational methods associated with R-R laws, methods we have begun to use in the development of our attitudinal questionnaire. It may be surprising that the R-R approach is quite effective. Even a novice in the field can construct a test capable of accounting for about 50 percent of the variance in the conditioning situation. This approach can be as objective as any other: it is simply a case of allowing the implications of experimental results to dictate next steps, wherever these steps may take us. If we get lost venturing into relatively uncharted areas of psychology in this way, we are sophisticated enough, when we discover that we need new concepts, to approach them from a known operational base. In my opinion, we now have the methodology to fulfill our obligation to attempt to make systematic and experimental sense of much more of the field of psychology than we had in the past. I suspect that the study of something as apparently trivial, artificial, sterile and limited as the conditioned eyeblink can contribute to the accomplishment of this objective.

47

A Stimulus-Response Analysis of Anxiety and Its Role as a Reinforcing Agent[1]

O. H. MOWRER

Within recent decades an important change has taken place in the scientific view of anxiety (fear),[2] its genesis, and its phychological significance. Writing in 1890, William James stoutly supported the then current supposition that anxiety was an *instinctive* ("idiopathic") reaction to certain objects or situations, which might or might not represent real danger. To the extent that the instinctively given, predetermined objects of anxiety were indeed dangerous, anxiety reactions had biological utility and could be accounted for as an evolutionary product of the struggle for existence. On the other hand, there were, James assumed, also anxiety reactions that were altogether senseless and which, conjecturally, came about through Nature's imperfect wisdom. But in all cases, an anxiety reaction was regarded as phylogenetically fixed and unlearned. The fact that children may show no fear of a given type of object, e.g., live frogs, during the first year of life but may later manifest such a reaction, James attributed to the "ripening" of the fear-of-live frogs instinct; and the fact that such fears, once they have "ripened," may also disappear he explained on the assumption that all instincts, after putting in an appearance and, as it were, placing themselves at the individual's disposal, tend to undergo a kind of obliviscence or decay unless taken advantage of and made "habitual."

Some years later John B. Watson (1928) demonstrated experimentally that, contrary to the Jamesian view, most human fears are specifically relatable to and dependent upon individual experience. Starting with the reaction of infants to loud sounds or loss of physical support, which he refused to call "instinctive" but did not hesitate to regard as "unlearned" or "reflexive," Watson was able to show, by means of Pav-

[1] Reprinted with permission from *Psychological Review,* 1939, 46.
[2] Psychoanalytic writers sometimes differentiate between anxiety and fear on the grounds that fear has a consciously perceived object and anxiety does not. Although this distinction may be useful for some purposes, these two terms will be used in the present paper as strictly synonymous.

lov's conditioning technique, that an indefinitely wide range of other stimuli, if associated with this reaction, could be made to acquire the capacity to elicit unmistakably fearful behavior. This was an important discovery, but it appears to have involved a basic fallacy. Watson overlooked the fact that "loud sounds" are intrinsically *painful,* and he also overlooked the fact that "loss of physical support," although not painful in its own right, is almost certain to be followed by some form of stimulation (incident to the stopping of the body's fall) that is painful. The so-called fearful reaction to loss of support—if not confused with an actual pain reaction—is, therefore, in all probability itself a learned (conditioned) reaction, which means that, according to Watson's observations, human infants show no innate *fear* responses whatever, merely innate *pain* responses.

Freud seems to have seen the problem in this light from the outset and accordingly posited that *all* anxiety (fear) reactions are probably learned; his hypothesis, when recast in stimulus-response terminology, runs as follows. A so-called "traumatic" ("painful") stimulus (arising either from external injury, of whatever kind, or from severe organic need) impinges upon the organism and produces a more or less violent defense (striving) reaction. Furthermore, such a stimulus-response sequence is usually preceded or accompanied by originally "indifferent" stimuli which, however, after one or more temporally contiguous associations with the traumatic stimulus, begin to be perceived as "danger signals," i.e., acquire the capacity to elicit an "anxiety" reaction. This latter reaction, which may or may not be grossly observable, has two outstanding characteristics: (1) it creates or, perhaps more accurately, consists of a state of heightened tension (or "attention") and a more or less specific readiness for (expectation of) the impending traumatic stimulus; and (2), by virtue of the fact that such a state of tension is itself a form of discomfort, it adaptively motivates the organism to escape from the danger situation, thereby lessening the intensity of the tension (anxiety) and also probably decreasing the chances of encountering the traumatic stimulus. In short, *anxiety (fear) is the conditioned form of the pain reaction,* which has the highly useful function of motivating and reinforcing behavior that tends to avoid or prevent the recurrence of the pain-producing (unconditioned) stimulus.

In the mentalistic terminology that he characteristically employs, Freud (1936) has formulated this view of anxiety formation and its adaptational significance as follows:

Now it is an important advance in self-protection when this traumatic situation of helplessness [discomfort] is not merely awaited but is foreseen, anticipated. Let us call the situation in which resides the cause of this anticipation the danger situation; it is in this latter that the signal of anxiety is given. What this means is: I anticipate that a situation of helplessness [discomfort] will come about, or the present situation reminds me of one of the traumatic experiences which I have previously undergone. Hence I will anticipate this trauma; I will act as if it were already present as long as there is still time to avert it. Anxiety, therefore, is the expectation of the trauma on the one hand, and on the other, an attentuated repetition of it [pp. 149–150].

Affective [anxiety] states are incorporated into the life of the psyche as precipitates of primal traumatic experiences, and are evoked in similar situations like memory symbols [p. 23]. Anxiety is undeniably related to expectation; one feels anxiety lest something occur [pp. 146–147].

According to views expressed elsewhere by Freud, expectation and anxiety lie along a continuum, with the former merging into the latter at the point at which it becomes uncomfortably intense, i.e., begins to take on motivational properties in its own right. The preparatory, expectant character of anxiety is likely, however, to be obscured by the fact that danger situations sometimes arise and pass so quickly that they are over before the anxiety reaction—involving, as it does, not only an augmentation of neuro-muscular readiness and tension but also a general mobilization of the physical energies needed to sustain strenuous action—has had an opportunity to occur. The result is that in situations in which danger is so highly transitory, as, for example, in near-accidents in motor traffic, anxiety is commonly experienced, somewhat paradoxically, *after* the danger is past and therefore gives the appearance of being indeed a useless, wasted reaction (cf. James). It must not be overlooked, however, that situations of this kind are more or less anomalous. The fact that in a given situation the element of danger disappears before flight, for which the anxiety-preparedness is most appropriate, has had time to occur, does not, of course, mean that anxiety-preparedness in the face of danger is not in general a very adaptive reaction.

As early as 1903, Pavlov expressed a point of view that bears a striking resemblance to the position taken by Freud in this connection. He said: "The importance of the remote signs (signals) of objects can be easily recognized in the movement reaction of the animal. By means of distant and even accidental characteristics of objects the animal seeks his food, avoids enemies, etc." (cf. Pavlov, 1938, p. 52). Again, a quarter of a century later, Pavlov (1927) wrote as follows:

"It is pretty evident that under natural conditions the normal animal must respond not only to stimuli which themselves bring immediate benefit or harm, but also to other physical or chemical agencies—waves of sound, light, and the like—which in themselves only *signal* the approach of these stimuli; though it is not the sight and sound of the beast of prey which is in itself harmful to the smaller animal, but its teeth and claws" (p. 14).

Although both Pavlov and Freud thus clearly recognize the biological utility of anticipatory reactions to danger signals, there is an important difference in their viewpoints. Pavlov emphasizes the mechanism of simple stimulus substitution (conditioning). According to his hypothesis, a danger signal (the conditioned stimulus) comes to elicit essentially the same "movement reaction" that has previously been produced by actual trauma (the unconditioned stimulus). It is true that the blink of the eyelids to a threatening visual stimulus is not greatly unlike the reaction made to direct corneal irritation. A dog may learn to flex its leg in response to a formerly neutral stimulus so as to simulate the flexion produced by an electric shock administered to its paw. And a small child may for a time make very much the same type of withdrawal reactions to the sight of a flame that it makes to actual contact with it. However, any attempt to establish this pattern of stimulus substitution as the prototype of all learning places severe restrictions on the limits of adaptive behavior: it implies that the only reactions that can become attached to formerly unrelated stimuli (i.e., can be learned) are those which already occur more or less reflexly to some other type of stimulation.

According to the conception of anxiety proposed by Freud, on the other hand, a danger signal may come to produce any of an infinite variety of reactions that are wholly unlike the reaction that occurs to the actual trauma of which the signal is premonitory. Freud assumes that the first and most immediate response to a danger signal is not a complete, overt reaction, as Pavlov implies, but an implicit state of tension and augmented preparedness for action, which he calls "anxiety." This state of affairs, being itself a source of discomfort, may then motivate innumerable random acts, from which will be selected and fixated (by the law of effect) the behavior that most effectively reduces the anxiety. Anxiety is thus to be regarded as a motivating and reinforcing (fixating) agent, similar to hunger, thirst, sex, temperature deviations, and the many other forms of discomfort that harass living organisms, which is, however, presumably distinctive in that it is derived from (based upon anticipation of) these other, more basic forms of discomfort.

By and large, behavior that reduces anxiety also operates to lessen the danger that it presages. An antelope that scents a panther is likely not only to feel less uneasy (anxious) if it moves out of the range of the odor of the panther but is also likely to be in fact somewhat safer. A primitive village that is threatened by marauding men or beasts sleeps better after it has surrounded itself with a deep moat or a sturdy stockade. And a modern mother is made emotionally more comfortable after her child has been properly vaccinated against a dreaded disease. This capacity to be made uncomfortable by the mere prospect of traumatic experiences, in advance of their actual occurrence (or recurrence), and to be motivated thereby to take realistic precautions against them, is unquestionably a tremendously important and useful psychological mechanism, and the fact that the forward-looking, anxiety-arousing propensity of the human mind is more highly developed than it is in lower animals probably accounts for many of man's unique accomplishments. But it also accounts for some of his most conspicuous failures.

The ostrich has become a proverbial object of contempt and a symbol of stupidity because of its alleged tendency, when frightened, to put its head in the sand, thereby calming its emotional agitation but not in the slightest degree altering the danger situation in its objective aspects. Such relevant scientific inquiry as has been carried out indicates, however, that infra-human organisms are ordinarily more realistic in this respect than are human beings. For example, if a dog learns to avoid an electric shock by lifting its foreleg in response to a tone, it will give up this response entirely when it discovers that the tone is no longer followed by shock if the response is not made. Human beings, on the other hand, are notoriously prone to engage in all manner of magical, superstitious, and propitiatory acts, which undoubtedly relieve dread and uncertainty (at least temporarily) but which have a highly questionable value in controlling real events. The remarkable persistence of such practices may be due, at least in part, to the fact that they are followed relatively promptly by anxiety-reduction, whereas their experienced futility at the reality level may come many hours or days or even months later. The persistence of certain forms of "unrealistic" anxiety-reinforced behavior may also be due to the fact that in most societies there seem always to be some individuals who are able and ready to derive an easy living by fostering beliefs on the part of others in "unrealistic" dangers. For the common man protection against such "dangers" consists of whatever type of behavior the bogey-makers choose to say is "safe" (and which furthers their own interests).

Yet other forms of "unrealistic" anxiety-reinforced behavior are to be observed in the symptomatic acts of the psychoneuroses. According to Freud (1936, p. 111) anxiety is in fact "the fundamental phenomenon and the central problem of neurosis." He further says:

"Since we have reduced the development of anxiety to a response to situations of danger, we shall prefer to say that the symptoms are created in order to remove or rescue the ego from the situation of danger. . . . We can also say, in supplement to this, that the development of anxiety induces symptom formation—nay more, it is a *sine qua non* thereof, for if the ego did not forcibly arouse the pleasure-pain mechanism through the development of anxiety, it would not acquire the power to put a stop to the danger-threatening process elaborated in the id" (pp. 112–113).

Willoughby (1935), in a scholarly, well-documented paper, has previously stressed the similarity of magical rites (including religion) and neurotic symptoms and has shown that both types of behavior spring from the common propensity of human beings to deal with their anxieties unrealistically, i.e., by means which diminish emotional discomfort but do not adaptively alter external realities. This excellent study has, in the present writer's opinion, only one important weakness: it takes as its point of departure what Freud has called his "first theory" of anxiety formation . . . which he subsequently abandoned for the one outlined above. In brief, Freud's earlier supposition was that anxiety arose whenever a strong organic drive or impulse was prevented from discharging through its accustomed motor outlets. According to this view, inhibition was the primary state, anxiety the resultant. In all his more recent writings, on the other hand, Freud takes the position, here also adopted, that anxiety (as a reaction to a "danger signal") is primal and that inhibition, of anxiety-arousing, danger-producing impulses, is a consequence. Reaction mechanisms (magic, symptoms, etc.) that contribute to this end tend, for reasons already given, to be reinforced and perpetuated. Willoughby's analysis is not of necessity predicated upon Freud's original view of anxiety formation and would seem to gain rather than lose cogency if based instead upon his more recent formulations.

Magical and neurotic practices constitute a very perplexing and challenging problem from the point of view of traditional psychological theory; but, as Allport (1937) has recently pointed out, so also do many other types of human activity that are commonly regarded as both rational and normal. Allport rightly stresses the inadequacies of the conditioned-reflex concept as a comprehensive explanation of learning and personality development in general. He also justly criticizes the view that all human conduct is to be accounted for in terms of trial-and-error striving to eliminate immediately felt organic needs. The plain fact is that much of modern man's most energetic behavior occurs when his organic needs are ostensibly well satisfied. In an attempt to account for this state of affairs, without, on the other hand, falling back on a forthright mentalistic type of approach, Allport elaborates the view, previously advanced by Woodworth, that habits themselves have an on-going character, independent of the motivation that originally brought them into being, and that this type of habit-momentum constitutes a form of self-sustained motivation. Allport calls this the principle of "functional autonomy" and relies heavily upon it in developing his system of the "psychology of personality."

In the estimation of the present writer, "functional autonomy" is on a par with "perpetual motion." Its author clearly perceives an important psychological problem, but it seems unlikely that his is a scientifically tenable solution to it. The position here taken is that human beings (and also other living organs to varying degrees) can be motivated either by organic pressures (needs) that are currently present and felt *or* by the mere anticipation of such pressures and that those habits tend to be acquired and perpetuated (reinforced) which effect a reduction in *either* of these two types of motivation. This view rests upon and is but an extended application of the well-founded law of effect and involves no assumptions that are not empirically verifiable. It has the further advantage that it is consistent with common-sense impressions and practices and at the same time serves as a useful integrational device at the scientific level.

The present analysis of anxiety (anticipation, expectancy) and its role in shaping both "adaptive" and "mal-adaptive" behavior in human beings is also consistent with the growing tendency to eliminate the distinction between learning through "punishment" and learning through "reward." The earlier view was that so-called punishment "stamped out" habits and that reward "stamped" them in. This distinction now appears to have been spurious and to have depended upon a selectivity of emphasis or interest (Mowrer, 1938). If an individual is motivated by an internal discomfort or need (produced by his own metabolic processes), and if another individual provides the means of eliminating it, and if, in the process, the first individual acquires new behavior, this is called learning through "reward." But if a second individual supplies the need (by inflicting or threatening to inflict some form of discomfort), and if the affected individual supplies the means of eliminating this discomfort (by flight, inactivity, propitiation, compliance, or the like), and if, in the process, this individual acquires new behavior, then this is called learning through "punishment." The truth of the matter seems to be that all learning presupposes (1) an increase of motivation (striving) and (2) a decrease of motivation (success) and that the essential features of the process are much the same, regardless of the specific source of motivation or of the particular circumstances of its elimination.

There is, however, one practical consideration to be taken into account. Although learning through "punishment" does not seem to differ basically from learning through "reward," inter-personal relationships are likely to be affected very differently in the two cases. If the method of "reward" is employed, inter-personal relationships are likely to be made more "positive" (i.e., approach tendencies will be strengthened); whereas, if the method of "punishment" is employed, inter-personal relationships are likely to be made more "negative" (i.e., avoidance tendencies will be strengthened). From a purely social point of view, it is therefore preferable to employ the method of "reward," whenever this is possible; but "punishment" may have to be resorted to if no *organic* needs are present to be "rewarded" or if means of rewarding them are not available. Punishment (or the threat of punishment, i.e., anxiety) is particularly convenient in that it can be produced instantly; but this advantage is accompanied by disadvantages which cannot be safely disregarded. . . .

Even the practical basis for distinguishing between learning through reward and through punishment just suggested becomes tenuous when one considers the type of situation in which one person withholds from another an expected reward. This, in one sense, is a form of "punishment," and yet its effectiveness is based upon the principle of "reward." This complicated state of affairs seems especially likely to arise in the parent-child relationship and has implications that have been but slightly explored in stimulus-response terms.

SUMMARY

In contrast to the older view, which held that anxiety (fear) was an instinctive reaction to phylogenetically predetermined objects or situations, the position here taken is that anxiety is a learned response, occurring to "signals" (conditioned stimuli) that are premonitory of (i.e., have in the past been followed by) situations of injury or pain (unconditioned stimuli). Anxiety is thus basically anticipatory in nature and has great biological utility in that it adaptively motivates living organisms to deal with (prepare for or flee from) traumatic events in advance of their actual occurrence, thereby diminishing their harmful effects. However, experienced anxiety does not always vary in direct proportion to the objective danger in a given situation, with the result that living organisms, and human beings in particular, show tendencies to behave "irrationally," i.e., to have anxiety in situations that are not dangerous or to have no anxiety in situations that are dangerous. Such a "disproportionality of affect" may come about for a variety of reasons, and the analysis of these reasons throws light upon such diverse phenomena as magic, superstition, social exploitation, and the psychoneuroses.

Moreover, by positing anxiety as a kind of connecting link between complete well-being and active organic discomfort or injury, it is possible to reconcile the fact that much, perhaps most, of the day-to-day behavior of civilized human beings is not prompted by simultaneously active organic drives and the fact that the law of effect (principle of learning through motivation-reduction) is apparently one of the best-established of psychological principles. This is accomplished by assuming (a) that anxiety, i.e., mere anticipation of actual organic need or injury, may effectively motivate human beings and (b) that reduction of anxiety may serve powerfully to reinforce behavior that brings about such a state of "relief" or "security." Anxiety, although derived from more basic forms of motivation, is thus regarded as functioning in an essentially parallel manner as far as its role as an activating and reinforcing agent is concerned. This analysis is consistent with the common sense view in such matters and does not conflict with any known empirical fact. Finally, it has the advantage of being open to objective investigation and of giving rise to a host of problems that have scarcely been touched experimentally.

References

ALBERTS, E., & EHRENFREUND, D., 1951. Transposition in children as a function of age. *J. exp. Psychol., 41,* 30–38.

ALLPORT, G. W., 1937. *Personality.* New York: Holt, Rinehart and Winston.

AMSEL, A., 1949. Selective association and the anticipatory response mechanism as explanatory concepts in learning. *J. exp. Psychol., 39,* 785–799.

ANDERSSON, B., 1951. The effect and localization of electrical stimulation of certain parts of the brain stem in sheep and goats. *Acta Physiol. Scand., 23,* 8–23.

ANDERSSON, B., 1952. Polydipsia caused by intrahypothalamic injections of hypertonic NaCl solutions. *Experientia, 8,* 157.

ANDERSSON, B., 1953. The effect of injections of hypertonic NaCl solutions into different parts of the hypothalamus of goats. *Acta Physiol. Scand., 28,* 188–201.

ANDERSSON, B., & WYRWICKA, W., 1957. The elicitation of a drinking motor conditioned reaction by electrical stimulation of the hypothalamic "drinking area" in the goat. *Acta Physiol. Scand., 41,* 194–198.

ANNAU, Z., & KAMIN, L. J., 1961. The conditioned emotional response as a function of intensity of the US. *J. comp. physiol. Psychol., 54,* 428–432.

ANTAL, J., & KEMENY, A., 1964. The rate of elaboration of alimentary and defensive reflexes in group conditioning. *Physiologia Bohemoslovenica, 13,* 110–115.

ARMINGTON, J. C., & MITNICK, L. L., 1959. Electroencephalogram and sleep deprivation. *J. appl. Psychol., 14,* 247–250.

ASRATYAN, E. A., 1949. *I. P. Pavlov, his life and work.* Moscow: Foreign Languages Publishing House.

AZRIN, N. H., 1958. Some effects of noise on human behavior. *J. exp. Anal. Behav., 1,* 183–199.

AZRIN, N. H., 1964. Aggression. Paper presented at the American Psychological Association convention, Los Angeles.

AZRIN, N. H., & HOLZ, W. C., 1961. Punishment during fixed-interval reinforcement. *J. exp. Anal. Behav., 4,* 343–347.

AZRIN, N. H., & HUTCHINSON, R. R., 1963. Unpublished study.

AZRIN, N. H., HUTCHINSON, R. R., & HAKE, D., 1963. Pain-induced fighting in the squirrel monkey. *J. exp. Anal. Behav., 6,* 620–621.

AZRIN, N. H., HUTCHINSON, R. R., & SALLERY, R. D., 1964. Pain-aggression toward inanimate objects. *J. exp. Anal. Behav., 7,* 223–228.

AZRIN, N. H., ULRICH, R. E., HUTCHINSON, R. R., & NORMAN, D. G., 1964. Effect of shock-duration on shock-induced fighting. *J. exp. Anal. Behav., 7,* 9–11.

References

BABKIN, B. P., 1949. *Pavlov: A Biography*. Chicago: University of Chicago Press.

BAILEY, C. J., 1955. The effectiveness of drives as cues. *J. comp. physiol. Psychol., 48*, 183–187.

BAILEY, C. J., & PORTER, L. W., 1955. Relevant cues in a drive discrimination in cats. *J. comp. physiol. Psychol., 48*, 180–182.

BAKER, L. E., 1938. The pupillary response conditioned to subliminal auditory stimuli. *Psychol. Monogr., 50*, No. 3 (Whole No. 223).

BAKER, R. A., & LAWRENCE, D. H., 1951. The differential effects of simultaneous and successive stimulus presentation on transposition. *J. comp. physiol. Psychol., 44*, 378–382.

BARD, P., 1950. Central nervous mechanisms for the expression of anger in animals. In M. L. Reymert (Ed.), *Feelings and emotions*. New York: McGraw-Hill.

BARNES, G. W., 1956. Conditioned stimulus intensity and temporal factors in spaced-trial classical conditioning. *J. exp. Psychol., 51*, 192–198.

BARRY, H., III, 1958. Effects of strength of drive on learning and on extinction. *J. exp. Psychol., 55*, 473–481.

BARTLEY, S. H., 1941. *Vision*. New York: Van Nostrand.

BASS, B., 1958. Gradients in response percentage as indices of nonspatial generalization. *J. exp. Psychol., 56*, 278–281.

BASS, M. J., & HULL, C. L., 1934. The irradiation of a tactile conditioned reflex in man. *J. comp. Psychol., 17*, 47–65.

BEACH, F. A., & JAYNES, J. 1954. Effects of early experience upon the behavior of animals. *Psychol. Bull., 51*, 239–263.

BECHTEREV, V., 1933. *General principles of human reflexology*, trans. by E. and W. Murphy. London: Hutchinson.

BECK, E. C., & DOTY, R. W., 1957. Conditioned flexion reflexes acquired during combined catalepsy and de-efferentation. *J. comp. physiol. Psychol., 50*, 211–216.

BEEMAN, E., 1947. The effect of male hormone on aggressive behavior in mice. *Physiol. Zool., 20*, 373–405.

BEIER, D. C., 1940. Conditioned cardiovascular responses and suggestions for the treatment of cardiac neuroses. *J. exp. Psychol., 26*, 311–321.

BERGMANN, G., & SPENCE, K. W., 1941. Operationism and theory in psychology. *Psychol. Rev., 48*, 1–14.

BERKUN, M. M., KESSEN, M. L., & MILLER, N. E., 1952. Hunger-reducing effects of food by stomach fistula versus food by mouth measured by a consummatory response. *J. comp. physiol. Psychol., 45*, 550–554.

BERNHARD, C. G., 1939. Experimental studies on conditioned salivary reflexes in children. *Acta Paediatrica, 23*, 118–128.

BERNSTEIN, A. L., 1934. Temporal factors in the formation of conditioned eyelid reactions in human subjects. *J. gen. Psychol., 10*, 173–197.

BEVAN, W., DAVIS, F., & LEVY, W., 1960. The relation of castration, androgen therapy and pre-test fighting experience to competitive aggression in the male C57 BL/10 mice. *Animal Behav., 8*, 1–2.

BICKEL, A., 1897. Uber der einfluss der sensiblen nerven der labirynthe and die bevegungen der thiere. *Plugers Archiv., 67*.

BILLS, M. A., 1920. The lag of visual sensation in its relation to wavelength and intensity of light. *Psychol. Monogr., 28,* No. 5 (Whole No. 127).

BINDRA, D., PATERSON, A. L., & STRZELECKI, JOANNA, 1955. The relation between anxiety and conditioning. *Canad. J. Psychol., 9,* 1–5.

BITTERMAN, M. E., & HOLTZMAN, W. H., 1952. Conditioning and extinction of the galvanic skin response as a function of anxiety. *J. abnorm. soc. Psychol., 47,* 615–623.

BLACK, A. H., & LANG, W. M., 1964. Cardiac conditioning and skeletal responding in curarized dogs. *Psychol. Rev., 71,* 80–85.

BLOUGH, D. S., 1957. Spectral sensitivity in the pigeon. *J. opt. Soc. Amer., 47,* 827–833.

BONEAU, C. A., 1958. The interstimulus interval and the latency of the conditioned eyelid response. *J. exp. Psychol., 56,* 464–472.

BORING, E. G., 1942. *Sensation and perception in the history of experimental psychology.* New York: Appleton-Century-Crofts.

BRADY, J. V., 1962. Psychophysiology of emotional behavior. In A. Bachrach (Ed.), *Experimental foundations of clinical psychology.* New York: Basic Books.

BRIDGER, W. H., 1960. Signal systems and the development of cognitive functions. In M. A. B. Brazier (Ed.), *The central nervous system and behavior.* New York: Transcript of Third Conference, Josiah Macy, Jr. Foundation. Pp. 425–456.

BRIDGER, W. H., 1964. Contributions of conditioning principles to psychiatry. In *Pavlovian conditioning and psychiatry,* Symposium No. 9, 181–198.

BRIDGER, W. H., & GANTT, W. H., 1956. The effect of mescaline on differentiated conditional reflexes. *Amer. J. Psychiat., 113,* 352.

BRIDGER, W. H., & MANDEL, I. J., 1964. A comparison of GSR fear responses produced by threat and electric shock. *J. psychiat. Res., 2,* 31–40.

BRIERTON, G. R., STACHNIK, T. J., & ULRICH, R. E., 1964. Unpublished study.

BRIERTON, G. R., ULRICH, R. E., & WOLFF, P. C., 1964. Unpublished study.

BROBECK, J. R., 1946. Mechanism of the development of obesity in animals with hypothalamic lesions. *Physiol. Revs., 26,* 541–559.

BROGDEN, W. J., 1939. The effect of frequency of reinforcement upon the level of conditioning. *J. exp. Psychol., 24,* 419–431.

BROWN, J. S., 1942. The generalization of approach responses as a function of stimulus intensity and strength of motivation. *J. comp. Psychol., 33,* 209–226.

BROWN, J. S., 1948. Gradients of approach and avoidance responses and their relation to levels of motivation. *J. comp. physiol. Psychol., 41,* 450–465.

BROWN, J. S., & JACOBS, A., 1949. The role of fear in the motivation and acquisition of responses. *J. exp. Psychol., 39,* 747–759.

BROWN, J. S., BILODEAU, E. A., & BARON, M. R., 1951. Bidirectional gradients in the strength of a generalized voluntary response to stimuli on a visual-spatial dimension. *J. exp. Psychol., 41,* 52–61.

BROWN, J. S., CLARK, F. R., & STEIN, L., 1958. A new technique for studying spatial generalization with voluntary responses. *J. exp. Psychol., 55,* 359–362.

References

Brown, J. S., Kalish, H. I., & Farber, I. E., 1951. Conditioned fear as revealed by magnitude of startle response to an auditory stimulus. *J. exp. Psychol., 41,* 317–328.

Brown, T., 1846. *The philosophy of the human mind.* London: Hallowell, Glazier, Masters, & Smith.

Bruner, J. S., Matter, J., & Papanek, M. L., 1955. Breadth of learning as a function of drive level and mechanization. *Psychol. Rev., 62,* 1–10.

Bugelski, R., 1938. Extinction with and without sub-goal reinforcement. *J. comp. Psychol., 26,* 121–133.

Campbell, B. A., & Kraeling, D., 1954. Response strength as a function of drive level during training and extinction. *J. comp. physiol. Psychol., 47,* 101–103.

Campbell, B. A., & Sheffield, F. D., 1953. Relation of random activity to food deprivation. *J. comp. physiol. Psychol., 46,* 320–322.

Carr, H. A., 1925. *Psychology, a study of mental activity.* New York: Longmans.

Carter, L. F., 1941. Intensity of conditioned stimulus and rate of conditioning. *J. exp. Psychol., 28,* 481–490.

Cason, H., 1922a. The conditioned eyelid reaction. *J. exp. Psychol., 5,* 153–196.

Cason, H., 1922b. The conditioned pupillary reaction. *J. exp. Psychol., 5,* 108–146.

Cason, H., 1937. The organic nature of fatigue. *Amer. J. Psychol., 47,* 337–342.

Collias, N. W., 1944. Aggressive behavior among vertebrate animals. *Physiol. Zool., 17,* 83–123.

Cook, S. W., & Harris, R. E., 1937. The verbal conditioning of the galvanic skin reflex. *J. exp. Psychol., 21,* 202–210.

Coons, E. E., 1963. Motivational correlates of eating elicited by electrical stimulation in the hypothalamic feeding area. Unpublished doctoral dissertation, Yale University.

Coons, E. E., Fonberg, E., & Miller, N. E. 1963. How hypothalamic and cingulate lesions affect the rate of rewarding self-stimulation. Paper read at 1963 meetings, Eastern Psychological Association.

Cotton, J. W., 1953. Running time as a function of amount of food deprivation. *J. exp. Psychol., 46,* 188–198.

Courvoisier, S., 1956. Pharmacodynamic basis for the use of chlorpromazine in psychiatry. *J. clin. exp. Psychopath., 17,* 25.

Covain, M. R., 1949. Rate of emotional stress in the survival of adrenalectomized rats given replacement therapy. *J. clin. Endocrinol., 9,* 678.

Crespi, L. P., 1942. Quantitative variation of incentive and performance in the white rat. *Amer. J. Psychol., 55,* 467–517.

Cuff, N. B., 1929. The law of use. *J. educ. Psychol., 20,* 438–447.

Culler, E., & Mettler, F., 1934. Conditioned reflexes in a decorticate dog. *J. comp. Psychol., 18,* 291–303.

Daniel, W. J., 1943. An experimental note on O'Kelly-Steckle reaction. *J. comp. Psychol., 35,* 267–268.

Davis, J. D., & Miller, N. E., 1963. Fear and pain: their effect on self-injection of amobarbital sodium by rats. *Science, 141,* 1286–1287.
Delgado, J. M. R., Roberts, W. W., & Miller, N. E., 1954. Learning motivated by electrical stimulation of the brain. *Amer. J. Physiol., 179,* 587–593.
Dodge, R., 1926. A pendulum-photochronograph. *J. exp. Psychol., 9,* 155–161.
Dollard, J., & Miller, N. E., 1950. *Personality and psychotherapy.* New York: McGraw-Hill.
Drazin, D. H., 1961. Effects of foreperiod, foreperiod variability and probability of stimulus occurrence on simple reaction time. *J. exp. Psychol., 62,* 43–51.
Dubos, R. J., & Schaedler, R. W., 1961. The effect of bacterial endotoxins on the water intake and body weight of mice. *J. exp. Med., 112,* 921–934.
Dufort, R. H., & Kimble, G. A., 1958. Ready signals and the effect of interpolated UCS presentations in eyelid conditioning. *J. exp. Psychol., 56,* 1–7.

Egger, M. D., & Miller, N. E., 1962. Secondary reinforcement in rats as a function of information value and reliability of the stimulus. *J. exp. Psychol., 64,* 97–104.
Egger, M. D., & Miller, N. E., 1963. When is reward reinforcing? An experimental study of the information hypothesis. *J. comp. physiol. Psychol., 56,* 132–137.
Ehrenfreund, D., 1952. A study of the transposition gradient. *J. exp. Psychol., 43,* 81–87.
Eisman, E., 1956. An investigation of the parameters defining drive (D). *J. exp. Psychol., 52,* 85–89.
Eisman, E., Asimow, A., & Maltzman, I., 1956. Habit strength as a function of drive in a brightness discrimination problem. *J. exp. Psychol., 52,* 58–64.
Elliott, M. H., 1930. Some determining factors in maze performance. *Amer. J. Psychol., 42,* 315–317.
Eninger, M. U., 1951. The rate of learning a tone–no-tone discrimination as a function of the tone duration at the time of the choicepoint response. *J. exp. Psychol., 41,* 440–445.
Estes, W. K., 1943. Discriminative conditioning. I. A discriminative property of conditioned anticipation. *J. exp. Psychol., 32,* 150–155.
Estes, W. K., 1948. Discriminative conditioning. II. Effects of a Pavlovian conditioned stimulus upon a subsequently established operant response. *J. exp. Psychol., 38,* 173–177.
Estes, W. K., 1950. Toward a statistical theory of learning. *Psychol. Rev., 57,* 94–107.
Evans, W. O., 1961. Two factors affecting stimulus generalization on a spatial dimension. *J. exp. Psychol., 61,* 142–149.

Farris, H. D., 1963. Behavioral development, social organization and conditioning of courting behavior in the Japanese quail (*Coturnix coturnix japonica*). Unpublished doctoral dissertation, Michigan State University.

FEATHER, B. W., 1965a. Semantic generalization of classically conditioned responses: a review. *Psychol. Bull., 63,* 425–441.
FEATHER, B. W., 1965b. Human salivary conditioning. Unpublished doctoral dissertation, Duke University.
FEIRSTEIN, A. R., & MILLER, N. E., 1963. Learning to resist pain and fear: effects of electric shock before versus after reaching goal. *J. comp. physiol. Psychol., 56,* 797–800.
FINAN, J. L., 1940. Quantitative studies of motivation. I. Strength of conditioning in rats under varying degrees of hunger. *J. comp. Psychol., 29,* 119–134.
FINESINGER, J. E., & SUTHERLAND, G. F., 1939. The salivary conditional reflex in man. *Transactions of the American Neurological Association, 50.*
FINESINGER, J. E., SUTHERLAND, G. F., & MCGUIRE, F. F., 1942. The positive conditional salivary reflex in psychoneurotic patients. *Amer. J. Psychiat., 99,* 61–74.
FLORY, R. K., ULRICH, R. E., & WOLFF, P. C. (in press). Effects of visual deprivation on fighting behavior. *Psychol. Rec.*
FOLEY, J. P., 1935. A critical note on certain experimental work on the conditioned response. *J. gen. Psychol., 12,* 443–445.
FOWLER, W. R., 1964. The interstimulus interval and schedule of reinforcement in eyelid conditioning. Unpublished doctoral dissertation, Duke University.
FREEMAN, G. L., 1930. The galvanic phenomenon and conditioned responses. *J. gen. Psychol., 3,* 529–539.
FRENCH, T. M., 1933. Interrelations between psychoanalysis and the experimental work of Pavlov. *Amer. J. Psychiat., 12,* 1165–1203.
FREUD, S., 1936. *The problem of anxiety.* New York: Norton.
FREUD, S., 1956. The unconscious. In *Collected papers,* Vol. 4. London: Hogarth.
FRICK, F. C., SCHOENFELD, W. N., & KELLER, F. S., 1948. Apparatus designed for introductory psychology at Columbia College. *Amer. J. Psychol., 61,* 409–414.
FRICK, G. C., 1948. An analysis of an operant discrimination. *J. Psychol., 26,* 93–123.
FROLOV, Y. (n. d.). *Work and the brain.* Moscow: Foreign Languages Publishing House.

GANTT, W. H., 1949. Psychosexuality in animals. In P. H. Hoch and J. Zubin (Eds.), *Psychosexual development in health and disease.* New York: Grune & Stratton. Pp. 33–51.
GARCIA, J., KIMMELDORF, D. J., & KOELLING, R. A., 1955. Conditioned aversion to saccharin resulting from exposure to gamma radiation. *Science, 122,* 157–158.
GASTAUT, H., 1958. Some aspects of the neurophysiological basis of conditioned reflexes and behavior. In G. E. W. Wolstenholme and C. M. O'Connor (Eds.), *Neurological basis of behavior.* London: Ciba Foundation.

GELLERMANN, L. W., 1933. Form discrimination in chimpanzees and two-year-old children: I. Discrimination of form *per se*. II. Form versus background. *J. genet. Psychol.*, 42, 3–50.

GILBERT, T. F., 1958. Fundamental dimensional properties of the operant. *Psychol. Rev.*, 65, 272–282.

GIRDEN, E., 1942. Generalized conditioned responses under curare and erythroidine. *J. exp. Psychol.*, 31, 105–119.

GIRDEN, E., & CULLER, E., 1937. Conditioned responses in curarized striate muscle in dogs. *J. comp. Psychol.*, 23, 261–274.

GIRDEN, E., METTLER, F. A., FINCH, G., & CULLER, E., 1936. Conditioned responses in a decorticate dog to acoustic, thermal, and tactile stimulation. *J. comp. Psychol.*, 21, 367–385.

GLEY, E., & MENDELSSOHN, M., 1915. Some experiments on the conditioned salivary reflex among men. *Comptes Rendus de la Societe de Biologie*, 78, 645–649.

GORSKA, T., JANKOWSKA, E., & KOZAK, W., 1961. The effect of deafferentation on instrumental (type II) cleaning reflex in cats. *Acta Biol. Exper.*, 21, 207–217.

GRANT, D. A., 1964. Classical and operant conditioning. In A. W. Melton (Ed.), *Categories of human learning*. New York: Academic.

GRETHER, W. F., 1938. Pseudo-conditioning without paired stimulation encountered in attempted backward conditioning. *J. comp. Psychol.*, 25, 91–96.

GRICE, G. R., 1948a. The acquisition of a visual discrimination habit following response to a single stimulus. *J. exp. Psychol.*, 38, 633–642.

GRICE, G. R., 1948b. The relation of secondary reinforcement to delayed reward in visual discrimination learning. *J. exp. Psychol.*, 38, 1–16.

GRICE, G. R., 1949. Visual discrimination learning with simultaneous and successive presentation of stimuli. *J. comp. physiol. Psychol.*, 42, 365–373.

GRICE, G. R., & HUNTER, J. J., 1964. Stimulus intensity effects depend upon the type of experimental design. *Psychol. Rev.*, 71, 247–256.

GRICE, G. R., & SALTZ, E., 1950. The generalization of an instrumental response to stimuli varying in the size dimension. *J. exp. Psychol.*, 40, 702–708.

GRINGS, W. W., 1960. Preparatory set variables related to classical conditioning of autonomic responses. *Psychol. Rev.*, 67, 243–252.

GROSSMAN, S. P., 1960. Eating or drinking elicited by direct adrenergic or cholinergic stimulation of hypothalamus. *Science*, 132, 301–302.

GROSSMAN, S. P., 1962a. Direct adrenergic and cholinergic stimulation of hypothalamic mechanism. *Amer. J. Physiol.*, 202, 872–882.

GROSSMAN, S. P., 1962b. Effects of adrenergic and cholinergic blocking agents on hypothalamic mechanisms. *Amer. J. Physiol.*, 202, 1230–1236.

GULLIKSEN, H., 1934. A rational equation of the learning curve based on Thorndike's law of effect. *J. gen. Psychol.*, 11, 395–434.

GULLIKSEN, H., & WOLFLE, D. L., 1937. A rational theory of discrimination learning. *Psychometrika*, 2, 68.

GULLIKSEN, H., & WOLFLE, D. L., 1938. A theory of learning and transfer: II. *Psychometrika, 3,* 225–251.
GUTHRIE, E. R., 1930. Conditioning as a principle of learning. *Psychol. Rev., 37,* 412–428.
GUTHRIE, E. R., 1933a. On the nature of psychological explanations. *Psychol. Rev., 40,* 124–137.
GUTHRIE, E. R., 1933b. Association as a function of time interval. *Psychol. Rev., 40,* 355–367.
GUTHRIE, E. R., 1934a. Pavlov's theory of conditioning. *Psychol. Rev., 41,* 199–209.
GUTHRIE, E. R., 1934b. Reward and punishment. *Psychol. Rev., 41,* 450–460.
GUTHRIE, E. R., 1935. *The psychology of learning.* New York: Harper & Brothers.
GUTHRIE, E. R., 1936. Psychological principles and scientific truth. *Proc. 25th Anniv. Grad. Stud. U. S. C.,* 104–115.
GUTHRIE, E. R., 1937. Tolman on associative learning. *Psychol. Rev., 44,* 525–528.
GUTHRIE, E. R., 1938. *The psychology of human conflict.* New York: Harper & Row.
GUTHRIE, E. R., 1940a. Association and the law of effect. *Psychol. Rev., 47,* 127–148.
GUTHRIE, E. R., 1940b. Review of "organizing and memorizing." *Psychol. Bull., 37,* 820–823.
GUTHRIE, E. R., 1942a. Conditioning: a theory of learning in terms of stimulus, response, and association. *Forty-first Yearbook of the National Society for the Study of Education,* Part II. Bloomington: Public School Publishing, pp. 17–60.
GUTHRIE, E. R., 1942b. The principle of associative learning. In *Philosophical essays in honor of Edgar Arthur Singer, Jr.* Philadelphia: University of Pennsylvania Press, pp. 109–117.
GUTHRIE, E. R., 1946a. The conditioned response. *Encycl. Psychol.,* Philosophical Library.
GUTHRIE, E. R., 1946b. Psychological facts and psychological theory. *Psychol. Bull., 43,* 1–20.
GUTHRIE, E. R., 1946c. Recency or effect: a reply to Captain O'Connor. *Harv. Educ. Rev., 16,* 286–289.
GUTHRIE, E. R., 1952. *The psychology of learning.* (Rev. ed.) New York: Harper & Row.
GUTHRIE, E. R., & HORTON, G. P., 1937. A study of the cat in the puzzle box. *Psychol. Bull., 34,* 774.
GUTHRIE, E. R., & HORTON, G. P., 1946. *Cats in a puzzle box.* New York: Holt, Rinehart and Winston.
GUTHRIE, E. R., & YACORZYNSKI, G. K., 1937. A comparative study of involuntary and voluntary conditioned responses. *J. gen. Psychol., 16,* 235–257.
GUTTMAN, N., 1953. Operant conditioning, extinction, and periodic reinforcement in relation to concentration of sucrose used as reinforcing agent. *J. exp. Psychol., 46,* 213–224.

GUTTMAN, N., & KALISH, H. I., 1956. Discriminability and stimulus generalization. *J. exp. Psychol., 51,* 79–88.
GWINN, G. T., 1951. Resistance to extinction of learned fear-drives. *J. exp. Psychol., 42,* 6–12.

HANSON, H. M., 1959. Effects of discrimination training on stimulus generalization. *J. exp. Psychol., 58,* 321–334.
HARLOW, H. F., & STAGNER, R., 1933. Effect of complete striate muscle paralysis upon the learning process. *J. exp. Psychol., 16,* 283–294.
HARTMAN, T. F., & GRANT, D. A., 1962. Effect of pattern of reinforcement and verbal information on acquisition, extinction and spontaneous recovery of the eyelid CR. *J. exp. Psychol., 63,* 217–226.
HARTMAN, T. F., GRANT, D. A., & ROSS, L. E., 1960. An investigation of the latency of "instructed voluntary" eyelid responses. *Psychol. Rep., 7,* 305–311.
HEBB, D. O., 1956. The distinction between "classical" and "instrumental." *Canad. J. Psychol., 10,* 165–166.
HERON, W., DOANE, B. K., & SCOTT, T. H., 1956. Visual disturbances after prolonged perceptual deprivation. *Canad. J. Psychol., 10,* 13.
HESS, W. R., 1954. *Das zwischenhirn: syndrone, lokalisationem, functionem.* (2nd ed.) Basel, Switzerland: Schwabe.
HILGARD, E. R., 1931. Conditioned eyelid reactions to a light stimulus based on the reflex wink to sound. *Psychol. Monogr., 41,* No. 1 (Whole No. 184).
HILGARD, E. R., 1933a. Modification of reflexes and conditioned reactions. *J. gen. Psychol., 9,* 210–215.
HILGARD, E. R., 1933b. Reinforcement and inhibition of eyelid reflexes. *J. gen. Psychol., 8,* 85–113.
HILGARD, E. R., 1936a. The nature of the conditioned response: I. The case for and against stimulus substitution. *Psychol. Rev., 43,* 366–385.
HILGARD, E. R., 1936b. The nature of the conditioned response: II. Alternatives to stimulus-substitution. *Psychol. Rev., 43,* 547–564.
HILGARD, E. R., 1937. The relationship between the conditioned response and conventional learning experiments. *Psychol. Bull., 34,* 61–102.
HILGARD, E. R., 1948. *Theories of learning.* New York: Appleton-Century-Crofts.
HILGARD, E. R., 1951. Methods and procedures in the study of learning. In S. S. Stevens (Ed.), *Handbook of experimental psychology.* New York: Wiley.
HILGARD, E. R., 1956. *Theories of learning.* (Rev. ed.) New York: Appleton-Century-Crofts.
HILGARD, E. R., & CAMPBELL, A. A., 1936. The course of acquisition and retention of conditioned eyelid responses in man. *J. exp. Psychol., 19,* 227–247.
HILGARD, E. R., CAMPBELL, A. A., & SEARS, W. N., 1937. Conditioned discrimination: the development of discrimination with and without verbal report. *Amer. J. Psychol., 49,* 564–580.

HILGARD, E. R., CAMPBELL, R. K., & SEARS, W. N., 1938. Conditioned discrimination: the effect of knowledge of stimulus relationships. *Amer. J. Psychol., 51,* 498–506.
HILGARD, E. R., DUTTON, C. E., & HELMICK, J. S., 1949. Attempted pupillary conditioning at four stimulus intervals. *J. exp. Psychol., 39,* 683–689.
HILGARD, E. R., & HUMPHREYS, L. G., 1938a. The effect of supporting and antagonistic voluntary instructions on conditioned discrimination. *J. exp. Psychol., 22,* 291–304.
HILGARD, E. R., & HUMPHREYS, L. G., 1938b. The retention of conditioned discrimination in man. *J. gen. Psychol., 19,* 111–125.
HILGARD, E. R., & MARQUIS, D. G., 1935. Acquisition, extinction, and retention of conditioned lid responses to light in dogs. *J. comp. Psychol., 19,* 29–58.
HILGARD, E. R., & MARQUIS, D. G., 1940. *Conditioning and learning.* New York: Appleton-Century-Crofts.
HILGARD, E. R., MILLER, J., & OHLSON, J. A., 1941. Three attempts to secure pupillary conditioning to auditory stimuli near the absolute threshold. *J. exp. Psychol., 29,* 89–103.
HILLMAN, B., HUNTER, W. W., & KIMBLE, G. A., 1953. The effect of drive level on the maze performance of the white rat. *J. comp. physiol. Psychol., 46,* 87–89.
HNIK, P., 1956. Motor function disturbances and excitability changes following deafferentation. *Physiologia Bohemo-slovenica, 5,* 305.
HOBHOUSE, L. T., 1901. *Mind in evolution.* New York: Macmillan.
HOLLANDER, F. (Ed.), 1955. The regulation of hunger and appetite. *Ann. N. Y. Acad. Sci., 63,* 1.
HOLMES, J. E., & MILLER, N. E., 1963. Effects of bacterial endotoxin on water intake, food intake, and body temperature in the albino rat. *J. exp. Med., 118,* 649–658.
HOLST, E. V., 1954. Relations between the central nervous system and the peripheral organs. *Brit. J. Animal Behav., 2,* 89–94.
HOLZ, W. C., AZRIN, N. H., & ULRICH, R. E., 1963. Punishment of temporally spaced responding. *J. exp. Anal. Behav., 6,* 115–122.
HONIG, W. K., 1962. Prediction of preference, transposition, and transposition-reversal from the generalization gradient. *J. exp. Psychol., 64,* 239–248.
HONIG, W. K., THOMAS, D. R., & GUTTMAN, N., 1959. Differential effects of continuous extinction and discrimination training on the generalization gradient. *J. exp. Psychol., 58,* 145–152.
HORENSTEIN, B., 1951. Performance of conditioned responses as a function of strength of hunger drive. *J. comp. physiol. Psychol., 44,* 210–224.
HORTON, G. P., & GUTHRIE, E. R., 1938. A further study of the cat in the puzzle box. *Psychol. Bull., 36,* 521.
HOVLAND, C. I., 1936. "Inhibition of reinforcement" and the phenomena of experimental extinction. *Proc. Nat. Acad. Sci., 22,* 430–433.
HOVLAND, C. I., 1937a. The generalization of conditioned responses: I. The sensory generalization of conditioned responses with varying frequencies of tone. *J. gen. Psychol., 17,* 125–148.

HOVLAND, C. I., 1937b. The generalization of conditioned responses: II. The sensory generalization of conditioned responses with varying intensities of tone. *J. genet. Psychol., 51,* 279–291.

HUDGINS, C. V., 1933. Conditioning and the voluntary control of the pupillary light reflex. *J. gen. Psychol., 8,* 3–51.

HUDGINS, C. V., 1935. Steckle and Renshaw on the conditioned iridic reflex: a discussion. *J. gen. Psychol., 12,* 208–214.

HUDGINS, C. V., & HUNTER, W. S., 1934. Voluntary activity from the standpoint of behaviorism. *J. gen Psychol., 10,* 198–203.

HULL, C. L., 1929. A functional interpretation of the conditioned reflex. *Psychol. Rev., 36,* 498–511.

HULL, C. L., 1930. Knowledge and purpose as habit mechanisms. *Psychol. Rev., 37,* 511–525.

HULL, C. L., 1932. The goal gradient hypothesis and maze learning. *Psychol. Rev., 39,* 25–43.

HULL, C. L., 1933. Differential habituation to internal stimuli in the albino rat. *J. comp. Psychol., 16,* 255–273.

HULL, C. L., 1934a. The concept of the habit-family hierarchy and maze learning. *Psychol. Rev., 41,* Part I, 33–52; Part II, 134–152.

HULL, C. L., 1934b. Learning: II. The factor of the conditioned reflex. In C. Murchison (Ed.), *A handbook of general experimental psychology.* Worcester, Mass.: Clark University Press. Pp. 382–455.

HULL, C. L., 1934c. The rat's speed of locomotion gradient in the approach to food. *J. comp. Psychol., 17,* 393–422.

HULL, C. L., 1935. The conflicting psychologies of learning—a way out. *Psychol. Rev., 42,* 491–516.

HULL, C. L., 1937. Mind, mechanism, and adaptive behavior. *Psychol. Rev., 44,* 1–32.

HULL, C. L., 1943. *Principles of behavior.* New York: Appleton-Century-Crofts.

HULL, C. L., 1947. The problem of primary stimulus generalization. *Psychol. Rev., 54,* 120–134.

HULL, C. L., 1949. Stimulus intensity dynamism (V) and stimulus generalization. *Psychol. Rev., 56,* 67–76.

HULL, C. L., 1951. *Essentials of behavior.* New Haven: Yale University Press.

HULL, C. L., 1952. *A behavior system: an introduction to behavior theory concerning the individual organism.* New Haven: Yale University Press.

HUMPHREYS, L. G., 1939. Generalization as a function of method of reinforcement. *J. exp. Psychol., 25,* 261–272.

HUMPHREYS, L. G., 1943. Measures of strength of conditioned eyelid responses. *J. gen. Psychol., 29,* 101–111.

HUNTER, W. S., 1934. Learning, IV: Experimental studies of learning. In C. Murchison (Ed.), *A handbook of general experimental psychology.* Worcester, Mass.: Clark University Press. Pp. 497–570.

HUNTER, W. S., 1935. Conditioning and extinction in the rat. *Brit. J. Psychol., 26,* 135–148.

HUNTER, W. S., & HUDGINS, C. V., 1934. Voluntary activity from the standpoint of behaviorism. *J. gen. Psychol., 10,* 198–204.

IWAMA, K., & ABE, M., 1952. Electroencephalographic study of conditioned salivary reflexes in human subjects. *The Tohoku Journal of Experimental Medicine, 56,* 345–355.

IWAMA, K., & SHINJO, T., 1950. A method for leading off action currents from human salivary gland and for recording velocity of secretion. *The Tohoku Journal of Experimental Medicine, 52,* 223–229.

JABBUR, S. J., & TOWE, A. L., 1960. Effect of pyramidal tract activity on dorsal column nuclei. *Science, 132,* 547.

JACOBSON, E., 1929. *Progressive relaxation.* Chicago: University of Chicago Press.

JAMES, W., 1890. *Principles of psychology.* New York: Holt, Rinehart and Winston.

JAMES, W. T., 1934a. A conditioned avoiding posture of the dog. *Psychol. Bull., 31,* 730.

JAMES, W. T., 1934b. A conditioned response of two escape reflex systems of the guinea pig and the significance of the study for comparative work. *J. genet. Psychol., 44,* 449–453.

JANKOWSKA, E., 1957. Ruchowe (instrumentalne) odruchy warunkowe deaferentowanej konczyny u kotow. *Acta Physiol. Pol., 8,* 360.

JANKOWSKA, E., 1959. Instrumental scratch reflex of the deafferentated limb in cats and rats. *Acta Biol. Exper., 19,* 233.

JASPER, H. H., & SMIRNOV, G. D. (Eds.), 1960. *The Moscow colloquium on electroencephalography of higher nervous activity.* Supplement No. 13. The International Journal of Electroencephalography and Clinical Neurophysiology. Montreal: The EEG Journal.

JENKINS, J. J., & HANRATTY, J. A., 1949. Drive intensity discrimination in the albino rat. *J. comp. physiol. Psychol., 42,* 228–232.

JENKINS, W. O., PASCAL, G. R., & WALKER, R. W., JR., 1958. Deprivation and generalization. *J. exp. Psychol., 56,* 274–277.

JENSEN, D. D., 1961. Operationism and the question "Is this behavior learned or innate?" *Behaviour, 17,* 1–8.

JERSILD, A., 1929. Primacy, recency, frequency, and vividness. *J. exp. Psychol., 12,* 58–70.

JOHN, E. R., 1958. Electrophysiological correlates of avoidance conditioning in the cat. In *The central nervous system and behavior.* Transcript of First Conference, Josiah Macy, Jr. Foundation. New York.

JONES, J., 1962. Contiguity and reinforcement in aversive conditioning. *Psychol. Rev., 69,* 176–186.

JONES, LOUISE F., 1939. A study of human salivary conditioning. *J. exp. Psychol., 24,* 305–317.

JOUVET, M., 1960. Telencephalic and rhombencephalic sleep in the cat. In G. E. W. Wolstenholme and C. M. O'Connor (Eds.), *The nature of sleep.* London: Ciba Foundation.

KALISH, H. I., & GUTTMAN, N., 1957. Stimulus generalization after equal training on two stimuli. *J. exp. Psychol., 53,* 139–144.

KAMIN, L. J., 1956. The effects of termination of the CS and avoidance of the US on avoidance learning. *J. comp. physiol. Psychol., 49,* 420–424.

KAMIN, L. J., 1957. The gradient of delay of secondary reward in avoidance learning. *J. comp. physiol. Psychol., 50,* 445–449.

KAMIN, L. J., 1961. Trace conditioning of the conditioned emotional response. *J. comp. physiol. Psychol., 54,* 149–153.

KAMIN, L. J., & SCHAUB, R. E., 1963. Effects of conditioned stimulus intensity on the conditioned emotional response. *J. comp. physiol. Psychol., 56,* 502–507.

KAPPAUF, W. E., & SCHLOSBERG, H., 1937. Conditioned responses in the white rat. III. Conditioning as a function of the length of the period of delay. *J. genet. Psychol., 50,* 27–45.

KELLER, F. S., 1941. Light aversion in the white rat. *Psychol. Res., 4,* 235–250.

KELLER, F. S., & SCHOENFELD, W. N., 1950. *Principles of psychology.* New York: Appleton-Century-Crofts.

KELLEY, T. L., 1928. *Crossroads in the mind of man.* Stanford: Stanford University Press.

KENDLER, H. H., 1945. Drive interaction: II. Experimental analysis of the role of drive in learning theory. *J. exp. Psychol., 35,* 188–198.

KENDLER, H. H., 1946. The influence of simultaneous hunger and thirst drives upon the learning of two opposed spatial responses of the white rat. *J. exp. Psychol., 36,* 212–220.

KENDLER, H. H., 1951. Reflections and confessions of a reinforcement theorist. *Psychol. Rev., 58,* 368–374.

KENDLER, H. H., & UNDERWOOD, B., 1948. The role of reward in conditioning theory. *Psychol. Rev., 55,* 209–215.

KENDLER, T. S., 1950. An experimental investigation of transposition as a function of the difference between training and test stimuli. *J. exp. Psychol., 40,* 552–562.

KESSEN, W., 1953. Response strength and conditioned stimulus intensity. *J. exp. Psychol., 45,* 82–86.

KILLAM, L. R., & KILLAM, E. K., 1956. The action of lysergic acid diethylamide on the central afferent system in the cat. *J. Pharmacol. exp. Therapeutics, 116,* 35.

KIMBLE, G. A., 1947. Conditioning as a function of the time between conditioned and unconditioned stimuli. *J. exp. Psychol., 37,* 1–15.

KIMBLE, G. A., 1951. Behavior strength as a function of the intensity of the hunger drive. *J. exp. Psychol., 41,* 341–348.

KIMBLE, G. A., 1961a. Pavlovian conference on higher nervous activity. Discussion: Part VI. *Ann. N. Y. Acad. Sci., 92,* 1189–1192.

KIMBLE, G. A., 1961b. *Hilgard and Marquis' conditioning and learning.* (2nd ed.) New York: Appleton-Century-Crofts.

KIMBLE, G. A., 1964. Categories of learning and the problem of definition. In A. W. Melton (Ed.), *Categories of human learning.* New York: Academic.

KIMBLE, G. A., & OST, J. W. P., 1961. A conditioned inhibitory process in eyelid conditioning. *J. exp. Psychol., 61,* 150–156.

KIMBLE, G. A., & PENNYPACKER, H. S., 1963. Eyelid conditioning in young and aged subjects. *J. genet. Psychol., 103,* 283–289.
KIMMEL, H. D., 1959. Amount of conditioning and intensity of conditioned stimulus. *J. exp. Psychol., 58,* 283–288.
KIMMEL, H. D., 1961. Inhibitory factors in classical conditioning. Colloquium given at Duke University in May.
KIMMEL, H. D., & GREENE, W. A., 1964. Disinhibition in GSR conditioning as a function of the number of CS-UCS trials and the temporal location of the novel stimulus. *J. exp. Psychol., 68,* 567–572.
KIMMEL, H. D., & HILL, FRANCES A., 1960. Operant conditioning of the GSR. *Psychol. Repts., 7,* 555–562.
KIMMEL, H. D., & PENNYPACKER, H. S., 1962. Conditioned diminution of the UCR as a function of the number of reinforcements. *J. exp. Psychol., 64,* 20–23.
KING, MARGARET S., KIMBLE, G. A., GORMAN, J., & KING, R. A., 1961. Replication report: two failures to reproduce effects of anxiety on eyelid conditioning. *J. exp. Psychol., 62,* 532–533.
KLEITMAN, N., & CRISLER, G., 1927. A quantitative study of a salivary conditioned reflex. *Amer. J. Psychol., 79,* 571–614.
KLÜVER, H., 1933. *Behavior mechanisms in monkeys.* Chicago: University of Chicago Press.
KNAPP, H. D., TAUB, E., & BERMAN, A. J., 1958. Effect of deafferentation on a conditioned avoidance response. *Science, 128,* 842.
KOCH, S., 1944. Hull's principles of behavior. A special review. *Psychol. Bull., 41,* 269–286.
KOCH, S., 1954. Clark L. Hull. In Estes *et al., Modern learning theory.* New York: Appleton-Century-Crofts.
KOCH, S., & DANIEL, W. J., 1942. The effect of satiation on the behavior mediated by a habit of maximum strength. *J. exp. Psychol., 30,* 93–113.
KOHLER, W., 1925. *The mentality of apes.* New York: Harcourt, Brace & World.
KOHN, M., 1951. Satiation of hunger from food injected directly into the stomach versus food ingested by mouth. *J. comp. physiol. Psychol., 44,* 412–422.
KONORSKI, J., 1948. *Conditioned reflexes and neuron organization.* New York: Cambridge University Press.
KONORSKI, J., & MILLER, S., 1933. Podstawy fizjologicznej teorii ruchow nabytych. *Ruchowe odruchy warunkowe.* Warszawa.
KONORSKI, J., & MILLER, S., 1936. Uslownyje refleksy dwigatelnogo analizatora. *Trudy fiziol. Lab. Pavlova, 6,* 119.
KONORSKI, J., & SZWEJKOWSKA, G., 1952. Chronic extinction and restoration of conditioned reflexes. IV. *Acta Biol. Exper., 16,* 95–113.
KONORSKI, J., & WYRWICKA, W., 1952. Hamowanie nastepcze w odruchach warunkowych analizatora ruchowego. (Inhibitory after-effect in conditioned reflexes of the motor analyser) Polish text with an English summary. *Acta Physiol. Pol., 3,* 63–84.
KOSUPKIN, J. M., & OLMSTEAD, J. M. D., 1943. Slowing of the heart as a conditioned reflex in the rabbit. *Amer. J. Physiol., 139,* 550–552.

Krasnagorsky, N., 1926. Die letzten fortschritte in der methodik der erforschung der bedingten reflexe an kindern. *Jahrbuch fur Kinderheilkunde, 114,* 255–267.

Krasne, F. B., 1962. General disruption resulting from electrical stimulus of ventromedial hypothalamus. *Science, 138,* 822–823.

Krechevsky, I., 1932. "Hypotheses" versus "chance" in the pre-solution period in sensory discrimination-learning. *Univ. Calif. Publ. Psychol., 6,* 27–44.

Krechevsky, I., 1937a. Brain mechanisms and variability. I. Variability within a means-end-readiness. *J. comp. Psychol., 23,* 121–138.

Krechevsky, I., 1937b. Brain mechanisms and variability. II. Variability where no learning is involved. *J. comp. Psychol., 23,* 139–163.

Krechevsky, I., 1937c. Brain mechanisms and variability. III. Limitations of the effect of cortical injury upon variability. *J. comp. Psychol., 23,* 351–364.

Krechevsky, I., 1938. A study of the continuity of the problem solving process. *Psychol. Rev., 45,* 107–133.

Kupalov, P. S., & Murav'era, 1960. Pathological irradiation of the inhibition process. Privately circulated background material for Pavlovian conference on higher nervous activity. New York.

Kuypers, H. G. J. M., 1960. Central cortical projections to motor and somatosensory cell groups. *Brain, 83,* 161.

Lashley, K. S., 1916. Reflex secretion of the human parotid gland. *J. exp. Psychol., 1,* 461–493.

Lashley, K. S., 1929. Learning: I. Nervous-mechanisms of learning. In *The foundations of experimental psychology.* Worcester, Mass.: Clark University Press. Pp. 524–563.

Lashley, K. S., & Wade, M., 1946. The Pavlovian theory of generalization. *Psychol. Rev., 53,* 72–87.

Lassek, A. M., 1953. Inactivation of voluntary motor function following rhizotomy. *J. Neuropath. exp. Neurol., 12,* 83.

Lawson, R., 1960. *Learning and behavior.* New York: Macmillan.

Lazarus, R. S., & McCleary, R. A., 1951. Autonomic discrimination without awareness: a study of subception. *Psychol. Rev., 58,* 113–122.

Leeper, R., 1935. The role of motivation in learning: a study of the phenomenon of differential motivational control of the utilization of habits. *J. genet. Psychol., 46,* 3–40.

Lentz, A. K., 1935. Salivary conditioned reflexes in normal and insane subjects; relation to degree of consciousness of subject. *L'Encephale, 30,* 394–440.

Lepley, W. M., 1932. A theory of serial learning and forgetting based upon conditioned reflex principles. *Psychol. Rev., 39,* 279–288.

Lepley, W. M., 1934. Serial reactions considered as conditioned reactions. *Psychol. Monogr., 46,* No. 1 (Whole No. 205).

Levi, W. M., 1957. *The pigeon.* Sumter, S. C.: Levi.

Levine, S., 1953. The role of irrelevant drive stimuli in learning. *J. exp. Psychol., 45,* 410–416.

Lewin, K., 1933. Environmental forces. In C. Murchison (Ed.), *A handbook of child psychology.* (2nd ed. rev.) Worcester, Mass.: Clark University Press. Pp. 590–625.

LEWIN, K., 1935. *A dynamic theory of personality,* trans. by D. K. Adams and K. E. Zener. New York: McGraw-Hill.

LEWIN, K., 1936. *Principles of topological psychology.* New York: McGraw-Hill.

LEWIS, D. J., & COTTON, J. W., 1957. Learning and performance as a function of drive strength during acquisition and extinction. *J. comp. physiol. Psychol., 50,* 189–194.

LIDDELL, H. S., JAMES, W. T., & ANDERSON, O. D., 1934. The comparative physiology of the conditioned motor reflex. *Comp. psychol. Monogr., 11,* No. 1, 1–89.

LINDQUIST, E. F., 1947. Goodness of fit of trend curves and significance of trend differences. *Psychometrika, 12,* 65–78.

LINDQUIST, E. F., 1953. *Design and analysis of experiments in psychology and education.* Boston: Houghton Mifflin.

LINDSLEY, D. B., & SASSAMAN, W. H., 1938. Autonomic activity and brain potentials associated with "voluntary" control of the pilomotors (mm. arrectores pilorum). *J. Neurophysiol., 1,* 342–349.

LIU, IN MAO, 1964. A theory of classical conditioning. *Psychol. Rev., 71,* 408–411.

LIVINGSTONE, R. B., 1959. Central control of receptors and sensory transmission systems. In J. Field, H. W. Magoun, and V. E. Hall (Eds.), *Handbook of physiology, Section 1: Neurophysiology.* Vol. 1. Washington: American Physiological Society.

LOGAN, F. A., 1956. A micromolar approach to behavior theory. *Psychol. Rev., 63,* 63–73.

LORGE, I., 1936. Irrelevant rewards in animal learning. *J. comp. Psychol., 21,* 105–128.

LURIA, A. R., & VINOGRADOVA, O. S., 1959. Objective investigation of the dynamics of semantic systems. *Brit. J. Psychol., 50,* 89–105.

MCALLISTER, W. R., 1953. The effect on eyelid conditioning of shifting the CS-US interval. *J. exp. Psychol., 45,* 423–428.

MCALLISTER, W. R., & MCALLISTER, D. E., 1960. The influence of the ready signal and unpaired UCS presentations on eyelid conditioning. *J. exp. Psychol., 60,* 30–35.

MCDONALD, ANNETTE, 1946. The effect of adaptation to the unconditioned stimulus upon the formation of conditioned avoidance responses. *J. exp. Psychol., 36,* 1–12.

MCDOUGALL, W., 1904. The variation of the intensity of visual sensations with the duration of the stimulus. *Brit. J. Psychol., 1,* 151–189.

MACDUFF, M. M., 1946. The effect on retention of varying degrees of motivation during learning. *J. comp. Psychol., 39,* 207–240.

MCGEOCH, J. A., 1942. *The psychology of human learning.* New York and London: Longmans.

MCNEMAR, Q., 1955. *Psychological statistics.* New York: Wiley.

MAGNI, P., MELZACK, R., MORUZZI, G., & SMITH, C. J., 1959. Direct pyramidal influences on the dorsal-column nuclei. *Arch. ital. Biol., 97,* 357.

MALCOLM, J. L., 1958. The electrical activity of cortical neurones in relation to behaviour, as studied with microelectrodes in unrestrained cats. In

G. E. W. Wolstenholme and C. M. O'Connor (Eds.), *Neurological basis of behavior*. London: Ciba Foundation.

MALMO, R. E., 1963. On central and autonomic nervous system mechanisms in conditioning, learning, and performance. *Canad. J. Psychol., 17*, 1–36.

MARQUIS, D. P., 1931. Can conditioned responses be established in the newborn infant? *J. genet. Psychol., 39*, 479–492.

MARQUIS, D., & HILGARD, E., 1937. Conditioned responses to light in monkeys after removal of the occipital lobes. *Brain, 60*, 1.

MARRAZZI, A. S., & HART, E. R., 1955. Relationship of hallucinogens to adrenergic cerebral neurohumors. *Science, 121*, 365.

MARTINO, G., 1939. The conditioned reflex of blinking. *J. Neurophysiol., 2*, 173–177.

MASSERMAN, J. H., 1941. Is the hypothalamus a center of emotion? *Psychosom. Med., 3*, 3–25.

MATEER, F., 1918. *Child behavior*. Boston: Badger.

MAY, M. A., 1948. Experimentally acquired drives. *J. exp. Psychol., 38*, 66–77.

MENZIES, R., 1937. Conditioned vasomotor responses in human subjects. *J. Psychol., 4*, 75–120.

MILLER, N. E., 1948a. Studies of fear as an acquirable drive: I. Fear as motivation and fear-reduction as reinforcement in the learning of new responses. *J. exp. Psychol., 38*, 89–101.

MILLER, N. E., 1948b. Theory and experiment relating psychoanalytic displacement to stimulus response generalization. *J. abnorm. soc. Psychol., 43*, 155–178.

MILLER, N. E., 1951a. Comments on multiple-process conceptions of learning. *Psychol. Rev., 58*, 375–381.

MILLER, N. E., 1951b. Learnable drives and rewards. In S. S. Stevens (Ed.), *Handbook of experimental psychology*. New York: Wiley. Pp. 435–472.

MILLER, N. E., 1955. Shortcomings of food consumption as a measure of hunger; results from other behavioral techniques. *Ann. N. Y. Acad. Sci., 63*, 141–143.

MILLER, N. E., 1956. Effects of drugs on motivation: the value of using a variety of measures. *Ann. N. Y. Acad. Sci., 65*, 318–333.

MILLER, N. E., 1957. Experiments on motivation: studies combining psychological, physiological and pharmacological techniques. *Science, 126*, 1271–1278.

MILLER, N. E., 1958. Objective techniques for studying motivational effects of drugs on animals. In S. Garattini and V. Ghetti (Eds.), *Psychotropic drugs*. London: Cleaver Hume Press.

MILLER, N. E., 1959. Liberalization of basic S-R concepts: extensions to conflict behavior, motivation and social learning. In S. Koch (Ed.), *Psychology: a study of a science*, Study 1, Vol. 2. New York: McGraw-Hill. Pp. 196–292.

MILLER, N. E., 1960a. Some motivational effects of brain stimulation and drugs. *Fed. Proc., 19*, 846–854.

MILLER, N. E., 1960b. Learning resistance to pain and fear: effects of overlearning, exposure and rewarded exposure in context. *J. exp. Psychol., 60*, 137–145.

MILLER, N. E., 1961a. Some recent studies of conflict behavior and drugs. *Amer. Psychologist, 16*, 12–24.

MILLER, N. E., 1961b. Integration of neurophysiological and behavioral research. *Ann. N. Y. Acad. Sci., 92,* 830–839.
MILLER, N. E., 1961c. Analytical studies of drive and reward. *Amer. Psychologist, 16,* 739–754.
MILLER, N. E., 1961d. Animal experiments on emotionally induced ulcers. Vol. 3. Montreal: Proc. World Congress Psychiatry (June 4–10). Pp. 213–219.
MILLER, N. E., 1961e. Learning and perception motivated by direct stimulation of the brain. Implications for theories of reinforcement. In D. E. Sheer (Ed.), *Electrical stimulation of the brain: subcortical integrative systems.* Houston: University of Texas Press.
MILLER, N. E., 1963a. Some reflections on the law of effect produce a new alternative to drive reduction. *Nebraska symposium on motivation.* Lincoln: University of Nebraska Press. Pp. 65–112.
MILLER, N. E., 1963b. Some motivational effects of electrical and chemical stimulation of the brain. *Electroenceph. clin. Neurophysiol.,* suppl., *24,* 247–259.
MILLER, N. E., 1964. Some implications of modern behavior theory for personality change and psychotherapy. In P. Worchel and D. Byrne (Eds.), *Personality change.* New York: Wiley.
MILLER, N. E. (in press). An experimental analysis of motivational effects of amobarbital sodium. In H. Steinberg, A. U. S. de Reuck and E. J. Knight (Eds.), *Ciba Foundation symposium, jointly with co-ordinating committee for symposia on drug action, on animal behaviour and drug action.* London: J. & A. Churchill.
MILLER, N. E., BAILEY, C. J., & STEVENSON, J. A., 1950. Decreased "hunger" but increased food intake resulting from hypothalamic lesions. *Science, 112,* 256–259.
MILLER, N. E., & DOLLARD, J. C., 1941. *Social learning and imitation.* New Haven: Yale University Press.
MILLER, N. E., GOTTESMAN, K. S., & EMERY, N., 1964. Dose-response to carbachol and norepinephrine in rat's hypothalamus. *Amer. J. Physiol.*
MILLER, N. E., & KESSEN, M. L., 1952. Reward effects of food via stomach fistula compared with those of food via mouth. *J. comp. physiol. Psychol., 45,* 555–564.
MILLER, N. E., & MILES, W. R., 1935. Effect of caffeine on the running speed of hungry, satiated, and frustrated rats. *J. comp. Psychol., 20,* 397–412.
MILLER, N. E., SAMPLINER, R. I., & WOODROW, P., 1957. Thirst-reducing effects of water by stomach fistula vs. water by mouth measured by both a consummatory and an instrumental response. *J. comp. physiol. Psychol., 50,* 1–5.
MILLER, N. E., & STEVENSON, S. S., 1936. Agitated behavior of rats during extinction and a curve of spontaneous recovery. *J. comp. Psychol., 21,* 205–231.
MILLER, W. E., 1948. Theory and experiment relating psychoanalytic displacement to stimulus-response generalization. *J. abnorm. soc. Psychol., 43,* 155–178.
MONTGOMERY, K. C., & SEGALL, M., 1955. Discrimination learning based upon the exploratory drive. *J. comp. physiol. Psychol., 48,* 225–228.

Moore, A. U., & Marcuse, F. L., 1945. Salivary, cardiac and motor indices of conditioning in two sows. *J. comp. Psychol., 38,* 1–16.

Moore, S. W., & Gormezano, I., 1961. Yoked comparisons of instrumental and classical eyelid conditioning. *J. exp. Psychol., 62,* 552–559.

Morgan, C. L., 1930. *Mind at the crossways.* New York: Holt, Rinehart and Winston.

Moss, F. A., 1934. The effect of drugs and internal secretions on animal behavior. In F. A. Moss (Ed.), *Comparative psychology.* New York: Prentice-Hall. Pp. 113–148.

Mowrer, O. H., 1938. Preparatory set (expectancy)—a determinant in motivation and learning. *Psychol. Rev., 45,* 62–91.

Mowrer, O. H., 1939. A stimulus-response analysis of anxiety and its role as a reinforcing agent. *Psychol. Rev., 46,* 553–565.

Mowrer, O. H., 1940. An experimental analogue of "regression" with incidental observations on "reaction-formation." *J. abnorm. soc. Psychol., 35,* 56–87.

Mowrer, O. H., 1947. On the dual nature of learning—a reinterpretation of "conditioning" and "problem solving." *Harv. educ. Rev., 17,* 102–148. (Reprinted in Mowrer, O. H., 1950. *Learning theory and personality dynamics.* New York: Ronald. Pp. 222–274.)

Mowrer, O. H., 1951. Two-factor learning theory: summary and comment. *Psychol. Rev., 58,* 350–354.

Mowrer, O. H., 1956. Two-factor learning theory reconsidered with special reference to secondary reinforcement and the concept of habit. *Psychol. Rev., 63,* 114–128.

Mowrer, O. H., 1960. *Learning theory and behavior.* New York: Wiley.

Mowrer, O. H., & Lamoreaux, R. R., 1942. Avoidance conditioning and signal duration—a study of secondary motivation and reward. *Psychol. Monogr., 54,* No. 5 (Whole No. 247).

Muenzinger, K. F., 1934. Motivation in learning. I. Electric shock for correct response in the visual discrimination habit. *J. comp. Psychol., 17,* 267–277.

Muenzinger, K. F., & Dove, C. C., 1937. Serial learning: I. Gradients of uniformity and variability produced by success and failure of single responses. *J. gen. Psychol., 16,* 403–414.

Muenzinger, K. F., & Gentry, E., 1931. Tone discrimination in white rats. *J. comp. Psychol., 12,* 195–206.

Myers, A. K., & Miller, N. E., 1954. Failure to find a learned drive based on hunger; evidence for learning motivated by "exploration." *J. comp. physiol. Psychol., 47,* 419–427.

Nagaty, M. O., 1951. Effect of food reward immediately preceding performance of an instrumental conditioned response on extinction of that response. *J. exp. Psychol., 42,* 333–340.

Nicholls, Margaret F., & Kimble, G. A., 1964. Effect of instructions upon eyelid conditioning. *J. exp. Psychol., 67,* 400–402.

Nissen, H. W., 1951. Phylogenetic comparisons. In S. S. Stevens (Ed.), *Handbook of experimental psychology.* New York: Wiley.

NOTTERMAN, J. M., SCHOENFELD, W. N., & BERSH, P. J., 1952. Conditioned heart rate response in human beings during experimental anxiety. *J. comp. physiol. Psychol., 45,* 1–8.

NOVIN, D., & MILLER, N. E., 1962. Failure to condition thirst induced by feeding dry food to hungry rats. *J. comp. physiol. Psychol., 55,* 373–374.

NOWLIS, V., & NOWLIS, H. H., 1956. The description and analysis of mood. *Ann. N. Y. Acad. Sci., 65,* 345–355.

O'KELLY, L. E., & STECKLE, L. C., 1939. A note on long-enduring emotional responses in the rat. *J. Psychol., 8,* 125–131.

O'KELLY, L. I., & MEYER, A. W., JR., 1948. Studies in motivation and retention. I. Retention of a simple habit. *J. comp. Psychol., 41,* 466–478.

OLDS, J., & MILNER, P., 1954. Positive reinforcement produced by electrical stimulation of septal area and other regions of rat brain. *J. comp. physiol. Psychol., 47,* 419–427.

OMINSKY, M., & KIMBLE, G. A., 1966. Anxiety and eyelid conditioning. *J. exp. Psychol., 71,* 471–472.

ORBELI, L. A., & KUNSTMAN, K. J., 1924. Oposledstwach deafferentacii zadnich konecznosti u sobak. *Izw. Inst. im. Leshafta, 9,* 187.

OSGOOD, C. E., 1953. *Method and theory in experimental psychology.* New York: Oxford University Press.

OSGOOD, C. E., SUCI, G. J., & TANNENBAUM, P. H., 1957. *The measurement of meaning.* Urbana: University of Illinois Press.

PAVLOV, I. P., 1910. *The work of the digestive glands* (2nd ed.), trans. by W. H. Thompson. London: Griffin.

PAVLOV, I. P., 1927. *Conditioned reflexes,* trans. by G. V. Anrep. London: Oxford University Press.

PAVLOV, I. P., 1928. *Lectures on conditioned reflexes,* trans. by W. H. Gantt. New York: International Publishers.

PAVLOV, I. P., 1932. The reply of a physiologist to psychologists. *Psychol. Rev., 39,* 91–127.

PAVLOV, I. P., 1955. *Selected works.* Moscow: Foreign Language Publishing House.

PEELE, T. L., 1954. *The neuroanatomical basis for clinical neurology.* New York: McGraw-Hill.

PENNYPACKER, H. S., 1961. Inhibitory factors in classical conditioning. Unpublished major area paper, Duke University.

PENNYPACKER, H. S., 1964. External inhibition of the conditioned eyelid reflex. *J. exp. Psychol., 67,* 33–40.

PENNYPACKER, H. S., & KIMMEL, H. D., 1961. Conditioned diminution of the UCR as a function of the number of reinforcements. *Amer. Psychologist, 16,* 442. (Abstract)

PENNYPACKER, H. S., KING, F. A., ACHENBACH, K. E., & ROBERTS, L. (in press). An apparatus and procedure for conditioning the eyeblink reflex of the squirrel monkey. *J. exp. Anal. Behav.*

PERIN, C. T., 1942. Behavior potentiality as a joint function of the amount of training and degree of hunger at the time of extinction. *J. exp. Psychol., 30,* 93–113.

PETERSON, J., 1917. Frequency and recency in maze learning by white rats. *J. Anim. Behav., 7,* 338–364.
PETERSON, J., 1922. Learning when frequency and recency factors are negative. *J. Exp. Psychol., 5,* 270–300.
PIAGET, J., 1951. *Play, dreams and imitation in childhood.* New York: Norton.
PLATONOV, K., 1959. *The word as a physiological and therapeutic factor.* Moscow: Foreign Languages Publishing House.
PURPURA, D. P., 1956. Electrophysiological analysis of psychotogenic drug action. *Arch. Neurol. Psychiat., 75,* 122.

RABEN, M. W., 1949. The white rat's discrimination of differences in intensity of illumination measured by a running response. *J. comp. physiol. Psychol., 42,* 254–272.
RANSON, S. W., 1928. The role of the dorsal roots in muscle tonus. *Arch. Neurol. Psychiat., 19,* 201.
RANSON, S. W., HINSEY, J. C., & TAYLOR, L. A., 1929. The crossed extensor reflex in deafferentated muscle. *Amer. J. Physiol., 8,* 52.
RAZRAN, G., 1933. Conditioned responses in children; a behavioral and quantitative critical review of experimental studies. *Arch. Psychol., N. Y., 23* (148), 3–120.
RAZRAN, G., 1934. Conditioned withdrawal responses with shock as the conditioning stimulus in adult human subjects. *Psychol. Bull., 31,* 111–143.
RAZRAN, G., 1935. Conditioned responses: an experimental study and a theoretical analysis. *Arch. Psychol., N. Y., 28,* 1–124.
RAZRAN, G., 1936. Attitudinal control of human conditioning. *J. Psychol., 2,* 327–337.
RAZRAN, G., 1939. Conditioning and attitudes. *J. exp. Psychol., 24,* 215–226.
RAZRAN, G., 1949. Stimulus generalization of conditioned responses. *Psychol. Bull., 46,* 337–365.
RAZRAN, G., 1957. The dominance-contiguity theory of the acquisition of classical conditioning. *Psychol. Bull., 54,* 1–46.
RAZRAN, G., 1961. The observable unconscious and the inferrable conscious in current Soviet psychophysiology: interoceptive conditioning, semantic conditioning, and the orienting reflex. *Psychol. Rev., 68,* 81–147 (Whole issue No. 2).
REED, H. J., 1927. The essential laws of learning or association. *Psychol. Rev., 34,* 107–115.
RENNER, K. E., 1964. Delay of reinforcement. A historical review. *Psychol. Bull., 61,* 341–361.
REYNOLDS, B., 1945. The acquisition of a trace conditioned response as a function of the magnitude of the stimulus trace. *J. exp. Psychol., 35,* 15–30.
REYNOLDS, B., 1949. The relationship between the strength of a habit and the degree of drive present during acquisition. *J. exp. Psychol., 39,* 296–305.
REYNOLDS, G. S., 1961. Behavioral contrast. *J. exp. Anal. Behav., 4,* 57–71.
REYNOLDS, G. S., CATANIA, A. C., & SKINNER, B. F., 1963. Conditioned and unconditioned aggression in pigeons. *J. exp. Anal. Behav., 1,* 73–75.

REYNOLDS, W. F., 1958. Acquisition and extinction of the conditioned eyelid response following partial and continuous reinforcement. *J. exp. Psychol., 55,* 335–341.

RICHTER, C. P., 1922. A behavioristic study of the activity of the rat. *Psychol. Monogr., 1,* No. 2.

RICHTER, C. P., 1950. Domestication of the Norway rat and its implications for the problem of stress. In Harold G. Wolff, *et al.* (Eds.), *Life stress and bodily disease.* Pp. 19–47. (Assoc. for Research in Nervous and Mental Diseases, Vol. 29) Baltimore: Williams & Wilkins.

RIGGS, L. A., 1941. Continuous and reproducible records of the electrical activity of the human retina. *Proc. Soc. exp. Biol. Med., 48,* 204–207.

RILEY, D. A., RING, K., & THOMAS, J., 1960. The effect of stimulus comparison on discrimination learning and transposition. *J. comp. physiol. Psychol., 54,* 415–421.

ROBERTS, W. W., 1958a. Rapid escape learning without avoidance learning motivated by hypothalamic stimulation in cats. *J. comp. physiol. Psychol., 51,* 391–399.

ROBERTS, W. W., 1958b. Both rewarding and punishing effects from stimulation of posterior hypothalamus of cat with same electrode at same intensity. *J. comp. physiol. Psychol., 51,* 400–407.

RODNICK, E. H., 1937a. Characteristics of delayed and trace conditioned responses. *J. exp. Psychol., 20,* 409–425.

RODNICK, E. H., 1937b. Does the interval of delay of conditioned responses possess inhibitory properties? *J. exp. Psychol., 20,* 507–527.

ROESSLER, R. L., & BROGDEN, W. J., 1943. Conditioned differentiation of vasoconstriction to subvocal stimuli. *Amer. J. Psychol., 56,* 78–86.

ROSENZWEIG, M. R., 1959. Salivary conditioning before Pavlov. *Amer. J. Psychol., 72,* 628–633.

ROWLAND, V., 1957. Differential electroencephalographic response to conditioned auditory stimuli in arousal from sleep. *EEG clin. Neurophysiol., 9,* 585–594.

RUCH, F. L., 1941. *Psychology and life.* New York: Scott, Foresman.

SCHLOSBERG, H., 1928. A study of the conditioned patellar reflex. *J. exp. Psychol., 11,* 468–494.

SCHLOSBERG, H., 1932. An investigation of certain factors related to ease of conditioning. *J. gen. Psychol., 7,* 328–342.

SCHLOSBERG, H., 1934a. A preliminary description of the behavior of the white rat in a simple conditioned response situation. *Psychol. Bull., 31,* 615–616.

SCHLOSBERG, H., 1934b. A quantitative study of certain factors influencing the rate and depth of conditioning in the white rat. *Psychol. Bull., 31,* 732.

SCHLOSBERG, H., 1934c. Conditioned responses in the white rat. *J. genet. Psychol., 45,* 303–335.

SCHLOSBERG, H., 1936. Conditioned responses in the white rat. II. Conditioned responses based upon a shock to the foreleg. *J. genet. Psychol., 49,* 107–138.

SCHLOSBERG, H., 1937. The relationship between success and the laws of conditioning. *Psychol. Rev., 44,* 379–394.

SCHLOSBERG, H., & KAPPAUF, W. E., 1935. The role of "effect" in conditioned leg withdrawal. *Psychol. Bull., 32,* 562.

SCHLOSBERG, H., & KAPPAUF, W. E., 1937. Conditioned responses in the white rat. III. Conditioning as a function of the length of the period of delay. *J. genet. Psychol., 50,* 27–45.

SCHLOSBERG, H., & SOLOMON, R. L., 1943. Latency of response in a choice discrimination. *J. exp. Psychol., 33,* 22–39.

SCHOENFELD, W. N., 1947. Unpublished study.

SCHOENFELD, W. N., 1950. An experimental approach to anxiety, escape, and avoidance behavior. In P. H. Hoch and J. Zubin (Eds.), *Anxiety.* New York: Grune & Stratton.

SCHWARTZ, L., 1960. Conditioned reflexes to verbal stimuli. *Problems Psychol., 1,* 36.

SCOTT, H. D., 1930. Hypnosis and the conditioned reflex. *J. gen. Psychol., 4,* 113–130.

SCOTT, J. P., 1958. *Aggression.* Chicago: The University of Chicago Press.

SCOTT, J. P., & FREDERICSON, E., 1951. The causes of fighting in mice and rats. *Physiol. Zool., 24,* 273–309.

SEARS, R. R., 1934. Effect of optic lobe ablation on the visuomotor behavior of goldfish. *J. comp. Psychol., 17,* 233–265.

SECHENOV, I. M., 1935. *Collected works.* Moscow: State Publishing House.

SECHENOV, I. M. (n. d.—based on Russian edition dated 1952–1956) *Selected physiological and psychological works.* Moscow: Foreign Languages Publishing House.

SEWARD, J. P., 1945. Aggressive behavior in the rat. I. General characteristics; age and sex differences. II. An attempt to establish a dominance hierarchy. III. The role of frustration. IV. Submission as determined by conditioning, extinction, and disuse. *J. comp. Psychol., 38,* 175–197.

SHEFFIELD, F. D., 1949. Hilgard's critique of Guthrie. *Psychol. Rev., 56,* 284–291.

SHEFFIELD, F. D., 1951. The contiguity principle in learning theory. *Psychol. Rev., 58,* 362–367.

SHEFFIELD, F. D., & ROBY, T. B., 1950. Reward value of a nonnutritive sweet taste. *J. comp. physiol. Psychol., 43,* 471–481.

SHEFFIELD, VIRGINIA, 1949. Extinction as a function of partial reinforcement and distribution of practice. *J. exp. Psychol., 39,* 511–526.

SHERRINGTON, C. S., 1947. *The integrative action of the nervous system.* New Haven: The Yale University Press.

SHIPLEY, W. C., 1933. An apparent transfer of conditioning. *J. gen. Psychol., 8,* 382–391.

SHOBEN, E., 1949. Psychotherapy as a problem in learning theory. *Psychol. Bull., 46,* 366.

SIDMAN, M., 1953. Avoidance conditioning with brief shock and no exteroceptive warning signal. *Science, 118,* 157–158.

SIEGEL, P. S., & STEINBERG, M., 1949. Activity level as a function of hunger. *J. comp. physiol. Psychol., 42,* 413–416.

SIEGEL, S., 1956. *Nonparametric statistics for the behavioral sciences.* New York: McGraw-Hill.

SIVADJIAN, J., 1934. Etude pharmacologique d'un reflex conditionee. Paris: *Comptes rendus hebdomadaires des seances de l'Academie des sciences, 199,* 884.

SKINNER, B. F., 1931. The concept of the reflex in the description of behavior. *J. gen. Psychol., 5,* 427–458.

SKINNER, B. F., 1932. Drive and reflex strength. *J. gen. Psychol., 6,* 38–48.

SKINNER, B. F., 1935. Two types of conditioned reflex and a pseudo type. *J. gen. Psychol., 12,* 66–77.

SKINNER, B. F., 1938. *The behavior of organisms; an experimental analysis.* New York: Appleton-Century-Crofts.

SKINNER, B. F., 1947. An automatic shocking grid apparatus for continuous use. *J. comp. Psychol., 40,* 305–307.

SKINNER, B. F., 1953. *Science and human behavior.* New York: Macmillan.

SKINNER, B. F., 1959. An experimental analysis of certain emotions. *J. exp. Anal. Behav., 2,* 264.

SMITH, K., 1964a. Curare drugs and total paralysis. *Psychol. Rev., 71,* 77–79.

SMITH, K., 1964b. Comment on the paper by Black and Lang. *Psychol. Rev., 71,* 86.

SMITH, O. A., 1956. Stimulation of lateral and medial hypothalamus and food intake in the rat. *Anat. Record, 124,* 363–364.

SMITH, S., & HOSKING, E., 1955. *Birds fighting.* London: Faber.

SOLOMON, R. L., & BRUSH, E., 1956. Experimentally derived conceptions of anxiety and aversion. In M. R. Jones (Ed.), *Nebraska symposium on motivation.* Lincoln: University of Nebraska Press. Pp. 212–305.

SOLOMON, R. L., & WYNNE, L. C., 1954. Traumatic avoidance learning: the principles of anxiety conservation and partial irreversibility. *Psychol. Rev., 61,* 353–385.

SOLTYSIK, S., 1960. Studies on the avoidance conditioning. II. Differentiation and extinction of avoidance reflexes. *Acta Biol. Exper., 20,* 171.

SOLTYSIK, S., & KOWALSKA, M., 1960. Studies on the avoidance conditioning. I. Relations between cardiac (type I) and motor (type II) effects in the avoidance reflex. *Acta Biol. Exper., 20,* 157.

SPEARMAN, C., 1927. *The nature of "intelligence" and the principles of cognition.* London: Macmillan.

SPENCE, K. W., 1936. The nature of discrimination learning in animals. *Psychol. Rev., 43,* 427–449.

SPENCE, K. W., 1937. The differential response in animals to stimuli varying within a single dimension. *Psychol. Rev., 44,* 430–444.

SPENCE, K. W., 1941. Failure of transposition in size-discrimination of chimpanzees. *Amer. J. Psychol., 54,* 223–229.

SPENCE, K. W., 1942a. The basis of solution by chimpanzees of the intermediate size problem. *J. exp. Psychol., 31,* 257–271.

SPENCE, K. W., 1942b. Theoretical interpretations of learning. In F. A. Moss (Ed.), *Comparative psychology.* New York: Prentice-Hall.

SPENCE, K. W., 1947. The role of secondary reinforcement in delayed reward learning. *Psychol. Rev., 54,* 1–8.

SPENCE, K. W., 1950. Cognitive vs. stimulus-response theories of learning. *Psychol. Rev., 57,* 159–172.

SPENCE, K. W., 1953. Learning and performance in eyelid conditioning as a function of the intensity of the UCS. *J. exp. Psychol., 45,* 57–63.

SPENCE, K. W., 1954. The relation of response latency and speed to the intervening variables and N in S-R theory. *Psychol. Rev., 61,* 209–216.

SPENCE, K. W., 1956. *Behavior theory and conditioning.* New Haven: Yale University Press.

SPENCE, K. W., 1964. Anxiety (drive) level and performance in eyelid conditioning. *Psychol. Bull., 61,* 129–139.

SPENCE, K. W., & ROSS, L. E., 1959. A methodological study of the form and latency of eyelid responses in conditioning. *J. exp. Psychol., 58,* 376–385.

SPENCE, K. W., & RUNQUIST, W. N., 1958. Temporal effects of conditioned fear on the eyelid reflex. *J. exp. Psychol., 55,* 613–616.

STECKLE, L. C., 1936. Two additional attempts to condition the pupillary reflex. *J. gen. Psychol., 15,* 369–377.

STECKLE, L. C., & RENSHAW, S., 1934. An investigation of the conditioned iridic reflex. *J. gen. Psychol., 11,* 3–23.

STEWART, M. A., STERN, J. A., WINOKUR, G., & FREDMAN, S., 1961. An analysis of GSR conditioning. *Psychol. Rev., 68,* 60–67.

STRASSBURGER, R. C., 1950. Resistance to extinction of a conditioned operant as related to drive level at reinforcement. *J. exp. Psychol., 40,* 473–487.

SUTHERLAND, G. F., 1962. Salivary conditional reflexes in man. *Recent Advances in Biological Psychiatry, 4,* 29–37.

SUTHERLAND, G. F., & KATZ, RUTH A., 1961. Apparatus for study of salivary conditional reflex in man. *J. appl. Physiology, 16,* 740–741.

SWITZER, S. A., 1930. Backward conditioning of the lid reflex. *J. exp. Psychol., 13,* 76–97.

SWITZER, S. A., 1933. Disinhibition of the conditioned galvanic skin response. *J. gen. Psychol., 9,* 77–100.

TAYLOR, H. C., 1933. A conditioned change in vocal pitch. *J. gen. Psychol., 8,* 465–467.

TEASDALL, R. B., & STAVRAKY, G. W., 1953. Responses of deafferented spinal neurones to corticospinal impulses. *J. Neurophysiol., 16,* 367.

TEDESCHI, R. E., TEDISCHI, D. H., MUCHA, A., COOK, L., MATTIS, P. A., & FELLOWS, E. J., 1959. Effects of various centrally acting drugs on fighting behavior of mice. *J. pharm. exp. Therapeutics, 125,* 28–31.

TEEL, K. S., 1952. Habit strength as a function of motivation during learning. *J. comp. physiol. Psychol., 45,* 188–191.

TEITELBAUM, P., & EPSTEIN, A. N., 1962. The lateral hypothalamic syndrome: recovery of feeding and drinking after lateral hypothalamic lesions. *Psychol. Rev., 69,* 74–90.

TENEN, S. S., & MILLER, N. E., 1964. Strength of electrical stimulation of lateral hypothalamus, food deprivation, and tolerance for quinine in food. *J. comp. physiol. Psychol., 58,* 55–62.

THOMAS, D. R., & KING, R. A., 1959. Stimulus generalization as a function of level of motivation. *J. exp. Psychol., 57,* 323–328.

References

THOMPSON, R., 1955. Transposition in the white rat as a function of stimulus comparison. *J. exp. Psychol., 50,* 185–190.
THORNDIKE, E. L., 1898. *Animal intelligence.* New York: Macmillan.
THORNDIKE, E. L., 1903. *Educational psychology.* New York: Lemike and Buechner.
THORNDIKE, E. L., 1911. *Animal intelligence.* (rev. ed.) New York: Macmillan.
THORNDIKE, E. L., 1913. *The psychology of learning.* New York: Teachers College, Columbia University.
THORNDIKE, E. L., 1923. *Educational psychology,* Vol. III; *Mental Work and Fatigue; Individual Differences and their Causes.* New York: Teachers College, Columbia University.
THORNDIKE, E. L., 1927a. A fundamental theorem in modifiability. *Proc. Nat. Acad. Sci., 13,* 14–18.
THORNDIKE, E. L., 1927b. *The Measurement of Intelligence.* New York: Teachers College, Columbia University.
THORNDIKE, E. L., 1931. *Human learning.* New York: Century.
THORNDIKE, E. L., 1932. *Educational psychology.* New York: Teachers College, Columbia University.
THORNDIKE, E. L., 1935. *Wants, interest and attitudes.* New York: Century.
THORNDIKE, E. L., et al., 1932. *The fundamentals of learning.* New York: Teachers College, Columbia University.
THURSTONE, L. L., 1919. The learning curve equation. *Psychol. Monogr., 26,* No. 3 (Whole No. 114).
THURSTONE, L. L., 1935. *The vectors of mind.* Chicago: University of Chicago Press.
TINBERGEN, N., 1951. *The study of instinct.* Oxford: Clarendon Press.
TINBERGEN, N., 1953. *Social behavior in animals.* New York: Wiley.
TOLMAN, E. C., 1922. A new formula for behaviorism. *Psychol. Rev., 29,* 44–53.
TOLMAN, E. C., 1923. A behavioristic account of the emotions. *Psychol. Rev., 30,* 217–227.
TOLMAN, E. C., 1925. Purpose and cognition: the determiners of animal learning. *Psychol. Rev., 32,* 285–297.
TOLMAN, E. C., 1926. A behavioristic theory of ideas. *Psychol. Rev., 33,* 352–369.
TOLMAN, E. C., 1927. A behaviorist's definition of consciousness. *Psychol. Rev., 34,* 433–439.
TOLMAN, E. C., 1933. The law of effect: a reply to Dr. Goodenough. *J. exp. Psychol., 16,* 459–462.
TOLMAN, E. C., 1934. Theories of learning. In F. A. Moss (Ed.), *Comparative psychology.* New York: Prentice-Hall.
TOLMAN, E. C., 1935. Psychology versus immediate experience. *Philosophy of Science, 2,* 356–380.
TOLMAN, E. C., 1938. The determiners of behavior at a choice point. *Psychol. Rev., 45,* 1–41.
TOLMAN, E. C., 1948. Cognitive maps in rats and men. *Psychol. Rev., 55,* 189–208.
TOLMAN, E. C., 1949. There is more than one kind of learning. *Psychol. Rev., 56,* 144–155.

Tolman, E. C., & Brunswik, E., 1935. The organism and the causal texture of the environment. *Psychol. Rev., 42,* 43–77.

Tyron, R. C., 1935. A theory of psychological components—an alternative to "mathematical factors." *Psychol. Rev., 42,* 425–454.

Turner, Barbara B., 1963. The effects of a ready signal upon eyelid conditioning. Unpublished doctoral dissertation, Duke University.

Turner, L. H., & Solomon, R. L., 1962. Human traumatic avoidance conditioning. *Psychol. Monogr., 76,* No. 40 (Whole No. 559).

Ulrich, R. E., 1961. Reflexive fighting in response to aversive stimulation. *Dissert. Abstr., 22,* 4421.

Ulrich, R. E., 1962. Unpublished study.

Ulrich, R. E., & Azrin, N. H., 1962. Reflexive fighting in response to aversive stimulation. *J. exp. Anal. Behav., 5,* 511–520.

Ulrich, R. E., & Craine, W. H., 1964. Behavior: persistence of shock-induced aggression. *Science, 143,* 971–973.

Ulrich, R. E., Johnston, M., Richardson, J., & Wolff, P. C., 1963. The operant conditioning of fighting behavior in rats. *Psychol. Rec., 13,* 465–470.

Ulrich, R. E., Stachnik, T. J., Brierton, G. R., & Mabry, J. H., 1964. Unpublished study.

Ulrich, R. E., Wolff, P. C., & Azrin, N. H., 1964. Shock as an elicitor of intra- and inter-species fighting behavior. *Animal Behav., 12,* 14–15.

Walker, K. C., 1942. Effects of a discriminative stimulus transferred to a previously unassociated response. *J. exp. Psychol., 31,* 312–321.

Warden, C. J., 1924. Primacy and recency as factors in cul-de-sac elimination in a stylus maze. *J. exp. Psychol., 7,* 98–116.

Warden, C. J., & Cummings, S. B., 1929. Primacy and recency factors in animal motor learning. *J. genet. Psychol., 36,* 240–256.

Waters, R. H., 1936. Equivalence of response in learning. *Psychol. Bull., 33,* 798–799.

Waters, R. H., 1937. The principle of least effort in learning. *J. gen. Psychol., 16,* 3–20.

Watson, J. B., 1914. *Behavior: an introduction to comparative psychology.* New York: Holt, Rinehart and Winston.

Watson, J. B., 1916. The place of the conditioned-reflex in psychology. *Psychol. Rev., 23,* 89–116.

Watson, S. B., 1925. *Behaviorism.* New York: Horton.

Watson, J. B., 1928. Experimental studies on the growth of the emotions. In *Psychologies of 1925.* Worcester, Mass.: Clark University Press. Pp. 37–57.

Wedell, C. H., Taylor, F. V., & Skolnick, A., 1940. An attempt to condition the pupillary response. *J. exp. Psychol., 27,* 517–531.

Welch, L., & Kubis, J., 1947. The effect of anxiety on the conditioning rate and stability of the PGR. *J. Psychol., 23,* 83–91.

Wenger, M. A., 1936. External inhibition and disinhibition produced by duplicate stimuli. *Amer. J. Psychol., 48,* 446–456.

Wenger, M. A., 1937. A criticism of Pavlov's concept of internal inhibition. *Psychol. Rev., 44,* 297–312.

WICKENS, D., 1959. Conditioning to complex stimuli. *Amer. Psychologist, 14,* 180.
WILEY, L. E., & WILEY, A. M., 1937. Studies in learning function. *Psychometrika, 2,* 1–20.
WILLETT, R. A., 1960. Measures of learning and conditioning. In H. J. Eysenck (Ed.), *Experiments in personality.* Vol. 2. London: Routledge. Pp. 167–174.
WILLIAMS, G. W., & O'BRIEN, C., 1937. The effect of sodium phenobarbital on the learning behavior of white rats. *J. comp. Psychol., 23,* 457–474.
WILLOUGHBY, R. R., 1935. Magic and cognate phenomena: an hypothesis. In *A handbook of social psychology.* Worcester, Mass.: Clark University Press. Pp. 461–519.
WILSON, W. R., 1924. Principles of selection in "trial and error" learning. *Psychol. Rev., 31,* 150–160.
WINER, J., 1962. *Statistical principles in experimental design.* New York: McGraw-Hill.
WING, K., & SMITH, K., 1942. The role of the optic cortex in the dog in the determination of functional properties of conditioned reactions to light. *J. exp. Psychol., 31,* 478.
WINNICK, WILMA A., & HUNT, J. McV., 1951. The effect of an extra stimulus upon strength of response during acquisition and extinction. *J. exp. Psychol., 41,* 205–215.
WOLF, G., & MILLER, N. E., 1964. Lateral hypothalamic lesions: effects on drinking elicited by carbachol in preoptic area and posterior hypothalamus. *Science, 143,* 585–586.
WOLFLE, H. M., 1930. Time factors in conditioning finger-withdrawal. *J. gen. Psychol., 4,* 372–378.
WOLFLE, H. M., 1932. Conditioning as a function of the interval between the conditioned and the original stimulus. *J. gen. Psychol., 7,* 80–103.
WOLPE, J., 1958. *Psychotherapy by reciprocal inhibition.* Stanford: Stanford University Press.
WOOD, D. M., & OBRIST, P. A., 1964. Effects of controlled and uncontrolled respiration on the conditioned heart rate response in humans. *J. exp. Psychol., 68,* 221–229.
WOODWORTH, R. S., 1947. Reënforcement of perception. *Amer. J. Psychol., 60,* 119–124.
WYRWICKA, W., 1950. The effect of diminished alimentary excitability upon conditioned reflexes of the second type. *Acta Biol. Exper., 15,* 205–214.
WYRWICKA, W., 1952. On the mechanism of the motor conditioned reaction. *Acta Biol. Exper., 16,* 131–137.
WYRWICKA, W., 1956. On the effect of experimental situation upon the course of motor conditioned reflex. *Acta Biol. Exper., 17,* 189–203.
WYRWICKA, W., 1957. Wstepne badania nad wplywem uszkodzen podwzgorza na pokarmowe ruchowe odruchy warunkowe u krolikow. (The effect of hypothalamic lesions on alimentary motor conditioned reflexes in rabbits.) *Acta Physiol. Pol., 8,* 575–576.
WYRWICKA, W., 1958. Studies on the effects of the conditioned stimulus applied against various experimental background. *Acta Biol. Exper., 18,* 175–193.

WYRWICKA, W., DOBRZECKA, C., & TARNECKI, R., 1959. On the instrumental conditioned reaction evoked by electrical stimulation of the hypothalamus. *Science, 130,* 336–337.

YAMAGUCHI, H. G., 1951. Drive (D) as a function of hours of hunger (h). *J. exp. Psychol., 42,* 108–117.
YOSHIOKA, J. G., 1928. Pattern vs. frequency and recency factors in maze learning. *J. genet. Psychol., 35,* 193–200.
YOSHIOKA, J. G., 1929. Weber's law in the discrimination of maze distance by the white rat. *Univ. Calif. Publications in Psychol., 4,* 155–184.
YOSHIOKA, J. G., 1930. Frequency factors in habit formation. *J. comp. Psychol., 11,* 37–49.
YOUTZ, R. E. P., 1938a. Reinforcement, extinction, and spontaneous recovery in a non-Pavlovian reaction. *J. exp. Psychol., 22,* 305–318.
YOUTZ, R. E. P., 1938b. The change with time of a Thorndikian response in the rat. *J. exp. Psychol., 23,* 128–140.
YOUTZ, R. E. P., 1939. The weakening of one Thorndikian response following the extinction of another. *J. exp. Psychol., 24,* 294–304.

ZEAMAN, D., 1949. Response latency as a function of the amount of reinforcement. *J. exp. Psychol., 39,* 466–483.
ZELENY, G., & KADYKOV, B., 1938. Contribution to the study of conditioned reflexes in the dog after cortical extirpation. *Psychol. Abstr., 12,* No. 5829.
ZENER, K., 1937. The significance of behavior accompanying conditioned salivary secretion for theories of the conditioned response. *Amer. J. Psychol., 50,* 384–403.
ZENER, K., & MCCURDY, H. G., 1939. An analysis of motivational factors in conditioned behavior: I. The differential effect of changes in hunger upon conditioned, unconditioned, and spontaneous salivary secretion. *J. Psychol., 8,* 321–350.